Networking Systems Design and Development

IT MANAGEMENT TITLES
FROM AUERBACH PUBLICATIONS AND CRC PRESS

The Executive MBA in Information Security
John J. Trinckes, Jr
ISBN: 978-1-4398-1007-1

The Decision Model: A Business Logic Framework Linking Business and Technology
Barbara von Halle and Larry Goldberg
ISBN: 978-1-4200-8281-4

The SIM Guide to Enterprise Architecture
Leon Kappelman, ed.
ISBN: 978-1-4398-1113-9

Lean Six Sigma Secrets for the CIO
William Bentley and Peter T. Davis
ISBN: 978-1-4398-0379-0

Building an Enterprise-Wide Business Continuity Program
Kelley Okolita
ISBN: 978-1-4200-8864-9

Marketing IT Products and Services
Jessica Keyes
ISBN: 978-1-4398-0319-6

Cloud Computing: Implementation, Management, and Security
John W. Rittinghouse and James F. Ransome
ISBN: 978-1-4398-0680-7

Data Protection: Governance, Risk Management, and Compliance
David G. Hill
ISBN: 978-1-4398-0692-0

Strategic Data Warehousing: Achieving Alignment with Business
Neera Bhansali
ISBN: 978-1-4200-8394-1

Mobile Enterprise Transition and Management
Bhuvan Unhelkar
ISBN: 978-1-4200-7827-5

The Green and Virtual Data Center
Greg Schulz
ISBN: 978-1-4200-8666-9

The Effective CIO
Eric J. Brown, Jr. and William A. Yarberry
ISBN: 978-1-4200-6460-5

Business Resumption Planning, Second Edition
Leo A. Wrobel
ISBN: 978-0-8493-1459-9

IT Auditing and Sarbanes-Oxley Compliance: Key Strategies for Business Improvement
Dimitris N. Chorafas
ISBN: 978-1-4200-8617-1

Best Practices in Business Technology Management
Stephen J. Andriole
ISBN: 978-1-4200-6333-2

Leading IT Projects: The IT Manager's Guide
Jessica Keyes
ISBN: 978-1-4200-7082-8

Knowledge Retention: Strategies and Solutions
Jay Liebowitz
ISBN: 978-1-4200-6465-0

The Business Value of IT
Michael D. S. Harris, David Herron, and Stasia Iwanicki
ISBN: 978-1-4200-6474-2

Service-Oriented Architecture: SOA Strategy, Methodology, and Technology
James P. Lawler and H. Howell-Barber
ISBN: 978-1-4200-4500-0

Service Oriented Enterprises
Setrag Khoshafian
ISBN: 978-0-8493-5360-4

Networking Systems Design and Development

Lee Chao

CRC Press is an imprint of the
Taylor & Francis Group, an **Informa** business
AN AUERBACH BOOK

CRC Press
Taylor & Francis Group
6000 Broken Sound Parkway NW, Suite 300
Boca Raton, FL 33487-2742

International Standard Book Number: 978-1-4200-9159-5 (Hardback)

Library of Congress Cataloging-in-Publication Data

Chao, Lee, 1951-
Networking systems design and development / Lee Chao.
p. cm.
Includes index.
ISBN 978-1-4200-9159-5 (hardcover : alk. paper)
1. Computer networks. I. Title.

TK5105.5.C45939 2010
004.6--dc22 2009041624

Visit the Taylor & Francis Web site at
http://www.taylorandfrancis.com

and the CRC Press Web site at
http://www.crcpress.com

Contents

Preface

Today's E-commerce is built on various types of networks. The IT industry requires our students to understand how network systems are used to transmit business information across the world. The present online teaching/learning environment also requires that networking textbooks be able to handle new challenges. The author of the book has been motivated by the following factors.

Motivation

More and more universities support Web based teaching and learning. It is difficult to teach technology-based online courses because these courses often require hands-on practice on certain IT products. It is not easy to find a textbook that teaches networking theories as well as hands-on skills online.

Almost every major university has Linux computer labs to support hands-on practice in the computer science and information systems curriculum. There are demands for textbooks that are designed to directly utilize these Linux computer labs for teaching networking-related courses.

The job market now requires IT professionals to understand networking theories and have hands-on skills for solving real-world network problems. However, theory-based networking textbooks often cover inadequate hands-on practice, and books for hands-on practice may not systematically cover networking concepts. Therefore, many of our students and instructors prefer a textbook that integrates both the theories and hands-on practice within the same book.

By considering the fact that most of our students are beginners in the field of networking, and they may take networking classes online, a textbook should be easy to follow, and the instructions for the hands-on practice should be step-by-step. The textbook should also include instructions on setting up the lab environment at home.

With the above motivation, this book is designed with the following objectives to help instructors, students, and IT professionals to get a quick start in developing network systems.

Objectives of the Book

Online teaching/learning has become mainstream among higher education institutions. More and more courses in various fields have been offered online. However, for many universities, it is challenging to offer networking-related courses online due to the requirement of lab activities. The first goal of this book is to provide a networking textbook that is suitable for online teaching and learning in a lab environment and for IT professionals' self study of Linux networking-related topics.

The second goal of this book is to prepare students and IT professionals to get ready for developing network systems with the Linux operating system. An enterprise network system involves network design, implementation, and management. This book covers the knowledge related to all these three aspects. It is designed to provide the necessary conceptual knowledge and hands-on skills for developing a fully functioning network system with open source materials. The content covered in this book helps readers to create network systems that can be used for daily business activities.

Another intention of this book is to help readers understand how a network works. It is written so that the networking concepts are introduced in an orderly fashion and progress step by step.

Features of the Book

To achieve its goals, this book is designed with the following features.

- *Self-contained content:* For the convenience of readers, the book is self-contained. It includes some necessary basic networking concepts and theories, and hands-on activities, as well as the information about Linux networking tools.
- *Suitable for self-study:* This book provides detailed instruction that is suitable for self-study. It does not just state the networking concepts and theories, but explains them through examples, illustrations, and hands-on activities.
- *Designed for online teaching:* The book is specially designed for online teaching. All the lab activities can be done on a student's home computer through the use of virtual machine technologies.
- *A wide range of coverage:* This book covers various types of networks: wired networks, wireless networks, and mobile networks. It discusses Linux-based networking on both the server side and the client side.
- *Linux technology:* The development of a Linux network system costs almost nothing for the reader. Ubuntu GUN/Linux is used for all the lab activities. Ubuntu is known by its features such as versatility, power, and ease of use.
- *Step-by-step instructions:* For the hands-on activities, the book provides step-by-step instructions and illustrations so that even beginners can follow. The book gives directions on setting up the virtual lab environment for hands-on practice.
- *Real-world approach:* Examples, illustrations, and hands-on practice projects are included in each chapter of this book. These materials are designed for helping readers gain confidence and skills in developing a network system that can be used in a real-world business.
- *Supplementary materials:* To assist teaching and learning, the book provides review questions and case study projects to enhance readers' understanding. A solution manual and PowerPoint presentations are also provided.

With these features, the book can be used for a one-semester networking course. It is also suitable for IT professionals who do self-study on Linux networking.

Organization of the Book

There are twelve chapters in this book. Each chapter consists of an introduction, main body of the chapter, summary, review questions, and case study projects. In each chapter, one or more hands-on activities are provided for readers to enhance understanding and gain practical skills.

Chapter 1 covers two topics, the network architectures and the Linux operating system. First, this chapter introduces two commonly used network architectures, Open Systems Interconnection (OSI) and TCP/IP. The second topic is about the Linux operating system. After giving a brief history of the Linux operating system, this chapter introduces several well-known Linux distributions. It also describes how Linux is used to support networking. The hands-on activity in this chapter demonstrates the installation of Ubuntu Linux.

As described in Chapter 1, each layer in the TCP/IP architecture has its own set of protocols to perform network tasks. Chapter 2 provides more detailed information about the commonly known protocols in the layers of application, transport, Internet, and network interface. After the discussion of these protocols, this chapter investigates the relationships among the protocols in each layer and provides a protocol graph to show how the protocols are related. The hands-on activity examines the tools and services provided by the Ubuntu Linux operating system.

After learning about the protocols and their relationships, readers are ready to explore networks and network devices. To prepare for network design and development, Chapter 3 first provides information about the types of networks and their features. Then, it discusses the network media used to transmit data over networks. It describes how data are transmitted through different types of media. In Chapter 3, readers also learn about network devices used by local area networks and wide area networks. Chapter 3 covers network devices such as network interface cards, switches that can be used to link multiple computers in a network, and routers used to link multiple networks so that computers on different networks can communicate with each other. Through the hands-on practice, readers can learn how to use network tools to configure network interface cards and test network connection by following the step-by-step instruction.

After learning about the basics of networks and network devices, readers can now look into network design. Chapter 4 discusses network design–related issues. It first talks about how to collect requirement information from customers. Then, it discusses how to design a network to meet the requirements. A network model is used to determine if the future network will meet the requirements. For computers and other network devices to communicate with each other, each host in a network must be assigned an IP address. Chapter 4 looks at how IP addresses are used to form a network. It explains why subnetting and supernetting are necessary. Then, it introduces the theory of subnetting and supernetting. For subnetting and supernetting, readers first learn about IP conversion between the binary system and the decimal system. Chapter 4 shows how to divide a network into several small networks and how to form a larger network with several smaller networks. The calculation of subnet masks, subnet network IDs, and IP addresses for the hosts in a subnet is taught in this chapter, which also discusses the calculation of the number of subnets and the number of hosts in a subnet. The discussion includes both the IPv4 version and IPv6 version of the IP protocol. The hands-on practice in this chapter explores IPv6 on Linux. It illustrates how to develop a simple IPv6 Linux network.

Once a network is designed and developed, various network services will be created to help the network administrator manage the network. Chapter 5 discusses several commonly used network services in more detail. It first looks at the user authentication service and describes how user information is stored by the Linux operating system. Through the first hands-on activity, readers can learn how to create a user account and how to assign privileges to the user account. The second network service discussed in this chapter is called DHCP. DHCP is the service that can automatically assign an IP address to a computer or network device soon after it is linked to a network. Through the second hands-on activity, readers learn how to implement the DHCP service to automatically assign IP addresses. The third service covered in Chapter 5 is the name service called Domain Name System (DNS). DNS is used to translate the name assigned to a computer to an

IP address, and vice versa. In this way, users can access computers by using meaningful computer names instead of IP addresses. Through the third hands-on activity, readers can learn how to implement the DNS service on a private network.

In a large enterprise-level network, there are multiple networks interconnected to one another. A router is a device that links multiple networks. Chapter 6 discusses various tasks that can be accomplished by a router. Readers learn about router-related concepts and how a router works. Chapter 6 provides a number of examples that demonstrate how a router can dynamically update its routing table and identify optimal routes to destinations. Two routing table update methods, static and dynamic, are discussed in this chapter. For the dynamic method, the chapter provides the information of several commonly used routing protocols. It also shows the reader how to construct a router with the tools provided by the Linux operating system. Through the hands-on practice, readers learn how to physically create a router with Linux. They also learn how to connect multiple networks with routers that are used to pass network traffic from one network to another. In addition, the hands-on practice demonstrates how the routing table is updated dynamically.

In the real world, network resources are shared by hundreds and even thousands of users simultaneously. Chapter 7 shows how to share the network resources and how to remotely access those network resources. First, this chapter introduces the service called NFS which allows the hosts on a Linux network or UNIX like network to share files, directories, and even hard drives. The installation and configuration of NFS services are discussed in detail. Through the hands-on practice in this chapter, readers learn how to let two Linux computers share their files. In an enterprise environment, network resources are shared by the networks running on various operating systems. The second topic in Chapter 7 is about sharing network resources with a network operated on Windows operating systems. It introduces Samba technology for sharing network resources with a Windows network. In the hands-on practice, readers learn how to access a Linux server from a Windows client and share the files of the Linux server. The third topic is about remote access. Readers learn how to set up a Virtual Private Network (VPN) service that allows users to remotely log on to a private network. This chapter introduces various VPN products and the tunneling protocols used in VPN services. VPN configuration related issues are also discussed in this chapter. Through the hands-on practice, the reader can learn how to set up a VPN service with the Linux utilities and determine if the user can remotely access the computers on a private network through the VPN. The last topic is the Network Address Translation (NAT) service. It discusses different types of NAT applications and how translation is carried out in these NAT applications. It also looks at the configuration of NAT. Through the hands-on practice, readers learn how to set up a NAT service so that the computers on a private network can use the same public IP address to access the Internet.

The Internet can be considered a global network consisting of various types of individual networks. Services created for the Internet are globalized services. Universities and companies depend on Internet services for globalized online education and e-commerce. Readers will learn about Internet-based services in Chapter 8. The discussion of the Web server and its services is the first topic of Chapter 8. The second topic deals with the FTP server and FTP services that allow users to share files on the Internet. Readers will learn how to install and configure FTP services. The third topic in Chapter 8 is e-mail service. Through the hands-on practice, readers will learn about Linux e-mail server installation, configuration, and management.

Once a network is up and running, network security is the top concern of users and network managers. Chapter 9 addresses the issues of implementing network security measures with the Linux operating system. The first topic in Chapter 9 deals with issues related to network security such as security policies, hacker attacks and computer viruses, and commonly used security measures. The next topic is the introduction of some security technologies. These network technologies are used to protect private networks and data being transmitted through public networks. The last topic is about firewalls. Various firewalls and their functions are examined. Through the hands-on practice, readers learn how to install and configure some network security software such as SSL, SSH, and firewalls by following the step-by-step instruction.

Chapter 10 introduces several tools for managing network resources. It first discusses some command-based and GUI-based utilities that manage users and groups. This chapter focuses on the development of the directory service with Lightweight Directory Access Protocol (LDAP). LDAP is a powerful tool for managing users, computers, and other network resources for an enterprise-level network. Through the hands-on practice, readers learn how to develop an LDAP service for network user authentication. The next topic in this chapter is about the issues related to kernel and driver maintenance. The hands-on practice shows readers how to customize the Linux kernel by adding new network functions.

The discussion in Chapter 11 focuses on the Linux wireless network system. Readers will learn about wireless network technologies and how a wireless network works. This chapter examines the tools for wireless network construction and configuration. To develop a successful Linux wireless network, one needs to resolve the hardware compatibility issue first. This chapter provides detailed information on Linux compatible wireless network devices and drivers. The hands-on practice illustrates how to build a wireless network.

The last chapter in this book is about the Linux mobile network. In Chapter 12, readers will learn about mobile Linux and mobile network–related topics. This chapter first introduces mobile Linux and its features. It also provides information about mobile Linux architecture, kernel, user interface, and utilities used for configuring mobile networks. The next topic is about mobile devices such as PDAs, cell phones, and other mobile devices. Then, this chapter discusses mobile networks. It describes how mobile networks evolve from the first generation to the fourth generation. The hands-on practice in this chapter demonstrates how to configure a mobile network modem with Ubuntu Linux. The hands-on practice also illustrates how to set up a personal computer to run the mobile Linux operating system on a virtual machine.

One or more hands-on activities are included in each of the chapters. It is recommended that readers complete the activities in the previous chapters before starting a hands-on activity in the next chapter because some of these activities may depend on the ones in previous chapters.

For the real-world network solution, this book shows that creating a fully functioning network system does not have to be expensive. The book demonstrates to students and IT professionals how to take advantage of Linux to develop a fully functioning network system with minimum cost. It shows how to properly design, implement, and manage network systems. It also provides enough technical details to help students and IT professionals develop networks of their own. The book introduces a number of open-source networking tools that can make networking more efficient and flexible.

Acknowledgments

The author would like to thank his students and Dr. Jenny Huang for their participation in the book proofreading process. They thoroughly reviewed the book content and tested the hands-on activities throughout the book. They contributed constructive recommendations for improving the quality of the book. They also corrected a number of typos in the writing.

The author's thanks also go to the wonderful editorial staff members and other personnel at Auerbach Publications of Taylor & Francis Group for their support of this project. Especially, the author truly appreciates the encouragement and collaboration from John Wyzalek, senior acquisitions editor, and Jennifer Ahringer, project coordinator. The book would not be possible without their inspiration and great effort.

The Author

Lee Chao, Ph.D., is currently a professor in the Science, Technology, Engineering, and Mathematics Division, University of Houston–Victoria. He received his Ph.D. from the University of Wyoming. Dr. Chao has been teaching IT courses for over 18 years. His current research interests are networking and technology-based teaching. He is also the author of over a dozen research articles and books in various areas of IT.

Chapter 1

Linux Networking Overview

Objectives

- Get an overview of the Linux operating system.
- Understand the role of Linux in networking.
- Learn about the process of implementing networks with Linux.
- Journey through the Linux operating system installation process.

1.1 Introduction

In this information age, computer networks are the essential component in supporting communication among computers. The infrastructure of an information system employs the Internet, wide area networks, and local area networks as building blocks. Networks allow computers located thousands of miles apart to communicate with one another. With networks, companies can communicate with their customers across the world. A Web-based teaching system allows students in rural areas to remotely access the course materials stored on a server on a campus located in a major city. People around the world can get their morning news through computers linked to the Internet. Nowadays, networks are used everywhere to support our daily life and business activities.

To meet the ever-increasing needs of better and faster networks, new network technologies have been invented at a rapid pace. With the invention of the ARPANET network in the 1970s, the Internet era began. Then, the layered network architecture was invented by IBM for data communication. In 1974, Ethernet technology was invented by Xerox for local area networks. Ethernet technology is still widely used by today's computer networks. In 1984, Integrated Services Digital Network (ISDN) was created to support digital telephones. High-speed broadband technology was invented between 1997 and 1998. This technology has made Internet connections significantly faster.

Since the 1990s, wireless network technology has become mature. Wi-Fi is the commonly used technology for wireless local area networks. Worldwide Interoperability for Microwave Access (WiMAX) is the technology used for wireless metropolitan area networks. Various technologies have also been developed for mobile device networks. Global System for Mobile communication (GSM) is the most used technology for mobile phone communication. Personal Communications Service (PCS) is another popular technology for the mobile phone service in North America. Bluetooth is a wireless technology for wireless personal area networks (PANs) that can connect devices such as mobile phones, laptops, PCs, printers, digital cameras, and video game consoles.

Since the year 2000, gigabit network technology has become popular. It increases network transmission speed from 10/100 to 1000 Mbps. Starting from the year 2006, twisted-pair network cables could run 10-Gigabit Ethernet technology, which is 10 times as fast as gigabit technology.

The fast-developing network industry has a great impact on economies around the world. Many giant network-related technology companies have been formed since the 1970s. For network equipment, there are some well-known companies such as Cisco, Nortel, Alcatel-Lucent, 3COM, and Juniper. For network operating systems, there are Microsoft, IBM, Hewlett-Packard (HP), and various Linux distributions. There are several famous telecommunication companies such as AT&T, Verizon, Sprint, and T-Mobile. There are also computer companies such as HP, Dell, Acer, and Lenovo that sell network equipment and provide network services. These are all international companies, and they have contributed a large portion of a country's GDP, such as India.

Due to the importance of networks for information systems, networking theory and practice are included in today's computer science and information systems curricula. Developing a network system requires a lot of knowledge of various fields such as computer engineering, computer security, operating systems, telecommunication, and Internet development. To construct a network system for a real-life business requires a thorough understanding of the theories in network design, implementation, and management. It also requires IT professionals to have hands-on skills in using technologies involved in network development and management. It is the goal of this book to provide necessary knowledge and skills to design, implement, and manage network systems with the open source product Linux.

1.2 Overview of Linux Operating Systems

Computer networking is the process of interconnecting a group of computers so that they can communicate with one another. In this process, one has to deal with the issues of how to connect these computers with network devices and network transmission media such as cables, radio waves, or other media. After the computers are physically linked, it is also important to make the software on one computer to communicate with the software on another computer. This is where an operating system plays an important role. Often, network-capable operating systems or other network software are used to configure the network devices so that the computers can send and receive data through a network. Network-capable operating systems can also be used to manage network devices and the communication software associated with these devices.

Many operating systems are able to accomplish networking tasks. For example, the enterprise version of Linux, the Microsoft Windows server operating system, and various versions of UNIX operating systems can all be used to develop and manage networks. Among these operating systems, Linux is mostly a free, open source product. Although some of the distributions may charge a small fee on some commercial versions of their Linux products, the cost is still much less than proprietary operating systems. In spite of being free, Linux does not lack functionalities in handling networking tasks. In fact, Linux is powerful and versatile when handling networking tasks. In the following subsections, we will overview the Linux operating system and examine the network utilities provided by Linux.

1.2.1 Brief History

Linux is an open source UNIX like operating system originally developed to run on personal computers with the 32-bit Intel 386 architecture. In 1991, Linus Torvalds, a computer science student from the University of Helsinki, developed an operating system kernel with a multithreaded file system for his new personal computer with an 80386 processor. In 1992, he made a prerelease version of Linux available to the public. This prerelease version of Linux was a combination of his work with some existing free software such as the multiple language compiler GCC, the debugger GDB, and the text editor GNU. The first version of Linux was made available to the public in 1994 under the GNU General Public License, which guarantees that Linux is free to the general public. Linux quickly became a popular operating system for Intel 386 personal computers. Although Linux is often used as the name for the entire operating system, the operating system is a combination of the Linux kernel with other open source software. Especially, GNU has contributed significantly to the operating system. The real name of the operating system should be GNU/Linux. Because Linux has become a popular name, we will continue to use the name Linux if there is no conflict. Each time we use the name Linux, we mean GNU/Linux.

Because Linux is an open source operating system, many enthusiastic programmers have contributed to the Linux operating system. These contributions have made Linux a fully functioning operating system. The following is a brief time line of the Linux development process:

- 1987—MINIX, released by Andrew S. Tanenbaum, was created for personal computers with the Intel 8086 microprocessor.
- 1992—By rewriting MINIX, Linus Torvalds published the prerelease version of Linux, which was created for personal computers with the Intel 80386 microprocessor.
- 1994—Red Hat Linux was introduced.
- 1996—The first GUI-based desktop environment, K Desktop Environment (KDE), was introduced for the Linux operating system.
- 2001—The Linux operating system was chosen for supercomputing.
- 2005—Linux was used by four of the five fastest supercomputers as their operating system.
- 2006—Led by Motorola, the Linux Mobile (LiMo) Foundation was formed, and the Linux-based handset was developed by Motorola.
- 2008—Led by Google, the Open Handset Alliance developed the Android Linux mobile operating system, which has been used to power the T-Mobile's G1 phone.

After years of development, various versions of Linux have been created. As an operating system for personal computers, Linux is fast and efficient. As a server operating system, Linux supports 64-bit symmetric multiprocessing, which is an ideal environment for large databases and enterprise-scale network management. In recent years, Linux has also been developed into an operating system for mobile devices. In general, Linux is a stable, secure, and versatile operating system. With these advantages, Linux has become one of the fastest-growing operating systems. Nowadays, Linux is widely used on servers, personal computers, supercomputers, mobile phones, PDAs, and network routers. These are certainly good reasons why Linux has been chosen by many to be the operating system for developing and managing their networks.

1.2.2 Linux Distributions

The Linux operating system was developed by a group of volunteers led by Linus Torvalds. It is a combination of the Linux kernel, a file system, and a lot of other open source software that handles tasks such as text editing, network management, and GUI-based desktop environment development. The Linux kernel is frequently upgraded. Every time the latest version of the Linux kernel becomes available, one can integrate it with other open source software packages to form a full-fledged operating system. Based on their individual needs, many do-it-yourself fans create their own customized perfect operating systems in this way. Many vendors have realized that they can make a profit by integrating open source packages with the Linux kernel. These vendors first create a file system, then download the necessary open source code, compile the source code, synchronize the components included in Linux, make installation CDs, write a user's manual, and provide technical support. These vendors provide free or commercial Linux packages called Linux distributions. Due to its popularity, the Linux operating system is assembled by many Linux companies and user communities such as Red Hat, Novell, and Canonical Ltd. These Linux distributions are fully supported by several major hardware and software vendors such as Dell, Hewlett-Packard, IBM, Novell, and Sun Microsystems. The following are some major Linux distributions:

1. *Ubuntu Linux:* Ubuntu is a major Linux distribution sponsored by Canonical Ltd., a private company from South Africa. Its operating systems are easy to use, free, regularly updated, versatile, and have a large user base. Ubuntu is updated every 6 months. It provides both the desktop and server editions of the Linux operating system. Unlike many other Linux distributions that often make the enterprise editions of Linux commercial products, both the desktop and server editions of the Ubuntu Linux operating system are free. Ubuntu installation is quick and simple. Ubuntu Linux is available on a live CD, so live hard disk installation is possible. The live installation first tests the compatibility of the hardware, and then the CD can be booted into a fully functioning Linux operating system with applications and services.

   The server edition of Ubuntu Linux includes the LAMP (Linux, Apache, MySQL, and PHP) package, which can be automatically installed during the server installation process. This feature can really save a lot of time for system administrators. The automatic installation process provides better security and reduces the risk of misconfiguration.

   In addition to the server edition, Ubuntu also provides a desktop-oriented operating system. The Ubuntu desktop edition is specially designed to meet the needs of personal computers. It is one of the top Linux desktop operating systems on the market. Various desktop application utilities are included in the Ubuntu desktop operating system. For example, Ubuntu includes many utilities for handling multimedia content such as photo editing and media editing tools. It also includes e-mail and the latest Web browsing technology. For the management of the desktop environment, the Ubuntu desktop operating system provides various tools for searching, calendaring, Web form spellchecking, phishing detection, and system administration. It also includes many desktop application software packages such as the office suite OpenOffice.org, the instant messenger Pidgin, and graphics editor GIMP. It has the Personal Package Archive (PPA) service, which is used to build and publish packages for the Low-Power Intel Architecture (LPIA), which is the architecture optimized for battery-powered devices. The LPIA is a platform for the development of the Ubuntu Mobile and Embedded edition. The Ubuntu Mobile and Embedded edition runs video and sound, and offers fast and rich browsing on the Mobile Internet Device (MID) platform. The Ubuntu Mobile and Embedded edition can run with small memory and storage space. It also delivers fast boot time and resume time.

The aforementioned Ubuntu editions can handle a wide range of computing tasks, from supercomputers to hand-held mobile devices. In recent years, Ubuntu Linux has been gaining attraction among users. Many personal computer companies, such as Dell, have begun to offer Ubuntu as one of the optional operating systems for their customers. These companies also provide technical support for Ubuntu to their customers through Ubuntu's sponsor company, Canonical.

2. *SUSE Linux:* SUSE is also a major Linux distribution owned by Novell, which is a well-known network software company. SUSE provides both open source and proprietary products. The open source version of SUSE Linux, openSUSE, is a popular operating system, mainly for desktop and notebook computers. In the SUSE Linux family, openSUSE is the most-used operating system. It includes many application software packages, such as OpenOffice.org for creating and managing document files. OpenOffice.org is compatible with many other document formats such as Microsoft Office and Adobe Portable Document Format (PDF). The search software Beagle included in SUSE Linux can be used to search application files, e-mail, instant messages, and Web pages with keywords. SUSE Linux also bundles several multimedia software packages such as K3b for CD/DVD burning, Amarok for audio playback, Kaffeine for movie playback, RealPlayer, and the Xgl graphical environment, which provides a 3-D graphical desktop environment.

   SUSE Linux also has commercial Linux products such as SUSE Linux Enterprise Server (SLES) and SUSE Linux Enterprise Desktop (SLED) that target enterprise computing environments. Both of these products include technical support and contain some software from proprietary sources. SLES supports over 2000 application software packages as well as more than 1000 open source software packages. These two products are designed for the business environment. In addition to being able to run on the x86 platform, both SLES and SLED are able to run on other major server platforms such as PowerPC, Itanium 2, and so on. The commercial editions of SUSE Linux, are sold through several major hardware vendors such as IBM, HP, Sun Microsystems, Dell, and SGI. These vendors are also certified to provide technical support for the commercial editions of SUSE Linux. They install, configure, and thoroughly test SLES and SLED for their customers to make sure that the products are stable and optimized for performance. Unlike the open source of SUSE Linux, which is upgraded very often, SLES is upgraded roughly every 2 years and each version is supported for a life cycle of 7 years. In this way, SLES can retain its stability, which is important for a server operating system.

   One of the advantages of SUSE Linux is that it can interact with many services provided by other proprietary products such as Microsoft Active Directory, Novell GroupWise, Lotus Domino, and Microsoft Exchange Server. The SUSE Linux operating system can coexist with Microsoft Windows. It supports the Windows NTFS file system and Windows-specific modems for remote access. The virtualization technology provided by the combination of SUSE and Xen allows other operating systems to run on the Linux operating system, which creates an environment for software testing and development. These features make SUSE Linux suitable for the enterprise environment, which requires Linux to interact with a variety of applications and operating systems from other vendors. This is why SUSE Linux is chosen as the Linux solution by many global companies such as Walmart, BMW, and Casio.

3. *Red Hat Linux:* The Red Hat company was founded in 1993. Since then, Red Hat Linux has become a major Linux distribution, especially in supporting the enterprise-level computing environment. Red Hat Linux provides both the open source and the proprietary editions of the Linux operating system; each serves a different purpose.

   Fedora is the open source edition of the Linux operating system supported by both Red Hat employees and the user community. Fedora is updated about every 4 to 6 months to keep up with the newest technology. Because Fedora is an open source product, Red Hat Linux does not provide much technical support and training. Once a fault is detected in the software, Fedora relies on the user community and individual Red Hat employees to fix the problem. Although Fedora is a fully functioning operating system, it is less tested and, therefore, it is less stable. Fedora is a good platform for developers and inventors to fix problems and to extend Linux functionalities. Fedora is free for everyone and is the most downloaded Red Hat product.

   Red Hat Enterprise Linux is the commercial version of the Linux operating system supported by Red Hat, which provides the convenient 24x7 within 1 hour response service. Red Hat also organizes all the necessary software into packages for users to conveniently download them. The training for using Red Hat Enterprise Linux is provided by the Red Hat company and many consulting companies in various formats, including classroom, on-site, and e-learning. Red Hat Enterprise Linux is upgraded at a much slower pace. With about every three new upgrades of Fedora, there will typically be one upgrade of Red Hat Enterprise Linux. This makes Red Hat Enterprise Linux more stable, but also makes it slower in keeping up with the newest products on the market. As a commercial product, each version of Red Hat Enterprise Linux is fully supported by the Red Hat company for 7 years since its release. Red Hat Enterprise Linux also includes some proprietary software so that it can work with some commercial application software from Oracle, CA, and IBM. Red Hat Enterprise Linux is also widely supported by many computer hardware companies such as Dell, HP, and IBM. In addition to being able to run on the x86 platform, Red Hat Enterprise Linux can also run on other platforms, such as Itanium 2, POWER, zSeries, S/390, and SPARC.
4. *Debian Linux:* Debian is also a major Linux distribution. It started in 1993. Debian only includes open source software in its version of the Linux operating system. Debian is a comprehensive operating system that includes 18,000 precompiled open source programs. Debian's strict open source policy has influenced some other Linux distributions. For example, Ubuntu, which is considered by many as an extension of Debian, also conforms to the open source policy. Although Debian follows a strict open source policy, it is still supported on major computation platforms such as x86, POWER, SPARC, HP PA_RISC, and so on.

   Unlike the aforementioned three Linux distributions that have the server edition for servers and the desktop edition for personal computers, Debian can handle both server and desktop tasks. As an all-in-one operating system, Debian can significantly cut down the workload on system development and management time in an enterprise-level environment. When dealing with the same operating system on both servers and personal computers, it is much easier to handle tasks such as system installation, system configuration, software update, technical support, and troubleshooting.

   Also, unlike some other Linux distributions that rely only on the user community to test the free versions of their products, the newly released version of the Debian operating system is rigorously tested by Debian. The thoroughly tested Debian Linux operating system is a more stable system than some other distributions' open source Linux operating systems. Debian has a slower release cycle for better stability and quality in the new version. Due to its stability, Debian Linux is suitable for use as a server operating system. When used as a server operating system, Debian Linux is so stable that system administrators may not need to reboot the system for a long time.

Debian is also known for its strong technical support. When Debian receives e-mail asking for assistance, it usually responds to that e-mail within 15 min. To help users upgrade, install, and remove packages between major releases, Debian provides an integrated package management system that can help users maintain dependent packages automatically. In this way, it can eliminate orphan files and incompatible products during the system update process. Also, Debian allows users to update the Linux operating system with the latest programs, tools, and security patches over the Internet by executing a single command, or through a scheduler configured for automatic update.

Debian Linux is an efficient operating system. It does not require many computing resources, such as a fast and big CPU, RAM, video card, hard disk, and so on. It may be able to run on a Pentium III personal computer with a 4 GB hard drive. Even though it uses fewer computing resources, the Debian Linux operating system can still achieve fairly decent performance gain. If a computer does not have enough resources, Debian can run across multiple computers.

5. *Knoppix Linux:* Knoppix is an interesting Linux operating system that is run directly from a CD. Knoppix is an extension of the Debian version of Linux and is designed to be bootable on a CD or DVD. The executable code of the Linux operating system is compressed on a CD that can hold 2 GB code or on a DVD that can hold up to 8 GB code. The executable code can also be stored on a bootable USB device such as a USB flash drive. By running on a CD or DVD, Knoppix has to deal with the hardware devices installed on various host computer systems. The Knoppix Linux operating system needs be compatible with as many hardware devices as possible. To accomplish this goal, Knoppix provides an extensive hardware detection program that can work with most computer systems and network devices with no configuration required. The hardware detection program can detect various peripheral devices, including video cards, network interface cards, hard drives, and USB devices.

   Knoppix is also a very efficient operating system. It does not need a lot of RAM and can even run on an x86 personal computer with 128 MB RAM. It is easy to carry Knoppix Linux around and boot the operating system on an existing host computer system without changing anything on the host. During the operation, Knoppix saves the modified or new files to the local hard drive, USB flash drive, or temporarily on memory. This is why Knoppix is often used to rescue a crashed computer system. After booting Knoppix from a CD, the user can fix the problem that caused the crash by, for example, correcting a wrongly configured file on the host computer. Knoppix can also save valuable data on a crashed computer to a different hard drive and then reinstall the host operating system.
6. *Android Linux:* Android Linux was initiated by Google. It is being continually developed by the Open Handset Alliance, which consists of over 30 hardware, software, and telecom companies. Android Linux's main target is the cell phone market. It is designed to have the features that meet the requirements of mobile devices. It is an open source product, including an operating system as well as an application software development platform. It allows mobile device makers to develop their own application software for mobile phones.

   Android is a versatile operating system that is capable of handling tasks for different types of phones such as voice phones, camera phones, multimedia phones, game phones, and so on. The operating system included in Android is capable of multitasking. It handles multiple processes running on the same mobile device. For example, when a phone rings, the phone process passes the caller's information to the display process so that the caller ID can be displayed on screen. Among these processes, one process can call the methods defined in other processes. The objects can also be passed from one process to another process. The middleware included in Android is used to handle transactions between processes.

Android application software developers can work with low-end processors to reduce the cost of hardware. Its wide-ranging compatibility enables the developer to use low-cost off-the-shelf Linux applications. It also has the application development utilities such as the device emulator and Eclipse IDE for software development. It has tools for debugging and performance profiling. The application development platform also includes the Java programming language. With Java, third-party application software developers can create utilities and services for mobile devices. To further help the developers, Android also includes various built-in libraries.

In today's cell phone market, Android is a well-known mobile Linux operating system. To meet the requirements of cell phones, Android is designed to handle tasks such as e-mail processing, touch screen control, Adobe Flash display, connecting personal network devices, and so on. Android includes an e-mail client, Short Message Service (SMS), calendar, map, browser, contacts, and so on. These applications in Android are all written in the Java programming language.

The foregoing discussion has indicated that Linux is an efficient, low-cost, versatile, open source operating system. Many hardware and software companies are centered around Linux. More and more IT companies, such as Sun and IBM, preinstall the Linux operating system on their servers, workstations, as well as personal computers. Based on customers' requests, major computer hardware companies such as Dell, Lenovo, and HP also preinstall the Linux operating system on their laptop and desktop computers.

In the foregoing text, we have discussed several major Linux distributions. There are hundreds of other Linux distributions, each with its own specialties. With so many choices, it is hard to decide which one to pick. The selection of a Linux distribution depends on the tasks to be accomplished. For most networking-related tasks, Linux distributions such as Ubuntu, SUSE, Red Hat, and Debian Linux should be able to do the job. For mobile devices, the Linux distributions such as Ubuntu and Android are good choices. Because Ubuntu Linux has desktop, server, and mobile editions, it has something out there for every type of networking task. Besides, we can also benefit from its great features such as being easy to use, completely free, and versatile. Therefore, Ubuntu Linux will be our choice for the hands-on practice included in this book.

Further discussion about other Linux distributions is beyond the scope of this book. Next, we will focus on Linux networking capabilities and services.

1.3 Linux Networking

The previous section briefly gave an overview of the Linux operating system. This section will focus on the introduction of Linux networking features and services. It will introduce the major components in a network system. We will take a look at how the network functionalities are designed and implemented in Linux. The Linux network management tools will also be introduced in this section.

1.3.1 Linux Network Architecture

A network consists of a set of computers and network devices linked by physical media so that these computers are able to exchange data with each other. A network can be as small as two computers connected by a copper wire or as large as the Internet, which links millions of computers and network devices. For computers to be able to communicate with each other through physical media, the Linux operating system provides four major components: application, service, protocol, and adapter.

To implement a network system that can best handle data transmission tasks on various networks, a network model, also called network architecture, is developed to give network designers an overview of the network system that will be built. The network architecture includes the major components for the network and the interfaces between them. To conveniently display the components and interfaces, network architecture is often presented as a layered system. The network components provided by Linux can be presented as a layered model (Figure 1.1).

Application software and tools form a service interface between users and the Linux kernel. The application software and tools manage data exchange through the network. They handle users' requests for file transfer, database query, and message exchange. The application service interface will determine if the data to be exchanged are available and if the network resources are adequate for data transmission.

The Linux kernel handles the data delivery between the network adapter and application software. In the Linux Kernel, the network management component is used to manage network operations. For example, when incoming data arrive, the network management component will collect, identify, and forward it to a process for further handling.

A network protocol serves as a service interface between the application software and the network driver. It includes a set of rules that determine the meanings and forms of information exchanged between two different computers in a network, just as the grammar of a language is used by two people to exchange information. The tasks to be performed by the protocol may include error detection, data formatting, defining how data is sent, and defining how data is received. There are hundreds of protocols supported by the Linux operating system; each of them handles a specific type of information. There will be more discussion of the commonly used protocols in later chapters.

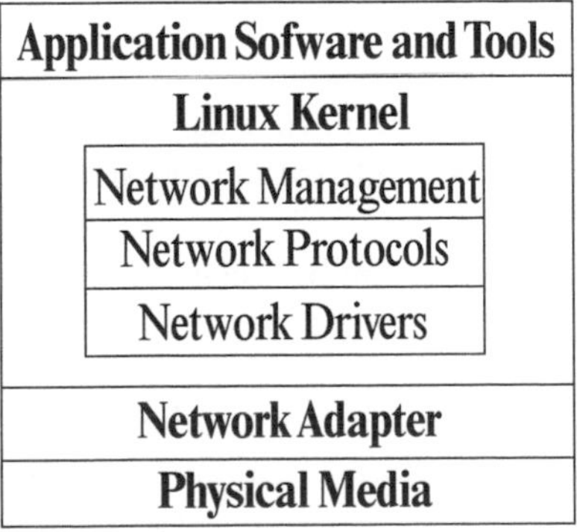

Figure 1.1 Linux network architecture.

A network driver serves as an interface that allows the Linux kernel to communicate with the network adapter hardware. When a network device driver is installed, it will register itself and get ready to exchange data between the software and hardware. The driver initializes an interface that can communicate with the network adapter and handle the I/O interrupts. It is able to manage buffers, communicate with network protocols, as well as interact with the operating system. The network driver is also designed to handle tasks such as resolving network addresses, maintaining network traffic, and reporting error statistics.

A network adapter serves as an interface between the Linux kernel and the physical media. Originally, the network adapter was an Ethernet network interface card for personal computers. Today, network adapters can also mean wireless network gear, PCMCIA cards, USB network devices, and software-based virtual network adapters. Electrical signals are formed in a network adapter, which will specify the transmission rate and the shape and strength of binary signals. A network adapter physically sends and receives binary electrical signals to and from transmission media. It communicates with its peer network adapter through a low-level hardware addressing system. The network adapter verifies the destination address information included in the binary signals on the physical media. If the destination address matches the hardware address of the receiver's network adapter, the network adapter will inform the Linux kernel on the receiver's computer to get ready to process the incoming binary signals.

The physical media provides a service interface between two network hosts such as computers or other network devices. This interface transmits electrical signals that represent binary bits to remote hosts through the media such as copper cables, fiber glass, radio waves, etc. This interface defines the media types and how the hardware is connected.

The specific network architecture described in the preceding text can be further abstracted into a more general network architecture that can be used by a wide range of network systems. There are two general network architectures, Open Systems Interconnection (OSI) architecture and Internet architecture. Developed by the International Organization for Standardization (ISO), OSI is a network architecture that defines the communication process between two computers. OSI categorizes the entire communication process into the seven layers shown in Figure 1.2.

Starting from the top, the application layer in the OSI network architecture handles requests for file transfer, database query, message exchange, and so on, which can be handled by some application-level protocols.

The presentation layer in the OSI network architecture handles the data formats exchanged between two applications. The tasks to be handled by this layer can be data compression, data encryption, video streaming, data format conversion, and so on.

The session layer manages the communication session established between two applications such as a conference call or remote connection to a database server. It starts, manages, and terminates the session, which includes tasks such as the request and response of a data transmission process between applications.

The transport layer handles the connection between two hosts. This layer performs tasks such as error checking, network flow control, transporting data, and establishing, managing, and terminating connections.

The network layer handles message routing to another network node. This is the layer that works with routers and network logical address configuration tools. Routable protocols are used to handle the tasks in this layer.

The data-link layer is often implemented in the network card driver. It specifies the beginning and ending of a data transmission unit. Logical source and destination addresses are converted to

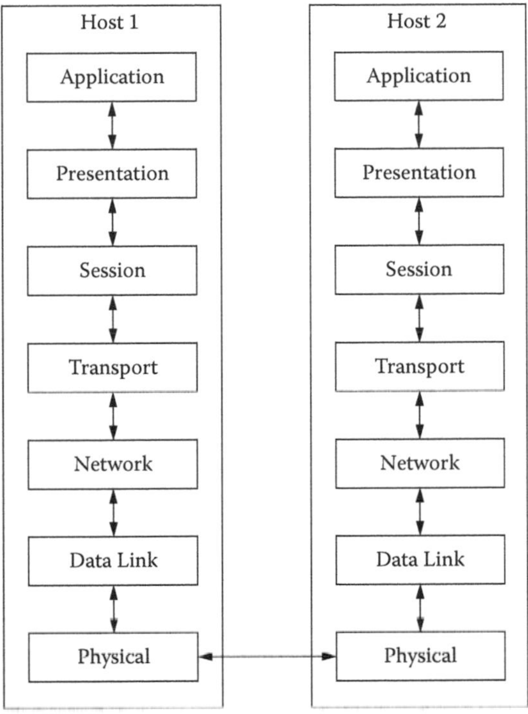

Figure 1.2 OSI network architecture.

hardware addresses in this layer so that packets can be delivered to the designated receivers. This layer also detects and corrects errors that may occur during the data transmission in the physical layer.

The physical layer transmits electrical binary signals over the physical media that link two hosts. When an electrical binary signal arrives from the physical media, the physical layer passes the binary signals up to the data-link layer.

The foregoing presents a general picture of the OSI architecture for data exchange between two applications connected by a network. The other commonly used network architecture, Internet architecture, is designed for modeling data exchange through the Internet. This architecture is built around the Transmission Control Protocol and Internet Protocol (TCP/IP). Therefore, the Internet architecture is also called the TCP/IP architecture, which combines the application layer, the presentation layer, and the session layer in the OSI architecture into one application layer. It still keeps the transport layer. The network layer in the OSI architecture becomes the Internet layer in the TCP/IP architecture. The OSI data-link layer and the physical layer are combined into the network interface layer in the TCP/IP architecture. Figure 1.3 shows the flowchart illustration of the TCP/IP architecture.

The OSI network architecture has been adopted by the U.S. government. Companies that manufacture network software and hardware for the U.S. government need to show their compliance with the OSI network architecture. On the other hand, the TCP/IP architecture has been adopted by network systems governed by the Berkeley UNIX operating system as well as the Microsoft Windows Server operating system.

Linux is a UNIX like operating system. Therefore, a Linux-based network system can be implemented by closely following the TCP/IP network architecture. The application layer in

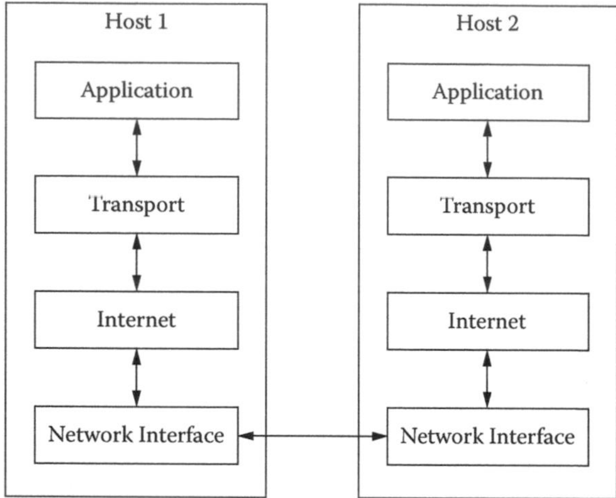

Figure 1.3 TCP/IP network architecture.

the TCP/IP network architecture is similar to the layer of application software and tools in Figure 1.1. Application software and tools in Figure 1.1 are often used to carry out tasks such as data compression, data encryption, video streaming, and data format conversion. The network management tools in Linux applications can handle tasks related to session establishment, maintenance, and termination. The tasks in the transport layer in the TCP/IP network architecture can be done by Transmission Control Protocol (TCP), which handles data transmission error checking, network flow control, and establishing, managing, and terminating a connection between two hosts. TCP is included in the network protocols component in Figure 1.1. The Internet layer in the TCP/IP network architecture includes routable protocols such as the IP protocol. These protocols are also included in the network protocols component in Figure 1.1. The network interface layer of the TCP/IP network architecture converts packets into binary electrical signals or vice versa. It sends or receives electronic binary signals through the physical media. It also performs low-level error checking and converts logical addresses to hardware addresses or vice versa so that a connection between two hosts on the network can be established. This layer includes the components of network drivers, network adapters, and physical media listed in Figure 1.1.

The foregoing brief discussion has illustrated data communication in a Linux network system. Network architecture shows how data is exchanged between two applications on a network. It serves as a model of the complicated data communication process. Detailed discussions of the aforementioned components will be presented in later chapters. Next, we will take a look at the networking tasks and network tools included in the Linux operating system.

1.3.2 Linux Networking Tasks and Network Tools

Linux distributions often include various network tools in their Linux operating system packages. These network tools can be used to build or manage networks. They can be used for network configuration, troubleshooting, monitoring, remote access, and security management. The following are networking tasks that can be accomplished with Linux network tools:

- *Network device and service configuration:* Network devices need to be properly configured before they can exchange data. The Linux operating system provides various tools to configure network devices and network services. Most of the text-based network configuration tools are portable from one Linux distribution's product to another Linux distribution's product. Some Linux distributions also provide GUI tools that are often specific to their own Linux distributions.
- *Network troubleshooting:* The Linux operating system provides tools that can assist network troubleshooting, such as determining if a network interface card is properly configured and if data can reach designated destinations. These tools can analyze the collected information and provide guidelines for network administrators to fix network problems.
- *Network monitoring:* The Linux operating system includes some network monitoring tools that can be used to assist troubleshooting and enforcing network security measures. These tools can be used to capture and analyze network traffic.
- *Network security:* The network security management tools included in the Linux operating system can be used to detect network security vulnerabilities and enforce security measures. These tools can help network administrators to configure firewalls, detect hacker intrusion, download and install antivirus upgrades and service packs, set up permissions, create user accounts, and so on.
- *Remote access:* Tools are provided by the Linux operating system to establish remote access. Some of these tools also include remote access management functionalities that can help network administrators set up remote access authentication criteria and set up permissions for individual users to remotely access network resources.
- *Management reporting:* Linux also provides tools for collecting network statistics and generating reports about operations of a network. The reports may include network faults, security vulnerabilities, and analyses of network statistics. Some of the sophisticated reports also include tables, charts, and animations to illustrate the dynamic change in a network.
- *Managing users and network resources:* One of the commonly performed network tasks is the management of users and network resources. The directory service is such a tool; it stores information about user accounts, computers, and other network devices. The directory is usually hosted by the Linux operating system to perform user authentication. When a user logs on to an operating system, the username and password will be used to match the user information stored in the directory. If the information provided by the user matches the information stored in the directory, he or she will be allowed to log on to the computer system or network device.

The network tools included in the Linux operating system provide an inexpensive, easy-to-use, and flexible solution for network configuration and management. In later chapters, there will be more detailed coverage of how to use the tools included in Linux to accomplish these tasks. The first step in carrying out the Linux networking tasks is to install and configure the Linux operating system to make it ready for other networking tasks.

Activity 1.1 Linux Installation

The installation of the Linux operating system can be done in two ways. The first method is to install Linux on a computer that will have Linux as its only operating system. If Linux is used to manage the real-world network or a student has spare computers at home, this is the way to go.

The second method is to install Linux on a virtual machine or as a dual-boot operating system. In a situation where the Linux operating system is used to support network-related courses, due to limited resources, one computer lab is often required to support multiple courses. Each course may need a different operating system. In this case, multiple operating systems will be installed on a single computer. Students often use their own personal computers for hands-on practice. Again, a student's computer needs to support multiple courses. If a student has only one computer that is already running another operating system, the student may consider installing Linux on a virtual machine.

As mentioned before, Linux has various distributions that may have their own specialties. Among the Linux products, Ubuntu is a 100% free product, and it can serve as an operating system for a server, personal computer, and mobile device. Ubuntu is also known for its easy-to-use features. Therefore, Ubuntu Linux will be used to demonstrate the installation process in this section. The installation of the operating systems of other Linux distributions is similar.

INSTALLATION PREPARATION

A successful installation of the Linux operating system requires careful planning. First, we need to decide where and how to obtain the Linux operating system. Before the installation, you should collect information about the host computer on which Linux will be installed. The computer hardware such as the CPU, RAM, hard disks, and network interface card should meet the requirements of the Linux operating system to be installed. Based on the requirements, you should decide which components should be installed.

1. *Getting Linux:* Each Linux distribution has its own Web site for downloading the open source version. Users can also get Linux on CDs mailed by the Linux distributions or third-party companies that create CDs for the Linux distributions. It is necessary to install Linux with CDs if there is no Internet connection linked to the Linux distribution's Web site. There may be a small cost for the CDs, and shipping and handling.

   As an example, let us consider downloading Ubuntu Linux from the Web site, http://www.ubuntu.com.

   From the download Web site, users can choose to download the desktop edition of Ubuntu or the server edition of Ubuntu. In our case, both of the editions will be downloaded. The following are the steps to download the Ubuntu operating system:

   - Surfing to the Ubuntu Web site, click the **Get Ubuntu** link. Click the **Download Now** link.
   - You will be prompted to select which version to download and a download location. For example, you may choose the version **Desktop Edition Ubuntu 8.10** and specify the download location at **United States MIT Media Lab**. You may also specify the computer architecture as the **32-bit version**.
   - Then, click the button **Begin Download**. If the downloading process does not start in 15 seconds, click the link **launch the download**.
   - In the File Download dialog box, click the **Save** button. The ISO image file to be downloaded is about 700 MB. It may take some time to download the file.

   After the Ubuntu image file is downloaded, it can be burned into a CD or DVD for installation. To burn an ISO image file on Microsoft Windows Vista, you can use Roxio Creator. To do so, right-click the newly downloaded file and select **Open With** and then **Roxio Creator** from the pop-up menu. Insert a blank CD-R or DVD-R disk, and click the **Burn Image** button.

   Ubuntu recommends the free software Infra Recorder for Windows users, which can be downloaded from the Web site http://infrarecorder.sourceforge.net.

   After Infra Recorder is downloaded and installed, follow the steps below to burn the ISO image file to a DVD.

   - Insert a recordable DVD into a DVD burner.
   - Start Infra Recorder, and click **Action** on the menu bar. Then select **Burn Image**.

- Find the Ubuntu image file in the Open dialog.
- Click the **Open** button to open the Burning Image dialog. Click **OK** to start the burning process.

After the image-burning process is completed, the DVD will be automatically ejected. Mark the DVD as Ubuntu GNU/Linux. Now, the downloading process is completed. In addition to the desktop edition and server edition, Ubuntu also offers the following editions:

- *Kubuntu:* This edition uses the popular KDE desktop environment instead of the default GNOME desktop environment. Until recently, KDE has been the number one choice for the Linux desktop environment for many years.
- *Xubuntu:* This edition uses the Xfce desktop environment, which is a simple and fast desktop environment.
- *Eubuntu:* Eubuntu is designed for the education environment. It is easy-to-use for students of all ages. More education and game software are added to this edition.
- *Gobuntu:* This edition only includes the open source software. It has no firmware, drivers, and applications. This edition is for developers to construct a free software distribution on top of Ubuntu.
- *Ubuntu Mobile:* Ubuntu Mobile is an edition designed for Internet mobile devices and tasks such as Web browsing, e-mail, media, cameras, VoIP, instant messaging, GPS, blogging, digital TVs, gaming, and so on. This edition is finger friendly and touch driven.

Users can select the edition that best fits their needs. In the following, we will investigate the hardware requirements for hosting the Ubuntu operating system.

2. *System requirements:* In general, the hardware requirements for the installation of Linux are moderate. The system requirements for installing Ubuntu depend on which edition of the operating system will be installed. More system resources are required for the desktop operating system than for the server operating system. Also, a live CD requires more memory. For the desktop operating system, the following should be adequate:
   - *Processor:* Ubuntu can be installed on a personal computer with a 700 MHz x86 processor or better.
   - *Hard drive:* Ubuntu needs 8 GB of available storage space on the hard disk to keep the files for the desktop operating system. You may need 10 GB for the hands-on practice in this book.
   - *Memory:* If the Linux operating system runs on the hard drive, the minimum requirement for memory is 256 MB.
   - *CD/DVD:* For data exchange, running multimedia materials, or installing the operating system stored on a CD or DVD, a CD-ROM/CD-RW drive or DVD-ROM/DVD-RW drive is required.
   - *USB controller:* It is used for USB devices.
   - *Network interface card:* For connecting to the Internet or carrying out installation through a network, an Ethernet network interface card is required. You may need two network interface cards for the hands-on practice in this book.
   - *Graphics card:* Running the Ubuntu Linux desktop operating system requires a graphics card with 1024×768 pixel resolution or better.
   - *Sound card:* A high-quality sound card is also necessary for running multimedia software.

   The system requirements for the server operating system are relatively less because servers are not designed to handle multimedia. The following are the system requirements for the server operating system:

   - A personal computer with a 300 MHz x86 processor will be able to run the server operating system.
   - The server operating system needs a minimum of 64 MB memory.
   - 500 MB of disk space can be used to store the necessary configuration files.
   - There is a lower requirement on the graphics card. A VGA graphics card capable of 640×480 pixel resolution is adequate.
   - The server operating system also needs a CD-ROM drive.

More memory is needed when running Ubuntu Linux on a live CD. The minimum memory requirement is 384 MB RAM.

These requirements for different editions of Ubuntu can be met by even an old Pentium III personal computer. Ubuntu can also be installed on computers constructed with other platforms such as the following:

- The i386 compatible Intel and AMD platforms such as 64-bit AMD, Athlon64, Opteron, Xeon, and so on.
- Sun UltraSPARC platforms.

After making sure that the system requirements are met for installing Ubuntu, you are ready to install the software that has been downloaded and burned on a DVD. The installation procedure will be covered in the next section.

LINUX INSTALLATION

In this section, the process of Linux installation will be discussed. During the installation process, the user will be prompted to specify the following information:

- Language used by the operating system
- Time zone setting
- Keyboard setting
- Partition setting
- User setting

Partition setting is the most complicated step in the installation process. Users will be asked to specify the swap space and the file system, which includes folders such as the following:

- /, which denotes the directory for the root user
- **/home**, which denotes the user's home directory
- **/boot**, which denotes the directory that contains files used by the bootstrap loader LILO, kernel images, and so on
- **/usr**, which denotes the directory for application files, help files, and libraries
- **/dev**, which denotes the directory for device files of disk drives, serial ports, and so on
- **/etc**, which denotes the directory for storing configuration files that are specific to the machine
- **/var**, which denotes the directory for files that are dynamic and are frequently being changed, such as mail-, news-, log-, and man-page-related files

Basically, there are two choices. The installation process can automatically create partitions and the file system by using the entire hard disk space, or the user can manually create the partitions and the file system based on specific needs. If the computer is to be configured so that it can run both the Windows operating system and the Linux operating system, one should choose the manual configuration option.

Some Linux installation programs allow the user to resize the current partitions on the current computer system to make room for the Linux installation. During the manual installation, the user needs to decide the size of the swap partition and the size of the directories in the file system. The swap space is used as virtual memory when the amount of physical memory is used up. Normally, the size of the swap space can be set to be 1.5 times of the physical memory. If the user often works with large files that require a lot of memory such as multimedia files, the user should increase the size of the swap space.

The sizes of directories depend on how the Linux operating system will be used. For hands-on practice in a network-related course, 512 MB is usually adequate for most of the directories except the directory /usr. If one decides to have a complete installation, the size of /usr should be large enough to store all application files. It may take several gigabytes of space to hold these files. The user also needs to decide the file system type. The file system type ext3 or ext2 should be the choice for the Linux operating system.

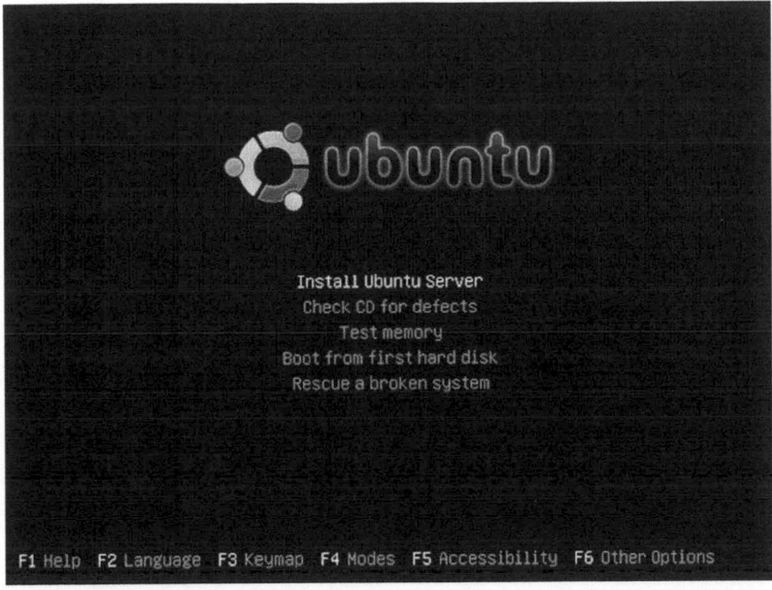

Figure 1.4 Ubuntu installation option list.

The installation of Linux also requires the user to create one or more user accounts. The hands-on practice in the networking courses requires students to have a root account, which is the system administrator's account. For these courses, regular user accounts are also needed.

Next, Ubuntu Linux will be used as an example to illustrate the installation process. Suppose that you have a personal computer or a virtual machine that meets the foregoing system requirements. The following are the step-by-step instructions for installing Ubuntu:

1. Start a personal computer, and insert the Ubuntu server edition DVD (created in the previous section) into the DVD drive. Then restart the personal computer.
2. After the computer is restarted. You will be prompted to choose the installation task from a text menu (Figure 1.4). Select **Install Ubuntu Server**, and press the **Enter** key.
3. On the next page, you will choose the language for the operating system. In this example, **English** is selected (Figure 1.5). Press the **Enter** key. On the next page, you will be asked to select the type of English. Select **United States,** and press the **Enter** key.
4. Next, you will be prompted to specify the keyboard (Figure 1.6). When asked if the keyboard layout should be detected, select **No** and press the **Enter** key.
5. On the next page, select **USA** for the origin of the keyboard and press the **Enter** key. When prompted for the keyboard layout, select **USA** and press the **Enter** key.
6. The installation process will now begin. If you have multiple network interface cards on your computer, you will be asked to select the primary network interface for the installation. Select **eth0,** and press the **Enter** key.
7. The next page will ask you to give a host name for the computer. For example, you may enter **ubuntu-server** as the host name (Figure 1.7). Use the **Tab** key to select **<Continue>,** and press **Enter.**
8. The next page asks you to specify the time zone; select the time zone (Figure 1.8), and press the **Enter** key.
9. As mentioned earlier, you can either manually partition the hard drive or let the installation software partition the hard drive automatically. In our example, let us suppose the entire hard drive will be used for Ubuntu Linux. So, select the option **Guided—use entire disk** (Figure 1.9).

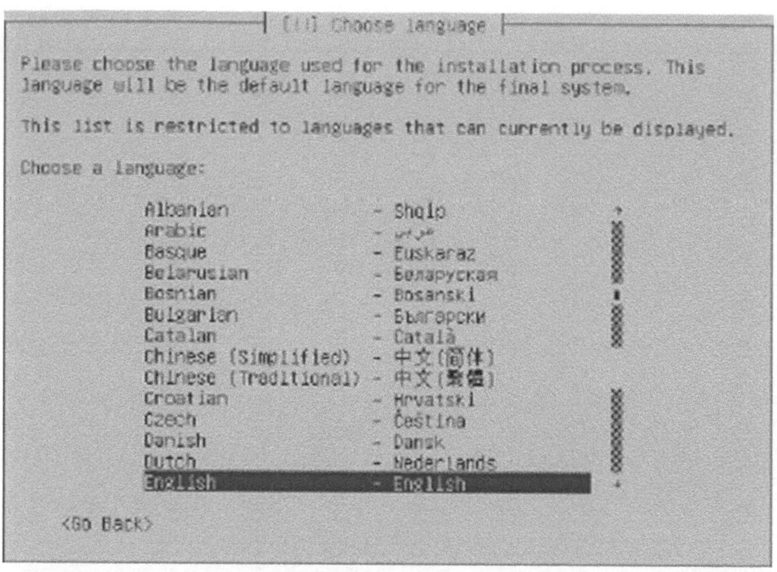

Figure 1.5 Specifying language used by Linux.

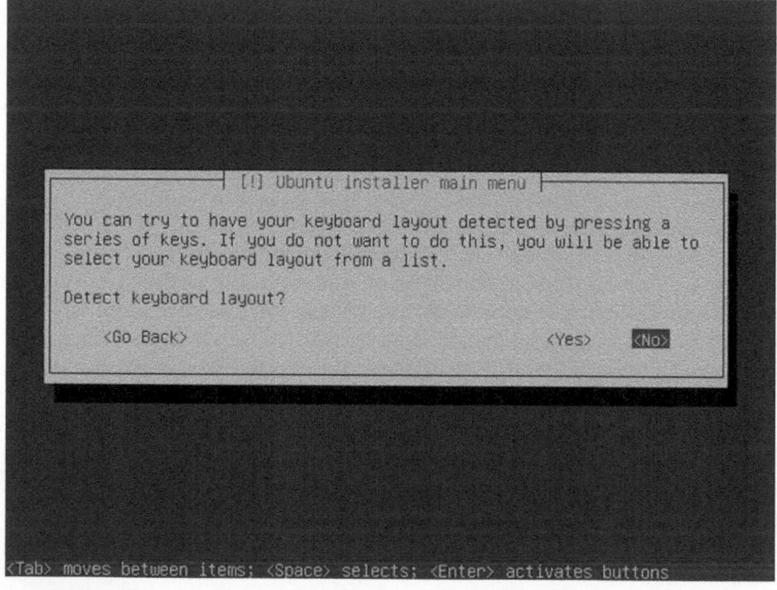

Figure 1.6 Specifying keyboard layout.

When prompted, select the hard drive to partition, and press the **Enter** key. The next page displays the partitions to be created and a warning message that all the data on the selected hard drive will be destroyed if you continue (Figure 1.10).

When asked if you want to write the changes to disks, use the left arrow key to select **Yes,** and press **Enter** to create the partitions.

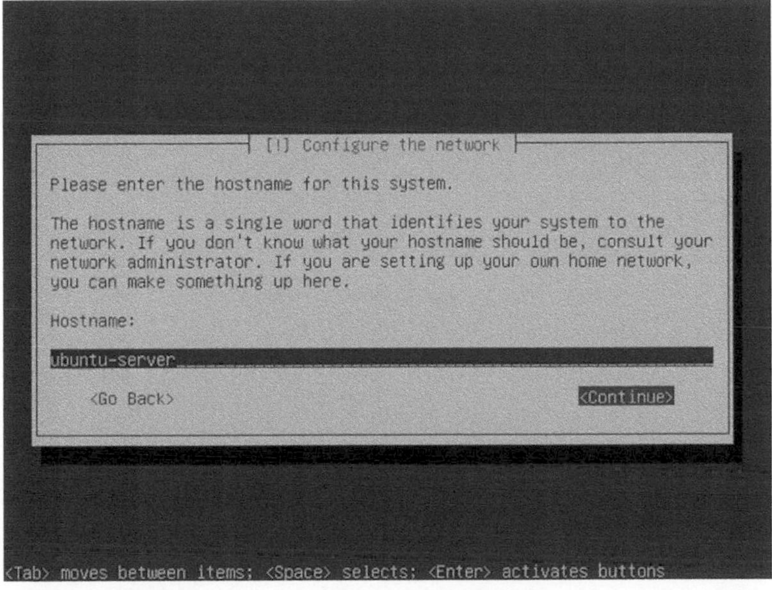

Figure 1.7 Specifying host name.

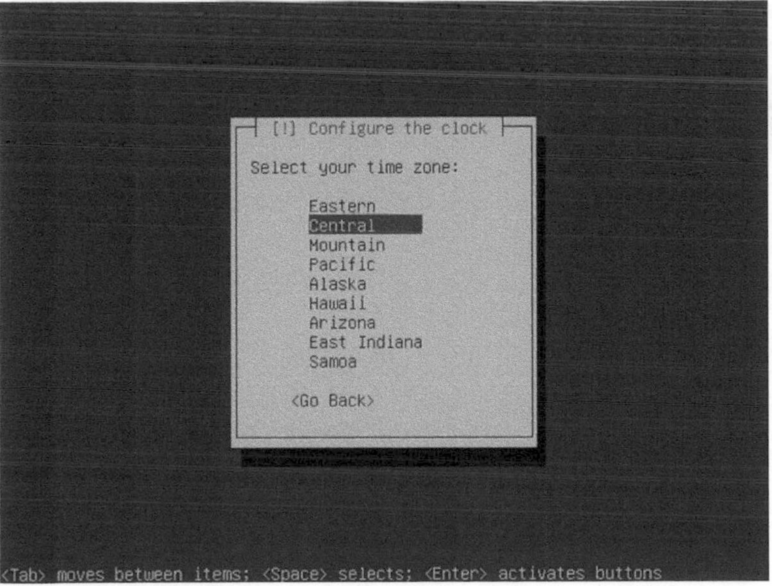

Figure 1.8 Setting time zone.

10. The next page will prompt you to create a new user account. In this example, you can set the full name of the user as **student** (Figure 1.11). Use the **Tab** key to move the cursor to **<Continue>,** and press the **Enter** key. Also, set the username as **student** on the next page.
11. Enter the password **ubuntu** for the user, and use the **Tab** key to select **<Continue>** and press the **Enter** key. Confirm the password by entering it again.

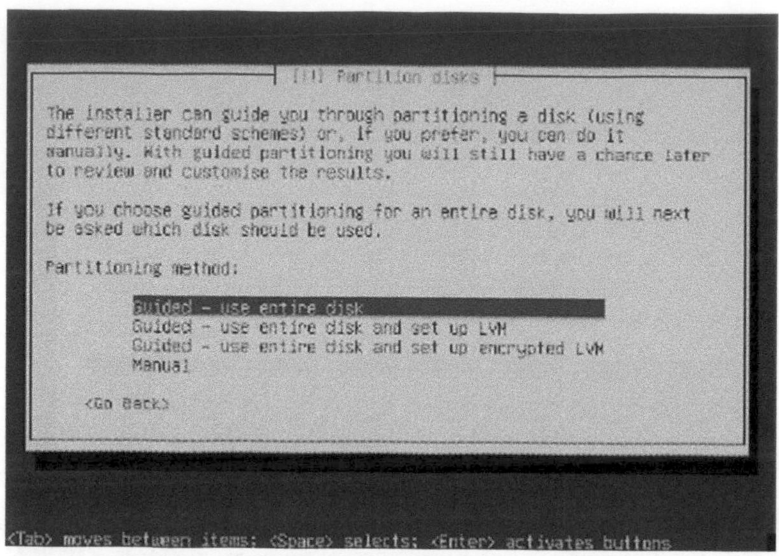

Figure 1.9 Specifying partitioning method.

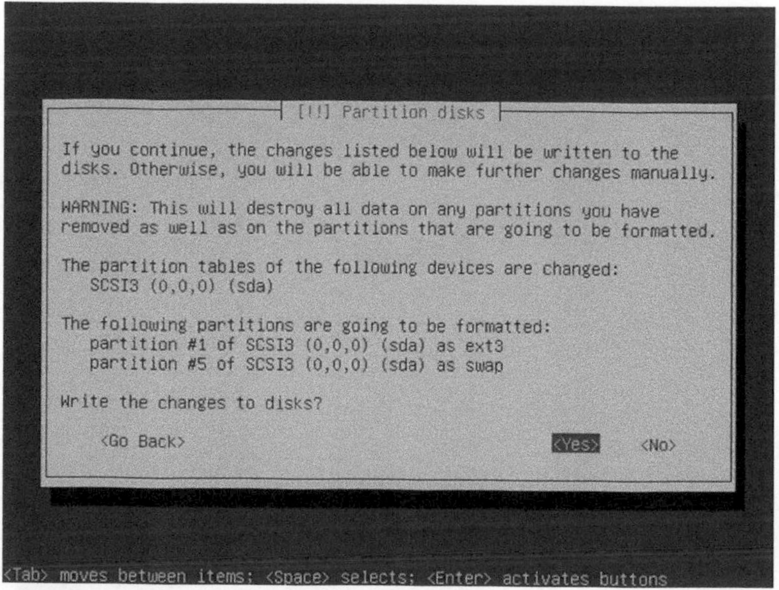

Figure 1.10 Partitions to be created and warning message.

12. The next page asks if you would like to set up an encrypted private directory. Keep the default selection **No,** and press the **Enter** key.
13. The next page asks you to enter the HTTP proxy information. Leave the message blank, use the **Tab** key to select **<Continue>**, and press the **Enter** key.
14. The next page prompts you to make a decision on how to download and install the security update. Use the arrow key to select **Install security update automatically,** and press the **Enter** key.

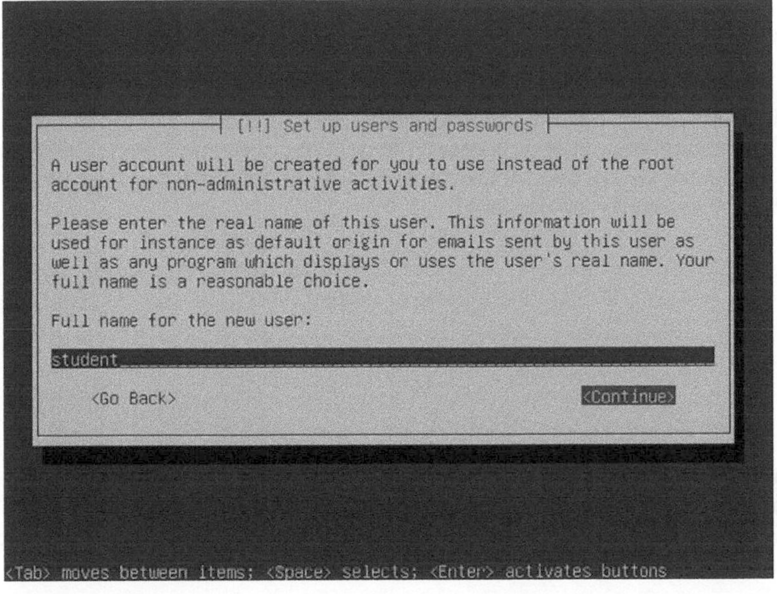

Figure 1.11 Setting username.

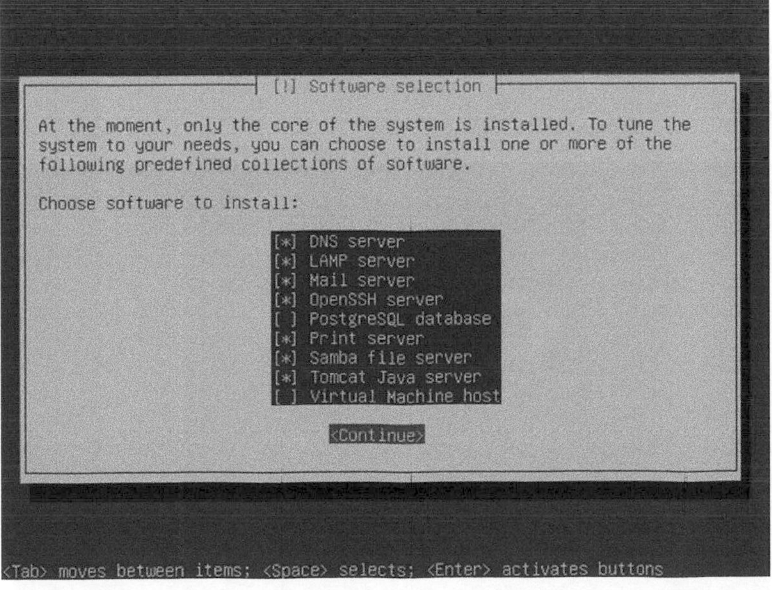

Figure 1.12 Installation of application software.

15. Next, you will be prompted to choose the application software. Use the space bar and arrow key to select the software (Figure 1.12). Then, use the **Tab** key to select **<Continue>,** and press the **Enter** key.
16. If **LAMP server** is selected for installation, you will be prompted to enter the password for the MySQL root account. Enter **ubuntu** as the password for MySQL. If **Mail server** is selected for installation, you will be prompted to specify the type of mail configuration.

Select **Internet Site** for the general type of mail configuration, and press the **Enter** key. On the next page, accept the default system mail name, use the **Tab** key to select **<Continue>**, and press the **Enter** key.

After the installation of the application software is completed, select **Finish the Installation**. Use the **Tab** key to select **<Continue>,** and press the **Enter** key to finish the installation. After the system is restarted, the Ubuntu operating system will be on the personal computer. To log on to the new system, press the **Enter** key to get the prompt for entering the username and password.

17. You can log on the system with username **student** and password **ubuntu**. When prompted to choose between the options **moved** or **copied**, you may want to choose the option **copied**.
18. To log off, execute the command

```
sudo init 0
```

You now have your own computer running Ubuntu Linux Server Edition.

The installation of the desktop edition of Ubuntu is similar. With the help of the GUI tools, the installation is relatively simple. The following are the instructions for installing the desktop edition of Ubuntu Linux:

1. Download the desktop edition of Ubuntu at the Web site http://www.ubuntu.com. Save the downloaded file to a CD or DVD.
2. Insert the Ubuntu desktop edition DVD into the CD/DVD drive. Then restart the personal computer.
3. After the computer restarts, you will be prompted to specify the language. Select **English** and press the **Enter** key.
4. Choose the installation task from the list of options (Figure 1.13). Select the **Install Ubuntu** link to start the installation process.

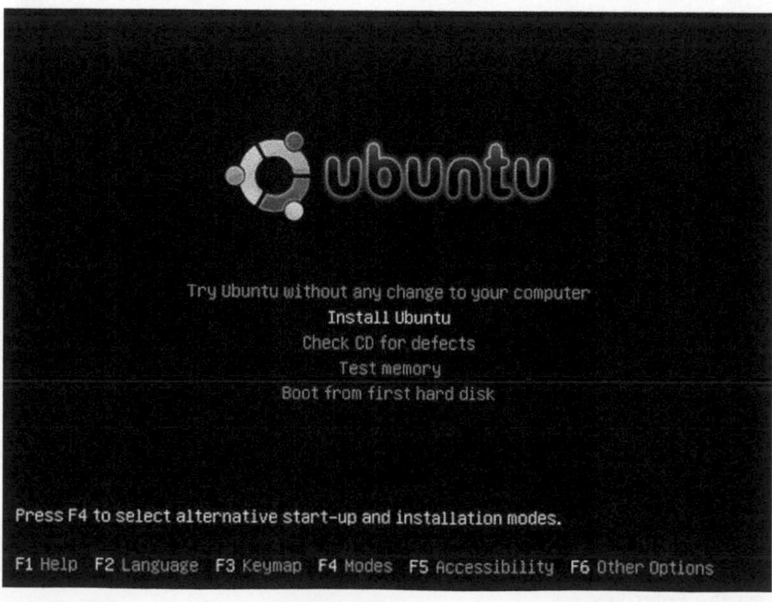

Figure 1.13 Installation of desktop edition of Ubuntu Linux.

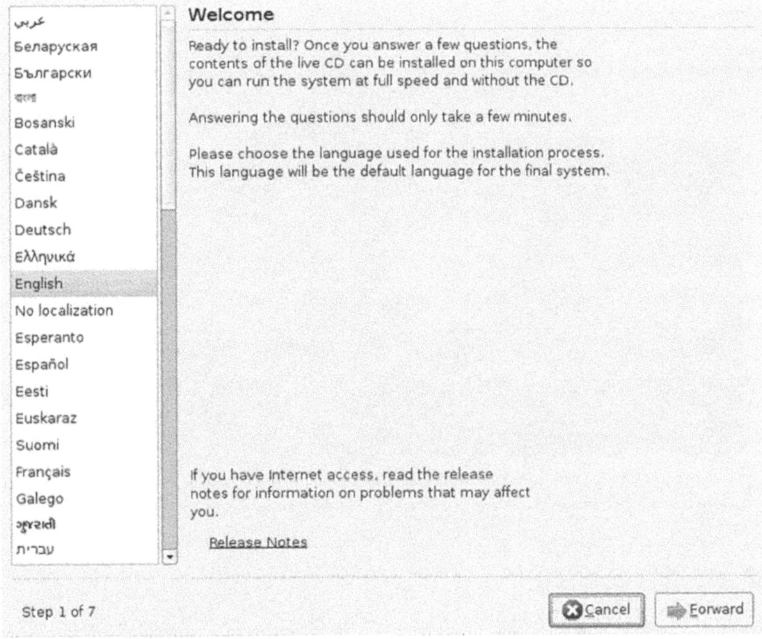

Figure 1.14 Language specification.

5. The desktop edition installation process comprises seven steps. The first step is to specify the language. The default is **English** (Figure 1.14). Accept the default, and click **Forward**.
6. The second step is to determine the time zone. Select a city in your time zone (Figure 1.15), and click **Forward.**
7. The third step of the installation process is to determine the keyboard layout. The default keyboard layout is **USA** (Figure 1.16). Select the keyboard layout of your choice, or simply use the default setting. Click **Forward** to go to the next step.
8. The fourth step is to determine how the hard drive is used for the installation of Ubuntu Linux. You have the choice of using the entire hard drive for installing the operating system, using the largest continuous free space of the hard drive, or configuring the hard drive manually. If you do not want to overwrite the existing operating system and need to have more control over how Ubuntu Linux should use the hard drive space, you may choose to manually configure the hard drive. For the manual configuration, Ubuntu will show you how much free space is available for the installation. If there is not much space available, you can shrink the hard drive space occupied by the existing operating system with the Edit Partition tool provided by Ubuntu Linux. This is a great advantage of Ubuntu Linux. You do not need to purchase another software package for hard drive repartitioning. Once you have enough free space for the installation, you will need to create some partitions to host the file system. The detailed information on manual installation of the Linux operating system can be found in most introductory Linux operating system books. For our hands-on practice, we simply choose to use all of the hard drive (Figure 1.17). Then, click **Forward** to move to the next page.
9. Step 5 is to configure the user account. In this hands-on activity, the username is **student**, the password is **ubuntu**, and the computer name of your choice is shown in Figure 1.18.
10 After clicking the **Forward** button, you will see information about the installation (see Figure 1.19.) This is your last chance to go back to adjust your configuration. If you are satisfied with the information presented to you, click **Install** to complete the installation.
11. After this step, your computer will restart.

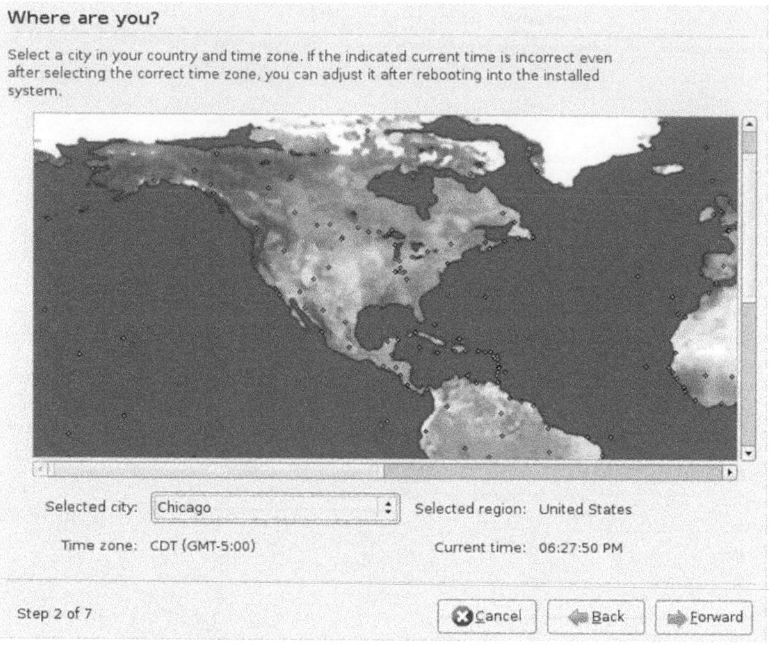

Figure 1.15 Time zone specification.

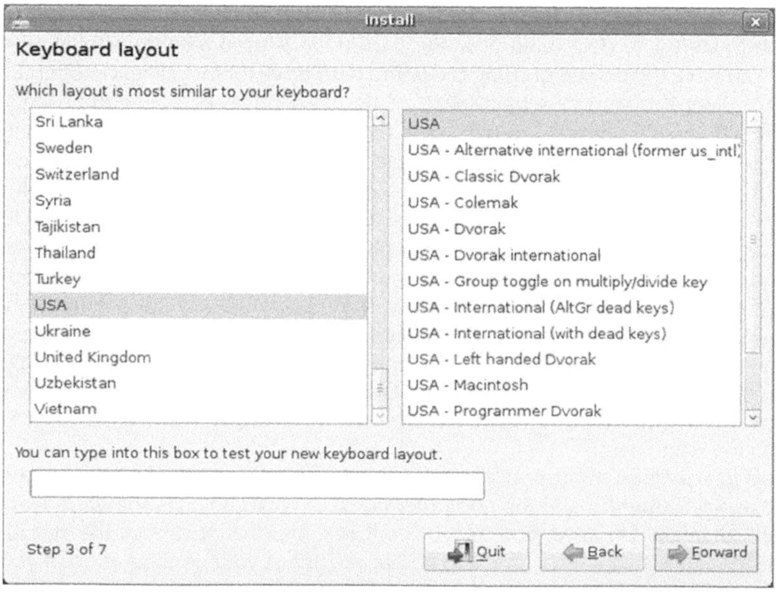

Install

Keyboard layout

Which layout is most similar to your keyboard?

Sri Lanka
Sweden
Switzerland
Syria
Tajikistan
Thailand
Turkey
USA
Ukraine
United Kingdom
Uzbekistan
Vietnam

USA
USA - Alternative international (former us_intl)
USA - Classic Dvorak
USA - Colemak
USA - Dvorak
USA - Dvorak international
USA - Group toggle on multiply/divide key
USA - International (AltGr dead keys)
USA - International (with dead keys)
USA - Left handed Dvorak
USA - Macintosh
USA - Programmer Dvorak

You can type into this box to test your new keyboard layout.

Step 3 of 7

Quit Back Forward

Figure 1.16 Keyboard layout specification.

Figure 1.17 Disk space specification.

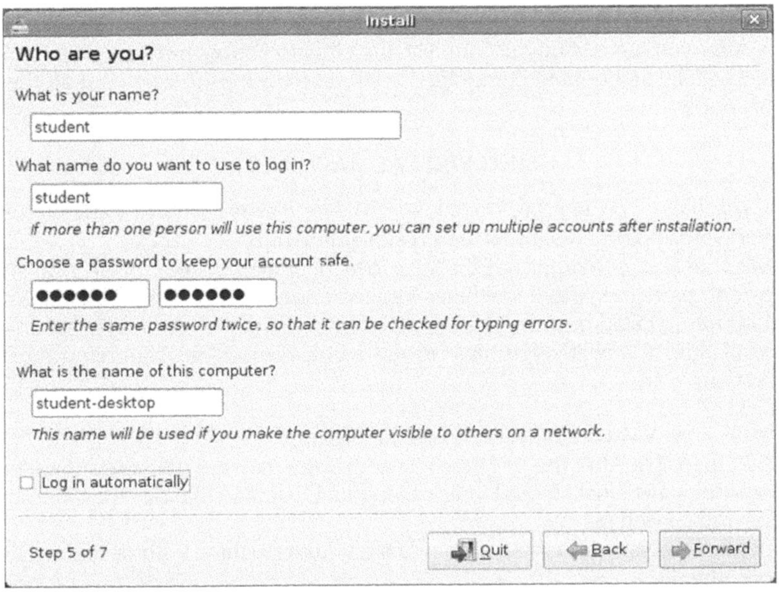

Figure 1.18 User account specification.

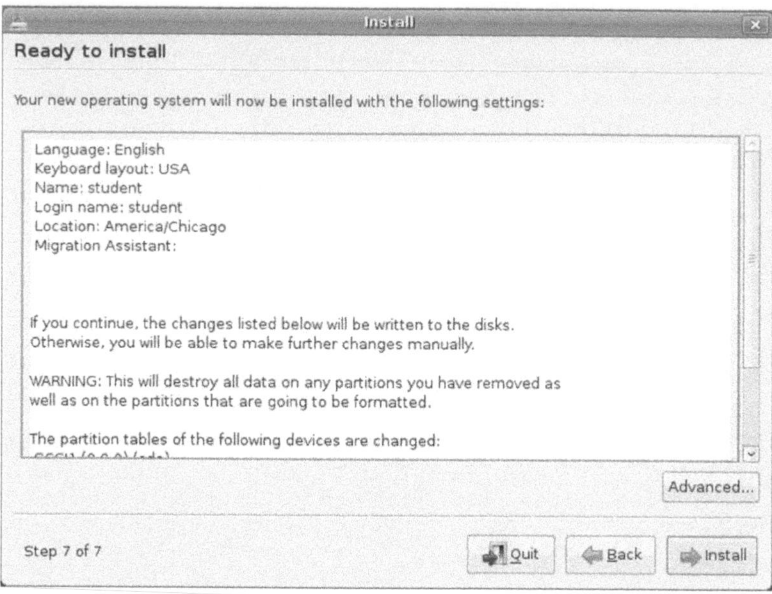

Figure 1.19 Configuration information.

12. After the system is rebooted, you can log on the system with username **student** and password **ubuntu**. When prompted to choose the options **moved** or **copied**, you may want to choose the option **copied**.
13. To log off, execute the command

```
sudo init 0
```

You now have your own computer running Ubuntu Linux Desktop Edition. The foregoing procedure shows that it is relatively easy to install Ubuntu Linux on a personal computer or on a virtual machine. After you successfully accomplish the Ubuntu Linux operating system installation, you will have two fully functioning computers or virtual machines to carry out all the hands-on practice in this book.

USING VIRTUAL MACHINES

To run virtual machines, you need to download VMware Player from the Web site http://www.vmware.com/download/player. Its installation is straightforward.

Assume that your host computer has the Windows operating system. After VMware Player is installed, copy and paste the virtual machines into the folder named Virtual Machines automatically created by the installation process in the Document folder or the folder specified by you during the installation. It is relatively simple to run a virtual machine. The following steps show you how to do that:

1. Double-click the **VMware Player** icon on the desktop.
2. Click the **Open** link. After the VMware Player dialog is opened, find the subfolder that contains the virtual machines. Double-click the virtual machine that has the extension .vmx to start the virtual machine.
3. After a virtual machine is started, log on to the virtual machine with username **student** and password **ubuntu**.

Now, we are ready to begin a grand tour of the available Linux network tools. The hands-on activity in Chapter 2 will explore these tools.

1.4 Book Framework

This section provides an overview of what will be covered in this book and how its content is organized. We will take a look at the concepts and hands-on practice to be covered in each chapter and how the content in one chapter is related to other chapters.

This book includes 12 chapters. Each chapter includes an introduction to the content of that chapter, the main body of the chapter, a summary section, and a review questions section. Each chapter also includes hands-on activities to help readers practice the skills of developing a network for a real-world business.

Chapter 1 introduces the network architectures and the Linux operating system. Two commonly used network architectures, Open Systems Interconnection (OSI) and TCP/IP, are discussed in this chapter. In later chapters, each layer of these network architectures is discussed in more detail. This chapter gives a brief history of the Linux operating system. It introduces several well-known Linux distributions and discusses how Linux is used to support networking. For the hands-on activity, this chapter demonstrates the installation of Ubuntu Linux.

Chapter 2 reviews networking protocols in general. Each layer in the TCP/IP architecture has its own set of protocols to carry out network tasks. This chapter first introduces the commonly known protocols in the layers of application, transport, Internet, and network interface. Then, it examines the relationships among the protocols in each layer and draws a protocol graph to give a bird's-eye view of how the protocols are related. The hands-on activity for this chapter allows readers to explore the tools and services provided by the Linux operating system.

Once readers have learned about the functionalities of the protocols, the next task is to study some basic concepts about network design and development. Chapter 3 first provides information about the types of networks and their features. The second topic discussed in Chapter 3 is about network media used to transmit data in a network. The types of network media and how data is transmitted through the media are discussed in detail. Next, the chapter introduces network devices used by local area and wide area networks. Among the network devices, network interface cards are first discussed. Then, this chapter introduces switches that can be used to link multiple computers in a network. Routers are also explored in this chapter. A router is used to link multiple networks so that computers on different networks can communicate with each other. For hands-on practice, this chapter provides step-by-step instructions to illustrate how to use network tools to configure network interface cards and test network connection.

Building a network at the enterprise level often requires careful design of the future network. Chapter 4 discusses how to design a network so that computers and other network devices can communicate with each other. Chapter 4 deals with the issues on how IP addresses are used to form a network. To design a network that meets the requirements, network modeling is first introduced in Chapter 4. Then, the issues related to the IP address assignment are discussed. Both IPv4 and IPv6 are examined in this chapter. The concepts of subnets are also introduced in Chapter 4. Subnets can make networks more efficient and more secure. This chapter discusses why subnetting is necessary. Then, it covers subnetting theory and IP conversion between the binary system and the decimal system. The calculation of subnet masks, subnet network IDs, and IP addresses for the hosts in a subnet is also taught in this chapter. The next topic is about the method of calculating the number of subnets and the number of hosts in a subnet. For hands-on practice, this chapter explores IPv6 on Linux. With the tools provided by Linux, a simple IPv6 Linux network is built during the hands-on practice.

Once a network is created, it must be supported by various network services. Chapter 5 examines several commonly used network services in more detail. The first topic covered by this chapter is the user authentication service. This chapter shows how user information is stored. Through the first hands-on activity, the chapter illustrates how to create a user account and how to assign privileges to it. Then, this chapter discusses the service that can automatically assign an IP address to a computer or network device as soon as the computer or network device joins a network. The second hands-on activity demonstrates how to implement the DHCP service to automatically assign IP addresses. The next topic is about name services. A name service translates the name assigned to a computer to an IP address, and vice versa. The name service allows computers to be accessed by using names. The third hands-on activity in this chapter implements the DNS service on a private network. A DNS server can be used to search the IP address for a given name, and vice versa.

Chapter 6 is devoted to an important network device, the router. This chapter starts with an explanation of what a router can do. It lists various tasks that can be accomplished by a router. Router-related theories and concepts are introduced. They are used to explain how a router works. Through examples, this chapter demonstrates how a router can dynamically update its routing table and identify optimal routes to destinations. The next topic in Chapter 6 is the construction of a router with tools provided by the Linux operating system. This chapter introduces two methods, static and dynamic, to update routing tables. For the dynamic method, the chapter provides the information about different routing protocols. It also provides hands-on practice in physically creating a router with Linux. A routing protocol is used to implement dynamic routing. In the hands-on practice, Linux routers are used to connect multiple networks and to pass packets from one network to another. The hands-on practice demonstrates how the routing table is updated dynamically.

On an enterprise-level network, network resources are shared by hundreds and even thousands of users simultaneously. Chapter 7 discusses how to share network resources and how to remotely access them. The first topic in this chapter is about NFS services, which allow the hosts on a UNIX like network to share files, directories, and even hard drives. The chapter discusses the installation and configuration of NFS services. The hands-on practice demonstrates how the files are shared by two Linux computers. In an enterprise environment, various operating systems are used on personal computers. To share a network with Windows operating systems, this chapter introduces Samba technology. Through the hands-on practice, readers can access a Linux server from a Windows client and share the files stored on the Linux computer. Next, this chapter illustrates how to set up a virtual private network (VPN) service to allow users to remotely log on to a private network. This chapter provides information about VPN tunneling protocols and various VPN products. It also discusses some VPN configuration issues. The hands-on activities in this chapter include setting up a VPN with the Linux utilities and verifying that one can remotely access the computers on a private network through the VPN. The last topic in this chapter is the Network Address Translation (NAT) service. The chapter describes various NAT applications and explains how the translation can be done. Some NAT configuration issues are also discussed. The hands-on practice shows how to set up a NAT service to allow the computers on a private network to share the same public IP address to access the Internet.

Companies need to extend their business through the Internet. Chapter 8 discusses network issues related to the Internet. The first topic covered in Chapter 8 is the installation and configuration of a Web server and the security measures related to the Web server. The next topic is about FTP services. It deals with the installation and configuration of FTP services. E-mail service is also discussed in this chapter, which includes e-mail server installation, configuration, and management.

Network security is the top concern for any network. Chapter 9 deals with the issues of implementing network security measures with the Linux operating system. It first discusses security-related issues such as security policies, various types of hacker attacks and computer viruses, and commonly used security measures. Then, this chapter introduces some security technologies used to protect private networks and data being transmitted over public networks. Firewall protection is another topic covered in Chapter 9. As part of the hands-on practice, step-by-step instructions on installing and configuring network security software, such as SSL and SSH, and firewalls, are given in this chapter.

Chapter 10 is about network resource management. The first management task is network user account management. It includes command-based and GUI-based utilities for managing users and groups. The development of the directory service with Lightweight Directory Access Protocol (LDAP) is discussed in detail. The first hands-on practice illustrates the development of LDAP for network user authentication. Then, the chapter discusses network device resource management. Issues related to kernel and driver maintenance are explored. The last hands-on activity illustrates the process of customizing the Linux kernel.

Chapter 11 discusses wireless network systems. The topics covered in this chapter include wireless network technologies. Tools for developing wireless networks are also included. This chapter illustrates wireless network configuration. It provides detailed information on Linux-compatible wireless network devices and drivers. Setting up a wireless network is the hands-on practice for this chapter.

Chapter 12 focuses on mobile-Linux and mobile-network-related topics. One of the main topics in this chapter is mobile Linux features and mobile-Linux-related issues such as mobile Linux architecture, kernel, user interface, and utilities for configuring mobile networks. Then, this chapter introduces mobile devices, including PDAs, cell phones, and other mobile devices. The mobile network is another important topic in this chapter. The last hands-on practice demonstrates how to set up a personal computer to run the virtual machine installed with the mobile Linux operating system for supporting applications on mobile devices.

1.5 Summary

This chapter gave an introduction to Linux networking. It first provided an overview of the Linux operating system. It then gave a brief history of Linux. It also provided information about Linux distributions. This chapter reviewed the Linux network architecture. Two abstract network models were introduced in this chapter. It then described the role of Linux in developing network systems. By putting the topics covered by each chapter together, this chapter also outlined the framework of the book.

The chapter showed that Linux is a powerful solution for developing a sophisticated network system. The hands-on practice walked the reader through the process of installing both the server edition and the desktop edition of Ubuntu Linux on two computers. Once the Linux operating system is installed, we are in a position to discover how Linux is used to accomplish various networking tasks.

Review Questions

1. Originally, who developed the Linux kernel and for what platform?
2. Why is GNU/Linux a better name for the Linux operating system?
3. What computing environments do SLES and SLED target?
4. What are the editions provided by Ubuntu Linux?
5. Which Linux distribution has an all-in-one package that includes both the server edition and the desktop edition?
6. Which Linux distribution mentioned in this chapter has one of the first Linux operating systems designed for mobile devices?
7. Describe the application layer in the OSI network architecture.
8. What tasks can be handled by the transport layer in the OSI network architecture?
9. What tasks can be handled by the network layer in the OSI network architecture?
10. What layers in the OSI network architecture are included in the application layer of the TCP/IP network architecture?
11. What layers in the OSI network architecture are included in the network interface layer of the TCP/IP network architecture?
12. What tasks can be accomplished by Transmission Control Protocol (TCP) in the transport layer?
13. In which layer of the TCP/IP network architecture is IP?
14. Network drivers are in which layer of the TCP/IP network architecture?
15. What tasks can be accomplished by the network security tools provided by the Linux operating system?

Chapter 2

Network Protocols

Objectives

- Learn about the protocols used in the TCP/IP architecture.
- Understand the relationship among the protocols.
- Investigate network tools.

2.1 Introduction

As described in Chapter 1, a protocol is the language used by a network for communication. A network uses different protocols to accomplish different tasks. In the later chapters, the concept of network protocols will be mentioned frequently. Before we can create and manage a network, we need to know how these network protocols work, what their responsibilities are, and how they are related. In this chapter, we will take a closer look at these protocols. This chapter first provides the information about each of these protocols in detail. Then, we will investigate how these protocols are related in the TCP/IP architecture. During network operation, Linux provides various tools for managing these protocols. This is why Linux is such a key component in network implementation and management. In the hands-on practice included in this chapter, we are going to investigate the network management tools included in Ubuntu Linux.

In Chapter 1, we have mentioned that a Linux-based network system can be implemented by closely following the TCP/IP network architecture. There are four layers in the TCP/IP architecture: the application layer, transport layer, Internet layer, and network interface layer. Each layer in the TCP/IP architecture includes several protocols that perform certain tasks. In the following, we will introduce the commonly known protocols in each of the layers.

2.2 Application Layer Protocols

The application layer takes care of the communication between application software installed on two hosts on a network, such as a conference call or remote connection of a database server. Protocols included in this layer are used to establish, terminate, and manage the sessions that handle requests and responses between the two hosts. In the application layer of the TCP/IP architecture, protocols also perform tasks such as data compression, data encryption, video streaming, and data format conversion. The commonly known network protocols in the application layer are Hypertext Transfer Protocol (HTTP), File Transfer Protocol (FTP), Dynamic Host Configuration Protocol (DHCP), Simple Mail Transfer Protocol (SMTP), Post Office Protocol version 3 (POP3), Internet Message Access Protocol (IMAP), Telecommunication Network (Telnet), Secure Shell (SSH), Lightweight Directory Access Protocol (LDAP), and Simple Network Management Protocol (SNMP).

To distinguish between the services provided by the protocols and application software, a port number is assigned to a service. For example, HTTP handles the message sent to port 80, FTP works with the message sent to port 21, and MySQL uses port 3306. Linux supports all these application protocols. Detailed descriptions of these protocols follow:

1. *Hypertext Transfer Protocol (HTTP):* HTTP is the protocol used for transferring data between Web browsers and Web servers. It can transfer data in various formats such as text, graphic images, sound, video, and other multimedia files. HTTP has a set of commands that handle how a Web browser requests the data provided by a Web server and how the server responds to the request from the Web browser. HTTP can also handle how a Web browser uploads files to a Web server. For example, to request a Web page, the user enters the Web page URL and presses the enter key, and the Web browser immediately sends an HTTP GET command to the Web server at port 80. After finding the requested Web page, the Web server will return the page to the Web browser. If the user uploads a file to a Web server, an HTTP PUT command will be used by the Web browser. In addition to telling the Web server how to respond to a request from the client, HTTP can instruct the Web server to pass data to other applications or scripts on the server. Web servers use interfaces such as Common Gateway Interface (CGI) and Internet Server Application Programming Interface (ISAPI) to pass data to other applications and scripts.
2. *File Transfer Protocol (FTP):* FTP is a protocol that can be used to exchange files between computers on a network. It can be used to download files from a Web site or upload files to a Web server. Users can use FTP commands to get, put, delete, rename, move, and copy files. If allowed, users are able to access the public file folders hosted by a FTP server through the anonymous account. The file transfer process starts with a request from an FTP client. Based on the client's request, a set of commands is formed. The client request will be forwarded to the FTP server through the port 21, to which the FTP server listens.

   FTP is simple, but has some security and performance problems. FTP transmits files in cleartext, which means that hackers can easily intercept and read the content sent by FTP. To initialize a file transfer, FTP needs to execute several commands, which delays the transfer process. FTP uses different connections to control data transmission; this can also slow down the transmission process. Both HTTP and FTP can be used to transmit files. However, FTP is less appealing owing to its weakness in security and performance.
3. *Dynamic Host Configuration Protocol (DHCP):* DHCP is a protocol that can be used to automatically assign network parameters to a computer or network device. The commonly used

network address parameters are the IP address, the subnet mask, the addresses for the default gateway and DNS server, and so on. Later chapters will provide more information about these parameters. Manually entering these network address parameters for each computer or network device in a large network can be very tedious. DHCP greatly reduces the amount of configuration time spent on these computers and network devices.

Here is how DHCP works. If a client computer is configured to receive network parameters from a DHCP server, during the boot time, it sends out a broadcast message to look for the DHCP server on the same network. After the DHCP server receives the request broadcasted by the client computer on the network, it will offer a set of network parameters to the client computer. Once the client computer receives the offer from the DHCP server, it will respond to the DHCP server with a message accepting the offer. If multiple DHCP servers give offers to the same client computer, the client computer will inform the DHCP servers about which offer has been selected. Then, the chosen DHCP server sends an acknowledgement to the client computer and informs the client computer that it can use the network parameters now.

4. *Simple Mail Transfer Protocol (SMTP):* SMTP is a protocol used by e-mail clients to send messages to e-mail servers. It can also transmit e-mail messages between two e-mail servers. However, SMTP is not used to receive messages from e-mail servers for reading owing to its limited ability to queue messages at the receiving end.

   SMTP is a simple text-based protocol that has only about ten commands, to reduce bandwidth and improve performance. The SMTP client connects to the SMTP server through port 25. As a simple protocol, SMTP has no authentication measure to verify who is sending the message. It is unable to check if the message is sent by the real sender or someone else. To improve security and performance, we can use Enhanced Simple Mail Transfer Protocol (ESMTP), which adds many features for authentication, reducing bandwidth, and error recovery.
5. *Post Office Protocol version 3 (POP3):* POP3 is one of the protocols used for receiving e-mail messages. POP3 can be used to check the mail box on an e-mail server and download e-mail from the server for reading. POP3 does not support sending messages. Most of the e-mail client software and Web browsers include POP3.

   After the e-mail messages are downloaded from the server, they will be removed from the e-mail server, which is a less desired feature of POP3. POP3 uses port 110 for the e-mail information exchange. The disadvantage of POP3 is that it only supports a single inbox and does not support multiple folders on the e-mail server.
6. *Internet Message Access Protocol (IMAP):* IMAP can also be used for receiving e-mail messages. The advantage of IMAP is that it supports multiple folders on the server side. For users who keep a lot of e-mail messages, multiple folders are truly useful in organizing the messages. IMAP also allows users to select which messages to download. IMAP operates on port 143, through which a local client can exchange e-mail messages with an e-mail server.
7. *Telecommunication Network (Telnet):* Telnet can be used to remotely access UNIX and Linux systems, or a network device such as a switch. The Telnet protocol defines how the information can be exchanged between the Telnet server and the client. Telnet does not support a GUI. All the information exchanged through Telnet is in the text format. Once the user logs on to the server, he or she can access the application software or even perform some system administration tasks based on the privilege assigned. Telnet communicates with the server through port number 23. Created in 1969, Telnet is not secure. It transmits data in cleartext. Telnet does not support authentication and encryption measures to secure the

content exchanged on the network. It has been gradually replaced by more secure protocols such as Secure Shell (SSH).

8. *Secure Shell (SSH):* SSH is a network protocol used to securely exchange information on the network. Like Telnet, SSH allows users to log on to a remote host, execute commands, and transfer files. Better than Telnet, SSH supports strong authentication and encryption, which can protect the network from attacks such as IP spoofing or IP source routing. The authentication accepts connection only from trusted hosts. The encryption provided by SSH protects the confidentiality of the data. During transmission, SSH establishes a secure channel between two hosts on the network. By default, SSH uses port 22 for information exchange.
9. *Lightweight Directory Access Protocol (LDAP)*: LDAP can be used to manage the directory service that stores, organizes, and authenticates information about network users and network resources. With LDAP, the network administrator can manage network objects such as users, groups, computers, printers, files, domains, and organization units. The content in the directory service is stored on a tree substructure and is arranged according to the organization's structure. LDAP is often used by other services, such as the Web service and e-mail service for authentication.
10. *Simple Network Management Protocol (SNMP):* SNMP can be used to improve network performance, detect and correct network problems, and monitor network activities. Network operating systems and network management software use SNMP to accomplish network management tasks. SNMP has some commands that can be used to obtain information from network devices and control the behavior of network devices. The information about network devices and software is stored in a management information base (MIB). In the MIB, the names of network objects and information about their locations are stored on a tree structure and are coded in the Abstract Syntax Notation Number One (ASN.1) language. ASN.1 code provides a standard representation of the network objects that SNMP can access. SNMP only has minimum security measures, called SNMP Community Strings, to protect the data being transmitted.

These are just a few application layer protocols. In later chapters, more information will be provided about some of the application layer protocols when we use them. The list of application protocols introduced in this book is by no mean a complete list. There are over 70 protocols in the application layer.

2.3 Transport Layer Protocols

The application layer protocols do not directly contact the application layer on the other end of a network. They directly interact with the protocols in the transport layer. The protocols in the transport layer prepare the network transmission. They break the data to be transmitted into small units called packets. The transport layer protocols also handle tasks such as data transmission error checking, network flow control, and establishing, managing, and terminating a connection between two hosts. They are responsible for processing requests from the application layer and issuing them to the Internet layer in the TCP/IP architecture. The protocols in the application layer communicate through dedicated ports. The transport layer protocols have the ability to identify the ports so that the packets can be delivered to the proper ports of the destinations. Transmission Control Protocol (TCP) and User Datagram Protocol (UDP) are two well-known transport layer protocols.

2.3.1 Transmission Control Protocol (TCP)

TCP is a commonly used core transport layer protocol. The following are some of the features that make TCP such an important protocol:

- *Connection orientation:* TCP accepts the connection request from the application layer protocol and then creates a reliable connection. This feature makes sure that the connection is established and both hosts agree to communicate before sending data.
- *Point-to-point communication:* TCP views the ports as the connection end points.
- *Complete reliability:* TCP guarantees that no data will be lost during the transmission.
- *Full-duplex communication:* This feature allows simultaneous communication in both directions, just like a two-lane road with one lane for each direction.
- *Three-way handshake connection:* TCP uses the 3-way handshake process to initiate and terminate a connection. The 3-way handshake guarantees that the connection is reliable and the termination is graceful.

TCP performs the following tasks in order to support the aforementioned features:

- Dividing the data to be transmitted over a network into small units called packets
- Implementing the 3-way handshake with a 3-packet process to establish and terminate a reliable connection between the ports hosted by two network hosts
- During the transmission process, controlling the flow of packets by using a window mechanism
- Controlling network congestion by determining the proper packet transmission rate based on the network capacity
- Tracking packets and making sure that all the packets arrive at the destination host
- Keeping the transmitted packets in order so that the packets can be reassembled back to the original file
- Computing and verifying the checksum for transmission error detection
- Checking if there are transmission errors and resending the packets that have transmission errors or are lost during the transmission
- Discarding the duplicated packets mistakenly re-sent by TCP

In the next few paragraphs, let us dig a little deeper to see how exactly TCP can get the foregoing tasks done.

The data block to be transmitted over a network will be divided into small units. Packets are used because

- The protocol and hardware involved in a transmission need time to coordinate the transmission.
- When multiple computers share the same network media, these computers transmit packets in turns. The use of packets ensures that each computer gets equal chances to transmit.

Packets are formed by adding additional information to these small data units. In general, besides a data unit, which is called a payload, a packet also includes a header and a trailer. The following briefly describes each component of a packet.

A header includes information about the data to be transmitted and the network to carry out the transmission. It may include the following:

- The source and destination addresses used for delivering a packet to the destination host and for receiving the response from the destination host
- A packet sequence number to identify the packet
- Synchronization bits that can be turned on and off to synchronize network transmission
- A packet type indicator to identify the type of information to be carried by the packet
- The length of the packet that represents the size of the packet

The preceding is the basic information usually included in the header. In practice, the header of a protocol may include more or less information than the foregoing. For a complicated protocol such as TCP, more information is included in the header. The following is a diagram of the TCP header (Figure 2.1). In the diagram, each row represents a unit of 32 binary bits transmitted through a network.

A brief description of each field in the diagram follows:

- Source Port and Destination Port: Identify the end points of a TCP connection.
- Sequence Number: This number is assigned to the outgoing packet. It is used for reordering packets and computing acknowledgement numbers.
- Acknowledgement Number: This number is an increment of the received sequence number and is sent after the sequence number is received.
- Data Offset: This field specifies the size of a TCP header. The minimum size is 20 bytes, and the maximum size is 60 bytes.
- Reserved: This field is reserved for future use.
- Control Bits: This field has six information control bits, including the URG for validating the urgent pointer, the SYN and ACK for establishing a reliable connection, PSH for sending data out, RST for resetting a connection, and FIN for terminating a connection.
- Window: This field specifies the size of the receiving window. The size is determined by the buffer space available for the incoming data.
- Checksum: Checksum is used to check if the header is damaged during the transmission.

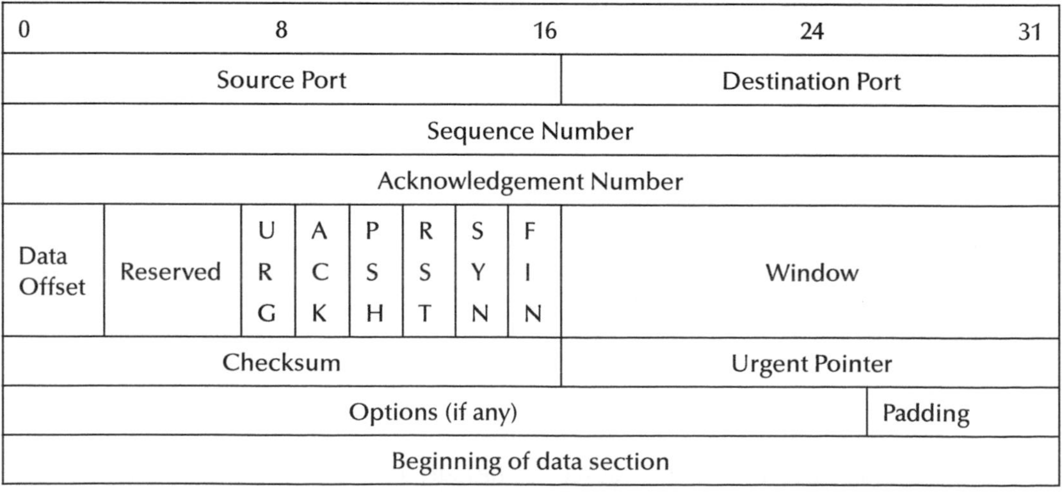

Figure 2.1 TCP header diagram.

- Urgent Pointer: The field contains a pointer that points to urgent data. This field will be processed if the URG control bit is turned on.
- Options: This field specifies various TCP options such as the maximum segment size and the window scale.
- Padding: The padding field is used to create a 32-bit boundary between the header and the data section.

Next to the header section is the data section, which typically contains from 1000 to 1500 bytes of message. The data section is also called the payload or packet body. Depending on the size of the data, the length of the data section may vary. If a packet has a fixed length, the data section will be padded with blanks.

Next to the data section is the packet trailer that indicates the end of a packet. The trailer may also include an error-checking mechanism called cyclic redundancy check (CRC). CRC can be very useful for detecting damaged binary signals or binary bits caused by hardware failure. During transmission, binary signals can be wrongly altered by outside interference. CRC is also good for detecting this type of transmission error.

The implementation of the 3-way handshake is done through a 3-packet process, illustrated in Figure 2.2. The following are steps used by the 3-way handshake process:

- To establish a connection, the 3-way handshake process is begun by Host A, which first sends a packet to Host B with the SYN bit turned on. The turned-on SYN bit indicates that the packet is asking for a connection negotiation. In addition to the SYN bit, the first packet also contains the sequence number, say *x*, called the Initial Send Sequence (ISS), and several network connection parameters. The first packet is sometimes called the SYN packet.
- Once Host B receives the SYN packet, it will return a packet to Host A with both the ACK and SYN bits turned on. The turned-on ACK bit is an acknowledgement of the request for the connection negotiation from Host A. The second packet also contains an

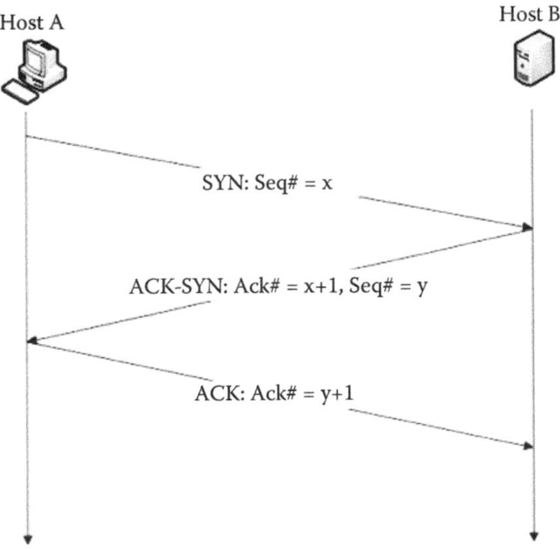

Figure 2.2 Three-way handshake process.

acknowledgement sequence number that equals $x + 1$, another sequence number such as y, and a set of possibly revised network connection parameters. The second packet is also called the ACK-SYN packet.

- Once the ACK-SYN packet is sent to Host A, it will decide if it is going to accept the terms sent by Host B. If so, Host A will return a packet with the ACK bit turned on, and the acknowledgement number is updated to $y + 1$. Once the third package arrives at Host B, the data transmission process can be started.

Similarly, the 3-way handshake process can be applied to the process of terminating a connection. It provides a graceful way to disconnect the communication between two hosts.

When a packet gets lost or delayed, TCP provides a retransmit mechanism to resend the packet. After sending out a packet, TCP on the sender side will wait for the acknowledgement from the receiver. If TCP does not hear from the receiver after waiting for a certain amount of time, it will start its retransmit mechanism. The timeout period is estimated by TCP to adapt to the transmission rate on the network. TCP measures the round-trip time for sending a packet and getting the acknowledgement back. It then calculates the estimated mean and standard deviation of the measures of the round-trip time. The timeout for retransmission can be determined by the following rules:

- When measures of the round-trip time remain close to the mean, the timeout for retransmission can be a time period value that is slightly larger than the mean. In this way, TCP can wait long enough for most of the sending–receiving round trips to complete before retransmission.
- When the measures of the round-trip time vary significantly from the mean, the timeout value can be set as the mean plus twice the standard deviation. Such a timeout period is long enough for 95% of the round-trip transmissions to complete their journeys, and can adapt to various network traffic environments.

After the timeout period is over, TCP assumes that the packet is lost and sends the packet again.

During packet transmission, there could be a situation where the sender sends data in a much faster rate than the rate that the receiver can handle. TCP provides a window mechanism to control the flow of packets so that the receiver is not overwhelmed. Once a connection is established between two hosts, the receiver will create a buffer to store the incoming data. The available buffer is also called the *window*. It is necessary for the sender to adjust the packet transmission rate according to the size of the window on the receiver's side. The notification about the buffer size is also called the *window advertisement*. When the receiver receives the packet from the sender, it will send a window advertisement to the sender with the acknowledgement. Every time the receiver receives a packet, it will recalculate the available buffer size. When the buffer is full, the receiver will send a zero window advertisement to inform the sender to stop sending packets. The sender can start sending data again after the receiver informs the sender with a positive window advertisement.

During packet transmission, packets can be delayed or lost if many packets are crowded in one section of a network. Such a phenomenon is called *network congestion*. When the packets get delayed or lost, TCP's resend mechanism will resend those packets, which will add more traffic on the network. In the end, little or no meaningful communication can be carried out by the network. Such a phenomenon is called *network congestion collapse*. TCP includes several congestion control mechanisms to resolve the network congestion problem. One of the solutions is to adjust the packet transmission rate according to the packet loss rate. When packets get lost or delayed during the transmission, instead of resending all the missing packets immediately, TCP will resend one packet first. If the acknowledgement from the receiver indicates no packet loss during the transmission, TCP will double the retransmission rate. If there is no packet loss during the transmission, TCP will double the retransmission rate again. By doing this, the exponential retransmission rate will quickly reach about half of the advertised window size. After that, if there is still no packet loss, TCP will increase the retransmission rate linearly until the entire retransmission process is complete. In this way, TCP can control how much traffic to add on the network, and reduce the network congestion.

The foregoing discussion has briefly stated how the TCP protocol handles various packet transmission tasks. In addition to TCP, UDP is another important protocol included in the transport layer. A brief discussion of UDP follows.

2.3.2 User Datagram Protocol (UDP)

Similar to TCP, UDP is also a transport layer protocol used to send and receive messages over a network. Unlike TCP, UDP is a protocol that does not provide mechanisms to establish a reliable connection between two network hosts before transmitting packets. Also, it does not provide a transmission error correction mechanism. UDP delivers packets in a connectionless manner, which is a process that resembles the mail delivery. UDP simply sends and receives packets from one port to another port over the network. Although UDP has better performance than TCP, UDP is a less reliable protocol. Therefore, UDP is often used in situations that do not require guaranteed delivery, such as broadcasting messages over the network. It can also be used in network applications and services that require fast and efficient message exchange. UDP is commonly used in network applications and services such as online games, Trivial File Transfer Protocol (TFTP), and Domain Name System (DNS). UDP is also the protocol used to transmit data for streaming media applications such as Voice-over-IP (VoIP) and IP Television (IPTV).

In the foregoing, two main transport layer protocols, TCP and UDP, are introduced. In addition to TCP and UDP, there are a few dozen other less known transport layer protocols. If necessary, we will look at some other transport layer protocols in later chapters. In the TCP/IP architecture, the transport protocols handle service requests from the application protocols and issue the service requests to the protocols in the Internet layer. In the next section, we will discuss the protocols in the Internet layer.

2.4 Internet Layer Protocols

The Internet layer is the interface between the transport layer and network interface layer. The protocols in the Internet layer process requests from the protocols in the transport layer and issue the service requests to the protocols in the network interface layer. The protocols in the Internet layer are used to deliver packets from a source host to a destination host across a network. The well-known Internet layer protocol is the Internet Protocol (IP), which is a core protocol in the TCP/IP architecture. On a network, information exchange is carried out by the IP protocol. Another significant Internet layer protocol is the Internet Control Message Protocol (ICMP) used by network operating systems to get responses from remote hosts. The Address Resolution Protocol (ARP) relates an IP address with its hardware address, and IP Security (IPSec) is for securing IP communication. This layer also includes various Internet routing protocols such as the Open

Shortest Path First (OSPF) protocol, Routing Information Protocol (RIP), and Border Gateway Protocol (BGP).

2.4.1 Internet Protocol (IP)

IP provides the fundamental delivery service. It uses a connectionless method to deliver packets. With connectionless delivery, IP does not use the 3-way handshake to create a reliable connection from end to end. It also does not provide the mechanism to control the transmission flow and check transmission errors. IP relies on TCP to provide the connection-oriented service to accomplish these tasks. IP formats packets, called Internet packets, so that these packets can be delivered across the Internet. The Internet packet is also called a *datagram*. Two versions of IP, IPv4 and IPv6, are used on the Internet.

IPv4 is the current version of IP, which is widely deployed for delivering data across the Internet. IPv4 uses a 32-bit binary number to specify the address for each network host. This means that IPv4 can identify at most 2^{32} = 4,294,967,296 network devices uniquely. However, not all the 32-bit numbers are available for identifying hosts. Some of these numbers are used for identifying networks, for broadcasting in different networks, and for multicasting. As the number of hosts on the Internet grows exponentially, we are facing a shortage of numbers that can be allocated by IPv4 to address the hosts on the Internet. Because IPv4 is also a data-oriented protocol, it is not able to provide specific paths for transmitting audio and video signals. In many ways, IPv4 is not very efficient. For example, IPv4 broadcasts messages over the entire network to contact an unknown host instead of focusing on a small group of hosts that possibly include the potential receiver.

The limitations of IPv4 have stimulated research into and deployment of IPv6, which is the next-generation IP protocol. IPv6 uses 128-bit binary numbers to identify the hosts on the Internet. The set of 2^{128} binary numbers is large enough to avoid running out of host identification numbers for many generations to come. IPv6 is also designed to be able to establish an optimized path to transmit the audio and video signals over the Internet. IPv6 can also simplify the network configuration and management tasks.

The general format of an Internet packet is shown in Figure 2.3.

The header in Figure 2.3 contains information for sending data across a network. The amount of data that can be sent by an Internet packet may vary depending on the specification of an application. For IPv4, the maximum size of an Internet packet is 64K bytes, including both the data and the header.

Because IP is designed to carry data across the Internet, it must be able to deliver a packet through heterogeneous networks. To accommodate heterogeneity, IP must accomplish the following tasks:

- Format packets with an addressing scheme.
- Pass data from one network to another network.
- Fragment packets into smaller packets to pass through the networks that have low data transmission rates, and reassemble the fragments at the ultimate destinations.

Header	Data Section

Figure 2.3 General format of Internet packet.

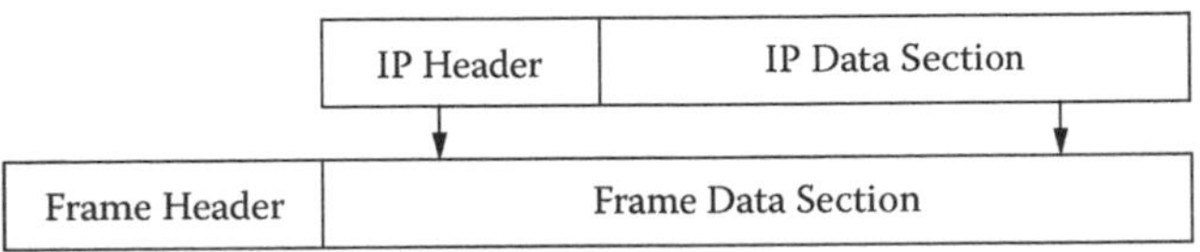

Figure 2.4 Encapsulation of IP datagram.

To deliver packets across the Internet, IP must format the packets with destination addresses so that it will know where to deliver them. Also, to get a response from the receiver, IP must format a packet with the sender's address, called the *source address*. The address of each host on the Internet must be unique. Both the source and destination addresses are included in an IP packet in the form of IP addresses. An IP address is assigned to each network device, such as a network interface card, by the network administrator.

A frame is a packet formed by a specific network hardware technology in the network interface layer. Different types of networks form different types of frames. Frames are used to carry Internet packets, or datagrams, through different types of networks. The process of loading a datagram to a frame is called *encapsulation*. Figure 2.4 illustrates the encapsulation process.

If the destination host is located within the same network, the frame will carry the datagram to its destination. On the other hand, if the destination host is located on a different network, the frame can only carry the datagram to the border between two networks, where the datagram will be reloaded to a different type of frame formed by another network and continue its journey. In this way, the datagram can be carried through different types of networks.

To deliver data across the Internet, a datagram may need to travel through several networks to get to the destination. Each network has its own specification of the value of the maximum transmission unit (MTU). The MTU refers to the maximum amount of data that a frame can carry. It may happen that the MTU of a network in the middle of the delivery path is less than that of the network to which the sender belongs, so the amount of data originally loaded by the sender is too much to be carried by the frame formed by the network with the lower MTU. In this case, the originally loaded data will be divided into smaller units so that the amount of data in each unit is less than that specified by the MTU. The process of dividing the data into small units is called *fragmentation*. The header of each fragment is so constructed that all the fragments can be reassembled into the original datagram. Because the fragments are transmitted through different routes to the ultimate destination, it is difficult to reassemble them in the middle of the delivery path. Therefore, the fragments are reassembled at the ultimate destination.

An IP header is constructed in such a way that it can accomplish the foregoing tasks. Figure 2.5 shows how the IP header for IPv4 is constructed.

The following briefly describes some of the fields in the IP header structure:

- H. Len: This field specifies the length of the IP packet header. The header contains a minimum of five words, and each word consists of 32 bits. Therefore, the smallest IP header contains 20 bytes of information.
- Type of Service: This field is used to specify whether a datagram passes through a route with the minimum delay, the maximum throughput, the maximum reliability, or the minimum cost.
- Total Length: This field contains the length of a datagram, including both the header and the data.

<table>
<tr><td>0</td><td>4</td><td></td><td>16</td><td>19</td><td>31</td></tr>
<tr><td>Version</td><td>H-Len</td><td>Type of Service</td><td colspan="3">Total Length</td></tr>
<tr><td colspan="3">Identification</td><td>Flags</td><td colspan="2">Fragment Offset</td></tr>
<tr><td colspan="2">Time To Live</td><td>Protocol</td><td colspan="3">Header Checksum</td></tr>
<tr><td colspan="6">Source IP Address</td></tr>
<tr><td colspan="6">Destination IP Address</td></tr>
<tr><td colspan="5">IP Options (if any)</td><td>Padding</td></tr>
<tr><td colspan="6">Beginning of Data Section</td></tr>
</table>

Figure 2.5 IP header structure.

- Identification: This field is used to identify the datagram to which the fragments belong. Together with the source address, the value in the identification field can be used to reassemble the original datagram.
- Flags: The value in this field is used to set and display fragment-related properties.
- Fragment Offset: This field is used to instruct the receiver how to reassemble a fragmented datagram.
- Time to Live (TTL): This field contains a number that represents the lifetime of a datagram. Each time a datagram passes a network, the lifetime number will be reduced by one. When the lifetime number is decremented to zero, the datagram is discarded. TTL can be used to prevent a datagram from traveling in a loop formed with several networks.
- Protocol: This field specifies the protocol to be encapsulated.
- Header Checksum: This field contains an IP header checksum that is used to check whether the bits in the header have been altered during the transmission.
- Source Address and Destination Address: These two fields contain the sender's and receiver's IP addresses.
- Options: This field specifies various IP options, such as MTU replay and experimental flow control.
- Padding: This field is used to create a 32-bit boundary between the header and the data section.

In the preceding text, we briefly discussed the tasks that can be accomplished by the protocol IP and the IP header structure. In the TCP/IP architecture, TCP and IP are the core protocols. These two protocols are often used together and are denoted as TCP/IP. The Internet layer also includes several other protocols, which will be introduced next.

2.4.2 Internet Control Message Protocol (ICMP)

ICMP is the protocol used to report network operation status and errors. The following are some of the tasks that can be accomplished by ICMP:

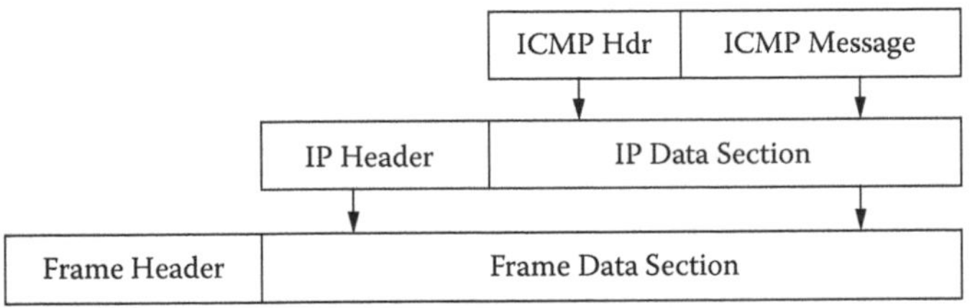

Figure 2.6 Internet Control Message Protocol (ICMP) encapsulation.

- Report network status: ICMP can be used to carry the reply for an echo request message back to the sender. ICMP can also be used to report how packets are redirected to different networks.
- Report network errors: ICMP can be used to report network problems; for example, a host, a port, or a network is unreachable. ICMP also carries the network parameters that indicate a network is not functioning properly.
- Report network congestion: When a receiving device on a network cannot process the received data fast enough, ICMP will deliver a Source Quench message to the sender for adjustment. ICMP can also be used to detect the MTU of a network. It will carry the response to a MTU probe back to the sender.
- Assist network troubleshooting: A network management command such as ping uses ICMP to test if a packet can be sent to a dedicated destination. ICMP can also report the round-trip time and the percentage of packet loss during the transmission. The command tracer-oute uses ICMP to provide a report about the networks the packets have passed through. The report also includes the TTL value. When TTL drops to zero, ICMP will return the "time expire" message.

ICMP uses an IP datagram to carry a message through different networks. To deliver an ICMP message, a network device creates an IP datagram first and then encapsulates the ICMP message in the IP datagram (Figure 2.6).

2.4.3 Address Resolution Protocol (ARP)

ARP is another commonly known protocol in the Internet layer. ARP resolves the IP address used by an IP packet to the hardware address (also called MAC address) used by a frame packet. To deliver an IP packet to the destination specified by the destination IP address included in the header of the IP packet, the destination IP address needs to be converted into the destination hardware address used by a frame. When the frame reaches the destination network, each host in the network compares its hardware address with the destination hardware address included in the frame. If there is a match, the frame will be processed by the destination host. It is crucial to resolve the IP address to the hardware address correctly. Otherwise, the frame will not be able to find its destination.

There are several ways to resolve IP addresses to hardware addresses. One commonly used address resolution scheme is called *message exchange*, which can be accomplished in three steps. When a host needs to resolve an IP address, it will first broadcast a message to ask which host has the hardware address that is related to the IP address. All the hosts in the destination network will

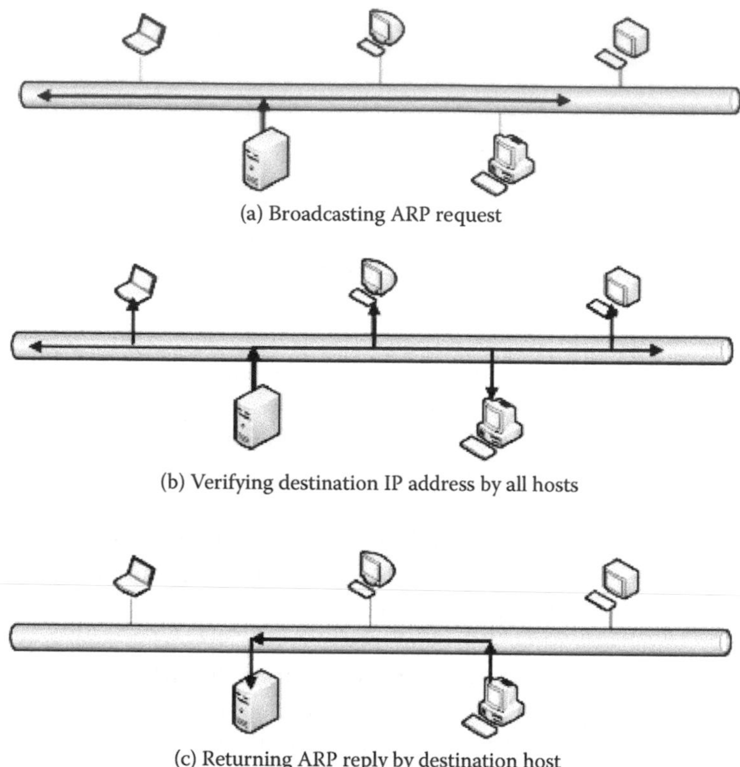

(a) Broadcasting ARP request
(b) Verifying destination IP address by all hosts
(c) Returning ARP reply by destination host

Figure 2.7 Message exchange process.

receive the broadcasted ARP request. After a host finds the match in the IP address, it will respond with an ARP reply that contains the corresponding hardware address to the host that issued the ARP request. After the ARP reply arrives, the host that issued the ARP request will place the hardware address in the destination address field in the header of the frame to be sent to the destination host. Then the frame is ready to be sent. Figure 2.7 illustrates the three-step process.

As a protocol, ARP determines how address resolution messages should be formatted and how to handle the resolution messages. To make ARP more efficient in resolving IP addresses to hardware addresses, the host operating system saves the mapping of IP address and hardware address pairs in a cache. Next time, if a host needs to resolve an IP address to a hardware address, it will search the cache first. If there is no match in the cache, then the host will start the message exchange process.

2.4.4 IP Security (IPSec)

While traveling across a network, an IP packet can be read by unauthorized individuals or intentionally altered by hackers. IPSec is a set of protocols that provides authentication, encryption, and a digital signature mechanism for securing TCP/IP communication. IPSec authentication makes sure that the computers or network devices on both ends of a communication path are trusted. It also hides the IP address after a secure connection is established. IPSec encryption makes the content carried by IP packets unreadable. Even if the IP packets are captured by hackers during the transmission, the hackers will not be able to get the content. The IPSec digital signature can make sure that the content of an IP packet has not been altered during the transmission. IPSec is an Internet layer protocol and, therefore, it can protect the protocols in the transport layer and application layer so that those protocols do not have to have their own protection. IPSec can also work with security protocols such as SSH in the layers above the Internet layer. The disadvantage of IPSec is that it slows down the traffic on a network.

2.4.5 Internet Routing Protocols

The Internet layer includes several Internet routing protocols such as Routing Information Protocol (RIP), Open Shortest Path First (OSPF) protocol, and Border Gateway Protocol (BGP). These protocols are used to create and update routing tables, which store information about the routes from one network to other networks on the Internet. The routing protocols can also be used to calculate the best path from one network to another and advertise routes for dynamic routing.

BGP is the protocol used to manage the routing table, which contains the information about autonomous systems, each of which includes networks that adopt the same routing policy. Each Internet service provider (ISP) may create its own autonomous system. BGP is often used by ISPs to establish routing among themselves. The Internet routing protocol that manages routes among autonomous systems is also called Exterior Gateway Protocol (EGP). If an Internet routing protocol is used within an autonomous system, it is called Interior Gateway Protocol (IGP). BGP supports many functionalities to accomplish the routing tasks. The following are some of them:

- BGP is a type of EGP as well as IGP.
- BGP allows the sender and receiver to negotiate routing policies.
- BGP uses TCP for updating the routing table. Therefore, BGP is reliable.
- BGP can define an autonomous system as a transit system that allows network traffic to pass through or as a stub system that blocks the network traffic to be delivered through the autonomous system.
- BGP dynamically updates neighboring autonomous routing tables.
- BGP can be used to program routing policies and route filters.
- BGP allows users to inject specific routes into the routing table.

RIP is a commonly used Internet routing protocol within an autonomous system. RIP is a simple protocol and requires very little configuration. However, updating routing tables by RIP takes a lot of network resources. Therefore, RIP is usually used in small projects or for educational purposes. The following are some of the RIP features:

- RIP is used as IGP.
- RIP uses UDP to exchange messages, which is faster but less reliable.
- RIP does not check transmission faults and errors while updating routing tables.
- RIP uses broadcasting to update routing tables, which takes less effort. On the other hand, using broadcasting for updating routing tables is less efficient.
- RIP measures the distance of a route by counting how many networks the route traverses. RIP can measure up to 15 networks. This feature makes RIP a protocol that updates routing tables locally.
- To update the routing tables hosted by servers or network routing devices on a network, every 30 seconds, each RIP broadcasts a packet that contains a complete routing table for

other routing tables to update themselves. Broadcasting a routing table every 30 seconds can significantly slow down the network's performance if the network contains many routing tables and each routing table has a large number of items. Therefore, RIP is not designed for large networks.

The Open Shortest Path First (OSPF) protocol is also an Internet routing protocol used within an autonomous system. OSPF is designed to handle the routing needs of large companies and ISPs. The OSPF protocol has the following features:

- OSPF is used as IGP.
- Its hierarchical structure allows it to handle the updating of large numbers of routing tables. It can divide a large autonomous system into areas and allow the updating of routing tables within each area. The use of areas can significantly reduce the size of routing tables.
- It uses Dijkstra's algorithm to calculate the shortest path inside each area. The criteria of the shortest path can be specified by the network administrator.
- It can efficiently assign IP addresses to networks and the hosts in a network.
- It provides the authentication mechanism to secure the routing table information exchange.
- It can import routes created by other routing protocols.
- It uses multicasting within an area for updating routing tables. Multicasting is more efficient than broadcasting.
- When exchanging messages for updating routing tables, OSPF only sends what has been changed in a routing table to other routing tables in an area for updating their table content. Changes are sent only when they occur, not every 30 seconds.

The foregoing features show that the OSPF protocol is a more sophisticated Internet routing protocol. The disadvantages of OSPF are that it requires more computing power, and it takes more time for one to learn how to configure the protocol.

2.5 Network Interface Layer Protocols

The network interface layer contains protocols that are implemented by combining the hardware and software. Some textbooks split the network interface layer into two layers. One is the network interface layer that contains protocols that form frames and the other is the physical layer, which includes the network hardware. Here, hardware such as a network interface card and software such as a network device driver are combined into a single network interface layer. More than a dozen protocols and network technologies are included in this layer. The commonly used protocols and network technologies in the network interface layer are Point-to-Point Tunneling Protocol (PPTP), Layer 2 Tunneling Protocol (L2TP), Point-to-Point Protocol (PPP), Ethernet, Wireless Fidelity (Wi-Fi), Worldwide Interoperability for Microwave Access (WiMAX), network interface card, twisted-pair cable, optical fiber, electromagnetic radio wave, and more.

The network interface layer converts packets into raw binary bits and transfers the bits across the network media. The bits are then organized into code words and converted into physical electronic signals. The physical signals are transmitted to the destination host linked by the network media. At the destination host, these physical electronic signals are reorganized into packets for protocols in the upper layers to process. Although many protocols in the network interface layer do not check for transmission errors, some of the protocols in this layer may have the mechanism to verify if the physical electronic signals have been correctly transferred to the destination:

1. *Point-to-Point Tunneling Protocol (PPTP):* PPTP is a protocol that supports virtual private network connections. PPTP was jointly developed by several companies such as Microsoft, 3COM, US Robotics, and others. Linux has supported PPTP since the release of its version 2.6.14 kernel in 2005. One of the advantages of PPTP is that it is simple to configure. By using PPTP, users can securely remotely access their companies' or universities' network devices and computers through the Internet. PPTP provides both user authentication and encryption to secure communication on the Internet. There is some concern that PPTP only authenticates users but not network devices and computers involved in a VPN connection. This means that the end points of the VPN connection may not be truly authenticated. For better security, one can consider using L2TP.
2. *Layer 2 Tunneling Protocol (L2TP):* L2TP is used to carry insecure traffic over the Internet. It can also be used to support the virtual private network (VPN) connection. The data to be transmitted are encapsulated into L2TP packets. L2TP does not provide an encryption mechanism. To protect data confidentiality, L2TP uses IPSec for data encryption. An L2TP packet is encapsulated into an IPSec packet and transmitted over the public Internet. The disadvantage of L2TP/IPSec is that it requires more configuration. Both the VPN client and server need to be configured to use the IPSec authentication. On the other hand, L2TP/IPSec improves authentication by providing both user-level and computer-level authentication.
3. *Point-to-Point Protocol (PPP):* PPP is a protocol commonly used for transferring Internet packets over a serial link such as a telephone line or an optical link. The TCP/IP protocols do not work well over a serial link. Therefore, PPP is designed for this purpose. This protocol is used by ISPs to connect their customers to the Internet through dialup services. It provides error checking and authentication mechanisms.
4. *Ethernet:* Ethernet is a network interface layer technology for transmitting data over the network media. Ethernet technology has two components. The first component specifies the format of the frames to be transmitted across a network. The frames are used to carry IP packets across the network media. The second component defines the wiring and signaling standards. In an Ethernet network, network media such as cables are designed to follow Ethernet standards. The network hardware used to connect to the cables, such as cable plugs and network interface cards, are also designed to follow Ethernet wiring and signaling standards. Ethernet technology is widely used in wired networks. In recent years, wireless technology has been increasingly using Ethernet. Originally, the transmission rate supported by Ethernet technology was 10 Mbps. Ethernet technology has been improving, and Fast Ethernet supports 100 Mbps transmission rate. Gigabit Ethernet technology can support the transmission rates of up to 1000 Mbps. Recently, 10G Gigabit Ethernet has become available. All these Ethernet technologies share the same frame format, so they communicate with protocols in the Internet layer in the same way.
5. *Wireless Fidelity (Wi-Fi):* Wi-Fi is a protocol used for short-distance wireless communication. It is commonly used in local area networks, cordless phones, video games, and so on. Wi-Fi network interface cards or other Wi-Fi network devices are commonly installed in laptop computers and mobile devices. Through radio waves, computers and mobile devices can communicate with access points, which typically provide local area network and Internet access services. Wi-Fi access points are available in many public locations such as student dormitories, restaurants, airports, and hotels. Wi-Fi technology makes networking more

flexible, and it can reduce network deployment cost by avoiding the cabling process. The main disadvantages of Wi-Fi are the short communication range, lower performance than the wired network, and some security concerns.

6. *Worldwide Interoperability for Microwave Access (WiMAX):* WiMAX is a wireless communication protocol. It is known for its efficient use of bandwidth, better ability to prevent interference, and higher data transmission over longer distances. It can cover an area of 50 km radius. It is designed to be able to download data at the rate of 75 Mbps and to upload data at the rate of 25 Mbps.

   There are two types of WiMAX: fixed WiMAX and mobile WiMAX. Fixed WiMAX technology is used to provide Internet access to residents. Fixed WiMAX does not support mobile devices. Mobile WiMAX technology provides both fixed and mobile services. It is in its initial deployment stage.

7. *Network interface card (NIC):* This is one of the technologies included in the network interface layer. Physically, one side of an NIC is connected to a computer bus, and the other side is connected to a network medium. A computer bus is an array of wires with a connector on each end of the bus. The computer bus shared by different electrical devices is used to transmit electric signals from one device to another device. Through NICs, frames can be passed on to network media such as copper wire, fiber-optic cable, or radio waves for wireless networks. Each NIC has a unique serial number and is often used as the hardware address.

   During the transmission process, after a frame is formed, the CPU sends it through the computer bus and informs the NIC to transmit the data. The NIC handles all the details of frame transmission and reception, such as accessing network media and sending electronic signals. During the receiving process, the CPU allocates buffer space in memory and tells the NIC to read the incoming frame. The NIC waits for all the parts of the frame to arrive and verifies the checksum. If there is no error, the NIC will compare the destination address in the received frame with its own hardware address. If there is a match, the NIC will inform the CPU to process the frame and make a copy of the frame in memory. If the hardware address does not match the destination address, the received frame will be discarded. The interaction with the CPU is handled by the network card driver, which is either installed with the operating system or installed by a network administrator manually. Logically, in TCP/IP architecture, the network card driver is the interface between the Internet layer and the network interface layer.

8. *Twisted-pair cable:* This is a type of wire that is used to transmit electronic signals to the destination host. A pair of insulated copper wires is twisted together to form this kind of cable so that it can minimize the electric interference. The use of copper wire is due to its low resistance to electric currents.

9. *Optical fiber:* Optical fiber is a type of flexible glass fiber that can be used to transmit data to a remote destination. To transmit data over optical fiber, the sender converts the data into light pulses and transmits light pulses by using a light emitting diode (LED). When the light pulses reach the destination, a phototransistor detects them and converts them into electric current. The receiver converts the electric current into data. Compared with copper wire, optical fiber has the following advantages:
   - Optical fiber transmits light, which is not susceptible to electric interference.
   - Optical fiber can transmit light pulses much faster than copper wire can transmit electric signals.

- Optical fiber can transmit data over much longer distances than copper wire because a light pulse suffers very little degradation during long-distance travel.
- Light can be encoded with much more information than electric current.

The disadvantage of optical fiber is that it is difficult to install and repair.

10 *Electromagnetic radio waves:* Electromagnetic radio waves can be used to transmit data over the air. The sender and receiver do not have to be physically wired. The transition is done between antennae. The radio waves can be converted into binary signals, or vice versa. Different types of mobile devices use different sections of radio wave frequencies. For example, Wi-Fi uses frequencies between 2.4 and 5.6 GHz. The higher the frequency, the faster the transmission rate.

The preceding text briefly introduced some of the network interface layer protocols and technologies. Frames are formed in this layer and are transmitted over the network media in raw binary bits. The network interface layer is responsible for transferring data between two hosts in a network and interacting with the protocols in the Internet layer. In the next section, we will take a closer look at how these protocols relate to each other.

2.6 Network Protocol Graph

Before we get into the details of network construction, let us overview how network protocols are related in the TCP/IP architecture. To help the reader get a birds eye view of relationships, a protocol graph will be displayed in this section to illustrate how the protocols are related.

The protocols in the application layer are used to perform tasks to handle requests or responses for applications. These protocols run on the top layer of the TCP/IP architecture, and they cannot travel through a network by themselves. To get to a destination host in a network, a message in an application layer protocol needs to be chopped into small units and carried by another protocol to the destination. To reach the destination host, one also needs protocols such as TCP to create a connection between two hosts on the network. Also, there are many protocols at each layer of the TCP/IP architecture. They may be related to different protocols in the neighboring layers. Figure 2.8 illustrates the relationships among these protocols.

As shown in Figure 2.8, when a client sends a request to a server for certain information or activities by using an application layer protocol, the request will be passed on to a transport protocol such as TCP. Then, TCP will establish a reliable connection to the port dedicated to the application on the server. Most of the application protocols interact with TCP. Some protocols such as SNMP and DHCP run on UDP. IP specifically formats the Internet packets and delivers them to the destination host across the Internet. IP itself does not create the connection to a remote host. IP relies on TCP to establish the connection and control the data flow. IP uses ICMP to get error messages from remote hosts. On the other hand, protocols such as ICMP and ARP use IP to transport messages. To deliver an Internet packet or datagram, IP depends on the protocols or technologies in the network interface layer. For example, to transmit an Internet packet across an Ethernet network, the Internet packet will be carried by the frame formed by Ethernet technology. The frame is then converted by a network interface card to binary signals that are transmitted by electric currents, light pulses, or electromagnetic radio waves to the remote destination. Once the binary signals reach the destination host, the network interface card will verify the destination

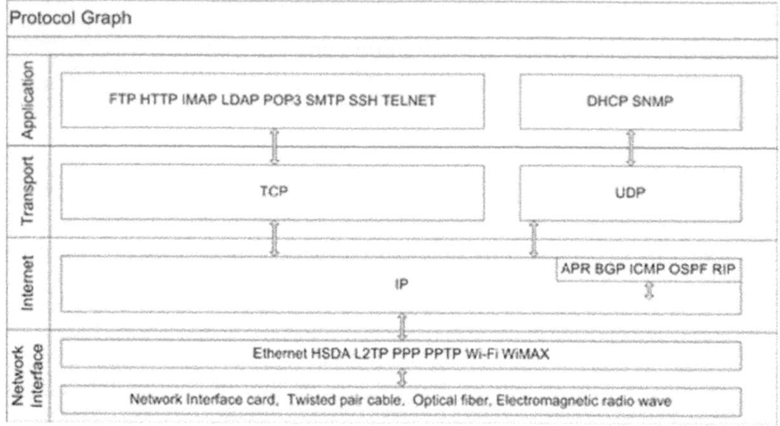

Figure 2.8 Protocol graph.

Table 2.1 Communication Ports

Application Layer Protocol	*Port Number*	*Transport Layer Protocol*
FTP	21	TCP
HTTP	80	TCP
IMAP	143	TCP
LDAP	389	TCP
POP3	110	TCP
SMTP	25	TCP
SSH	22	TCP
Telnet	23	TCP
DHCP	67	UDP
SNMP	161	UDP

address with its own hardware address. If there is a match, the binary signals will be reassembled to get the Internet packet back. At the destination, TCP will perform error checking and decide if a resend is necessary. After the request is sent to the server, the TCP on the server side picks up the request and forwards the message to the protocol related to the application server program through the corresponding port. Table 2.1 lists the port numbers used by the application layer protocols to communicate with the transport layer protocols mentioned in Figure 2.8.

In the foregoing text, we have investigated the relationships among some commonly used protocols in each layer of the TCP/IP architecture through a graph. Most of these protocols are supported by Linux. In the next section, we will examine some network tools and services provided by Linux.

Activity 2.1 Exploring Network Tools and Services

In Chapter 1, we installed Ubuntu. In this lab activity, we will explore some of the networking services and tools provided by Ubuntu. Before beginning the exploration, we assume that two virtual machines are created, one for the desktop edition of Ubuntu and the other for the server edition. The two editions may be installed on two different computers.

Ubuntu provides tools and services for accomplishing the following tasks:

- Configuration of wired network connection
- Configuration of wireless network connection
- Configuration of mobile broadband connection
- Configuration of DSL connection
- Configuration of e-mail client
- Network management

Let us begin with the computer on which the desktop edition of Ubuntu is installed. This computer is also referred to as the client machine. In the following, we will start with the tools for configuring network interface cards.

CONFIGURATION OF WIRED NETWORK CONNECTION

Our first task is to explore the GUI network configuration tool for a wired connection. To do so, follow these steps:

1. Start the client machine, and log on to it with the username **student** and password **ubuntu**.
2. After you have logged on to the client machine, on top of the screen, click the **System** menu, **Preferences**, and then **Network Configuration**.
3. The Network Connections dialog opens. This dialog includes five tabs, each of which is used for a specific type of network configuration task. The types of network connections that can be configured in this dialog are wired, wireless, mobile broadband, VPN, and DSL.
4. Click the **Wired** tab. You will see two links, Auto eth3 and Auto eth2 (Figure 2.9). eth2 and eth3 are the names of two network interface cards on the client machine.
5. Under the Wired tab, click the **Auto eth2** link. To edit the configuration of eth2, click the **Edit** button to open the Editing Auto eth2 dialog shown in Figure 2.10. You can see the MAC address (hardware address) of the network interface card and the setting for Maximum Transmission Unit (MTU).
6. Click the **IPv4 Settings** tab to get the dialog shown in Figure 2.11. As indicated in Figure 2.11, the client computer gets its IP address automatically from a DHCP server.
7. Click the **Method** drop-down list, and select **Manual**. As shown in Figure 2.12, you will be prompted to enter the network connection configuration for the client machine, including the following:
   - The IP address for the client machine under the Address tab
   - The netmask for the network where the client computer is located
   - The IP address for the Gateway used to access other networks
   - The IP address of the Domain Name System (DNS) server that is used to resolve IP addresses from host names, and vice versa
   - The name of the search domain that includes a set of network resources such as applications, users, network devices, and so on

The concepts of netmask, gateway, DNS, and domain will be discussed later in other chapters. Now that we have explored the GUI network configuration tool for a wired connection, click the **Cancel** button to quit.

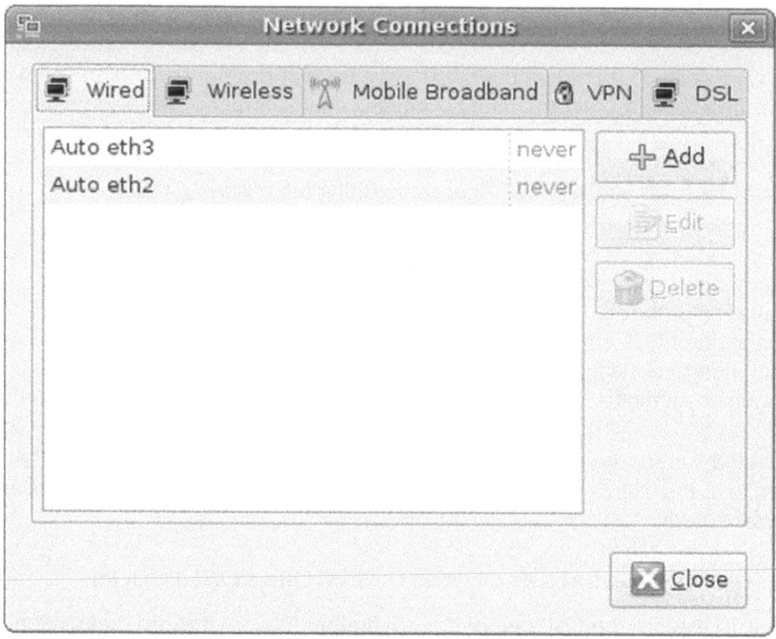

Figure 2.9 Configuration of wired connection.

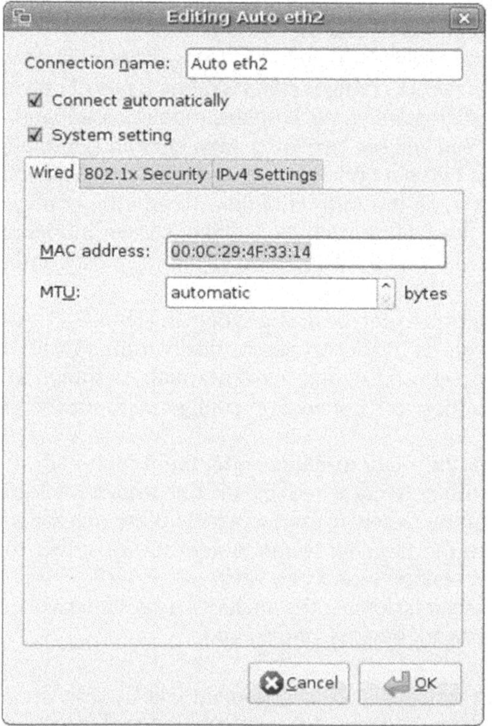

Figure 2.10 Settings of wired connection.

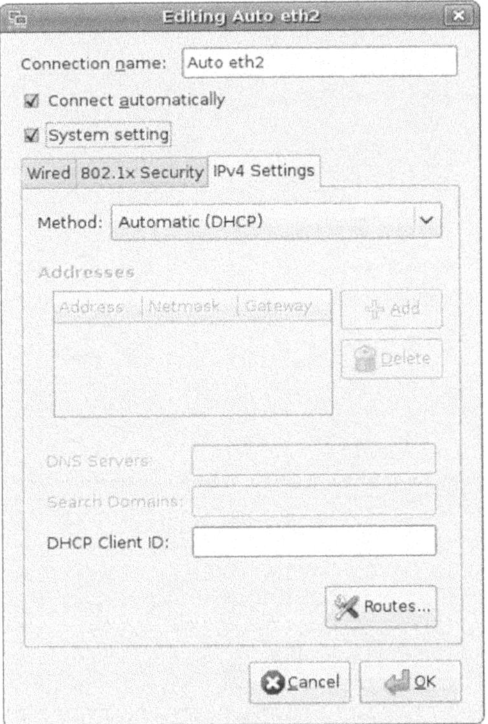

Figure 2.11 IPv4 setting for wired network connection.

CONFIGURATION OF WIRELESS NETWORK CONNECTION

Our next task is to explore the GUI network configuration tool for a wireless connection. To do so, follow these steps:

1. Click the **Wireless** tab (Figure 2.13) in the Network Connections dialog. Under the Wireless tab, you can find the configuration of wireless network connections. If your computer has a Linux-compatible wireless network interface card, it will show up under this tab.
2. Click the **Add** button to open the Editing Wireless connection 1 dialog shown in Figure 2.14.
3. As shown in Figure 2.14, you are prompted to enter information about the following items:
   - The wireless Service Set Identifier (SSID)
   - The wireless network service mode
   - The Basic Service Set Identifier (BSSID)
   - The MAC address
   - The setting for Maximum Transmission Unit (MTU)

Now that we have finished our exploration of wireless connection configuration, click **Cancel** to exit. Terms such as SSID, wireless network service mode, and configuration of wireless network connection will be discussed in later chapters.

CONFIGURATION OF MOBILE BROADBAND CONNECTION

Our next task is to explore the GUI network configuration tool for a mobile broadband connection. To do so, follow these steps:

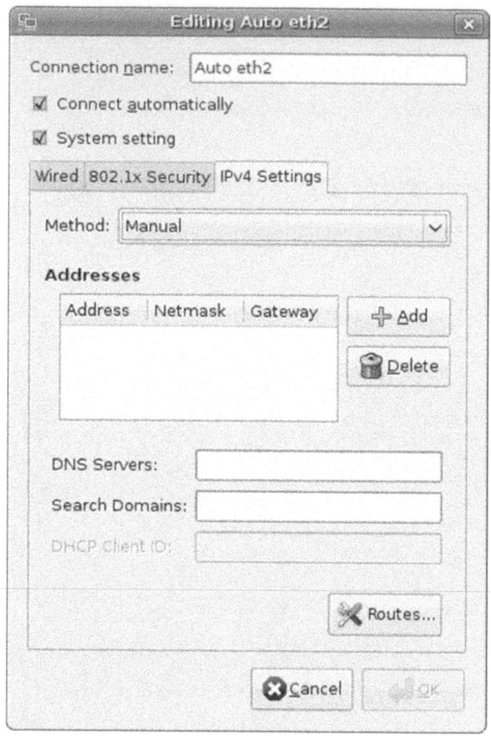

Figure 2.12 Manual configuration of network connection.

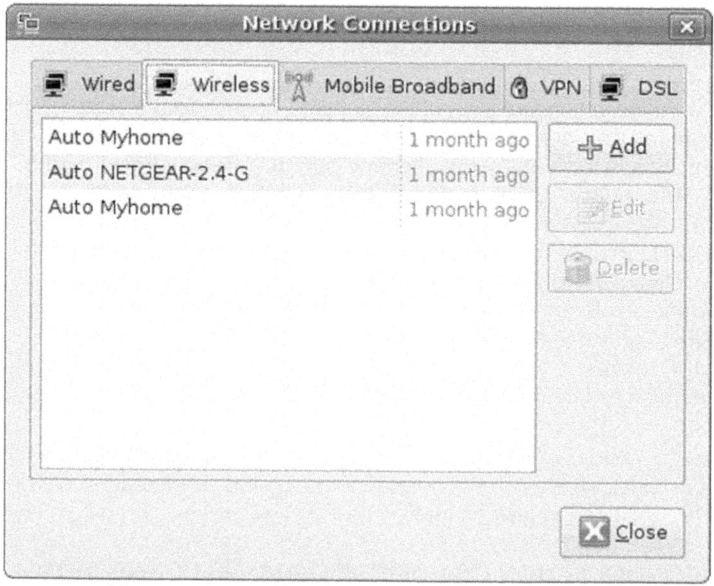

Figure 2.13 Configuration of wireless connection.

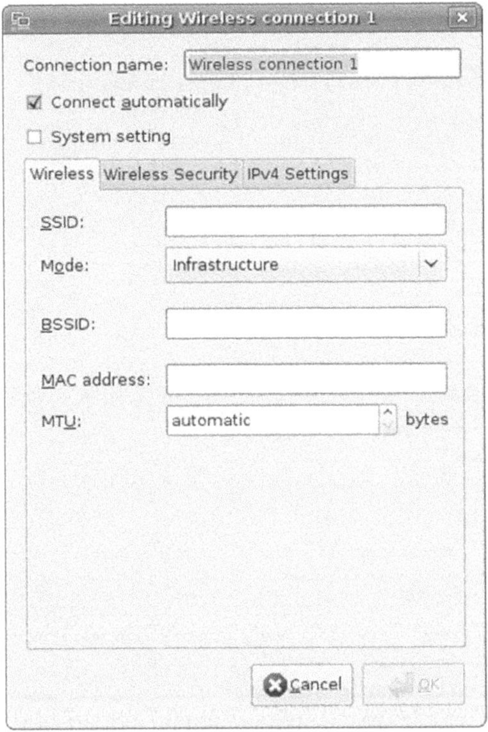

Figure 2.14 New wireless connection specification.

1. Click the **Mobile Broadband** tab. Under the Mobile Broadband tab, click the **Add** button to start the New Mobile Broadband Connection wizard.
2. Click the **Forward** button on the Welcome page to go to the Service Provider page shown in Figure 2.15. You should be able to see some mobile broadband service providers' names listed on this page.
3. Select **T-Mobile (Internet),** and click the **Forward** button to go to the Summary page. Click the button **Apply** to specify T-Mobile as the service provider (Figure 2.16).
4. Click the **Edit** button. Under the Mobile Broadband tab, you can configure the user account (Figure 2.17).
5. Click the tab **Point-to-Point Protocol (PPP).** PPP is a protocol used for transmitting packets over a serial line that connects the modem to an ISP for a dial-up connection. This dialog allows you to configure the settings for authentication and data compression (Figure 2.18). Click **Cancel** after you finish the exploration.

CONFIGURATION OF DSL CONNECTION

Our next task is to explore the GUI network configuration tool for a DSL connection to access the Internet. To do so, follow this instruction:

> Click the **DSL** tab. As shown in Figure 2.19, you will be prompted to enter the DSL account information. Click **Cancel** when you finish the exploration.

CONFIGURATION OF E-MAIL CLIENT

E-mail is one of the applications on the client side. The e-mail client packages commonly used by users of Ubuntu desktop computers are Evolution and Thunderbird. The e-mail client software can

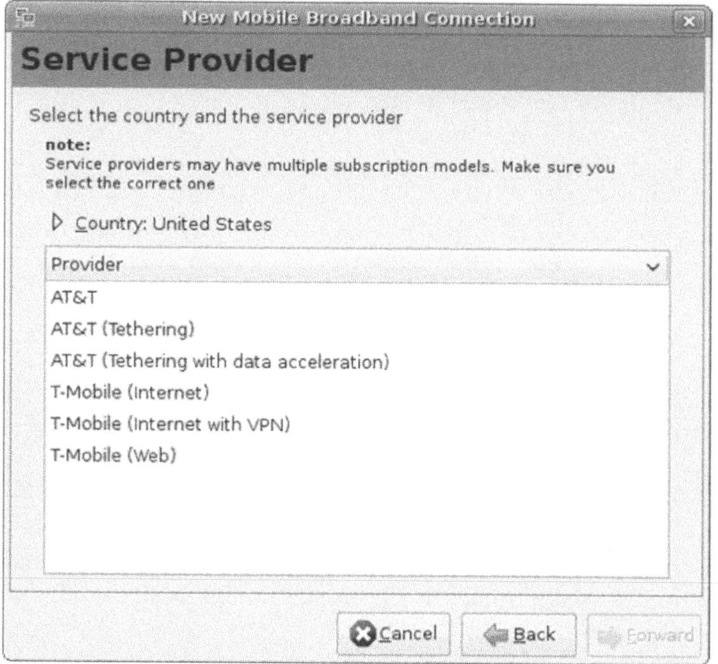

Figure 2.15 Configuration of service provider for mobile broadband.

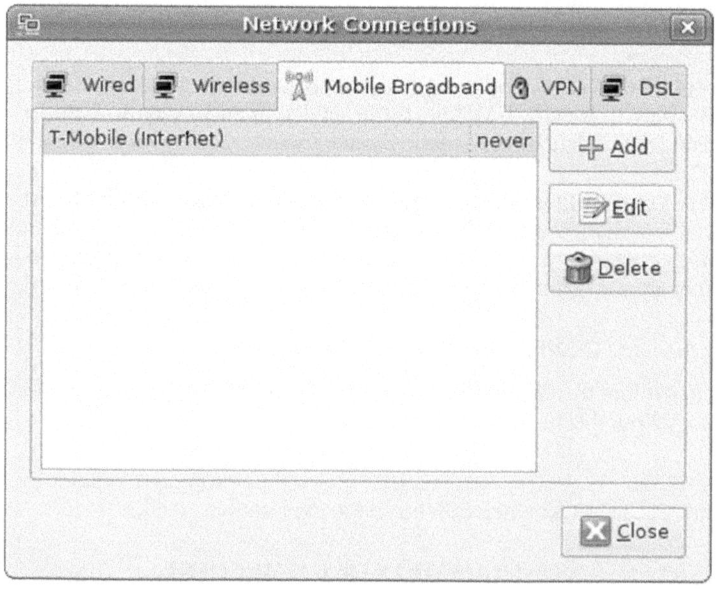

Figure 2.16 Specified mobile broadband service provider.

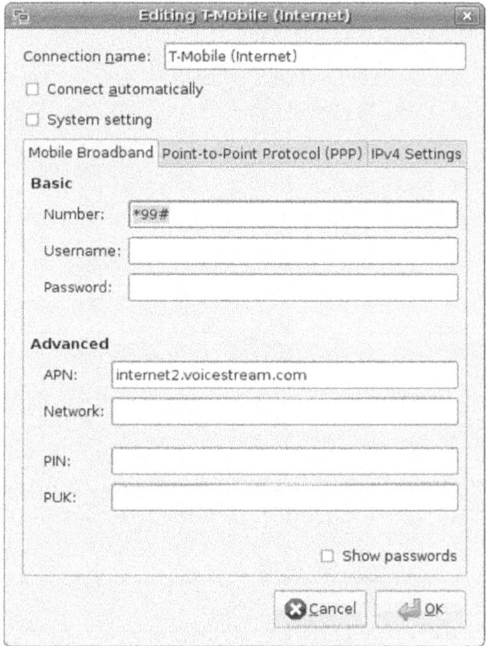

Figure 2.17 Configuration of user account for mobile broadband.

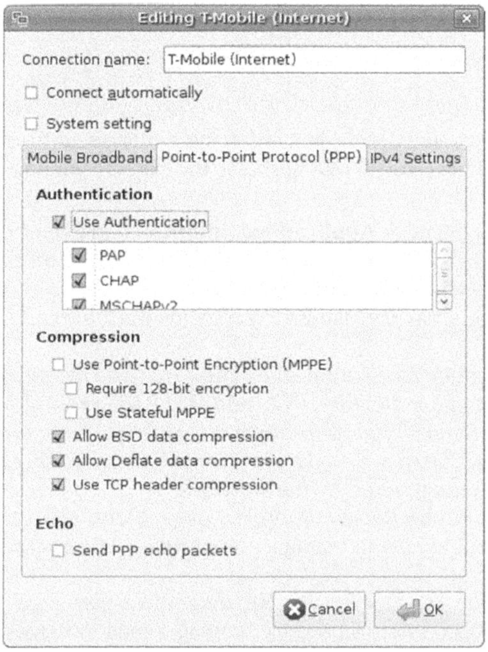

Figure 2.18 Configuration of PPP for dial-up connection.

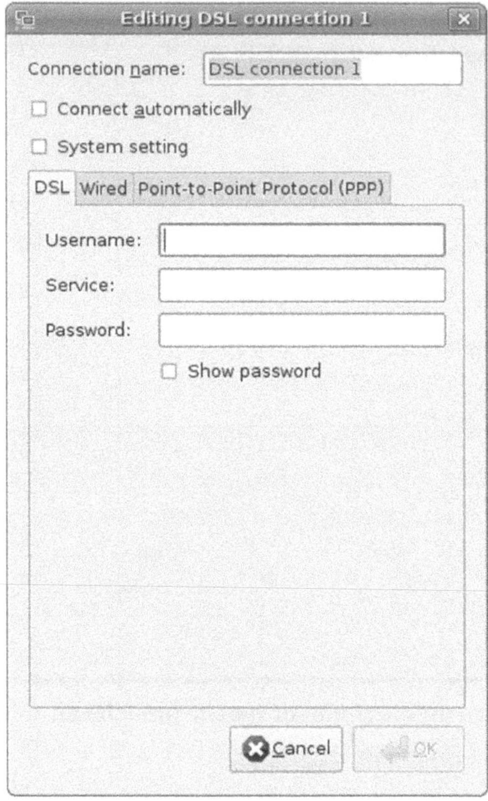

Figure 2.19 Configuration of DSL connection.

be used to manage e-mail accounts, including enforcing e-mail security, organizing e-mail folders, and setting up e-mail accounts. The following shows the steps for setting up an e-mail account:

1. To start the e-mail client, click **Applications**, **Internet**, and **Evolution Mail.**
2. On the Welcome page, click the **Forward** button. You will be prompted to restore from the backup. On this page, click **Forward** again.
3. On the Identity page shown in Figure 2.20, enter the username and e-mail address for identification.
4. After entering the identity information, click **Forward** to go the Receiving Email page shown in Figure 2.21. As mentioned earlier, POP and IMAP are protocols used to receive e-mail. Select **POP** from the Server Type drop-down list, and enter your e-mail server such as **plus.pop.mail.yahoo.com**. You may also decide if e-mail messages should be encrypted or if the password should be remembered by the software.
5. Click **Forward** to go to the Receiving option page. Here, you can specify how to check new e-mail messages and how to manage e-mail storage. Check the option **Leave messages on server.**
6. Click **Forward** to go to Sending Email page shown in Figure 2.22. As mentioned earlier in this chapter, the protocol SMTP is used for sending e-mail messages. Therefore, select **SMTP** in the Server Type drop-down list. In the Server text box, enter **plus.smtp.mail.yahoo.com** as

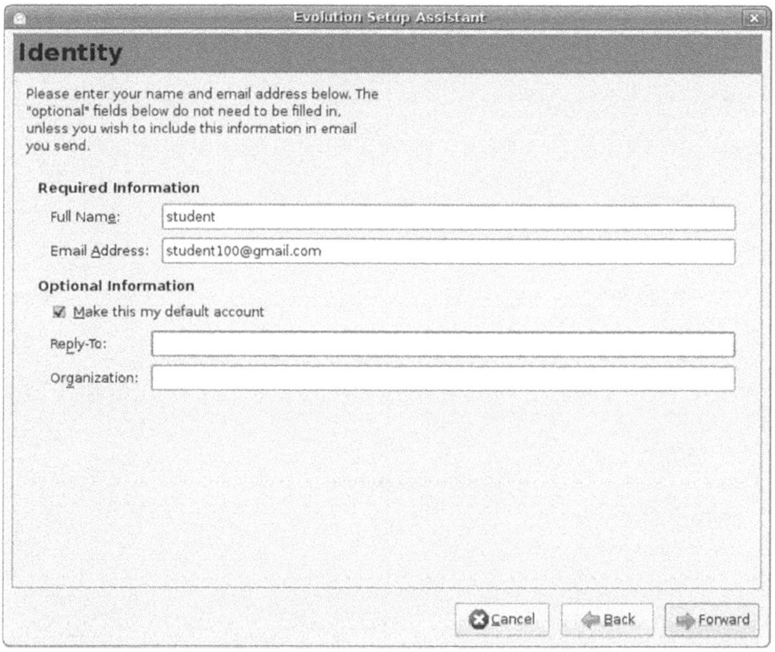

Figure 2.20 Configuration of e-mail identity.

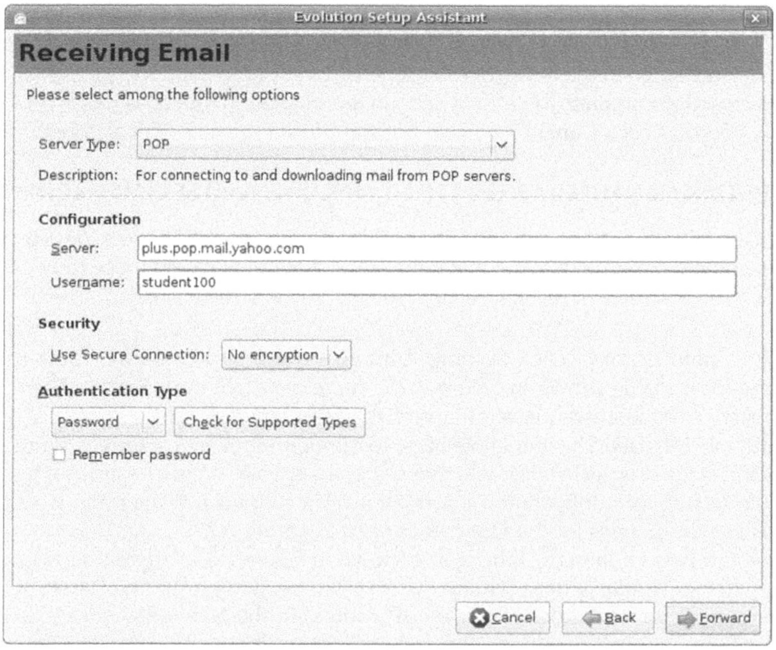

Figure 2.21 Configurations of e-mail receiving properties.

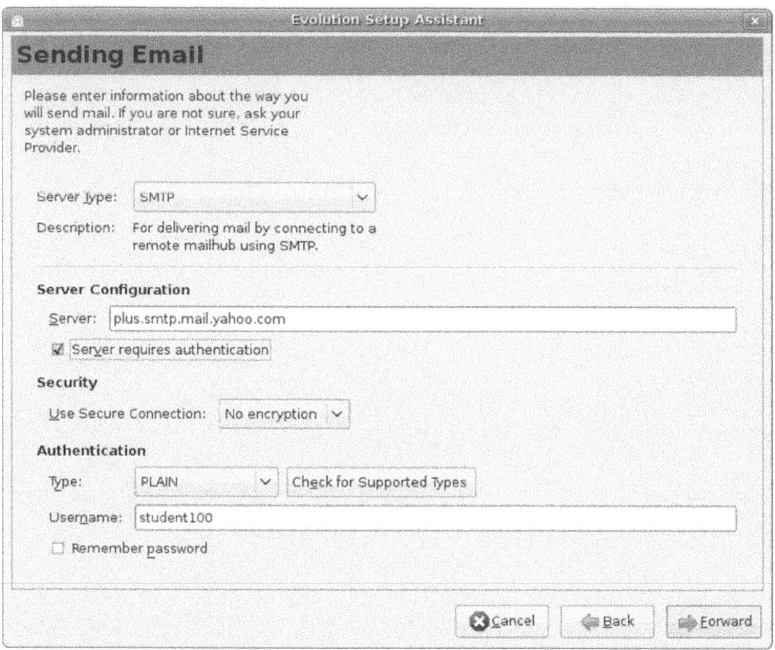

Figure 2.22 Configuration of e-mail sending properties.

the server name. In this page you may also be able to configure security- and authentication-related properties.

7. Click **Forward** to go to the page Account Management. You can use the default e-mail account or enter a new e-mail account for display purposes.
8. Click **Forward** to go to the Timezone page. Select your time zone for the e-mail account.
9. Click **Forward** to complete the e-mail account configuration. Because this is only a demonstration, you may click **Cancel** if you do not want to set up an e-mail account.

NETWORK MANAGEMENT ON CLIENT MACHINE AND SERVER MACHINE

For network management, Ubuntu provides several frequently used GUI tools to help client users with the management of networks. The following steps show how to use these network management tools:

1. On the Ubuntu desktop, click **System**, **Administration**, and **Network Tools** to open the Network Tools dialog shown in Figure 2.23. There are eight tabs. Each of them is used to accomplish a frequently requested network management task.
2. Click the tab **Devices.** This tab allows you to configure network interface cards. From the Network Device drop-down list, you can select a network interface card, such as **Ethernet Interface (eth2)**, for configuration information. After a network interface card is elected, you will see the settings for the Ethernet card eth2 (Figure 2.23).
3. Click the tab **Ping** to open the Ping dialog shown in Figure 2.24. Ping is a network tool used to verify if a particular a network interface card is working properly. It uses ICMP to get responses from network hosts. Enter the IP address in the Network Address text box, and click the **Ping** button. You will see the response from the specified network interface card. You can also specify how many requests to send. The default is five requests each time you execute a ping command.
4. Click the **Netstat** tab. As shown in Figure 2.25, under this tab, you are able to view the content of the routing table, the currently active network service, and the multicast information.

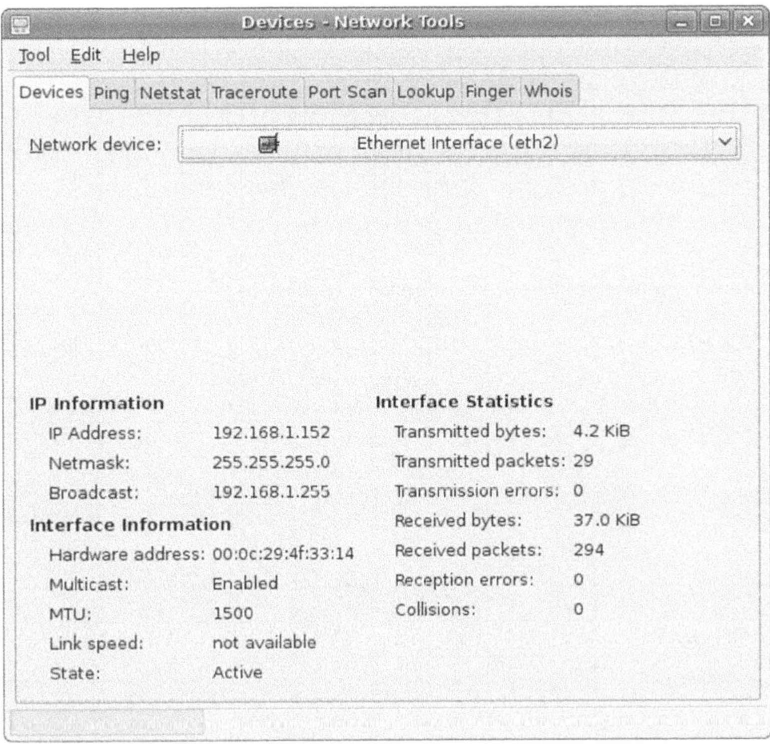

Figure 2.23 Network Tools dialog box.

Click one of the options such as **Routing Table Information** and click the **Netstat** button; the related information will be displayed in this dialog.

5. Click the **Traceroute** tab. Under this tab, you can use the traceroute command to trace the route of an IP packet that is traveling through networks. By using ICMP, traceroute can display information about each network included in the route to the destination. Enter an IP address and click the Trace button; you will get the result shown in Figure 2.26.
6. Click the **Port Scan** tab. As shown in Figure 2.27, this dialog allows you to find out what ports are available on a network host. Enter the IP address of the remote host, and click the button **Scan**; you will get a list of open ports.
7. Click the **Lookup** tab. This dialog allows you to search for the information about a computer system, network connection, and other information. As shown in Figure 2.28, you can enter the IP address of a computer you want to look for and select the information type such as Internet Address. Then, click the **Lookup** button.
8. Click the **Finger** tab (Figure 2.29). The finger command can be used to find information about a user on a computer including login name and other information in the user's profile. Enter the username and IP address of a network host, and then click the **Finger** button to get the information you want.
9. Click the **Whois** tab, and you will see the dialog box shown in Figure 2.30. Whois allows you to find out the domain owner for a given domain name such as www.mycollege.edu.

In addition to these user-friendly GUI tools, users can also perform some network tasks in the command terminal. For example, to view the existing network interface card configuration, you may execute the following steps:

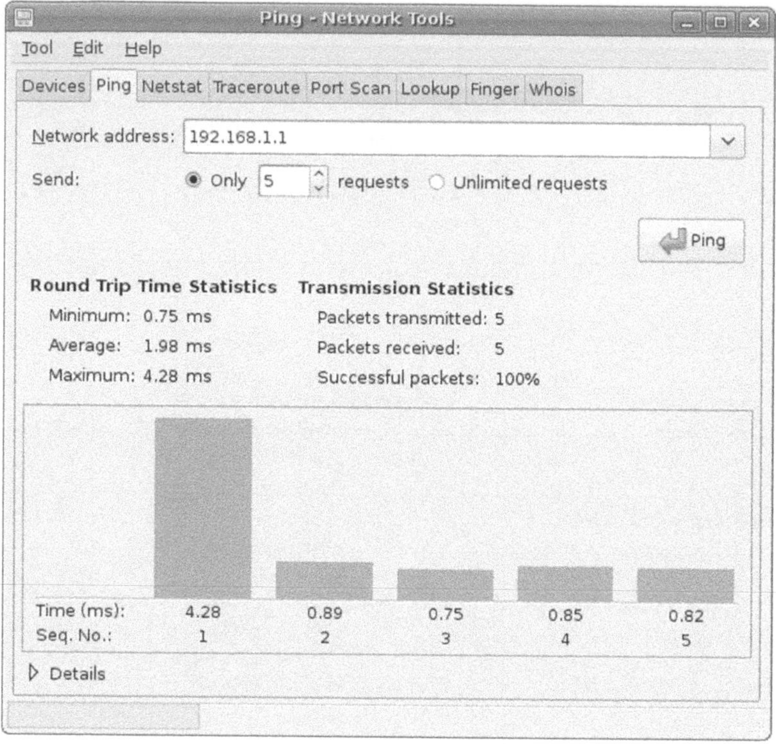

Figure 2.24 Ping dialog box.

1. Start the computer with the Ubuntu desktop operating system installed on it. On the desktop, click **Applications**, **Accessories**, and **Terminal** to open the terminal for entering commands.
2. For example, to view the configuration of the existing network interface card, you may enter the command:

   ```
   sudo ifconfig
   ```

   For security purposes, you will be prompted to enter the password. Enter the password **ubuntu** and press the **Enter** key, and you will see information similar to that displayed in Figure 2.31. In the preceding command, sudo means "superuser do." If you log in as root, which is the superuser, all you need to do is to enter the command ifconfig in the terminal and press **Enter.**
3. The GUI network tools shown previously include two commonly used commands, ping and traceroute. You can also run these two commands in the terminal. To run the traceroute command, you need to install the traceroute program first. The first command in the following code is used to install the traceroute program, the second one is to ping an IP address 5 times, and the third one to run the traceroute command:

   ```
   sudo apt-get install traceroute
   ping -c 5 192.168.1.151
   traceroute 192.168.1.151
   ```

   The execution result of the ping and traceroute commands is displayed in Figure 2.32.

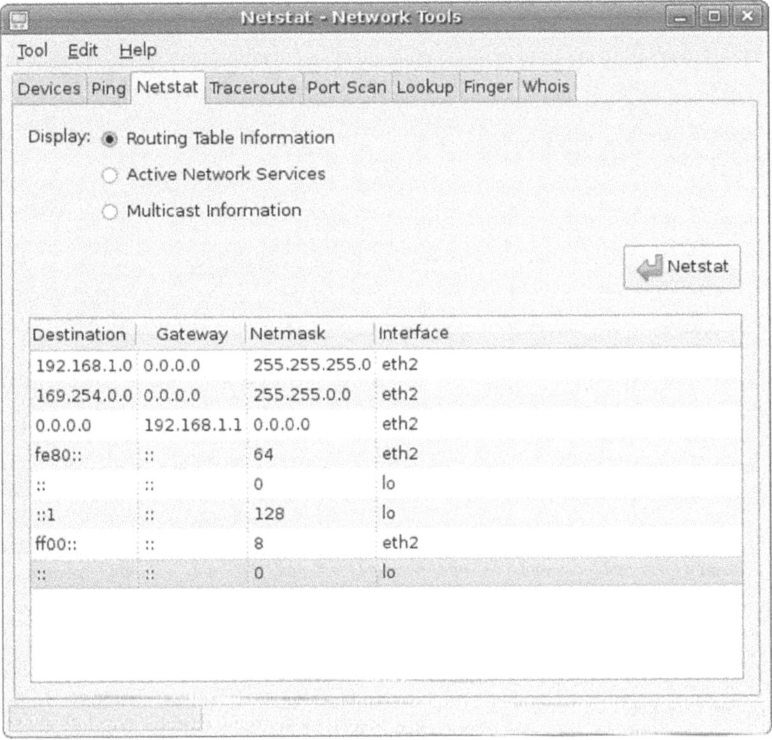

Figure 2.25 Netstat dialog box.

Commands are run in the terminal for network tasks in the server edition of Ubuntu Linux. The following steps show you how to run commands on the Ubuntu server:

1. Start the computer with the Ubuntu server operating system installed. Log in as **student** with password **ubuntu**.
2. Then, run a few commands. For example, in the terminal, you can assign the Ethernet network an IP address and display the IP address with the following two commands:

```
sudo ifconfig eth1 192.168.1.200
sudo ifconfig
```

3. The result is shown in Figure 2.33.

By default, Ubuntu does not implement the root account, to make the operating system more secure. For many network tasks, the root privilege is required to run certain commands. You either place "sudo" in front of a command, or enable the root account by running the command:

```
sudo passwd root
```

You will be prompted to enter the password. Enter **ubuntu** as the password. To disable the root account, enter the following command:

```
sudo passwd -l root
```

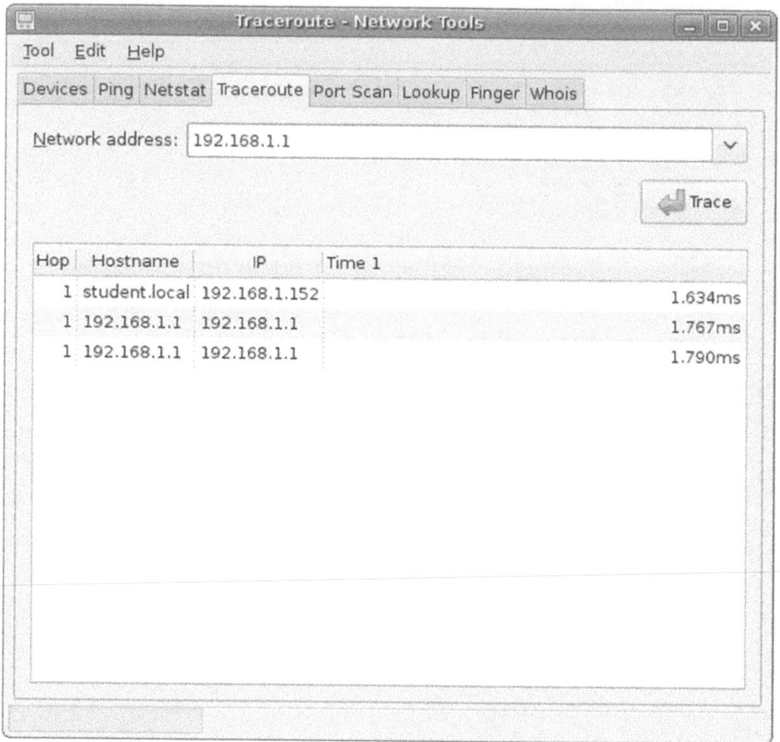

Figure 2.26 Traceroute dialog box.

In this section, we have briefly explored several commonly used network tools included in Ubuntu. The user-friendly GUI network tools make network tasks easy to handle. These network tools will be used in later chapters to develop network systems.

2.7 Summary

This chapter gave an introduction to some of the commonly used protocols in the TCP/IP architecture. These protocols are designed and implemented to allow a host to communicate with another host through a network. This chapter showed that protocols play a key role in delivering data over a network. The relationships among these protocols were illustrated through a protocol graph in this chapter. As hands-on practice, we explored various network management tools included in the Ubuntu Linux operating system. These tools make Linux the control center for a network system. Now that you have learned the properties and usage of the protocols, our next task, in Chapter 3, is to investigate the types of networks and the design and development issues related to these networks.

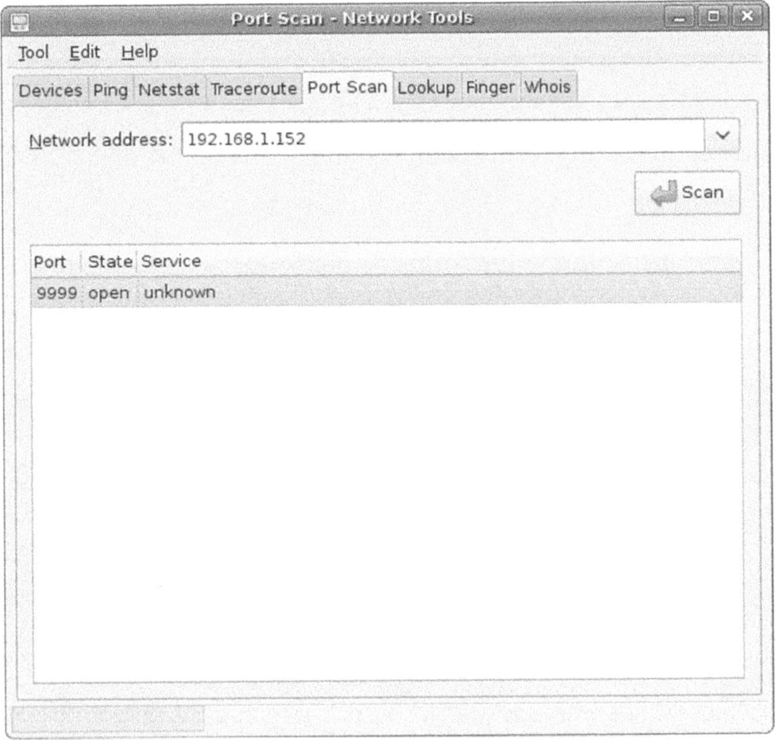

Figure 2.27 Port Scan dialog box.

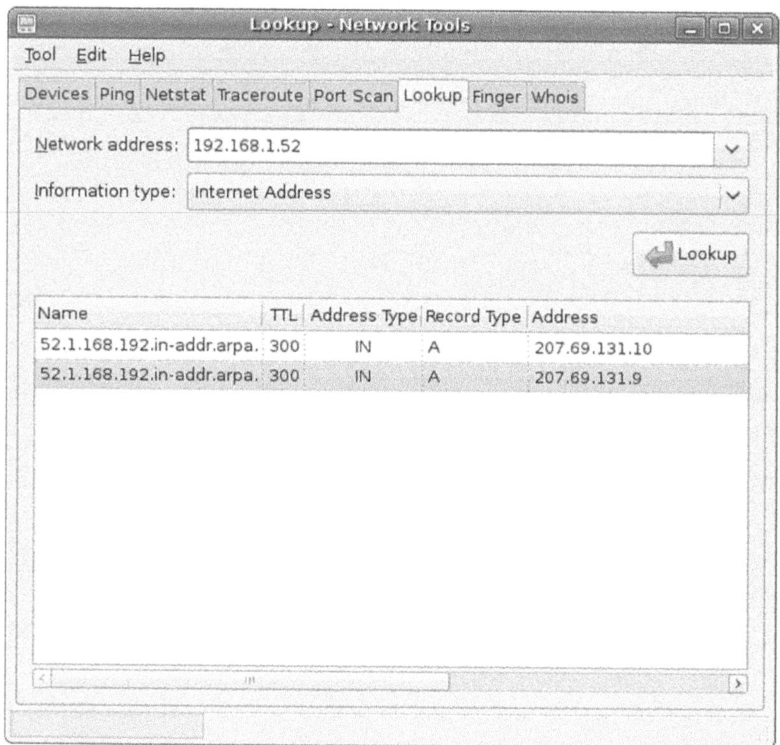

Figure 2.28 Lookup dialog box.

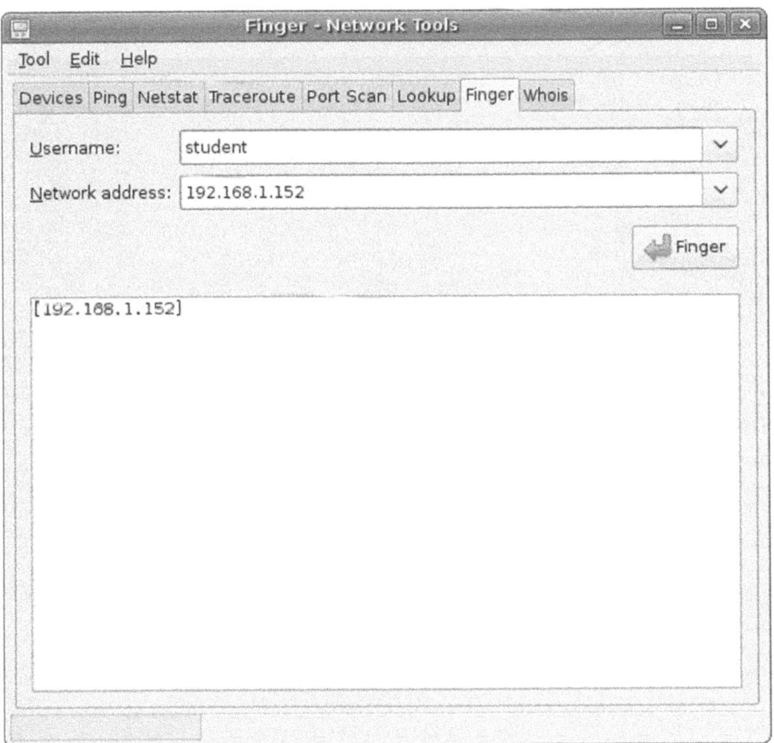

Figure 2.29 Finger dialog box.

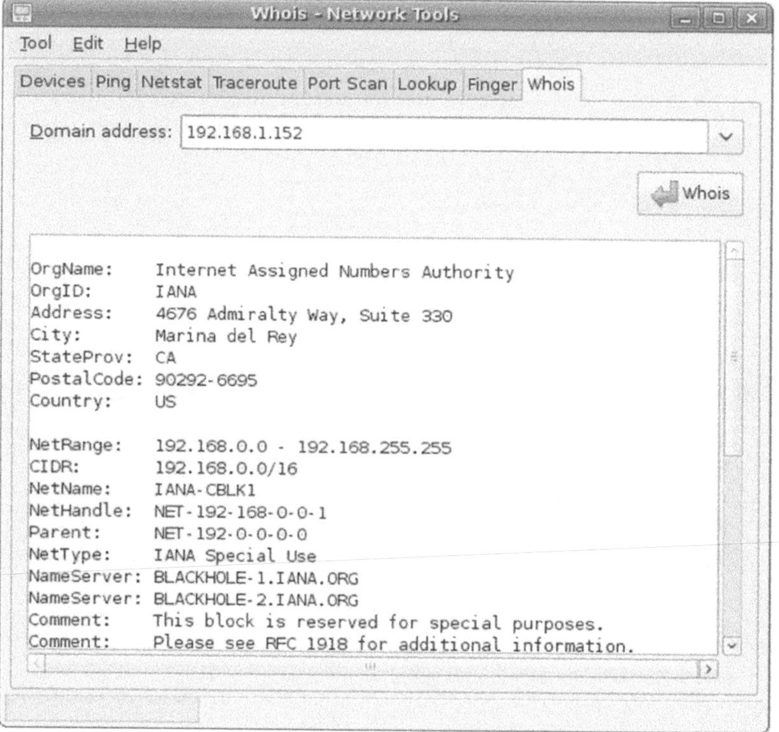

Figure 2.30 Whois dialog box.

```
student@student: ~
File  Edit  View  Terminal  Tabs  Help
student@student:~$ sudo ifconfig
[sudo] password for student:
eth2      Link encap:Ethernet  HWaddr 00:0c:29:4f:33:14
          inet addr:192.168.1.152  Bcast:192.168.1.255  Mask:255.255.255.0
          inet6 addr: fe80::20c:29ff:fe4f:3314/64 Scope:Link
          UP BROADCAST RUNNING MULTICAST  MTU:1500  Metric:1
          RX packets:65897 errors:0 dropped:0 overruns:0 frame:0
          TX packets:65652 errors:0 dropped:0 overruns:0 carrier:0
          collisions:0 txqueuelen:1000
          RX bytes:3978292 (3.9 MB)  TX bytes:4864115 (4.8 MB)
          Interrupt:19 Base address:0x2000

eth3      Link encap:Ethernet  HWaddr 00:0c:29:4f:33:1e
          UP BROADCAST MULTICAST  MTU:1500  Metric:1
          RX packets:0 errors:0 dropped:0 overruns:0 frame:0
          TX packets:0 errors:0 dropped:0 overruns:0 carrier:0
          collisions:0 txqueuelen:1000
          RX bytes:0 (0.0 B)  TX bytes:0 (0.0 B)
          Interrupt:16 Base address:0x2080

lo        Link encap:Local Loopback
          inet addr:127.0.0.1  Mask:255.0.0.0
          inet6 addr: ::1/128 Scope:Host
          UP LOOPBACK RUNNING  MTU:16436  Metric:1
```

Figure 2.31 Executing command ifconfig.

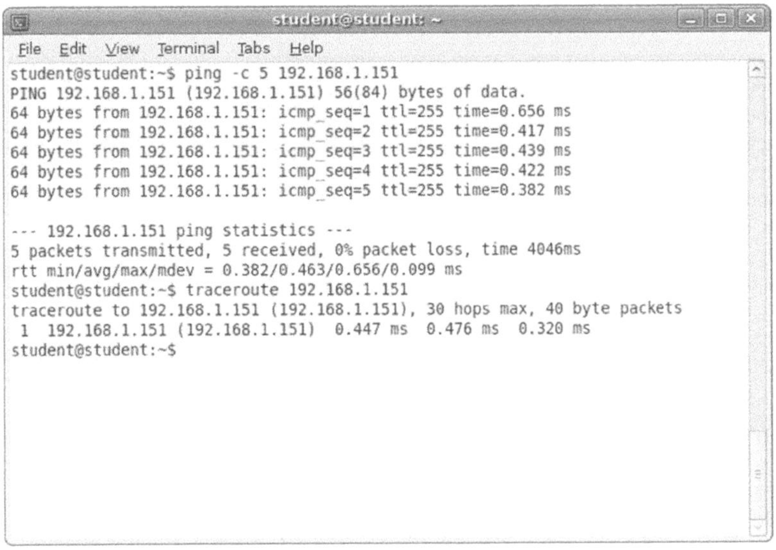

```
student@student: ~
File  Edit  View  Terminal  Tabs  Help
student@student:~$ ping -c 5 192.168.1.151
PING 192.168.1.151 (192.168.1.151) 56(84) bytes of data.
64 bytes from 192.168.1.151: icmp_seq=1 ttl=255 time=0.656 ms
64 bytes from 192.168.1.151: icmp_seq=2 ttl=255 time=0.417 ms
64 bytes from 192.168.1.151: icmp_seq=3 ttl=255 time=0.439 ms
64 bytes from 192.168.1.151: icmp_seq=4 ttl=255 time=0.422 ms
64 bytes from 192.168.1.151: icmp_seq=5 ttl=255 time=0.382 ms

--- 192.168.1.151 ping statistics ---
5 packets transmitted, 5 received, 0% packet loss, time 4046ms
rtt min/avg/max/mdev = 0.382/0.463/0.656/0.099 ms
student@student:~$ traceroute 192.168.1.151
traceroute to 192.168.1.151 (192.168.1.151), 30 hops max, 40 byte packets
 1  192.168.1.151 (192.168.1.151)  0.447 ms  0.476 ms  0.320 ms
student@student:~$
```

Figure 2.32 Executing ping and traceroute commands.

```
Ubuntu_Server  VMware Player ▾  CD-ROM (IDE 1:0)  Floppy  Ethernet ▾
student@ubuntuLab:~$ sudo ifconfig eth0 192.168.1.200
SIOCSIFADDR: No such device
eth0: ERROR while getting interface flags: No such device
student@ubuntuLab:~$ sudo ifconfig eth1 192.168.1.200
student@ubuntuLab:~$ sudo ifconfig
eth1      Link encap:Ethernet  HWaddr 00:0C:29:DF:2D:24
          inet addr:192.168.1.200  Bcast:192.168.1.255  Mask:255.255.255.0
          inet6 addr: fe80::20c:29ff:fedf:2d24/64 Scope:Link
          UP BROADCAST RUNNING MULTICAST  MTU:1500  Metric:1
          RX packets:0 errors:0 dropped:0 overruns:0 frame:0
          TX packets:27 errors:0 dropped:0 overruns:0 carrier:0
          collisions:0 txqueuelen:1000
          RX bytes:0 (0.0 b)  TX bytes:2943 (2.8 KB)
          Interrupt:16 Base address:0x1400

lo        Link encap:Local Loopback
          inet addr:127.0.0.1  Mask:255.0.0.0
          inet6 addr: ::1/128 Scope:Host
          UP LOOPBACK RUNNING  MTU:16436  Metric:1
          RX packets:93 errors:0 dropped:0 overruns:0 frame:0
          TX packets:93 errors:0 dropped:0 overruns:0 carrier:0
          collisions:0 txqueuelen:0
          RX bytes:40237 (39.2 KB)  TX bytes:40237 (39.2 KB)

student@ubuntuLab:~$ _
To direct input to this virtual machine, press Ctrl+G     VMware Player
```

Figure 2.33 Executing commands on Ubuntu server edition.

Review Questions

1. Name some commonly known application layer protocols.
2. What is HTTP and what do we use it for?
3. What is DHCP used for?
4. The protocols SMTP, POP3, and IMAP are e-mail-related protocols. What are the differences among these protocols?
5. What makes SSH safer than Telnet?
6. What can the network administrator do with LDAP?
7. What are the TCP features mentioned in this chapter?
8. What tasks mentioned in this chapter can be handled by TCP?
9. What is included in a TCP header?
10. How does TCP decide the timeout to resend a packet?
11. What is the difference between UDP and TCP?
12. Name some commonly used protocols in the Internet layer.
13. Why do we need to replace IPv4 with IPv6?
14. What are the tasks mentioned in this chapter that can be accomplished by IP?
15 What is encapsulation?
16 How can ICMP packets be transmitted across heterogeneous networks?
17 Describe the differences among the IP routing protocols, RIP, OSPF, and BGP.
18 What is the concern when we use PPTP for a virtual private network?
19 Describe the two components included in Ethernet.
20 Compared with copper wire, what are the advantages of optical fiber?

Case Study Projects

The following are two network projects that involve the investigation of the existing networks in your university or workplace. You may investigate the network you currently are able to access by yourself, or ask the network administrator to help.

Case Study Project 2.1. List at least 10 network protocols used by your network, and briefly describe each of them.

Case Study Project 2.2. List at least 10 network tools that are currently used in managing your network. Provide information such as the tasks that can be accomplished by the tools, manufacturer information, and the advantages and disadvantages of these tools.

Chapter 3

Network Technologies

Objectives

- Learn about different types of networks.
- Understand the technologies used in the networks.
- Construct local area networks.

3.1 Introduction

In Chapter 2, the protocols in each layer of the TCP/IP architecture were discussed in detail. These protocols will be used to develop and manage different types of networks by various network technologies. In addition to the concepts of protocols, which are languages used for communication, to be able to develop and manage networks with Linux, you also need to know more about the network itself. In this chapter, we will first explore various types of networks. We will study the concepts of networks such as local area networks (LANs), wide area networks (WANs), wireless networks, and the Internet. For each type of network, we will examine the technologies used to construct the network. After you have learned about the networks, the next step is to learn about the network devices used to implement the networks. We will investigate the network devices such as network interface cards (NICs), switching devices, and network routing devices. We will look into how these devices are put together to physically construct a network. For hands-on practice, this chapter provides step-by-step instructions on how to create a LAN with two computers configured to communicate with each other on the network. Network tools illustrated in Chapter 2 will be used to configure the NICs and to test the network connection.

3.2 Network Types

As mentioned in the previous chapters, the Linux operating system plays an important role in constructing and managing networks. Linux can be integrated in various types of networks. To be able to construct networks with Linux, you need to understand the concepts about, and the technologies used in, networks. Based on network scales, functionalities, and how the hosts are connected, networks can be categorized as LAN, WAN, and the Internet. Similar to WANs, there are also campus area networks (CANs) and metropolitan networks (MANs). In addition to the wired connection, a LAN, CAN, MAN, and WAN can also be implemented with wireless technology. In the following, we will take a closer look at LAN, WAN, Internet, and wireless networks.

3.2.1 Local Area Network

A LAN is the type of network that links the computers and network devices located in a building or a room. The digital signals used in a LAN cannot travel very far, say, not more than 200 m. On the other hand, the data transmission speed of a LAN is usually higher than that of other types of networks. The hardware and software used in a LAN are, in general, less expensive than that used by other types of networks. A LAN is owned by its creator in an organization and is usually built in such a way as to prevent access by people outside the organization. The goal of the LAN is to allow a group of network devices and computers to share the resources on a network. There are several LAN technologies, such as Ethernet, Token Ring, Fiber Distributed Data Interface (FDDI), and Fibre Channel, that can be used to implement a LAN.

3.2.1.1 Ethernet

The most popular LAN technology is Ethernet. Originally, the Ethernet network was constructed on a bus system (Figure 3.1).

In this system, each host on an Ethernet bus is connected to a transceiver that converts the digital signals used by computer equipment to analog signals used by analog hardware, or vice versa. At each end of the bus, a terminator absorbs the electric signals that reach it. In this way, terminators prevent electric signals from bouncing back to cause collision with other electric signals. After years of development, the functionalities of the transceiver and terminator were built into a small network device called a *hub*. Computers and network devices are linked to a hub with twisted-pair cables (Figure 3.2).

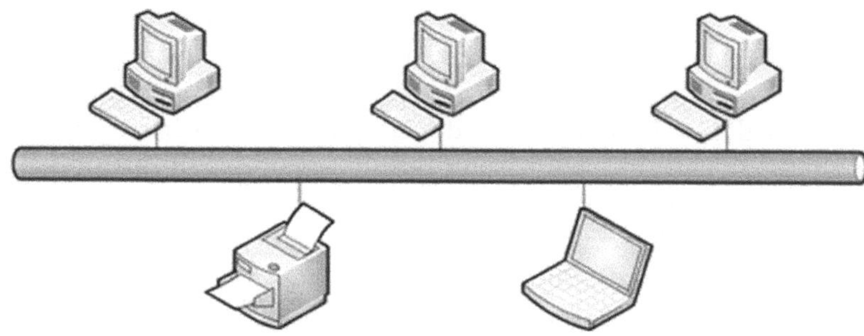

Figure 3.1 Ethernet bus.

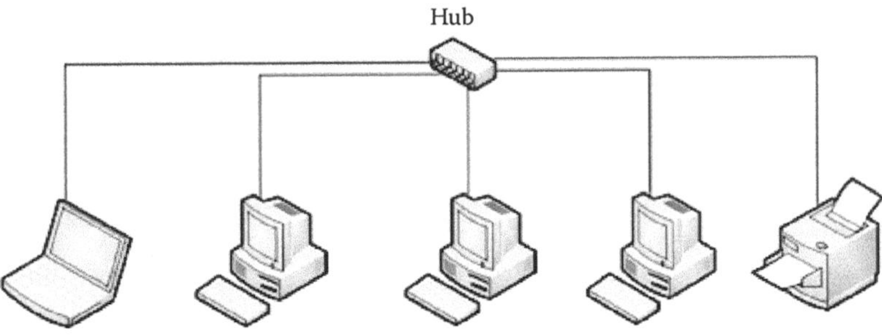

Figure 3.2 Twisted-pair Ethernet.

As illustrated in Figures 3.1 and 3.2, multiple computers share a bus or a hub. While one computer is sending a frame to another computer across the bus or hub, other computers are waiting until the process is done, so that one of them can send another frame. To send a frame across a bus or hub, the first thing a sender needs to do is check if another computer is sending a frame. The technology to determine when a computer can send a frame is called Carrier Sense Multiple Access (CSMA). There is a small chance that two computers will send their frames simultaneously, without knowing that the other one is sending a frame too. In such a case, a collision occurs, which damages both frames. The technology to detect a collision is called Collision Detect (CD). After a collision is detected, both computers will wait for a random delay period and then try to resend the frames.

It was mentioned in Chapter 2 that a frame is used to carry an IP packet across a network constructed with a specific technology such as Ethernet. Frames are network technology specific. For Ethernet, a frame has the format shown in Figure 3.3.

The preamble section in Figure 3.3 is used to provide a pause time during which the receiver's hardware can get ready for the next incoming signal. The length of the preamble section is 8 bytes. Considering that 1 byte is 8 bits, 8-byte preamble data contains 64 bits of zeros or ones to synchronize with the signal frequency before the transmission of the data in the header. An Ethernet frame contains both the destination hardware address and the source hardware address, each of which has a 6-byte length. The frame type section is used to identify the type of the content, such as IPv4 or network games, in the payload section. The section length is 2 bytes (16 bits), which can be used to identify thousands of data content types. The payload section contains 46 to 1500 bytes of data. The last section contains 4 bytes of CRC code used to verify if an error occurred during transmission.

There are different versions of Ethernet frames. The Ethernet frame introduced earlier has a format that matches the commonly used Ethernet versions 1.0 and 2.0, which include the 16-bit frame type section. It is the most common Ethernet version, having the ability to directly handle IP packets.

	<----------header---------->				
8 bytes	6 bytes	6 bytes	2 bytes	46–1500 bytes	4 bytes
Preamble	Destination Address	Source Address	Frame Type	Payload	CRC

Figure 3.3 Ethernet frame.

<---------LLC--------->	<---------------------SNAP--------------------->	
3 bytes	3 bytes	2 bytes
Type Field Indicator	Organization Identifier	Type Identifier

Figure 3.4 IEEE 802.2 LLC/SNAP frame header.

There are other versions of Ethernet frames, such as the IEEE 802.2 LLC/SNAP frame. There are some technologies that may not specify the frame type section to provide the content type information. In this case, the IEEE 802.2 LLC/SNAP frame allows the sender and receiver to use the first few bytes of the payload section to identify the content type. LLC stands for Logical Link Control, which is used to indicate that a type field follows. SNAP stands for SubNetwork Attachment Point, which contains two fields: the first one is used to identify the organization, and the second one is used to identify the content type defined by the organization. Figure 3.4 illustrates the fields in the IEEE 802.2 LLC/SNAP frame header.

Ethernet technology can also be used to transmit data over a wireless network such as Wi-Fi. The discussion of Wi-Fi will be given in the wireless network section. Ethernet is the dominant LAN technology for wired networks. There are some other LAN technologies such as Token Ring, FDDI, and many others that have been used in the past. On the other hand, there are some newly developed LAN technologies such as Fibre Channel. We will discuss Fibre Channel in the following section.

3.2.1.2 Fibre Channel

Unlike Ethernet, which is a general LAN technology, Fibre Channel is a LAN technology often used to connect network hosts to a network storage device such as a storage area network (SAN). It is also used internally in a network storage device to connect storage drives to storage controllers. The data transmission rate can reach as high as 10 Gbps. Fibre Channel supports point-to-point connection between the storage device and other network devices such as external hard drive arrays, computers, and printers.

The communication among devices linked by Fibre Channel can be controlled by an arbitrated loop. If a host wants to send data, it will first send an arbitrate frame, which is used to inform other hosts on the network. The host can begin to send data only if it gets the arbitrate frame back. If multiple hosts send arbitrate frames at the same time, the sender with the lowest hardware address wins the competition. The sender that wins the arbitration will send data first and wait for all other hosts in the competition to get their chance to send data before it can send data again. The arbitrated loop allows as many as 127 devices to be connected to the network.

Fibre Channel can be implemented on fiber-optic cables as well as twisted-pair cables. When implemented over twisted-pair cables, Fibre Channel can only reach the hosts that are short distances away. When implemented on fiber-optic cables, Fibre Channel can reach the hosts 10 km away. Using fiber-optic cables also allows over 16 million devices to be linked to the network. However, using fiber-optic cables requires expensive switches. A disadvantage of Fibre Channel is the lack of compatibility among Fibre Channel manufacturers.

In practice, many LAN segments can be connected to form a larger network. The commonly used network devices for linking small network segments include one or more hubs or switches used to link computers together. On the other hand, a switch or hub often links upward to another

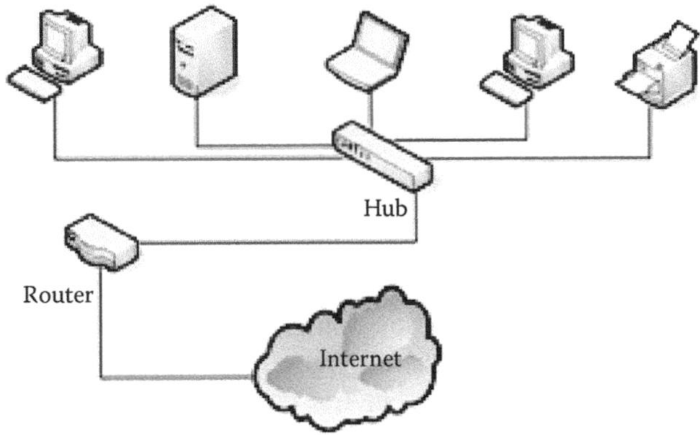

Figure 3.5 Simple LAN segment.

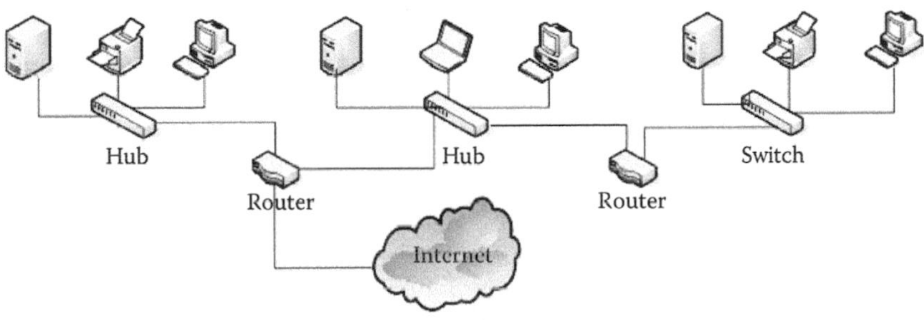

Figure 3.6 Multiple LAN segments linked by two routers.

switch, hub, router, cable modem, or a DSL modem. Switches and routers will be further discussed later in this chapter. Figure 3.5 shows a simple LAN segment. It consists of desktop computers, a server, a laptop computer, and a network printer. A hub is used to link computers and network devices together. As a network device, a switch can be used to link computers and network devices together as the hub does.

Multiple LAN segments can be linked together by routers or bridges so that data can be forwarded from one LAN segment to another. Figure 3.6 shows three LAN segments that are linked by two routers.

For a large LAN, multiple switches, hubs, routers, and other network devices are included. Over a physical LAN, virtual LANs (VLANs) can also be created for better resource management. A VLAN can group a set of computers so that they communicate with one another as if they were on the same network segment, even though they are physically located on different LAN segments. With VLAN technology, multiple VLAN segments can be created on a physical segment. VLAN technology can be used to limit the network traffic to a specific VLAN segment. It provides the flexibility of reconfiguring the network structure without physically relocating the computers and network devices. It can also be used to improve network security and manageability.

Linux supports various LAN technologies by providing tools for network device configuration and for testing the network connection. It also provides tools for network monitoring and security management. Later in this chapter, a hands-on activity will illustrate how to develop a LAN that links a client computer to a server computer.

3.2.2 Wide Area Network

When a network can be scaled to a large geographical area with multiple sites, each site has a large number of hosts, and the large number of hosts can communicate simultaneously, such a network can be called a *wide area network* (WAN). Scalability is a key factor of a WAN. A network that can link network hosts in a large geographical area but is only limited to a few hosts may not be qualified as a WAN.

To be able to expand to a large geographical area and allow multiple network hosts to communicate simultaneously, WANs depend on telephone companies or Internet service providers to carry out the telecommunication services. Compared with a LAN, the transmission on a WAN through telecommunication devices is usually slower. The following is a description of several commonly used WAN technologies:

- X.25: It is an early WAN technology. It was created even before personal computers. The limitation of X.25 technology is its low performance.
- Integrated Services Digital Network (ISDN): ISDN is a dial-up technology that can be used for communication between two WAN sites. It is very much like a digital telephone technology.
- Frame Relay: As the name indicates, Frame Relay is the WAN technology that relays frames from one LAN segment to another remote LAN segment. Therefore, it is designed to handle up to an 8000-byte data block, with a transmission rate up to 100 Mbps.
- Switched Multimegabit Data Service (SMDS): SMDS is a technology that is specially designed for data transmission in LAN and WAN. It can transmit a frame that contains 53 bytes of data. Its data transmission rate is faster than that of Frame Relay.
- Asynchronous Transfer Mode (ATM): ATM is another WAN or LAN technology designed to handle telephone service as well as data transmission. It is a hardware-based technology; therefore, it can achieve a much higher transmission rate. In theory, the transmission rate of ATM may reach as high as 10 Gbps.
- Synchronous Optical Network (SONET): SONET is a WAN technology that is designed for data communication over fiber-optic cable. The transmission rates of SONET range from 51.84 Mbps to 2.5 Gbps. It can combine packets with different formats into a single data format for the transmission over fiber-optic cable. Large companies can take advantage of this feature. In a large company, it is possible that the data communication service is handled by multiple WAN technologies. SONET simplifies packet transmission between two different technologies.

All the preceding technologies belong to the network interface layer. They are used to directly interact with the network media for data transmission. The commonly used methods for linking two sites in a WAN are listed as follows:

1. *Leased telephone line:* A leased telephone line is used to link two sites. The wire and the equipment at each end of the connection are provided by the telephone company.
2. *Circuit switching:* Unlike the leased telephone line connection, this kind of connection can be initialized when requested. When data transmission is requested by the sender, a call to

the receiver's number is dialed. After the data transmission is completed, the connection will be terminated. The WAN technology of ISDN uses circuit switching.

3. *Packet switching:* Packet switching is a WAN or LAN technology. When used in a WAN, it allows multiple WAN sites to share a network constructed by telecommunication companies. Different from circuit switching, packet switching has its end nodes connected all the time so that data can be sent at any time. Packets are transmitted through packet switches. A packet switch has two sets of ports. One set is used to link to other packet switches, and the other set is used to link to the hosts on the LAN segment attached to the packet switch. At a packet switch, packets are queued or buffered. Based on the destination address carried by a packet, the packet switch determines if the packet should be sent to the attached LAN segment or be forwarded to another packet switch. Packet switching can efficiently use the shared network, and the operating cost of packet switching is, in general, lower than that of other types of technology. Packet switching is used by many WAN technologies such as X.25, Frame Relay, and SONET. Packet switching is also used by the Internet as well as LANs.
4. *Cell switching:* Like packet switching, cell switching also delivers packets to destination hosts. The difference is that cell switching delivers data in cells. Unlike packets, cells have a fixed size of 53 bytes. Both SMDS and ATM use cell switching for data transmission.

WAN hardware devices and cables are owned by telecommunication companies, and LAN segments are owned by a company or university. Several devices are used to link LAN segments to telephone lines or fiber-optic cables owned by telecommunication companies. The packet switch mentioned in packet switching is this type of device. Figure 3.7 shows the use of packet switches in a WAN.

A remote access server can be used to link an external WAN network to the LAN segments in a WAN. Figure 3.8 illustrates a WAN formed with access servers.

When the sites in a WAN are connected through telephone lines, modems are used to convert digital signals used by computers to analog signals transmitted by telephone lines. At the destinations, the analog signals will be converted back to digital signals by the modems. Figure 3.9 illustrates the usage of modems.

It is more common for the sites of a WAN to be connected through a digital telephone circuit called T-series. Some of the popular T-series connections are T1, T2, and T3. T-series lines are made of optical fiber and can carry much more data than traditional copper telephone

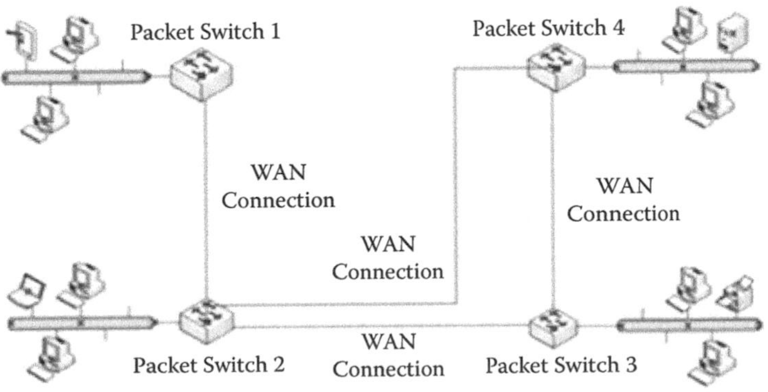

Figure 3.7 WAN formed with packet switches.

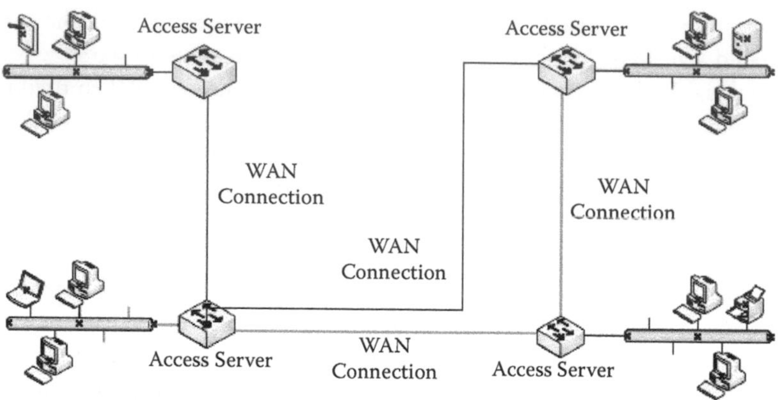

Figure 3.8 WAN formed with remote access servers.

Figure 3.9 Connecting to WAN through modems.

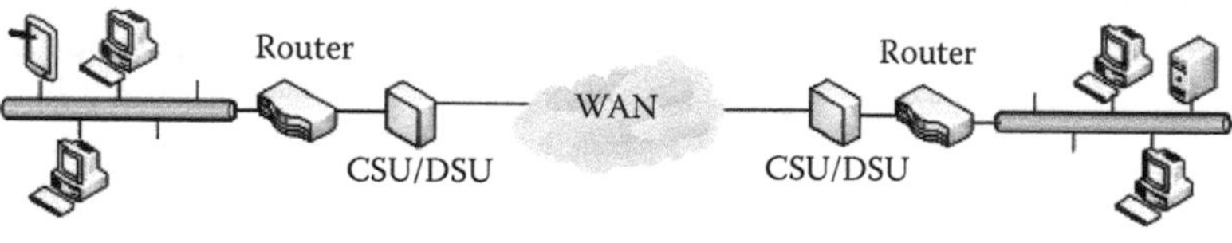

Figure 3.10 Connecting to WAN through CSU/DSU.

lines. When a T-series line is used to connect WAN sites, a digital-interface device unit called CSU/DSU is used to connect a router on a LAN segment to the T-series line. CSU/DSU stands for Channel Service Unit/Data Service Unit; CSU/DSU is used to convert a LAN frame to a frame that meets the T-series standards, and vice versa. CSU is the device that sends or receives data to or from T-series lines and provides loopback signals for testing. DSU is the device that handles frame conversion from LAN standards such as RS-232C and RS-449 to the T-series standards. Figure 3.10 illustrates the usage of CSU/DSU in the implementation of a WAN.

The sites in a WAN can also be connected with ISDN technology, which is a digital telephone service over traditional copper telephone lines. The transmission rate of ISDN is 64 Kbps, which is a much slower speed than that of the T-series lines. ISDN terminal adapters are used to connect a LAN segment to a telephone line. The usage of ISDN terminal adapters is illustrated in Figure 3.11.

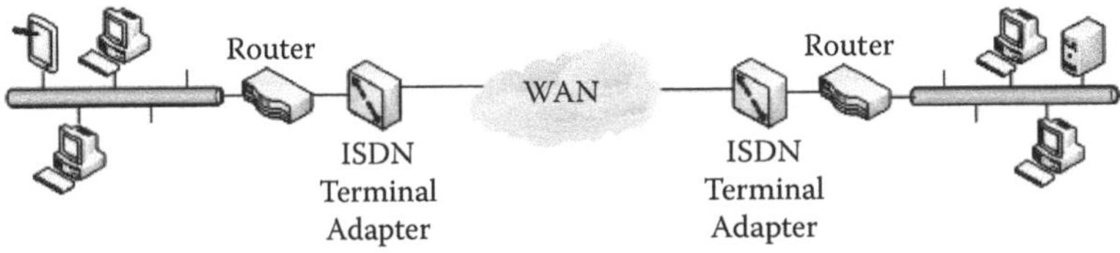

Figure 3.11 Connecting to WAN through ISDN terminal adapters.

WAN technologies are usually developed and managed by telecommunication companies. Data are transmitted through telephone lines or fiber-optic cables, which are often considered as the public network. To be able to transmit a company's private data over the public network, a virtual private network is developed to achieve this goal. Encryption and authentication technologies are used to make private data unreadable even if data packets are captured by hackers over the public network.

Many of these WAN technologies have Linux drivers so that Linux can be involved in WAN management and WAN device configuration. Linux can also be used to handle protocols used by these WAN technologies.

3.2.3 Internet

The Internet is used to connect a large number of heterogeneous LANs and WANs to form a worldwide accessible computer network. The creation of the Internet was motivated by the fact that the networks created with different technologies and different configurations were not able to communicate directly. There was a great demand for a uniform network technology to allow international enterprises and millions of smaller companies, academic institutions, and government organizations to communicate worldwide. To meet this demand, hardware and software have been developed to allow packets to be delivered from one type of network to another. For example, the router is one such key network device that delivers packets through different types of networks. Also, TCP and IP are network protocols that can hide differences in network technologies from application software. In this way, application software can treat the Internet as a uniform network and leave TCP/IP to deal with the differences in network technologies. The Internet-capable application layer protocols such as Hypertext Transfer Protocol (HTTP) and File Transfer Protocol (FTP) all rely on TCP/IP to communicate over the Internet. The combination of the router and TCP/IP makes communication possible among networks constructed with different types of technologies.

As the name indicates, the Internet is a network of networks with different technologies. The hosts on the Internet are connected in many different ways. The computers at students' homes are connected to the Internet through an ISP. The ISPs themselves are part of the global network constructed by telecommunication companies. The global network is built to reach many different regions throughout the world. It communicates with the regional network through an access point called point of presence (POP). A POP is the point that separates the global network from the regional network. It can be a telecommunication facility rented by an ISP for accessing the global network, or it can be any facility used to access the Internet such as a dial-up server, router, or ATM switch. Usually, an ISP may have thousands of POPs to keep up with the demand for Internet access. These POPs are connected by fiber-optic cables. ISPs are not the only companies that provide POPs for local regions; some large companies can also provide POPs for their local users.

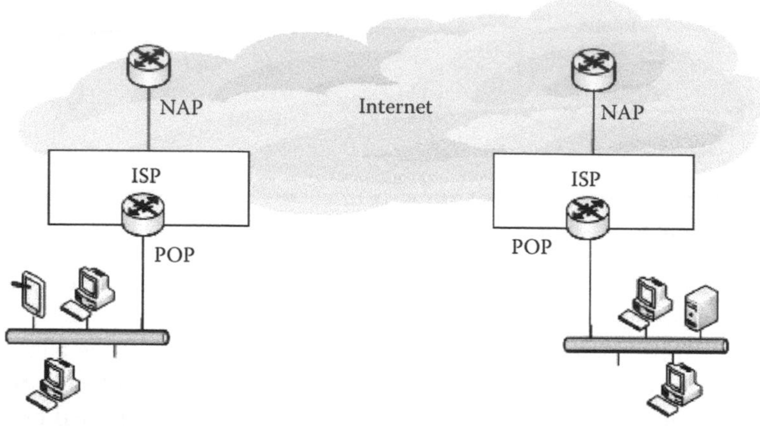

Figure 3.12 Overview of the Internet's structure.

Computers within each ISP are able to communicate with each other through the interconnected POPs. To reach the computers in other ISPs, a higher level of communication is needed. At the higher level, ISPs are able to access the global network through a network access point (NAP), which is the major Internet interconnection point. An ISP can reach another ISP through NAPs. Some of the major international enterprises may also access the Internet through NAPs. In this way, every computer on the Internet is able to communicate with every other computer. Figure 3.12 is an overview of the Internet's structure.

Fiber-optic cables are used to construct the backbone of the global network, which either follows the T-series standards with transmission rates from 1.544 Mbps to 45 Mbps or the faster Optical Carrier (OC) standards with transmission rates from 155 Mbps to 2.488 Gbps. Originally, the backbone of the global network was jointly developed by the National Science Foundation (NSF), IBM, MCI, and Merit. Nowadays, many international enterprises have their own high-capacity backbone connections. These backbone connections are linked through NAPs. Once a computer in a LAN is connected to the Internet through a POP, the computer and the LAN become part of the Internet. Although the LAN becomes part of the Internet, no one else owns this part of the network except the company or individual who created the LAN. Therefore, no one completely owns the entire Internet.

Due to the lack of centralized control on the Internet and the openness of Internet protocols, the size of the Internet has been growing exponentially. Today's Internet includes millions of networks and supports various applications such as World Wide Web, e-mail, online chats, online games, text messaging, file transfer, Web logging, Internet phones, Internet TVs, and so on. The Internet has changed the way of teaching and learning at universities and the way of doing business. It also has greatly impacted the structure of social life.

The Linux operating system is designed to support the Internet in many ways. In addition to supporting various protocols used by the Internet technology, it can be used to host Web servers and other Internet-capable servers. Linux supports various Internet access services such as dial-up and DSL. Internet applications such as the Internet e-mail and Web browser are also supported by Linux.

3.2.4 Wireless Network

As wireless network technologies improve, wireless networks are becoming more and more popular due to its flexibility, mobility, maintainability, and scalability. The cost of wireless network devices has been lowered significantly, and the speed of transmission has been notably improved. The construction cost of a wireless network can be much lower than that of a wired network because no cabling is necessary. A wireless network can be operated using radio waves, microwave, and infrared. Based on these transmission media, several wireless technologies, such as Wi-Fi, WiMAX, and Bluetooth, have been developed. More details about wireless networks will be given in Chapter 11.

Most recent versions of Linux handle the wireless computing environment very well. With the Linux, one can configure wireless network devices such as wireless network interface cards (NICs) and wireless network routers. Linux provides tools to assist the wireless connection to find an access point. It has strong support for wireless security measures such as authentication and encryption.

In this section, several different types of networks have been introduced. We looked at the features of LAN, WAN, Internet, and wireless networks. We examined how data are transmitted in these networks. Data transmission is carried out over various network media. In the next section, we will take a closer look at some of the commonly used network media.

3.3 Network Media

In this section, we are going to take a look at topics related to network media. Various materials can be used to transmit binary electrical signals from sender to receiver. We will describe the features of these materials. For long-distance transmission, the binary signals must be reshaped so that they can go all the way to their destinations. When multiple users are sharing the same network media for data transmission, the binary signals also need to be treated so that the signals sent by each user can be identified at their destination. This section will also discuss the technologies used to treat the binary electrical signals.

3.3.1 Modulation

To transmit data over network media, the data will be first converted into binary code. The binary code is then represented by electric pulses, which are transmitted through network media such as copper wire. The problem is that an electric pulse cannot travel very far. To overcome this problem, a carrier, which is a continuously oscillating electric current, is used to carry a binary signal for long distances. The continuously oscillating electrical current is known to propagate long distances without losing much of its energy.

To carry a binary signal, the amplitude, frequency, or phase of a carrier has to be modified so that the zeros and ones are distinguishable in the continuously oscillating electric current. Such modification of a carrier is called *modulation*. Figure 3.13 illustrates an amplitude modulation process.

By changing the frequency, we can modulate a carrier for data transmission. Figure 3.14 illustrates the idea of frequency modulation. Similarly, by changing the phase of the carrier's waves, we will be able to transmit the binary code through a medium.

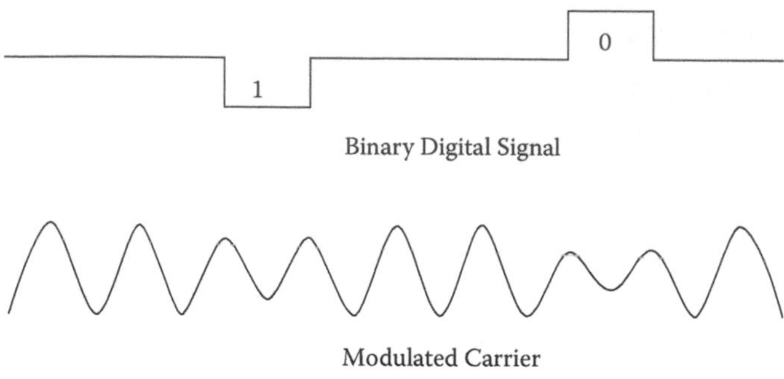

Figure 3.13 Illustration of amplitude modulation.

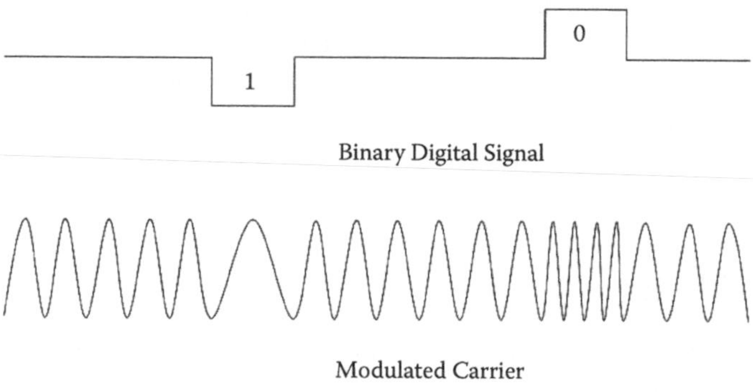

Figure 3.14 Illustration of frequency modulation.

3.3.2 Multiplexing

By using different carriers, multiple, separate communication paths can share a single medium without interference. For example, each sender and receiver pair on the network can use a carrier with a particular frequency to exchange messages. The process of sharing a single medium by using multiple carriers with different frequencies is called *frequency division multiplexing*. Using frequencies is not the only way to distinguish carriers. Optical fiber uses light for data transmission. Therefore, colors can be used to separate different carriers. This process is called *color division multiplexing*, or technically, *wavelength division multiplying*. Letting multiple carriers take turns to send signals is another way to share a medium. This process is called *time division multiplexing*. With multiplexing techniques, communication over a single medium can be made much more efficient.

3.3.3 Twisted-Pair Wire

As mentioned in Chapter 2, copper wire, optical fiber, and radio waves are commonly used network media for transmitting frames from one host to another on a network. The choice of network media depends on the requirements of the network and issues related to cost, performance, and reliability.

Table 3.1 Transmission Rates of Ethernet Technologies

Ethernet	*Transmission Rate (Mbps)*
10Base-T	10
100Base-T	100
1000Base-T or Gigabit Ethernet	1,000
10 Gigabit Ethernet	10,000

Table 3.2 Twisted-Pair Cable Categories

Category	*Bandwidth (MHz)*	*Usage*
5	100	Can be used on 10Base-T and 100Base-T Ethernet networks. May not be suitable for Gigabit Ethernet.
5E	100	Can be used for 10Base-T, 100Base-T, and Gigabit Ethernet networks.
6	250	Can be used for 10Base-T, 100Base-T, Gigabit Ethernet networks and 10 Gigabit Ethernet networks with limited distance.
6a	500	Can be used for 10Base-T, 100Base-T, Gigabit Ethernet networks and 10 Gigabit Ethernet networks up to 100 m.
7	600	This is a feature of the 10 Gigabit Ethernet technology designed for 10 Gigabit Ethernet networks over 100 m. Its transmission rate can possibly reach 100 Gbps over 70 m.

The twisted-pair wire is the commonly used network medium to connect computers and network devices on a LAN. Ethernet can transmit data with various transmission rates over twisted-pair wires. Table 3.1 lists the Ethernet technologies and their transmission rates.

Ethernet uses twisted-pair wires, which can be made of copper. A twisted-pair cable links two computers by plugging the cable into the RJ45 network connector on each of the computers. Ethernet supports twisted-pair cables in various transmission speeds. The twisted-pair cables can be classified into several categories. Table 3.2 lists some of the cable categories.

3.3.4 Optical Fiber

Optical fiber is made of a transparent glass string or plastic string. Through optical fiber, light is used to transmit data. Thousands of optical fibers can be enclosed in one cable wrapped with a plastic outer layer. There are two types of optical fibers: multimode fiber and single-mode fiber. The multimode fiber supports multiple light propagation paths in one optical fiber. It is used for short-distance communication. The single-mode fiber supports a single light propagation path. For the communication over 200 m, a single-mode fiber-optic cable should be considered. Compared with copper wires, fiber-optic cables can deliver data over much longer distances with a much faster transmission rate due to the following features:

- More fibers can be bundled into one cable due to the lighter weight and thinner diameter of the optical fiber.
- Optical fiber uses light to transmit data. Therefore, it is immune to electrical interference.
- Modulating data signals into carriers can be done faster with light. The modulation rate can be as high as 40 Gbps. Therefore, a single optical fiber can carry much more data than a copper wire.
- During data transmission, light suffers less degradation. Therefore, optical fiber can transmit data to longer distance with better quality.
- It takes less electric power to propagate light in optical fiber.
- Because it uses light, optical fiber does not cause electric sparks, which can be dangerous in some sensitive environments.

These features make optical fiber suitable for data transmission, especially for long-distance communication. Because of these advantages, optical fiber has been used to construct the backbone of the global network since as early as 1987. Optical fiber has been used for digital telephone services. The T-series standards mentioned earlier are standards for digital telephone services. Information on T-series is listed in Table 3.3.

The first Internet backbone project was built based on the T1 standard. As the amount of data on the Internet grows, the T-series standards are not enough for today's data transmission requirements. New standards have been created for optical carriers. These standards are called OC standards. Table 3.4 provides some information about the commonly used OC standards.

Table 3.3 T-Series Standards

Name	*Transmission Rate (Mbps)*	*Number of Voice Circuits Supported*
T1	1.544	24
T2	6.312	96
T3	44.736	672

Table 3.4 Optical Carrier (OC) Standards

Name	*Transmission Rate (Mbps)*	*Number of Voice Circuits Supported*
OC-1	51.840	810
OC-3	155.520	2430
OC-12	622.080	9720
OC-24	1,244.160	19440
OC-48	2,488.320	38880
OC-192	9,953.280	155520
OC-768	39,813.12	622080

As seen in Table 3.4, OC-768 has nearly a 40 Gbps data transmission rate. The OC-768 standard has been used in constructing today's backbone projects for the global network. Such types of backbone projects will provide a full range of services for the Internet-based communication needs of various types of businesses and home users.

The disadvantage of optical fiber is that it is difficult to handle light signals at each end of a fiber-optic cable. Specially designed equipment has to be used to handle the data-converting tasks at each end of a fiber-optic cable.

3.3.5 Wireless Transmission Media

The media used to transmit data through a wireless network are radio, microwave, and infrared. These wireless transmission media have their own specified frequency range and wavelength. The lower a frequency is, the longer the wavelength. A carrier with higher frequency has a better ability to resist interference and has a higher transmission rate. A carrier with lower frequency can easily get around a physical obstacle.

Most wireless communication employs radio waves. The radio wave frequency range of a wireless network can be as low as 9 kHz (kilohertz) or as high as thousands of gigahertz (GHz). At 9 kHz, the wavelength is about 21 km. For radio waves with frequencies at the high end, the wavelength can be as short as 1 mm. Various types of wireless devices make use of radio waves in different sections. Table 3.5 describes the sections of radio waves that are commonly used in wireless networks.

From Table 3.5, microwave is a radio wave with frequency at the high end of the radio wave spectrum, including UHF, SHF, and EHF signals. Because of its high frequency, microwave can be used to carry data 50 km away with much more bandwidth than other sections of radio waves.

As the frequency increases to higher than 300 GHz, which is the upper bound of radio wave frequencies, the signal takes on other forms such as infrared, visible light, ultraviolet, x-ray, and so on.

Table 3.5 Radio Frequencies

Name	*Symbol*	*Frequency Range*	*Application*
Low frequency	LF	30–300 kHz	AM radio, navigation
Medium frequency	MF	300–3000 kHz	AM radio, navigation
High frequency	HF	3–30 MHz	Shortwave broadcasting
Very high frequency	VHF	30–300 MHz	FM radio, TV, aviation
Ultra high frequency	UHF	300–3000 MHz	TV, mobile phone, wireless network, microwave
Super high frequency	SHF	3–30 GHz	Wireless network, radar, satellite, microwave
Extremely high frequency	EHF	30–300 GHz	High-speed and high-bandwidth microwave communication

3.4 Network Devices

In addition to computers and network media, many other types of network devices are needed in a network. These devices are used to mediate data in a network. In this section, you will learn about some commonly used network devices, including network interface cards (NICs), switches, and routers. These devices play a very important role in a network. When you construct a network, proper selection of the network devices is vital for the success of network-based computing.

3.4.1 Network Interface Cards

In a network, each computer or network device with memory and a CPU must have one or more NICs installed in it to link to the network media. An NIC can be used as the interface between a computer and a network medium. It allows computers and network devices to communicate with one another through cables or radio waves wirelessly.

After a CPU forms a packet in memory, it informs the NIC to transmit the packet. The NIC is built in such a way that it can directly access memory. It can transmit and receive binary signals by interacting with memory without getting the CPU involved. It knows the formats of network frames, so it can convert binary code to electric signals, or vice versa. It also handles packet transmission through the network media. While the NIC prepares and transmits the packet, the CPU can continue to do other tasks. After finishing the packet transmission, the NIC informs the CPU. On the receiving side, the NIC places the received packet in memory and informs the CPU to process the packet.

An NIC has a built-in ROM chip that contains a unique hardware address burned into it. The 48-bit hardware address is provided by the NIC manufacturer and is used as the manufacturer ID and the product serial number. The first 24 bits are related to the manufacturer's identification and is therefore called the Organizationally Unique Identifier (OUI). The Institute of Electrical and Electronics Engineers (IEEE) assigns unique hardware addresses to NIC manufacturers for their products. In a network, the hardware address is used as a network host ID. The sender and receiver's hardware addresses are included in a frame for information exchange.

There are various types of NICs depending on which network interface layer protocol is used by a card. For a wired network, the most popular type of NIC is built with the Ethernet protocol. The performance of Ethernet NICs matches the data transmission rates listed in Table 3.1. Therefore, an Ethernet NIC can be categorized as a 10Base-T Ethernet NIC, which can handle data transmission rates up to 10 Mbps; a Fast Ethernet NIC, which can handle data transmission rates up to 100 Mbps; a Gigabit Ethernet NIC, which can handle data transmission rates up to 1,000 Mbps; or a 10 Gigabit Ethernet NIC, which can handle data transmission rates up to 10,000 Mbps. For wireless networks, various NICs are built to match the Wi-Fi standards.

Usually, an NIC is constructed on a plug-in PCI or PCMCIA card that can be plugged into the system bus on a motherboard. Some computers have one or more built-in NICs on the motherboard. Therefore, an NIC is also called a *network interface controller*. It can be built on an ExpressCard, which is thinner, lighter, and faster than a PCMCIA card. There are also USB- and Wi-Fi-based NICs. A Wi-Fi-enabled NIC has a built-in transmitter/receiver unit, and it does not need a cable connection port. Some NICs support both wired and wireless connections.

When selecting an NIC for constructing a network, one needs to make sure that the NIC matches the capability of the other network devices and the networked computer. To transmit data with a higher transmission rate, the use of the NIC alone may not achieve the goal. The network media and other network devices such as switches and routers are also required to be capable of handling the higher data transmission rate. Also, one needs to be aware that the NIC for a wired network is not compatible with that used in a wireless network. Most of the newer NICs are backward compatible with older version NICs that are based on the same type of technology.

Linux supports various NICs that are connected to different types of network media. Drivers for NICs are included in the Linux operating system. During the system boot process, the Linux kernel detects the NIC for a specific network medium and automatically loads the driver to handle the network medium. Linux also includes management tools for different types of NICs.

3.4.2 Network Switches

As mentioned earlier, for multiple computers or network devices to communicate with each other, the computers need to be connected to a hub. A hub has multiple RJ45 ports, each of which can be plugged with a twisted-pair wire that is connected to a network host at the other end of the wire. Because a hub is simulating a network medium, it only allows one pair of hosts to communicate at one time even though it may have multiple ports. Similar to a hub, a switch is also used to connect multiple computers or network devices so that they can communicate with each other. The difference between a switch and a hub is that a switch allows multiple pairs of hosts to communicate at the same time. For example, if a switch has 126 ports that are linked to hosts, it allows 63 pairs of hosts to communicate at the same time, whereas a hub with 126 ports only allows one communication at a time. Therefore, compared with a hub, a switch is a much more efficient device. Switches also support full-duplex transmission, which allows data transmission in both directions simultaneously. Full-duplex transmission can transmit twice as much data in a network that uses only switches to connect hosts.

There are different types of switches. When a switch is used to connect hosts in a LAN, it is called a LAN switch. When a switch is used to link multiple LAN segments, it is called a Layer 3 switch. The following describes these types of switches:

1. *LAN switch:* In a LAN, a switch links hosts by acting as a distribution center. All the hosts in a LAN communicate with the switch, not directly with one another. Computers and network devices that are connected to a switch often form a LAN. Therefore, a switch is used to form a LAN or to connect multiple LANs. The IT industry is fast developing, and requirements for network services change with advances made by the IT industry. It is not an easy task to reconstruct the physical network from time to time to meet ever-changing requirements. For greater flexibility, security, and reliability, VLANs are created, to reconstruct networks without changing the existing networks physically. Switches can be configured to allow multiple LANs to coexist on a single switch.

   In a LAN, when a host sends a packet to another host, the packet is first sent to a switch connected to the host. There are several ways to handle the packet by a switch. The two commonly used methods are cut-through switching and store-and-forward switching. To process the incoming packet, the cut-through switching method stores the 6 bytes of the destination address, reads the destination address, and then forwards the packet to the destination. This method increases performance but decreases reliability. The store-and-forward switching method is used to improve reliability. The switch saves the whole packet to a temporary memory called *buffer* after the packet arrives. Then, the switch checks the CRC code to verify if there was any error during the transmission. If there was no error, the switch reads the destination hardware address included in the packet, and then forwards the packet to the receiver. Otherwise, the packet is discarded.

2. *Layer 3 switch:* If a switch has the capability of forwarding packets to a receiver located in a different LAN segment, the switch is called a Layer 3 switch. The term Layer 3 comes from the third layer of the Open Systems Interconnections (OSI) network architecture, which is the network layer in the OSI architecture or the Internet layer in the TCP/IP architecture. Normally, the functionality of a switch is performed by the protocols in the second layer of the OSI model, which is the data-link layer in the OSI architecture or the network interface layer in TCP/IP architecture. In the network interface layer, a switch can identify the destination host by checking the destination hardware address included in a frame. Working in layer 2, a switch can achieve a much better performance. On the other hand, a Layer 2 switch does not keep track of information about networks. In the Internet layer, IP is designed to carry data through different types of networks. With IP, a Layer 3 switch is able to look up routes in a routing table and forward data to a different network. It can also perform other routing functionalities such as determining the best route, recalculating the checksum, and making decisions on the value of Time To Live (TTL). To improve performance, a Layer 3 switch implements routing capability with hardware. It is even capable of dynamically reprogramming the hardware after the routing information is updated. Because it implements routing functionality, a Layer 3 switch in general is faster than a router.

3.4.3 Network Routing Equipment

A router is a key network component used to forward data from one network to other networks. As the Internet is a global network including thousands of LANs and WANs, communication over the Internet depends on routers to deliver messages from network to network. A router serves as a gateway for data distribution among networks. Through routers, data from LANs owned by individual organizations can be passed to the Internet, or vice versa. Various routers are designed to handle tasks at different levels, from wireless routers used for home networks to routers that can handle the exchange of messages for the backbone of a global network or anything in between. The following briefly describes the routers at different levels:

1. *Broadband Internet access router:* This type of router is used to link a home network or a small business network to the Internet. Such a router can be built for a wired network or a wireless network or for both. Usually, this kind of router can only link one network to the Internet. That makes this type of router affordable, simple to set up, and easy to use. The routing table can be manually configured through the GUI tools provided by the router. Some routers support Gigabit Ethernet technology or wireless technology. Users can use this type of router for e-mail, Web surfing, online gaming, file exchange, and hosting a VoIP telephone. At the high end, this type of router may also include security measures such as firewalls and content filters. It may also support the connection to certain types of WANs and remote access mechanisms such as a VPN. Some routers support the quality-of-service (QoS) feature, which can prioritize network traffic to keep the multimedia application running smoothly.
2. *Router for medium-sized business:* This type of router is designed to support the needs of a branch office or a medium-sized business for communicating through multiple internal LANs, the Internet, or intranet. It supports both wired and wireless connections. Usually, it provides two or more Gigabit Ethernet ports for connecting two or more LANs. It also provides options to connect the LANs to a broad range of WANs or the Internet. For dynamically updating the routing table, the interior gateway protocols (IGPs) such as the Routing

Information Protocol (RIP) or Open Shortest Path First (OSPF) protocol are used in this type of router. Some configuration is required, especially when the OSPF protocol is used in a router. This type of router usually supports dozens or hundreds of VPN tunnels for remote access. Some high-end routers in this category support one or more T-1 connections. They support the remote site telephone call services by providing ports for the Public Switched Telephone Network (PSTN) or Private Branch Exchange (PBX). Various security management tools are often included with these routers to help network managers detect network vulnerabilities and to implement security measures. For wired connections, routers in this category may provide a technology called Power over Ethernet (PoE). PoE is used to provide electricity to network hardware over the Ethernet Category 5 or higher cables. Therefore, there is no need to install an extra AC power cord and outlet.

3. *Router for large-sized business:* This type of router serves the needs of a large enterprise or organization. It provides integrated service for various types of data transmission including data, telephone, Web conferencing, and wireless communication. It supports thousands of VPN tunnels for remote access. Multiple Gigabit Ethernet ports are provided to connect a large number of LAN segments. Through the router, an enterprise is able to connect to a wide range of WANs or the Internet. One or more T-3 connections are usually supported by this type of router. The router supports hundreds of IP phone connections. OSPF is the protocol used for this type of router to dynamically update the routing table and to optimize the path from a sender to a receiver located in different networks. Also, it is recommended that the protocol BGP should be run at least on this type of router. The router provides its own uninterruptible power supply (UPS) to prevent the damage caused by power outages. It uses the Power over Ethernet (PoE) technology to support direct electric currents to other network hardware. The router in this category often includes abundant security management tools for protecting networks linked to the router.
4. *Edge aggregation router:* This type of router serves at the edge of an enterprise internal network and a public network. This type of router is used on the backbone of a global network. It is able to handle millions of transactions simultaneously. Routers in this category are often run on multiple CPUs for parallel processing. They use Multiprotocol Label Switching (MPLS) technology to transmit data through LANs and WANs created with various technologies such as Ethernet, Frame Relay, and ATM. With MPLS, frames created with different technologies can be encapsulated and delivered. MPLS also provides tools for connection management. It turns various types of LANs and WANs into a single network infrastructure and integrates the data service, Web conferencing, and the IP telephone service into a unified service. Routers with MPLS are capable of determining the optimal route to deliver data based on network policies developed on the basis of network characteristics such as network traffic flows, bandwidth of a network, queuing priorities, and the optimal route between sender and receiver. MPLS is also the preferred technology to provide QoS service in IP networks. This type of router is a high-performance router. Fast optical fibers, such as the OC-48 or OC-192 optical fibers, are used to link an edge aggregation router to other routers. In addition to its high performance, this type of router is also highly reliable. Technologies such as redundant power supplies, resilient fabric, standby route processors, and alarm modules are included for improving reliability. The router is so reliable that it is often qualified as a carrier-class router that can achieve 99.999% availability. It also includes various tools for security, network management, IP telephones, and Web conferencing.

A computer with Linux installed can also be configured as a fully functioning router. When used with other network devices, the Linux router can be used to distribute data among different networks.

In this section, various types of routers were introduced. Routers are a key device for the Internet. To construct a company's network, the design team needs to carefully select routers that meet the requirements. Companies can purchase routers from network equipment manufacturers or simply convert a Linux computer to a router. More technical details about router development will be covered in later chapters.

Activity 3.1 Implementation of a Simple LAN

In this chapter, you have learned about various networks and some of the major types of network equipment. With the knowledge gained in this chapter, you are ready to create a simple network with the tools provided by the Ubuntu Linux operating system. In the hands-on activity, you will create a private network with two computers assigned to you: one has the desktop edition and the other has the server edition of Ubuntu. When you finish the hands-on practice, the two computers should be able to communicate with each other. The following are the major tasks to be accomplished in this hands-on practice:

- Check the existing network configuration.
- Configure the NICs.
- Test the newly created private network.

In the following subsections, step-by-step instructions are provided to guide you through the creation of the private network. The hands-on activity is based on the virtual machines included in the DVD. If you have installed Ubuntu on your own computer, the screenshots may be slightly different. Each of the virtual machines included in the DVD has two NICs. The first one is used to link to the network in the laboratory or in your home, and the second one is used to create a simple private network between the server virtual machine and the client virtual machine. In this hands-on activity, we will focus on the configuration of the second NIC.

CHECK EXISTING NETWORK CONFIGURATION WITH GUI TOOLS

There are several ways to view the existing network configuration. You can either view the configuration by using network GUI tools or by executing commands in the terminal window. During the hands-on practice in Chapter 2, you learned how to use the tools Network Configuration and Network Tools to configure and display the settings for a network connection. This hands-on activity will show you how to get the information about the network connection with a new GUI tool. In the following, let us start with the client computer assigned to you:

1. Boot the client machine that has the desktop edition of Ubuntu.
2. Log on to the client machine with username **student** and password **ubuntu**.
3. The new GUI tool used to configure and display the network connection is called NetworkManager. The icon for NetworkManager is displayed at the upper-right corner of the desktop screen. It is an overlapping dark computer monitor image (Figure 3.15).
4. To display information about the existing network connection, click on the **NetworkManager** icon; you will get the result shown in Figure 3.16. You can see in Figure 3.16 that only the wired Ethernet network interface cards **Auto eth2** and **Auto eth3** are active and available for configuration. (On your computer, it is more likely that you will see Auto eth0 and Auto eth1, depending on how the virtual machines are created.)
5. Right-click the **NetworkManager** icon; the pop-up menu will be opened (Figure 3.17). From the pop-up menu, you will see the links to Connection Information, Edit Connections, and

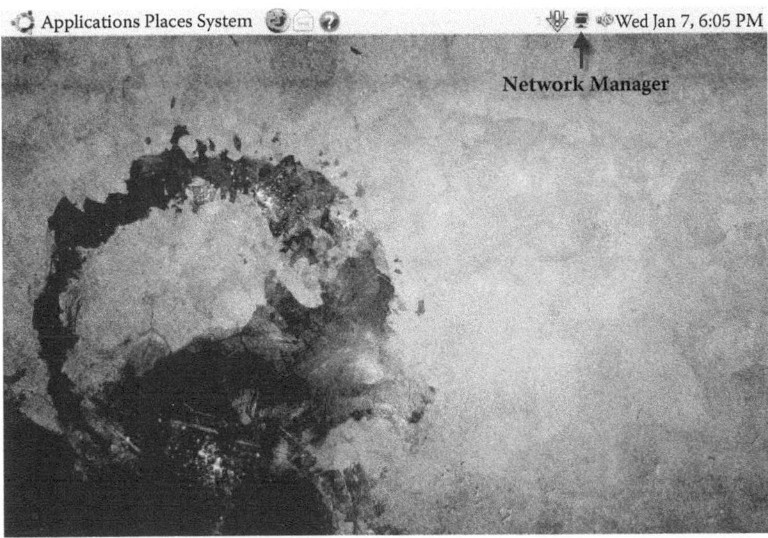

Figure 3.15 Opening network manager.

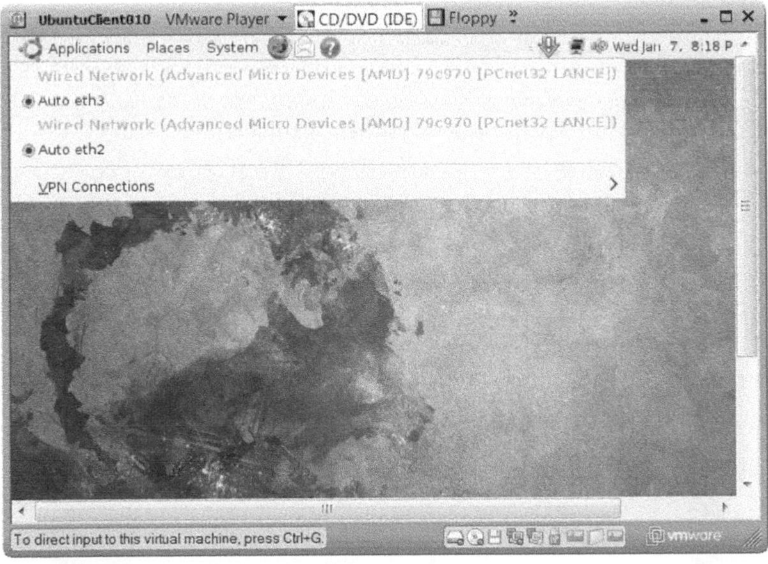

Figure 3.16 Available network connections.

About (which contains the information about NetworkManager), and the check mark indicating that the networking is enabled.

6. To edit the network connection, click the link **Edit Connections** to open the Network Connections dialog shown in Figure 3.18.
7. Assume that you use the NIC eth3 for communication between the private network and the server machine. To view the configuration for eth3, select **Auto eth3** in the Network Connections dialog, and click the **Edit** button to open the **Editing Auto eth3** dialog shown in Figure 3.19.

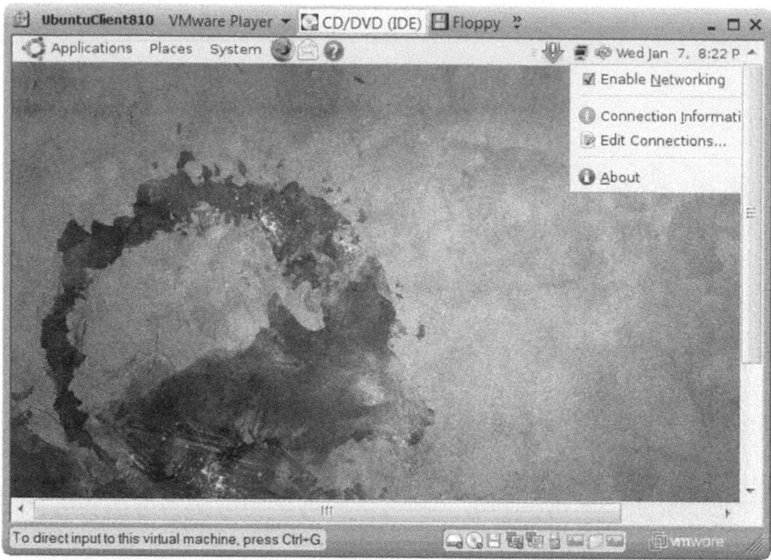

Figure 3.17 NetworkManager pop-up menu.

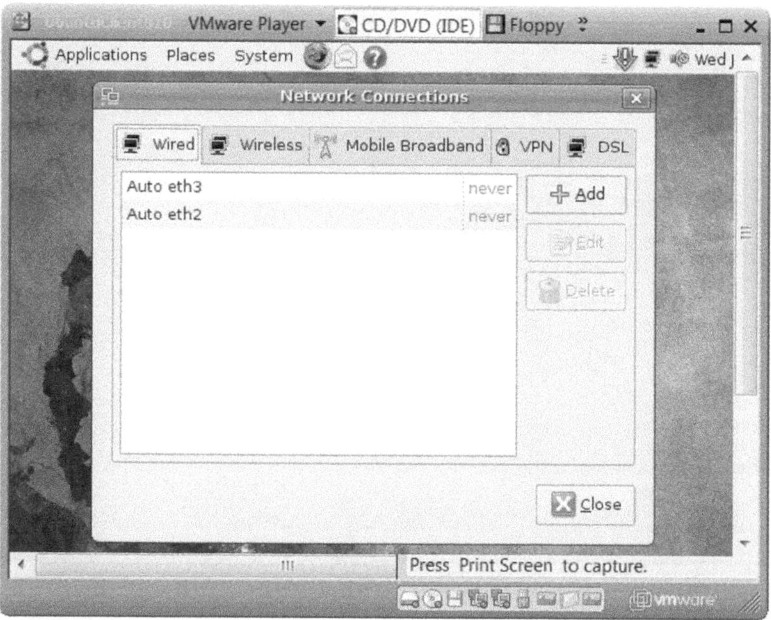

Figure 3.18 Network Connections dialog.

8. Click the **IPv4 Settings** tab in the Editing Auto eth3 dialog. You should be able to see the current configuration for eth3 (Figure 3.20). According to Figure 3.20, eth3 is currently configured to automatically get its IP address from a DHCP server.

Next, we are going to change the current settings of the Ethernet NIC eth3.

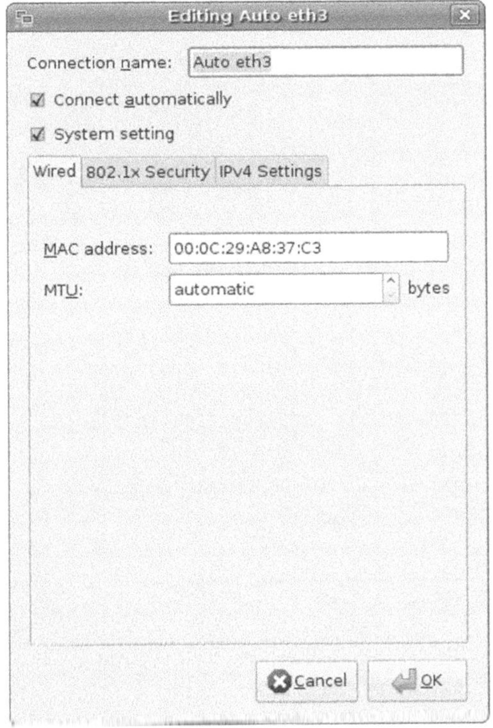

Figure 3.19 Editing Auto eth3 dialog.

CONFIGURE NETWORK INTERFACE CARD ETH3

You can manually configure the NIC eth3 to have a static IP address. For Ubuntu 8.10, using GUI tools to manually assign a static IP address to an NIC is bit complicated. The previous version of Ubuntu involved no such inconvenience. In this section, you will go through the configuration process in detail by following these steps:

1. The first task is to reconfigure the NIC named Auto eth3 so that it cannot automatically get its IP address from a DHCP server. To do so, continue from Figure 3.20, select **Link-Local Only** from the Method drop-down list. Also, uncheck the options **Connect automatically** and **System setting** (Figure 3.21).
2. The next step is to get the MAC address of the NIC called eth3. Click the tab **Wired**, and you should see the display shown in Figure 3.19. Highlight the address in the MAC address field, and press the **Ctrl+C** key combination to copy the MAC address. Click **OK** to accept the settings, and go back to the Network Connections dialog.
3. In the next step, you will add a new name for the NIC, which has the MAC address copied from the previous step. To do so, click the **Add** button in the Network Connections dialog. You should see an empty editing dialog. Paste the MAC address into the MAC address field, and enter the settings shown in Figure 3.22. The new connection name is **Private Client,** and the option **Connect automatically** is checked.
4. The next step is to manually assign an IP address to the NIC Private Client. To do so, click the tab **IPv4 Settings**. Select **Manual** in the Method drop-down list. As shown in Figure 3.23, you are prompted to enter the settings. The settings for the NIC Private Client are given in Table 3.6.

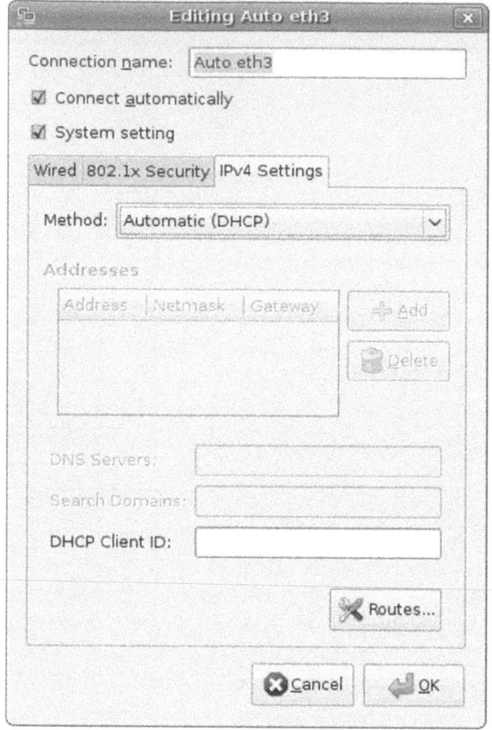

Figure 3.20 Current IPv4 settings for eth3.

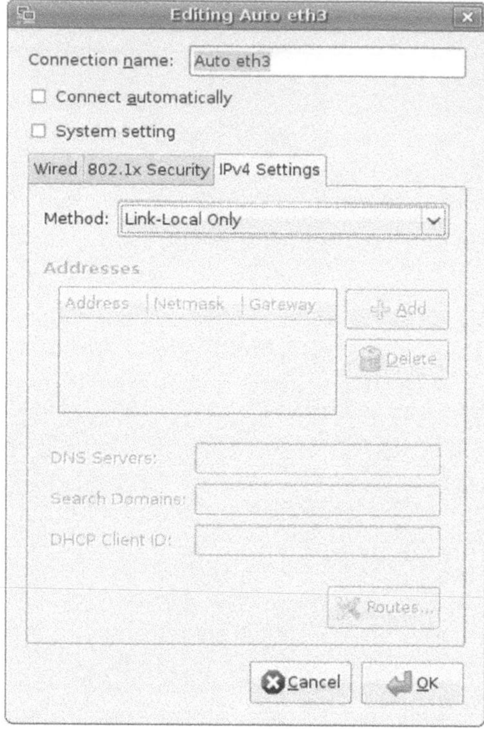

Figure 3.21 Reconfiguration of Auto eth3.

5. To enter the settings for the Ethernet NIC Private Client, click the button **Add**. Enter the settings listed in Table 3.6. You will get the result shown in Figure 3.24. Make sure that the option **Connect automatically** is checked.

   The IP address 192.168.2.2 is for internal use, and the subnet mask entered is used for Class C IPv4. More information about the IP address and subnet mask will be given in Chapter 4. The gateway IP address is for the router. Assume that the router to another network is 192.168.2.1. As we have not configured the DNS and domain yet, we will leave those two fields blank. The router, DNS, and domain will be further covered in later chapters. Enter the settings, and click **OK** to complete the configuration.
6. To activate the NIC Private Client, click the NetworkManager icon, and click the option **Private Client** (Figure 3.25).
7. You can verify the result of the configuration by using the network tools introduced in the hands-on practice in Chapter 2. To do so, click the **System** menu, **Administration**, and **Network Tools**. From the Network Device drop-down list, select **Ethernet Interface (eth3)**. You should get the result shown in Figure 3.26.
8. You can verify the configuration with a command that is a more portable way to check a network connection. You can open a terminal window by clicking **Applications**, **Accessories**, and **Terminal**. After the terminal window is opened, enter the command:

   ```
   sudo ifconfig
   ```

   You should be able to see the output shown in Figure 3.27. Note that both Ethernet NICs should have IP addresses. In Figure 3.27, the IP address for the eth2 NIC is 192.168.1.153, which is automatically obtained from the DHCP server, and the IP address for eth3 is.

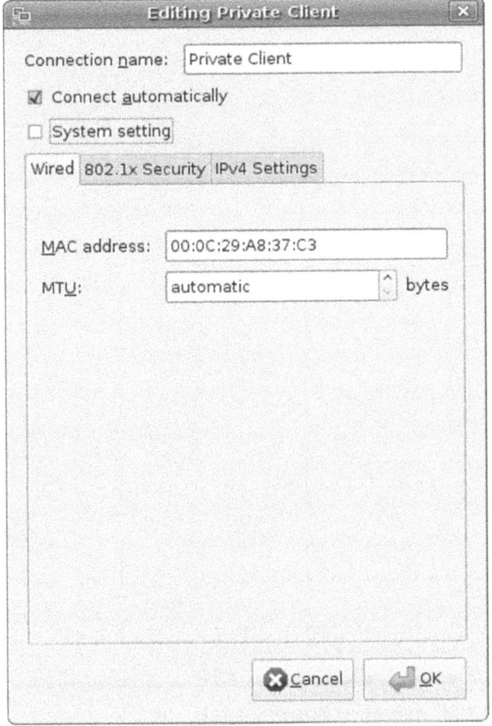

Figure 3.22 Configuration of private client.

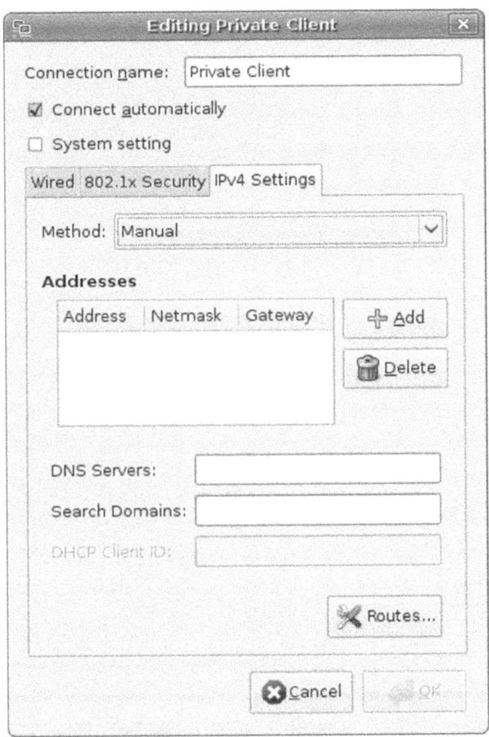

Figure 3.23 Manual configuration dialog.

Table 3.6 Configuration Activities for Private Client

Item	*Setting*
Address	192.168.2.2
Netmask	255.255.255.0
Gateway	192.168.2.1

the static IP address 192.168.2.2. (The IP address for the eth2 NIC may be different on your computer.)

Thus far, you have configured the second NIC with a fixed IP address with the GUI tool. You can also configure it with commands that will be illustrated next.

CONFIGURE NIC WITH COMMANDS

To be able to create a simple network between server and client, you also need to configure the server computer. In this section, you will learn how to configure the Ethernet NIC with commands and the text editor nano. The configuration process will be demonstrated on the server machine. Use the following steps to configure the second NIC on the server machine:

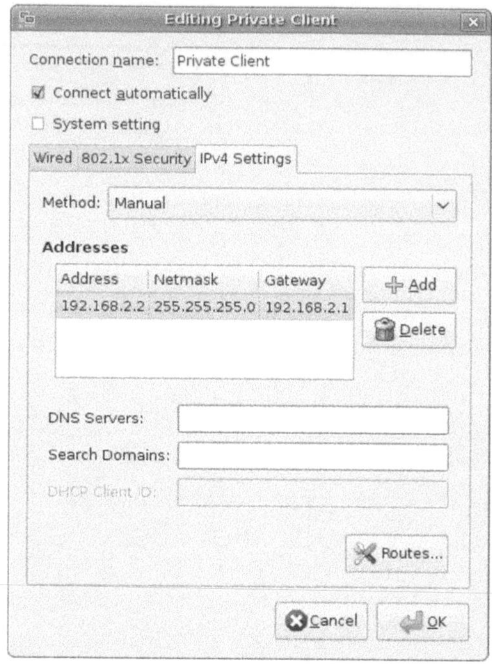

Figure 3.24 Result of new configuration of Ethernet NIC private client.

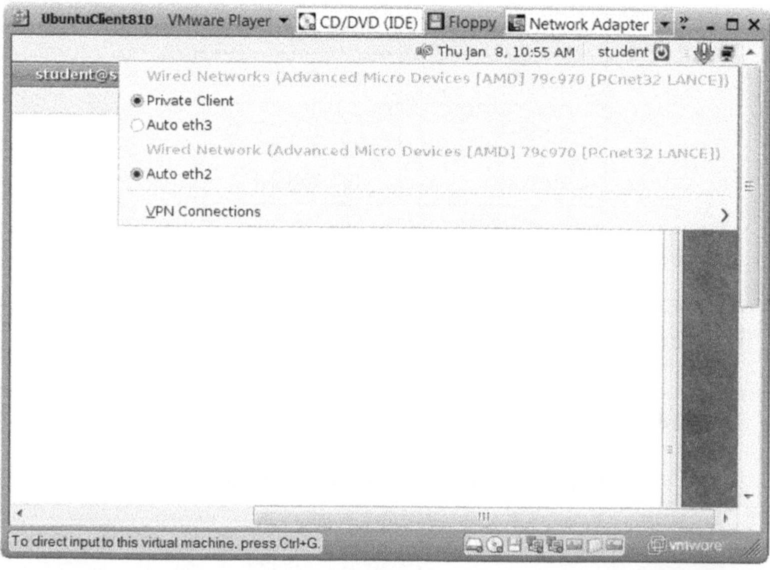

Figure 3.25 Enabling private client connection.

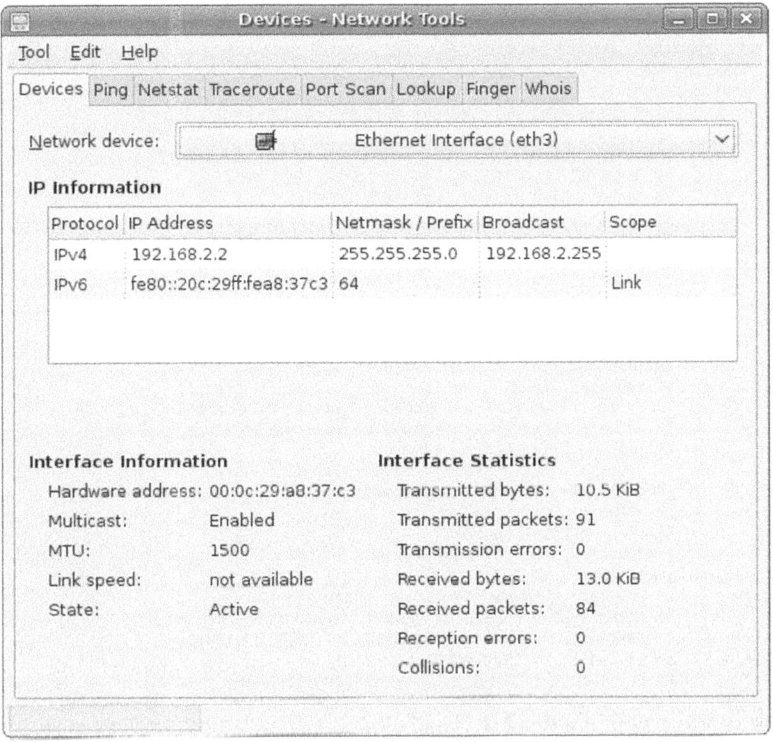

Figure 3.26 Private client configuration.

1. Start the computer that has the server edition of Ubuntu installed. Log in with username **student** and password **ubuntu**.
2. If you want to configure the second NIC to have a static IP address, you need to edit the file /etc/network/interfaces with the nano editor. To open the file with the nano editor, enter the following command:

```
sudo nano /etc/network/interfaces
```

3. After the file is opened, move the cursor below the last row. Type the following code:

```
# eth1 configuration
auto eth1
iface eth1 inet static
address 192.168.2.1
netmask 255.255.255.0
network 192.168.2.0
broadcast 192.168.2.255
```

Figure 3.28 shows the code entered in the nano text editor.

4. After the code is typed, press the **Ctrl+X** key combination to exit the editor. When asked if you want to save the file, press the key **Y**. Then press the **Enter** key to exit the nano text editor.
5. You may verify the configuration by entering the following commands.

```
sudo /etc/init.d/networking restart
sudo ifconfig
```

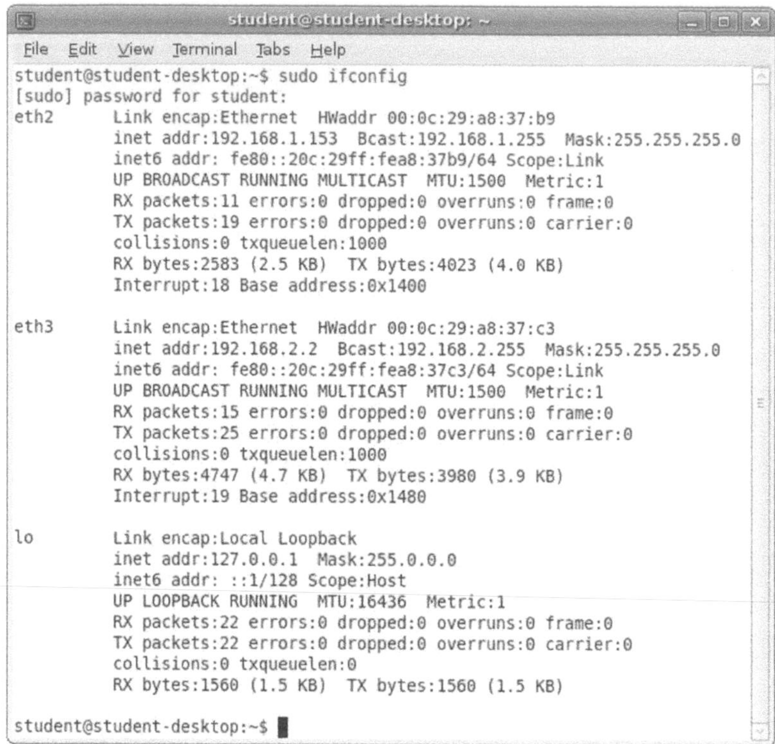

Figure 3.27 Result of configuration for private client NIC.

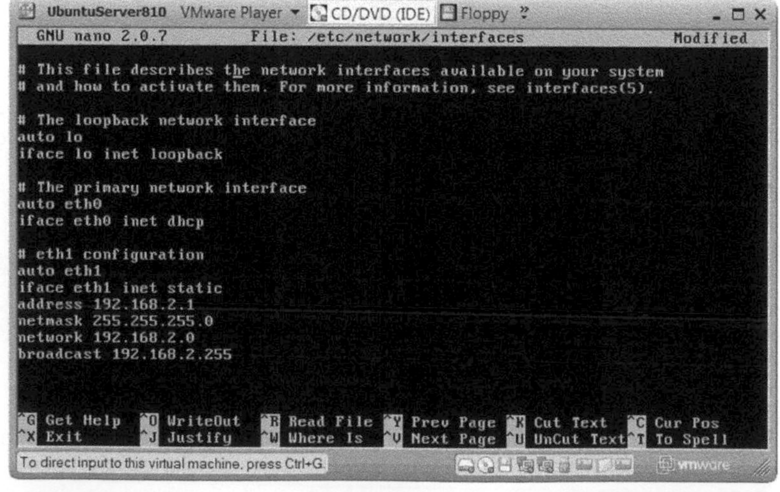

Figure 3.28 Configuration of eth1.

```
UbuntuServer810  VMware Player ▾  CD/DVD (IDE)  Floppy
          TX packets:57 errors:0 dropped:0 overruns:0 carrier:0
          collisions:0 txqueuelen:1000
          RX bytes:7362 (7.3 KB)  TX bytes:7682 (7.6 KB)
          Interrupt:18 Base address:0x1400

eth1      Link encap:Ethernet  HWaddr 00:0c:29:36:14:94
          inet addr:192.168.2.1  Bcast:192.168.2.255  Mask:255.255.255.0
          inet6 addr: fe80::20c:29ff:fe36:1494/64 Scope:Link
          UP BROADCAST RUNNING MULTICAST  MTU:1500  Metric:1
          RX packets:33 errors:0 dropped:0 overruns:0 frame:0
          TX packets:41 errors:0 dropped:0 overruns:0 carrier:0
          collisions:0 txqueuelen:1000
          RX bytes:5312 (5.3 KB)  TX bytes:5876 (5.8 KB)
          Interrupt:19 Base address:0x1480

lo        Link encap:Local Loopback
          inet addr:127.0.0.1  Mask:255.0.0.0
          inet6 addr: ::1/128 Scope:Host
          UP LOOPBACK RUNNING  MTU:16436  Metric:1
          RX packets:13 errors:0 dropped:0 overruns:0 frame:0
          TX packets:13 errors:0 dropped:0 overruns:0 carrier:0
          collisions:0 txqueuelen:0
          RX bytes:728 (728.0 B)  TX bytes:728 (728.0 B)

student@ubuntu-server:~$ _
To direct input to this virtual machine, press Ctrl+G.
```

Figure 3.29 Result of eth1 configuration.

You should be able to see the result displayed in Figure 3.29. If you cannot see the information about eth1 in the display, you may have a MAC address conflict. Some of you who use virtual machines for the hands-on practice may have copied the virtual machines from elsewhere. If so, there may be a conflict between the MAC addresses originally assigned to your NICs and the new MAC addresses assigned to your virtual machine at the new location. If so, you need to remove the persistent rule file from the Linux operating system. To do so, first make a copy of the file /etc/udev/rules.d/70-persistant-net.rules with the following command:

```
sudo cp /etc/udev/rules.d/70-persistent-net.rules /etc/udev/
rules.d/70-persistent-net.rules-old
```

After you have copied the file, run the following command to remove the file:

```
sudo rm /etc/udev/rules.d/70-persistent-net.rules
```

For the configuration to take effect, you need to reboot the system by entering the following command:

```
sudo reboot
```

After your system is rebooted, run the following command to verify the configuration:

```
sudo ifconfig
```

This time, you should be able to see the information regarding eth1 displayed on-screen (Figure 3.29).

TEST NEWLY CREATED PRIVATE NETWORK

After the second NIC on both client and server computers are configured, these two computers should be able to communicate with each other. The following steps show you how to test the simple network between server and client:

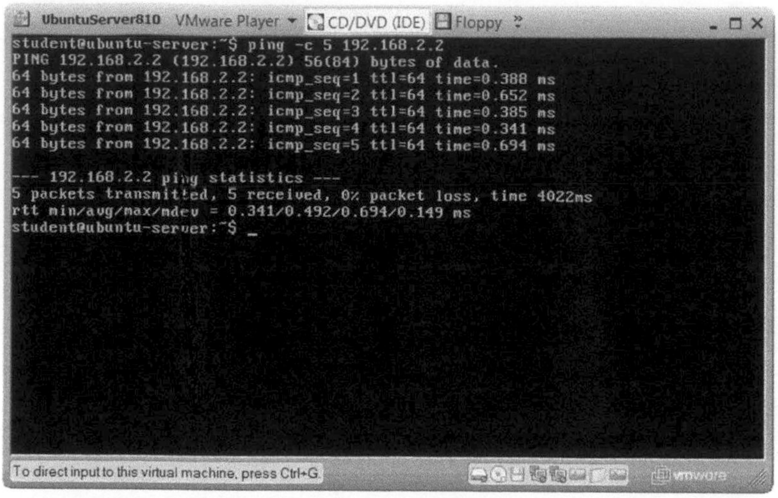

Figure 3.30 Testing connection between server and client computers.

1. Suppose the client computer is still on. To test the connection between client and server, you may execute the ping command, which uses ICMP to get a response from the receiver. Type the following command:

   ```
   ping -c 5 192.168.2.2
   ```

   In the aforementioned command, -c 5 indicates that five responses will be displayed on screen. 192.168.2.2 is the IP address of the client computer.
2. Press the **Enter** key to run this command. If everything works properly, you should be able to see the output shown in Figure 3.30.

In this hands-on activity, you created a simple network between client and server computers. In later chapters, some of our hands-on activities will be carried out on this simple network created here. Make sure that the network is working properly before you move on to the next project.

3.6 Summary

In this chapter, we investigated three aspects of network infrastructure. To create a network for an organization's information system, designers, technicians, and network administrators need to know the type of network, the network devices to be used to send and receive data, and the network media to be used to connect network devices for distributing data in the network. This chapter should serve to inform professionals involved in network construction about the capabilities and limitations of each type of network. The networks discussed in this chapter are LANs, WANs, the Internet, and wireless networks. This chapter provided information about various networks and explains how each type of network gets the job done. It also described various types of network media such as twisted wire, optical fiber, radio wave, and infrared. It provided information on the specifications of these network media.

This chapter also covered the commonly used network devices. It discussed network devices such as NICs, switches, and routers. The focus of this chapter was on two major devices, switches, and routers. Different types of switches and routers were examined. This chapter showed that a successful network relies on good network design, network media used for connecting computers, and network devices for data distribution.

In the hands-on activity of this chapter, you created a simple network that connects two hosts: the client computer and the server computer. The GUI tool called NetworkManager was used for configuring the network connection. Another way to configure NIC settings is to use commands and a text editor such as nano. The nano text editor was used to modify the network configuration files. To create a network on a bigger scale, we need to know more about IP address and subnet masks, and how they can be used to form subnets. These topics will be covered in Chapter 4.

Review Questions

1. What is the most popular LAN technology?
2. Describe how an Ethernet frame is constructed.
3. What are the CSMA and CD technologies?
4. What are the advantages of a VLAN?
5. Which WAN technology can reach transmission rates of up to 10 Gbps?
6. Which WAN technology is using circuit switching technology?
7. Explain why a packet switch uses two sets of ports.
8. What are CSU and DSU?
9. What is the Internet?
10. How can hosts in private LANs communicate through the Internet?
11. What is a POP?
12. What are the two key technologies that make communication over the Internet possible?
13. On the Internet, how can an ISP reach another ISP?
14. What is the range of data transmission rates for the T-series standards?
15. Name three commonly used wireless transmission media.
16. Name three types of commonly used wireless technologies.
17. Why do we need modulation?
18. What is the difference between a hub and a switch?
19. What are the advantages of a Layer 3 switch?
20. What are the reasons for an edge aggregation router to use MPLS?

Case Study Projects

The following are two network projects that involve the investigation of the existing network in your university or workplace. You may investigate the network you are currently able to access by yourself, or ask the network administrator to help.

Case Study Project 3.1. Write a report on the type of network used at your university or at your home. Describe the technology used by the network for accessing the Internet.

Case Study Project 3.2. Investigate what network media are used for your university's network. Write a paragraph explaining why the network technology at your university should be upgraded to a better technology, or why it should not.

Chapter 4

Network Design

Objectives

- Become familiar with network design strategies.
- Learn about IP addresses.
- Understand subnets.
- Know how to design networks with subnets.

4.1 Introduction

In the previous chapters, you have learned about the TCP/IP protocols and various types of networks. You also know that each computer on the Internet must have an IP address, and a router must have two or more IP addresses to connect two or more networks.

To physically create a network, we need to resolve some issues such as which IP address should be given to which host, how to group a set of hosts so that they can exchange information within the group, and how many hosts can be linked to a network, and so on. These questions can be addressed during the network design process. The requirements of a network infrastructure will be investigated in the network design process. Based on the requirements, decisions will be made regarding how the hosts in the network are addressed and how they can be linked in the network. In this chapter, we will first go through the network modeling process. Along the way, we will discuss issues related to network modeling. We will take a closer look at issues such as assigning IP addresses. The concept of subnets will also be discussed in this chapter. Examples related to the calculation of subnets will be given. We will also discuss issues related to the coexistence of IPv4 and IPv6. For hands-on practice, this chapter will explore IPv6 on Linux. You will carry out a hands-on activity on testing the support for IPv6 by the Linux operating system and using some simple IPv6-based network tools.

4.2 Network Design

Before a network can be physically built, it must be carefully designed logically, especially if it is a large-scale network project. The network design process includes several steps. The following are some of the major steps in the design phase:

- Investigation of the requirements for the future network
- Development of a logical network model, which should include the specifications for the protocols, applications, network media, and network devices
- Development of an IP addressing and routing strategy
- Development of a security policy
- Based on the logical network, development of a plan for the physical implementation of the network

In the following subsections, we will go through each of the major steps in the network design process.

4.2.1 Requirement Investigation

The design process starts with an investigation of the needs of the future network. The designers need to find out what network services should be provided by the network, collect information about the existing network, and determine the type of network needed to meet the requirements of the users. The following are some of the commonly used methods to collect information:

- Prepare a list of questions about the needs of the future network.
- Interview the users, technicians, and network administrators.
- Observe how the existing network works, and document the network devices used in the current network.
- Review documents about the operation of the existing network.

Once the information is collected, the designers will categorize and analyze the information. By carefully reviewing the collected information, the designers will be able identify the service and support needed for the new network. For future reference, they should document information about the needs.

4.2.2 Logical Network Model

After the designers find out what the needs are, they will decide which network infrastructure to use and draft an implementation plan. But first, they will create a logical model to represent the future network infrastructure. The benefit of developing a logical model first is huge. The logical model can be used to verify that the network to be developed will meet the users' requirements. Also, it is easy to make modifications to a network infrastructure on the logical model. For a large network, the commonly used network model is the Cisco hierarchical network design model. This model has three layers: the core layer, the distribution layer, and the access layer.

The core layer serves as the backbone of a network infrastructure. Depending on the needs, the core layer can be constructed as a LAN, MAN, or WAN. In the TCP/IP architecture, the core layer belongs to the network interface layer. The basic requirement for the core layer is that it should be a network with better performance and better reliability than the networks for the other layers. High-performance switches and network media are commonly used to link the network devices for this layer. The designers should carefully check if there are weak components in the core layer. Redundancy is a commonly used method to improve reliability. It guarantees that there are two or more paths to reach the distribution layer. Using high-performance network software and hardware can significantly improve performance. During the design process, the designers should always keep these factors in mind.

The distribution layer consists of data distribution network devices such as switches and routers. When communicating with the core layer, the routers convert each frame to one that is acceptable by the core layer, because the core layer has only switches. The hosts in the access layer communicate with each other through the distribution layer. The distribution layer defines the broadcast domain and blocks the local network traffic to be passed on to another distribution layer. Therefore, the access control service, proxy server, and security management are often located in this layer. Subnets are often defined in the distribution layer. Routers are used to connect these subnets. Later in this chapter, more information about subnets will be provided. In this layer, the designers need to make decisions on which routing protocols to use based on the requirements for scalability and performance. Often, network operating systems that host network management software are installed in this layer. Security application software programs such as antivirus software and firewall systems are also included in this layer.

The access layer consists of network hosts such as personal computers, mobile devices, and printers. This is the layer that allows users to access the network. Reliability and performance are not as superior as those for the core layer. Desktop operating systems or operating systems for mobile devices are more likely to be installed in this layer. Also, network-based application software, such as the database client and VPN client, is also installed in this layer. The network device commonly used in this layer is the layer 2 switch, which has no routing capability. The layer 2 switches are used to form LANs in the access layer. Figure 4.1 illustrates the three-layer modeling concept.

Based on the three-layer network model, the designers will specify the details of the network media and the network devices used in each layer. For example, when considering the devices used in the distribution layer, the designers need to decide what type of router should be used. If performance is a concern, the designers should choose hardware routers, which provide better

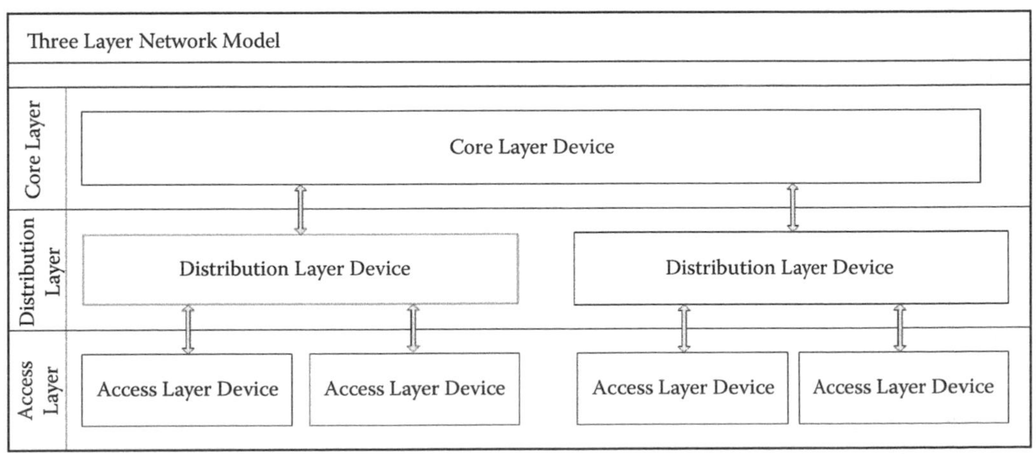

Figure 4.1 Three-layer network model.

performance. In a large organization, it is common for hardware routers to be used to direct network traffic and convert packets from one type of frame to another. On the other hand, if cost is a concern, a software router is often implemented with a server operating system. In small companies, software routers are commonly used to handle lighter network traffic.

After the specifications are entered for the devices in each of the three layers, the designers should verify if the requirements of the network are fulfilled. Often, it takes several rounds of modification before a satisfactory result is achieved.

4.2.3 IP Addressing and Routing Strategy

An enterprise-level network often includes a large number of computers and multiple LAN segments. The designers need to come up with an IP addressing strategy to decide how the IP addresses should be assigned to the LAN segments and network hosts. The designers should make decisions regarding the following options:

- Use either public IP addresses or private IP addresses for hosts and subnets.
- Make decisions regarding the number of subnets and the number of hosts in each subnet.
- Choose either classless or classful IP addresses.
- Determine whether to use a hierarchical routing infrastructure or a flat routing infrastructure.
- Decide whether to use the variable-length subnet mask.
- Determine whether to use supernets.
- Decide if a host should be assigned a static IP address or automatically assigned a dynamic IP address.
- Reserve a range of static IP addresses for servers and routers.

After the designers sketch the IP addressing plan for the local and global networks, they need to come up with a routing strategy to interconnect the networks. The designers may need to make the following decisions:

- Determine which routing protocols to use to deliver packets to destinations.
- Based on the routing functionalities, divide the networks into routing areas, and define routing autonomous regions and routing boundaries.
- Decide if routers should be updated statically or dynamically.
- Make a decision on how soon the routers should be updated.
- Specify the features of the routing equipment to be used to physically link networks.

Addressing and routing together outline the whole picture about the connections of the networks to be developed. Some of the IP-addressing-related topics will be discussed later this chapter. More information about routing will be given in Chapter 6.

4.2.4 Security Policy

To properly manage user authentication and authorization, the designers need to identify user groups and priorities to be assigned to these groups. They also need to consider ways to prevent virus infection and prevent hackers from penetrating the private network. The security policy is created by a team that consists of an organization's administrators, network managers, and user representatives. It is a set of guidelines on how to protect the network.

The security policy includes a list of security measures to protect the network. The content of the security policy is related to data confidentiality, integrity, and availability as described in the following:

- *Confidentiality:* Make sure that confidential information is not viewed by unauthorized individuals.
- *Integrity:* Make sure that confidential information is not intentionally or unintentionally altered. The data being transmitted on the network should not be modified.
- *Availability:* Make sure that the data is available to the authorized users whenever they need them.

The security policy addresses these issues by providing a set of rules. When developing a new network, these rules should be strictly followed.

Confidential information can be compromised by making it available to unauthorized individuals through unprotected disks, networks, and portable media such as CDs, e-mail, documents, and even word of mouth. The security policy should address the issue of how to protect the data on these media.

Most of the older protocols such FTP and Telnet transmit data in cleartext. Hackers can easily capture the data content carried by these protocols. The designers should consider protecting the data transmitted over the Internet with technologies such as Secure Sockets Layer (SSL). SSL can be used to establish an authenticated connection between the sender and the receiver. It can also encrypt data to protect it from hackers. The designers need to specify which application layer protocols of the TCP/IP architecture should be protected with SSL.

In addition to the security policy, the network designers also need to determine at which layer of the TCP/IP architecture the security measures should be enforced. For example, if authentication and encryption are enforced at the network interface layer, the security measures can also protect the protocols and applications above the network interface layer. This means that once the security measures are enforced in the network interface layer, there is no need to enforce them at each individual application in the application layer. However, enforcing security in the network interface layer will slow down performance. Therefore, the designers need to decide on issues such as this.

There are two ways in which the integrity of data can be damaged. During transmission, data may be altered unintentionally by electrical spikes or other interference. Protocols that use the checksum or CRC can detect this type of error. Data can also be altered intentionally. To prevent data from being intentionally altered by unauthorized individuals, security measures such as digital signature and packet-level protection should be considered by the designers. Security measures such as the Message Authentication Code (MAC) can also be used to protect data integrity.

To make data available to qualified users whenever they need them is another major concern to be considered during the design process. Based on the security policy, the designers can do two things to improve availability. The first is to correctly identify the user groups so that the designers can properly design the access layer devices. The second is to consider adding redundancy to reduce downtime. Using some of the following measures may help improve availability:

- Creating a network so that each of the devices in the network can be accessed through multiple routes. When one route to a device is out of order, the device can still be accessed through other routes. A network with such structure is often called a *mesh network*.
- Device redundancy is another way to improve availability. The network server can be replicated to multiple computers. Using dual-homing Ethernet switches in a network is another

way to improve availability. By using Virtual Router Redundancy Protocol (VRRP) technology, one can treat a group of routers as a single virtual router that can serve as a gateway for LAN segments. Even if one of the routers in the group fails, the gateway to the LAN is still available.
- Constructing a grid system for an international organization is another way to improve availability. The grid system allows hosts to use network devices at different locations. In case the devices at one location fail, the hosts can still use the devices at the other locations. The grid system can not only improve availability but can also improve performance significantly by balancing the computing load of multiple sites.

A well-managed network can also improve availability. During the design process, the designers may need to consider adding some services and facilities to improve the network's availability:

- Adding more tools for network monitoring, and troubleshooting hardware or software problems.
- Adding more backup and restoration facilities such as creating a Redundant Array of Independent Disks (RAID) system with multiple hard drives.
- Adding more spare devices for critical network devices such as routers, switches, and network servers.
- Adding an uninterruptible power supply (UPS) system to critical network devices to prevent power outage from shutting them down. The UPS system can also be used to reduce the damage caused by electricity spikes.

In the foregoing, several issues related to the security policy have been discussed. The security-related technologies are recommended for protecting the network infrastructure. These technologies should be specified in the logical network model. When physically implementing a network, the security-related hardware and software should be properly configured, and one should make sure that these technologies work properly before the network can be accessed by the public.

4.2.5 Planning for Physical Implementation

Based on the logical network model, the designers should come up with a plan to transform the network on paper into a physically existing network. The designers need to allocate the budget, organize the construction team, identify the product suppliers, contact the consulting companies, and get support from the administrators. Often, the designers need to balance the needs and the cost. If the budget and other resources are limited, it is necessary to revise the logical network model to lower the cost.

To implement a large-scale network system, thorough planning is a key step for success. Based on the logical model, the designers will work with the administrators to allocate the resources for the network project. The designers should find out the following:

- What is the estimated total cost, including the equipment cost and the labor cost?
- Is the funding enough for the project? If not, is there an alternative solution that meets the requirements of the network?
- Are skilled technicians available to construct the entire network? If not, what is the cost of outsourcing the workload to consulting companies?

After all the questions are answered and all the problems are resolved, it is time to organize a team for the task of network construction. To help the construction team achieve its goals, the following tasks should be included in the implementation plan:

- A time line should be drafted to guide the network implementation progress. The time line should indicate what tasks can be done simultaneously and what tasks should be done before other tasks.
- It is also helpful to personalize the job assignments so that everyone in the construction team is clear about his or her responsibility.
- If the project is implemented at multiple sites, the construction team should have a plan for collaboration among these sites.
- In the plan, the room and building information should also be included so that the construction team can decide where to connect the wire.
- After the network servers, switches, and routers are put in place, there should be a plan regarding the configuration of these devices according the logical network model.
- Lastly, the plan should include regulations on the network-testing process. The devices in all the three layers of the network logical model should be thoroughly tested before the network can be made available to the public. Make sure that all the devices in the access layer can reach each other.

The plan should be well documented and available to all the construction team members. During the planning for physical implementation, the designers should come up with specifications about servers, client computers, network devices, and software. There are many choices in the selection of technologies. Many factors can influence the selection. Linux and many other open source applications are good candidates for consideration. Once Linux is chosen for constructing the network, the designers need to specify details regarding the vendor contact information, Web sites to download software from, the compatibility of Linux with the existing network infrastructure, the versions of the software, requirements for hardware and software, the installation process, and the Internet service provider (ISP). The specifications should be documented for future reference.

4.3 IP Addressing

As mentioned earlier, every host on the Internet should have a unique IP address. IP addressing is a critical part of making the Internet work properly. The Internet consists of thousands of networks that may be created with various technologies. Physically, the networks created with different technologies are not compatible. The hardware addresses are not numerous enough to uniquely identify the hosts on the Internet, because they are coded differently in different technologies. Therefore, we must come up with a unified addressing scheme, which is the IP addressing scheme. An IP address is independent of physical structure. In this section, we will discuss how IP addresses are formed and how they are classified. We will also examine some specially defined IP addresses used for different purposes.

4.3.1 IPv4 IP Addressing

For IPv4, an IP address is a unique 32-bit binary number. This allows IPv4 to identify 2^{32} objects. In IPv4, the 32 binary bits are divided into two parts. The first part is called the prefix, which is

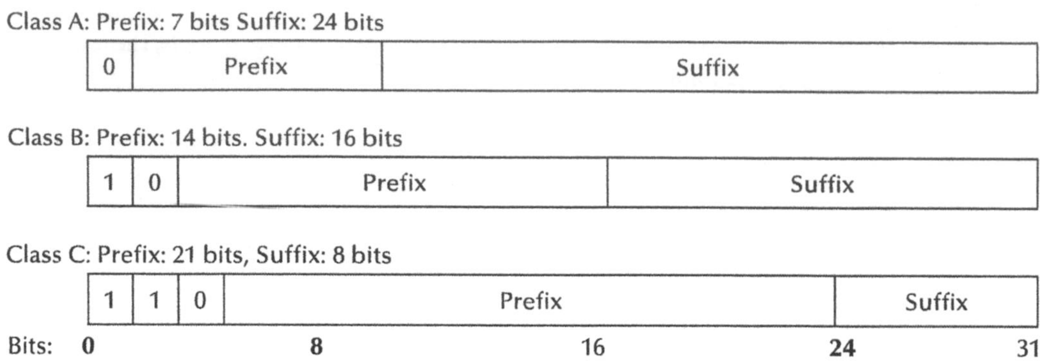

Figure 4.2 Classes of IPv4 addresses.

used to identify the networks. The second part is called the suffix which is used to identify the hosts in a network. For a large network that has a large number of hosts, the IP addresses should be formed with more bits in the suffix and fewer bits in the prefix. On the other hand, for a small network that links a small number of hosts, the IP addresses can be formed by using fewer bits in the suffix section and more bits in the prefix section.

Among the thousands of networks that form the Internet, a few are very large networks, such as those run by ISPs, and many of them are small networks, such as those run by small companies. To efficiently use these IP addresses, the IPv4 IP addresses are categorized into different classes so that a network designer can choose an IP address from the proper class based on the size of the network. Figure 4.2 shows how the prefix and suffix are divided in each class.

In Figure 4.2, the binary code in front of the prefix is used as the class ID. That is, if an IP address starts with the 0 bit, it is a Class A IP address. Similarly, if an IP address starts with the two bits 10, it is a Class B IP address; and if an IP address starts with 110, it is a Class C IP address. IPv4 also includes Class D and Class E IP addresses. The IP addresses in Class D are used for multicasting. Class D uses the identification code 1110. The IP addresses in Class E are reserved for future use. The class ID for Class E is 1111. Both Class D and Class E are not as widely used as the three primary classes, Class A, Class B, and Class C. Therefore, they are less known by users. Because this type of IP addressing scheme divides IP addresses into different classes, it is called classful IP addressing.

Table 4.1 lists the number of networks and the number of hosts that can be identified by each of the three primary classes.

Although computers use binary numbers for their operations, they are difficult for humans to use. When users interact with computers, decimal numbers are used. When represented by

Table 4.1 Number of Networks and Hosts Identified by Each Class

Class	*Number of Networks*	*Number of Hosts*
Class A	$2^7 = 128$	$2^{24} = 16777216$
Class B	$2^{14} = 16384$	$2^{16} = 65536$
Class C	$2^{21} = 2097152$	$2^8 = 256$

Table 4.2 Decimal Value of the 1 Bit in An Octet

Octet Column	*7*	*6*	*5*	*4*	*3*	*2*	*1*	*0*
Decimal value	$2^7 = 128$	$2^6 = 64$	$2^5 = 32$	$2^4 = 16$	$2^3 = 8$	$2^2 = 4$	$2^1 = 2$	$2^0 = 1$

decimal numbers, the 32 binary bits are divided into four groups with each group having 8 bits; each such group is called an octet. Each octet is often represented by a decimal number. Table 4.2 shows the decimal values corresponding to various positions of the 1 bit in an octet.

In Table 4.2, one can easily convert a binary number to a corresponding decimal number. For example, for the binary number 10010101 in an octet, you should use the binary value to multiply the corresponding decimal value, as shown below, and then add the products together. The sum is the corresponding decimal value of the binary number 10010101:

$$1\times2^7 + 0\times2^6 + 0\times2^5 + 1\times2^4 + 0\times2^3 + 1\times2^2 + 0\times2^1 + 1\times2^0$$

$$= 128 + 0 + 0 + 16 + 0 + 4 + 0 + 1$$

$$= 149$$

For each octet, the smallest binary number is 00000000, which has the corresponding decimal number 0. The largest binary value in an octet is 1111111. We can find out from Table 4.2 that the corresponding decimal value is 255. That is, the decimal value for an octet cannot go beyond 255.

By representing each octet with a decimal number, a 32-bit IP address can be represented by four decimal numbers separated by three dots. Table 4.3 gives some examples of IP addresses represented by both binary numbers and decimal numbers.

As shown in Table 4.3, it is much easier to work with decimal IP addresses. Because Class A uses the first octet as the prefix, a Class A decimal IP address uses the first number to identify the network. Similarly, Class B uses the first two octets as the prefix. Therefore, a decimal IP address in Class B uses the first two numbers as the network ID. Class C uses the first three octets as the prefix, which means that the first three numbers in a decimal IP address in Class C are used as the network ID.

One small inconvenience of a decimal IP address is that we can no longer see the class identification bit. Excluding the Class A identification bit, Class A uses seven binary bits in the first octet to identify a network. This means that Class A can only identify 128 networks. Because a decimal Class A IP address uses the first number as the network identifier, the first number of all the decimal IP addresses in Class A has a value between 0 and 127. Similarly, because a Class B IP address uses the first two binary digits as a class identifier, six digits are available for network identification in the first octet. The six binary digits can be represented by decimal numbers from 0 to 64. Thus, following the numbers used by Class A IP addresses, Class B IP addresses have decimal

Table 4.3 Examples of IP Addresses

32-Bit Binary IP Address	*Decimal IP Address*
10101100 00010000 00000000 00000110	172.16.0.6
00001010 00000100 10011011 00000000	10.4.155.0
11000000 10101000 00000001 00010000	192.168.1.16

Table 4.4 Range of Values for the First Octet

Class	*Range of Values in the First Number*
Class A	0–127
Class B	128–191
Class C	192–223

values between 128 and 191 for the first decimal number. Again, the first decimal number in a Class C IP address has a value ranging between 192 and 223, which is the range represented by the five remaining binary digits in the first octet. Table 4.4 lists the range of decimal values used by the first number of an IP address for each class.

By looking at the first decimal number in an IP address, we can easily identify the class to which the address belongs. For example, we easily tell that the IP address 192.168.1.16 is a Class C IP address, and 10.4.155.0 is a Class A IP address.

4.3.2 Special IP Addresses

IPv4 has some IP addresses reserved for special purposes. These special IP addresses usually represent network IDs, broadcast addresses, loopback IP address for testing, and computer IP addresses for booting computers. These special IP addresses are never assigned to regular hosts.

In the previous section, we mentioned that Class A decimal IP addresses use the first number as the prefix and the last three numbers as the suffix, Class B decimal IP addresses use the first two numbers as the prefix and the last two numbers as the suffix, and Class C decimal IP addresses use the first three numbers as the prefix and the last number as the suffix. Therefore, by filling the suffix portion of a decimal IP address with 0's, we have the IP address for a network shown in Table 4.5.

Network IP addresses are used by a router to establish an optimal route from one host to another. Therefore, we do not want to assign network IP addresses to regular hosts, which may confuse the router. The network IP addresses for subnets have no nice pattern, as shown in Table 4.5. Some of the network IP addresses for subnets are just like regular IP addresses. We need to be very careful not to assign subnet IP addresses to regular hosts. Later, we will discuss subnets in this chapter.

Through broadcasting, messages can be sent to all the hosts in a network. Broadcasting can also be used to find a host with an unknown IP address. Broadcasting to a specific network can be done through a dedicated broadcast IP address. For the three primary classes, the broadcast IP addresses can be formed by keeping the numbers used for the prefix and filling the suffix with the number 255. The number 255 represents an octet with all 1's. There is a special broadcast IP

Table 4.5 Network IP Addresses

Class	*Examples of Host IP Address*	*Network IP Address*
Class A	10.1.1.11	10.0.0.0
Class B	172.16.6.21	172.16.0.0
Class C	192.168.1.16	192.168.1.0

Table 4.6 Broadcast IP Addresses

Class	*Examples of IP Address*	*Broadcast IP Address*
Class A	10.1.1.11	10.255.255.255
Class B	172.16.6.21	172.16.255.255
Class C	192.168.1.16	192.168.1.255
Local	—	255.255.255.255

address that has 255 in both the prefix and suffix portions of a decimal IP address. This broadcast IP address is only used to broadcast in a local network. Table 4.6 shows how these broadcast IP addresses are formed.

Again, a broadcast IP address should not be assigned to a regular host. The broadcast IP address patterns shown in Table 4.6 only apply to the IP addresses in the three primary classes. When applied to subnets, the broadcast IP addresses may not follow the patterns illustrated in Table 4.6.

The local broadcast IP address 255.255.255.255 is used during a computer's startup process if the computer does not know the network IP address. To communicate with other hosts on a network, the computer also needs to know its own IP address, called the source IP address. However, during the startup process, the computer does not know its own IP address yet. In this case, the specific IP address 0.0.0.0 is assigned to "this" computer so that the computer can complete its startup process. When used in a routing table, 0.0.0.0 represents "this" network. However, the broadcast IP address 255.255.255.255 is more preferred for "this" network.

To test network-based application software, usually the client and server need to be installed on two separate computers linked by a network. The IP addresses, one for the client and one for the server, are used for the communication between client and server. However, by using a specially assigned loopback IP address, the test can be done on a single computer. A loopback IP address starts with the number 127. For example, the commonly used first loopback IP address is 127.0.0.1. The word *localhost* is the reserved name for the loopback IP address. The word *localhost* is also used as the default Web page for a computer. To test if localhost is the default Web page, you can enter the URL http://localhost on the computer's Web browser. After the Enter key is pressed, the name localhost is translated to 127.0.0.1. Then, the computer's default Web page will be displayed on screen.

In the foregoing text, several reserved special IP addresses have been discussed. Again, none of these special IP addresses should be assigned to regular hosts. Also, we cannot use one type of special IP address for other purposes, such as using a loopback IP address for a network ID.

4.3.3 Private and Public IP Addressing

As mentioned earlier, IP addresses are used to identify hosts on the Internet. Therefore, they should be publicity accessible. On the other hand, many institutions have their own Intranets, which are not supposed to be accessed by the public. To allow the hosts on an Intranet to be able to communicate with each other, three blocks of IP addresses are reserved as private IP addresses for internal use. Table 4.7 lists all the three blocks of private IP addresses.

Table 4.7 Private IP Addresses

Block	*Block Range*	*Available IP Addresses*
Class A block	10.0.0.0–10.255.255.255	16,777,216
Class B block	172.16.0.0–172.31.255.255	1,048,576
Class C block	192.168.0.0–192.168.255.255	65,536

These private IP addresses cannot be recognized on the Internet. Therefore, each individual company does not need to worry about its private IP addresses conflicting with those of other companies. For example, the IP address 10.1.1.11 can be used by multiple companies internally if only it does not cause conflict internally. For those who have built a home network, the IP address starts with 192.168, commonly used for a private IP address. To allow computers with private IP addresses to access the Internet, the private IP addresses need to be translated into public IP addresses assigned by ISPs. Network Address Translation (NAT) is the kind of technology that can get the job done.

Some computers are configured to automatically receive an IP address from a DHCP server. However, it often happens that a DHCP server is unable to deliver the IP address to a DHCP client due to a network problem or error in the configuration of the DHCP server. In such a case, the DHCP client is assigned an Automatic Private IP Addressing (APIPA) IP address. APIPA includes IP addresses ranging from 169.254.0.1 to 169.254.255.254. Again, these IP addresses are not recognizable on the Internet. Once the network or DHCP server problem is fixed, the APIPA IP address will be automatically replaced by the one delivered from the DHCP server.

This discussion is based on IPv4. The specifications for IPv6 are different. IPv6 will be discussed in the next section.

4.3.4 IPv6 Addressing

As mentioned in Chapter 2, IPv4 has almost run out of IP addresses. For IPv6, an IP address is a unique 128-bit binary number. IPv6 supports 2^{128} distinct IP addresses, which is such a large number that we do not need to worry about running out of IP addresses for many generations to come.

Because an address in IPv6 has 128 binary bits, even decimal numbers are not convenient for such a large number. Therefore, an IPv6 address is represented by eight hexadecimal numbers separated by the character ":". For example, an IPv6 IP address may look like this:

43AC:0000:740A:0000:0000:0000:0000:97CC

Even though represented in the hexadecimal system, an IPv6 address is still not easy to remember for most users. To further simplify it, the consecutive zero sets can be compressed as follows:

43AC:0:740A::97CC

Providing more IP addresses is not the only improvement. There are many other good reasons to use IPv6. The following are some IPv6 features:

- IPv6 supports a large number of IP addresses.
- IPv6 has a flexible header structure that can minimize header overhead.

- IPv6 supports a hierarchical addressing and routing infrastructure, to reduce the load on backbone routers.
- IPv6 does not support broadcasting. Instead, it supports the more efficient unicast, multicast, and anycast.
- IPv6 can create a high-quality path between the sender and the receiver for transmitting multimedia content.
- IPv6 has the built-in encryption service for data security.

Normally, an IPv6 packet contains a 40-byte base header. Additional extension headers can be added for transmitting data in different protocols (Figure 4.3). For example, to transmit TCP data, it simply adds a TCP header to the base header. Such a flexible header structure allows IPv6 to quickly accommodate new features. An existing protocol need not be rewritten to support new features. It simply adds one or more extension headers to support the new features once they become available.

To enhance routing and scaling, IPv6 addresses are organized into a hierarchical system. The idea of using a hierarchical system in IPv6 was borrowed from the telephone system, which starts with the country code, area code, prefix, and line number. On this system, the longer a phone number is, the farther the phone is from the local area. Similarly, an IPv6 address has three levels: public topology, site topology, and interface identifier (Figure 4.4).

- *Public topology:* The public topology is the leftmost 48-bit section of an IPv6 IP address. It is used to identify a site and is assigned by an ISP to provide access to the IPv6 Internet.
- *Site topology:* The next 16-bit section is the site topology, which is used to identify the subnets within an organization.
- *Interface identifier:* The next 64-bit section is the interface identifier, which identifies an NIC. The interface identifier can be either automatically configured based on the NIC's hardware address or manually configured.
- The three-level hierarchical system is more efficient for address allocation; it can reduce the latency for routing lookup.

Broadcasting in IPv4 can generate a lot of network traffic. Instead of using broadcasting, IPv6 uses three types of addresses: unicast, multicast, and anycast.

Base Header 40 bytes	Optional Extension Header 1	...	Optional Extension Header N	Payload

Figure 4.3 Flexible IPv6 header structure.

Public Topology	*Site Topology*	*Interface Identifier*
48 Bits Global routing prefix	16 Bits Subnet ID	64 Bits Interface ID

Figure 4.4 Three-level hierarchical system.

4.3.4.1 Unicast IP Address

When messages are exchanged between a sender and a receiver over a network, the information exchange process is called *unicast*. A unicast IP address is used for an individual host on a network. There are five types of unicast IP addresses.

Global unicast addresses in IPv6 are similar to public IP addresses in IPv4. They are IPv6-Internet-accessible IP addresses. For a unicast IP address, the three-level hierarchical system can be specifically formed as shown in Figure 4.5.

The prefix code 001 indicates that the IP address is a global unicast address. The size of the global routing prefix is 45 bits for a global unicast address.

Link-local addresses in IPv6 are similar to ARIPA IP addresses in IPv4, which has the network ID 169.254.0.0. The structure of a link-local address is shown in Figure 4.6.

Site-local addresses in IPv6 are similar to those private addresses with the network IDs 10.0.0.0, 172.16.0.0, and 192.168.0.0. Site-local addresses are used for intranets and are not accessible through the Internet. Similar to private addresses, site-local addresses can also be used in subnets. The structure of a site-local address is given in Figure 4.7.

Similar to IPv4, IPv6 also reserves some special addresses, including the loopback address and the unspecified address:

- *Loopback address:* An IPv6 loopback address is similar to an IPv4 loopback address. The IPv6 loopback looks like ::1 or 0:0:0:0:0:0:0:1.
- *Unspecified address:* An IPv6 unspecified address is similar to the 0.0.0.0 in IPv4 used for "this" computer. The IPv6 unspecified address looks like :: or 0:0:0:0:0:0:0:0.

Compatibility addresses are used to help the migration from IPv4 to IPv6. These addresses are compatible with both the IPv4 and IPv6 standards. Table 4.8 lists some types of compatibility addresses.

	Public Topology	*Site Topology*	*Interface Identifier*
001	48 Bits Global routing prefix	16 Bits Subnet ID	64 Bits Interface ID

Figure 4.5 Global unicast hierarchical system.

	54 Zero Bits	64 Bits
1111 1110 10	0000000000...0000000000	Interface ID

Figure 4.6 Link-local address structure.

	36 Zero Bits	16 Bits	64 Bits
1111 1110 11	000...000	Subnet ID	Interface ID

Figure 4.7 Site-local address structure.

Table 4.8 Compatibility Addresses

Address Name	*Expression*	*Usage*
IPv4-compatible address	0:0:0:0:0:0:w.x.y.z or ::w.x.y.zwhere w.x.y.z is the 32-bit IPv4 address	Used by IPv6/IPv4 hosts to communicate with IPv4 routers
IPv4-mapped address	0:0:0:0:0:FFFF:w.x.y.z or ::FFFF:w.x.y.z where w.x.y.z is the 32-bit IPv4 address	Used internally to represent IPv4 addresses for IPv6 applications
6to4 address	2002:wwxx:yyzz:[subnetId]:[interfaceId] where wwxx:yyzz is the embedded IPv4 address in the HEX format	Allows IPv6 packets to be transmitted over an IPv4 network
ISATAP address	::0:5EFE:w.x.y.z where w.x.y.z is the 32-bit IPv4 address	Used by two IPv6/IPv4 hosts to communicate with each other over an IPv4 intranet
Teredo address	2001:0000:[serverId]:[flag]:[UDP port number]:[public IPv4 address] All values are in the HEX format	Used by IPv6/IPv4 hosts located behind IPv4 NAT devices

With these compatibility addresses, IPv6 can work with the existing IPv4 Internet without the reconfiguration of explicit tunnels.

4.3.4.2 Multicast

Multicast is for communication between a single sender and multiple receivers. A multicast address is used to identify a group of hosts. The hosts can join or leave a multicast group at any time. During a multicast process, IPv6 hosts listen for multicast traffic dedicated to the group. The packets in the multicast traffic use the multicast address as its destination address. The packets are then sent to all the hosts in the group identified by the multicast address. The structure of a multicast address is shown in Figure 4.8.

In Figure 4.8, the Transient flag, or T flag, is defined in the 4-bit Flag field. The T can be set to 0 to indicate that the multicast address is assigned permanently by the Internet Assigned Numbers Authority (IANA), or set to 1 to indicate that the multicast address is not assigned permanently by the IANA. The 4-bit scope defines the scope that a multicast address can cover. The commonly defined scope values are defined in Table 4.9.

	4 Bits	4 Bits	112 Bits
1111 1111	Flag	Scope	Multicast Group Address

Figure 4.8 Multicast address structure.

Table 4.9 Scope Definition

Scope Value	*Definition*
1	Node-local scope
2	Link-local scope
5	Site-local scope
8	Organization-local scope
14	Global scope

There are several specially assigned multicast group addresses. For example, the multicast group address FF02:0:0:0:0:0:1 is for "all hosts" in the link-local scope, and the multicast address FF05:0:0:0:0:0:2 is for "all routers" in the site-local scope.

4.3.4.3 Anycast

Anycast is for the communication between any sender and one of the receivers in a group of hosts. Anycast is used when a request from a sender can be answered by a group of devices. Each of the devices in the group can handle the job equally well, and the sender has no preference on which device should handle the task. Anycast selects the device that is easiest to reach for handling the task.

An anycast address is used as the destination address in a packet. Up to now, the anycast address has been assigned to a router that serves as the gateway of a group. There is a specially designed anycast address structure. Anycast addresses are chosen from the unicast address pool. Anycast addresses are the same as unicast addresses. When a unicast address is assigned to a group of devices, an anycast address is created automatically.

The newer versions of Linux provide complete support for both IPv4 and IPv6. The patches for supporting IPv6 have been included in the Linux kernel version 2.6.x or later. The new features related to IPv6 for mobile networking are also under development.

4.4 Subnets

Subnetting is the process of dividing a network into several smaller networks. Within a subnet, all hosts have the same network ID in their IP addresses. With subnets, a physical network can be divided into logical units. The hosts in each unit can directly communicate with each other and use the same router to communicate with the hosts in the other subnets. Local broadcasting is limited within a subnet. There are several reasons to divide a network into subnets.

4.4.1 Reasons for Using Subnets

As mentioned earlier, in order to efficiently use IPv4 addresses, three IP address classes have been created. Each network in Class A can have at most 16,777,216 hosts, each network in Class B can have at most 65,536 hosts, and each network in Class C can have at most 256 IP addresses. A designer can, based on a company's size, choose which class to use. Suppose that a company has 5,000 hosts; its size is larger than what a Class C network can handle and is much smaller than what a Class B network can handle. If the company assigns addresses in Class B, there will be about 60,000 unused IP addresses. To reduce the number of unused hosts, a network in a class should be further divided into smaller subnets.

There are more reasons for subnets. Subnets are often used to improve network performance. Hosting a large number of computers in a network will increase the chance of collisions. The number of collisions can be reduced if the network is divided into subnets, and each subnet has a smaller number of hosts.

Broadcasting is the process of sending packets to each of the hosts on a network. The more computers a network has, the heavier the network traffic that will be caused by broadcasting. Subnetting again can be used to reduce the number of hosts in a network. With fewer computers in a network, there will be less broadcasting traffic.

Another reason for using subnets is that it strengthens network security control. Routers are used to separate subnets. They do not forward broadcasting packets to other subnets. Routers can also be configured to control network traffic. They can be configured to block certain protocols or certain hosts from accessing certain networks. Therefore, one can use subnets to protect a group of hosts from being accessed by unauthorized personnel.

Subnets can be constructed hierarchically. A subnet can be divided into several smaller subnets. Such a network structure can be used by large organizations to match their organization's infrastructure. A company may have multiple sites, buildings, departments, and offices. The company may want its networks to be constructed to mirror its physical and geographical structures. Subnets can be used to implement the network structure at the site, building, department, and office levels.

With subnets, the computers on a network at home or in an office can share one public IP address to access the Internet. In this way, we can reduce the cost of paying the ISP for public IP addresses. Also, we can save a number of public IPv4 addresses for other important uses.

Routing can also be simplified with subnets. A subnet with a single public IP address can be represented in a routing table with a single row, so the routing table in each router that is connected to the subnet can be simplified.

Splitting a network into smaller subnets involves calculating the bits of IP addresses to determine the range of the subnets. During the subnetting process, the size of the prefix and suffix in an IP address will be recalculated to meet the requirements. One also needs to reconfigure the network so that the routers are able to recognize the new subnets. The following are some topics related to the construction of subnets. We will start with an introduction to subnet masks.

4.4.2 Subnet Masks

A subnet mask is a string of 32-bit binary code used to determine which part of an IP address is used as the network ID. Similar to an IP address, these 32 bits are divided into four octets. Each octet includes eight binary bits. A subnet mask can also be represented by decimal numbers. Four decimal numbers are separated with three dots. Table 4.10 shows some examples of subnet masks.

Unlike IP addresses, the leftmost bits in a subnet mask must be a sequence of consecutive 1's and rightmost bits must be consecutive 0's. Table 4.11 gives a few examples of invalid subnet masks.

As mentioned earlier, Class A uses the first octet as the prefix used to identify a network, Class B uses the first two octets as the prefix, and Class C uses the first three octets as the prefix. For Class A, Class B, and Class C, the subnet masks are listed in Table 4.12.

For other subnets, the masks do not have a nice pattern, as shown in Table 4.12. The designer often needs to manually calculate a subnet mask based on the number of hosts to be included in the subnet. From Table 4.12, one can see that 1's are used to represent the prefix in a subnet mask,

Table 4.10 Examples of Subnet Masks

Binary Subnet Mask	*Decimal Subnet Mask*
11111111 00000000 00000000 00000000	255.0.0.0
11111111 11111111 00000000 00000000	255.255.0.0
11111111 11111111 11111111 00000000	255.255.255.0
11111111 11111111 11100000 00000000	255.255.224.0
11111111 11111111 11111111 11110000	255.255.255.240

Table 4.11 Invalid Subnet Masks

Binary	*Decimal*
11111111 00000101 00000000 00000000	255.5.0.0
11111111 11111100 11111111 00000000	255.252.255.0
10000000 11111111 11111111 00000000	128.255.255.0
11111111 11111111 11111111 11110001	255.255.255.241

Table 4.12 Examples of Subnet Masks in Classes A, B, and C

Class	*Binary Subnet Mask*	*Decimal Subnet Mask*
Class A	11111111 00000000 00000000 00000000	255.0.0.0
Class B	11111111 11111111 00000000 00000000	255.255.0.0
Class C	11111111 11111111 11111111 00000000	255.255.255.0

Table 4.13 Subnet Mask for Subnet with Maximum of 1024 Hosts

Binary	*Decimal*
11111111 11111111 11111100 00000000	255.255.252.0

and 0's are used to represent the suffix. As mentioned earlier, the suffix is used to represent the host ID. The number of bits in the suffix can decide the maximum number of hosts that can be identified. Thus, to support a subnet that is able to host 600 computers and other network devices, we need the suffix to have ten bits so that 2^{10} = 1024 hosts can be identified by the subnet. Therefore, one needs a subnet mask that looks like the one listed in Table 4.13.

Subnet masks are used to identify network IDs through the AND operation on binary numbers. Table 4.14 illustrate how the AND operation is performed.

That is, 0 AND 0 = 0, 0 AND 1 = 0, 1 AND 0 = 0, or 1 AND 1 = 1. With the AND operation, one can extract the network ID out of an IP address.

Table 4.14 AND Operation

Bit 1	*Bit 2*	*AND output*
0	0	0
0	1	0
1	0	0
1	1	1

Table 4.15 Extracting Network ID with Subnet Mask and AND Operation

	Binary	*Decimal*
IP address	11000000 10101000 00000001 00001011	192.168.1.11
Subnet mask	11111111 11111111 11111111 00000000	255.255.255.0
AND result	11000000 10101000 00000001 00000000	192.168.1.0

The following is an example that shows how to get the network ID from a given IP address. Suppose the Class C IP address is 192.168.1.11 and the subnet mask is 255.255.255.0. The result of the AND operation is given in Table 4.15.

As expected, the result of AND is 192.168.1.0, which is the network ID for the IP address 192.168.1.11. From Table 4.15, one can see that if any binary bit is ANDed with a 1bit, the original bit will be left unchanged. Any binary bit ANDed with a "0" bit will be changed to 0. This is how the network ID is extracted from an IP address.

4.4.3 Network Subnetting

If one needs to subnet a network in Class A, Class B, or Class C, all that the person needs to do is to turn some of the 0 bits in a subnet mask into 1 bits. In this way, the number of 0 bits is reduced and the number of 1 bits is increased; that is, there will be fewer hosts in each subnet and there will be more subnets to be created. The following are some examples to demonstrate the subnetting process.

Example 1

Suppose that you have a Class B network with the network ID 172.5.0.0. You would like to divide this standard Class B network into four possible subnets. The subnetting process is summarized in Table 4.16.

As shown in Table 4.16, to subnet a network into four possible subnets, we need to turn the first two leftmost zeros in the suffix section of the original subnet mask to two 1's. The reason to turn the two 0 bits to 1 bits is $4 = 2^2$, where the exponential value 2 is the number of bits needed to get four subnets from the original network. In general, the exponential value *n* in the formula

$$N = 2^n$$

Table 4.16 Subnetting Class B Network

	Binary	*Decimal*
Original network ID	10101100 00000101 00000000 00000000	172.5.0.0
Original subnet mask	11111111 11111111 00000000 00000000	255.255.0.0
New subnet mask	11111111 11111111 11000000 00000000	255.255.192.0
New subnet ID	10101100 00000101 00000000 00000000	172.5.0.0
	10101100 00000101 01000000 00000000	172.5.64.0
	10101100 00000101 10000000 00000000	172.5.128.0
	10101100 00000101 11000000 00000000	172.5.192.0

equals the number of bits that need to be changed, and N is the number of subnets to be generated. Note that we mentioned there are four possible subnets. In the classful IPv4 IP address system, the first and last one among the resulting subnet IDs are reserved and should not be assigned to any of the subnets. In this case, only two subnets are actually available. Therefore, the formula

$$2^n - 2$$

is often used to calculate the number of subnets. Because $n = 2$ in our example, then $2^2 - 2 = 2$ subnets are actually formed for the classful IPv4 network.

The formula $2^n - 2$ is also used to calculate the number of hosts in each subnet. In this formula, the number n is the number of 0's in the new subnet mask. In our example, the new subnet mask has 14 zeros. Therefore, the number of hosts in each subnet is

$$2^{14} - 2 = 16382$$

Example 2

For the given IP address 192.168.1.131 and the subnet mask 255.255.255.248, determine the network ID and broadcast IP address for the subnet that contains the given IP address. Also, find how many subnets and how many hosts in each subnet can be specified by the subnet mask 255.255.255.248.

Because the IP address 192.168.1.131 starts with the decimal number 192, it is an IP address that belongs to Class C. The subnetting process is to create subnets under a standard Class C network. Therefore, some of the 0 bits in the fourth octet of the standard Class C subnet mask will be changed to 1. The subnetting process is summarized in Table 4.17.

Table 4.17 Subnet Identified by the Fourth Octet

	Binary	*Decimal*
IP address	11000000 10101000 00000001 10000011	192.168.1.131
Subnet mask	11111111 11111111 11111111 11111000	255.255.255.248
Subnet ID	11000000 10101000 00000001 10000000	192.168.1.128
Broadcast	11000000 10101000 00000001 10000111	192.168.1.135

From the subnet mask, we can see that the rightmost three bits are 0 bits; this means that the number of hosts in each subnet is

$$2^3 - 2 = 6$$

Compared with the standard Class C subnet mask, this subnet mask has turned five 0 bits into 1 bits in the last octet; the number of subnets can be calculated with the following formula:

$$2^5 - 2 = 30$$

To calculate the subnet ID for the subnet that contains the given IP address 192.168.1.131, one can AND the IP address with the subnet mask. The result of the IP address ANDing the subnet mask is

```
    11000000 10101000 00000001 10000011
AND 11111111 11111111 11111111 11111000
    11000000 10101000 00000001 10000000
```

When representing the AND result in decimal from, the ID of the subnet (which contains the IP address 192.168.1.131) is 192.168.1.128.

By turning the binary digits in the suffix of the IP address to 1, we have the broadcast IP address. Because the rightmost three bits belong to the suffix, we then have the broadcast address in the following binary:

11000000 10101000 00000001 10000111

The corresponding decimal broadcast address is 192.168.1.135.

Note that the subnet ID is 192.168.1.128, which does not have the traditional format in which all the digits corresponding to the suffix are set to zero. Similarly, the broadcast address 192.168.1.135 does not necessarily have all the bits corresponding to the suffix set to "1" bits or 255 in decimal.

Example 3

For the given IP address 172.16.7.171 and the subnet mask 255.255.252.0, determine the network ID and broadcast IP address for the subnet that contains the given IP address. Also, find how many subnets and how many hosts in each subnet can be specified by the subnet mask 255.255.252.0.

Because the IP address 172.16.7.171 starts with the decimal number 172, it is an IP address that belongs to Class B. The subnetting process is to create subnets under a standard Class B network. Therefore, some of the 0 bits in the third octet of the standard Class B subnet mask will be changed to 1 bits. The subnetting process is summarized in Table 4.18.

Table 4.18 Subnet Identified by the Third Octet

	Binary	*Decimal*
IP address	10101100 00010000 00000111 10101011	172.16.7.171
Subnet mask	11111111 11111111 11111100 00000000	255.255.252.0
Subnet ID	10101100 00010000 00000100 00000000	172.16.4.0
Broadcast	10101100 00010000 00000111 11111111	172.16.7.255

From the subnet mask, we can see that the rightmost ten bits are 0 bits; this means that the number of hosts in each subnet is

$$2^{10} - 2 = 1022$$

Compared with the standard Class B subnet mask, this subnet mask has turned six 0 bits in the third octet into 1 bits; the number of subnets can be calculated with the following formula:

$$2^{6} - 2 = 62$$

To calculate the network ID for the subnet that contains the given IP address 172.16.7.171, you may need to AND the IP address with the subnet mask just as you did in the previous example. The result of the IP address ANDing the subnet mask is

```
    10101100 00010000 00000111 10101011
AND 11111111 11111111 11111100 00000000
    10101100 00010000 00000100 00000000
```

After converting the preceding result to a decimal number, we have 172.16.4.0 as the ID for the subnet that contains the IP address 172.16.7.171.

To obtain the broadcast IP address, one needs to change all the bits in the suffix of the given IP address to 1 bits. Because the rightmost ten bits belong to the suffix, we then have the broadcast address in the following binary:

10101100 00010000 00000111 11111111

The corresponding decimal broadcast address is 172.16.7.255.

Example 4

For the given IP address 10.33.1.11 and the subnet mask 255.224.0.0, determine the network ID and broadcast IP address for the subnet that contains the given IP address. Also, find how many subnets and how many hosts in each subnet can be specified by the subnet mask 255.224.0.0.

Because the IP address 10.33.1.11 starts with the decimal number 10, it is an IP address that belongs to Class A. The subnetting process is to create subnets under a standard Class A network. Therefore, some of the 0 bits in the second octet of the standard Class A subnet mask will be changed to 1 bits. The subnetting process is summarized in Table 4.19.

Table 4.19 Subnet Identified by the Second Octet

	Binary	*Decimal*
IP address	00001010 00100001 00000001 00001011	10.33.1.11
Subnet mask	11111111 11100000 00000000 00000000	255.224.0.0
Subnet ID	00001010 00100000 00000000 00000000	10.32.0.0
Broadcast	00001010 00111111 11111111 11111111	10.63.255.255

From the subnet mask, we can see that the rightmost 21 bits are 0 bits; this means that the number of hosts in each subnet is

$$2^{21} - 2 = 2097150$$

Compared with the standard Class A subnet mask, this subnet mask has turned three 0 bits in the second octet into 1 bits; the number of subnets can be calculated with the following formula:

$$2^3 - 2 = 6$$

To calculate the network ID for the subnet that contains the given IP address 10.33.1.11, you may need to AND the IP address with the subnet mask just as you did in the previous examples. The result of the IP address ANDing the subnet mask is

00001010 00100001 00000001 00001011

AND 11111111 11100000 00000000 00000000

00001010 00100000 00000000 00000000

After converting this result to a decimal number, we have 10.32.0.0 as the subnet ID that contains the IP address 10.33.1.11.

To obtain the broadcast IP address, one needs to change all the bits in the suffix of the given IP address to "1" bits. Because the rightmost 21 bits belong to the suffix, we then have the broadcast address in the following binary:

00001010 00111111 11111111 11111111

The corresponding decimal broadcast address is 10.63.255.255.

Example 5

Create a subnet under a standard Class B network so that the subnet is just large enough to include both of the IP addresses 172.5.17.16 and 172.5.30.192.

Because the IP address 172.5.17.16 starts with the decimal number 172, it is an IP address that belongs to Class B. To create subnets under a standard Class B network, you need to change some of the 0 bits in the third octet of the Class B subnet mask to 1 bit. You should have enough 0 bits in the third octet to include both 17 and 30. The difference between 30 and 17 is 13. You need to use a number that is the power of 2 to cover 13. The smallest of such a number is $2^4 = 16$. The power is 4, which means that you need four 0 bits in the third octet of the subnet mask. The subnetting process is summarized in Table 4.20.

Table 4.20 Subnet Including Both 172.5.17.16 and 172.5.30.192

	Binary	*Decimal*
IP address	10101100 00000101 00010001 00010000	172.5.17.16
IP address	10101100 00000101 00011110 11000000	172.5.30.192
Subnet mask	11111111 11111111 11110000 00000000	255.255.240.0
Subnet ID	10101100 00000101 00010000 00000000	172.5.16.0

When ANDing both the IP addresses

10101100 00000101 00010001 00010000

10101100 00000101 00011110 11000000

with the subnet mask

11111111 11111111 11110000 00000000

you will see that they have the same subnet ID:

10101100 00000101 00010000 00000000

This means that both IP addresses 172.5.17.16 and 172.5.30.192 belong to the same subnet.

Example 6

If you want to create a subnet that includes the IP address 172.5.59.32 with the subnet mask 255.255.248.0, what is the range of IP addresses in the subnet?

Converting the IP address 172.5.59.32 to binary format:

10101100 00000101 00111011 00100000

The binary representation of the subnet mask 255.255.248.0 is

11111111 11111111 11111000 00000000

AND the IP address with the subnet mask, and you have

10101100 00000101 00111011 00100000

AND 11111111 11111111 11111000 00000000

10101100 00000101 00111000 00000000

Thus, the subnet ID is

10101100 00000101 00111000 00000000

The range of IP addresses for the subnet starts with the subnet ID. Converting the binary form of the foregoing subnet ID to the decimal form, we have the subnet ID 172.5.56.0, which is the first IP address in the subnet. The three 0 bits in the third octet of the subnet mask indicates that there are $2^3 = 8$ values in the third octet that can be used for hosts. Starting with the number 56, count 8 times and you have the last number (63). Thus, the range for the third octet is from 56 to 63. In a subnet, the last IP address is reserved for broadcasting. In this example, the binary form of the broadcast address is

10101100 00000101 00111111 11111111

The corresponding decimal broadcast address is 172.18.63.255. Therefore, the subnet has IP addresses ranging from 172.18.56.0 to 172.18.63.255.

4.4.4 Classless Inter-Domain Routing (CIDR)

As mentioned in the previous section, there are several reasons for subnetting the standard Class A, Class B, and Class C networks. A subnet mask is used to define a subnet by specifying the number of subnets and the number of hosts in the subnet. Like subnetting, CIDR is another way to allocate IP addresses. Class A, Class B, and Class C use the fixed 8-bit, 16-bit, and 24-bit prefixes. As a more flexible alternative, CIDR uses prefixes between 0 and 32 bits. That is, CIDR can define networks to have hosts from 0 to 2^{32}. This makes the IP address assignment much more efficient, so that each network can closely meet the needs of an organization. With a more flexible prefix, CIDR is used by many to replace the traditional Class A, Class B, and Class C addresses.

CIDR defines a network with the combination of an IP address and a network mask with the format

xxx.xxx.xxx.xxx/N

where xxx.xxx.xxx.xxx is the IP address and N represents the network mask, which is the number of bits used by the prefix. For example, 172.5.17.0/28 and 192.168.1.131/28 define two networks. Each network uses 28 bits for the prefix. This means that the suffix has 4 bits. Therefore, each network has

$$2^4 - 2 = 14$$

hosts. The 172.5.17.0/28 network has the network ID 172.5.17.0, which has the binary equivalent

10101100 00000101 00010001 00000000

and its broadcast IP address is 172.5.17.15 with the binary equivalent

10101100 00000101 00010001 00001111

Thus, the range of IP addresses allocated by the 172.5.17.0/28 network is from 172.5.17.0 to 172.5.17.15.

Similarly, 192.168.1.131/28 has the binary equivalent

11000000 10101000 00000001 10000011

To get the network ID, you can turn all the 1 bits in the suffix into 0. Then, you have the network ID 192.168.1.128 with the binary equivalent

11000000 10101000 00000001 10000000

and the broadcast IP address 192.168.1.143 with the binary equivalent

11000000 10101000 00000001 10001111

Then, we have the IP range starting from 192.168.1.128 to 192.168.1.143.

The network mask N is closely related to the subnet mask. For example, for the IP address 128.10.0.0 with the subnet mask 255.255.255.0 and the binary equivalent

11111111 11111111 11111111 00000000

you have the prefix with twenty-four 1 bits in the subnet mask. The corresponding CIDR notation is 128.0.0.0/24. The network mask is 24, matching the number of 1's in the prefix of the subnet mask. Conversely, one can easily find the subnet mask for a given CIDR notation. For example, for the given CIDR notation 128.0.0.0/19, the number of 1 bits in the prefix is 19. The binary form of the subnet mask is

11111111 11111111 11100000 00000000

The corresponding decimal subnet mask is 255.255.224.0.

As we have seen so far, CIDR is flexible and efficient. Many network devices such as routers are built to support CIDR. CIDR addressing allows route aggregation, which organizes a routing table in a hierarchical way so that the routing table can be simplified by summarizing the routes across the Internet. Route aggregation can also be used by routers to support private networks.

Activity 4.1 IPv6 on Linux

Earlier in this chapter, it was mentioned that IPv6 is the way to go for the future. It is certainly worth exploring how Linux supports IPv6 and how IPv6 comes into play in a networking process. Linux has supported IPv6 since the release of its 2.2.x kernel. The updated support for IPv6 is included in kernel 2.6.x or later. In this hands-on activity, you will perform the following hands-on practice related to IPv6:

- Verifying if the Linux operating system that you are using supports IPv6
- Verifying if the IPv6-related functionalities are enabled on your operating system
- Displaying IPv6 addresses
- Using IPv6 network tools
- Disabling IPv6

CHECKING THE AVAILABILITY OF IPV6

Most recent Linux operating systems support IPv6. In this hands-on activity, you will check if the operating system that you are using supports IPv6. Because two machines are used in the hands-on practice, one with the desktop edition of Ubuntu Linux and the other with the server edition of Ubuntu Linux installed on it, verification will be done on both machines. Let us start with the server edition of Ubuntu Linux:

1. Start the server machine, and log on with username **student** and password **ubuntu**.
2. If your Linux kernel supports IPv6, you should have the file if_inet6 in the folder /proc/net/. To verify this, enter the command

   ```
   ls /proc/net/
   ```

   If you see the file if_inet6 shown in Figure 4.9, your Linux kernel supports IPv6.
3. Similarly, after you log on to the machine on which the desktop edition of Ubuntu Linux is installed, click **Places** and **Documents**. Then, double-click the **File System** node, the **proc** folder, and the **net** folder. You should be able to find the file if_inet6 (Figure 4.10) if IPv6 is supported by your operating system.

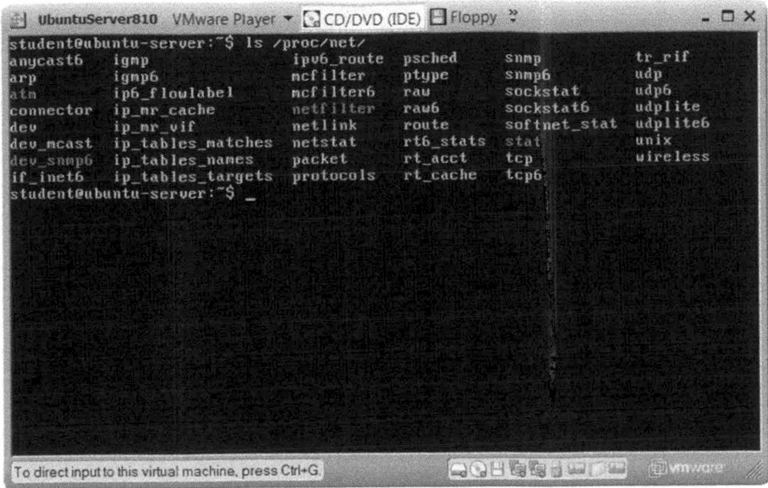

Figure 4.9 Checking the support for IPv6 on Ubuntu server.

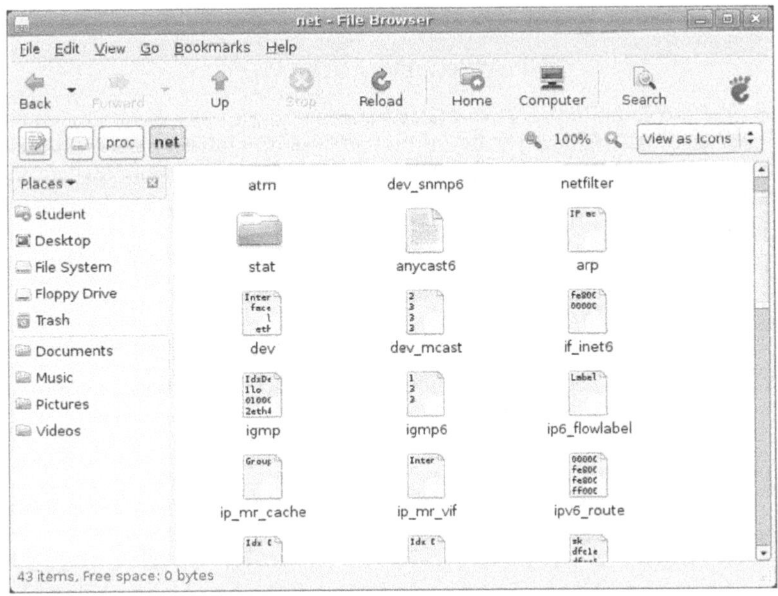

Figure 4.10 Checking the support for IPv6 on Ubuntu client.

CHECKING THE READINESS OF IPV6

To test if IPv6 is loaded, you may run the following command:

```
test -f /proc/net/if_inet6 && echo "IPv6 is loaded" || "IPv6 is not loaded"
```

If you see the echo "IPv6 is loaded" as shown in Figure 4.11, your system is ready to support IPv6 capabilities.

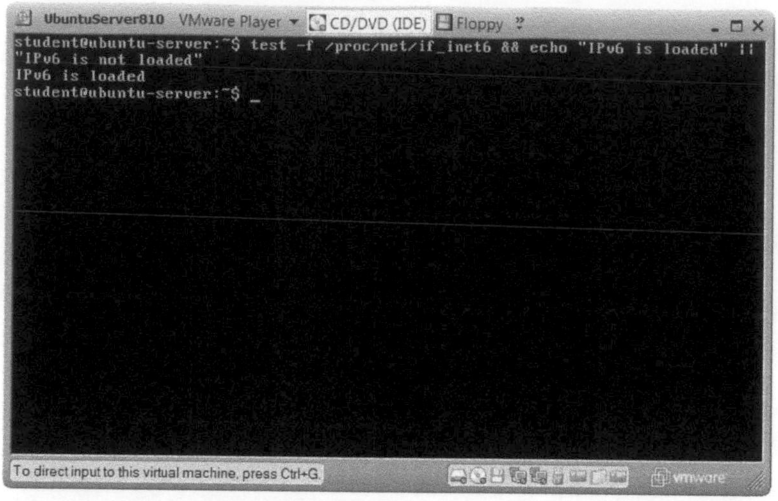

Figure 4.11 Testing the readiness of IPv6.

Similarly, on the Ubuntu client machine, you can open a terminal and run the test command shown in Figure 4.11.

DISPLAYING IPV6 ADDRESSES

In this section, you are going to use several IPv6-based network tools. You will first check if the network interface card is configured with an IPv6 address. Once you have the IP addresses of your machines, you will test the connection with IPv6 connection testing tools such as ping6 and traceroute6. These tools can be used to

- Test if a host is reachable through the network connection.
- Trace the route to the destination host.
- Display the transmitted TCP/IP packets.

Your first task is to display all your IPv6 addresses on your machine. To do so, perform the following steps:

1. Log on to your server machine, and enter the following command:

   ```
   cat /proc/net/if_inet6
   ```

   The output will list the IPv6 IP addresses for the loopback and two network interface cards similar to those displayed in Figure 4.12.

2. You can also use the following command to display the IPv6 addresses:

   ```
   sudo ifconfig
   ```

   The output will show you all the IPv6 and IPv4 addresses.
3. On the client machine, you can find the IPv6 addresses through the GUI tool called Network Tools. After logging on to the client machine, click **System**, **Administration**, and **Network Tools**. In the Network device drop-down list, you can select a network device, for example, **Ethernet Interface (eth3)**. You should be able to see the output shown in Figure 4.13.

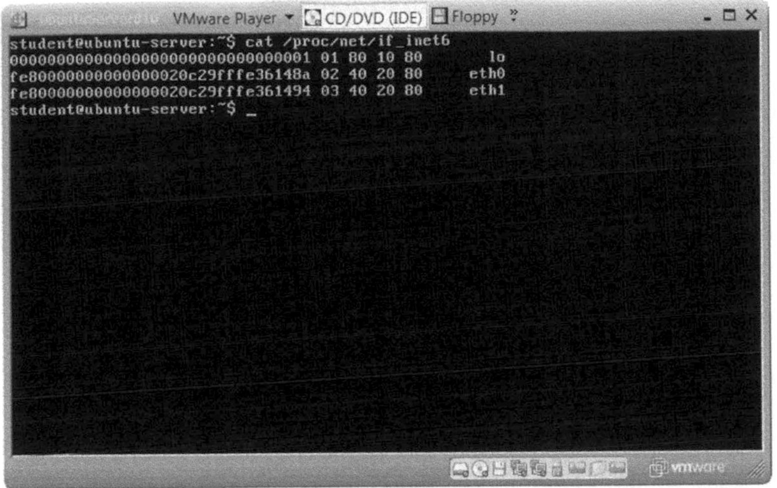

Figure 4.12 Displaying IPv6 addresses on Ubuntu server.

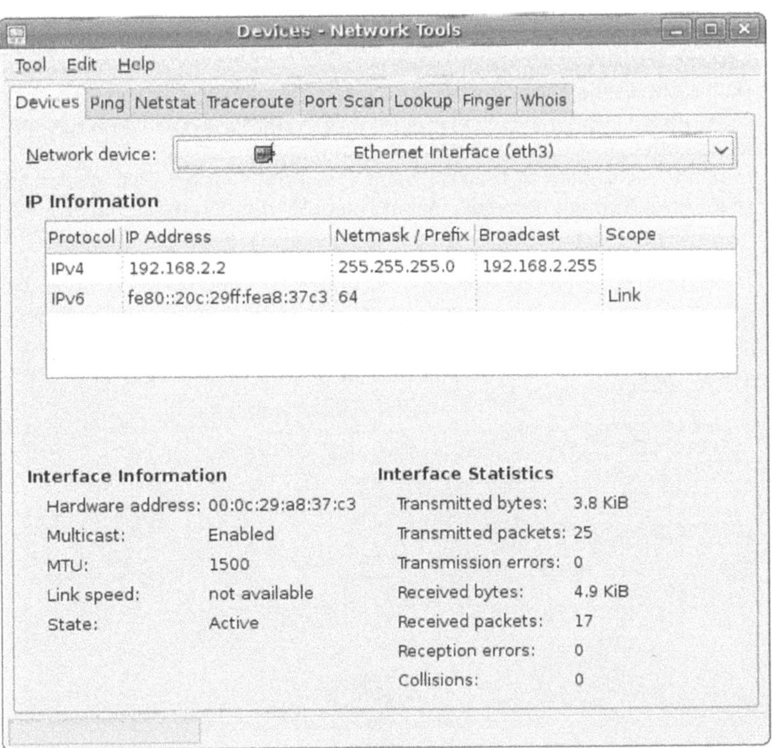

Figure 4.13 Displaying IPv6 addresses on Ubuntu client.

USING IPV6 NETWORK TOOLS

In the previous chapter, the command ping was used to test network connections. This command uses the protocol ICMP to get a response from a destination device. The corresponding ICMP version for IPv6 is ICMPv6, which is used by the commands ping6 and traceroute6. The following steps demonstrate the use of these commands:

1. In the previous section, the IPv6 address for the network interface card eth1 on the server machine was displayed. The first task is to ping the address for eth1 on the server to test if eth1 can respond to the ping6 command. Enter the following command (Note that, on your computer, the IPv6 address will be different. In the following command, use your own IPv6 address.):

   ```
   ping6 -I eth1 -c 5 fe80::20c:29ff:fe36:1494
   ```

   In this command, the option "I" refers to the Interface through which the sender sends the requests to the receiver. Also, the option "c" is the count of echoes to be displayed on the screen, and the number 5 after "-c" indicates that five requests are sent to the receiver. The result of ping6 is displayed in Figure 4.14. The output shows that the network interface card eth3 is working properly.
2. On the client machine, you can run the same command to test the connection between the client machine and the server machine. To do so, you need to log on to the client machine and open a terminal by click **Applications**, **Accessories**, and **Terminal**. Enter the following command to ping the server:

   ```
   ping6 -I eth3 -c 5 fe80::20c:29ff:fe36:1494
   ```

   You should see the output shown in Figure 4.15.

   The output shows that the connection between the client and server is working properly. Because the private NIC on the client is named eth3, the sender's interface in the command is specified as eth3.
3. The command traceroute6 is used to trace the route that an IPv6 packet travels from sender to receiver through networks. As an example, the command traceroute6 is used to

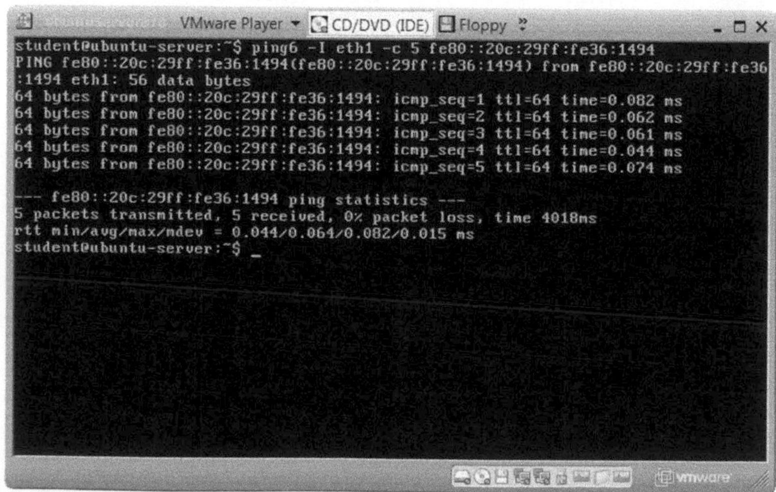

Figure 4.14 Use of ping6 command.

```
student@student-desktop: ~
File  Edit  View  Terminal  Tabs  Help
student@student-desktop:~$ ping6 -I eth3 -c 5 fe80::20c:29ff:fe36:1494
PING fe80::20c:29ff:fe36:1494(fe80::20c:29ff:fe36:1494) from fe80::20c:29ff:fea8
:37c3 eth3: 56 data bytes
64 bytes from fe80::20c:29ff:fe36:1494: icmp_seq=1 ttl=64 time=9.35 ms
64 bytes from fe80::20c:29ff:fe36:1494: icmp_seq=2 ttl=64 time=0.497 ms
64 bytes from fe80::20c:29ff:fe36:1494: icmp_seq=3 ttl=64 time=0.908 ms
64 bytes from fe80::20c:29ff:fe36:1494: icmp_seq=4 ttl=64 time=0.449 ms
64 bytes from fe80::20c:29ff:fe36:1494: icmp_seq=5 ttl=64 time=0.421 ms

--- fe80::20c:29ff:fe36:1494 ping statistics ---
5 packets transmitted, 5 received, 0% packet loss, time 4045ms
rtt min/avg/max/mdev = 0.421/2.326/9.359/3.521 ms
student@student-desktop:~$
```

Figure 4.15 Testing connection between client and server.

trace the route between client machine and server machine. Enter the following command in the terminal on the client machine:

```
sudo traceroute6 -i eth3 fe80::20c:29ff:fe36:1494
```

In this command, the IPv6 address is the server machine's IP address. The option "i" is used to identify the network interface card used to send the request. The result is displayed in Figure 4.16.

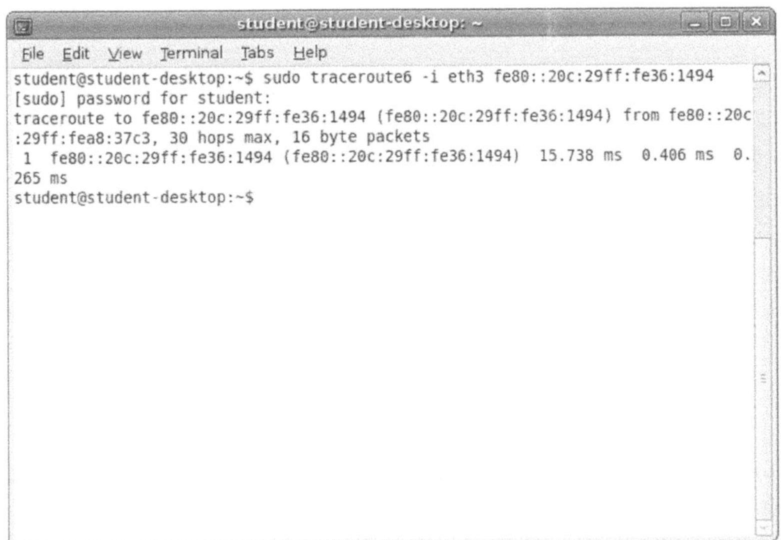

```
student@student-desktop: ~
File  Edit  View  Terminal  Tabs  Help
student@student-desktop:~$ sudo traceroute6 -i eth3 fe80::20c:29ff:fe36:1494
[sudo] password for student:
traceroute to fe80::20c:29ff:fe36:1494 (fe80::20c:29ff:fe36:1494) from fe80::20c
:29ff:fea8:37c3, 30 hops max, 16 byte packets
 1  fe80::20c:29ff:fe36:1494 (fe80::20c:29ff:fe36:1494)  15.738 ms  0.406 ms  0.
265 ms
student@student-desktop:~$
```

Figure 4.16 Tracing route from client to server.

DISABLING IPV6

By default, many Linux distributions have IPv6 enabled. Due to compatibility issues, the enabled IPv6 may cause some Internet connection problems. Users may experience problems in DNS resolution and network/Internet connection. By disabling IPv6, some of the problems can be resolved. The following are the steps to disable IPv6:

1. Suppose that you are still logged on to the client machine. All you need to do is to edit the aliases file. To do so, open a terminal window by clicking **Applications**, **Accessories**, and **Terminal**. Then, run the following command (see Figure 4.17):

   ```
   sudo gedit /etc/modprobe.d/aliases
   ```

2. In the text editor, find the line

   ```
   alias net-pf-10 ipv6
   ```

   Comment the line out with the # sign, and add the new line:

   ```
   alias net-pf-10 off
   ```

   shown in Figure 4.18. Click the **Save** button on the toolbar to save the change.
3. On the server machine, you can use the nano editor to edit the content in the file aliases. Suppose that you are still logged on to the server machine. Execute the following command:

   ```
   sudo nano /etc/modprobe.d/aliases
   ```

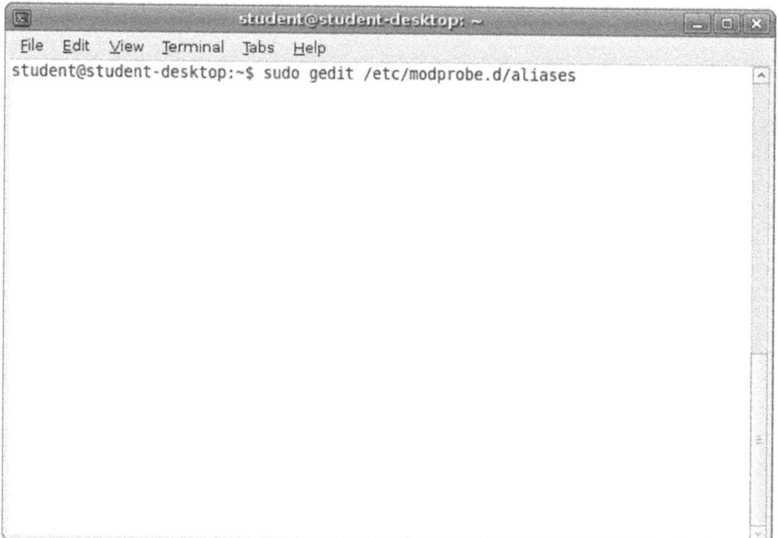

Figure 4.17 Searching for the aliases file on Ubuntu client.

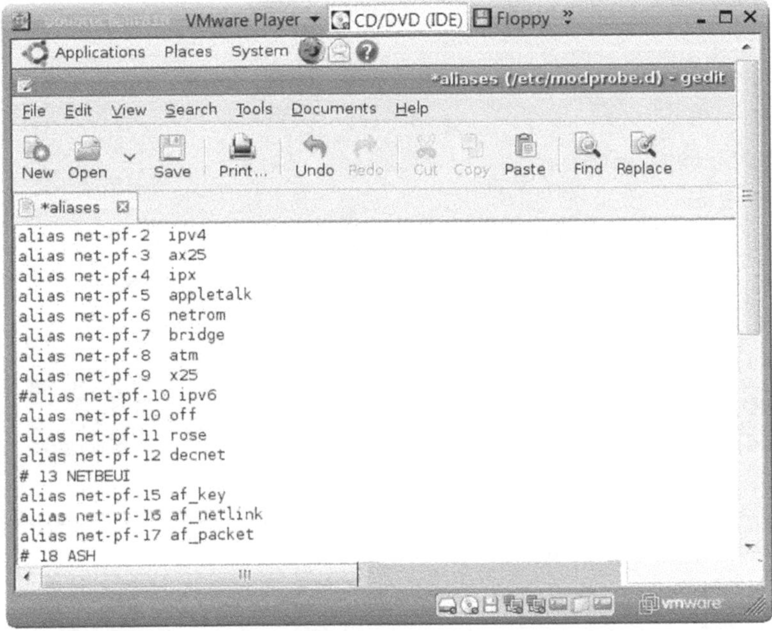

Figure 4.18 Disabling IPv6 on Ubuntu client.

4. Again, comment out the following line:

```
alias net-pf-10 ipv6
```

   And add the new line

```
alias net-pf-10 off
```

   as shown in Figure 4.19.

   Press the **Ctrl+X** key combination. When asked if you would like to save the change, press the key **Y**. Then, press the **Enter** key complete the configuration.

5. After you finish editing, restart your computer. To see the effect, execute the following command:

```
sudo ifconfig
```

   As seen in Figure 4.20, the IPv6 IP address is removed.

During this hands-on activity, you explored some IPv6-related topics. You went through the process of verifying if IPv6 was supported and enabled by your operating system. You learned how to use some simple IPv6-based network tools to check the network connection and trace the route between sender and receiver. At the end of the activity, you learned how to disable IPv6 on your operating system.

```
UbuntuServer810  VMware Player ▾  CD/DVD (IDE)  Floppy
  GNU nano 2.0.7            File: /etc/modprobe.d/aliases                    Modified

# These are the standard aliases for devices and kernel drivers.
# This file does not need to be modified.
#
# Please file a bug against module-init-tools if a package needs a entry
# in this file.

# network protocols ##################################################################
alias net-pf-1  unix
alias net-pf-2  ipv4
alias net-pf-3  ax25
alias net-pf-4  ipx
alias net-pf-5  appletalk
alias net-pf-6  netrom
alias net-pf-7  bridge
alias net-pf-8  atm
alias net-pf-9  x25
#alias net-pf-10 ipv6
alias net-pf-10 off_
alias net-pf-11 rose
alias net-pf-12 decnet

^G Get Help   ^O WriteOut   ^R Read File  ^Y Prev Page  ^K Cut Text   ^C Cur Pos
^X Exit       ^J Justify    ^W Where Is   ^V Next Page  ^U UnCut Text ^T To Spell
To direct input to this virtual machine, press Ctrl+G.                     vmware
```

Figure 4.19 Disabling IPv6 on Ubuntu server.

```
UbuntuServer810  VMware Player ▾  CD/DVD (IDE)  Floppy
          UP BROADCAST RUNNING MULTICAST  MTU:1500  Metric:1
          RX packets:42 errors:0 dropped:0 overruns:0 frame:0
          TX packets:50 errors:0 dropped:0 overruns:0 carrier:0
          collisions:0 txqueuelen:1000
          RX bytes:6539 (6.5 KB)  TX bytes:6383 (6.3 KB)
          Interrupt:18 Base address:0x1400

eth1      Link encap:Ethernet  HWaddr 00:0c:29:36:14:94
          inet addr:192.168.2.1  Bcast:192.168.2.255  Mask:255.255.255.0
          UP BROADCAST RUNNING MULTICAST  MTU:1500  Metric:1
          RX packets:34 errors:0 dropped:0 overruns:0 frame:0
          TX packets:35 errors:0 dropped:0 overruns:0 carrier:0
          collisions:0 txqueuelen:1000
          RX bytes:4638 (4.6 KB)  TX bytes:4674 (4.6 KB)
          Interrupt:19 Base address:0x1480

lo        Link encap:Local Loopback
          inet addr:127.0.0.1  Mask:255.0.0.0
          UP LOOPBACK RUNNING  MTU:16436  Metric:1
          RX packets:12 errors:0 dropped:0 overruns:0 frame:0
          TX packets:12 errors:0 dropped:0 overruns:0 carrier:0
          collisions:0 txqueuelen:0
          RX bytes:548 (548.0 B)  TX bytes:548 (548.0 B)

student@ubuntu-server:~$ _
To direct input to this virtual machine, press Ctrl+G.                     vmware
```

Figure 4.20 No IPv6 IP address used by eth1.

4.6 Summary

This chapter investigated some network-design-related topics. It started with strategies for investigating the requirements for a future network. As pointed out in this chapter, understanding the needs of an information system is a key step toward developing a successful network. To make sure that the users' needs are met, a logical model should be created first to verify if the proposed network can meet the requirements. This chapter provided a guideline for creating a logical network model.

To be able to identify the hosts linked to a network, network designers should come up with a network addressing plan so that each host can be properly assigned a unique address. The chapter introduced both IPv4 and IPv6 addressing schemes. It clarified the difference between classful and classless IP addresses.

To be able to use network resources more efficiently, the method of subnetting has been introduced. This chapter explained why one needs subnetting to make a network's operation more efficient and secure. Through several examples, this chapter demonstrated how to calculate subnet masks and how to perform other subnet related calculations.

In the hands-on activity of this chapter, you explored IPv6, which is supported by the Ubuntu Linux operating system. The hands-on practice illustrated how Linux supports IPv6. It also demonstrated how to check the network connection and trace the route of data transmission with IPv6 network tools. Lastly, the hands-on practice showed how to disable IPv6 to resolve compatibility problems.

Now that you have learned about the basic concepts and have created a basic network to link a client machine to a server machine, the next task is to develop some network services. In the next chapter, you will learn how to create some network services with the tools provided by Linux.

Review Questions

1. List some of the major tasks that should be accomplished in the design phase.
2. What are the layers in the Cisco hierarchical network design model?
3. To determine how IP addresses should be assigned, what are the decisions a designer has to make?
4. Who should be included in creating a security policy?
5. What are the prefix and suffix of an IP address?
6. List the number of networks and number of hosts that can be specified by each of the primary classes.
7. For the given binary number 11010111, find its corresponding decimal value.
8. For the given binary IP address 00001011 00001100 10011011 00000010, what is the corresponding decimal IP address?
9. What is the range of decimal values for the first octet of an IP address in each primary class?
10. What are the network IDs for the IP addresses 10.134.155.20, 172.6.23.10, and 192.168.2.11?
11. What are the dedicated broadcast addresses for the IP addresses 10.134.155.20, 172.6.23.10, and 192.168.2.11?
12. Lists all the three blocks of private IP addresses.
13. What are the improvements of IPv6 over IPv4?
14. What are the subnet masks for the three primary classes?
15. For the IP address 192.168.171.65 and the subnet mask 255.255.255.252, determine the network ID and broadcast IP address for the subnet that contains the given IP address. Also, find how many subnets and how many hosts in each subnet can be specified by the subnet mask 255.255.255.252.
16. For the IP address 172.16.20.0 and the subnet mask 255.255.248.0, determine the network ID and broadcast IP address for the subnet that contains the given IP address. Also, find how many subnets and how many hosts in each subnet can be specified by the subnet mask 255.255.248.0.
17. For the IP address 10.33.4.211 and the subnet mask 255.224.0.0, determine the network ID and broadcast IP address for the subnet that contains the given IP address. Also, find how many subnets and how many hosts in each subnet can be specified by the subnet mask 255.224.0.0.
18. Create a subnet under a standard Class B network so that the subnet is large enough to include both the IP addresses 129.5.18.116 and 129.5.29.12. What is the ID for the subnet that includes both these IP addresses?
19. For the given IP address 192.168.200.74 and subnet mask 255.255.255.240, what is the equivalent CIDR expression?
20. For the given CIDR expression 128.10.0.0/19, find the equivalent subnet mask.

Case Study Projects

The following are two network projects that involve the investigation of IPv6 and CIDR.

Case Study Project 4.1. Write a report on the investigation of IPv6, including the following topics:

- The current IPv6 implementation status in the world.
- The hardware and software requirements for implementing IPv6 for a small business.
- What are the difficulties of implementing IPv6 for a small business?
- How do you solve these problems?

Case Study Project 4.2. Investigate how CIDR addressing is used in routers. How can the use of CIDR simplify routing tables?

Chapter 5

Network Services

Objectives

- Set up user accounts.
- Install and configure DHCP service.
- Install and configure Domain Name System (DNS).

5.1 Introduction

In the three previous chapters, our focus has been on the network-architecture and network-design-related topics. Starting with this chapter, we will pay more attention to the networking process. In this chapter, we will create several network services with the tools provided by the Linux operating system. The services to be covered in this chapter include user account management, DHCP service, and DNS service. Through the hands-on practice, this chapter will illustrate how to develop and manage these services with the Ubuntu Linux operating system.

Our first task in this chapter is to create user accounts and assign permissions to the user accounts. Manually configuring IP addresses for the computers on a network can be time consuming. To reduce the time spent on IP address configuration, this chapter introduces the DHCP service, which automates the IP address configuration process. The name service is a key component for accessing the Internet. To access a Web site, we must know the name of the Web site, which is related to the IP address of the machine hosting the Web server. This chapter will discuss the configuration and management of a DNS server, which is used to resolve the IP address for a given name or vice versa. This chapter will provide more hands-on practice than the previous chapters. The hands-on practice includes setting up the administrator account, DHCP service, and DNS service.

5.2 User Accounts

The Linux operating system allows multiple users to log on to the same computer simultaneously. It also allows each user to perform several tasks at the same time. That is why Linux is a multiuser and multitask operating system by nature. Being this kind of operating system, Linux often provides sophisticated user management tools to help the network administrator create user accounts and manage users. For user account management, there are two components, user and group, in Linux.

5.2.1 Users and Groups

Each user can be identified by a username and password. Based on the privileges assigned to users, they can be categorized as administrative users, desktop users, and unprivileged users. The administrative user accounts are normally created by the operating system during the installation process. Administrative users possess certain privileges that enable them to perform tasks that require access to system files. In Linux, the system administrator, called root, is an administrative user. The account for the root user is automatically created during the Linux system installation process. The root user has all the privileges. The root is the most powerful and yet the most dangerous account. Inexperienced users with root privileges can often damage system files. Desktop user accounts are usually created by the system administrator. Regular users are often prevented from dealing with the system files directly. These users are allowed to access certain application software and to access the files created by themselves. Unprivileged users are guests to the operating system. Although everyone can use the unprivileged user account to access the system, unprivileged users have very few privileges. They are prevented from accessing most services and application software. For security reasons, the unprivileged user account should be disabled by default.

When the account for a user is created, the user is assigned a user identification number (UID). A home directory is created for each user account. In the multiuser environment, the home directory for each user is protected from being accessed by other users. All the users' home directories are listed in the directory /home.

The group is another component in user management. Users who have the same privileges can be placed in the same group. The configuration can be done at the group level instead of dealing with each individual user. The use of groups can significantly reduce the amount of work for user account management. As with the user component, when a group is created, a group identification number (GID) is assigned to the group.

In Linux, the user account information and group information are stored in three configuration files: /etc/passwd, /etc/shadow, and /etc/group. A description of the three files follows:

1. */etc/passwd:* This is the file that stores the user account information such as the username, UID, GID, comments, home directory, as well as the default shell. Figure 5.1 shows the content of a /etc/passwd file.

   In Figure 5.1, each row contains information about a user. The last row contains information about the user named "student" (see Table 5.1.)

   The content in each column is as follows:

   - *Username:* This column contains the user's login name.
   - *Password:* The character *x* indicates that the file /etc/shadow has an encrypted password.
   - *UID:* The user identification number is stored in this column. The desktop user's UID starts from 1000. The UID the root user is 0.

```
news:x:9:9:news:/var/spool/news:/bin/sh
uucp:x:10:10:uucp:/var/spool/uucp:/bin/sh
proxy:x:13:13:proxy:/bin:/bin/sh
www-data:x:33:33:www-data:/var/www:/bin/sh
backup:x:34:34:backup:/var/backups:/bin/sh
list:x:38:38:Mailing List Manager:/var/list:/bin/sh
i re:x:39:39:ired:/var/run/i red:/bin/sh
gnats:x:41:41:Gnats Bug-Reporting System (admin):/var/lib/gnats:/bin/sh
nobody:x:65534:65534:nobody:/nonexistent:/bin/sh
dhcp:x:100:101::/nonexistent:/bin/false
syslog:x:101:102::/home/syslog:/bin/false
klog:x:102:103::/home/klog:/bin/false
messagebus:x:103:109::/var/run/dbus:/bin/false
hplip:x:104:7:HPLIP system user,,, :/var/run/hplip:/bin/false
avahi-autoipd:x:105:113:Avahi autoip daemon,,,:/var/lib/avahi-autoipd:/bin/false
avahi:x:106:114:Avahi mDNS daemon,,,:/var/run/avahi-daemon:/bin/false
haldaemon:x:107:116:Hardware abstraction layer,,,:/home/haldaemon:/bin/false
gdm:x:108:118:Gnome Display Manager:/var/lib/gdm:/bin/false
student:x:1000:1000:student,,,:/home/student:/bin/bash
```

Figure 5.1 Sample content in /etc/passwd file.

Table 5.1 Information of Last Row in /etc/passwd File

Username	*Password*	*UID*	*GID*	*Comments*	*Home Directory*	*Default Shell*
student	x	1000	1000	student, , ,	/home/student	/bin/bash

- *GID:* Group identification number. A user can belong to multiple groups. In that case, the user will have multiple GIDs.
- *Comments:* This column includes the user's full name as well as contact information such as the address and phone numbers.
- *Home directory:* This column contains the home directory created for the user. In this example, the home directory for the user student is /home/student.
- *Default shell:* The default shell is the interface that allows the user to execute commands. Usually, Linux uses bash as the default shell.

```
news:*:13801:0:99999:7:::
uucp:*:13801:0:99999:7:::
proxy:*:13801:0:99999:7:::
www-data:*:13801:0:99999:7:::
backup:*:13801:0:99999:7:::
list:*:13801:0:99999:7:::
ire:*:13801:0:99999:7:::
gnats:*:13801:0:99999:7:::
nobody:*:13801:0:99999:7:::
dhep:!:13801:0:99999:7:::
syslog:!:13801:0:99999:7:::
klog:!:13801:0:99999:7:::
messagebus:!:13801:0:99999:7:::
hplip:!:13801:0:99999:7:::
avahi-autoipd:!:13801:0:99999:7:::
avahi:!:13801:0:99999:7:::
haldaemon:!:13801:0:99999:7:::
gdm:!=13801:0:99999:7:::
student:$!$4YM0zSs7$0gpSPFS6BhKyRH7/f/HSr/:14010:0:99999:7:::
```

Figure 5.2 Sample content in /etc/shadow file.

As you can see, even the file name indicates that this is a password-related file. In fact, the passwords are encrypted and saved to another file called /etc/shadow.

2. */etc/shadow:* The encrypted passwords and related expiration information are stored in the /etc/shadow file. Only the root user or the user who is assigned the privilege can access the /etc/shadow file. The content of the /etc/shadow file is displayed in Figure 5.2.

   In Figure 5.2, the information in each row is related to a user. Table 5.2 lists information about the last row of the sample content stored in the /etc/shadow file.

   The content in each column is as follows:

- *Username:* This column contains the user's login name.
- *Encrypted password:* The password field contains the user's encrypted password. If the password is empty, the user can log on to the system without a password. If the character * or ! is displayed in the password field, then the user has an invalid password.
- *Last password change date:* The number of days since the last password change date, that is, Jan 1, 1970.

Table 5.2 Information about Last Row in /etc/shadow File

Username	*Student*
Encrypted password	$1$4YM0zSs7$0gp…
Last password change date	14010
Days after which password can be changed	0
Days after which password must be changed	99999
Days before password expires that user should be notified	7

- *Days after which password can be changed:* The number of days after which the user can change his or her password.
- *Days after which password must be changed:* The number of days after which the user must change his or her password.
- *Days before password expires that user should be notified:* The number of days before the user's password expires that the user should be notified that his or her password must be changed.

3. */etc/group:* This is the file that stores information about a group. Each row contains information such as the group name, group ID, and the list of group members for a given group (Figure 5.3).

   Table 5.3 explains the data in the columns included in the last row.

Similar to the explanation for the content in the /etc/passwd file, the Username column contains the user login name. The Password column has the character x, which indicates that the encrypted password is stored in the /etc/shadow file. The GID column contains the group identification number.

Activity 5.1 Creating a User Account

In this section, you are going to create a system administrator account. Because you will be the network administrator for the hands-on practice in the rest of the book, a system administrator account will be very convenient for you to accomplish a lot of administrative tasks. On the other hand, it is very risky to log in as a system administrator. The system files can be accidentally altered or deleted, which can crash an operating system. Also, the system administrator account may cause some concerns for the system's safety. For a real-life network environment, it is strongly recommended not to log on as a system administrator. When the administrator privilege is needed to execute a certain command, you can always use the keyword sudo to execute the command.

In this hands-on activity, you are going to create a system administrator account on the client machine as well as on the server machine. The following are the steps to create a user account with Ubuntu Linux:

1. Log on to the client machine with username **student** and password **ubuntu**.
2. On the menu bar, click **System**, **Administration**, and **Users and Groups** to open the User Settings dialog.
3. Click the **Unlock** button, enter the password **ubuntu**, and then press the **Enter** key to log into the User Settings dialog.

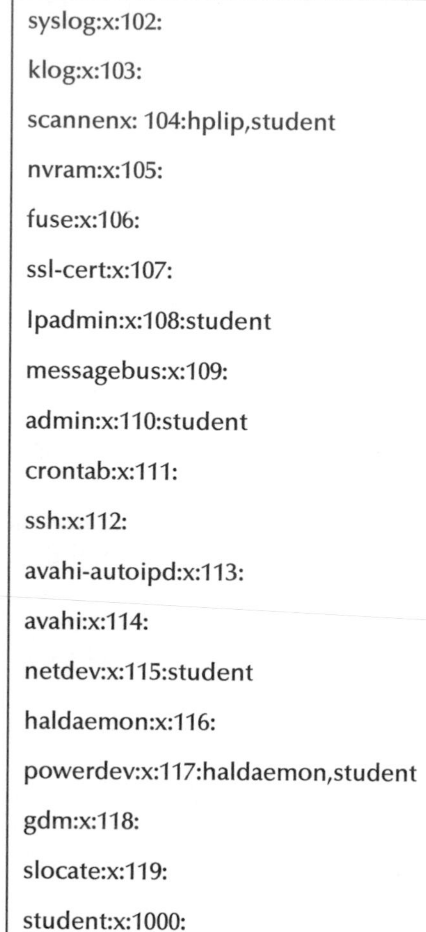

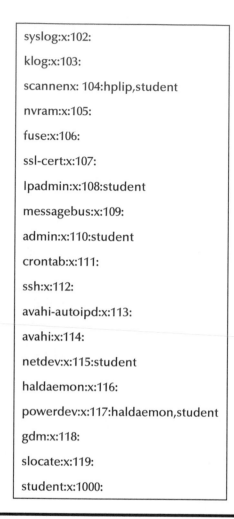

```
syslog:x:102:
klog:x:103:
scannenx: 104:hplip,student
nvram:x:105:
fuse:x:106:
ssl-cert:x:107:
lpadmin:x:108:student
messagebus:x:109:
admin:x:110:student
crontab:x:111:
ssh:x:112:
avahi-autoipd:x:113:
avahi:x:114:
netdev:x:115:student
haldaemon:x:116:
powerdev:x:117:haldaemon,student
gdm:x:118:
slocate:x:119:
student:x:1000:
```

Figure 5.3 Sample content in /etc/group file.

Table 5.3 Information about Last Row in the /etc/group File

Group Name	*Password*	*GID*
student	x	1000

4. Click the **Add User** button. When the New User Account dialog is opened, enter **studentadmin** as the username and **Student Administrator** as the real name. Select **Administrator** in the Profile drop-down list. Enter **ubuntu** as the password and then confirm it (Figure 5.4).
5. Click the **User Privileges** tab. As shown in Figure 5.5, all the check boxes are checked to give the studentadmin account all the privileges.
6. Click the **Advanced** tab. You will see the home directory, the shell, and the user ID that has been created for the user studentadmin. Select **root** from the main group drop-down list (Figure 5.6).

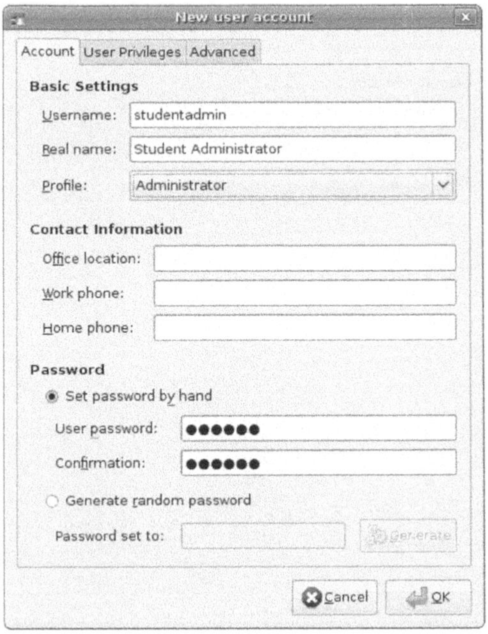

Figure 5.4 New user account.

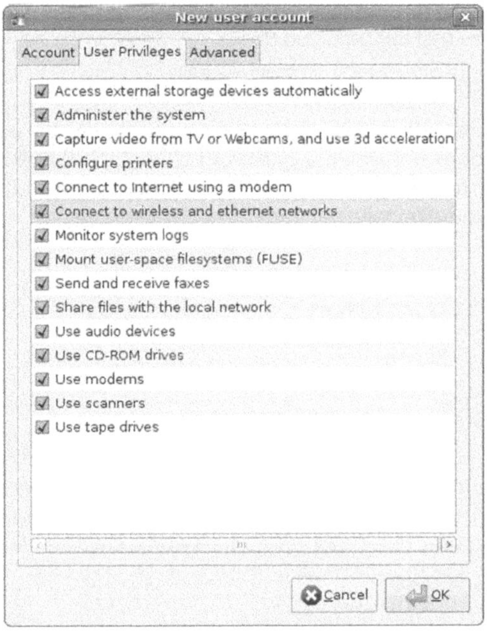

Figure 5.5 User privileges.

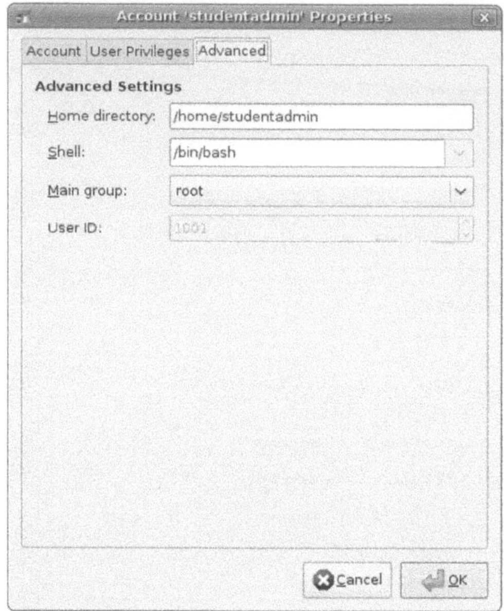

Figure 5.6 Advanced settings for new user.

7. Click **OK** to close the New User Account dialog. Then, click **Close** to close the User Settings dialog.
8. Reboot the system by clicking **System**, **Shut Down**, and **Restart**.
9. After the system is rebooted, log on with username **studentadmin** and password **ubuntu**.
10. To verify that the system administrator account is working properly, open the terminal window by clicking **Applications**, **Accessories**, and **Terminal**. Enter a command such as ifconfig and execute it. You can see that this time you do not need to use the keyword sudo to execute the command.

The other way to become a system administrator is to simply change the password of the root user. By default, Ubuntu Linux does not assign a password to root, so the user cannot log in as root. Changing the root's password allows the user to log in as root. In the following, you are going to do this on the server machine. The following are the steps to change the password for root on the server machine:

1. Log on to the server machine with username **student** and password **ubuntu**.
2. Enter the command:

   ```
   sudo passwd root
   ```

   Press the **Enter** key. You will be prompted to enter the password. Enter the password **ubuntu**. Then, you will be prompted to enter the new password for the user root. Enter the password **ubuntu** twice and press the **Enter** key. You should get the result shown in Figure 5.7.
3. To make sure that the user root does have a password, enter the following command:

   ```
   sudo grep root /etc/shadow
   ```

   Press the **Enter** key; you should have something similar to what is displayed in Figure 5.8.

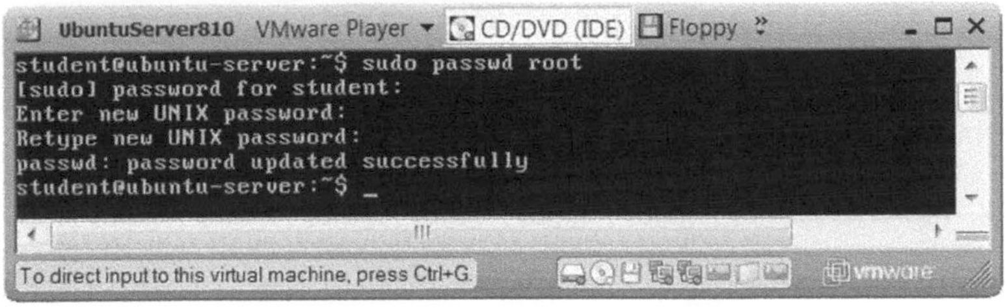

```
student@ubuntu-server:~$ sudo passwd root
[sudo] password for student:
Enter new UNIX password:
Retype new UNIX password:
passwd: password updated successfully
student@ubuntu-server:~$ _
```

Figure 5.7 Changing root password.

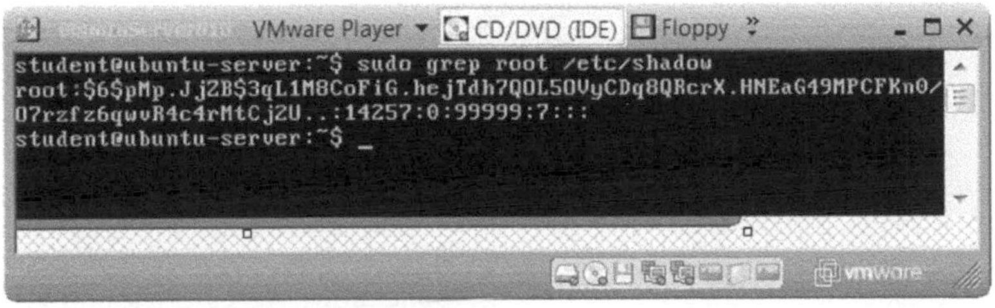

```
student@ubuntu-server:~$ sudo grep root /etc/shadow
root:$6$pMp.JjZB$3qL1M8CoFiG.hejTdh7QOL5OVyCDq8QRcrX.HNEaG49MPCFKn0/
O7rzfz6qwvR4c4rMtCj2U..:14257:0:99999:7:::
student@ubuntu-server:~$ _
```

Figure 5.8 Root account information.

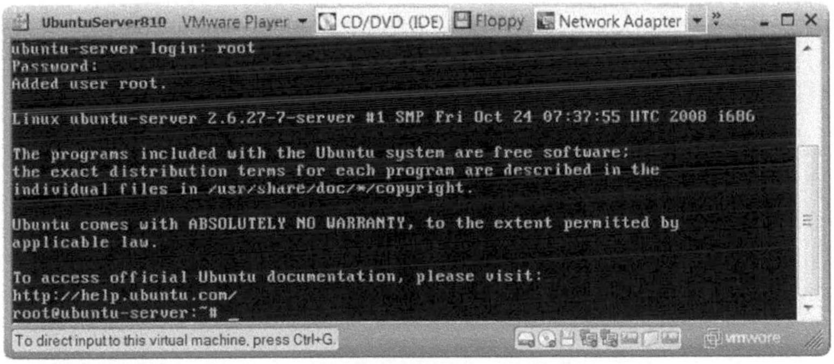

```
ubuntu-server login: root
Password:
Added user root.

Linux ubuntu-server 2.6.27-7-server #1 SMP Fri Oct 24 07:37:55 UTC 2008 i686

The programs included with the Ubuntu system are free software;
the exact distribution terms for each program are described in the
individual files in /usr/share/doc/*/copyright.

Ubuntu comes with ABSOLUTELY NO WARRANTY, to the extent permitted by
applicable law.

To access official Ubuntu documentation, please visit:
http://help.ubuntu.com/
root@ubuntu-server:~# _
```

Figure 5.9 Changed command prompt upon logging in as root user.

4. To verify if the newly created user account has the system administrator privilege, you need to reboot your system. To do so, execute the following command:

   ```
   sudo reboot
   ```

5. After the system has rebooted, log in with username **root** and the password **ubuntu**. Once you log in, note that the command prompt sign $ has been changed to #. This indicates that you are logged in as root (Figure 5.9).

As the root user, you are able to perform many tasks that cannot be done by a regular user.

Activity 5.2 Installing GUI Desktop on Server Machine

You have used the nano text editor for editing the file content. The GUI desktop includes a GUI-based text editor that is easy to use and is good for heavy editing tasks. Also, some of the tools used in later chapters may need the GUI interface. Although it is convenient to use GUI tools for many tasks, experienced professionals often prefer a text-based environment for efficiency, especially for servers. You can install a simple GNOME desktop on the server machine with the following steps:

1. Ensure that you are still on the server machine.
2. Execute the following command to update your server machine:

```
sudo apt-get update
```

3. To install the GNOME desktop, execute the following command:

```
sudo apt-get install ubuntu-desktop
```

4. The installation will take some time. Figure 5.10 shows that the installation is completed.
5. After the system is rebooted, log in with username **student** and password **ubuntu**. You should be able to see the GUI desktop shown in Figure 5.11.
6. The GUI desktop includes a text editor. Click **Applications**, **Accessories**, and **Text Editor** to open the text editor. Click the **Open** icon on the menu bar, and then click **File system**, **etc**, **network,** and **interfaces** to open the file /etc/network/interfaces (Figure 5.12).
7. The GUI-based text editor provides an environment in which editing tasks such as insert, update, and delete can be easily done. Click **File** and **Quit** to close the text editor.

5.3 Dynamic Host Configuration Protocol (DHCP)

As mentioned in Chapter 2, the Dynamic Host Configuration Protocol (DHCP) automates IP address configuration. During a computer's boot process, DHCP joins the computer to a network without requiring the network administrator to configure the IP address, subnet mask, default gateway, and name server. By using DHCP, the network administrator can save a lot of time on configuring network interface cards for computers or other network devices. In addition to saving configuration time, DHCP is also necessary for the wireless computing environment. A Wi-Fi access point assigns IP addresses and other network parameters to computers connected to the wireless network with DHCP.

5.3.1 Dynamic IP Address Assignment Process

DHCP uses a client-server approach to assign IP addresses. When a computer system boots up, it broadcasts a DHCP discovery packet with the broadcast address 255.255.255.255 to the local network. Once the broadcast packet reaches the DHCP server, the server offers a packet that contains the IP address, IP address lease time, subnet mask, and information about the default gateway. Multiple DHCP servers may offer their IP configuration packets to a DHCP client. The DHCP client will send a broadcast packet to inform all the servers about which offer has been accepted. Usually, DHCP takes the first offer. The chosen DHCP server sends a response back to indicate that the DHCP client is allowed to use the IP address for communication.

```
VMware Player ▾  CD/DVD (IDE)  Floppy
Setting up totem-plugins (2.24.3-0ubuntu1) ...

Setting up totem (2.24.3-0ubuntu1) ...
Setting up totem-mozilla (2.24.3-0ubuntu1) ...
Setting up tracker-search-tool (0.6.6-1ubuntu5.1) ...

Setting up tsclient (0.150-1ubuntu3) ...

Setting up update-notifier (0.71.8) ...

Setting up ubuntu-desktop (1.124) ...
Setting up vinagre (2.24.1-0ubuntu1.1) ...

Setting up vino (2.24.1-0ubuntu1) ...

Setting up gnome-pilot (2.0.15-2ubuntu4) ...

Setting up gnome-pilot-conduits (2.0.15-1.2) ...
Processing triggers for libc6 ...
ldconfig deferred processing now taking place
Processing triggers for python-support ...
Processing triggers for initramfs-tools ...
update-initramfs: Generating /boot/initrd.img-2.6.27-7-server
student@ubuntu-server:~$  * Reloading system log daemon...
```

Figure 5.10 Completed installation.

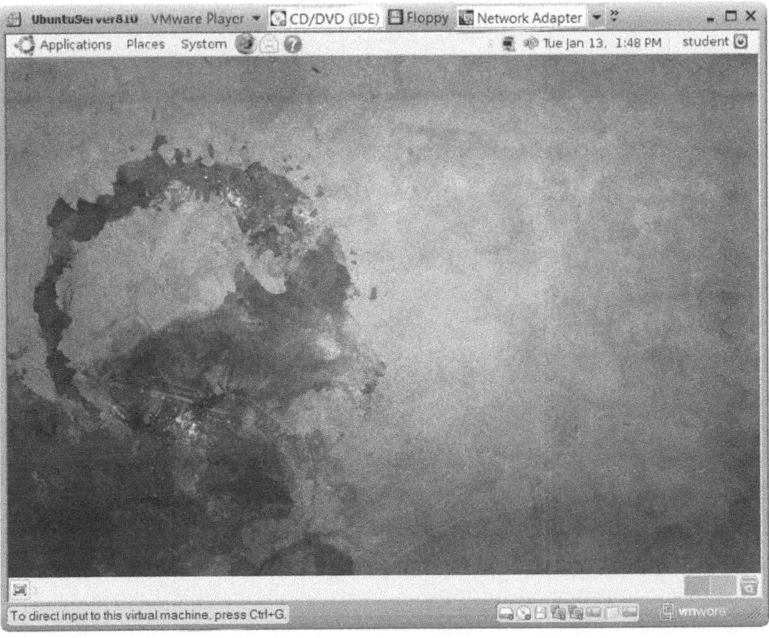

Figure 5.11 GUI desktop.

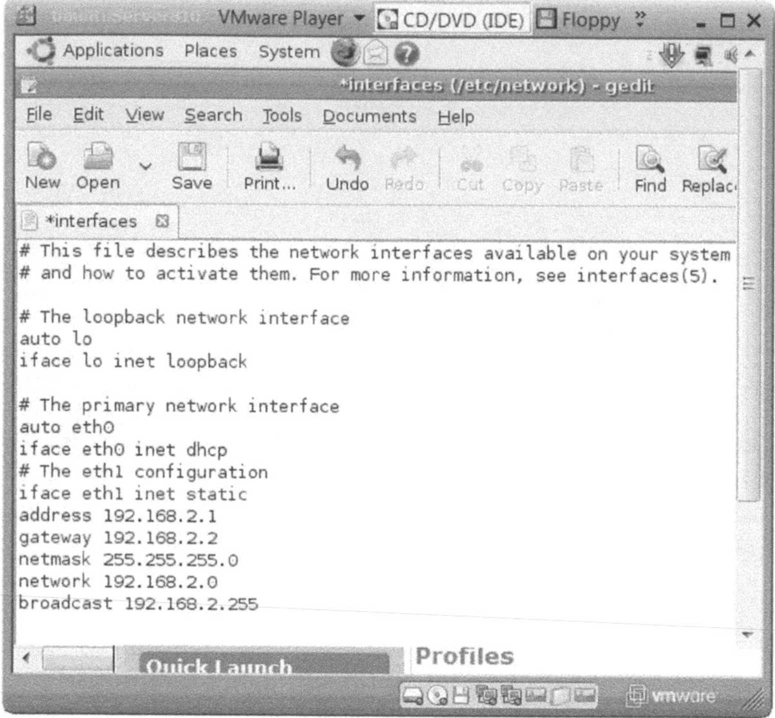

Figure 5.12 Opening the file etc/network/interfaces with the text editor.

The IP addresses assigned to computers can be either permanently leased or dynamically assigned. If a computer has a dynamically assigned IP address, it is not guaranteed to have the same IP address the next time it boots up. There are some situations in which a computer needs the same IP address assigned to it every time it is booted up. For example, some of the computers are so configured that they can be remotely accessed by many users. In such a case, a permanent IP address can help client computers to set up remote access. On the other hand, a dynamically assigned IP address is just fine for most computers. All that these computers need is to get an IP address to join the network. The expired IP addresses can be recycled and assigned to other computers.

During the configuration of a DHCP server, the user can specify the lease time period. After half of the lease time expires, the DHCP client can automatically issue a new request to the DHCP server. If the original DHCP server does not offer a new lease to the DHCP client, the DHCP client will broadcast to other DHCP servers for a new IP address. If there is no DHCP server available on the local network, the DHCP client will not be able to get an IP address automatically. Instead, it will get an APIPA IP address between 169.254.0.1 and 169.254.255.254. A host assigned an APIPA IP address, which can only be used by the host itself, is not allowed to join the local network.

It is possible for the computers in multiple subnets to share a DHCP server, by using a technology called DHCP Relay. The DHCP Relay Agent included in the Linux operating system can be used to relay DHCP requests from one network to another network where a DHCP server is located. The DHCP client's request is forwarded to a list of servers specified by the DHCP Relay Agent. The response of a DHCP server will be broadcast back to the network that has the sender.

```
# Sample /etc/dhcpd.conf
        default-lease-time 600;
        max-lease-time 7200;
        option subnet-mask 255.255.255.0;
        option broadcast-address 192.168.1.255;
        option routers 192.168.1.1;
        option domain-name "groupl.lab";
        option domain-name-servers 192.168.1.200;
        subnet 192.168.1.0 netmask 255.255.255.0 {
                range 192.168.1.210 192.168.1.240;
}
```

Figure 5.13 Content of DHCP configuration file.

5.3.2 DHCP Configuration

The Ubuntu Linux package includes both the DHCP server and client. The program dynamic host configuration protocol daemon (dhcpd) can act as a DHCP server. The DHCP client is automatically installed and configured by Ubuntu. Figure 5.13 shows the basic configuration for the DHCP server.

The first two lines of the code are related to the IP address lease time. The DHCP server will use the default lease time, which is 600 s, unless the user changes the default setting. If the user configures the lease time to be greater than the maximum lease time, the DHCP server will offer the maximum lease time. Then, there are several options for the underlying network. The user can enter information about the subnet mask, broadcast address, router's IP address, domain name, and IP address of the domain name server. The last line is about the range of IP addresses to be assigned to DHCP clients. To define the range, users need to specify the starting and ending IP addresses for the range. The IP addresses assigned in the range can come from different subnets. Thus, the users also need to specify the subnets where the IP addresses come from.

An IP address can be reserved for a DHCP client so that the client can always get the same IP address. The reservation can be done by relating an IP address to the hardware address of a network interface card. Figure 5.14 shows a sample code for reservation in a DHCP configuration file.

```
host clientl{
hardware ethernet aa:bb:cc:dd:ee:ff;
fixed-address 192.168.1.201;
}
```

Figure 5.14 Sample code for reservation in a DHCP configuration file.

In the code, aa:bb:cc:dd:ee:ff is the hardware address of the NIC on the DHCP client computer. The fixed IP address is assigned to that NIC. Do not mix the IP addresses in the DHCP range with the reserved IP addresses.

There are some other DHCP options, such as log file specification and updating the DNS server. Details will be given in the hands-on practice.

Activity 5.3 Installing and Configuring DHCP

The DHCP server file is included in the Ubuntu Linux package. The DHCP server is not installed by the default installation process. You need to manually install the DHCP server. The following are the steps used to install the DHCP server:

1. Log on to the server machine with username **student** and password **ubuntu**.
2. If the GUI desktop is installed on the server machine, to open the terminal window, click **Applications**, **Accessories**, and **Terminal**. Otherwise, you should already be in the terminal window.
3. Then, run the following command:

   ```
   sudo apt-get install dhcp3-server
   ```

   After the execution is completed, you should see the output shown in Figure 5.15.
4. As illustrated in Figure 5.15, automatically starting the DHCP service failed. This is because the DHCP server needs to be configured before it can be put into service. Before you change the content of the DHCP server files, you should backup the dhcp3-server file and the dhcpd.conf file, in case you need to get the original files back. To do so, enter the following command in the terminal window to make a backup copy:

   ```
   sudo cp /etc/default/dhcp3-server /etc/default/dhcp3-server_original
   sudo cp /etc/dhcp3/dhcpd.conf /etc/dhcp3/dhcpd.conf_original
   ```

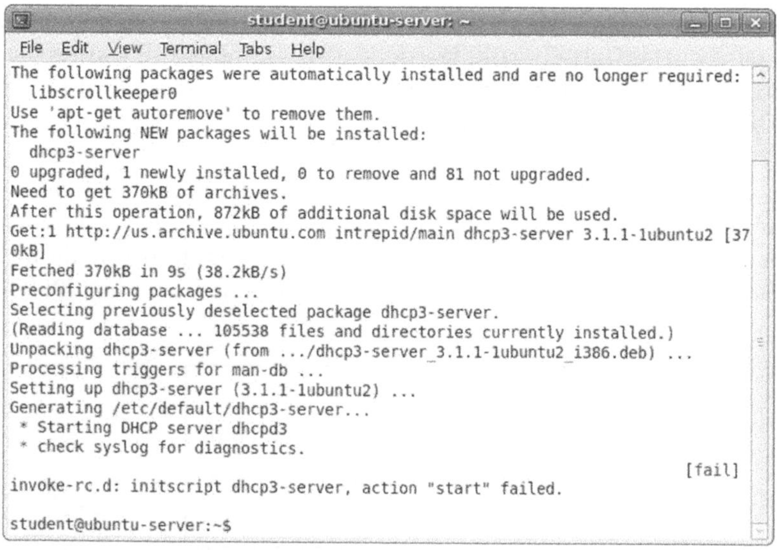

```
student@ubuntu-server: ~
File Edit View Terminal Tabs Help
The following packages were automatically installed and are no longer required:
  libscrollkeeper0
Use 'apt-get autoremove' to remove them.
The following NEW packages will be installed:
  dhcp3-server
0 upgraded, 1 newly installed, 0 to remove and 81 not upgraded.
Need to get 370kB of archives.
After this operation, 872kB of additional disk space will be used.
Get:1 http://us.archive.ubuntu.com intrepid/main dhcp3-server 3.1.1-1ubuntu2 [37
0kB]
Fetched 370kB in 9s (38.2kB/s)
Preconfiguring packages ...
Selecting previously deselected package dhcp3-server.
(Reading database ... 105538 files and directories currently installed.)
Unpacking dhcp3-server (from .../dhcp3-server_3.1.1-1ubuntu2_i386.deb) ...
Processing triggers for man-db ...
Setting up dhcp3-server (3.1.1-1ubuntu2) ...
Generating /etc/default/dhcp3-server...
 * Starting DHCP server dhcpd3
 * check syslog for diagnostics.
                                                                        [fail]
invoke-rc.d: initscript dhcp3-server, action "start" failed.

student@ubuntu-server:~$
```

Figure 5.15 Installation of DHCP server.

Next, you will configure the DHCP server by changing the content in the dhcp3-server file. Suppose you are working on your private network. For the hands-on practice in this book, the name of the NIC on the server machine is eth1 and the IP address is 192.168.2.1. For the client machine, the name of the NIC is eth3 and the IP address is 192.168.2.2. As mentioned in Chapter 3, each student or each group should have a unique number in the third octet of the IP address. Therefore, you may have a different number in the third octet for your private network. The following steps show how to configure the DHCP server. Again, make sure that the number in the third octet is the group number assigned by your instructor. The following code is used for Group 2:

1. Once you have backed up the DHCP server files, you can edit the file by entering the following command:

   ```
   sudo gedit /etc/dhcp3/dhcpd.conf
   ```

   Figure 5.16 shows the file content displayed in the text editor gedit.
2. The dhcpd.conf file provides some sample code. Because you are using private IP addresses, your first task is to comment out the section that is used for the Internet. Search for the following section, and comment out each line with the pound sign (#):

   ```
   ...
   option domain-name "example.org";
   option domain-name-servers ns1.example.org, ns2.example.org;

   default-lease-time 600;
   max-lease-time 7200;
   ...
   ```

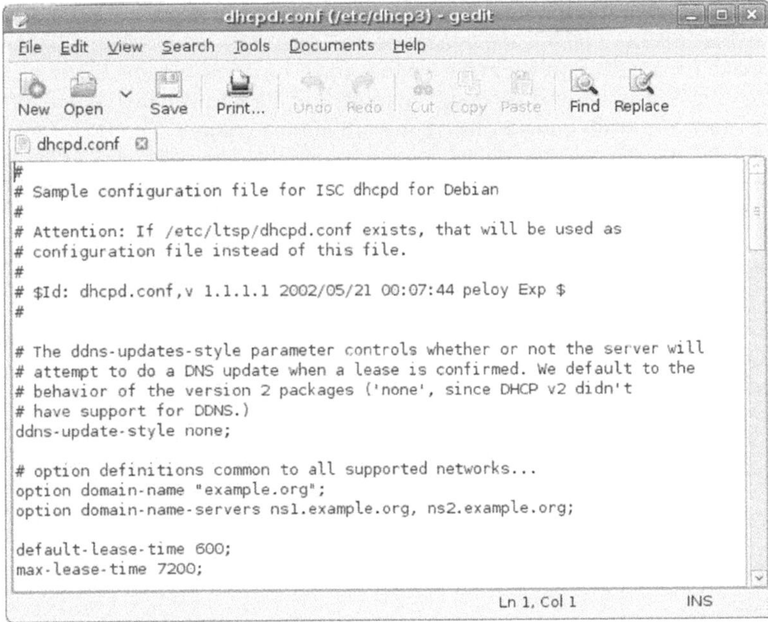

Figure 5.16 Content in dhcpd.conf file.

3. Next, search the section for private IP addresses:

```
...
# A slightly different configuration for an internal subnet.
#subnet 10.5.5.0 netmask 255.255.255.224 {
# range 10.5.5.26 10.5.5.30;
# option domain-name-servers ns1.internal.example.org;
# option domain-name "internal.example.org";
# option routers 10.5.5.1;
# option broadcast-address 10.5.5.31;
# default-lease-time 600;
# max-lease-time 7200;
#}
...
```

4. You may replace the preceding code with the following code (make sure that the number in the third octet is your group number if you work in the lab environment):

```
# A slightly different configuration for an internal subnet.
subnet 192.168.2.0 netmask 255.255.255.0 {
 range 192.168.2.100 192.168.2.200;
 option domain-name-servers 192.168.2.1;
 option domain-name "group2.lab";
 option routers 192.168.2.1;
 option broadcast-address 192.168.2.255;
 default-lease-time 600;
 max-lease-time 7200;
}
```

   Figure 5.17 shows the DHCP server configuration. In this configuration, the range of IP addresses to be assigned is from 192.168.2.100 to 192.168.2.200. The range is for the subnet 192.168.2.0 with the subnet mask 255.255.255.0. The IP address for the domain name server is 192.168.2.1, which is the IP address of the server machine. You will configure the server machine as a DNS server in the next section. The domain name is group2.lab, which will be configured in the next section. The router's IP address will be the one for the server machine, too. You will configure the router in the next chapter. The broadcast address is 192.168.2.255. Finally, take the default lease time and the default maximum lease time. The foregoing configuration is based on the assumption that it is for the network 192.168.2.0. If you are working with the network at home, the network ID, domain name, router IP address, DNS server IP address, and broadcast address may all be different. Before you can start the configuration, you need to collect all the preceding information about the network to which the DHCP server will be connected.
5. After you complete the configuration, click the **Save** icon on the menu bar. Click **File,** and select **Quit**.
6. You also need to configure the file dhcp3-server. To do so, enter the following command in the terminal window:

```
sudo gedit /etc/default/dhcp3-server
```

7. Change the line

```
INTERFACES=""
```

   to

```
INTERFACES="eth1"
```

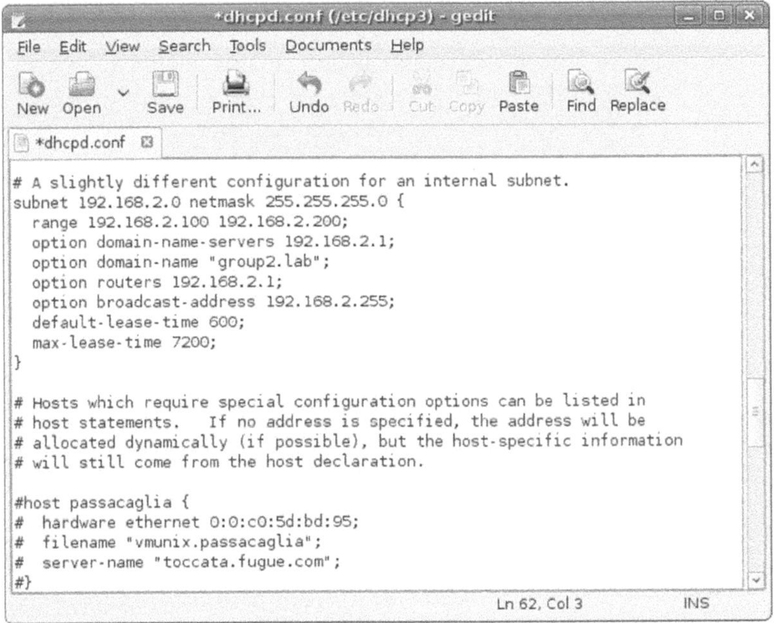

Figure 5.17 DHCP server configuration.

8. After you complete the configuration, click the **Save** icon on the menu bar. Click **File,** and select **Quit.**
9. You can now restart the DHCP server to allow the new configuration to take effect. Execute the following command to restart the DHCP server:

```
sudo /etc/init.d/dhcp3-server restart
```

Once the DHCP server is configured, you need to configure the DHCP client to receive the dynamic IP address from the DHCP server. Follow these steps to set up the client machine:

1. Log on to the client machine with username **student** and password **ubuntu**.
2. To make the private NIC on the client machine take the dynamic IP address, click **System**, **Preferences**, and **Network Configuration**. Select **Private Client** from the list. Then, click the **Edit** button.
3. When the Editing Private Client dialog opens, click the tab **IPv4 Settings**. Then, select **Automatic (DHCP)** from the Method drop-down list shown in Figure 5.18.
4. Click **OK** to complete the configuration.
5. To test if the DHCP client has received an IP address from the DHCP server, you may need to restart the client virtual machine by clicking the shutdown icon on the menu bar and selecting **Restart.**
6. After the system has rebooted, click the **System** menu, **Administration**, and **Network Tools**. From the Network device drop-down list, select **Ethernet Interface (eth3)**. As shown in Figure 5.19, eth3 has received the IP address 192.168.2.101 from the DHCP server.

To demonstrate how to configure the DHCP server to assign a client with a permanent IP address, you need to reconfigure the DHCP server with the following steps:

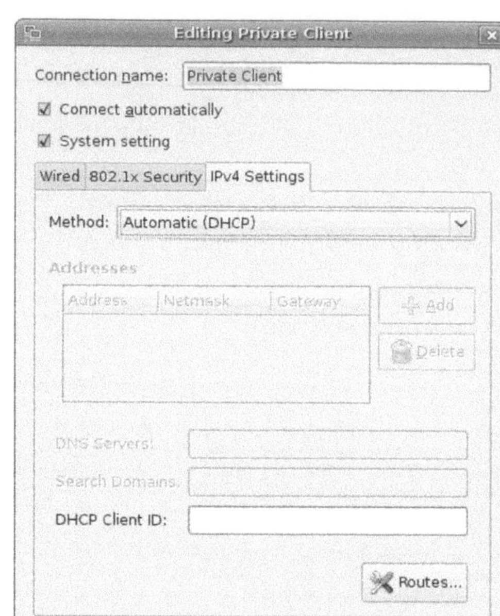

Figure 5.18 Configuring DHCP client.

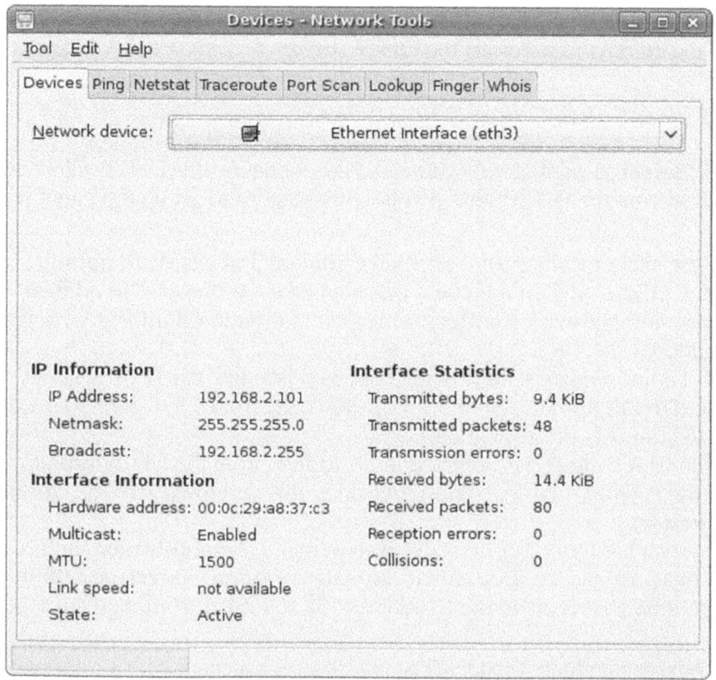

Figure 5.19 Dynamic IP address received from DHCP server.

1. First, you need to get the NIC's hardware address from the client machine. From Figure 5.19, you can see that the hardware address is 00:0c:29:a8:37:c3.
2. Assume that the server machine is still on. Enter the following command in the terminal window:

```
sudo gedit /etc/dhcp3/dhcpd.conf
```

3. Change the following section:

```
#host fantasia {
          #     hardware ethernet 08:00:07:26:c0:a5;
          #     fixed-address fantasia.fugue.com;
          #     }
```

to

```
host client1 {
                 hardware ethernet 00:0c:29:a8:37:c3;
                 fixed-address 192.168.2.99;
                 }
```

4. After you finish the configuration, click the **Save** icon on the menu bar. Click **File,** and select **Quit.**
5. Restart the DHCP server by entering the command:

```
sudo /etc/init.d/dhcp3-server restart
```

6. To see the effect of the configuration, restart the client virtual machine. After you log on to the client virtual machine, click the **System** menu, **Administration**, and **Network Tools**. From the Network device drop-down list, select **Ethernet Interface (eth3)**. As shown in Figure 5.20, the client machine has received the IP address 192.168.2.99 from the DHCP server.

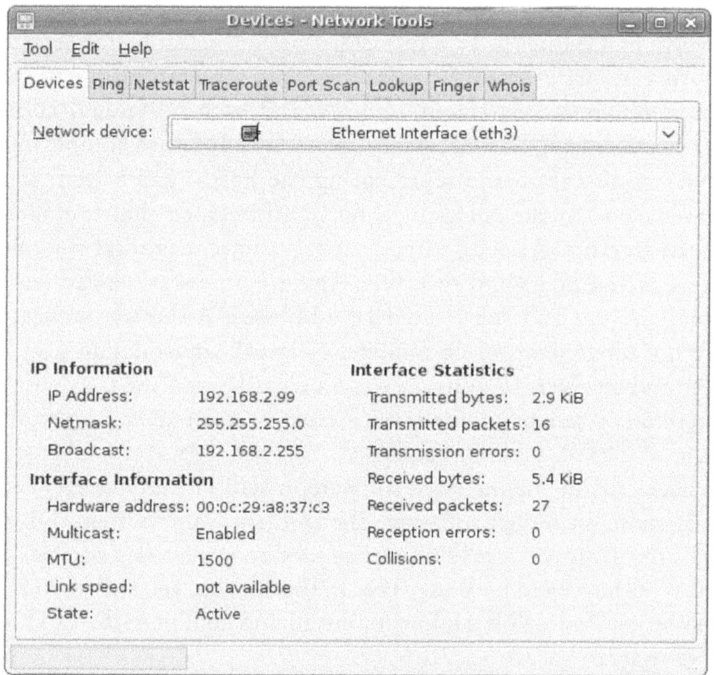

Figure 5.20 Fixed IP address received from DHCP server.

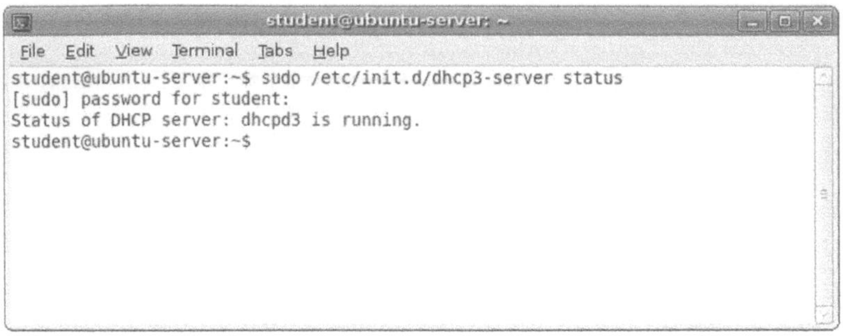

```
student@ubuntu-server:~$ sudo /etc/init.d/dhcp3-server status
[sudo] password for student:
Status of DHCP server: dhcpd3 is running.
student@ubuntu-server:~$
```

Figure 5.21 Status of DHCP server.

7. Through the above hands-on practice, you have created a DHCP server. There is one more task; you need to check if the DHCP server can automatically start every time the system reboots. Reboot the server machine. After the server machine is restarted, execute the following command in the terminal window:

```
sudo /etc/init.d/dhcp3-server status
```

You should be able to see the output shown in Figure 5.21. The DHCP server is up and running automatically.

5.4 Name Services

Name services resolve host names to IP addresses, and vice versa. Name services are essential for e-commerce. An enterprise network is organized as a hierarchical system based on the names of the company, sites, departments, offices, and each individual computer and network device. Name services are also necessary for today's Internet computing environment. Each Web server has a distinct name representing the host organization. It is necessary to resolve a Web server name to the corresponding IP address, so that the Web server can be accessed through the Internet. Also, all e-mail accounts have meaningful names so that users can easily identify e-mail senders and receivers. Again, name services are required to resolve the names of e-mail servers and the related IP addresses. Although names are convenient for users, they are not convenient for computers. Network transmission uses IP addresses to identify the sender and receiver. IP addresses can be easily identified, calculated, and stored by computers. Therefore, a reliable name service must be created and maintained to support the daily operation.

Once a name is entered in the interface software, it will be automatically translated into a related IP address by the name service software. The Domain Name System (DNS) is this type of software; it provides the name service. DNS can be used to resolve IP addresses for the hosts on the Internet as well as the hosts on a local network. In this section, you will learn about the services provided by a DNS server. You will learn how to install and configure the DNS service and how to manage the DNS server.

5.4.1 Naming Hierarchy

On the Internet, each host or Web site is assigned a name called a domain name. The domain name is a sequence of names separated with periods. For example:

myhost.mydepartment.mycompany.com

The domain name has a hierarchical structure. The name on the right has more general use than the one on the left. The rightmost name is called the top-level domain. There are only a limited number of such domains, each representing a main segment of the naming system. The commonly used top-level domains controlled by the Internet Corporation for Assigned Names and Numbers (ICANN) are listed in Table 5.4. The top-level domains can also be listed based on the country code. Table 5.5 illustrates some of the country-code-based top-level domains.

When an organization decides to participate in the domain name system so that it can be part of the Internet, the first thing that it needs to do is to decide which top-level domain to join. After the decision is made, the organization needs to apply for its name under the top-level domains. Once the name is approved by ICANN, the organization's name is registered under a selected top-level domain.

After the organization has registered its name in one of the top-level domains, it can add more layers to the hierarchical name system. The organization can add layers for all its departments, offices, and individual hosts under its name. It is free to create any layers and host names under the organization's name. There are up to 127 layers that can be created. Figure 5.22 demonstrates the naming hierarchy for a university.

Suppose that the math department has an online tutoring system. Each major subject of math is supported by a server for remote access. Then, the algebra server can be assigned the following domain name:

algebra.math.science.arts_sciences.university.edu

Table 5.4 Category-Based Top-Level Domains

Domain Name	*Category*
.com	Commercial
.edu	Education
.gov	Government
.org	Nonprofit Organization
.mil	Military
.net	Network Organization
.name	Individual User

Table 5.5 Country-Code-Based Top-Level Domains

Domain Name	*Category*
.us	United States
.au	Australia
.ca	Canada
.cn	China
.de	Germany
.ru	Russia
.uk	United Kingdom

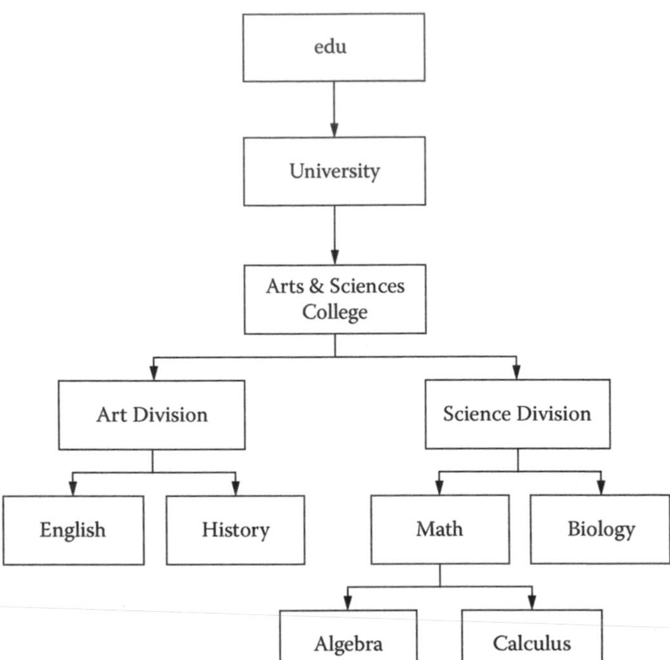

Figure 5.22 Example of naming hierarchy.

where edu is the top-level domain name and algebra is the computer's host name. It is required that the names within the same domain be unique. For example, within the edu domain, there should be no duplicated names.

Some enterprise-level companies may need multiple servers, each serving a special purpose. Some special-purpose servers, such as the mail server, ftp server, and Web server, are assigned well-known host names. Table 5.6 gives the names of these special-purpose servers.

Table 5.6 Host Names of Special-Purpose Servers

Server	*Host Name*
Mail	mail
FTP	ftp
Web	www

5.4.2 DNS Server Hierarchy

Computers or network devices on the Internet all have their own names, and these names all have IP addresses associated with them. There are billions of names that need to be converted to IP addresses, and vice versa. You may expect a large database to hold information about names and IP addresses and to manage their updates. For hosting such a large database, you also need powerful servers that can handle billions of requests every day. In fact, to store such large amounts of information, the database is distributed among many DNS servers. Another reason to distribute the database is that some companies may want to manage their own name resolution data for convenience and for security reasons. To host such a distributed database for name resolution, there will be a large number of DNS servers hierarchically arranged as a distributed system to match the name hierarchy.

In the DNS server hierarchy, a root server hosts the database that contains top-level domain names and IP addresses for the servers that host databases for these top-level domains. Each top-level DNS server host a database that contains information about organizations registered to the top-level DNS server. The information includes the organizations' domain names and the IP addresses of the organizations' DNS servers. Each organization's DNS server hosts a database that stores information about the layers below the organization layer.

5.4.3 Name Resolution Process

The process of finding the IP address for a given domain name is called a name resolution process. The process is also called a forward lookup process. In addition to the forward lookup process, DNS can also match the domain name to a given IP address. Such a process is called a reverse lookup process.

To demonstrate a name resolution process, let us consider an example. Suppose a user enters the following domain name in the Web browser URL text box:

lab.college.university.edu

After the user presses the Enter key, the Linux operating system first checks the file named "host" or something similar to "host" for the related IP address. If the file "host" contains the corresponding IP address, the name resolution is done. The IP address will be used by the client computer to communicate with the host named "lab." If there is no match, the operating system will check the DNS cache to see if there is a matched IP address. If not, the operating system on the client computer issues a name resolution request to the local DNS server whose IP address was specified during the configuration of the network interface card. If there is no matched IP address in the database hosted by the local DNS server, the request will be forwarded to the root server because each DNS server knows the root server's IP address. The root server contains all the major categories of domain names such as com, edu, or org. When a name resolution request comes, the root server checks the top-level domain names first. Once there is a match, the root server will return the IP address of the top-level domain server to the local DNS server. For example, if the top-level domain name is edu, the root server will return the IP address of the edu server to the local DNS server. Then, the local DNS server will issue a request to the edu DNS server. The edu server hosts the database that contains the names of universities registered under the edu top-level domain. If there is a match for the name of the university, then the IP address of the university's DNS server will be returned to the local DNS server. The local DNS server uses this returned IP address to send the request to the university's DNS server. The university's DNS server will check the college name and return the IP address of the college DNS server to the local DNS server. The local DNS server then uses the college's IP address sent by the university DNS server to send the request to the college DNS server. If the database hosted by the DNS server at the college layer has the IP address of the host name called lab requested by the client, the IP address will be returned to the local DNS server that issues the request. Then, the local DNS server will send the IP address to the client computer, and the client can use that IP address to communicate with the host lab in the college domain. Figure 5.23 illustrates the name resolution process in the hierarchical system.

Once the client computer gets the IP address for a given name, it caches the IP address with the domain name. Next time, to contact the same host, the client computer checks the cache first.

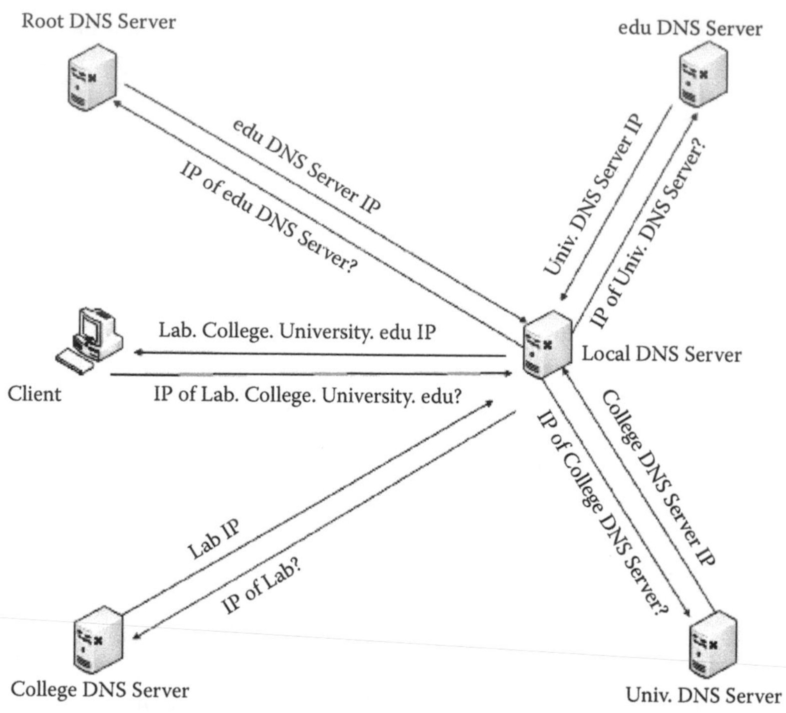

Figure 5.23 DNS name resolution process.

If there is a match, it gets the corresponding IP address from the cache in no time. In this case, the client computer does not need to send a request to the local DNS server.

5.4.4 DNS Zones

The entire DNS database is distributed to millions of DNS servers. Each DNS server only manages a portion of the entire DNS namespace; such a portion is called a DNS zone. To store DNS records, you need to first create a DNS zone on the DNS server. Then, you can add the DNS records manually or through a GUI interface. When the zone is created, two files are created: one is used to store the records for forward lookup and the other one is used to store the records for reverse lookup.

Once the zone is filled with DNS records, copies of the zone are often created and stored on different servers for fault tolerance. The copies can also be distributed to different DNS servers at different physical locations to reduce network traffic. The master zone (or the primary zone) is the originally created zone, and the slave zone (or the secondary zone) is the copy. The master zone and slave zones automatically synchronize the DNS information. The synchronization can be done by either replacing the slave zone with the entire master zone, or by updating the slave zone with changes made in the master zone.

5.4.5 Types of DNS Records

As mentioned earlier, the DNS database is distributed to millions of DNS servers. Each DNS server hosts its own database, which is part of the overall DNS database. Each record in the

Table 5.7 Types of DNS Records

Type	*Usage*
A	This is the Address type of record, which is used to bind a domain name to an IP address.
AAAA	It is the IPv6 Address type record.
MX	This is the Mail Exchange type of record, which provides information about a specified mail server.
NS	This is the Name Server type of record, which provides information about a specified DNS server.
PTR	This is the Pointer type record, which is used to resolve an IP address to a host name.
CNAME	This is the Canonical Name type of record, which is used to assign an alias to a host name.
SOA	This is the Start of Authority type of record, which provides configuration information about the domain for which this DNS server is responsible.

DNS database may include three basic fields, the domain name or IP address, the address type, and the record type. For example, in

```
group2  IN   A
```

group2 is the domain name, IN indicates an Internet address, and the type A indicates that the record is an Address type record. If the value in the first field is missing, the assumption is that it is the same as the value in the previous record. This field is often followed by optional parameters related to the third field.

There are various types of records in the DNS database. They have various functions: binding a domain name to an IP address, matching an e-mail address to an e-mail server, connecting hosts to local DNS servers, performing reverse lookup, and creating aliases for other domain names. The types of DNS records are summarized in Table 5.7.

The DNS records are stored in the DNS zone files. The following are some sample DNS records stored in one of the DNS zone files.

For the forward lookup, the sample zone file /etc/bind/zones/group2.lab.db contains the following DNS records:

```
$TTL 86400
@       IN  SOA    group2. root (
                   2 ; serial
                   28800 ; refresh
                   14400 ; retry
                   3600000 ; expire
                   86400 ; ttl
                   )
        IN  NS     192.168.2.200.
        IN   MX    10  mail.lab.net.
group2 IN  A       192.168.2.200
www     IN  CNAME  group2
```

In the first line, the directive $TTL defines the duration in seconds of how long the records may be cached. The value of the duration can also be hours, such as 3h, or days, such as 2d.
The next several lines show the SOA record, which contains a few items as shown:

```
@       IN SOA   group2. root (
                 2 ; serial
                 28800 ; refresh
                 14400 ; retry
                 3600000 ; expire
                 86400 ; ttl
                 )
```

The meanings of these records are listed as follows:

- @: This sign represents the host name of the DNS server, such as group2.lab.
- IN: This means the Internet. If the DNS server is on the Internet or Intranet, you should use IN.
- SOA: It indicates that the record is the Start of Authority type.
- group2.: This is the host name of the DNS server. It can be the name of an external DNS server.
- root: This is the e-mail address of the DNS server administrator.
- 2; serial: It is a serial number for checking if the DNS database has been updated recently.
- 28800 ; refresh: It is the time in seconds after which a slave DNS server will refresh its database by comparing its database with the master DNS database.
- 14400 ; retry: This is the time period in which a slave DNS server tries to reconnect to the master DNS server for database updates.
- 3600000 ; expire: This is the time period for a slave DNS server to give out domain information from its cached zone file in case the master DNS server cannot be contacted.
- 86400 ; ttl: This is the duration for which the slave DNS server should keep its cached zone file. The cached records are refreshed after this time.

The next two lines are about the DNS server and mail server:

```
IN    NS    192.168.2.200.
IN    MX    10 mail.lab.net.
```

The explanations for the items included in these two lines are as follows:

- NS: It indicates that the record is the Name Server type.
- 192.168.2.200.: This is the DNS server's IP address. Note that there is a "." at the end of the line. It means that the name is a qualified domain name. Without the final ".", the DNS server will automatically add a default domain name.
- MX: It indicates that the record is the Mail Exchange type.
- 10: This number is a preference number. If there are multiple MX records, the MX record with the smallest preference number has the highest priority and will be contacted first.
- mail.lab.net.: It is the qualified host name for the mail server.

The next line is

```
group2  IN A    192.168.2.200
```

The letter A indicates that the record is the Address type, which binds the name group2 to the IP address 192.168.2.200.

The next line

```
www      IN     CNAME       group2
```

is a Canonical Name type record. The keyword www is used as the alias for group2. If the group2 machine hosts a Web server, instead of using the domain name group2.lab, you can use the domain name www.lab, which is a more traditional name for a Web server.

For the reverse lookup, the sample zone file /etc/bind/zones/rev.2.168.192.in-addr.arpa contains the following DNS records:

```
$TTL 86400
@          IN    SOA group2.lab. root (
                 2 ; serial
                 28800 ; refresh
                 14400 ; retry
                 3600000 ; expire
                 86400 ; ttl
                 )
           IN    NS   192.168.2.200.
200        IN    PTR  group2.lab.
```

In the last line, the keyword PTR indicates that this is a Pointer type record. In the network 192.168.2, the host with ID 200 is assigned the domain name group2.lab.

In the foregoing paragraphs, several basic concepts related to DNS were introduced. The next section presents some hands-on practice on DNS-related topics to enhance understanding of the DNS service.

Activity 5.4 Installing and Configuring DNS with Linux

All the name resolution services can be done by a software called Berkeley Internet Name Domain (BIND). BIND knows all about the registration of new domain names and the translation between domain names and IP addresses. BIND has three components that can be used to handle name resolution tasks:

- *Name server (named):* A name server is used to translate domain names to IP addresses, and vice versa.
- *Resolver library:* It is a collection of programs used to query DNS zones based on the instruction given in the configuration file.
- *NSLOOKUP:* This is a utility that can be used for troubleshooting by looking up DNS records.

In the following hands-on exercise, you are going to configure your private network to use DNS with Ubuntu Linux. You will first install the software BIND, and then configure the BIND components to create DNS zones. Then, you will test the DNS configuration on both the server and client computers. To install and configure BIND, follow these steps:

1. Log on to the server machine with username **student** and password **ubuntu**.
2. Enter the following command in the terminal window to install BIND version 9:

   ```
   sudo apt-get install bind9 dnsutils
   ```

3. After the installation is completed, you will configure BIND by editing the file named.conf.local. To do so, enter the following command to open the file for configuration:

```
sudo gedit /etc/bind/named.conf.local
```

4. Once the file is opened, add the following code:

```
//The following code defines the forward lookup zone.

zone "group2.lab" {
type master;
file "/etc/bind/zones/group2.lab.db";
};

//The following code defines the reverse lookup zone.

zone "2.168.192.in-addr.arpa" {
type master;
file "/etc/bind/zones/rev.2.168.192.in-addr.arpa";
};
```

5. After you have entered the code, click the **Save** icon on the menu bar. Then, click the **File** menu, and select **Quit**.
6. In the preceding steps, you have specified two zones, one for the forward lookup and the other for the reverse lookup. Next, you will create a directory to host zone files. Enter the following command in the terminal window:

```
sudo mkdir /etc/bind/zones
```

7. Enter the following command to create a zone file for the forward lookup:

```
sudo gedit /etc/bind/zones/group2.lab.db
```

8. After the file is opened, enter the following code. Then, click **Save**. After the code is saved, click the **File** menu, and select **Quit**.

```
$TTL 86400
@     IN   SOA    group2.lab. root (
                  2 ; serial
                  28800 ; refresh
                  14400 ; retry
                  3600000 ; expire
                  86400 ; ttl
                  )
      IN   NS     192.168.2.1.
      IN   MX     10   group2.lab.
ns1   IN   A      192.168.2.1
www   IN   CNAME  ns1
```

9. Next, you will create a zone file for the reverse lookup. Enter the following command to create the zone file:

```
sudo gedit /etc/bind/zones/rev.2.168.192.in-addr.arpa
```

10. After the file is opened, enter the following code. Then, click **Save**. After the code is saved, click the **File** menu, and select **Quit**.

```
$TTL 86400
@          IN     SOA  group2.lab. root (
                  2009031001 ; serial
                  28800 ; refresh
                  14400 ; retry
                  3600000 ; expire
                  86400 ; ttl
                  )
           IN     NS   192.168.2.1.
1          IN     PTR  ns1.group2.lab.
```

11. After you have created these two zone files, you need to manually restart the BIND server. Enter the following to restart the BIND server:

```
sudo /etc/init.d/bind9 restart
```

12. After the BIND server is restarted, you need to let the resolver know where to search for the zone file and the IP address of the DNS server. To do so, enter the following command to open the configuration file of the resolver:

```
sudo gedit /etc/resolv.conf
```

13. After the file is opened, you may comment out the lines that are already in there. Then, enter the following lines:

```
search group2.lab
nameserver 192.168.2.1
```

    After the code is entered, click the **Save** menu. Then, click the **File** menu, and select **Quit**.
14. The last step is to test the BIND server. To do so, enter the following command:

```
nslookup
```

    When prompted, enter the name **ns1** and press the **Enter** key. The output should have the IP address 192.168.2.1 (Figure 5.24). After you get the IP address for the name www, enter the IP address **192.168.2.1** and press the **Enter** key. The output should give the domain name group2.lab shown in Figure 5.24. To quit nslookup, type **exit,** and press the **Enter** key.
15. Another easy way to test the DNS service is to use the tool called HOST. To resolve the IP address for the name www, enter the following commands in the terminal window:

```
host ns1
host www
host 192.168.2.1
```

    If everything works well, you should be able to see the output in Figure 5.25.

You may want to see if the DNS service works on the client computer. The following steps show how to conduct the test:

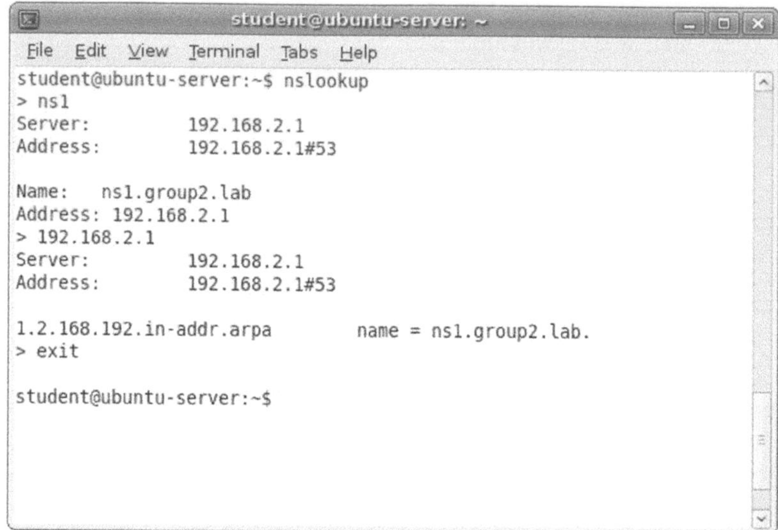

Figure 5.24 Testing DNS service with NSLOOKUP tool.

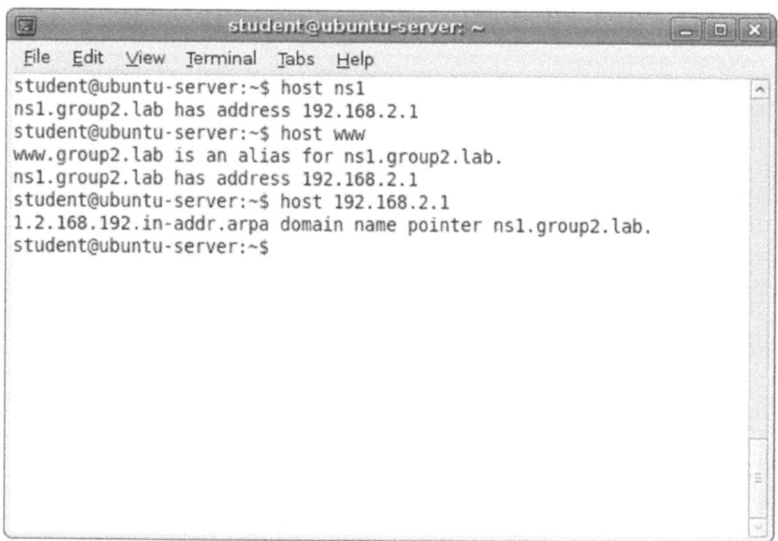

Figure 5.25 Testing DNS service with HOST tool.

1. Log on to your client computer with username **student** and password **ubuntu**.
2. Next, you need to tell the resolver where to search for the DNS server. To do so, first execute the following command in the terminal window:

```
sudo gedit /etc/resolv.conf
```

3. After the resolv.conf file is opened, make sure the following code is already in there. If both the client and server machines are on the same private network, Ubuntu Linux on the client

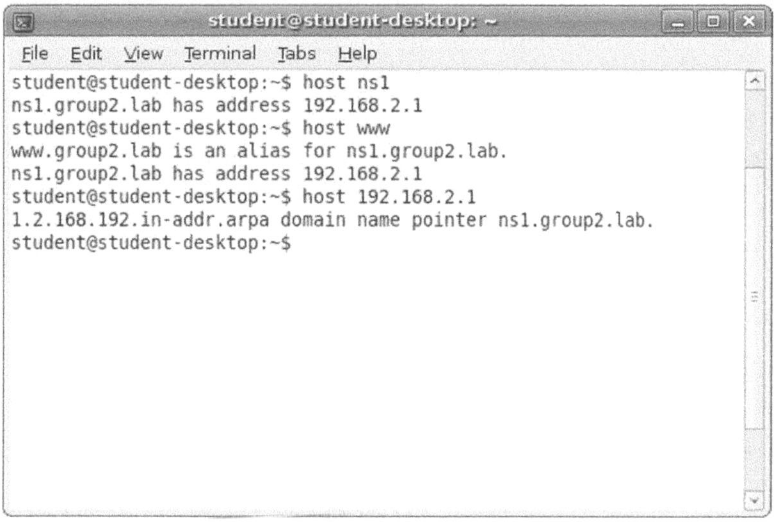
student@student-desktop: ~
File Edit View Terminal Tabs Help
student@student-desktop:~$ host ns1
ns1.group2.lab has address 192.168.2.1
student@student-desktop:~$ host www
www.group2.lab is an alias for ns1.group2.lab.
ns1.group2.lab has address 192.168.2.1
student@student-desktop:~$ host 192.168.2.1
1.2.168.192.in-addr.arpa domain name pointer ns1.group2.lab.
student@student-desktop:~$

Figure 5.26 Testing DNS service on client machine.

machine should pick up the content of the resolv.conf file on the server machine. If not, enter the following code and comment out other existing code:

```
search group2.lab
nameserver 192.168.2.1
```

After the code is entered, click the **Save** menu. Then, click the **File** menu, and select **Quit**.

4. To test the DNS service, execute the following commands, and you should get the results shown in Figure 5.26:

```
host ns1
host www
host 192.168.2.1
```

Next, you may want to assign your client machine a new name such as client1 on the DNS server. The following steps show you how to get the job done:

1. Assume that the server machine is still on. Enter the following command to open the forward lookup zone file:

```
sudo gedit /etc/bind/zones/group2.lab.db
```

2. After the file is opened, add the following code. Then, click **Save**. After the code is saved, click the **File** menu, and select **Quit**.

```
client1    IN    A    192.168.2.2
```

3. Next, you will create a zone file for the reverse lookup. Enter the following command to create the zone file:

```
sudo gedit /etc/bind/zones/rev.2.168.192.in-addr.arpa
```

4. After the zone file is opened, enter the following code. Then, click **Save**. After the code is saved, click **File,** and select **Quit**.

```
2          IN    PTR  client1.group2.lab.
```

5. After you have created the two zone files, you need to manually restart the DNS server, BIND. Enter the following command to restart the BIND server:

```
sudo /etc/init.d/bind9 restart
```

6. Now, go back to the client machine. Enter the following commands to test the DNS server:

```
host client1
host 192.168.2.2
```

   You should get the result shown in Figure 5.27.

In the foregoing procedure, you created a DNS server for hands-on practice. Note that the private IP address is assigned to the DNS server. Therefore, the DNS server can only be used in the intranet.

During this hands-on activity, you created a DNS service for your own private network. The file named.conf.local is configured to define the zone files for both forward and reverse lookup. Then, the zone file group2.lab.db is configured to include the records for the name server, the client, and the alias. This hands-on activity also defines the reverse lookup zone file. In the file resolv.conf, the search domain and the name server's IP address are provided so that the resolver knows where to query the zone file. At the end of the activity, instructions are given to show you how to test the DNS service. Two commonly used DNS testing tools, NSLOOKUP and HOST, are introduced in this hands-on activity.

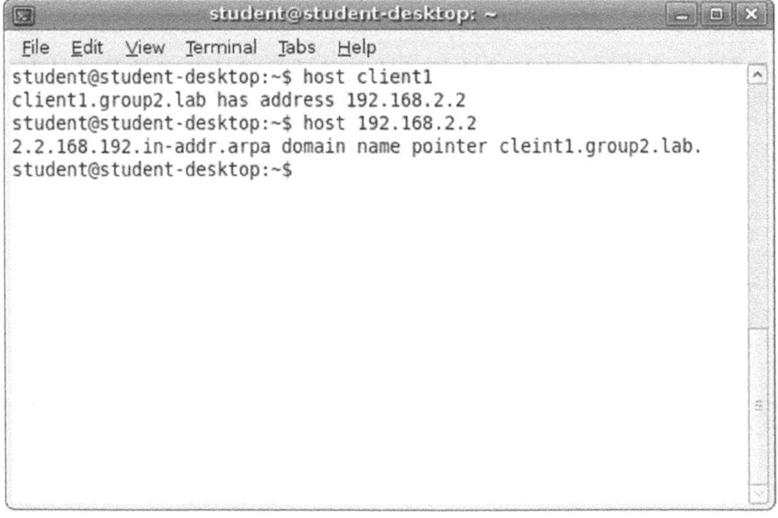

Figure 5.27 Testing name resolution for client machine.

5.5 Summary

This chapter examined some commonly used network services. Linux provides various tools for developing and managing these services. The first topic in this chapter was users and groups. User authentication is important for Linux because it allows multiple users to perform multiple tasks simultaneously. A group can be created to include users with the same authentication configuration. Using groups can significantly reduce the workload of the network administrator. The first hands-on activity in this chapter demonstrated how to create a network administrator account and assign the account the privileges to perform network administration tasks. The hands-on activity also briefly illustrated how to add the GNOME desktop on the server machine.

A way to reduce the network administrator's workload is to create a DHCP service to automatically assign IP addresses to network hosts. The DHCP service is necessary in a computing environment where computers join and leave a network frequently. With the DHCP service, each time a computer joins the network, the computer is automatically assigned an IP address. This chapter explained how DHCP automatically assigns IP addresses to computers. In the hands-on activity, the DHCP service was implemented on the private network constructed in the previous chapters.

The name service is essential for the Internet computing environment. All the Web sites are associated with human-friendly names. These names have to be resolved to IP addresses for network transmission. DNS provides such a service. This chapter presented the DNS hierarchy and the related hierarchical DNS server structure. DNS processes were also explained in this chapter. The DNS service performs forward lookup and reverse lookup to resolve the name to an IP address, and vice versa. The test of DNS can be done with the tools NSLOOKUP and HOST provided by Linux.

In addition to the DNS service, routing is another essential component of the Internet computing environment. Linux also includes various tools to help users route data from one network to another network. In the next chapter, you will learn how a router works and how you can use Linux to build routers.

Review Questions

1. How are users categorized?
2. In Linux, which user has all the privileges?
3. Why do we need groups for user management?
4. What is the command to change the root user's password on Ubuntu?
5. What are the three files mentioned in this chapter that contain information about a user's account and the user's group?
6. Explain the meaning of each column in the file /etc/passwd.
7. Explain the meaning of each column in the file /etc/shadow.
8. Describe the DHCP assigning process.
9. What are the benefits of using DHCP?
10. What are the values of the default lease time and the maximum lease time?
11. Why do we need the name service?
12. List at least five category-based top-level domains.
13. What is the maximum number of layers that can be added to the name hierarchy?
14. What is a root server?
15. What is a forward lookup process?

16. What is a reverse lookup process?
17. Before forwarding the name resolution request to the root server, what does the operating system need to check first?
18. What is the DNS zone?
19. What is an NS DNS record?
20. What is an SOA DNS record?

Case Study Projects

The following are two network projects that involve the investigation of DHCP and DNS.

Case Study Project 5.1. Investigate the DHCP configuration of your home network or workplace network.

Case Study Project 5.2. Describe the DNS configuration of your home network or workplace network.

Chapter 6

Routing

Objectives

- Understand routers.
- Build routers with Linux.
- Configure routers.

6.1 Introduction

As described earlier, a router is the key network device that links the various types of networks that make up the Internet. This chapter is devoted to this important network device. A router is considered by many to be a sophisticated network device. The goal of this chapter is to help readers understand this important network device through actually building a router by themselves.

A lot has been written on the theories and concepts of the services and functionalities provided by routers. Therefore, our first task in this chapter is to understand how a router works. Some theories and concepts will be introduced to explain how a router transmits a packet to its destination through an optimized route and how it computes this route.

After the theories and concepts related to routers are introduced, our next task is to build a router with the tools provided by Linux. Many routers are products of network device vendors such as Cisco. A router can also be built with Linux and a proper routing protocol. This chapter provides hands-on practice on how to physically create a router with Linux. Such a router can be used to connect two different networks and allow packets to be transmitted from one network to another. The hands-on practice will give readers an opportunity to explore router details and gain a deeper understanding of the router's functionalities.

6.2 Connecting Networks with Routers

Networks are often constructed so that they consist of multiple network segments, and they may be constructed with different network technologies. Especially, an enterprise-level network may include the Internet, WAN, and LAN technologies. On this type of network, the transmission of packets from one location to another location can be a challenging task. Routers are network devices used to pass packets from one network segment to another. In order to do so, a router must be able to perform the following tasks:

- It must be physically linked to two or more network segments and be able to handle the frames specified by these network segments.
- It must be able to store the information about the networks and routes to reach each network.
- It must be able to update information about the networks when there is change in the network structure and configuration.
- Based on the stored information, the router must be able to compute the shortest path to the destination network.
- During packet transmission, the router must be able to dynamically redefine its transmission so that it can comply with the constraints imposed by different networks.

Next, you will learn how routers can accomplish these tasks.

Physically similar to a computer, a router is a network device that includes a CPU and memory for sophisticated computation. It also includes two or more network interface cards to physically connect multiple networks. The network connection to a router is just like the connection to a computer on the network. Unlike a general-purpose computer, the computation on a router mainly focuses on creating and managing the routing table and searches for the shortest path to a destination.

When connected to a network segment, the network interface card must be configured to have the same network ID as the network segment so that the computers on the network segment can communicate with the network interface card installed on the router. Figure 6.1 illustrates how a router's network interface cards are configured.

As shown in Figure 6.1, for the network with ID 192.168.1.0, the router's network interface card connected to the network is configured to have the IP address 192.168.1.1. Any

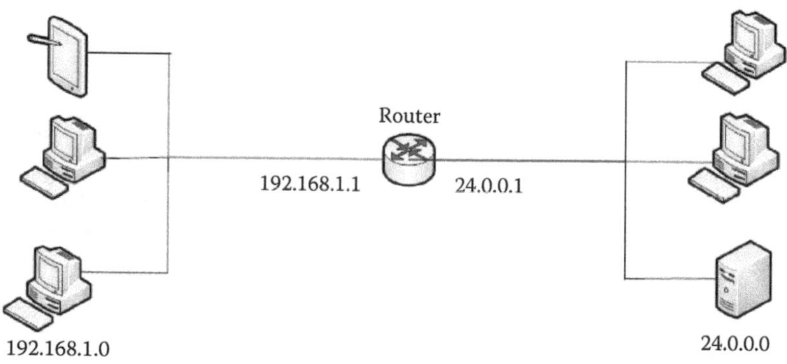

Figure 6.1 Connecting two network segments with router.

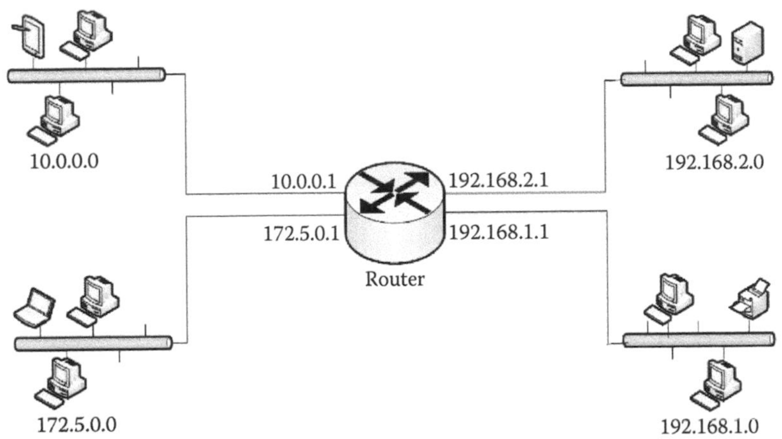

Figure 6.2 Connecting multiple network segments with router.

IP address that is valid for the network 192.168.1.0 can be assigned to the router's network interface card. However, because the IP address assigned to the router's interface card will be used by each of the hosts on the network, an easy-to-remember IP address should be assigned to the router's interface card. In our example, 192.168.1.1 is assigned to the router's network interface card.

The router in Figure 6.1 connects two networks with two network interface cards. By adding more network interface cards, a router can connect more networks (Figure 6.2). However, in a real-life situation, due to security, reliability, and performance reasons, an organization may not be willing to connect too many networks to a single router. Connecting too many networks to a router will cause performance bottlenecks. An error in the router may cause multiple networks to shut down, and a network virus may be passed on to each of the networks connected to the router.

The number of networks to be connected to a router depends on the organization's requirements for reliability, security, costs of routers, network capacities, and performance. It requires a careful balance to come up with a good design.

6.3 Routing Table

The information about networks is stored in the routing table. Each entry of a routing table is about a network, including the destination network ID, subnet mask, default gateway, network interface card, and so on (Table 6.1).

Table 6.1 Sample Routing Table

Destination	*Gateway*	*Genmask*	*Flags*	*Metric*	*Ref*	*Use*	*Iface*
192.168.1.0	*	255.255.255.0	U	0	0	0	eth0
127.0.0.0	0.0.0.0	255.0.0.0	U	0	0	0	lo
192.168.2.0	192.168.2.1	255.255.255.0	UG	100	0	0	eth1

The following is a brief explanation of the items in a routing table:

- *Destination:* It is the IP address of the destination network.
- *Gateway:* This is the IP address of a gateway. If no gateway is specified, use the symbol '*'. The value 0.0.0.0 or '*' means that the destination network is a directly connected network.
- *Genmask:* It is the subnet mask for the destination network.
- *Flags:* These are signals for a particular routing status. The commonly used flags are as follows.
  U: The route is up.
  G: The route uses an external gateway.
  R: The route is a reinstate route for dynamic routing.
  D: The router is dynamically installed.
  M: The route is modified.
  !: It indicates a rejecting route.
- *Metric:* It is the distance to the destination network. The distance can be measured by the number of networks crossed or other measures.
- *Ref:* It is the number of references to this route.
- *Use:* It gives a count of packets transmitted via this route.
- *Iface:* It is the name of the network interface card to which this route sends a packet.

The information stored in a routing table can be used to calculate the best path to deliver a packet to the destination network. Once the packet reaches a router, it examines the packet and compares the destination address of the packet with the entries stored in the routing table. If there is a match, the table content can be used to find the next router on the route to the destination network. Then, the router will deliver the packet to that router through the network that links the two routers. The trip on which a packet is delivered from one router to another is called a *hop*.

6.4 Updating Routing Table

When a network is added, dropped, or changed, the routing table needs to be updated. The routing protocol interacts with the routers in the neighborhood. Based on the information collected, the routing protocol recalculates the optimal route to each destination, and then updates the routing table. There are two ways to update a routing table. A routing table can be updated manually or dynamically. The routing is called *static* if the routing table's content remains unchanged unless it is changed manually by the network administrator. In dynamic routing, the routing table's content is updated by a routing protocol automatically.

In static routing, routes are manually entered in the routing table by the network administrator. This means that routing protocols are not needed for calculating the routes and updating the routing table. Static routing does not consume CPU power and network bandwidth. Therefore, it can improve a network's performance. On the other hand, static routing is not flexible. It does not keep up with the changes that occurred in a network's structure. Static routing is not fault tolerant. It is not able to find a new route to the destination if the static route is blocked because of network equipment failure. Also, it does not scale well to a large network with many routers. A large network with many routers can generate a large number of entries in the routing table; this can significantly add to the network administrator's workload.

The features of static routing make it suitable for a small network that has only a few routes that remain unchanged most of the time, for example, a home network that is only connected to the

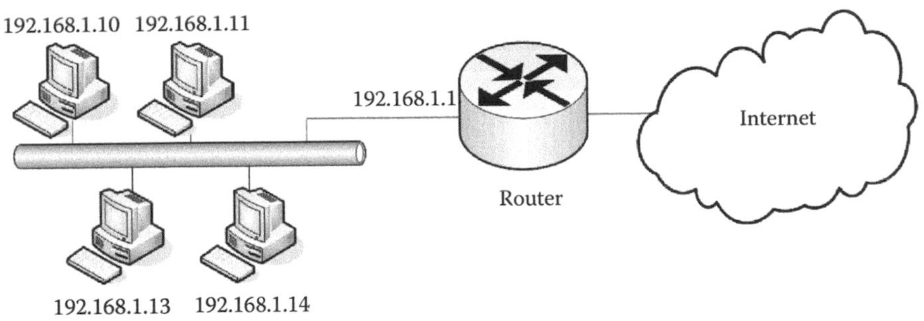

Figure 6.3 Home network.

Internet through one router (Figure 6.3). Although an IP packet may have a long journey to the destination on the Internet, it will first be sent to the router that directly connects the home network and the Internet. After the packet gets on the Internet, it will be sent to the ISP. From the ISP, there are other routers that will take care of the rest of journey. In this way, packets are delivered from this home computer to the ISP over the same route again and again. For this type of network, static routing is a better choice.

Because there is one network and one router connected to the Internet, the routing table can have as few as only two entries.

Table 6.2 Static Routing Table

Destination	*Gateway*	*Genmask*
192.168.1.0	*	255.255.255.0
default	192.168.1.1	0.0.0.0

In Table 6.2, the entries in the first row are about the route to the home network that is directly connected to the router. The home network has the ID 192.168.1.0. The second row in the routing table is the default route to the ISP. Each routing table can have one default route. A destination column may contain the keyword "default" on some systems or "0.0.0.0" on other systems for the default network. If the destination in an IP packet is not listed in the routing table, the packet will be sent to the gateway specified by the IP address in the default-gateway cell. This is why all the packets generated in the network 192.168.1.0 are sent to the router that has the network interface card configured with the IP address 192.168.1.1, no matter what the destination is.

While configuring the router, the user will be prompted to enter the information manually and then the configuration file will create the static routing table. After the static routing table is created, it will remain that way until the user changes the configuration manually.

Although static routing is good for networks such as the foregoing one, it is not suitable for networks that dynamically change their topologies and networks that may contain hundreds of routers. Once a network segment is added or removed, the change should be immediately updated in the routing table.

The routing table should be able to calculate the routes to new destinations. Then, the changes made in the routing table should be passed on to hundreds of other routers for them to update their routing tables. Obviously, it is impossible to do it manually. All this has to be done automatically by routing protocols. Therefore, dynamic routing is used on most of the routers. During the dynamic process, each router exchanges routing information with other routers in its neighborhood. The router will update its routing table dynamically if the routing tables on the other routers in the neighborhood have changed.

6.5 Route Calculation

One of the tasks during the routing table update is to determine the optimal route to a destination. The calculation of the optimal route is done by computer algorithms. The criteria of the optimal route can be time delay, average traffic, number of hops, and other costs. The computer algorithms are differentiated by the method used to determine the optimal route and the method used to exchange routing information. There are only two major algorithms for determining the optimal route; they are the link state (LS) routing algorithm and the distance vector (DV) routing algorithm.

6.5.1 Link State Routing Algorithm

The LS routing algorithm requires information about all other routers on the network and the cost of delivering packets from one router to another router in the network. The method builds a list of optimal routes to all the destinations in the network. For example, the routing protocol Open Shortest Path First (OSPF) is a link state protocol. When the LS routing algorithm is used, a routing protocol performs the following tasks:

- Sending messages to other routers to get their IP addresses.
- Measuring the cost of delivering packets to other routers. For example, you can use an echo packet to measure the time delay for transmitting a packet between two routers.
- Exchanging routing information with other routers on the network.
- Computing the optimal route between a pair of routers. The commonly used computer algorithm to accomplish this task is Dijkstra's shortest path algorithm.

By considering a router as a node, the connection between two routers as an edge, and the cost as the weight of an edge, a network can be represented by a mathematical object called a *weighted graph*. This graph shows the locations of routers on a network and the edges that connect them. Every edge is weighted with a number. The LS algorithms such as Dijkstra's shortest path algorithm require input values such as the number of routers and each router's ID, which is a unique number assigned to the router, as well as the weight assigned to each edge that connects two routers. With this input information, a routing protocol builds a graph of the network. Then, the graph is used to compute the shortest path between each pair of notes. Figure 6.4 illustrates a sample graph consisting of routers, links, and weights.

To examine the process of finding the optimal path from R1 to R6 with Dijkstra's shortest path algorithm, let us use the graph in Figure 6.4 as an example. R1 is considered the source node, and R6 is considered the sink node.

1. In the first step, create a four-column status record array to include all the nodes on the network and the status of the nodes. A node can be permanent or tentative. Initially, all the nodes are tentative except the source node as shown in Table 6.3.
2. In the second step, compare the weights of the links that directly connect the tentative nodes to the permanent node. Select the tentative node that has the least weight sum, and update the status record array by making the selected tentative node a permanent node. Once a node's status is changed as permanent, the node will not be used again in the process. For example, there is only one node, R4, which is directly connected to R1 in Figure 6.4. Update the status record array by changing the status of R4 as permanent

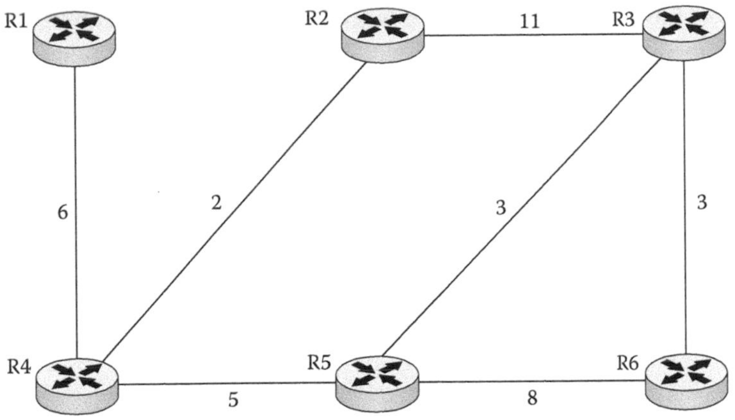

Figure 6.4 Routers and weighted links on a network.

Table 6.3 Initializing Status Record Array

Node	*Sum of Weights*	*Status*	*Previous*
R1	0	Permanent	
R2		Tentative	
R3		Tentative	
R4		Tentative	
R5		Tentative	
R6		Tentative	

Table 6.4 Updating Node R4 in Status Record Array

Node	*Sum of Weights*	*Status*	*Previous*
R1	0	Permanent	
R2		Tentative	
R3		Tentative	
R4	6	Permanent	R1
R5		Tentative	
R6		Tentative	

(Table 6.4). Because R1 is the permanent node previously linked to R4, add the node R1 in the column Previous.

3. If the status of the sink node is not permanent yet, repeat Step 2. This time, there are two tentative nodes, R2 and R5, which are directly linked to the permanent node R4 with the sum of weights 8 and 11, respectively. Therefore, update the status array table by changing

Table 6.5 Updating Node R2 in Status Record Array

Node	*Sum of Weights*	*Status*	*Previous*
R1	0	Permanent	
R2	6 + 2 = 8	Permanent	R4
R3		Tentative	
R4	6	Permanent	R1
R5	6 + 5 = 11	Tentative	
R6		Tentative	

Table 6.6 Updating Status Record Array of Node R5

Node	*Sum of Weights*	*Status*	*Previous*
R1	0	Permanent	
R2	6 + 2 = 8	Permanent	R4
R3	6 + 2 + 11 = 19	Tentative	
R4	6	Permanent	R1
R5	6 + 5 = 11	Permanent	R4
R6		Tentative	

the status of R2 to permanent (Table 6.5). Also, because R4 is the previous permanent node connected to R2, add the node R4 to the column Previous.

4. Repeat Step 2. This time, the tentative node R5 connected to the permanent note R4 has the smallest weight sum 11, and the tentative node R3 linked to the permanent node R2 has the weight sum 19. Therefore, update the status array by changing the status of R5 to permanent (Table 6.6). Because R5 is linked to the previous node R4, enter R4 in the Previous column.
5. Repeat Step 2. This time, two tentative nodes, R3 and R6, are directly linked to the permanent nodes, R5 and R2, respectively. There are two routes to R3: one is through R2, and the other is through R5. The route to R3 through R2 has the weight sum 19. The route to R3 through R5 has the weight sum 14. The route from R5 to R6 has the weight sum 19. Therefore, update the status array table by changing the status of R3 to permanent (Table 6.7). Because R5 is selected as the previous node for R3, add R5 to the Previous column.
6. Because the status of the sink node is not permanent yet, repeat Step 2. This time, only one tentative node, R6, is left. It is directly linked to the permanent node R5 with the weight sum 19 and linked to the permanent node R3 with the weight sum 17. Therefore, update the status array table by changing the status of R6 to permanent (Table 6.8). R3 is selected as the previous node, and it is added to the column Previous.
7. As shown in Table 6.8, the status of the sink node R6 is changed to permanent. The process can be stopped. From the sink node, trace back to the source by looking at the nodes in the Previous column. Starting from R6, its previous node is R3, the previous node for R3 is R5,

Table 6.7 Updating Status Record Array of Node R3

Node	*Sum of Weights*	*Status*	*Previous*
R1	0	Permanent	
R2	6 + 2 = 8	Permanent	R4
R3	6 + 5 + 3 = 14	Permanent	R5
R4	6	Permanent	R1
R5	6 + 5 = 11	Permanent	R4
R6	6 + 5 + 8 = 19	Tentative	

Table 6.8 Updating Status Record Array of Node R6

Node	*Sum of Weights*	*Status*	*Previous*
R1	0	Permanent	
R2	6 + 2 = 8	Permanent	R4
R3	6 + 5 + 3 = 14	Permanent	R5
R4	6	Permanent	R1
R5	6 + 5 = 11	Permanent	R4
R6	6 + 5 + 3 + 3 = 17	Permanent	R3

and so on. Tracing all the way back to R1, you have the following optimal route from the source node R1 to the sink node R6:

$$R1 \rightarrow R4 \rightarrow R5 \rightarrow R3 \rightarrow R6$$

The weight sum for this route is 17. In fact, there are other routes from R1 to R6, such as the route R1 → R4 → R5 → R6 with the weight sum 19, the route R1 → R4 → R2 → R3 → R6 with the weight sum 22, and the route R1 → R4 → R2 → R3 → R5 → R6 with the weight sum 30. By comparing the routes, the one selected by Dijkstra's shortest path algorithm has the optimal value.

The foregoing illustrates the use of Dijkstra's shortest path algorithm with a very simple example. In fact, by tracing the routes from R1 to R6, one may find the optimal route without using Dijkstra's shortest path algorithm. However, for a large network that frequently changes its topologies, Dijkstra's shortest path algorithm has to be used to update the routing table as soon as a change occurs. It can find the optimal route for each node that is connected to the source node.

In some cases, there is a tie between the weight sums of multiple edges, each of which connects a tentative node to a permanent node. In this case, update the status record array with any one of the edges, such as the edge with the tentative node that is ranked the lowest in the node array index. In the next few steps, because the rest of the tied weight sums are still smaller than other weight sums, the algorithm will take care of these tied weight sums and the Previous column will be updated with the tied node that generates a better result.

Dijkstra's shortest path algorithm should be run by each router on a network. Once the optimal routes have been created, each router on the network can build its own routing table with these optimal routes. To program Dijkstra's shortest path algorithm, you may follow the flowchart displayed in Figure 6.5.

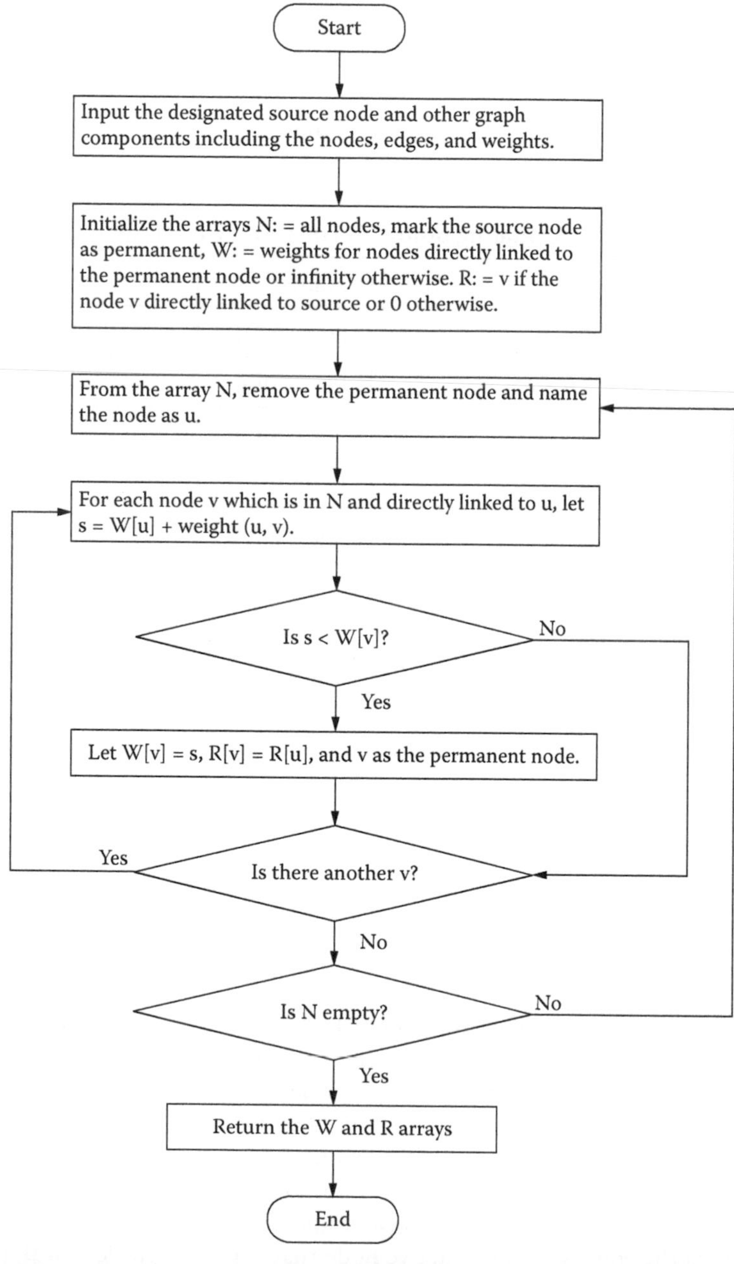

Figure 6.5 Flowchart of Dijkstra's shortest path algorithm.

Dijkstra's shortest path algorithm works well for small- or medium-sized networks. For large networks with many routers, it may take a lot of time for routers to run this algorithm. Also, this algorithm is very sensitive to the inaccuracy of the values input into it. For example, if the weight assigned to each edge is incorrect, the decision regarding the optimal route will be different. There are some alternative routing algorithms that are easier to process and less sensitive to the inaccuracy of the input values. The distance vector (DV) routing algorithm is this type of algorithm, and will be covered in the next section.

6.5.2 Distance Vector Routing Algorithm

As an alternative routing algorithm, the DV routing algorithm only needs information about the routers in the neighborhood. The algorithm does not need to know about every router on the network. The number of hops through which a packet is delivered to the destination is used as a measure of the optimal route. If a route uses fewer hops, that means it is a better route to the destination. The well-known Routing Information Protocol (RIP) is an example of protocols that use the DV algorithm.

To use the DV routing algorithm, a routing protocol in a network performs the following tasks:

- Each router saves the weights of the links directly connected to it in the routing table.
- Each router periodically sends the collected routing information, including destinations and weights, to the routers in its neighborhood.
- When a router receives routing information from the routers in the neighborhood, it examines the routing information to see if there are lower weights than those that are currently in use.
- If lower weights are used by the neighboring routers, the router updates its own routing table accordingly.

A router's routing table contains information such as the destination and weight of a route to a destination. As an example, let us consider the network displayed in Figure 6.4. The routing table for node R5 is given in Table 6.9.

During the updating process, R5 will send the destination and weight message to its direct neighboring routers R4, R3, and R6. When R4 receives the message from R5, it will update its own routing table accordingly and then send a message to R1, R2, and R5.

The updating of the routing table in Table 6.9 may cause a problem called count-to-infinity. Suppose the connection between R1 and R4 is broken and R5 does not know about it. After R4

Table 6.9 Routing Table on Node R5

Destination	*Weight*	*Next Hop*
R1	11	R4
R2	7	R4
R3	3	R3
R4	5	R4
R5	0	R5
R6	8	R6

receives the message from R5, it may think that there is another route linking R5 to R1 and, therefore, update its routing table by changing the weight for the link from R4 to R1 as 5 + 11 = 16. Then, R4 sends the updated routing table to R5. When R5 receives the message from R4, it realizes that the weight from itself to R1 needs to be changed; instead of 6 + 5 = 11, the weight from R5 to R1 should be 16 + 5 = 21. Then, R5 will send the updated message to R4. When R4 receives the updated message from R5, it will update its weight to R1 to 6 + 21 = 27. As this process keeps going, the weight to R1 will get larger and larger until the value is so large that the algorithm realizes that there is no connection between R1 and R4. The count-to-infinity problem can significantly slow down the routing table's updating performance. A technique called triggered update is used to solve the problem. When a connection is broken or a router crashes, the routers in the neighborhood will send the updated information to routers that are directly linked to them. The updated information includes setting infinity to those troubled routes and informing the neighbors to delete these routes.

To illustrate how the routing table is updated at each router, let us consider the network listed in Figure 6.4. Initially, each router only knows the direct neighboring routers. The route information at each router is shown in Table 6.10.

In Table 6.10, because no information is exchanged yet, each router only knows the weights from their direct neighboring routers. The number in a cell is the weight, and the grayed area indicates the optimal route to another router.

Assume that the routers start to exchange information of their routing tables with their neighboring routers. For instance, R1 sends its routing table to R4; R4 sends its routing table to R1, R2, and R5; R2 sends its routing table to R3 and R4; and so on. After the routers receive the messages from their neighbors, the routing tables are updated as shown in Table 6.11.

You can see that before the information exchange, R1 only knows it can reach R4. After the information exchange, R1 can reach R2 and R5 through R4. The weights from R4 to R2 and R5 are 2 and 5, respectively. Adding the weight from R1 to R4, the weight sum of the route from R1 to R2 is now updated to 6 + 2 = 8, and the weight sum for the route from R1 to R5 is 6 + 5 = 11.

Similarly, the weight sums for other routes can be updated accordingly. As seen in Table 6.11, from the router R2, there are two routes to the router R5. The first one is via R3, which has the weight sum 14 and the second one is via R4, which has the weight sum 7. The second route has a lower weight sum and, therefore, it is a better route from R2 to R5. Thus, in Table 6.11, the route from R2 to R5 via R4 is grayed out to indicate that this route is an optimal route. Similarly, if there are multiple routes between a pair of routers, you need to compare the weight sums and gray out the route with the lowest weight sum.

After each router updates its routing table, the routers will exchange routing information again. With the same rules as stated before, the routing table at each router is updated as shown in Table 6.12. In Table 6.11, the routes from R4 to R2, R3, R5, and R6 have the weights 2, 8, 5, and 13, respectively. Adding the weight from R1 to R4, in Table 6.12, the route from R1 to R2 is 6 + 2 = 8, from R1 to R3 is 6 + 8 = 14, from R1 to R5 is 6 + 5 = 11, and from R1 to R6 is 6 + 13 = 19. Similarly, you can add more routes and update the weight sums for these routes accordingly.

The contents of several tables have been changed. As long as the optimal routes can still be updated, the iteration cannot stop here. Make another update, and you will get the result shown in Table 6.13.

Because some of the tables still update their information, the DV needs to keep running. Iterate one more time, and you will get the result listed in Table 6.14.

This time, there is no new update on the optimal routes. The iteration process will tentatively stop until new updates are detected in the information exchange. Based on the optimal routes

Table 6.10 Initial Route Information at Each Router

From R1	*to R1*	*to R2*	*to R3*	*to R4*	*to R5*	*to R6*
via R1						
via R2						
via R3						
via R4				6		
via R5						
via R6						

From R2	*to R1*	*to R2*	*to R3*	*to R4*	*to R5*	*to R6*
via R1						
via R2						
via R3			11			
via R4				2		
via R5						
via R6						

From R3	*to R1*	*to R2*	*to R3*	*to R4*	*to R5*	*to R6*
via R1						
via R2		11				
via R3						
via R4						
via R5					3	
via R6						3

From R4	*to R1*	*to R2*	*to R3*	*to R4*	*to R5*	*to R6*
via R1	6					
via R2		2				
via R3						
via R4						
via R5					5	
via R6						

From R5	*to R1*	*to R2*	*to R3*	*to R4*	*to R5*	*to R6*
via R1						
via R2						
via R3			3			
via R4				5		
via R5						
via R6						8

From R6	*to R1*	*to R2*	*to R3*	*to R4*	*to R5*	*to R6*
via R1						
via R2						
via R3			3			
via R4						
via R5					8	
via R6						

discovered by the foregoing procedure, the routing tables can be constructed accordingly. For example, if router R1 wants to send a message to router R6, at the next hop, R1 will send the message to R4. At R4, to send the message to R6, R4 will send the message to R5. At R5, the next hop will be R3. Through R3, the message will be sent to R6. So, the optimal route is

$$R1 \rightarrow R4 \rightarrow R5 \rightarrow R3 \rightarrow R6$$

which is the same as the result derived by Dijkstra's shortest path algorithm.

Table 6.11 Updated Route Information after First Information Exchange

From R1	*to R1*	*to R2*	*to R3*	*to R4*	*to R5*	*to R6*
via R1						
via R2						
via R3						
via R4		8		6	11	
via R5						
via R6						

From R2	*to R1*	*to R2*	*to R3*	*to R4*	*to R5*	*to R6*
via R1						
via R2						
via R3			11		14	14
via R4	8			2	7	
via R5						
via R6						

From R3	*to R1*	*to R2*	*to R3*	*to R4*	*to R5*	*to R6*
via R1						
via R2		11		13		
via R3						
via R4						
via R5				8	3	11
via R6					11	3

From R4	*to R1*	*to R2*	*to R3*	*to R4*	*to R5*	*to R6*
via R1	6					
via R2		2	13			
via R3						
via R4						
via R5			8		5	13
via R6						

From R5	*to R1*	*to R2*	*to R3*	*to R4*	*to R5*	*to R6*
via R1						
via R2						
via R3		14	3			6
via R4	11	7		5		
via R5						
via R6			11			8

From R6	*to R1*	*to R2*	*to R3*	*to R4*	*to R5*	*to R6*
via R1						
via R2						
via R3		14	3		6	
via R4						
via R5			11	13	8	
via R6						

Each router updates its own routing table with the distance vector (DV) algorithm. To program the DV algorithm, you may follow the flowchart displayed in Figure 6.6.

The features of the DV algorithm make it suitable for a complicated network with many routers. A large network can be divided into regions. The routing table of each router includes destination and weight information about the routers in the same region and one router from each of the other regions. As an example, let us consider the network in Figure 6.7. The network consists of 17 routers. Without dividing it into regions, each routing table will consist of 17 entries. To simplify the routing tables, the network is divided into regions shown in Table 6.15.

Table 6.12 Updated Route Information after Second Information Exchange

From R1	*to R1*	*to R2*	*to R3*	*to R4*	*to R5*	*to R6*
via R1						
via R2						
via R3						
via R4		8	14	6	11	19
via R5						
via R6						

From R2	*to R1*	*to R2*	*to R3*	*to R4*	*to R5*	*to R6*
via R1						
via R2						
via R3			11	19	14	14
via R4	8		10	2	7	15
via R5						
via R6						

From R3	*to R1*	*to R2*	*to R3*	*to R4*	*to R5*	*to R6*
via R1						
via R2	19	11		13	18	25
via R3						
via R4						
via R5	14	10		8	3	9
via R6		17		16	9	3

From R4	*to R1*	*to R2*	*to R3*	*to R4*	*to R5*	*to R6*
via R1	6	14			17	
via R2	10	2	13		9	16
via R3						
via R4						
via R5	16	12	8		5	11
via R6						

From R5	*to R1*	*to R2*	*to R3*	*to R4*	*to R5*	*to R6*
via R1						
via R2						
via R3		14	3	11		6
via R4	11	7	13	5		18
via R5						
via R6		22	11	21		8

From R6	*to R1*	*to R2*	*to R3*	*to R4*	*to R5*	*to R6*
via R1						
via R2						
via R3		14	3	11	6	
via R4						
via R5	19	15	11	13	8	
via R6						

To simplify the discussion, let us assume that the weight for each edge is 1. Then, the routing table for the router R5 looks like the one in Table 6.16.

Instead of 17 entries, the routing table in Table 6.16 only has 7 entries. Because R5 belongs to Region 2, which includes two routers R5 and R6, the routing table includes these two routers in the Destination column. For the routers in the other regions, the routing table uses the region IDs as destinations and only sends updated messages to one of the routers in each region.

According to networking theory, the method introduced here is called *hierarchical routing*, which can significantly reduce a router's workload. The hierarchical routing method just illustrated

Table 6.13 Updated Route Information after Third Information Exchange

From R1	*to R1*	*to R2*	*to R3*	*to R4*	*to R5*	*to R6*
via R1						
via R2						
via R3						
via R4		8	14	6	11	17
via R5						
via R6						

From R2	*to R1*	*to R2*	*to R3*	*to R4*	*to R5*	*to R6*
via R1						
via R2						
via R3	25		11	19	14	14
via R4	8		10	2	7	13
via R5						
via R6						

From R3	*to R1*	*to R2*	*to R3*	*to R4*	*to R5*	*to R6*
via R1						
via R2	19	11		13	18	25
via R3						
via R4						
via R5	14	10		8	3	9
via R6	22	17		14	9	3

From R4	*to R1*	*to R2*	*to R3*	*to R4*	*to R5*	*to R6*
via R1	6	14	20		17	25
via R2	10	2	10		9	16
via R3						
via R4						
via R5	16	12	8		5	11
via R6						

From R5	*to R1*	*to R2*	*to R3*	*to R4*	*to R5*	*to R6*
via R1						
via R2						
via R3	17	13	3	11		6
via R4	11	7	13	5		16
via R5						
via R6	27	22	11	19		8

From R6	*to R1*	*to R2*	*to R3*	*to R4*	*to R5*	*to R6*
via R1						
via R2						
via R3	17	13	3	11	6	
via R4						
via R5	19	15	11	13	8	
via R6						

is a two-level hierarchical system. It allows more than two levels of regions for a large complicated enterprise-level network.

6.6 Routing across Networks

The earlier sections have shown how to create, compute, and update a routing table. Usually, a packet should be delivered via one of the routers listed in a routing table. When a packet arrives at a router, how does the router know via which router listed in the routing table to deliver the packet to a host in a different network? A router should ensure that the data can find its way to

Table 6.14 Updated Route Information after Fourth Information Exchange

From R1	*to R1*	*to R2*	*to R3*	*to R4*	*to R5*	*to R6*
via R1						
via R2						
via R3						
via R4		8	14	6	11	17
via R5						
via R6						

From R2	*to R1*	*to R2*	*to R3*	*to R4*	*to R5*	*to R6*
via R1						
via R2						
via R3	25		11	19	14	14
via R4	8		10	2	7	13
via R5						
via R6						

From R3	*to R1*	*to R2*	*to R3*	*to R4*	*to R5*	*to R6*
via R1						
via R2	19	11		13	18	24
via R3						
via R4						
via R5	14	10		8	3	9
via R6	20	16		14	9	3

From R4	*to R1*	*to R2*	*to R3*	*to R4*	*to R5*	*to R6*
via R1	6	14	20		17	23
via R2	10	2	12		9	15
via R3						
via R4						
via R5	16	12	8		5	11
via R6						

From R5	*to R1*	*to R2*	*to R3*	*to R4*	*to R5*	*to R6*
via R1						
via R2						
via R3	17	13	3	11		6
via R4	11	7	13	5		16
via R5						
via R6	23	19	9	17		8

From R6	*to R1*	*to R2*	*to R3*	*to R4*	*to R5*	*to R6*
via R1						
via R2						
via R3	17	13	3	11	6	
via R4						
via R5	19	15	11	13	8	
via R6						

the destination. Also, each network has its own data transmission capacity. How does the router determine the payload size acceptable by the networks along the path to the destination? This section is going to cover two topics that will give answers to these two questions:

- Identify the destination router from a given designation IP address.
- Dynamically adjust the payload size.

When a packet arrives at a router, it carries the destination IP address. The router needs to know which router is connected to the network that has the host with destination IP address. The column Genmask in Table 6.1 can be used to find the destination router. In the following, an

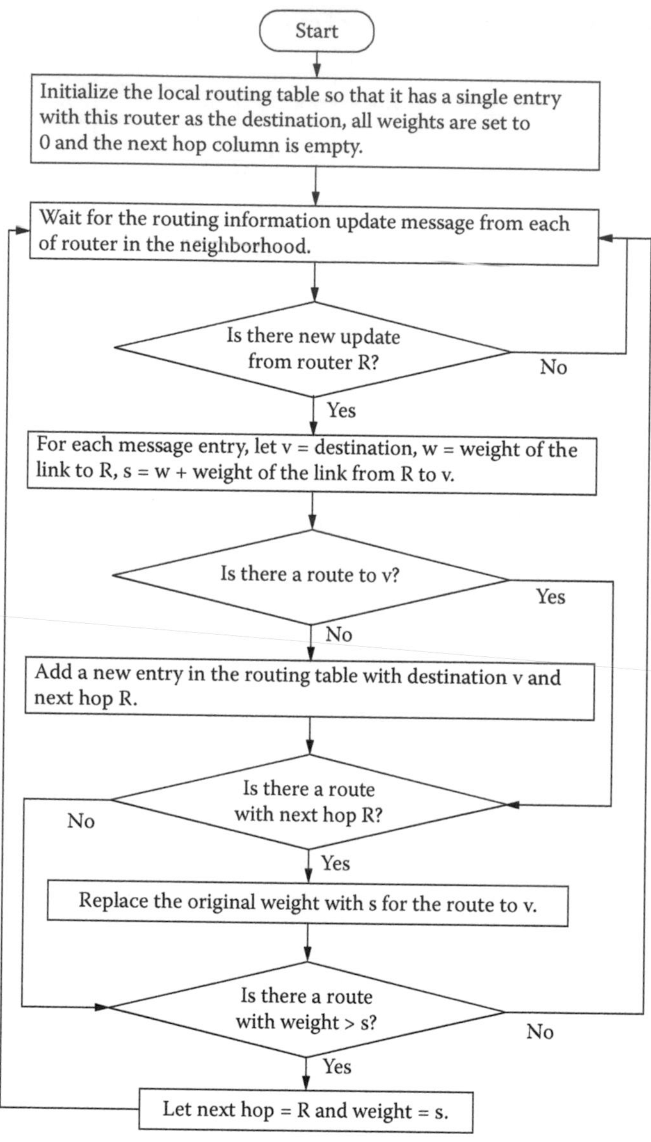

Figure 6.6 Flowchart of distance vector algorithm.

example is used to illustrate how the job can be accomplished. The sample network is given in Figure 6.8.

On each router, the routing table partially includes the information, as shown in Table 6.17 to Table 6.19, which can be used to figure out the destination router.

Suppose a sender sends a packet to the destination host with IP address 192.168.2.11 and suppose the packet arrives at router R3. Router R3 performs the AND operation on the destination IP address carried by the packet, with entries in the Genmask column as shown in Table 6.19. The result of the AND operation is listed in Table 6.20.

In Table 6.20, the AND operation is performed on the equivalent binary form of the IP address and subnet mask. The result of the AND operation is then converted back to the decimal

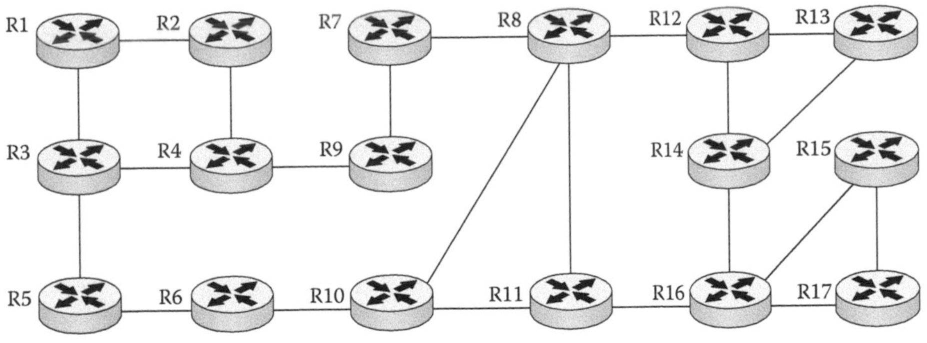

Figure 6.7 Large network with multiple regions.

Table 6.15 Regions, and Routers in Them

Region	*Router*
Region 1	R1, R2, R3, R4
Region 2	R5, R6
Region 3	R7, R9
Region 4	R8, R10, R11
Region 5	R12, R13, R14
Region 6	R15, R16, R17

Table 6.16 Routing Table on Router R5 with Regions

Destination	*Weight*	*Router to Contact*	*Next Hop*
R5	0	R5	R5
R6	1	R6	R6
Region 1	1	R3	R3
Region 3	3	R9	R3
Region 4	2	R10	R6
Region 5	4	R12	R6
Region 6	4	R16	R6

form. As indicated in Table 6.20, the AND operation result matches the destination 192.168.2.0. Therefore, the packet should be delivered to the corresponding next hop, 192.168.1.1.

To be able to deliver data to a host in a different network, a router should be able to pass the data carried by the frame from one network to the frame of another network. Also, the router should be able to dynamically adjust the payload size to match the network capacity constraints. The following briefly describes how a router can accomplish this task:

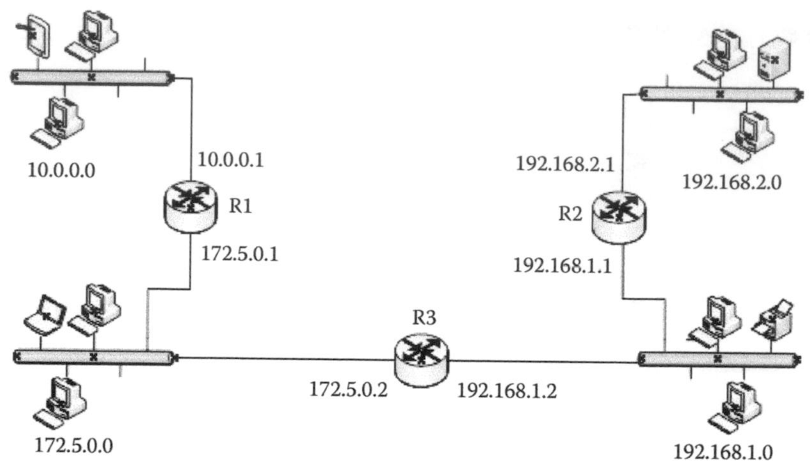

Figure 6.8 Sample network with three routers.

Table 6.17 Routing Table on Router R1

Destination	*Genmask*	*Next Hop*
10.0.0.0	255.0.0.0	Direct
172.5.0.0	255.255.0.0	Direct
192.168.2.0	255.255.255.0	172.5.0.2
192.168.1.0	255.255.255.0	172.5.0.2

Table 6.18 Routing Table on Router R2

Destination	*Genmask*	*Next Hop*
10.0.0.0	255.0.0.0	192.168.1.2
172.5.0.0	255.255.0.0	192.168.1.2
192.168.2.0	255.255.255.0	Direct
192.168.1.0	255.255.255.0	Direct

Table 6.19 Routing Table on Router R3

Destination	*Genmask*	*Next Hop*
10.0.0.0	255.0.0.0	172.5.0.1
172.5.0.0	255.255.0.0	Direct
192.168.2.0	255.255.255.0	192.168.1.1
192.168.1.0	255.255.255.0	Direct

Table 6.20 Result of AND Operation

Index	*Operation*	*Result*	*Explanation*
1	192.168.2.11 AND 255.0.0.0	192.0.0.0	No match to the destination 10.0.0.0
2	192.168.2.11 AND 255.255.0.0	192.168.0.0	No match to the destination 172.5.0.0
3	192.168.2.11 AND 255.255.255.0	192.168.2.0	Match to the destination 192.168.2.0
4	192.168.2.11 AND 255.255.255.0	192.168.2.0	No match to the destination 192.168.1.0

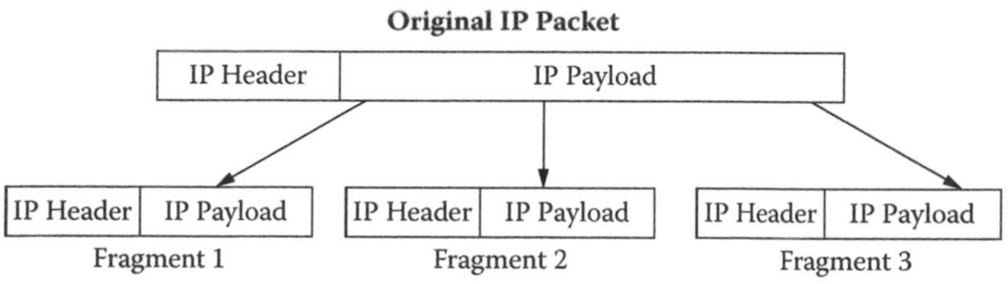

Figure 6.9 Fragmentation of IP packets.

1. *Forwarding packets from one network to another:* A frame created with one network technology will not work in other networks created with different technologies. To transmit an IP packet across multiple networks, the sender first encapsulates the IP packet in the frame created by the network where the sender belongs. When the frame reaches a router that is connected to another network, the router removes the IP packet from the frame and discards the frame. Then, the router encapsulates the IP packet in the frame created by another network technology and forwards the frame to another router in the path to the destination.
2. *Dynamically adjusting payload size:* Due to the different sizes of frames created by different networks, there is a chance that the size of the initial frame is much larger than the size of the frame created by a network in the middle of the transmission path. This means that the IP packet carried by the initial frame will not be able to be loaded onto that frame. In this case, the IP packet should be sliced into multiple smaller IP packets (Figure 6.9).

Each network has a parameter called the Maximum Transmission Unit (MTU), which specifies the maximum amount of data a frame can carry. The MTU is used by the router to determine how to slice a packet. During the journey to the destination, the packet can be fragmented more than once. The fragments will not be reassembled until it reaches the ultimate destination.

The foregoing sections have given a brief introduction on how a router works. As mentioned earlier, a router is a special-purpose computer that hosts routing software called a *routing protocol.* All the tasks mentioned earlier can be carried out by a routing protocol. When a routing protocol is installed on a Linux computer system, the computer can be used as a router. The following section will demonstrate how to build a router with Linux.

Activity 6.1 Routing with Linux

A router is used to connect two or more networks. To use a Linux computer system as a router, two or more network interface cards must be installed in the computer. Each card should be configured to have an IP address that matches the network to which the card connects.

In the computing environment for this hands-on activity, there is a private network with two hosts. Currently, these two hosts are configured to be on the same private network so that they can communicate with each other. Next, you will configure the hosts to be on different networks and allow them to communicate through routers. There are several ways to allow the hosts on different networks to communicate with each other. The following are three methods:

- Manually add a route to the routing table of the Linux computer system to allow a host on one network to communicate with another host on a different network.
- Use a ready-built hardware router to connect networks. For example, the DSL routers sold in computer stores can be used to connect private networks and the Internet.

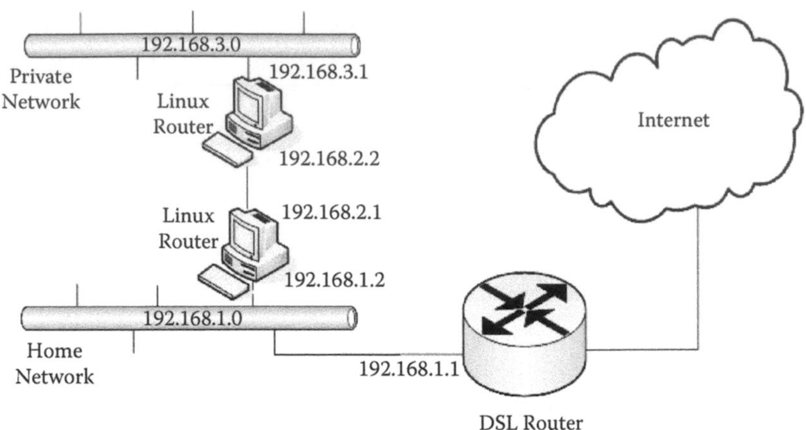

Figure 6.10 Connecting private network to home network.

- Download or create a routing protocol such as RIP for dynamic routing. After you install and configure the protocol on a Linux computer equipped with multiple network interface cards, you can turn a Linux computer system to a real router that allows multiple networks to communicate through it.

Suppose that at home you already have a home network that connects the computers at home to the Internet. Also, suppose that the network ID of your home network is 192.168.1.0 and the internal IP address of your DSL router is 192.168.1.1. If your home network configuration is different from this configuration, you may change the setting accordingly in the following hands-on activity. This activity is to construct Linux routers that can forward packets from one network to another network. Figure 6.10 shows how the Linux routers connect the private network to the home network.

In this hands-on activity, you will work on two projects. The first project is to manually add a route to forward packets from the 192.168.3.0 network to the 192.168.1.0 network, or vice versa. The second project is to change your Linux machines to routers by applying the RIP routing protocol.

Ubuntu provides a daemon called BIRD Internet Routing Daemon (BIRD), which serves as a dynamic Internet router. BIRD was developed by the math and physics faculty from Charles University in Prague. It is an open source product with the GNU General Public License. The daemon provides full support to many routing protocols such as OSPF, RIPv2 (No v1), and BGP. This daemon provides a configuration interface that makes the configuration relatively painless.

Before you change the network structure to that shown in Figure 6.10, you may want to install the routing protocol package by following these steps:

1. Log on to the server machine with username **student** and password **ubuntu**.
2. The installation process needs to access the Web site http://us.archive.ubuntu.com/. Make sure the server machine can access the Internet. If you work in a virtual machine computing environment, you may need to tentatively configure one of the two NICs to receive a dynamic IP address from the DSL router.
3. To install the daemon BIRD, execute the following command:

   ```
   sudo apt-get install bird
   ```

   When prompted to install "these packages without verification," enter the letter "y" (Figure 6.11).

student@ubuntul_ab:~$ sudo apt-get install bird
[sudo] password for student:
Reading package lists... Done
Building dependency tree
Reading state information... Done
The following NEW packages will be installed:
bird
0 upgraded, 1 newly installed, 0 to remove and 82 not upgraded.
Need to get 207kB of archives.
After unpacking 471kB of additional disk space will be used.
WARNING: The following packages cannot be authenticated!
bird
Install these packages without verification [y/N]? y
Get:l http://us.archive.ubuntu.com gutsy/universe bird 1.6.11-4 [207kB]
Fetched 207kB in 13s (15.5kB/s)
Selecting previously deselected package bird
(Reading database ... 64017 files and directories currently installed.)
Unpacking bird (from .../bird l.e.11-4 i386.deb) ...
Setting up bird (l.O.11-4) ...
Starting BIRD - Internet routing daemon: ok
student@ubuntul_ab: ~$

Figure 6.11 Installation of BIRD daemon.

4. Log on to the client machine with username **student** and password **ubuntu.**
5. Using the same steps, install the routing daemon bird to the client computer.

You are now ready to route packets from one network to another network. The following are step-by-step instructions for the two routing projects.

MANUALLY ADDING ROUTES TO ROUTING TABLE

Your first project is to manually add routes in the routing table. You will be using two routing-related commands. The first command is used to forward packets to the destination network 192.168.1.0. The iptables command has the following syntax:

```
iptables [-t <table-name>] <command> <chain-name> \
                           <parameter-1> <option-1> \
                           <parameter-n> <option-n>
```

The options in the angle brackets have the following meanings:

- The option <table-name> is used to specify a table other than the default filter table.
- The <command> option specifies an action to append or delete the rule specified by the <chain-name> option.
- The pairs of parameters and options decide how to process a packet if it matches the rule. Use the command iptable –help to see all the options.

The second command, **route add**, is used to add a route in the routing table. The command has the following syntax:

route add [**-net** | **-host** *destination*] [**netmask** *mask*] [**gw** *gateway*] [**metric** *n*] [**dev** *interface*]

The symbols used in the syntax have the following meanings:

- *Bold letter:* Words in bold are keywords.
- *Italic letter:* Words in italic are the values that need to be supplied by the user entering the command.
- *Square bracket:* Values included in a pair of square brackets are optional.
- *| sign:* This sign serves as the OR operator. You can use the value either on the left-hand side of the | sign or on its right-hand side.

The following are the steps to set forward routes and to add a router from the private network to the home network:

1. Log on to your client computer with username **student** and password **ubuntu.**
2. As shown in Figure 6.10, your client computer will be configured as a router to connect the networks 192.168.3.0 and 192.168.2.0. The two NICs on the client computer should be configured to have the IP addresses 192.168.3.1 for its eth3 NIC and 192.168.2.2 for its eth2 NIC. If you have Ubuntu 8.10 installed, the NIC configuration is a bit easier; you can edit the file /etc/network/interfaces. To do so, execute the following command:

   ```
   sudo gedit /etc/network/interfaces
   ```

   After the file is opened, add the configuration code shown in Figure 6.12.
3. To verify the NIC configuration on the client computer, execute the following commands:

   ```
   sudo /etc/init.d/networking restart
   ```

   and then

   ```
   sudo ifconfig
   ```

   The output should show that the NICs are configured (Figure 6.13). If you still get the dynamic IP address instead of the static IP address configured in the file /etc/network/interfaces, you may need to reboot your system. Then, verify the configuration again.

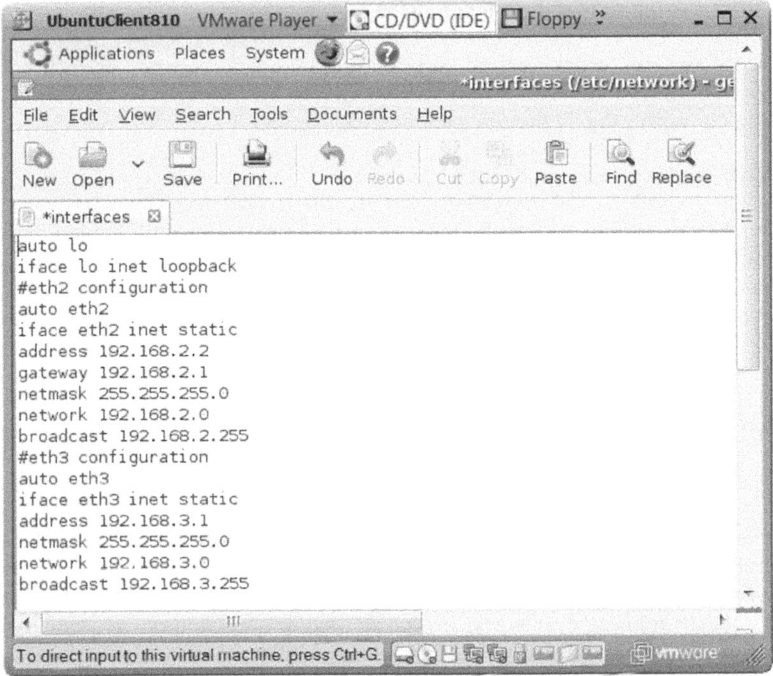

Figure 6.12 Editing NIC configuration on client machine.

```
student@student-desktop: ~
File Edit View Terminal Tabs Help
student@student-desktop:~$ sudo ifconfig
[sudo] password for student:
eth2      Link encap:Ethernet  HWaddr 00:0c:29:a8:37:b9
          inet addr:192.168.2.2  Bcast:192.168.2.255  Mask:255.255.255.0
          UP BROADCAST RUNNING MULTICAST  MTU:1500  Metric:1
          RX packets:122 errors:0 dropped:0 overruns:0 frame:0
          TX packets:31 errors:0 dropped:0 overruns:0 carrier:0
          collisions:0 txqueuelen:1000
          RX bytes:17878 (17.8 KB)  TX bytes:3833 (3.8 KB)
          Interrupt:18 Base address:0x1400

eth3      Link encap:Ethernet  HWaddr 00:0c:29:a8:37:c3
          inet addr:192.168.3.1  Bcast:192.168.3.255  Mask:255.255.255.0
          UP BROADCAST RUNNING MULTICAST  MTU:1500  Metric:1
          RX packets:113 errors:0 dropped:0 overruns:0 frame:0
          TX packets:17 errors:0 dropped:0 overruns:0 carrier:0
          collisions:0 txqueuelen:1000
          RX bytes:17110 (17.1 KB)  TX bytes:2685 (2.6 KB)
          Interrupt:19 Base address:0x1480

lo        Link encap:Local Loopback
          inet addr:127.0.0.1  Mask:255.0.0.0
          UP LOOPBACK RUNNING  MTU:16436  Metric:1
          RX packets:28 errors:0 dropped:0 overruns:0 frame:0
```

Figure 6.13 Client machine NIC configuration.

The NICs are now configured for the client machine. Now, let us check the server machine:

1. Log on to your server machine with username **student** and password **ubuntu**.
2. You should configure the NICs on the server machine according to Figure 6.10. Execute the following command to edit the file /etc/network/interfaces:

   ```
   sudo gedit /etc/network/interfaces
   ```

   The file should include the configuration for NICs eth0 and eth1, which are shown in Figure 6.14.
3. Save the configuration, and exit the editor. To verify, execute the following commands on the server machine:

   ```
   sudo /etc/init.d/networking restart
   ```

   and then

   ```
   sudo ifconfig
   ```

   After the commands are executed, you should be able to see the result of the configuration similar to the one in Figure 6.15. Note that the NICs eth0 and eth1 have the static IP addresses 192.168.1.2 and 192.168.2.1. Again, if you still get the dynamic IP address instead of the static IP address configured in the file /etc/network/interfaces, you may need to reboot your system. Then, verify the configuration again.

At this point, your server and client machines are ready to be configured as routers. The following steps take you through the configuration process:

1. Assume that your server machine is still on. Otherwise, log on to your server machine with username **student** and password **ubuntu**.
2. To view the content in the current routing table, enter the following command in the terminal window:

   ```
   route -n
   ```

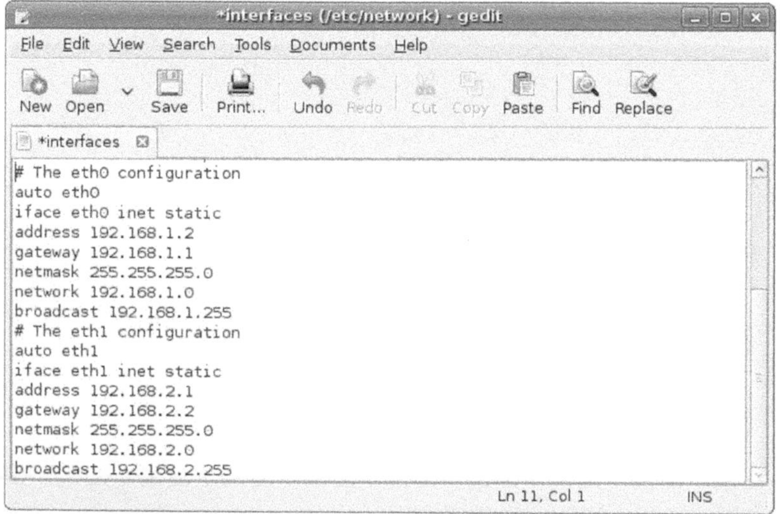

Figure 6.14 Editing NIC configuration on server machine.

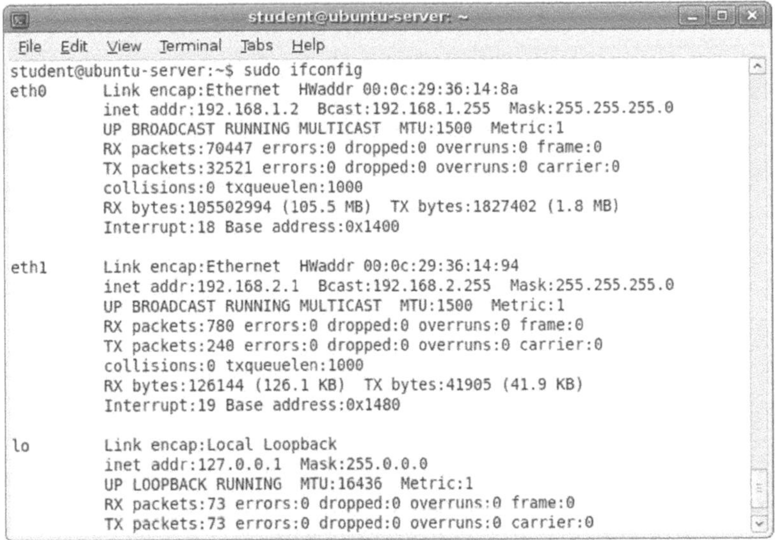

```
student@ubuntu-server: ~
File Edit View Terminal Tabs Help
student@ubuntu-server:~$ sudo ifconfig
eth0      Link encap:Ethernet  HWaddr 00:0c:29:36:14:8a
          inet addr:192.168.1.2  Bcast:192.168.1.255  Mask:255.255.255.0
          UP BROADCAST RUNNING MULTICAST  MTU:1500  Metric:1
          RX packets:70447 errors:0 dropped:0 overruns:0 frame:0
          TX packets:32521 errors:0 dropped:0 overruns:0 carrier:0
          collisions:0 txqueuelen:1000
          RX bytes:105502994 (105.5 MB)  TX bytes:1827402 (1.8 MB)
          Interrupt:18 Base address:0x1400

eth1      Link encap:Ethernet  HWaddr 00:0c:29:36:14:94
          inet addr:192.168.2.1  Bcast:192.168.2.255  Mask:255.255.255.0
          UP BROADCAST RUNNING MULTICAST  MTU:1500  Metric:1
          RX packets:780 errors:0 dropped:0 overruns:0 frame:0
          TX packets:240 errors:0 dropped:0 overruns:0 carrier:0
          collisions:0 txqueuelen:1000
          RX bytes:126144 (126.1 KB)  TX bytes:41905 (41.9 KB)
          Interrupt:19 Base address:0x1480

lo        Link encap:Local Loopback
          inet addr:127.0.0.1  Mask:255.0.0.0
          UP LOOPBACK RUNNING  MTU:16436  Metric:1
          RX packets:73 errors:0 dropped:0 overruns:0 frame:0
          TX packets:73 errors:0 dropped:0 overruns:0 carrier:0
```

Figure 6.15 Server machine NIC configuration.

```
student@ubuntu-server: ~
File Edit View Terminal Tabs Help
student@ubuntu-server:~$ route -n
Kernel IP routing table
Destination     Gateway         Genmask         Flags Metric Ref    Use Iface
192.168.2.0     0.0.0.0         255.255.255.0   U     0      0        0 eth1
192.168.1.0     0.0.0.0         255.255.255.0   U     0      0        0 eth0
169.254.0.0     0.0.0.0         255.255.0.0     U     1000   0        0 eth0
0.0.0.0         192.168.2.2     0.0.0.0         UG    100    0        0 eth1
0.0.0.0         192.168.1.1     0.0.0.0         UG    100    0        0 eth0
student@ubuntu-server:~$
```

Figure 6.16 Server machine's routing table.

The option –n is used to display the IP address in the output of the command. Otherwise, the host name will be displayed. Figure 6.16 shows the content in the routing table. There, two networks 192.168.1.0 and 192.168.2.0 are connected by the server machine through the network interface cards eth0 and eth1, respectively. As you can see, the server machine is connected to the networks 192.168.1.0 and 192.168.2.0. The gateway 192.168.1.1 is used to connect to the Internet.

3. You will not be able to ping the hosts on the 192.168.1.0 network from your client machine. To verify that, from the client, enter the command in the terminal window of your client machine to ping a host on the 192.168.1.0 network. Figure 6.17 shows the result of the ping command. In your lab or your home, the IP address for the host on the network 192.168.1.0 may be different. You need to change your command accordingly.
4. Back to the server machine, to forward a packet from the network 192.168.2.0 to the network 192.168.1.0, you may need to add a route in iptables. To do so, enter the following command:

```
sudo iptables -I FORWARD -j ACCEPT -s 192.168.0.0/24 -d 192.168.1.0/24
```

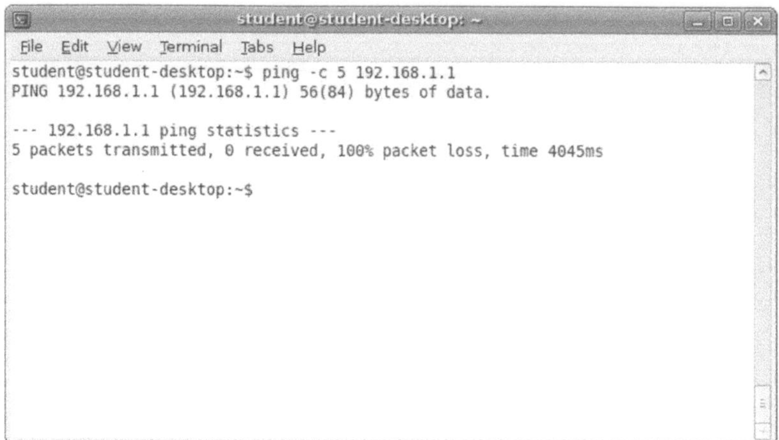

Figure 6.17 No route to the network 192.168.1.0.

The explanation for the preceding command is as follows:

- –I: Insert a rule.
- FORWARD: Forward a packet through a host.
- –j: If a packet matches a particular rule, jump to the specified target.
- ACCEPT: It is one of the targets of –j. It allows the packet through to its destination specified by the –d option.
- –s: It specifies the source from which the packet is sent.
- –d: It specifies the destination to which the packet is sent.

As you can see, the preceding command adds a rule that results in packets from all the Class C subnets of the network 192.168.0.0 being forwarded to the destination subnet 192.168.1.0.

5. After the rule is added to iptables, you need to enable the forwarding code in the kernel. For security reasons, by default, the kernel ignores the packets that are not directly sent to it. You need the root privilege to enable the forwarding code in the kernel. Enter the following command to become a root user:

```
su -
```

After entering the password **ubuntu**, enter the following command:

```
echo 1 > /proc/sys/net/ipv4/ip_forward
```

After the preceding command is executed, enter the following command:

```
exit
```

to go back to the student user environment.

6. Make sure that you can ping the IP address of a host in the network 192.168.1.0 from your client machine. Figure 6.18 gives the result of the ping command. As shown in Figure 6.18, the packets are successfully forwarded to the DSL router, which has the internal IP address 192.168.1.1.

If your gateway to the Internet is configured differently, the result in Figure 6.18 may be slightly different on your screen. What is important is that you are able to ping the Internet gateway on your home network from your 192.168.2.0 private network. Also, note that the

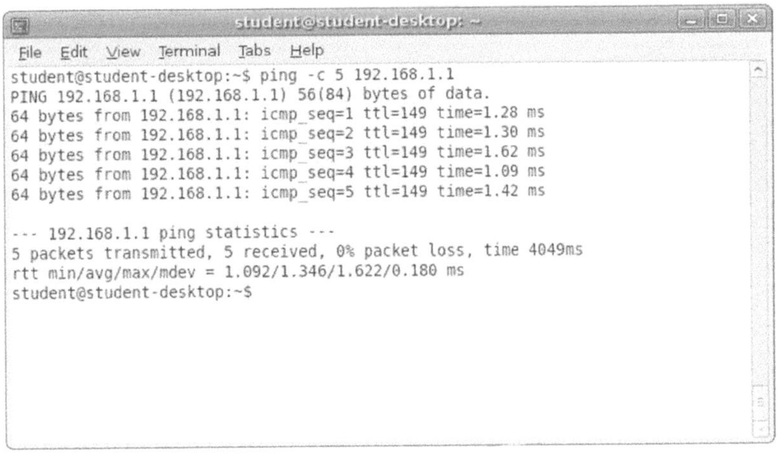

```
student@student-desktop: ~
File  Edit  View  Terminal  Tabs  Help
student@student-desktop:~$ ping -c 5 192.168.1.1
PING 192.168.1.1 (192.168.1.1) 56(84) bytes of data.
64 bytes from 192.168.1.1: icmp_seq=1 ttl=149 time=1.28 ms
64 bytes from 192.168.1.1: icmp_seq=2 ttl=149 time=1.30 ms
64 bytes from 192.168.1.1: icmp_seq=3 ttl=149 time=1.62 ms
64 bytes from 192.168.1.1: icmp_seq=4 ttl=149 time=1.09 ms
64 bytes from 192.168.1.1: icmp_seq=5 ttl=149 time=1.42 ms

--- 192.168.1.1 ping statistics ---
5 packets transmitted, 5 received, 0% packet loss, time 4049ms
rtt min/avg/max/mdev = 1.092/1.346/1.622/0.180 ms
student@student-desktop:~$
```

Figure 6.18 Result of ping to 192.168.1.1.

DSL router at your home should have a route through the gateway, such as 192.168.1.1, to your 192.168.1.0 network. In some lab environments on campus, the router that links the network in the lab to the campus network may be configured differently. You must ask the network administrator to add a route on that router to your 192.168.1.0 network through the gateway, say, 192.168.1.1.

DYNAMIC ROUTING

In the foregoing, you have learned to manually add and delete routes to and from a routing table. As mentioned earlier in this chapter, manual updation of routing tables cannot keep up with rapidly changing networks. In real-life situations, most routers use a routing protocol to automatically update routing tables.

The daemon "routed," which is installed with most Linux operating systems, runs the RIP routing protocol. When "routed" starts, the distance vector (DV) algorithm used by RIP sends a message to routers in the neighborhood to contact them. After routers in the neighborhood receive the contact information, they respond with the updated routing table information. Based on the updated information, the daemon "routed" updates its routing table.

The following steps show you how to install and configure RIP through the BIRD daemon:

1. Log on to the server machine with username **student** and password **ubuntu**.
2. Before you start the configuration process, you may want to back up the file bird.conf. To do so, enter the following command:

   ```
   sudo cp /etc/bird.conf /etc/bird.conf.old
   ```

   Most of the configuration will be done in the file bird.conf. In case this file is damaged, you can always recover it from the backup copy.
3. To configure the daemon BIRD, enter the following command:

   ```
   sudo gedit /etc/bird.conf
   ```

   When the bird.conf file opens, you will see the preconfigured examples and explanations in the file. In the configuration file, the symbol # at the beginning of each line indicates that the line is commented out. Also, the code included inside /* and */ is a comment, too. The configurable items are included in the { } brackets.

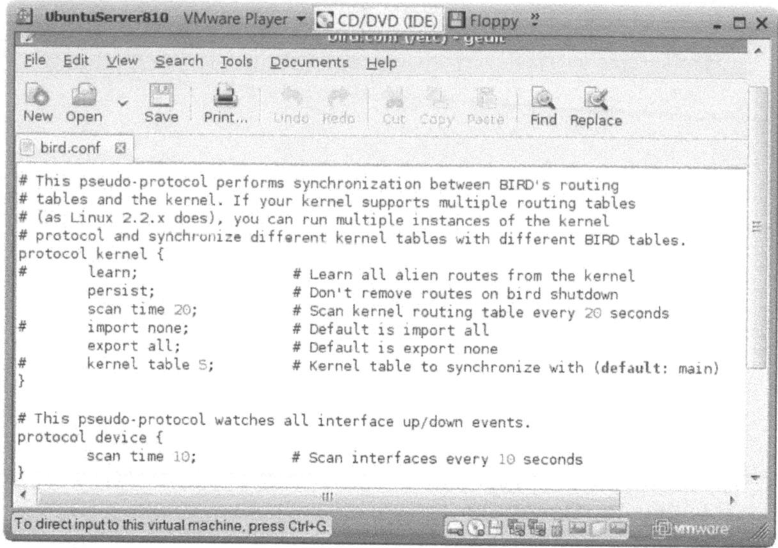

Figure 6.19 Protocol kernel configuration.

4. The configuration process starts with the protocol kernel block. Move the cursor down to the block (Figure 6.19).

   As shown in Figure 6.19, there are three lines in the protocol kernel block that are not commented out. Following each of these three lines, there is an explanation for the code. Let us keep these default settings.
5. Figure 6.19 also shows another configuration block, protocol device. This block controls the interface scan period. The default scan time is set to 10 s. Again, let us keep the default setting for this block.
6. The next configuration is for the RIP block shown in Figure 6.20.

To be able to properly configure RIP for the router, you need to get familiar with the items included in the configuration file. The following are the definitions and usage for the items shown in Figure 6.20:

- Preference: This item specifies the preference of the route generated by this protocol.
- Debug: The debug item has the options "all," "off," or one of the trace categories such as states, routes, filters, interfaces, events, and packets. If "all" is specified, all the trace messages will be printed. If one of the trace categories is specified, the trace messages in that category will be printed. The default value for debug is "off."
- Port: This item specifies the port number for communication. The default value is 1520.
- Period: This item specifies the update period in seconds. The default value is 30 s.
- Infinity: This item specifies a number to represent infinity. For RIP, the default infinity value is 16.
- Garbage time: This item specifies the time length before discarding inactive routes. The default value is 10.
- Interface: This is the item that specifies the network interface card for a router. For each network interface card, there are parameters that need to be specified. The first parameter is metric that has the default value 1. The second parameter is mode, which specifies how the network interface card communicates with others. The mode parameter has the options "multicast," "broadcast," "quiet," "nolisten," and "version1." If not specified, the default value for mode is "multicast." The options "broadcast" and "version1" are equivalent. The

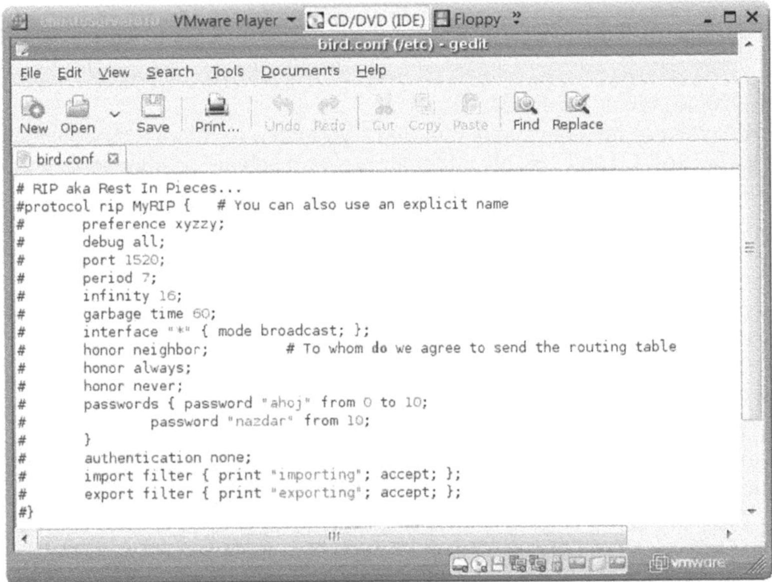

Figure 6.20 RIP block configuration.

option "quiet" means that there is no periodic message exchange with this network interface card. The option "nolisten" means that the network interface card does not listen to a message sent to it. The default value for interface is "none." In Figure 6.20, the symbol "*" means that all the network interface cards use the broadcast mode to communicate.

- Passwords: This item is used to specify the passwords used by this protocol in different time periods. As seen in Figure 6.20, two passwords are specified. The first password is "ahoj," which is used in the time period from 0 to 10. The second password is "nazdar," which is used in the time period from 10 and up.
- Honor: The item "honor" has three options: "always," "neighbor," and "never." A host may request for a routing table to be sent to it. The item "honor" specifies when the request should be honored. The default value is "never," which never honors such a request. However, if the request is from a host in a directly connected network, the value for the honor item can be specified as "always." It can also honor the request from a host in the neighborhood.
- Authentication: There are three options for the authentication method: none, plaintext, or md5. When none is specified, there is no authentication of transmitted packets. When plaintext is specified, the transmitted packets are authenticated by plaintext password. When md5 is specified, the packets are authenticated by the md5 cryptographic hash method. The default value for authentication is "none."
- Import: The import item has the options "all," "none," "filter name," "filter" {filter commands}, or "filter expression." Filter can be used to specify how to import routes from a protocol to the primary routing table. The default value for import is "all."
- Export: The export item has the same options as import. The export filter can be used to specify how to export routes from a routing table to the protocol. The default value for export is "none."

It should be advised that the use of nondefault values for the items, port, period, infinity, and garbage may cause incompatibility with the RFC standards.

Now that you have learned about the usage of the items included in the configuration file, you can configure the daemon BIRD to route packets between the networks 192.168.1.0 and 192.168.2.0 on the server machine, and between the networks 192.168.2.0 and 192.168.3.0 on the client machine. First, you need to prepare your private network for the routing configuration. The following are the preparatory steps:

1. Assume that the server machine is still on.
2. To see the effect of the configuration of BIRD, you need to remove the route between the networks 192.168.1.0 and 192.168.3.0 in the server machine's routing table. To do so, you may reboot the system by entering the following command:

   ```
   sudo reboot
   ```

3. To verify that the route has been removed, execute the following command to see that you are not able to ping 192.168.1.1 on the client machine:

   ```
   ping 192.168.1.1
   ```

After you have completed the preceding steps, you are ready to configure the daemon BIRD. The following is the step-by-step instruction for the configuration process:

1. Enter the following command in the terminal window of the server machine:

   ```
   sudo gedit /etc/bird.conf
   ```

2. After the bird.conf file is opened, configure the file according to Table 6.21. Figure 6.21 shows the result of the configuration.
3. Click the **Save** menu to save the file. Then, click **File** and **Quit** to complete the configuration.
4. Enter the following command in the terminal window:

   ```
   sudo birdc
   ```

Table 6.21 Configuration of bird.conf

Item	*Configuration*
debug	debug all;
port	port 1520;
period	period 7;
infinity	infinity 16;
garbage	garbage time 60;
interface	interface "eth0" { metric 3; mode broadcast; }, "eth1" { metric 2; mode broadcast; };
honor	honor neighbor;
authentication	authentication none;
import	import filter { print "importing"; accept; };
export	export filter { print "exporting"; accept; };

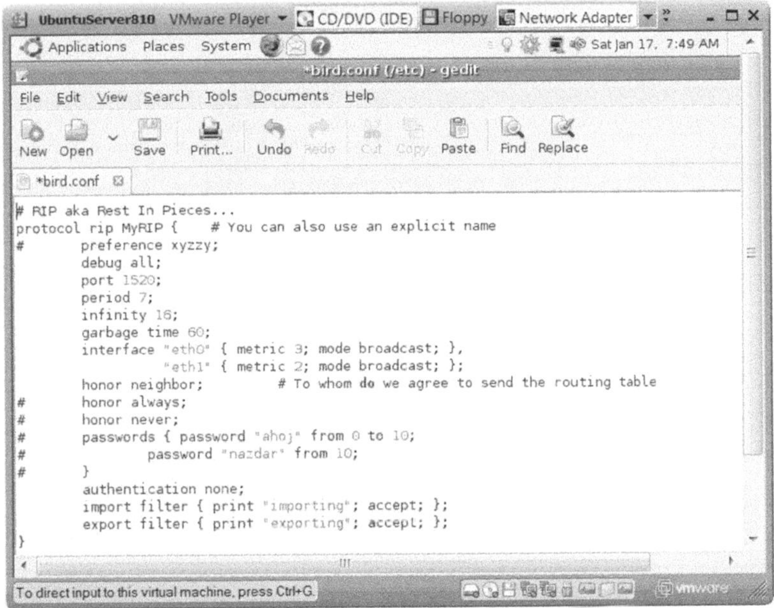

Figure 6.21 Configuration of bird.conf file on server machine.

You will be informed if there is a configuration error. You may enter the **?** command to get help.

5. You can now use birdc to configure the daemon BIRD by entering the following command:

```
configure
```

6. To check if the routing protocol RIP works, you need to enter the following command to see the routes in the routing table:

```
show route
```

Now, the routing table is modified as shown in Figure 6.22.

Now that you have completed the server-side configuration, you have your own router, which is the server machine. You need another router to communicate with the network 192.168.3.0. To do so, you will configure the client machine so it can be used as a router:

1. Similarly, you can configure the BIRD daemon on your client computer. Ensure that you use eth2 and eth3 for the configuration of the interface cards on the client machine. Figure 6.23 shows the configuration on the client computer.
2. Click the **Save** menu to save the file. Then, click **File** and **Quit** to complete the configuration.
3. Enter the following command in the terminal window:

```
sudo birdc
```

You will be informed if there is a configuration error.

```
student@ubuntu-server:~$ sudo birdc
BIRD 1.0.11 ready.
bird> ?
configure ["<file>"]                          Reload configuration
debug ...                                     Control protocol debugging
disable <protocol> | "<pattern>" | all        Disable protocol
down                                          Shut the daemon down
dump ...                                      Dump debugging information
echo [all | off | <mask>] [<buffer-size>]     Configure echoing of log messages
enable <protocol> | "<pattern>" | all         Enable protocol
exit                                          Exit the client
help                                          Description of the help system
quit                                          Quit the client
restart <protocol> | "<pattern>" | all        Restart protocol
show ...                                      Show status information
bird> configure
Reading configuration from /etc/bird.conf
Reconfigured.
bird> show route
192.168.1.0/24     dev eth0 [direct1 06:04] (240)
192.168.2.0/24     dev eth1 [direct1 06:04] (240)
127.0.0.0/8        dev lo [direct1 06:04] (240)
bird>
```

Figure 6.22 Routing table created by RIP on server machine.

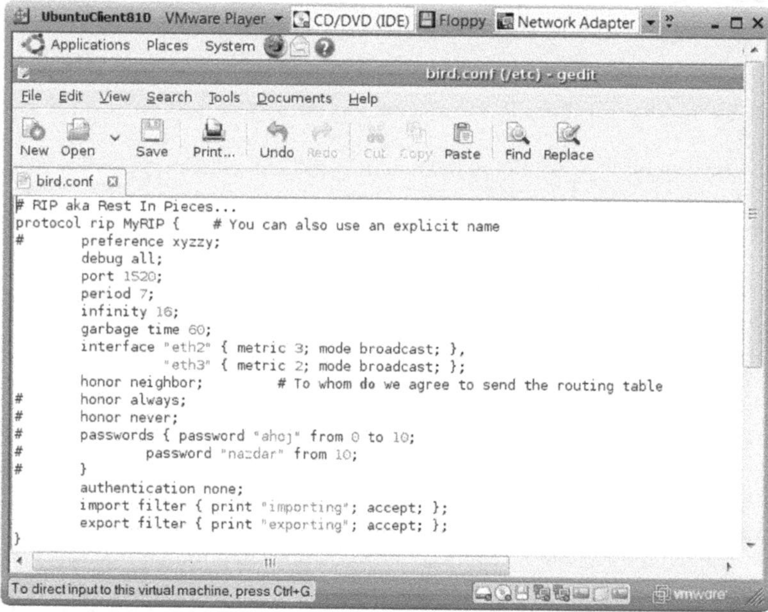

```
# RIP aka Rest In Pieces...
protocol rip MyRIP {     # You can also use an explicit name
#       preference xyzzy;
        debug all;
        port 1520;
        period 7;
        infinity 16;
        garbage time 60;
        interface "eth2" { metric 3; mode broadcast; },
                  "eth3" { metric 2; mode broadcast; };
        honor neighbor;          # To whom do we agree to send the routing table
#       honor always;
#       honor never;
#       passwords { password "ahoj" from 0 to 10;
#               password "nazdar" from 10;
#       }
        authentication none;
        import filter { print "importing"; accept; };
        export filter { print "exporting"; accept; };
}
```

Figure 6.23 Configuration of bird.conf file on client machine.

4. You can now use birdc to configure the daemon BIRD by entering the following command:

   ```
   configure
   ```

5. To check if the routing protocol RIP works, you need to enter the following command to see the routes in the routing table:

   ```
   show route
   ```

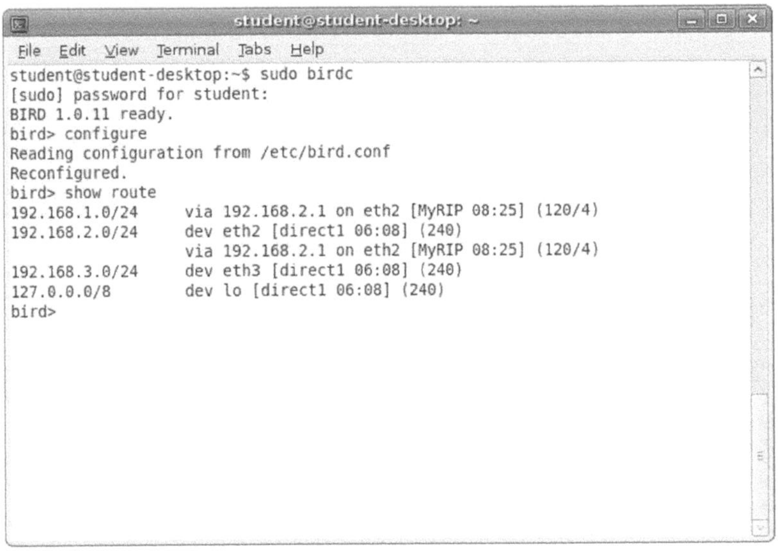

```
student@student-desktop: ~
File Edit View Terminal Tabs Help
student@student-desktop:~$ sudo birdc
[sudo] password for student:
BIRD 1.0.11 ready.
bird> configure
Reading configuration from /etc/bird.conf
Reconfigured.
bird> show route
192.168.1.0/24      via 192.168.2.1 on eth2 [MyRIP 08:25] (120/4)
192.168.2.0/24      dev eth2 [direct1 06:08] (240)
                    via 192.168.2.1 on eth2 [MyRIP 08:25] (120/4)
192.168.3.0/24      dev eth3 [direct1 06:08] (240)
127.0.0.0/8         dev lo [direct1 06:08] (240)
bird>
```

Figure 6.24 Routing table created by RIP on client machine.

Now, the routing table is modified as shown in Figure 6.24. Note that the network 192.168.1.0 has been automatically added to the routing table on the client machine by the protocol RIP.

After you have converted the client machine to a router, the routing table on the server machine should be automatically updated by RIP. Use the following steps to verify this:

1. Go back to your server machine. If the BIRD daemon configuration window is still open, enter the following command:

   ```
   show route
   ```

   As expected, upon comparing with Figure 6.22, you should see that an additional route to the network 192.168.3.0 has been added to the routing table (Figure 6.25).
2. Exit the BIRD configuration by executing the exit command.
3. Now, if you allow the server machine to forward packets, the networks 192.168.2.0 and 192.168.3.0 should be able to communicate with the network 192.168.1.0. To do so, enter the following command:

   ```
   su -
   ```

   After you enter the password **ubuntu**, enter the following command:

   ```
   echo 1 > /proc/sys/net/ipv4/ip_forward
   ```

   After the preceding command is executed, enter the command

   ```
   exit
   ```

   to go back to the student user environment.

```
student@ubuntu-server: ~
File  Edit  View  Terminal  Tabs  Help
disable <protocol> | "<pattern>" | all          Disable protocol
down                                            Shut the daemon down
dump ...                                        Dump debugging information
echo [all | off | <mask>] [<buffer-size>]       Configure echoing of log messages
enable <protocol> | "<pattern>" | all           Enable protocol
exit                                            Exit the client
help                                            Description of the help system
quit                                            Quit the client
restart <protocol> | "<pattern>" | all          Restart protocol
show ...                                        Show status information
bird> configure
Reading configuration from /etc/bird.conf
Reconfigured.
bird> show route
192.168.1.0/24      dev eth0 [direct1 06:04] (240)
192.168.2.0/24      dev eth1 [direct1 06:04] (240)
127.0.0.0/8         dev lo [direct1 06:04] (240)
bird> show route
192.168.1.0/24      dev eth0 [direct1 06:04] (240)
192.168.2.0/24      dev eth1 [direct1 06:04] (240)
                    via 192.168.2.2 on eth1 [MyRIP 08:40] (120/3)
192.168.3.0/24      via 192.168.2.2 on eth1 [MyRIP 08:40] (120/3)
127.0.0.0/8         dev lo [direct1 06:04] (240)
bird>
```

Figure 6.25 Updated routing table on server machine.

```
student@student-desktop: ~
File  Edit  View  Terminal  Tabs  Help
student@student-desktop:~$ ping -c 5 192.168.1.1
PING 192.168.1.1 (192.168.1.1) 56(84) bytes of data.
64 bytes from 192.168.1.1: icmp_seq=1 ttl=149 time=26.9 ms
64 bytes from 192.168.1.1: icmp_seq=2 ttl=149 time=1.18 ms
64 bytes from 192.168.1.1: icmp_seq=3 ttl=149 time=1.98 ms
64 bytes from 192.168.1.1: icmp_seq=4 ttl=149 time=1.14 ms
64 bytes from 192.168.1.1: icmp_seq=5 ttl=149 time=1.04 ms

--- 192.168.1.1 ping statistics ---
5 packets transmitted, 5 received, 0% packet loss, time 4050ms
rtt min/avg/max/mdev = 1.045/6.461/26.945/10.247 ms
student@student-desktop:~$
```

Figure 6.26 Testing router configuration.

4. Your client machine should be able communicate with 192.168.1.0 now. To verify this, go back to the client machine and exit the BIRD configuration. Now, execute the following command:

   ```
   ping -c 5 192.168.1.1
   ```

   As shown in Figure 6.26, the packets are delivered to the destination IP address 192.168.1.1.

In this hands-on activity, you have created your own routers with two Linux machines. You have experimented with both static and dynamic routing. During the hands-on activity, RIP has been used as the dynamic routing protocol. Although RIP has its limitations for enterprise-level networks, it is good for learning and for small businesses. Through this activity, you have learned about setting networks for router connection and about the configuration of routers. You can easily convert a surplus computer to a fully functioning router by installing Linux on it.

6.7 Summary

This chapter discussed routers in quite a bit of detail. As a major component in a network, routers are used to connect various networks to form the Internet. This chapter first illustrated how routers are used to connect different networks. It demonstrated how information is arranged in a routing table that is used to keep track of the information about the routes from one router to other routers.

During an operation, a routing table may need to be updated if the network topology changes. We discussed ways of updating routing tables. A routing table can be updated manually if the network is small and the network topology has few changes. If the network is large and its topology changes frequently, the routing table should be updated dynamically by using a dynamic routing protocol. The commonly used dynamic routing protocols are RIP, OSPF, and BGP, which dynamically update routing tables and find the shortest path from one router to another.

This chapter introduced two different ways to calculate the shortest path. The first one uses the link state routing algorithm, which can find the global optimal path between routers. The second one uses the distance vector routing algorithm, which calculates the shortest path with information provided by the routers in the neighborhood. This chapter also illustrated how a router determines the transmission rate for networks with different capacities.

For the hands-on practice, this chapter provided an activity that creates Linux routers with Ubuntu. With Ubuntu, a routing table can be updated manually and dynamically with routing protocols such as RIP. Although RIP is not suitable for a large network due to its limitations, it is a good choice for small businesses and for learning about routers.

After learning about routers, your next task is to deal with remote access and network resource sharing. Linux provides various tools to support the development of remote access and resource sharing. In Chapter 7, you will learn about remote access and network resource sharing.

Review Questions

1. What are the functions of a router?
2. When you try to determine how many networks should be linked together by a router, what are the criteria?
3. In a routing table, which symbol is used to represent the default network?
4. What are the measures that can be used for "metric" in a routing table?
5. What are the advantages of static routing?
6. What are the disadvantages of static routing?
7. Create a routing table for the DSL router that connects a Class C home network with ID 192.168.25.0 to the Internet.
8. Why do most routers use dynamic routing?
9. When a routing protocol uses the LS routing algorithm, what are the tasks that can be performed by the routing protocol?
10. For Figure 6.4, find the shortest path from R1 to R3 with Dijkstra's algorithm.
11. What are the disadvantages when you apply Dijkstra's algorithm to a complicated network system?
12. What are the advantages of the DV routing algorithm?

13. When a routing protocol uses the DV routing algorithm, what are the tasks that can be performed by the routing protocol?
14. How does hierarchical routing work?
15. Consider Figure 6.8. Suppose that a sender wants to send a message to the destination host with the IP address 10.0.0.2 and suppose that the packet arrives at the router R3. How does R3 determine the next hop?
16. How does a router forward a packet carried by a frame to another network that uses a different frame?
17. How does a router dynamically adjust the payload size?
18. Where can the fragmented packets be reassembled?
19. Describe three different ways to route a packet to a host in a different network.
20. What is BIRD?

Case Study Projects

The following are two networking projects that involve router development.

Case Study Project 6.1. By using the daemon BIRD, configure static routing to connect your home network to the Internet.

Case Study Project 6.2. By using BIRD, configure OSPF dynamic routing to connect two routers used in the hands-on activity in the chapter.

Chapter 7

Linux Network Resource Sharing

Objectives

- Establish Network File System (NFS).
- Set up Samba.
- Enable remote access with virtual private network (VPN).
- Understand Network Address Translation (NAT).

7.1 Introduction

Chapter 6 discussed routers, which are used to connect network segments. Once the network segments are connected with routers, computers from one network segment are able to access other computers located in different network segments. This allows the computers to share network resources such as files, storage devices, printing devices, and even network resources located in a different network segment. This chapter will cover some topics related to network resource sharing, such as the Network File System (NFS), Samba, virtual private network (VPN), and Network Address Translation (NAT). With these services, a Linux network can greatly improve its usability and flexibility. This chapter uses four sections to discuss these topics.

The first section provides an overview of the services provided by NFS and explains how it works. To help readers set up NFS, this section will introduce the configuration tools and demonstrate how to use these tools to configure an NFS service. The demonstration includes the configuration on both the server side and the client side. It also shows how a client can access the NFS server. The last topic to be covered by this section is related to NFS management, including NFS monitoring and troubleshooting.

The next section discusses the services provided by Samba, which allow a Linux network system to share network resources provided by a Microsoft network system. This section introduces the features provided by Samba. It discusses Samba Linux client support. It also demonstrates the configuration of the Samba server and client with the tools provided by Linux. The last topic in this section deals with Samba monitoring and testing.

Remote access to network resources through the Internet will be examined in the next section, which focuses on remote access through a VPN. To help readers understand how a VPN works, this section introduces some VPN-related concepts and describes how a VPN can securely transmit private data through the public Internet. Through some hands-on activities, this section shows how to set up a VPN server to enable remote access. It also demonstrates how to configure the VPN client so that the client can access network resources behind the VPN server. VPN service management and testing are also covered by this section.

The last topic to be discussed is the NAT service. Under this topic, an explanation is given as to how the NAT service allows multiple computers to share a routable IP address provided by an Internet service provider (ISP). The hands-on practice will illustrate how to install and configure the NAT service. In this section, you will also learn how to test and manage the NAT service.

In the following, let us take a tour to explore some network-resource-sharing technologies. The tour will start with NFS technology in the next section.

7.2 Network File System (NFS)

NFS technology, developed by Sun Microsystems, can be used to share files across a UNIX like network system. With NFS, users can share files, directories, and hard drives. NFS works like a client-server system. On the server side, an entire file system, or a portion of it, can be made available to qualified clients. On the client side, the client user can mount the exported file system on his or her own operating system so that the file system appears and behaves just like the one mounted on the local computer. This allows the user to access his or her own files from any computer on the network.

7.2.1 NSF Technology Overview

On a Linux network, the most often exported directory is /home, which is assigned to each user who has an account on the server. There are other partitions such as /usr or /lib that can be exported to the client machine. Figure 7.1 illustrates NFS technology.

In Figure 7.1, the NFS server exports the directory /home, and the client user mounts the /home directory on his or her own computer. The following is the procedure used by an NFS system:

1. When the client needs to access a file stored in the directory /home, it will contact the NSF server and ask the daemon portmap for the port number of the daemon mountd.
2. The daemon portmap responds to the client with the port number used by the daemon mountd.
3. After the client receives the port number, it will ask the daemon mountd for information about the directory /home.
4. The daemon mountd returns information about the directory /home to the client.
5. The client will ask portmap for the port number of the daemon nfsd, which is used to start the required kernel thread.

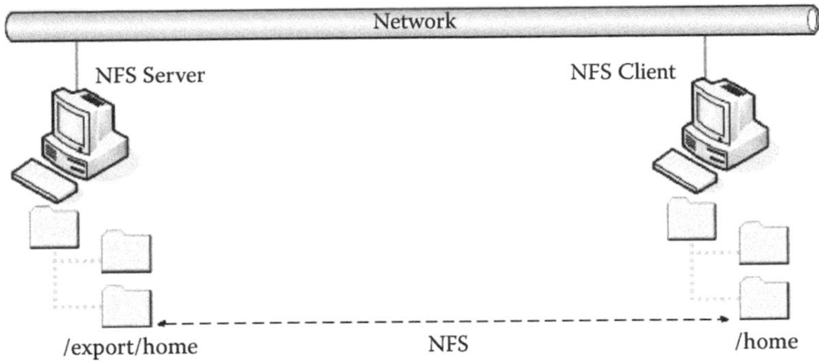

Figure 7.1 NFS technology.

6. The daemon portmap returns nfsd's port number to the client.
7. With the port number returned by portmap, the client sends the information on/home returned by the daemon mountd to nfsd, and asks nfsd for information on the requested file.
8. The daemon nfsd returns information about the requested file to the client.
9. With information returned by nfsd, the client can now work on the file exported by the NSF service.

One of the popular applications of NFS is the thin-client environment. In a thin-client network system, the client side has very limited data processing ability. Often, the client side does not have a hard drive to store data for computation. In this case, NFS provides a way to support the thin client by offering the home and other necessary directories to the client. In such an environment, many thin clients can share the hard drive hosted by the server. Nowadays, applications of NFS technology have been extended to the Internet. The Internet version of the NFS, WebNFS, is able to download large files in a short time and does not need to open and close connections to the server.

In addition to the thin-client network application, NFS has many other applications. The following are some of them:

- NFS allows multiple computers to share storage devices such as the CD-ROM drive, which may have a CD that stores drivers or other software to be shared by multiple computers.
- An NFS server can be used to store the home directories of all the employees in a company. In this way, each employee is able to work on his or her own home directory regardless of which computer in the network he or she is logged on to.

After the daemons for NFS are installed, our next task is to configure the NFS services. Topics related to their configuration are discussed in the next section.

7.2.2 NFS Configuration

The configuration process includes two parts. The first part is the server-side configuration, and the second part is the client-side configuration. Server-side configuration involves the following tasks:

- Install the NFS services.
- Check the status of the NFS daemon.
- Configure the file /etc/exports to specify the directories or partitions that should be exported.

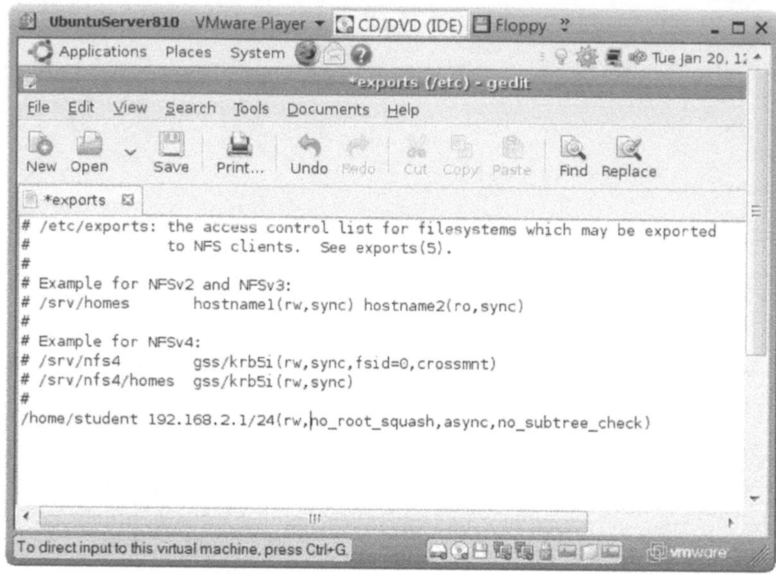

Figure 7.2 Entries in /etc/exports file.

- Set permissions in the /etc/exports file to specify which clients are allowed to access the exported materials. The access options can be specified.
- Start the NFS services.
- Configure the services to be available at boot time.

As seen from the foregoing tasks, the configuration is mostly done in the /etc/exports file. Figure 7.2 shows the entries in the /etc/exports file on the server machine.

Explanations for some of the commonly used terms and symbols in the /etc/exports file are listed in Table 7.1. You may find many other options by reading the manual page called export(5).

To be able to access the exported directories, some configuration needs to be done on the client side. The following are the client configuration tasks:

- Client-side configuration starts with checking if the service portmap has been started.
- If the service has been started, the next task is to mount the directories exported by the NFS server to the client computer. There are several options for the mount process. These options specify how the NFS client should behave after a server or network failure.

To illustrate the configuration of the server and client, in the following, we will perform a hands-on activity that demonstrates the process of developing an NFS service.

Activity 7.1 NFS Service

During this hands-on activity, you will experiment with NFS to share files and directories across a network. You will become familiar with the configuration tools provided by the Ubuntu Linux operating system. You will also deal with some of the issues involved in using NFS services. The following are the steps used to set up an NFS server:

Table 7.1 Items in /etc/exports File

Item	*Explanation*
/home/student	The directory name
host name	The host name of a client machine
192.168.2.0	The client network ID
ro	Read only
rw	Read and write
root_squash	Making sure that the root of a given computer does not have root permission for the file system
no_root_squash	Making sure that the root of a given computer has root permission for the file system
sync	Synchronizing NFS with the local file system
async	Opposite to sync. It speeds up the transfer, but may cause data corruption
subtree_check	When part of the volume is exported, it checks if the requested file is in the appropriate part of the volume
no_subtree_check	Disabling the subtree check to speed up the transfer

1. Log on to the server machine with username **student** and password **ubuntu**.
2. In Chapter 6, you changed the network structure during the hands-on practice. Your network may not be able to access the Internet at this point. To reconfigure the NIC so that you can access the Internet, execute the following command to edit the file /etc/network/interfaces:

   ```
   sudo gedit /etc/network/interfaces
   ```

   In earlier hands-on practice, you may have configured NIC eth1 to use the gateway 192.168.2.2 in the file /etc/network/interfaces. If so, comment the line out, and save the changes. In this way, you will be able to access the Internet through your home network. Also, if you have not completed the hands-on practice in Chapter 6, you may simply configure the eth0 NIC to take the dynamic IP address from the DHCP server built into your DSL router.
3. Enter the following command to install the NFS server:

   ```
   sudo apt-get install nfs-kernel-server nfs-common portmap
   ```

   Note that the hands-on activity in Chapter 6 or your network configuration may prevent you from accessing the Internet to download the files. If so, you may consider reconfiguring NIC eth0 to take the dynamic IP address from the DSL router with the following code in the file /etc/network/interfaces:

   ```
   auto eth0
   iface eth0 inet dhcp
   ```

You may also need to comment out the rest of configuration lines for eth0 and the line starting with the keyword gateway for eth1. Save the changes, and exit the file. Then, restart the network service with the following command or reboot the server machine:

```
sudo /etc/init.d/networking restart
```

After the packages are installed, you may need to change the NIC configuration back for the private network if necessary. You may also need to repeat the foregoing process for some later chapters.

4. To configure the NFS server, you need to edit the file /etc/exports. To do so, enter the following command:

```
sudo gedit /etc/exports
```

5. To allow every computer on the network 192.168.2.0 to be able to read and write files to the directory /home/student, add the following code at the end of the /etc/exports file:

```
/home/student 192.168.2.1/24(rw,no_root_squash,async,no_subtree_check)
```

6. Save the file, and quit. The configuration is shown in Figure 7.2.
7. After each modification to the /etc/exports file, you need to restart the NFS server. To do so, enter the following command:

```
sudo /etc/init.d/nfs-kernel-server restart
```

8. To make the change effective, enter the following command:

```
sudo exportfs -a
```

9. To verify that the directory is successfully exported, enter the following command:

```
sudo chmod 755 /home/student
sudo showmount -e 192.168.2.1
```

You should get the result shown in Figure 7.3.

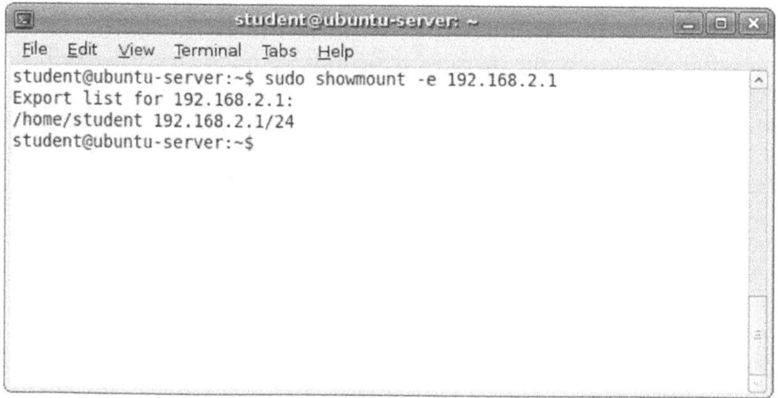

Figure 7.3 Exported directory /home/student.

Now, you have completed configuring of the NFS server. Next, you will configure the client machine. The following are the steps to get the job done:

1. First, you need to allow the server machine to forward packets from the client machine to the Internet. To do so, execute the following commands on the server machine:

   ```
   su -
   ```

   After entering the password **ubuntu**, enter the following command:

   ```
   echo 1 > /proc/sys/net/ipv4/ip_forward
   ```

   After the preceding command is executed, enter the command

   ```
   exit
   ```

   to go back to the student user environment.
2. Log on to the client machine with username **student** and password **ubuntu**.
3. Reconfigure the NIC eth2 to take the DHCP IP address from the server machine by executing the following command:

   ```
   sudo gedit /etc/network/interfaces
   ```

   After the file is opened, comment out the static configuration for eth2, and add the following two lines to configure the NIC eth2 to take the DHCP IP address from the server computer:

   ```
   auto eth2
   iface eth2 inet dhcp
   ```

   Your eth2 configuration should look like the one in Figure 7.4.

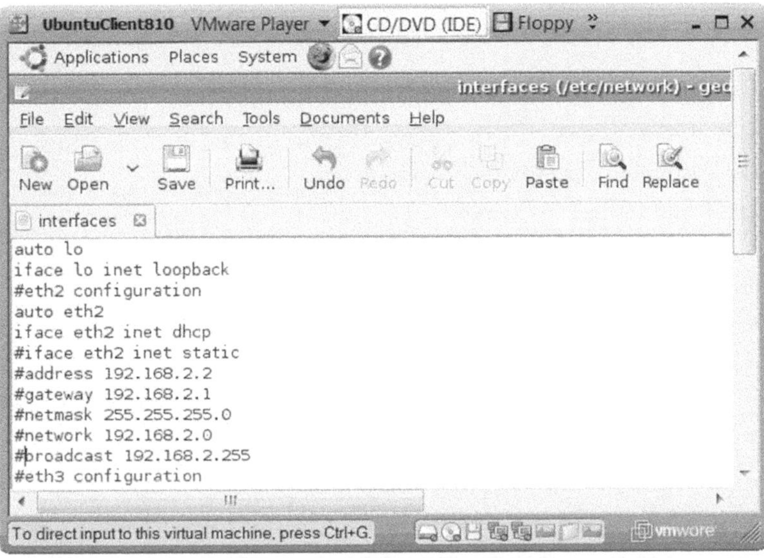

Figure 7.4 Reconfiguration of eth2.

4. Save the changes, and quit the editor. Execute the following command to make the change take effect:

```
sudo /etc/init.d/networking restart
```

The completion of the preceding steps will allow you to access the Internet from the client machine. Again, if you have not completed the hands-on activity in Chapter 6, you may simply configure the NIC eth3 to take the dynamic IP address from the DSL router on your home network so that your client computer can access the Internet.

5. To install the NFS client package, enter the following command:

```
sudo apt-get install portmap nfs-common
```

Again, if you cannot access the Internet, you may need to reconfigure the NIC to get the dynamic IP address from the DSL router.

6. To manually mount the /home/student directory posted by the NFS server, enter the following command:

```
sudo mount 192.168.2.1:/home/student /home/student
```

7. After you have successfully mounted the directory exported by the server, you may enter the following command to verify the result:

```
mount
```

As shown in Figure 7.5, you should be able to see that the directory 192.168.2.1:/home/student is mounted on the client machine.

8. To see if the directory /home/student has indeed come from the server, you can create a file by entering the following commands on the client machine:

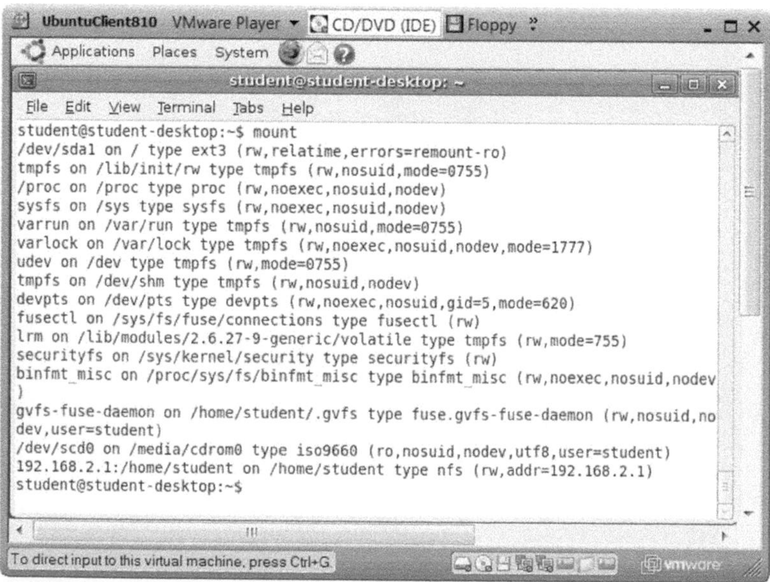

Figure 7.5 Currently mounted devices and directories on client machine.

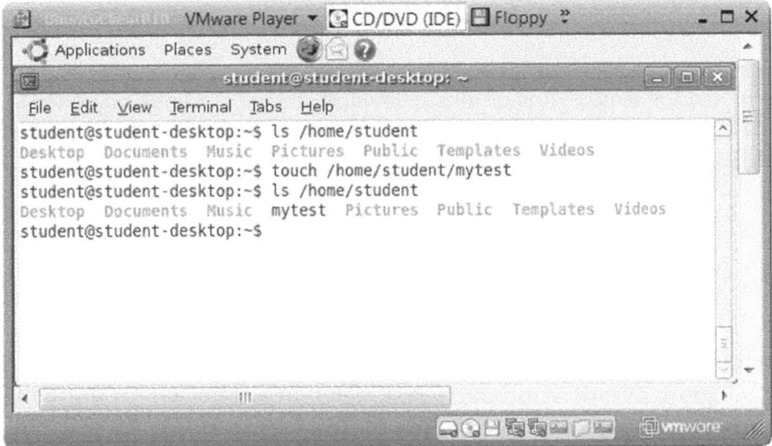

Figure 7.6 File mytest in /home/student directory.

```
ls /home/student
touch /home/student/mytest
ls /home/student
```

You can see that the file mytest is created in the directory /home/student (Figure 7.6).

9. To verify that the file mytest is actually created in the directory /home/student on the server machine, log on to the server and enter the following command:

```
ls /home/student
```

As shown in Figure 7.7, the file mytest is indeed created on the server machine.

In the foregoing, you have developed the NSF server and client. The hands-on activity has illustrated that the client machine can mount the directory /home/student on the server machine as its own directory. All the files created on the client machine will be automatically saved to

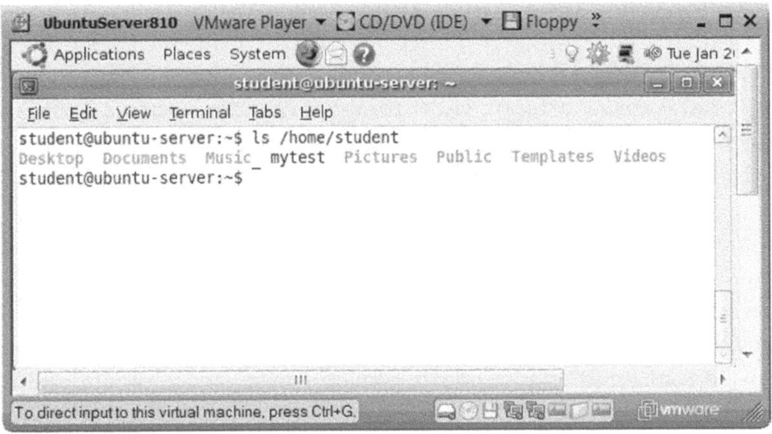

Figure 7.7 File mytest in /home/student directory on server machine.

the server machine. This allows the user to log on from any NFS client machine and work in the directory on the server machine. In the preceding hands-on activity, the mount process is not automatic. Every time you log on to a client machine, you need to execute the command mount. To be able to mount the remote /home/student directory at the boot time, you need to configure /etc/fstab on the client machine. Next, when the client machine reboots, the /home/student directory will be automatically mounted on the client machine.

7.3 Sharing Network with Windows

Similar to NFS, Samba is a software package that allows clients to access network resources such as files and printers through a network or the Internet. Especially, Samba allows Linux to communicate with Microsoft Windows products and many other UNIX operating systems. Samba implements client-server-based protocols, Server Message Block (SMB), and Common Internet File System (CIFS).

- *Server Message Block (SMB):* SMB is an application-level network protocol. It is commonly used to access shared files, printers, serial ports, and other network resources. SMB supports authenticated interprocess communication across a network. The SMB packets can be encapsulated in the TCP/IP packets to travel through a network. The main usage of SMB is to communicate with the network resources provided by Microsoft Windows.
- *Common Internet File System (CIFS):* CIFS is another application-level protocol. It defines rules to share files over the Internet. For example, it defines how to make a request to a file or to pass a message to application software running on a server through the Internet. To travel over the Internet, the CIFS packets are encapsulated in the SMB packets.

This section introduces the features of Samba. While discussing the concepts of Samba, we will examine how Samba works. The configuration of Samba will also be discussed. The hands-practice in this section will illustrate how to implement Samba on Linux computer systems. More details about Samba are given in the following subsections.

7.3.1 Samba Features and Applications

Through SMB, Samba enables a Linux server to support the Windows file system and printing service. Samba can also enable a Linux client to access Windows servers for sharing network resources. Through CIFS, Samba allows a wide range of applications, not just Web browsers, to share files over the Internet. The following are the features provided by Samba:

- Samba supports network services, such as Active Directory and printing services, provided by Microsoft Windows servers.
- Samba can set a Linux machine to be a member of the Active Directory domain.
- Samba provides security mechanisms, such as internal authentication, for data transmission.
- Samba can be configured as a Windows domain controller to authenticate the Windows client as well as the Linux client.
- Samba can work with older Windows products such as Windows NT.
- Samba allows the clients of various platforms, such as Microsoft Windows and different versions of the UNIX system, to share the same hard drive.

With these features, Samba can greatly expand its range of services to many other platforms in addition to Linux. Although Samba has a wide range of applications, it may not be necessary in some cases. For example:

- For a Linux network, resource sharing can be done through NFS. Here, Samba may not be necessary.
- When a Linux machine serves as a printing server and the printing server is shared by Windows clients, Samba is not necessary.
- When sharing a drive, a directory, or a file hosted by a Windows server, the Linux client only needs the plug-in called smbfs, instead of the entire Samba package.

A Linux computer with Samba installed on it can provide various services. The configuration of Samba to provide services will be discussed next.

7.3.2 Configuration of Samba Services

The Samba package has two components, Samba server and Samba client. When a Linux computer is used as a file and print server, the Samba server component should be installed. To make a Linux computer act as a Samba client, there are two options. You can either install the Samba client or the Samba plug-in smbfs.

Many Linux distributions include the Samba package. Samba installation is fairly simple. Once the Samba client is installed, it behaves like an FTP client. Through the Samba client, the user is able to search files and directories hosted by the server, send and retrieve files to or from the server, and so on.

Once installed, the Samba plug-in smbfs allows clients to mount network resources. After these network resources are mounted on the clients' computers, they behave as if they were hosted by the local computer. Therefore, many users prefer to use smbfs on the client computers. The installation of smbfs is straightforward.

After the Samba package is installed on a Linux computer, the next task is to configure Samba to provide services as a server or to access the services as a client. The configuration tasks may include the following:

- Create a user list and passwords for the users.
- Create user groups to make the user management task easier.
- Configure Samba as a server to manage services such as how files can be shared by clients, and so on.
- Configure Samba so that the Linux machine can be used as a domain controller.
- Configure the share securities such as user authentication and password protection.
- Configure Samba clients so that users can access the Samba server.
- Configure Samba clients to mount shared network resources.
- Change the options for starting and stopping a Samba service. The file used to start or stop a Samba service is /etc/init.d/samba.
- Configure the options for testing the Samba services.

The configuration of Samba can be done with commands or with GUI tools if they are provided by the Linux distributions. The configuration file used for the server-side configuration is /etc/samba/smb.conf. The file smb.conf is basically divided into two logical sections, the global section and share section. The share logical section can also be further divided into sections such as the printer section, home section, cdrom section, and so on. The following is an example of the /etc/samba/smb.conf file:

```
[global]
workgroup = mygroup
netbiosname = myname
os level = 2
security = user
......

[cdrom]
comment = Linux CD-ROM
path = /media/cdrom
locking = no
......

[home]
       comment = Home Directories
       browseable = no
       writable = yes
       valid users = %S
       create mode = 0664
......

[printers]
       comment = Printers
       path = /var/spool/samba
       printer = myprinter
       browseable = yes
       guest ok = yes
       writable = yes
       printable = yes
......
```

The [global] section contains the configuration of the network setup so that the Samba server is reachable by the clients via the protocol SMB. The following briefly describes the items included in the sample file:

- workgroup: The name of the workgroup to which your Samba server belongs.
- netbiosname: The DNS name assigned to your Samba server. If no DNS name is assigned, use myname instead.
- os level: The value that determines the relationship between the Samba server and the Windows server. The lower value is used to protect the Windows server from being taken over by the Samba server.
- security: The security level to be implemented. User is the default-level security. When the user level is specified, after a user is authenticated, the user can mount multiple share sections such as printer and home without additional authentication.

The options in the section [cdrom] specify how clients can share the CD-ROM drive on the Samba server. The options under this section in the sample smb.conf file have the following meanings:

- comment: The section description.
- path: The path to the CD-ROM device directory.
- locking: The locking control to determine if the locking requests by a client should be processed. When the value "yes" is specified, the server will process the locking request. For the [cdrom] section, the content on the CD is read-only, which does not need locking, so the value "no" is often used for the locking option.

The options in the section [home] specify how a user is connected to his or her own home directory. The following are explanations of those options:

- browseable: It specifies if the home directory is visible or invisible.
- valid user: The valid username. As soon as the user connects to the home directory, the value %S will be replaced by the username.
- create mask: It defines the permissions of a file created by Windows. The files created by Windows do not understand the UNIX permission system. The value 0664 indicates that all the files created by Windows will be assigned the 664 permission by default. The UNIX permission system is defined as

```
r="read permission"=4
w="write/edit permission"=2
x="execute permission"=1
```

Therefore, 664 means the owner of the file has read/write (4+2+0) permission, the users in the owner's group have read/write (4+2+0) permission, and the rest of the world has read-only (4+0+0) permission.

There are more options in each of the foregoing sections than those listed here. Interested readers can find the definitions for those options in the Linux manual.

Now that you have briefly learned about the Samba configuration file, the next task is to enhance the learning through hands-on practice. The following activity creates a Samba service.

Activity 7.2 Samba Service

In this hands-on activity, you will turn the server machine into a Linux file server. Then, you will configure a Windows Samba client to access shared network resources. Let us start with the server configuration:

- Log on to the server machine with username **student** and password **ubuntu**.
- For this activity, let us make a shared folder called myfolder in the directory /home/student with the GUI tool. To do so, click **Places,** and select the **Home Folder** on the pop-up menu.
- Once the Home Folder is opened, right-click inside the student folder pane, and select **Create Folder** on the pop-up menu. When prompted to change the folder name, enter **myfolder** as the folder name.
- After myfolder is created, right-click the **myfolder** icon, and select **Share Options** from the pop-up menu. Samba is included in Ubuntu Linux. If not, the message "Shared services are not installed" will show up on the pop-up menu. In this case, you should select the option "Install Windows network support (SMB)" and then click "Install services."
- If Samba is installed, the File Manager dialog will be opened for configuration. Check the **Share this folder** check box. You may also check the check box **Allow other people to write in this folder,** and enter the text **Samba test** in the comment text box shown in Figure 7.8.

Figure 7.8 Folder sharing on Windows network.

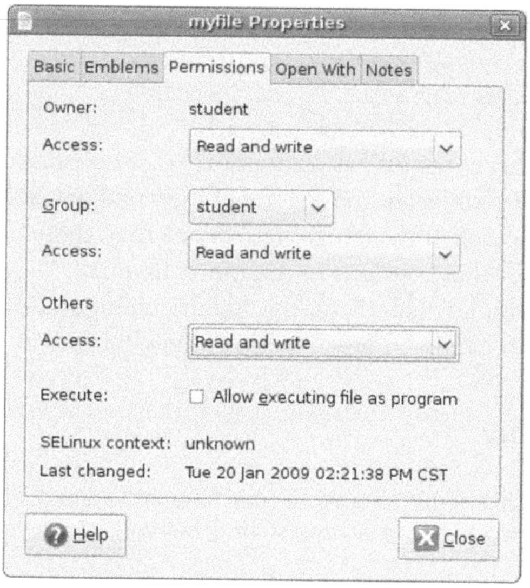

Figure 7.9 Configuring file permissions.

- Then, click the **Create Share** button to complete the configuration. You will be prompted to allow Nautilus to add permissions to the folder myfolder. Click the button **Add permissions automatically.**
- Double-click the newly created folder, **myfolder**. You will see that there is nothing in the folder. To create a file, right-click an empty spot inside the myfolder pane, and select **Create Document**; then select **Empty file**. After this, name the new file as **myfile.**
- To allow others to read from and write to the file, you can reset the permission to the file. Right-click the file **myfile,** and select **Properties**. Click the **Permissions** tab, and configure the permissions shown in Figure 7.9. Then, click **Close** to complete the configuration.

After the shared folder is configured on the server machine, your next task is to set up the Widows Samba client so that it can access the files in the shared folder myfolder:

1. Assume that your Linux virtual machine is running on a machine on which the Windows Vista operating system is installed as the host operating system. Also, assume that you are currently logged on to the Windows machine.
2. Click the **Start** menu, and select **Network** on the Start menu. If the server is properly configured, you should be able to see the server name UBUNTU-SERVER on the screen.
3. Double-click the **UBUNTU-SERVER** icon. You should be able to see the shared folder, myfolder, that was created earlier.
4. Double-click **myfolder**. When prompted, enter the username **student** and password **ubuntu**. Then, you will see the file myfile created on the server machine (Figure 7.10).
5. Right-click **myfile,** and select **Open** on the pop-up menu to open the **Open file** dialog. Click the **Open** button. You are prompted to select a program to open the file. In the **Open with** dialog, select **Notepad,** and click **OK**. The **Open file** dialog is started again; click the **Open** button to open the file myfile.
6. Type one or two words such as **Samba Test**. Click the **File** menu, and select **Exit**. When asked if you want to save the changes, click the **Yes** button.
7. Now, to verify that the file myfile is shared with the Linux machine, go back to the server machine. In the myfolder pane, double-click the file myfile. When prompted, click the **Display** button. You should be able to see the result displayed in Figure 7.11.

From the foregoing, you have learned how to share files between Linux and Windows. Our next project is to set up a VPN server for remote access.

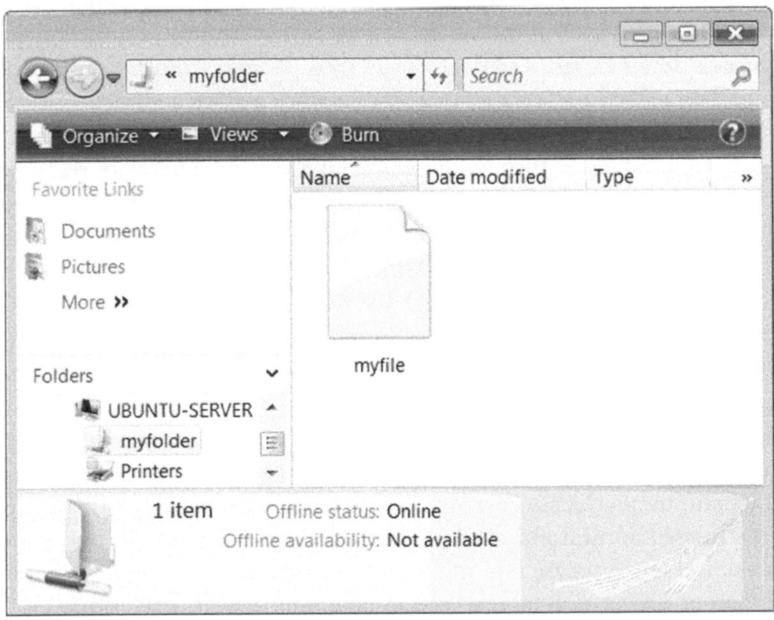

Figure 7.10 Remotely accessing shared file.

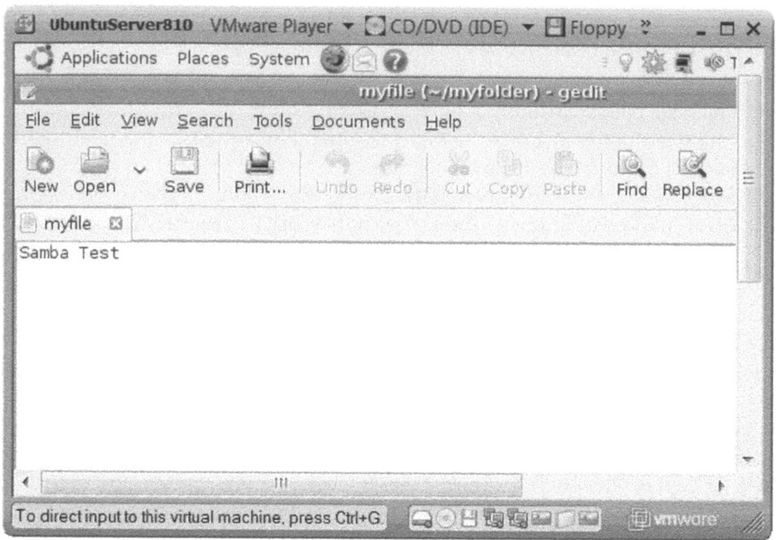

Figure 7.11 File sharing with Windows.

7.4 Remote Access through VPN

Remotely accessing services allows users to use network resources located at remote locations. Through networks, students at home can access course material posted on Web servers located on different campuses, salespeople from thousands of miles away are able to update their companies' databases as soon as a deal is closed, and doctors can treat patients from remote locations. Remote access has become a vital network service in today's network infrastructure.

To be able to access network resources at remote locations, local computers should be properly connected to the remote resources through networks. If the remote network resources are linked through the Internet, modems will be used to transform digital signals to analog signals. At the destinations, the analog signals will be transformed back to digital signals. Technologies such as DSL are used by modems to manage data transmission. For the communication between a user and a network resource, the data may go through the user's private network to the Internet. When the data reaches the destination, it will be transmitted from the Internet to another private network. To remotely access private networks through the Internet, there are two types of technologies: dial-up remote access and VPN remote access.

Dial-up remote access is a remote access technology designed for using the existing telephone network without changing the network's infrastructure. Because the telephone network has been established throughout the world, the cost of dial-up remote access is minimal. The dial-up remote access method is still used in rural and remote areas. On the other hand, the dial-up remote access technology has a slower transmission rate and is only suitable transmitting text-based content. On the server side, there is a modem pool installed to take multiple requests for access. The maintenance of the modem pool can be labor intensive and time consuming.

Another important remote access technology is VPN technology, which allows the user to access a private network through the Internet. When compared with dial-up remote access technology, VPN is a much faster and more secure solution. VPN can use the public Internet to deliver private data by encrypting the data. It can work with the broadband Internet technology to achieve a much higher transmission rate than dial-up technology can. Because VPN uses network interface cards, there is no extra network equipment to maintain. This makes the management of the VPN server much easier than using the dial-up modem pool. Due to these advantages, the focus of this section will be mostly on VPN technology. Later in this section, there will be some hands-on activities designed to configure the VPN client and VPN server.

There are some technologies that allow the user to remotely access the desktop of a computer. Virtual Network Computing (VNC) is this type of technology; VNC allows the user to log on to a remote computer and use its desktop to operate it. Similar to VNC technology, Remote Desktop Protocol (RDP) allows the user to access a computer running Microsoft Terminal Services. Many desktop versions of Linux provide applications such as rdesktop and vncviewer for remote desktop access.

This section started with an introduction to VPN technology. Later, the configuration of the VPN server and client will be covered in the hands-on practice. Remote desktop access will also be covered in the hands-on practice.

7.4.1 VPN Technology

VPN technology consists of VPN servers and VPN clients. To access a VPN server, the VPN client software must be installed on the user's computer and must be configured to be able to communicate with the VPN server. When the client tries to connect to the VPN server, the VPN client software connects to the VPN server with the tunneling protocol. When the VPN server receives the connection request, it checks the user's authentication information. If the user is authenticated, the VPN server will establish a secure connection to link the VPN client to the server. Before the data is transmitted, it will be encrypted. The encrypted data is transmitted through the secure connection to the receiver. At the receiver's end, the data will be decrypted. In this way, the private data is kept from being read and altered by an unauthorized person.

As mentioned earlier, the tunneling protocol is used to establish a connection between the VPN client and the VPN server. Packets are formed by the tunneling protocol, encapsulated in the IP protocol, and then transmitted through the Internet. The tunneling protocol also performs security-related tasks such as encryption and authentication. The tunneling protocol consists of three types of protocols:

- *Carrier protocol:* This kind of protocol carries private packets through a public network.
- *Encapsulating protocol:* This type of protocol encapsulates the private packets inside a carrier protocol. Later, three such protocols, IPSec, PPTP, and SSL, will be introduced.
- *Passenger protocol:* This type of protocol is not supported by the Internet and needs to be encapsulated in a carrier protocol.

Three popular tunneling protocols are available to handle the encapsulation tasks. The following subsections briefly describe these three protocols.

7.4.1.1 Internet Protocol Security (IPSec)

IPSec is a collection of related protocols used to ensure private and secure communication on a public network. By providing cryptographic security services, IPSec protects data integrity and confidentiality. Because IPSec is implemented in the Internet layer on the TCP/IP network architecture, it can protect the protocols implemented on top of the Internet layer, such as the protocols in the transport layer and the application layer. With the protection of IPSec, there is no need to enforce security measures on each individual application that uses TCP/IP. IPSec can be used as a complete VPN protocol by itself or used as an encryption utility with other VPN protocols.

Because IPSec is an older and well-established tunneling protocol, it has been implemented on various routers and network operating systems. It can provide a wide range of protection against the following:

- Attack from an untrusted network device
- Denial-of-service attack
- Packet sniffing
- Data corruption
- Data replay
- Data theft
- Data modification
- Identity theft
- Address spoofing

IPSec can be configured to protect the communication between subnets and between a host and a subnet. A disadvantage of IPSec is that it does not work well routing through a NAT service, which is the service used by many home networks and company private networks to access the Internet. Another disadvantage of IPSec is that it slows down the network traffic.

7.4.1.2 Secure Sockets Layer (SSL) VPN

SSL-based VPN is known for its ability to protect remote access from anywhere. Unlike IPSec VPN, which creates a tunnel between client and server, SSL-based VPN establishes a secure proxy connection from a client to a network resource. The proxy connection takes the client request first and authenticates the user. It forwards the request to the server only if the client is authenticated. In this way, SSL-based VPN can avoid a direct connection between the client and the network resource; this is safer approach than that of IPSec. SSL-based VPN uses the split tunneling approach. Simultaneously, split tunneling technology allows the client to access multiple servers such as file servers, database servers, mail servers, and other servers on a company's network through the VPN connection.

SSL-based VPN has flexible configuration options and provides better control of remote access so that it can assign different privileges to different clients. While establishing a tunnel, SSL-based VPN requires only a single TCP or UDP port. This feature enables SSL-based VPN to work easily with firewalls. SSL-based VPN is available for a wide range of operating systems, including Windows and different versions of the UNIX operating system.

Another advantage of SSL-based VPN is that there is no VPN client software to be installed and configured on the VPN client computer; this makes it more secure and simplifies the client-side configuration. For Linux, one of the mature SSL-based VPN packages is OpenVPN, which is an open source and feature-rich VPN package.

The disadvantage of SSL-based VPN is that it requires a browser on the client computer to allow active content so that the VPN can work properly. This makes the Web browser a target of malicious applets. Additional security enforcement is necessary to block unsigned activities and plug-ins. Another disadvantage is that it requires more configuration on the server side than IPSec.

7.4.1.3 Point-to-Point Tunneling Protocol (PPTP)

PPTP is a tunneling protocol jointly developed by Microsoft, 3COM, and some other companies. It is widely accepted and supported by different platforms such as Windows and Linux. One of PPTP's advantages is that it can work properly with the NAT service. This advantage is very important for students, whose computers are linked to private networks behind the NAT service. It is also important for small businesses and travelers, who often work on hotels' private networks behind the NAT service. PPTP is user-friendly and cost-effective. It is relatively easy to set up PPTP for the VPN service. It only requires a small portion of the bandwidth to operate PPTP. PPTP also supports a wide range of security measures for authentication, packet filtering, and encryption.

Despite its advantages, PPTP has some weaknesses. During data transmission, PPTP does not encrypt the control messages. This may raise some concerns about security. The connection established by PPTP may be vulnerable to hackers' attacks. The authentication of PPTP is based on the username and password. It does not authenticate the computer involved in the VPN process. This can cause a serious security problem. Hackers can set up a fake VPN server and redirect VPN traffic from the real VPN server to the fake VPN server and collect client information there without the clients' knowledge. For many serious uses, PPTP may not be secure enough. It has a problem working with firewalls. Also, for Linux users, PPTP requires kernel patches to perform encryption; this increases the complexity of setting up the VPN service.

Based on the usage of the VPN technology, tunneling can be voluntary or compulsory. Table 7.2 describes these two types of tunneling.

There are various VPN products on the market. Some of them are built into hardware, and others are software based. In general, VPN products can be categorized into three categories. Table 7.3 lists their advantages and disadvantages.

To overcome the disadvantages, each type of VPN product adds features normally seen in other types of products. For example, hardware-based VPN products include features offered by software-based VPN products. Software-based standalone VPN products support the features commonly seen in hardware-based VPN products.

VPN technology can also be categorized into two types based on connection. There are two kinds of connection, user-to-LAN connection and site-to-site connection. The user-to-LAN VPN is used for remote access to the VPN server. This type of connection allows clients to have secure and encrypted communication with the hosts on a private network through VPN technology. On

Table 7.2 Tunneling Types

Tunneling Type	*Function*	*Usage*
Voluntary tunneling	This type of tunneling allows a VPN client to handle the VPN connection. The client initiates the VPN connection and then creates a tunnel to a VPN server.	When VPN clients need to choose their own tunneling destinations, voluntary tunneling should be used.
Compulsory tunneling	This type of tunneling allows an ISP to handle the VPN connection. When a VPN client makes a request to the ISP, the ISP establishes a tunnel between the VPN client and a VPN server.	When a company outsources its VPN service to an ISP that deploys tunnels to serve the VPN clients in a local region, compulsory tunneling is used by the ISP.

Table 7.3 Advantage and Disadvantages of VPN Products

Product Type	*Advantage*	*Disadvantage*
Hardware-based VPN products	Hardware-based VPN products are secure and easy to use. They efficiently use the CPU processing power and provide the highest network throughput.	Hardware-based VPN products are less flexible.
Firewall-based VPN products	Firewall-based VPN products can restrict access to the internal network, perform network address translation, conduct authentication, support real-time alarm, protect the operating system, and support extensive logging.	Firewall-based VPN products, in general, have slower performance.
Software-based stand-alone VPN products	Software-based stand-alone VPN products are flexible. They can be used for the network with different types of routers and firewalls. They can tunnel traffic based on IP addresses and protocols. They can handle both VPN and non-VPN network traffic.	Software-based stand-alone VPN products require more configuration effort. They may require making changes in the routing table and the IP addressing scheme.

the client side, the client VPN software is installed and configured so that the client can access the VPN server anywhere and anytime.

The site-to-site connection allows companies or universities to link their private network sites located in different campuses through the public network such as the Internet. The site-to-site connection can be intranet-based or extranet-based. The Intranet-based connection connects one or more LANs to a private network within an organization's internal network. The extranet-based connection links LANs of one organization to the private network of another organization.

In the foregoing, various forms of VPN technology have been introduced. Our next task is to consider some issues related to configuration of the VPN service. The discussion is given in the next section.

7.4.2 VPN Configuration

The configuration of a VPN involves both server-side configuration and client-side configuration. Because the VPN communicates through network interface cards, you need to make sure that the network which links the client and server is functioning properly. On the server side, the configuration tasks include the following.:

- Install the VPN package, which is either included in a Linux package or downloaded from the Internet.
- Multiple network interface cards are used by the VPN server to connect to multiple networks. You need to specify the network interface card for each network.
- Specify if the VPN server can pass a dynamic IP address issued by the DHCP server to the VPN client. You can also specify if a client can get the same IP address each time the client connects to the VPN server.

- Specify if the VPN server can pass DNS information to the VPN client.
- Specify if password encryption or data encryption should be required.
- Specify how VPN server authentication should be performed.
- Specify the remote access policy that will be used to allow or deny remote access to a group of users.
- Specify which VPN tunneling protocol will be used to set up the VPN connection.
- Specify what types of remote access should be allowed, such as IP-based remote access and dial-up remote access.
- Specify if the connection is a user-to-LAN connection or a site-to-site connection.
- Specify how the firewall should be configured for the VPN connection.
- Specify how to share the network resources for the VPN connection.
- Restart the newly configured VPN service.

The configuration on the client side needs to perform the following tasks:

- Install the VPN client.
- Specify which VPN server to access.
- If multiple users can log on to the same client computer, specify which users can remotely access the VPN server through the client computer.
- Enable the VPN connection.
- Specify user authentication information by entering the user's username and password.
- Test the connection to the VPN server.

You will perform some of these configuration tasks in the following hands-on activity.

Activity 7.3 VPN Service

In this hands-on practice, you will first install and configure a VPN server. The VPN server will link two networks, 192.168.1.0 and 192.168.2.0. The 192.168.2.0 network is the virtual client network, and the 192.168.1.0 network is the private home network. PPTP will be used as the tunneling protocol. This will allow the Linux client on the virtual network to access the Windows computers on the home network.

CONFIGURATION OF VPN SERVER

This hands-on activity requires that both your server and client machines be able to access the Internet. If you have not completed the hands-on activity in Chapter 6, you may refer to Activity 7.1 to configure the eth0 and eth3 NICs accordingly. The following steps show you how to install and configure the VPN server on the server machine:

1. Log on to the server machine with username **student** and password **ubuntu**.
2. To install the protocol PPTP, make sure that the server machine has a working Internet connection, and execute the following command in the terminal window:

   ```
   sudo apt-get install pptpd
   ```

3. The configuration file is pptpd.conf. To open the file, execute the following command:

   ```
   sudo gedit /etc/pptpd.conf
   ```

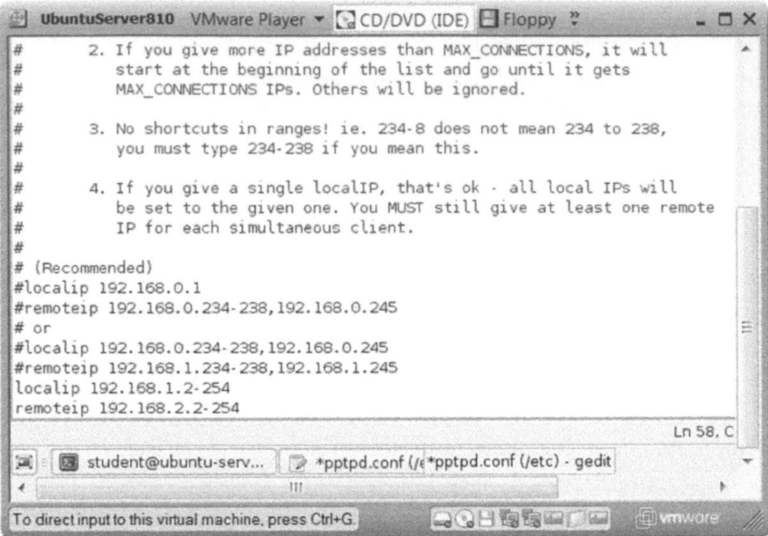

Figure 7.12 Configuration of localip and remoteip.

Table 7.4 User Authentication Information

Client	*Server*	*Secret*	*IP Address*
student	pptpd	ubuntu	*

4. Move the cursor to the bottom of the file, and configure the localip as 192.168.1.2-254, which includes all the hosts of the private network and the remoteip as 192.168.2.2-254, which includes all the hosts of the client network. The result is shown in Figure 7.12. Save the changes, and quit the text editor.
5. In this step, you will configure the VPN server to give permissions to the users on the client side. To do so, enter the following command:

```
sudo gedit /etc/ppp/chap-secrets
```

6. Enter the user's authentication information shown in Table 7.4. Save the configuration, and quit the text editor.
7. Restart pptpd by entering the following command:

```
/etc/init.d/pptpd restart
```

8. Upon rebooting your server machine, you may get an error message telling you that the name of the Web site for file downloading cannot be resolved. This may be because the server machine has blocked the request from the client for name resolution. To solve this problem, execute the following commands on the server machine. First, run

```
su -
```

After entering the password **ubuntu**, enter the following command:

```
echo 1 > /proc/sys/net/ipv4/ip_forward
```

After the preceding command is executed, run the command

```
exit
```

to go back to the student user environment.

You have now configured the VPN server. The VPN server is ready to take the connection request from the client.

The configuration of the client machine is covered in the next section.

CONFIGURATION OF CLIENT MACHINE

On the client side, you need to set up a connection to the VPN server. The following steps show you how to install and configure the VPN management package on the client machine:

1. Log on to the client machine with username **student** and password **ubuntu**.
2. Because you need to install the VPN Connection Manager package, make sure that your client machine is able to access the Internet. First, execute the following command on the client machine:

   ```
   sudo apt-get update
   ```

   As mentioned earlier in this chapter, you may need to reconfigure the NIC so that you can access the Internet in order to update your system.
3. First, you need to install the protocol PPTP on the client machine. To do so, execute the following command in the terminal window:

   ```
   sudo apt-get install network-manager-pptp
   ```

4. You may want to restart NetworkManager on your client machine. To do so, execute the following command:

   ```
   sudo NetworkManager restart
   ```

   Note that the NetworkManager icon may disappear during this lab activity. If that happens, you may need to configure the file /etc/NetworkManager/nm-system-settings.conf so that the following line is included in the file:

   ```
   managed=true
   ```

   Save the change, and exit the file. You may need to reboot the system for the command to take effect.
5. Once PPTP is installed on the client machine, your next task is to make sure that NetworkManager is working properly. After manually configuring the NICs in the file /etc/network/interfaces, the configuration done with the GUI tool NetworkManager in Ubuntu 8.10 may not function properly. The earlier versions of Ubuntu may not have this problem. To edit the file /etc/network/interfaces to remove the configuration done manually, execute the following command:

   ```
   sudo gedit /etc/network/interfaces
   ```

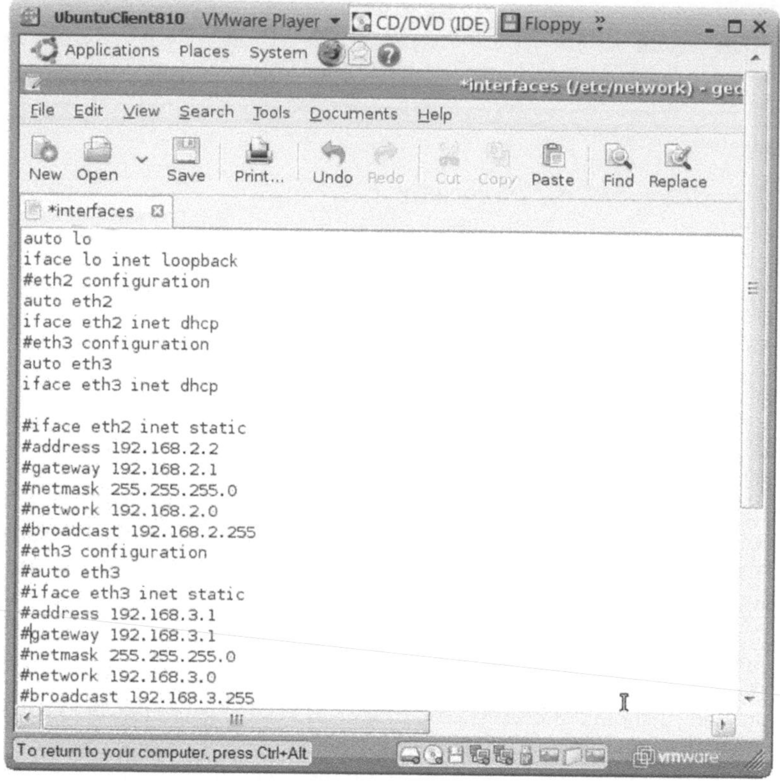

Figure 7.13 Configuration of eth2 and eth3 NICs.

6. Comment out the static configuration for the NICs eth2 and eth3. Add the DHCP configuration for eth2 and eth3 (Figure 7.13). Then, save the changes, and quit the text editor. To allow the configuration to take effect, you need to execute the following command:

```
sudo /etc/init.d/networking restart
```

7. You may also want to check the configuration of NICs with the GUI NIC configuration tools. Click the **System** menu, **Preferences**, **Network Configuration** to open the Network Connections dialog. Select **Auto eth3,** and click the **Edit** button.
8. Click the Wired tab, and configure eth3 (Figure 7.14). The MAC address will be different on your computer. If the MAC address is missing, you may run the sudo ifconfig command to get the MAC address (hardware address).
9. Click the IPv4 Settings tab, and configure the eth3 NIC (Figure 7.15). Then click **OK.**
10. Your next task is to configure the VPN client to connect to the VPN server. To configure the VPN connection, click the NetworkManager icon on your upper-right screen. Select **VPN Connections,** and then **Configure VPN** (Figure 7.16) to open the Network Connections dialog.
11. After the Network Connections dialog is opened, click the **Add** button. Then, configure the connection (Figure 7.17). The password is **ubuntu**. Click **OK.**
12. Click the button **Advanced**. Check the check box **Use Point-to-Point encryption (MPPE)**. Then, click the **OK** button. Click the **OK** button again. Then, close the Network Configuration dialog.

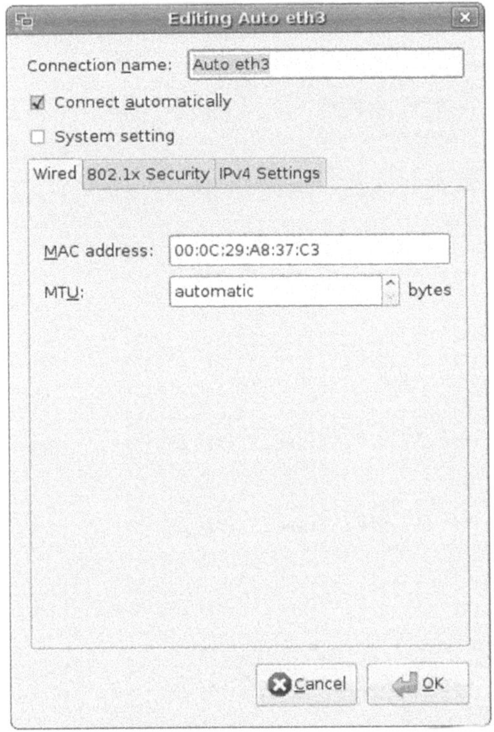

Figure 7.14 Wired configuration for eth3 NIC.

13. Click the **NetworkManager** icon. You will see that Lab VPN is added (Figure 7.18). Select **VPN Connections,** and then **Lab VPN**.
14. If the connection is successful, you should be able to see a golden lock on the NetworkManager icon. Click the NetworkManager icon; you will see that the client is connected to the VPN server (Figure 7.19).

NETWORK RESOURCES SHARING THROUGH VPN

Once you have successfully connected to the VPN server, you can share network resources on the private network. Suppose that on the network 192.168.1.0 there is Windows Server 2003, which can be accessed through the terminal service. Assume that Windows Server 2003 has a network with IP address 192.168.1.50. After the client machine on the network 192.168.2.0 logs on to the network 192.168.1.0, it should be able to log on to Windows Server 2003 through the terminal service. The following steps show how to share the desktop with the Windows computer on the private network:

1. Configure the Windows computer to accept the remote desktop connection. You may need to configure the computer's remote access properties. If you have Windows Server 2003 on your private network, right-click **My Computer,** and select **Properties**. When the Properties dialog is opened, click the **Remote** tab, and select the **Remote Desktop** option.
2. Assume that your client computer is still on. Click the **Applications** menu, select **Internet**, and then select **Terminal Server Client** to open the Terminal Server Client configuration dialog. Enter the Windows computer's IP address (e.g., 192.168.1.50), username, password, and the name of the workgroup used by your home network (Figure 7.20). You need to

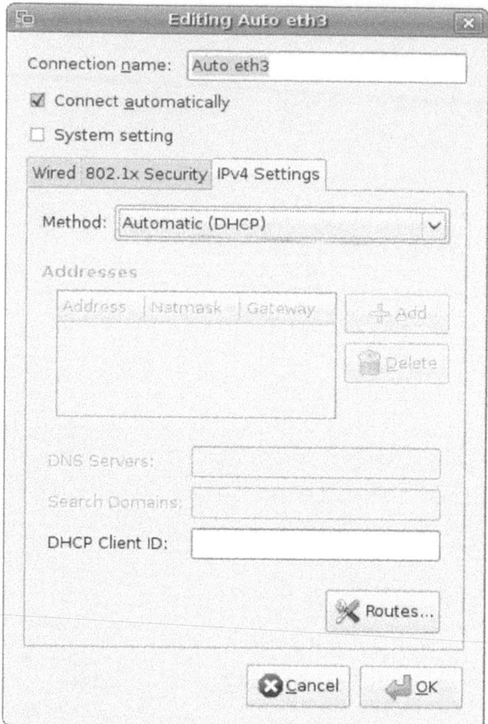

Figure 7.15 IPv4 configuration for eth3 NIC.

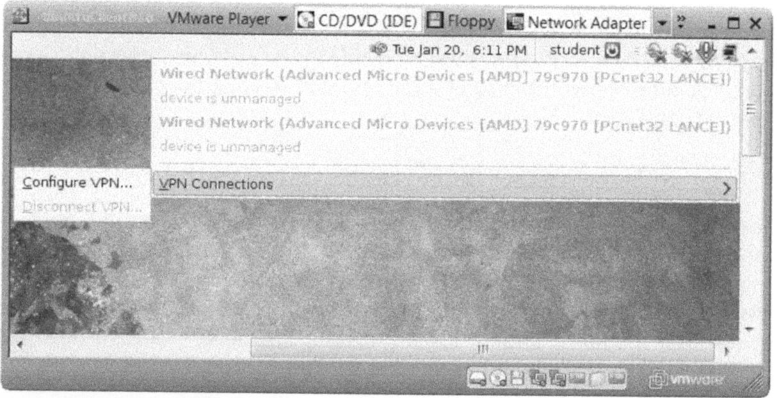

Figure 7.16 VPN configuration link.

configure the Terminal Server Client to match your home network. You may have different values from those displayed in Figure 7.20.

3. After the information is added, click the **Connect** button.
4. You should be able to see the desktop of the remote computer on your screen (Figure 7.21).

After you have logged on the remote desktop, you can run the programs on the remote computer. For example, you can complete a hands-on practice assignment on the remote computer in the campus computer lab from your home.

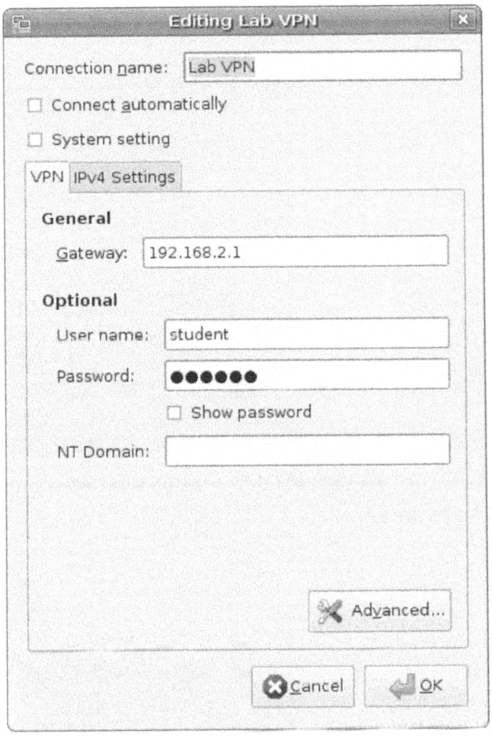

Editing Lab VPN

Connection name: Lab VPN

☐ Connect automatically

☐ System setting

VPN | IPv4 Settings

General

Gateway: 192.168.2.1

Optional

User name: student

Password: ●●●●●●

☐ Show password

NT Domain:

Advanced...

Cancel | OK

Figure 7.17 Lab VPN connection configuration.

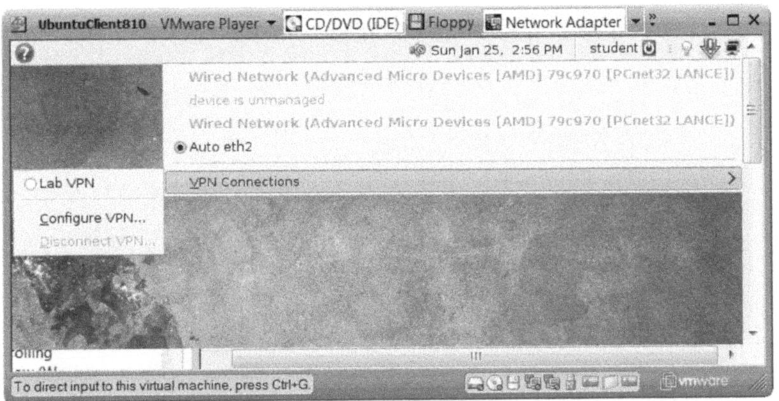

Figure 7.18 Lab VPN connection.

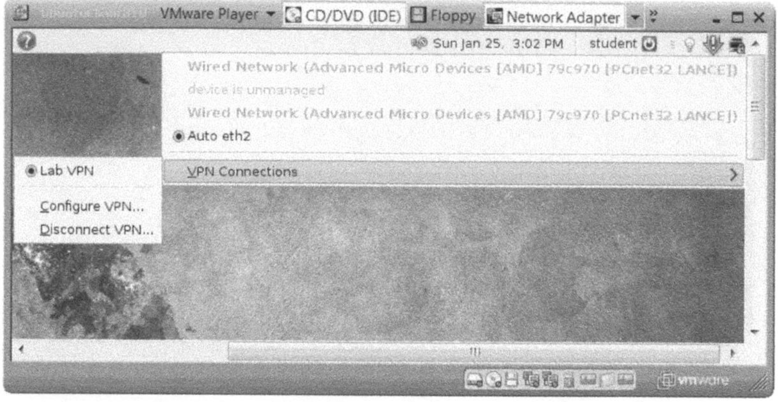

Figure 7.19 Connecting to VPN server.

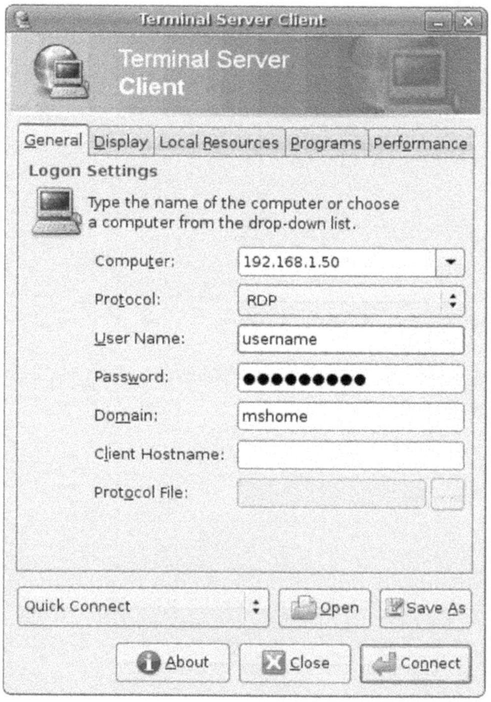

Figure 7.20 Terminal Server Client configuration dialog.

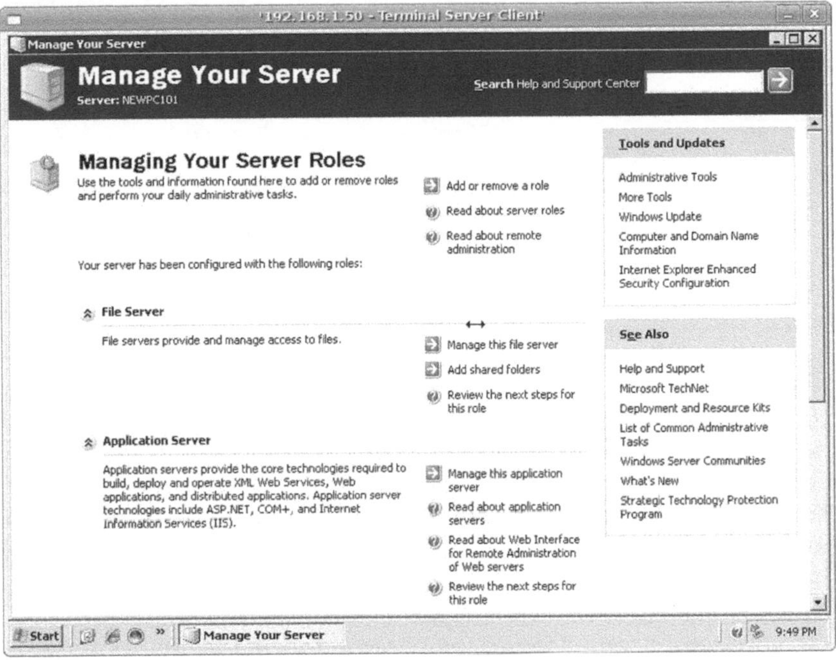

Figure 7.21 Remote desktop.

7.5 Network Address Translation (NAT)

In Chapter 4, in the discussion on IP addressing, it was mentioned that the IP addresses used by intranets and home networks are private IP addresses. The available private IP addresses are listed in Table 7.5.

Table 7.5 Available Private IP Addresses

Block	*Block Range*
Class A Block	10.0.0.0–10.255.255.255
Class B Block	172.16.0.0–172.31.255.255
Class C Block	192.168.0.0–192.168.255.255

As mentioned in Chapter 4, these IP addresses cannot be recognized on the Internet. To allow a computer with a private IP address to access the Internet, the private IP address has to be translated into a public IP address. NAT does the translation.

NAT can be built as a stand-alone device, or built into a router or a firewall, or implemented by a piece of software included in an operating system. Most of the Linux operating systems support NAT technology in one way or another. NAT technology will be discussed next.

7.5.1 NAT Technology

Developed by Cisco, NAT technology is often used by devices, such as firewalls or routers, that link a private network to a public network. When a computer on the private network sends a packet to a destination computer on the public network, the packet contains the private source IP address and the public destination IP address. When passing the packet from the private network to the public network, NAT replaces the private source IP address with the router's public NIC's

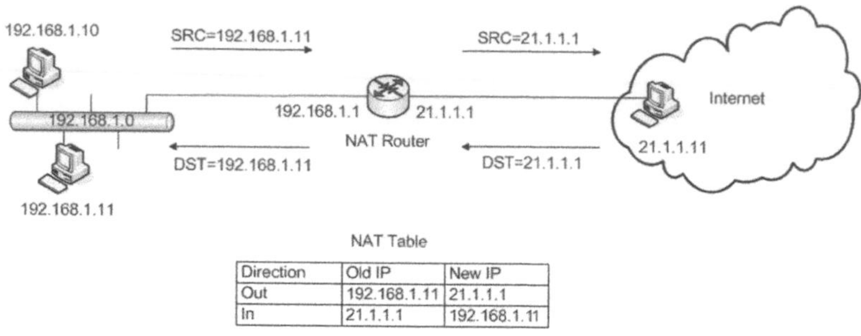

Figure 7.22 NAT translation.

IP address. On the Internet, the source address of the packet is the IP address of the public NIC. NAT uses a table to keep track of the original source IP address and the new source IP address, and the port number used by the transmission process. When the destination computer sends the response back, the destination IP address used by the packet will be the IP address of the public NIC of the router. At the router that connects the private network and the Internet, NAT finds the corresponding original private source IP address in the table and replaces the public IP address of the public NIC on the router with the original source IP address. Then, the return packet is sent to the original sender. Figure 7.22 shows how NAT does the translation for outbound and inbound traffic.

Figure 7.22 illustrates the communication between a computer with a private IP address and a computer with a public IP address.

When two computers on the same private network communicate with the same public computer, the NAT translation (Figure 7.22) will fail. When the public computer returns packets back to the computers on the private network, these packets will use the IP address of the router's public NIC as the destination IP address. When the packets reach the router, NAT translates the destination IP address back to the private IP addresses. However, in the NAT table, there are two private IP addresses corresponding to the same IP address for the router's public IP address. NAT will not be able to figure out which private computer a response packet should go to.

NAT is sophisticated enough to solve the problem by not only translating the IP addresses but also the port numbers used by TCP or UDP. Figure 7.23 illustrates the NAT translation process for multiple computers on the private network communicating with a computer on the public network.

In Figure 7.23, two computers with IP addresses 192.168.1.10 and 192.168.1.11 on the private network are communicating with the same computer on the public network. NAT replaces the source IP address of the packet sent by the computer with IP address 192.168.1.10 with IP address 21.1.1.1:1110. Similarly, the source IP address of the packet sent by the computer with IP address 192.168.1.11 is replaced with IP address 21.1.1.1:1111.

Later, when the computer with IP address 21.1.1.11 on the public network responds to the request carried by the packet with source IP address 21.1.1.1:1110, IP address 21.1.1.1:1110 will be used as the destination address. The same is true for the packet with source IP address 21.1.1.1:1111, which will be used as the destination IP address. The responding packets with destination IP address 21.1.1.1:1110 and the destination IP address 21.1.1.1:1111 are all sent back to the NAT router. If the destination address is 21.1.1.1:1110, NAT will translate it back to 192.168.1.10. Similarly, NAT will translate the destination address 21.1.1.1:1111 to 192.168.1.11. With the private destination addresses, the responding packets can be sent to the dedicated senders. When

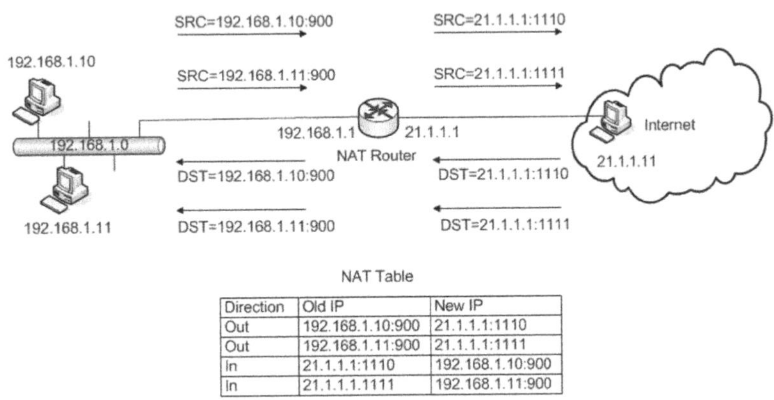

Direction	Old IP	New IP
Out	192.168.1.10:900	21.1.1.1:1110
Out	192.168.1.11:900	21.1.1.1:1111
In	21.1.1.1:1110	192.168.1.10:900
In	21.1.1.1.1111	192.168.1.11:900

Figure 7.23 NAT translation between a group of private computers and one public computer.

using port numbers to identify senders' source IP addresses, NAT is also called Network Address Port Translation (NAPT).

In the foregoing text, we briefly looked at how NAT works. The next section will provide some information on what NAT can do and how to configure NAT for different usages.

7.5.2 NAT Application and Configuration

Based on how you want to use it, NAT can be configured in several different ways. The common usages of NAT are as follows:

- The most common usage of NAT is to allow multiple computers on a private network to access the public network by sharing the same public IP address. This kind of network function is also called IP Masquerade or MASQ.
- With NAT, users on the public network can access the e-mail server or Web server installed on the private network.
- NAT can be used to redirect a packet to a different destination.

There are two ways to configure how to update a NAT table. The NAT table can be updated dynamically. With dynamic update, translations are added dynamically to the NAT table whenever they are available. During the configuration, you need to specify the timeout period for the translations added to the NAT table. After the timeout period, the out-of-date translations will be removed to keep the NAT table manageable. Another way to update the NAT table is by static update: Translations are manually added to the table and stay that way until they are manually modified.

To allow computers on a private network to access the public network, NAT can assign each computer on the private network a unique public IP address (Figure 7.22). This method can be implemented with static NAT, in which the NAT table is manually configured.

NAT can also allow a group of computers on a private network to share one public IP address (Figure 7.23). This second method is known as *overloading*. For the overloading method, the NAT table can be updated dynamically. If there are not many public IP addresses to spare, overloading is the method to use, so that multiple computers on a private network can share the same public IP address.

Sometimes, computers on the public network need to communicate with servers such as Web servers or e-mail servers, which are on private networks. In this case, the computers on the public network become the senders that initialize the communication. During the configuration of NAT, you need to specify the computers on the public network to communicate only with the dedicated Web servers or mail servers on the private networks. The static NAT table update is used to link the computers on the public network to dedicated servers on the private networks. To avoid all the inbound traffic being sent to the dedicated servers, the port numbers used by the servers are used to control the traffic. For example, you can configure all traffic with port number 80 to be sent to the Web server on the private network. Meanwhile, NAT allows computers on the private network to access computers on the public network through overloading. The dynamic method can be used to update the NAT table, except for those translations specified by the static update.

In some situations, servers may not use their popular default ports. For example, the default Web server communicates through port 80. The Web server can be configured to communicate through other ports, for example, port 8080. In such cases, NAT can be configured to translate the port number attached to the source IP address of a packet to a different port number. When NAT is used to redirect a packet to a different server, the static method can be used to configure the NAT translation process. The configuration of redirection should be done in both directions. For example, if an inbound packet has the source address 21.1.1.1:80, NAT should be configured to translate 21.1.1.1.:80 to 21.1.1.1:8080. On the other hand, NAT should be configured to translate outbound traffic with IP address 192.168.1.1:8080 to the IP address 21.1.1.1:80.

Having the ability to redirect network traffic, NAT can be used to control network traffic to dedicated destinations. For example, while replacing an existing server or router with a new one, if the new device has a different IP address or is on a different LAN segment, all the hosts on the client side need to be reconfigured to include the new IP address in the application software or network interface cards. If there are many hosts on the network, the reconfiguration is not an easy job. A simpler solution is to use NAT to redirect all the network traffic that goes to the old server or router to the IP address for the new device. In this way, the traffic will be forwarded to the new device without interrupting front-end users.

Because NAT is the interface between a private network and a public network, the first configuration task is to make sure that two NICs are installed and properly configured for each network. It is not necessary to let each host on the private network access the public network. When configuring NAT, you can specify the range of source IP addresses from the private network to be translated to the public IP address. Similarly, you can specify a list of available public IP addresses for the translation procedure.

The last step in the configuration process is to check if the NAT configuration works as required. You may test the connection linking the private and public networks by sending packets to a destination. If an error occurs, you can view the NAT table to see if it is a configuration error. You can also capture network traffic with network monitoring tools to identify the problem. Also, remember that if the IPSec protocol is used as the VPN tunneling protocol, it often will not work properly with NAT technology.

A hands-on activity is now provided for exploring the details of the configuration of NAT. Through this hands-on activity, you can get first-hand experience with NAT and enhance your understanding of NAT technology.

Activity 7.4 NAT Service

In this hands-on practice, you will implement the NAT service on the server machine. The server machine connects two networks identified by IDs 192.168.1.0 and 192.168.2.0. For demonstration purposes, you will configure the server machine to perform the NAT function. Consider the network 192.168.2.0 as the private network and the network 192.168.1.0 as the public network (it is not, however, a real public network). The following are the steps to configure NAT:

1. Log on to the server machine with username **student** and password **ubuntu**.
2. For the configuration of the server machine, you need to make sure that the server machine can forward a received packet. In Chapter 6, the server machine was configured to enable packet forwarding. To verify this, run the following command:

   ```
   sudo sysctl net.ipv4.ip_forward
   ```

   You should be able to see the result shown in Figure 7.24.

   If IP forwarding is not enabled (i.e., if the result is equal to 0), edit the configuration file by entering the following command:

   ```
   sudo gedit /etc/sysctl.conf
   ```

   When the file is opened, uncomment the line

   ```
   #net.ipv4.ip_forward=1
   ```

   by removing the # sign in front of the line. Then, restart the server machine, and run the preceding testing command.
3. Next, you need to enable "masquerade" in the routing table. To do so, execute the following command:

   ```
   sudo gedit /etc/rc.local
   ```

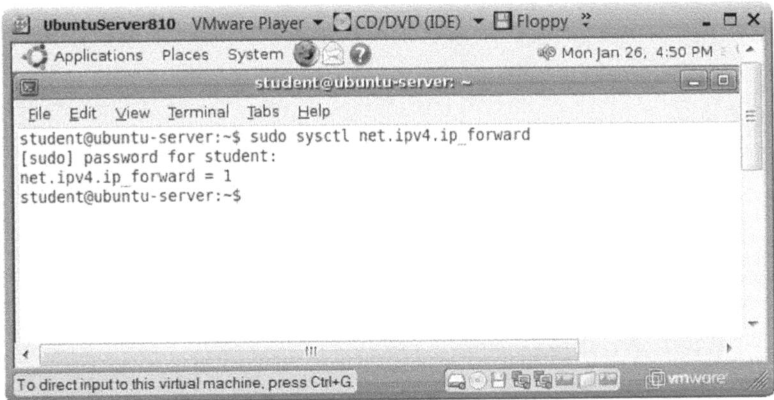

Figure 7.24 Verifying IP forwarding.

4. Add these two commands above the line exit 0:

```
/sbin/iptables -P FORWARD ACCEPT
/sbin/iptables -table nat -A POSTROUTING -o eth1 -j MASQUERADE
```

   Save the changes, and quit the editor. The options used in those two commands have the following meanings:
   - -P: Chain target
   - -A: Append
   - -o: Output NIC name
   - -j: Jump to a specified target
5. Then, reboot the server machine by executing the following command:

```
sudo reboot
```

Now, the NAT on the server is configured. Your next task is to configure the client machine. On the client side, you need to make sure that the client machine can communicate with the private NIC in the server machine. The following steps show you how to configure the client machine:

1. Log on to the client machine with username **student** and password **ubuntu.**
2. Configure the NIC eth2 on the client computer to take the static IP address 192.168.2.2. To do so, edit the following file:

```
sudo gedit /etc/network/interfaces
```

3. Comment out the lines for the DHCP configuration, and add the lines for static IP address shown as in Figure 7.25. Then, save the changes, and quit the editor.
4. To make the configuration take effect, execute the following command:

```
sudo /etc/init.d/networking restart
```

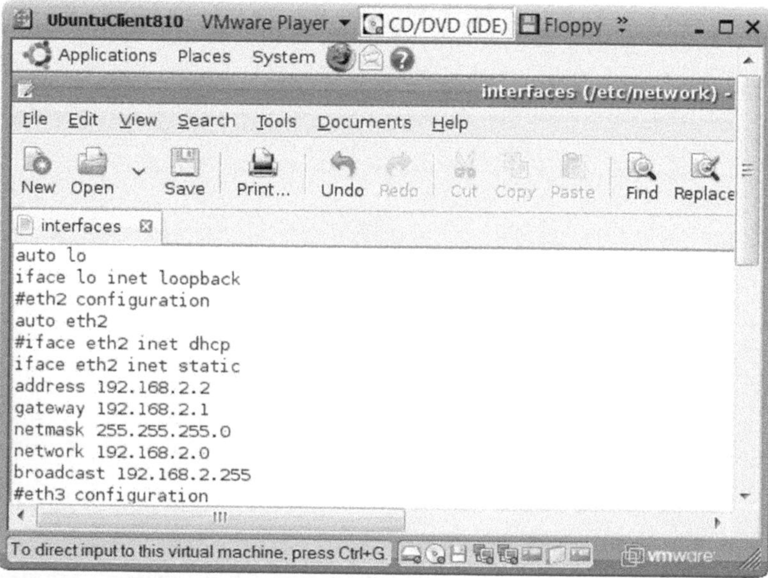

Figure 7.25 Static configuration of eth2 NIC.

5. To verify that the client machine can communicate with the server machine on the network 192.168.2.0, execute the following command:

```
ping -c 5 192.168.2.1
```

   You should be able to see the response from the server machine.
6. After the NIC on the client is configured, you may try to ping your DSL router. For example, run the following command:

```
ping -c 5 192.168.1.1
```

   You should be able see the response from your DSL router.
7. To verify that you can access the Internet from the network 192.168.2.0, start your Web browser and enter the URL:

   http://www.ubuntu.com/

   You should be able to get the result shown in Figure 7.26.

This hands-on practice has demonstrated how to configure NAT to allow computers on a private network to access the Internet. In the hands-on practice, the server machine is configured to allow IP forwarding. You also enabled masquerade on the server machine. On the client machine, the NIC on the client machine is configured so that you can ping the server machine from the client machine. After the configuration was completed, you were able to access the Internet from the client machine, which is on the private network 192.168.2.0.

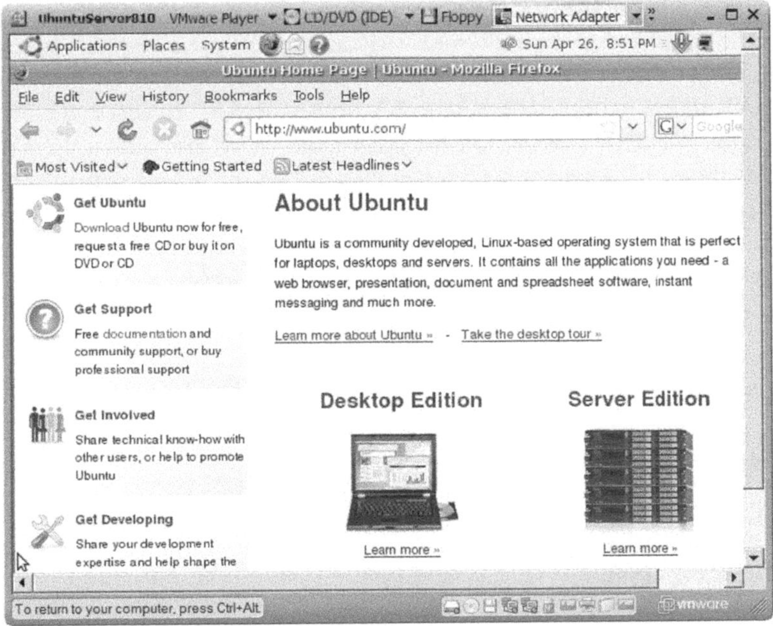

Figure 7.26 Result of NAT configuration.

7.6 Summary

This chapter discussed several network services that can be used to share network resources. On a UNIX like network, the Network File System (NFS) service allows network hosts to share files, directories, and hard drives exported by an NFS server. After an NFS client mounts the exported directories or hard drives, the user on that client computer can work on the files stored on the server as if these files were stored on the NFS client computer. NFS allows users to log on to a server from any computer on the network. With NFS, companies and universities can implement a thin-client network computing system, which greatly simplifies network management and reduces the cost of construction and management.

The second service introduced in this chapter was the Samba service, which allows Linux computers to share network resources such as files and printers with Windows computers. The Samba service also allows a wide range of applications to share files over the Internet. With Samba, Linux computers can become members of the Windows domain or can even become domain controllers to perform authentication tasks for Windows as well as Linux clients. Samba can also be configured to allow Linux computers and Windows computers to share the same hard drive.

VPN is a service that allows client computers to share network resources stored on a private network. Through the public Internet, users at home can log on to the computers on an organization's private network. VPN uses data encryption and authentication methods to protect the confidentiality and integrity of data. It has satisfactory performance. The configuration of VPN is relatively simple. This chapter also examined some VPN-related technologies. The hands-on practice dealt with the VPN configuration-related issues to enhance understanding of the VPN service.

The last topic covered in this chapter was NAT, which allows computers on private networks to access resources on a public network such as the Internet. With NAT, the private source IP address in a packet can be translated to a public source IP address. When a response is received, NAT translates the public destination IP address back to the private IP address. By properly translating IP addresses, NAT allows multiple computers on a private network to access the public network by sharing the same public IP address. On the other hand, NAT also allows users on the public network to access the e-mail server or Web server installed on the private network. NAT can also be used to redirect packets to different destinations.

Now that you have learned these network resource sharing and remote access services, your next task is to learn about the Web-related topics such as Web servers and browsers. Web-related topics will be covered in Chapter 8.

Review Questions

1. How does NFS work?
2. Briefly describe three NFS applications.
3. What are the NFS server configuration tasks?
4. Explain the meanings of the following parameters: root_squash, sync, and subtree_check in the file /etc/exports.
5. What are the NFS client configuration tasks?
6. What is Server Message Block (SMB)?
7. What are the features provided by Samba?
8. In what situations is Samba not necessary?
9. Why do users prefer to use smbfs on client computers?
10. What is the name of the Samba server configuration file? What are the logical sections included in the configuration file?

11. When compared with dial-up remote access, what are the advantages of a VPN?
12. How does a VPN work?
13. What are the three protocols used in a tunneling protocol?
14. When used as a tunneling protocol, what are the advantages and disadvantages of IPSec?
15. When used as a tunneling protocol, what are the advantages and disadvantages of the Secure Sockets Layer (SSL)?
16. When used as a tunneling protocol, what are the advantages and disadvantages of the Point-to-Point Tunneling Protocol (PPTP)?
17. How does NAT work?
18. Why do we need NAPT?
19. What are the common usages of NAT?
20. Describe two ways to update an NAT table.

Case Study Projects

The following are two networking projects that involve network resource sharing:

Case Study Project 7.1. Create a VPN server for your home network so that you can access your home network from school or the place where you work.

Case Study Project 7.2. Implement the NAT service for your home network so that all the computers on your home network can access the Internet.

Chapter 8

Internet Services

Objectives

- Set up Web servers, and develop Web-related services.
- Implement the FTP service.
- Install and configure e-mail services.

8.1 Introduction

The previous chapter covers topics related to network resource sharing and remote access. The technologies used for remote access link the private network to the public network, and vice versa. In this chapter, attention will be focused on services related to the public network, that is, the Internet. This chapter will cover some commonly used Internet technologies such as World Wide Web, File Transfer Protocol (FTP), and e-mail services. These public network services enable universities to implement online teaching and learning, and companies to carry out their business online. This chapter uses three sections to discuss these important Internet-related services.

The first section after the Introduction section in this chapter discusses World Wide Web (WWW)-related topics. We will first take a closer look at the Web server. This chapter will demonstrate how a Web server works. It will review different types of Web servers. It will provide information about Web server installation, configuration, implementation, and management. Some commonly used services provided by Web servers will also be examined. To enhance understanding of the World Wide Web, this chapter will include a hands-on activity for the reader to create his or her Web server.

The next section is about File Transfer Protocol (FTP). After a brief introduction to how FTP works, this section will introduce various FTP technologies. The advantages and disadvantages of FTP will also be examined. This section will discuss the issues related to FTP installation, configuration, and management. Later in this section, a hands-on activity will show the reader how to install and configure an FTP service with Ubuntu Linux.

The Linux operating system can be used to support various e-mail services. The next section of this chapter will introduce some commonly supported e-mail servers. It will get into some details on how an e-mail server works and how e-mail clients communicate with the e-mail server. After it has reviewed the concepts related to the e-mail server, this section will discuss installation and configuration procedures. It will take a closer look at the configuration files on the e-mail server and explain the meanings of the parameters in them. The installation and configuration on the e-mail client side will also be discussed. By following the step-by-step instructions in the hands-on practice, readers will learn how to set up an e-mail server and e-mail client.

The discussion will start with the Web. Details about Web server installation and configuration will be covered in the hands-on practice included in the following section.

8.2 Web Services

The World Wide Web, also known as the Web or WWW, is basically a system of interlinked hypertext documents. One can follow the link to go from document to document. The hypertext documents are also called Web pages. Each Web page on the Internet has a unique name, such as

http://www.google.com/intl/en/about.html

The unique name is called Universal Resource Locator (URL). A URL consists of four components. For example:

- *http:* The protocol used to handle requests.
- *www.google.com:* The Web server's name.
- */intl/en/:* The directory used to host the Web pages.
- *about.html:* The names of the files stored on the Web server. Sometimes, these files are also called *resources*.

In a Web system, the Internet links clients to Web servers, which deliver Web pages to the clients. Web pages are stored on server machines. Once a URL is entered into a Web browser, the browser will forward the Web server's name to a DNS server to get the server's IP address. With the returned IP address, the Web browser will establish a connection to the Web server on port 80. The protocol used to handle the request and response is called Hypertext Transfer Protocol (HTTP). The protocol HTTP will send the Web server a request for the file specified by the Web browser. When the client's request for a certain Web page arrives at the Web server, the Web server knows where to find the Web page by searching the path and file name. Once the file is found, it will be returned to the client by HTTP through the Internet. The client can view the Web page through the Web browser, which displays the content of the Web page in a predefined format, using a markup language such as HTML.

When Web server software such as Apache is installed on a server machine, the server machine becomes a Web server. The Linux operating system is a great platform for supporting Web server software as well as Web browsers, because of its strong secure features. The following will discuss Web-server-related topics.

8.2.1 Hypertext Transfer Protocol (HTTP)

The Web server software installed on a server machine can be used to process requests sent by a Web browser. The requests and responses are transmitted over the network by the HTTP protocol. HTTP can perform five basic operations:

- *HEAD:* This operation asks for status information about a Web page stored on a Web server.
- *GET:* This operation requests a specified Web page from a Web server.
- *POST:* The operation sends data to a Web server, which will insert the data in an application such as an HTML form.
- *PUT:* The operation uploads a Web page to a Web server, which will link the Web page to a specified URL.
- *OPTIONS:* This operation requests information about the available communication options.

HTTP also defines a few other operations that are not used as often as the foregoing operations. An HTTP server is required to implement at least the GET and HEAD operations.

8.2.2 Web Servers

Many of the Internet-related computing tasks are supported by Web servers, which use HTTP to communicate with Web browsers. In general, a Web server can perform the following tasks:

- Authenticate the client who is sending requests for certain Web pages.
- Accept the requests conveyed to it by HTTP.
- Verify the requests. If an error is detected, a message will be sent back to the client.
- Search for Web pages based on the requests. The Web pages and other resources are stored in a directory in the Linux file system. The path to the directory can be specified in the configuration file http.conf.
- Pass commands and data to port 80 in plaintext. To improve security, the Web server can use the protocol HTTPS to establish a secure connection between the client and server through port 443.
- For a dynamic Web page, compile and run programs to support dynamic activities.
- Prepare the response document to be returned by using HTTP.
- Compress the response document to reduce network traffic.
- Create virtual hosts to allow the same virtual machine to host multiple Web sites with different domain names.
- Log the receiving and responding processes.
- Perform bandwidth throttling to control the number of requests that a server can respond to during a specified time period.

The top five Web server software packages are Apache, Microsoft IIS, Google, Lighttpd, and Sun. Most Linux distributions include Web server software. Apache is the most used Web server software. Apache and Microsoft IIS together have over 85% market share. Apache is fully supported by Linux. Lighttpd is Web server software that is designed for speed-critical environments.

As Web server software, Apache can be used to deliver files, display Web pages, and manage Web sites on the Internet. In addition to delivering HTML documents to Web browsers, it can also deliver files in other formats such as audio, video, graphics, zip files, and computer programs. To handle the sophisticated computational logic, Apache can also be used to create, edit, and run code created with programming languages such as Perl, HyperText Preprocessor (PHP), Python, Ruby, and other scripting languages. Apache also allows the Web server administrator to manage user accounts, Web pages and other resources, and security measures.

Supported by Linux, Apache is often used with open source software packages such as the database management system MySQL, the programming languages PHP, Python, and Perl. Together, they form a powerful application development platform for developing Web-based applications.

To install, configure, and implement the Apache Web server software on a Linux server, you need to know the functions of the Apache Web server packages, for example, how to store resources, how to activate the Web server, how to run third-party code, and how to enforce security measures to protect the Web server.

The following are Apache Web server packages that can be installed on Linux computers:

- *apache2:* This Apache Web server package is used for basic installation.
- *apache2-prefork or apache-worker:* This Apache Web server package is designed for tasks that involve multiprocessing.
- *apache2-devel:* This package includes the tools to support module development and compilation of the third-party modules.
- *apache2-doc:* This package contains the Apache Web server documents.

After the Apache Web server is installed, you can enter the URL

http://localhost/

to check if the Apache server is activated. If the Apache example page does not show up, you need to activate the Apache Web server. Later, the hands-on practice will demonstrate how to activate the Apache server.

Apache can extend its functionalities by running a wide range of modules written in different programming languages such as Perl, PHP, Python, or Ruby. In fact, most Apache functions are handled by running various modules. Due to its capability of running a variety of modules, Apache can handle tasks beyond what a Web server can accomplish. For example, in addition to handling HTTP, Apache can handle the protocol POP3 for mail and FTP for file transfer.

A Web server is the interface between the public Internet and the private network. It is often an easier target for hackers to attach. Apache provides various functionalities to improve security. It allows users to disable an unused service or even an unused Web server. Apache can also limit access to directories that are used to store Web pages, other resources, and log files. It also upgrades itself in a timely manner against viruses and other vulnerabilities.

8.2.3 Web Server Configuration

The configuration of the Apache Web server can be done in the file /etc/apache2/apache2.conf. In this file, you can directly edit the configuration of directives, or include other files containing the configuration of directives. The following are some commonly used directives to be configured for the Apache Web server:

- *VirtualHost:* Apache supports virtual hosts, which allow a Web server host multiple Web sites on a single computer. The name of the default virtual host provided by Apache2 can be modified to a name that fits your requirements. You can also use the default virtual host as a template for quickly creating other Web sites. Information about the default virtual host is included in the file /etc/apache2/sites-available/default.
- *ServerAdmin:* This directive is used to specify the server administrator's e-mail address that will appear on the Web site. The default value for the SeverAdmin directive is webmaster@ localhost. In case an error occurs, the specified e-mail address will be displayed on the error report page so that the user can report the error to the Web server administrator. You can configure the ServerAdmin directive in the file /etc/apache2/sites-available.
- *Listen:* The Listen directive can be used to specify the port number to which the Web server should listen. You may also specify the IP address that the Web server should communicate with. If the IP address is not specified, Apache2 will communicate with the IP address of the host computer. The default port for a Web server is 80. You can configure the Listen directive in the file /etc/apache2/ports.conf.
- *ServerName:* This directive allows the user to specify the fully qualified domain name (FQDN) for the Web site. No FQDN is specified for the default virtual host. To give your Web site a specific name, you need to add the ServerName directive in the file /etc/apache2/sites-available/mysite and include this file in the configuration file /etc/apache2/apache2.conf.
- *ServerAlias:* To use the www prefix in the Web site name, you need to specify the directive ServerAlias. This directive can also be specified in the file /etc/apache2/sites-available/mysite.
- *DocumentRoot:* This directive specifies the directory where Web page files are stored. The directories where Web pages and other resources are stored vary from one Linux distribution to another. /var/www is called the document root directory. The files that are placed in the document root directory can be shared by other users through the Internet.
- *RedirectMatch:* If you want to use a different directory to store Web pages, you can specify RedirectMatch in the configuration file /etc/apache2/apache2.conf. Then, all requests for the Web pages will be redirected to that directory.
- *DirectoryIndex:* This directive specifies the directory index page. If specified, the directory index page will be displayed when a user enters a URL with / at the end of the directory name, such as http://www.servername.com/directoryname/. The default directory index page is index.html, which is specified in the file /etc/apache2/apache2.conf.
- *ErrorDocument:* This directive can be used to specify the error information page. For example, the commonly seen 404 error report for not being able to locate a Web page has the error information page /usr/share/apache2/error/HTTP_NOT_FOUND.html.var.
- *CustomLog:* This directive can be used to specify the directory that stores log files. The default directory for the Apache log is /var/log/apache2.
- *ErrorLog:* This directive is used to specify the directory that stores error log files. The default directory for the Apache log is again /var/log/apache2.
- *Directory:* It is used to configure options within a specified directory. The commonly used options that can be configured for a directory include ExecCGI for the execution of CGI scripts. The default directory for the CGI scripts is /usr/lib/cgi-bin. The Includes option allows an HTML file to include other files. If there is no DirectoryIndex directive specified,

the option index will display a list of the current directory's contents. The multiview option allows a resource to be displayed in multiple representations.

- *LockFile:* When the log files are saved to an NFS shared folder, the default path to the lock file should be updated accordingly. The directive can be used to specify a path to a directory on the local disk.
- *User:* The User directive can be used to specify user IDs.
- *LoadModule:* This directive adds modules to the list of active modules to extend the functionalities of the Web server.

There are many other options for the configuration of Apache. Detailed coverage of these options is beyond the scope of this book. To illustrate the configuration of Apache, a hands-on activity is created in the following section that demonstrates how to install and configure it.

Activity 8.1 Apache Web Server

This hands-on practice will show you how to set up the Apache Web server. By the end of the hands-on practice, you should have a working Web server. You will also have a chance to experiment with the configuration of a virtual host. The first task in this hands-on practice is to install Apache2. The following steps show you how to accomplish the installation tasks:

1. Log on to the server machine with username **student** and password **ubuntu.**
2. To install the Apache2 on the server machine, enter the following command:

   ```
   sudo apt-get install apache2
   ```

3. To make sure that the Web server is running, enter the following command:

   ```
   sudo /etc/init.d/apache2 restart
   ```

4. To make sure that the name service is working properly, enter the following command to open the configuration file of the resolver.

   ```
   sudo gedit /etc/resolv.conf
   ```

5. After the file is opened, overwrite the existing content in that file with the following lines:

   ```
   search group2.lab
   nameserver 192.168.2.1
   ```

   After the code is entered, click the **Save** menu. Then, click the **File** menu, and select **Quit.**
6. To view the default Web page for the Apache Web server, double-click the **Firefox Web Browser** icon, which is located on the menu bar.
7. Enter the following URL:

   http://ns1.group2.lab

   Press the **Enter** key, and you should be able to see the default Web page shown in Figure 8.1.

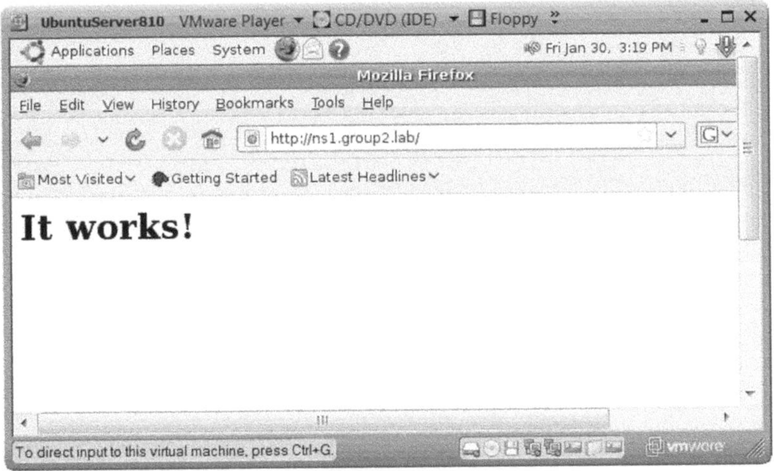

Figure 8.1 Default Web page.

In the foregoing steps, you have successfully installed the Apache Web server. You can access the Web server from the client machine. Follow these steps to access the newly created Apache Web server:

1. Log on to the client machine with username **student** and password **ubuntu**.
2. Make sure the name service is working properly. You need to check the configuration file resolv.conf by entering the following command:

```
sudo gedit /etc/resolv.conf
```

3. After the file is opened, overwrite the existing content in that file with the following lines:

```
search group2.lab
nameserver 192.168.2.1
```

   After the code is entered, click the **Save** menu. Then click the **File** menu, and select **Quit**.
4. Start the Web browser on the client machine by clicking the Firefox Web Browser icon on the menu bar. After the Web browser is opened, enter the following URL:

   http://ns1.group2.lab

   You will have the default Web page shown on the client machine (Figure 8.2).

Your next task is to experiment with a virtual host. You will create a virtual host called myvirtualhost on the same server machine. You can start your experiment by following these steps:

1. Log on to the server machine with username **student** and password **ubuntu**.
2. To find the IP address of the NIC eth0, execute the following command in the terminal window:

```
sudo ifconfig
```

   Record the IP address for the NIC eth0.

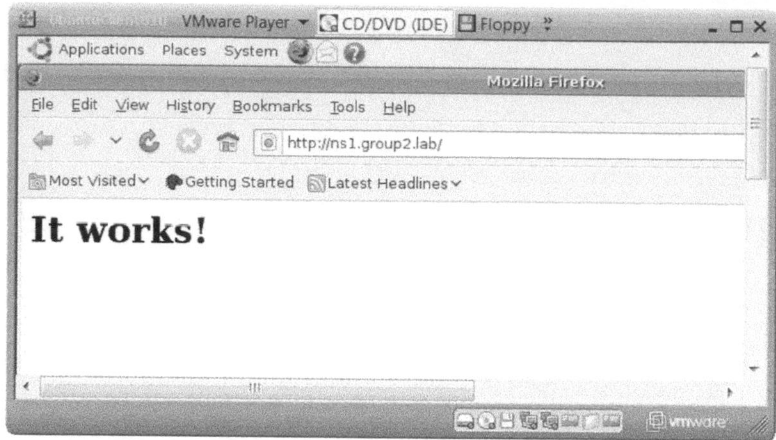

Figure 8.2 Accessing Apache Web server.

3. You will first create a virtual host configuration file in the directory /etc/apache2/sites-available. To do so, enter the following command to navigate to the directory /etc/apache2/sites-available:

```
cd /etc/apache2/sites-available
```

Then, execute the following command to recreate a configuration file called myvirtualhost.group2.lab.conf:

```
sudo gedit myvirtualhost.group2.lab.conf
```

4. You have just opened an empty file in which you can add the following configuration information for the VirtualHost directive. Here, we assume that the IP address for eth0 is 192.168.1.2.

```
<VirtualHost 192.168.1.2:80>
       ServerAdmin webmaster@ns1.group2.lab
       ServerName myvirtualhost.group2.lab
       ServerAlias www.myvirtualhost.group2.lab
       DocumentRoot /var/www/myvirtualhost/
       CustomLog /var/log/apache2/group2.lab.log combined
</VirtualHost>
```

Save the configuration and quit. The IP address in the VirtualHost tag is the IP address of the network interface card eth0. The IP address may be different on your computer.

5. After the configuration file is saved to the directory /etc/apache2/sites-available, you need to enable the configuration. To do so, enter the following command to navigate to the directory /etc/apache2/sites-enabled:

```
cd /etc/apache2/sites-enabled/
```

6. In the directory /etc/apache2/sites-enabled/, you can create a link to the file myvirtualhost.group2.lab.conf in the directory /etc/apache2/sites-available/. By doing so, you can enable the virtual host with the configuration specified in the file myvirtualhost.group2.lab. Use the following command to accomplish this task:

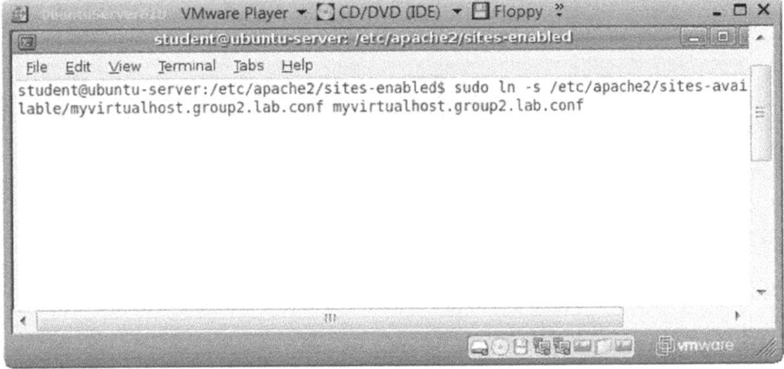

Figure 8.3 Linking to configuration file.

```
sudo ln -s /etc/apache2/sites-available/myvirtualhost.group2.lab.conf
myvirtualhost.group2.lab.conf
```

Be aware that there is a space between two file names, as shown in Figure 8.3.

The command ln -s symbolically links the enabled files in the directory /etc/apache2/sites-enabled/ to the available files in the directory /etc/apache2/sites-available/. The files in the directory /sites-available may not necessarily be enabled. By making a link, you can disable a virtual host in the directory /sites-enabled and still retain the configuration settings in the directory /sites-available.

7. To allow the client machine to view the virtual host's Web page, you need to assign a name for the server machine. To do so, you need to edit the file /etc/hosts. Enter the following command:

```
sudo gedit /etc/hosts
```

8. Add the names of the Web server after the name localhost, as shown in Figure 8.4. Save the changes and quit.

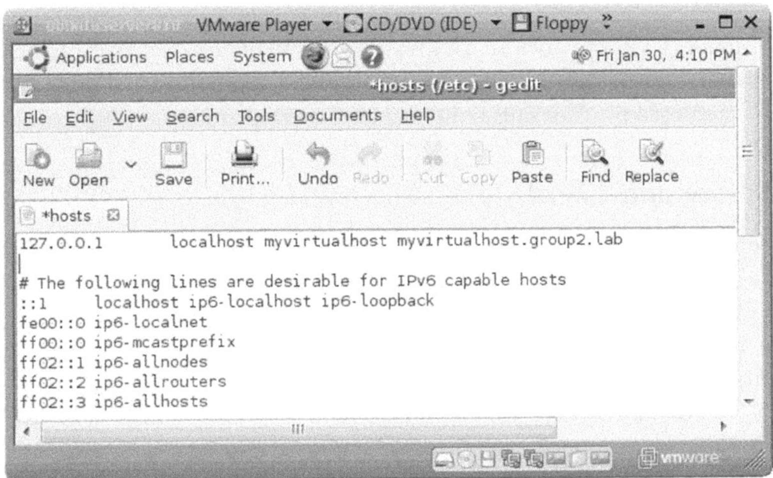

Figure 8.4 Naming server machine.

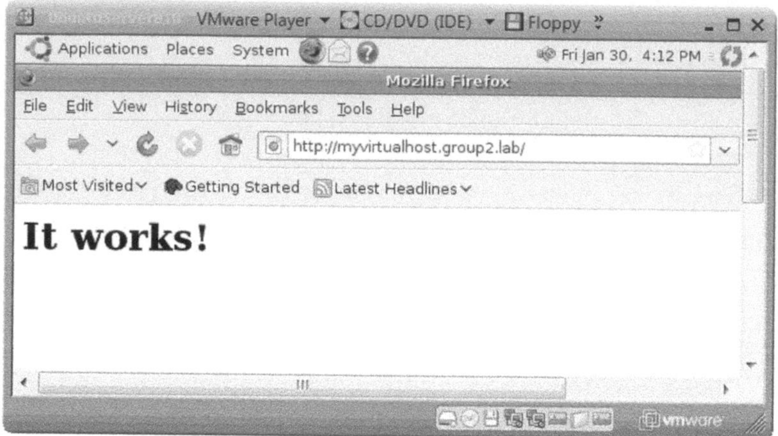

Figure 8.5 Testing virtual host.

9. You can now restart Apache by entering the following command:

```
sudo /etc/init.d/apache2 reload
```

10. To test the virtual host, click the Firefox Web browser icon on the menu bar. After the browser loads, enter the following URL:

```
http://myvirtualhost.group2.lab
```

You should be able to get the default Web page shown in Figure 8.5.

In the preceding activity, you have installed and configured the Apache2 Web server and the virtual host. In the next section, you are going to learn about another commonly used Web-based service, File Transfer Protocol (FTP).

8.3 File Transfer Service

File Transfer Protocol (FTP) provides an easy way to exchange files over the Internet. The advantages of FTP are that it is relatively easy to implement, and it is supported by most of the operating systems. FTP is often used by Web sites to upload and download files.

8.3.1 FTP Server and Client

There are two components in an FTP service, the FTP server and FTP client. The FTP server performs the following tasks:

- Hosting FTP sites that the client can access through the Internet
- Making files available for FTP clients to download
- Receiving connection requests from FTP clients
- Managing FTP user accounts
- Managing files and directories

For a client who has an account on the FTP server, he or she can log on to the FTP server with his or her username and password. The FTP server decides which files are available to the public and which files are kept private. It also decides when and where the public can access the files. Users with accounts on the FTP server may be allowed to access some of the protected files. Some FTP servers also allow anonymous clients to access them with minimal privileges, mostly just for downloading publicly available files. Sometimes, anonymous users are asked to submit their e-mail addresses as passwords to log on to FTP servers.

An FTP server can be accessed through a Web browser or through the FTP client software. The FTP client software allows users to upload and download files through the Internet. It allows users to search for files on both the FTP server machine and the FTP client machine. With the FTP client software, users can transfer files by simply dragging and dropping the files from the directory on the client side to the directory on the server side, and vice versa. The FTP client software allows users to transfer multiple files at once. It also provides tools for file management, user management, and security enforcement.

Web browsers are also used to access FTP servers for downloading files posted by the FTP servers. When users want to download files from an FTP server, they can enter the URL in a Web browser with the prefix ftp:// in front of the name of the FTP server instead of commonly seen http:// prefix.

8.3.2 FTP Connection

The connection that links an FTP client to an FTP server can be set in three different modes. Depending on the type of transaction, data can be transferred in the active, passive, or extended passive mode:

- *Active mode:* When initiating a connection, the FTP client sends a temporary port number to the FTP server so that the server can communicate with the client through that port number. On the server side, the FTP server binds that port to the default FTP port 20.
- *Passive mode:* In this mode, the FTP server opens a temporary port and sends the server's IP address to the FTP clients. On the client side, the temporary port will be bound to the port used by the client.
- *Extended passive mode:* This connection mode is similar to the passive mode. The difference is that the FTP server only opens a temporary port without sending the server's IP address to the FTP clients. The FTP client has to assume that the FTP connection is using the same IP address to which the client was originally connected.

8.3.3 FTP Commands

Once the connection is established between the FTP client and the FTP server, the user will be able to execute some commands to perform certain tasks. Table 8.1 lists some commonly used FTP commands and their usages.

8.3.4 FTP Configuration

The configuration of FTP can be done in the configuration file vsftpd.conf. In this file, you can configure the following activities performed by an FTP server:

Table 8.1 FTP Commands

Command	*Usage*
?	Displays a help message describing the FTP commands
append	Appends a local file to a file on a remote machine
ascii	Sets the file transfer type as ASCII
binary	Sets the file transfer type as binary
bye	Ends the file transfer session and exits the FTP environment
cd	Changes the working directory on the remote machine
cdup	Changes the working directory to the parent directory
close	Ends the file transfer session, but does not exit the FTP environment
delete	Deletes a file in the current directory on the remote machine
get	Copies a file from the remote machine to the local machine
help	Displays the help information, similar to the ? command
lcd	Changes the working directory on the local machine
ls	Lists the file names in the directory on the remote machine
mkdir	Makes a new directory on the remote machine
mget	Copies multiple files from the remote machine to the local machine
mput	Copies multiple files from the local machine to the remote machine
open	Opens a connection to a remote machine
put	Copies a file from the local machine to the remote machine
pwd	Displays the pathname of the current directory on the remote machine
quit	Ends the file transfer session and exits the FTP environment
rename	Renames a file on the remote machine
rmdir	Removes a directory on the remote machine
status	Displays the current status of the FTP environment

- *anonymous_enable:* It allows any remote user to log on to the FTP server with anonymous as username and the user's e-mail address as password. When this directive is set to NO, the anonymous login is disabled.
- *anon_root:* If the anonymous login is enabled, this directive specifies the default directory for the anonymous login. The default directory for anonymous is /var/ftp.
- *anon_upload_enable:* By default, the user with the anonymous login can only download files from the FTP server. When set to YES, the directive allows the anonymous account to upload files.

- *chroot_local_user:* To enhance security for the system, the chroot command redirects the root mount point / to a different directory. If this directive is set to YES, local users cannot access or name files outside their home directory.
- *xferlog_file:* By default, the FTP server stores the log file to the directory /var/log/vsftpd.log. This directive can specify a directory for storing log files.
- *userlist_deny or userlist_allow:* These directives deny or allow users listed in the userlist to log on to the FTP server.
- *ssl_enable:* This directive enables SSL. If access to the FTP server through the Internet is allowed, you have to set ssl_enable to YES to encrypt the data transmitted through the Internet.
- *local_enable:* If set to YES, this directive enables local users to log on to the FTP server.
- *write_enable:* If set to YES, this directive allows FTP commands such as STOR to write to the file system.

In the vsftpd.conf configuration file, there are many other directives that can be configured to specify activities. The comments in the file provide some information about these directives.

Activity 8.2 FTP Service

In this hands-on activity, you will develop an FTP service that allows the user to transfer files through a network. You will install and configure the FTP daemon vsftpd so that it can be used as an FTP server. The following are the steps to accomplish this task:

1. Log on to the server machine with username **student** and password **ubuntu**.
2. To install the daemon vsftpd, execute the following command:

   ```
   sudo apt-get install vsftpd
   ```

3. To configure the daemon vsftpd, you need to edit the file vsftpd.conf. Enter the following command to edit the file:

   ```
   sudo gedit /etc/vsftpd.conf
   ```

4. After the file is opened, remove the # sign in front of the following lines:

   ```
   local_enable=YES
   write_enable=YES
   chroot_local_user=YES
   ```

   Also, disable the anonymous logon to the FTP server by setting the anonymous_enable to No:

   ```
   anonymous_enable=NO
   ```

   Save the changes and quit.
5. Enter the following command to restart vsftpd:

   ```
   sudo /etc/init.d/vsftpd restart
   ```

These steps complete the configuration of the FTP server. You can now log on to the client machine to test the server:

Figure 8.6 Configuring server connection.

1. Log on to the client machine with username **student** and password **ubuntu**.
2. There is more than one way to connect to the FTP server. You can connect to the FTP server through the network server connection. Click the **Places** menu, and select **Connect to Server** to open the Connect to Server dialog.
3. In the Connect to Server dialog, select **FTP (with login)** from the Service type drop-down list, enter **ns1.group2.lab** in the Server text box, and enter **student** in the User Name text box shown in Figure 8.6.
4. Click the **Connect** button to open the Enter Password dialog shown in Figure 8.7.
5. Enter the password **ubuntu**, and click the **Connect** button. You should be able to see the content in the student user's home directory (Figure 8.8).
6. You can also access the FTP server through a Web browser. Open the Firefox Web browser, and enter the URL ftp://ns1.group2.lab. After entering the username **student** and password **ubuntu**, you should be able to connect to the FTP server (Figure 8.9).

Figure 8.9 shows the files that are available for the student user.

The foregoing hands-on practice has demonstrated the FTP installation and configuration process. As shown in the hands-on activity, the installation and configuration of an FTP service is fairly simple.

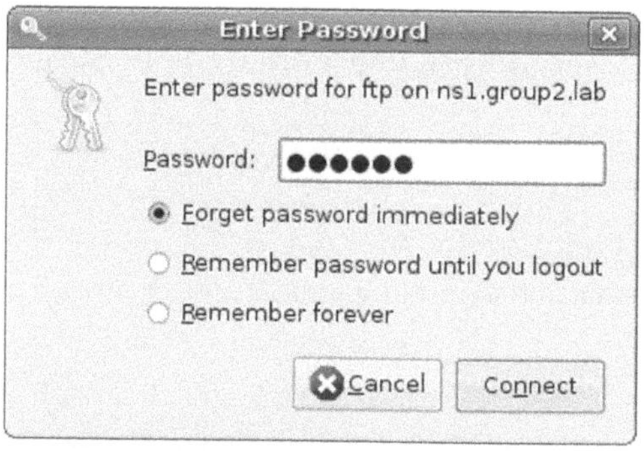

Figure 8.7 Entering password.

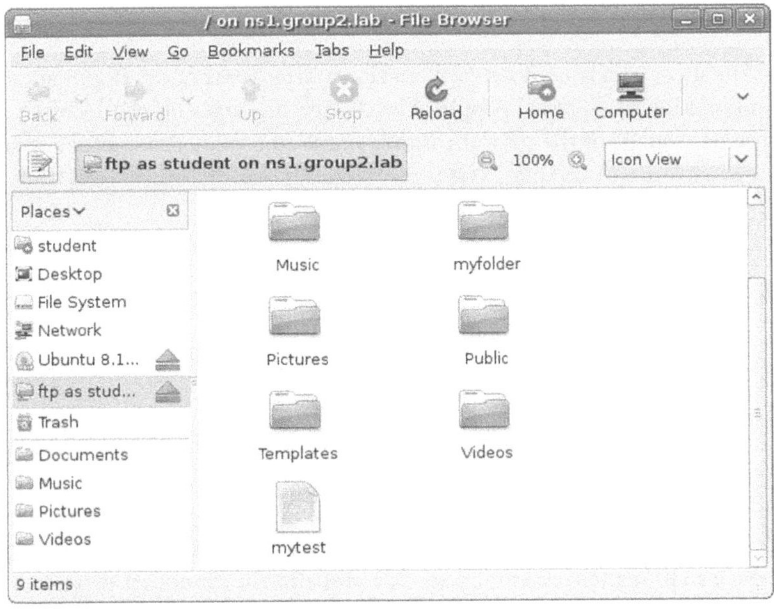

Figure 8.8 Content in home directory.

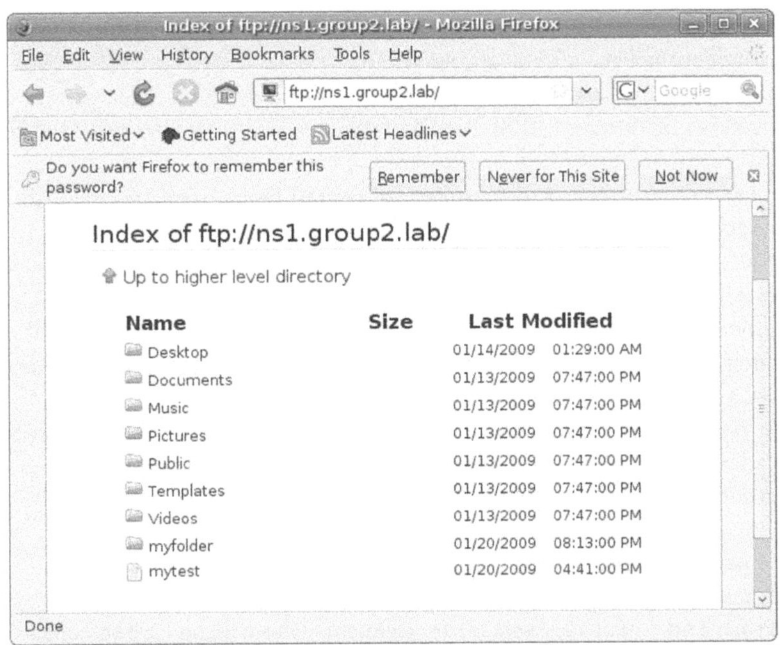

Figure 8.9 Connecting to FTP server through Web browser.

8.4 E-Mail Service

E-mail is one of the most widely used network services. After years of development, e-mail is now the main communication method for people to exchange messages on the Internet and on local networks. A large percentage of the network traffic is due to e-mail. An e-mail system is conceptually similar in some ways to the mail system: it includes the electronic version of the address, mailbox, letter, post office, sender, and receiver.

8.4.1 E-Mail System

The mailbox of e-mail is a private directory that stores all the messages received or sent. The name of the directory is often created by concatenating a user's last name and first name or the name selected by the user. In a large organization, the name of the e-mail mailbox can also be numbers automatically assigned by the e-mail software. Physically, the e-mail mailbox is a section of a hard drive where the e-mail messages are stored and protected.

E-mail mailboxes should be hosted by a computer that has enough memory, adequate hard drive space, good performance, and is equipped with an operating system that allows multiple users to access the e-mail mailboxes simultaneously and run the computer programs in the background. This type of computer is called an e-mail server. The e-mail server is like a post office where mail is collected from senders and distributed to receivers.

An e-mail server is a computer with the e-mail server software installed. All the e-mail mailboxes are kept on the hard drive of the e-mail server. In addition to sending and receiving e-mail messages, the e-mail server also manages all the e-mail mailboxes and cooperates with other e-mail servers. The e-mail server communicates through specific ports and carries out the following tasks:

- It maintains e-mail accounts. Each user who wants to have an e-mail mailbox on the server should have an e-mail account on the server.
- It hosts users' mailboxes, which are often files containing e-mail messages.
- It appends new e-mail messages to e-mail mailboxes and removes the e-mail messages that are deleted.
- The e-mail server receives e-mail messages submitted by its users and forwards them to the e-mail servers of the recipients.

An e-mail address has two parts. The first part is the name of the electronic mailbox, which should be uniquely defined on an e-mail server. The second part is the name of the e-mail server, which should be uniquely identified on the Internet. The sign @ is used to connect these two parts to uniquely identify a mailbox.

An e-mail message in an e-mail system is analogous to a letter in a mail system. It has two sections, the header and the body. The header is considered the envelope of the letter and contains the information such as the following:

- *From:* The name and e-mail address of the sender.
- *To:* The names and e-mail addresses of the recipients.
- *Cc:* The names and e-mail addresses of the recipients who will get carbon copies of the e-mail.
- *Bcc:* The names and e-mail addresses of the recipients who will get the blind carbon copies of the e-mail.

- *Date:* The date on which the message is sent.
- *Subject:* The subject of the message.

The body of an e-mail message contains the text and images. The actual content in an e-mail is in the body section.

E-mail senders and receivers use e-mail client software to specify and create, send, receive, and manage e-mails. Some well-known Linux e-mail client software programs are Evolution, Mozilla Thunderbird, and Kmail. There are also some Web-based e-mail interface packages such as Hotmail, Gmail, and Yahoo. Some application software programs such as database management systems and learning management systems are also able to help senders create and send e-mail messages, and help receivers retrieve e-mail messages from e-mail servers.

8.4.2 E-Mail Transfer

The e-mail delivery process starts with the creation of an e-mail message. With the e-mail client software, a sender can specify the e-mail message header and enter the content in the e-mail body. The sender can also attach additional files to include more information. The attachment can be used to deliver information in other formats other than the one used by the e-mail message. Video and audio files, word processing files, spreadsheets, database files, and so on, can be attached to the e-mail. After the e-mail message is created with the e-mail client software, the user can decide whether to send the e-mail message to the recipients or to save the e-mail message to the user's e-mail server, or both.

An e-mail server handles two types of traffic, outgoing traffic and incoming traffic. Outgoing traffic sends e-mail from the sender to an e-mail server or from an e-mail server to another e-mail server. Outgoing traffic is handled by the SMTP protocol.

Incoming traffic directs e-mail from an e-mail server to an e-mail receiver. Protocols such as POP3 and IMAP can be used to handle incoming traffic. These protocols allow e-mail receivers to view their mailboxes on e-mail servers and provide information about the e-mail mailboxes.

Figure 8.10 shows the e-mail delivery process. On the e-mail sender's computer, the user creates an e-mail message with the specified header and body. After the e-mail is sent, the following are some of the activities involved in the e-mail sending process:

1. The client e-mail software connects to the e-mail server with the SMTP protocol, which communicates through port 25.
2. After the connection is established, the client e-mail software sends an e-mail message that includes the header and body to the e-mail server.
3. Once the sender's e-mail server receives the e-mail message, it searches the e-mail header for the name of the destination specified by the sender. The e-mail server breaks the name into two parts, the receiver's name and the destination e-mail server's name.
4. If the receiver uses the same e-mail server as the sender, the e-mail server appends the e-mail message directly to the receiver's e-mail mailbox.
5. If the receiver uses a different e-mail server, the sender's e-mail server will forward the e-mail message to the e-mail server hosted by a remote computer with the SMTP protocol using port 25.
6. Once the receiver's e-mail server receives the e-mail message, it will append the e-mail message to the mailbox of the receiver.

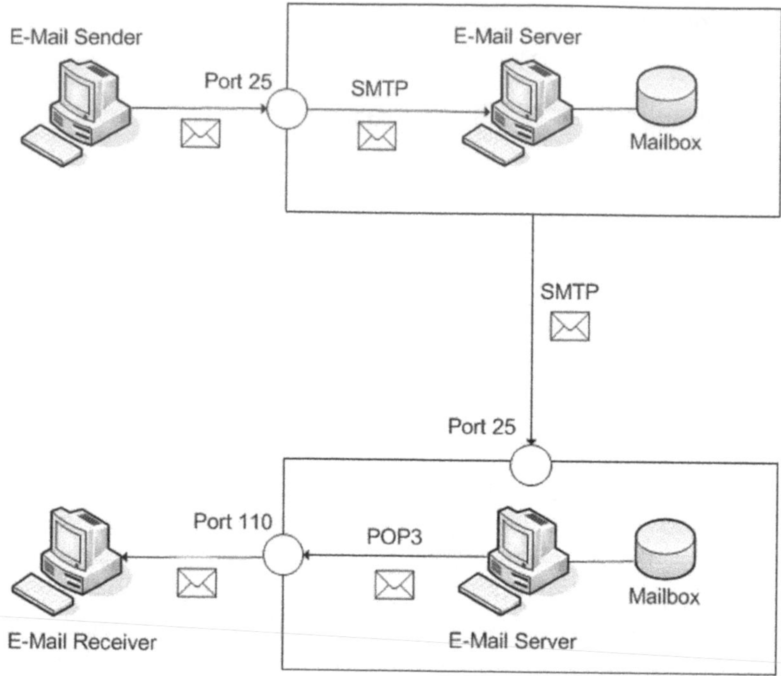

Figure 8.10 E-mail delivery process.

When a receiver wants to check his or her e-mail mailbox, the following tasks will be performed by the e-mail client software:

1. It will contact its e-mail server with the POP3 protocol, which communicates through port 110.
2. To obtain data using POP3, the user will be asked to enter the username and password for authentication.
3. After the user is authenticated, his or her mailbox will be open, and the e-mail client software will download a copy of the mailbox from the e-mail server and save it to the local computer.
4. The e-mail client software can display the mailbox in a table-like view. The header information can be presented in each row of the table.
5. The user can view new e-mail messages in the mailbox. Through the header, the receiver can view information such as the sender of the e-mail and the subject.
6. By reading the header information, the receiver can reply, forward, or delete the received e-mail message with the e-mail client software.

The receiver can also use the e-mail client software to download and display the mailbox, and reply, remove, and forward e-mail messages. If the user needs to keep some e-mail messages on the server and download the header only, the IMAP protocol should be used. Storing e-mail messages on the server allows the user to access the messages from any computer that connects to the server. IMAP allows the user to select specific e-mail messages to download and to create multiple directories for storing and organizing the e-mail messages. If the protocol IMAP is used for retrieving e-mail messages, port 143 should be used for communication.

If an e-mail message does not reach the destination e-mail server, it will be placed in a queue. After a period of time, the sender's e-mail server will try to send it again. Eventually, the sender's e-mail server will give up and inform the sender that the delivering process has failed.

8.4.3 E-Mail Service Configuration

As illustrated in the previous section, the delivery of e-mail messages from sender to receiver uses different protocols, e-mail client software, and e-mail server software. To make an e-mail service work properly, each of the components in an e-mail service system needs to be correctly configured so that they can work together. The configuration of an e-mail service needs to be done for both e-mail client software and e-mail server software:

1. *E-mail client:* On the client side, most of the e-mail client software programs are GUI based. The configuration of the e-mail client software may be slightly different depending on how the information is presented by GUI. In general, configuration of the e-mail client software may need to specify the following information:
   - The e-mail address or IP address of the e-mail server
   - User-account-related information such as username, domain, password, and other authentication-related settings
   - The message, such as the time period of the absence and instructions on how to get help, and the automatic reply when the user is away
   - The settings for the mailing list, including names, e-mail addresses, subjects, and the specification for the type of the list such as the announcement type or discussion type
   - The settings for the address book, including frequently used e-mail addresses, and settings on how the address book can be accessed
   - The languages to be used by the e-mail client software
   - The settings for e-mail-based applications such as electronic fax, Internet-based answering machine, Internet phone, and so on

   On the server side, the configuration of an e-mail server includes setting up the mail transfer agent, mail delivery agent, Web mail interface, and security measures, including antivirus, antispam, data encryption, and so on. The e-mail server configuration may also include specifying the settings for working with other application software such as firewalls, database management systems, and remote access tools. The following paragraphs provide more information about each area of the configuration.
2. *Mail transfer agent (MTA):* An MTA is an SMTP daemon that can transfer e-mail messages from one computer to another. An MTA can be used to forward e-mail messages to other e-mail servers. The well-known MTA packages are Exim, Microsoft Exchange Server, Postfix, and sendmail. The configuration of an MTA may need to specify the following items:
   - The name, domain, and IP address of the server that is used to host the MTA
   - The list of names and IP addresses of the destination e-mail servers specified for e-mail message forwarding
   - The settings for authentication and encryption
   - The specification for removing a connection and the waiting time period before reconnecting after a failed connection, and the number of reconnections allowed
   - The network interface cards connecting different networks
   - Trusted network resources such as computers, printers, routers, and so on

- Specified network services such as DNS servers, DHCP servers, file sharing, and address masquerading
- Configuration of network protocols such as SMTP, IPv4, and IPv6
- Restrictions to e-mail senders and receivers, and the interaction with SMTP clients
- Configuration of delivery status notification
- Settings for database support as well as settings for directory service support
- The antivirus scanner, the virus definition database, the method to handle infected e-mail, and the method to inform the sender about the virus infection
- The settings on spam blocking and the settings for spam identification based on factors such as keywords, characteristics, the sender's IP, and language used by the e-mail
- The settings for e-mail forwarding criteria, e-mail servers and user accounts for e-mail forwarding, and e-mail aliases used for forwarding
- The format for the mailboxes for storing e-mail, and the settings of the paths to the e-mail mailboxes for the users

The actual configuration of different MTA packages may vary. You need to check the user's manual for more specific information.

3. *Mail delivery agent (MDA):* An MDA is the software that delivers e-mail messages to recipients' mailboxes. As mentioned earlier, there are two protocols, IMAP and POP3, that are used to deliver e-messages from an e-mail server. The well-known Linux mail delivery agent packages are Dovecot, Procmail, and Maildrop. These packages serve as a POP3 and IMAP server. The configuration of the POP3 and IMAP server may include the specification of the following items:
   - The names, IP addresses, port numbers, and protocols of the outgoing e-mail server and the incoming e-mail server
   - User account information including user names and passwords for receiving e-mail messages from the e-mail server
   - Specification of the authentication method
   - Specification of the encryption method
   - Configuration for sorting and indexing
   - Support for the database and the directory service
   - Support for multiple plug-ins

   Both POP3 and IMAP4 are very well-known protocols for delivering e-mail messages to e-mail clients. Therefore, almost all of the e-mail client software and e-mail server software support theses two protocols.
4. *Web-based e-mail (Webmail):* Webmail allows users to access an e-mail server through a Web browser. Gmail, Hotmail, and Yahoo! Mail are well-known Webmail providers. If users' computers are connected to e-mail servers through the Internet, Webmail allows the users to access their e-mail servers anywhere and anytime. The configuration requires the following specifications:
   - The settings for IMAP mentioned in the previous paragraph
   - The specification for the outgoing e-mail
   - The type of authentication and encryption
   - The default location to store the files
   - The sorting method to be used to improve performance
   - The settings for the Apache Web server

After the configuration is done, you need to test the e-mail service. Make sure that users can access their e-mail mailboxes and are able to communicate with the e-mail server through the Internet. Correct all errors before the service is made available to the public.

Activity 8.3 E-Mail Service

In this hands-on activity, you are going to implement an e-mail system so that the e-mail client can submit or download e-mail to or from the e-mail server. You will install, configure, and test the e-mail server and client.

Let us start with the e-mail server. The e-mail server included in Ubuntu has two components, the mail transfer agent and the mail delivery agent. The mail transfer agent is called Postfix, which is used for transferring e-mail messages. The mail delivery agent is also called the IMAP and POP3 server. In Ubuntu, the IMAP and POP3 server is called Dovecot. The IMAP and POP3 server is used to communicate with the e-mail client software that is using POP3 and IMAP for retrieving e-mail messages. The following steps will walk you through the e-mail server installation process.

POSTFIX INSTALLATION AND CONFIGURATION

Postfix is the default MTA package included in Ubuntu. It is used to route e-mail. It is relatively easy to use and supports various types of security measures. Setting up Postfix consists of the following phases:

- Verifying the existence of the e-mail server
- Configuring the Simple Authentication and Security Layer (SASL) authentication methods
- Setting the Transport Layer Security (TLS) cryptographic mechanism
- Configuring Postfix to use SASL and TLS
- Testing Postfix

The installation and configuration of Postfix include the following steps:

1. Log on to the server machine with username **student** and password **ubuntu**.
2. The server version of Ubuntu includes the mail server. The installation performed in Chapter 1 should have the e-mail server installed. To verify, enter the following command to open the installation task package:

   ```
   sudo tasksel
   ```

3. Once the package is opened, you will see that the e-mail server is already installed (Figure 8.11).
4. After confirming that the e-mail server is installed, press the **tab** key to select **<OK>**. Then press the **Enter** key to exit tasksel.

Your next task is to configure the mail transfer agent Postfix. Follow these steps to accomplish the configuration task:

1. To configure Postfix, you need to enter the following command to start the configuration tool:

   ```
   sudo dpkg-reconfigure postfix
   ```

2. The starting page gives information about different types of e-mail configurations. After reading the information, press the **tab** key to select **<OK>**. Then press the **Enter** key to move to the next page.

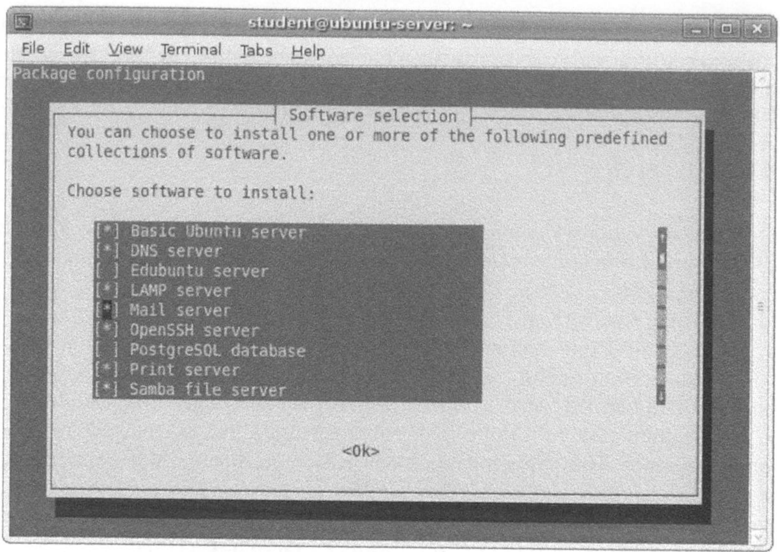

Figure 8.11 Installation of e-mail server.

3. On the next page, you are prompted to select the type of e-mail configuration. For the purpose of this hands-on practice, let us choose **Internet Site** by using the down arrow key. Press the **tab** key to select **<OK>**, and then press the **Enter** key to move to the next page.
4. This page prompts you to enter the name of the e-mail server. The name has to be a fully qualified domain name (FQDN). In our example, enter the following name:

   ```
   ns1.group2.lab
   ```

   After the name is entered, press the **tab** key to select **<OK>**, and then press the **Enter** key to move to the next page.
5. On this page, you will be asked to enter the root and postmaster mail recipient; you may leave it blank. Press the **tab** key to select **<OK>**, and then press the **Enter** key to move to the next page.
6. This page asks you to enter the other e-mail destinations. Enter the following names:

   ```
   ns1.group2.lab, localhost.localdomain, localhost
   ```

   Press the **tab** key to select **<OK>**, and then press the **Enter** key to move to the next page.
7. This page asks you if you want to force synchronous update on the mail queue. Accept the default **No**. Press the **Enter** key to move to the next page.
8. On this page, accept the default for the local networks. Press the **tab** key to select **<OK>**, and then press the **Enter** key to move to the next page.
9. This page asks whether you use Procmail to deliver local mail. Procmail is a mail processing utility that can be used to sort and filter e-mail messages. Accept the default selection **Yes**, and press the **Enter** key to move to the next page.
10. This page asks you to specify the limit that Postfix should place on mailbox files to prevent runaway software errors. Accept the default 0 for no limit. Press the **tab** key to select **<OK>**, and then press the **Enter** key to move to the next page.
11. Accept the default for the Local address extension character. Press the **tab** key to select **<OK>**, and then press the **Enter** key to move to the next page.
12. This page asks you to specify which network protocols to be enabled on the server. Select **all** to include both IPv4 and IPv6. Press the **tab** key to select **<OK>**, and then press the **Enter** key to complete the configuration.

Your next task is to configure the authentication settings. The authentication method to be used is the Simple Authentication and Security Layer (SASL), which is included in the Postfix package. With SASL, you can add authentication support to connection-based protocols such as SMTP in this example. You can either directly edit the file /etc/postfix/main.cf or use commands to configure the authentication settings. It is less risky to use commands for the configuration. The configuration can be done with the following steps:

1. Assume that your server machine is still on. Run the following command:

   ```
   sudo postconf -e 'smtpd_sasl_local_domain ='
   ```

   The preceding command is used to specify an identification domain name when passing a username to SASL. A user may be related to different domains or Web applications. The preceding command indicates that no name is specified for this purpose. The option -e means that the action is to edit the configuration of the file main.cf.
2. To enable the SASL authentication, enter the following command:

   ```
   sudo postconf -e 'smtpd_sasl_auth_enable = yes'
   ```

3. The next command is to specify that anonymous users are not allowed:

   ```
   sudo postconf -e 'smtpd_sasl_security_options = noanonymous'
   ```

4. The following command controls the interaction with SMTP clients. Some SMTP clients may not recognize the functionalities provided by Postfix.

   ```
   sudo postconf -e 'broken_sasl_auth_clients = yes'
   ```

   The value yes indicates that Postfix will advertise the SMTP authentication to the SMTP clients in a nonstandard way.
5. The following command specifies the restrictions to the recipients:

   ```
   sudo postconf -e 'smtpd_recipient_restrictions=
   permit_sasl_authenticated,permit_mynetworks,reject_unauth_destination'
   ```

6. The following command specifies that the e-mail server is to receive e-mail messages through all network interface cards:

   ```
   sudo postconf -e 'inet_interfaces = all'
   ```

7. You need the root privilege to access the file /etc/postfix/sasl/smtpd.conf. Enter the command to log in as root:

   ```
   su -
   ```

   Enter the password **ubuntu** to log in as root.
8. The next command adds the password-checking method saslauthd to the file /etc/postfix/sasl/smtpd.conf to notify SASL what the authentication method is. The echo command is used to display the message on the screen.

   ```
   echo 'pwcheck_method: saslauthd' >> /etc/postfix/sasl/smtpd.conf
   ```

9. The following command adds mech_list to the file /etc/postfix/sasl/smtpd.conf; mech_list is a list of supported authentication methods. After the keyword mech_list, the supported

authentication mechanisms plain and login are followed. These two mechanisms allow the users to access the server with their usernames and passwords in plaintext.

```
echo 'mech_list: plain login' >> /etc/postfix/sasl/smtpd.conf
```

10. Execute the following command to exit:

```
exit
```

In the foregoing steps, you have configured the authentication settings for the e-mail server. Your next job is to specify the cryptographic mechanism. Ubuntu supports several different cryptographic mechanisms. The one to be covered in this hands-on practice is the Transport Layer Security (TLS) encryption protocol. Similar to the Secure Sockets Layer (SSL), TLS can be used to secure the Internet connection by providing symmetric cipher encryption and a digital signature. The digital signature is a cryptographic mechanism used to authenticate the sender's message. The following steps illustrate the configuration of the digital signature mechanism supported by TLS:

1. Suppose that the server machine is still on. The first step is to generate an RSA private key. RSA is an algorithm for public-key cryptography. In Linux, the command genrsa can be used to generate an RSA key. To do so, enter the following command:

   ```
   sudo openssl genrsa -des3 -rand /etc/hosts -out smtpd.key 1024
   ```

   In this command, openssl is a cryptography tool that supports SSL and TLS. The options in the command have the following meanings:
   - -des3: It is an encryption algorithm that uses three 56-bit keys.
   - -rand: It is a file containing random data used as the seeds for generating random numbers.
   - -out: It specifies the output file name.

   The last number in the command is the length of the private key in bits.

   After you enter the command, you will be prompted to enter a new password. Type **ubuntu**, and press the **Enter** key. You will be asked to verify the password; type **ubuntu** again, and press the **Enter** key. Figure 8.12 illustrates the process of generating the RSA private key.
2. The next command changes the permission to the output file smtpd.key. The number 600 indicates that the owner of the file can read the file and also write to it. For security reasons, users from the same group as the owner and others are not allowed to access the file.

   ```
   sudo chmod 600 smtpd.key
   ```

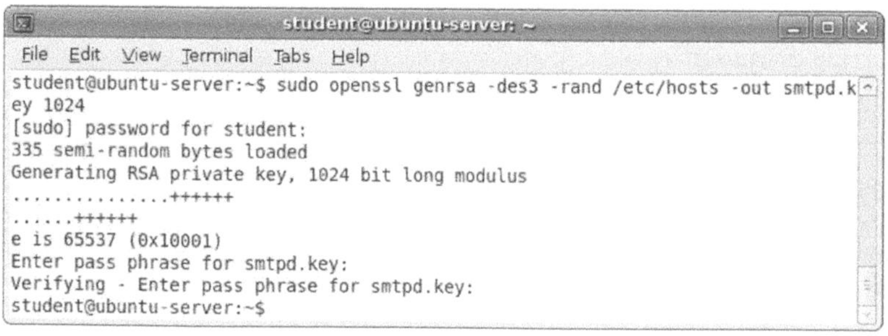

```
student@ubuntu-server: ~
File Edit View Terminal Tabs Help
student@ubuntu-server:~$ sudo openssl genrsa -des3 -rand /etc/hosts -out smtpd.k
ey 1024
[sudo] password for student:
335 semi-random bytes loaded
Generating RSA private key, 1024 bit long modulus
..............++++++
......++++++
e is 65537 (0x10001)
Enter pass phrase for smtpd.key:
Verifying - Enter pass phrase for smtpd.key:
student@ubuntu-server:~$
```

Figure 8.12 Generating RSA private key.

3. With the private key generated in Step 1, the command req is used to generate a certificate:

```
sudo openssl req -new -key smtpd.key -out smtpd.csr
```

In this command, the options have the following meanings:

- -new: This option is used to generate a new certificate request.
- -key: This option specifies the file containing the private key.
- -out: This option specifies the name of the output file.

After you press the **Enter** key, the command will ask a list of questions for the certificate (Figure 8.13). You may answer these questions depending on where you live and your affiliation. When prompted, enter **ubuntu** for the smtpd.key. Then, press the **Enter** key.

4. In the following, the x509 command is used to display certificate information and sign certificates. It can also be used to edit the certificate trust settings.

```
sudo openssl x509 -req -days 3650 -in smtpd.csr -signkey smtpd.key -out
smtpd.crt
```

In this command, the options have the following meanings:

- -req: This option specifies that a certificate request is expected.
- -days: This option specifies the certificate validation days.
- -in: This option specifies the name of the certificate input file.
- -signkey: This option allows the input file to be self-signed with the provided private key.
- -out: This option specifies the name of the output file.

After pressing the Enter key, you can see that the information you entered in the previous step is displayed on-screen. During the execution of the command, you will be asked for the password; enter **ubuntu** as the password. Figure 8.14 displays the result of the command execution process.

5. The next statement uses the rsa command to process RSA keys:

```
sudo openssl rsa -in smtpd.key -out smtpd.key.unencrypted
```

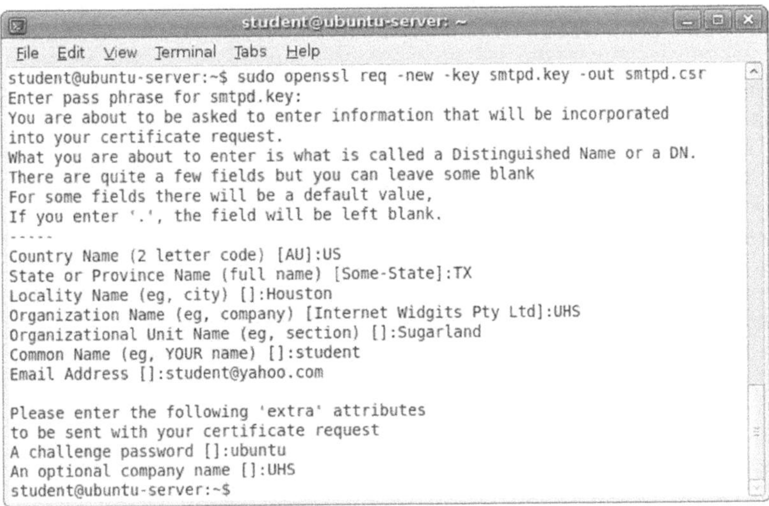

```
student@ubuntu-server:~$ sudo openssl req -new -key smtpd.key -out smtpd.csr
Enter pass phrase for smtpd.key:
You are about to be asked to enter information that will be incorporated
into your certificate request.
What you are about to enter is what is called a Distinguished Name or a DN.
There are quite a few fields but you can leave some blank
For some fields there will be a default value,
If you enter '.', the field will be left blank.
-----
Country Name (2 letter code) [AU]:US
State or Province Name (full name) [Some-State]:TX
Locality Name (eg, city) []:Houston
Organization Name (eg, company) [Internet Widgits Pty Ltd]:UHS
Organizational Unit Name (eg, section) []:Sugarland
Common Name (eg, YOUR name) []:student
Email Address []:student@yahoo.com

Please enter the following 'extra' attributes
to be sent with your certificate request
A challenge password []:ubuntu
An optional company name []:UHS
student@ubuntu-server:~$
```

Figure 8.13 Configuration of new certificate.

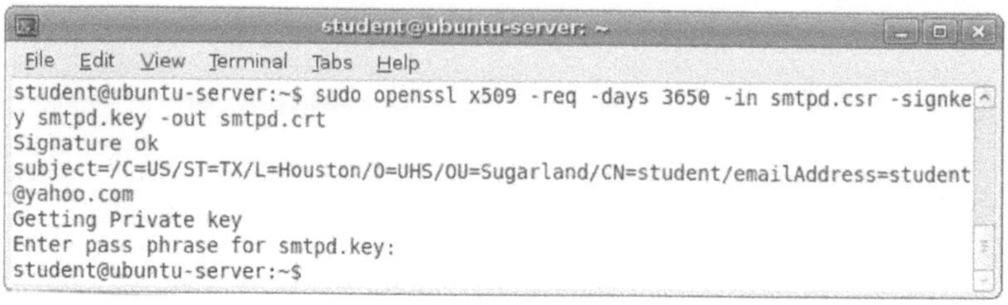

```
student@ubuntu-server:~$ sudo openssl x509 -req -days 3650 -in smtpd.csr -signke
y smtpd.key -out smtpd.crt
Signature ok
subject=/C=US/ST=TX/L=Houston/O=UHS/OU=Sugarland/CN=student/emailAddress=student
@yahoo.com
Getting Private key
Enter pass phrase for smtpd.key:
student@ubuntu-server:~$
```

Figure 8.14 Displaying certificate information.

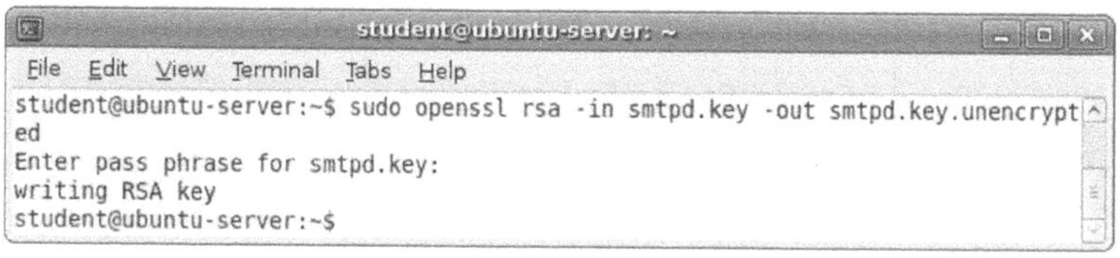

```
student@ubuntu-server:~$ sudo openssl rsa -in smtpd.key -out smtpd.key.unencrypt
ed
Enter pass phrase for smtpd.key:
writing RSA key
student@ubuntu-server:~$
```

Figure 8.15 Processing RSA key.

In this command, the options have the following meanings:

- -in: This option specifies the name of the input file containing the keys.
- -out: This option specifies the name of the key output file.

You will be prompted to enter the password. Enter **ubuntu** as the password (Figure 8.15).

6. The following statement renames the output file in the preceding step as smtpd.key:

```
sudo mv -f smtpd.key.unencrypted smtpd.key
```

The option -f specifies renaming of the file without prompting.

7. In the next statement, you will use the command req to create a self-signed certificate.

```
sudo openssl req -new -x509 -extensions v3_ca -keyout cakey.pem -out
cacert.pem -days 3650
```

The options used in the command have the following meanings:

- -new: This option is used to generate a new certificate request.
- -x509: This option outputs a self-signed certificate.
- -extensions: If the option –x509 is used, alternative sections to include certificate extensions can be specified.
- -keyout: This option specifies the name of the file to which the newly created private key will be saved.
- -out: This option specifies the name of the output file.
- -days: This option specifies the certificate validation days.

During the execution of the command, enter **ubuntu** when you are prompted to enter the value for PEM pass phrase. Similar to Step 3, enter the information for the sequence of prompts shown in Figure 8.16.

8. The mv command is used to move several files to the dedicated directories so that the digital signature process can find these files.

```
sudo mv smtpd.key /etc/ssl/private/
sudo mv smtpd.crt /etc/ssl/certs/
sudo mv cakey.pem /etc/ssl/private/
sudo mv cacert.pem /etc/ssl/certs/
```

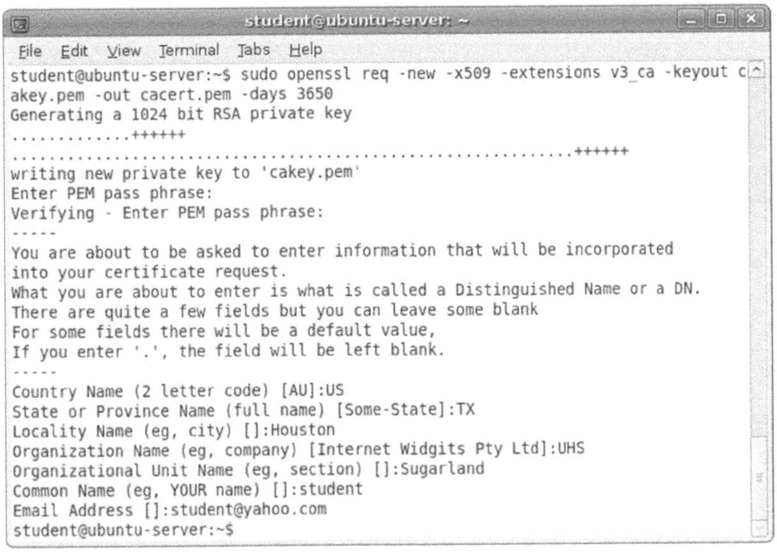

```
student@ubuntu-server: ~
File Edit View Terminal Tabs Help
student@ubuntu-server:~$ sudo openssl req -new -x509 -extensions v3_ca -keyout c
akey.pem -out cacert.pem -days 3650
Generating a 1024 bit RSA private key
............++++++
...........................................................++++++
writing new private key to 'cakey.pem'
Enter PEM pass phrase:
Verifying - Enter PEM pass phrase:
-----
You are about to be asked to enter information that will be incorporated
into your certificate request.
What you are about to enter is what is called a Distinguished Name or a DN.
There are quite a few fields but you can leave some blank
For some fields there will be a default value,
If you enter '.', the field will be left blank.
-----
Country Name (2 letter code) [AU]:US
State or Province Name (full name) [Some-State]:TX
Locality Name (eg, city) []:Houston
Organization Name (eg, company) [Internet Widgits Pty Ltd]:UHS
Organizational Unit Name (eg, section) []:Sugarland
Common Name (eg, YOUR name) []:student
Email Address []:student@yahoo.com
student@ubuntu-server:~$
```

Figure 8.16 Creating self-signed certificate.

So far, you have done the configuration for the SASL authentication mechanism and the digital signature. Sending an unencrypted authentication message through the network is a security risk. To enhance security, your next task is to configure Postfix so that it can provide TLS encryption for both incoming and outgoing e-mail messages. The following steps enable you to get the job done:

1. Assume that the server machine is still on. To be compatible with the Postfix versions that are not patched, Postfix is configured to accept the authentication without encryption. Enter the following command:

```
sudo postconf -e 'smtpd_tls_auth_only = no'
```

2. To use TLS when a remote SMTP server supports STARTTLS, which is the protocol used to establish TLS, enter the following command:

```
sudo postconf -e 'smtp_use_tls = yes'
```

3. The following command announces STARTTLS's support to SMTP clients:

```
sudo postconf -e 'smtpd_use_tls = yes'
```

4. When TLS is not already enabled for the remote SMTP server, the following command logs the host name of that server:

```
sudo postconf -e 'smtp_tls_note_starttls_offer = yes'
```

5. The following command specifies the Privacy Enhanced Mail (PEM) file that contains the RSA private key for the Postfix SMTP server. The PEM file contains the certificates or private keys, and is used to secure e-mail using public key cryptography.

```
sudo postconf -e 'smtpd_tls_key_file = /etc/ssl/private/smtpd.key'
```

6. The following command specifies the PEM file that contains the RSA certificate for the Postfix SMTP server. In addition, this file may also contain the private RSA key for the Postfix SMTP server.

```
sudo postconf -e 'smtpd_tls_cert_file = /etc/ssl/certs/smtpd.crt'
```

7. The following command assigns the CA certificate issued by the Postfix SMTP server:

```
sudo postconf -e 'smtpd_tls_CAfile = /etc/ssl/certs/cacert.pem'
```

8. At the logging level 1, the following command logs the TLS handshake and certificate information:

```
sudo postconf -e 'smtpd_tls_loglevel = 1'
```

9. This command requests the Postfix SMTP server to generate headers for the received messages:

```
sudo postconf -e 'smtpd_tls_received_header = yes'
```

10. The following command specifies the expiration time of the TLS session cache information:

```
sudo postconf -e 'smtpd_tls_session_cache_timeout = 3600s'
```

11. The next command specifies the external entropy source for the pseudorandom number generator's pool. The pool contains bits that have extremely strong random properties. The random number generator is used to provide random data for cryptographic keys. *Entropy* is a term used in information theory to measure the uncertainty associated with a random variable.

```
sudo postconf -e 'tls_random_source = dev:/dev/urandom'
```

12. The following command specifies the Internet host name of this e-mail server:

```
sudo postconf -e 'myhostname = ns1.group2.lab'
```

13. Now, all the commands have been entered. To verify this, you can display the content in the file /etc/postfix/main.cf by using the following command:

```
cat /etc/postfix/main.cf
```

14. If the items in the file /etc/postfix/main.cf are consistent with the foregoing commands, you may restart the Postfix daemon by using the following command:

```
sudo /etc/init.d/postfix start
```

If Postfix starts successfully, you have successfully configured the Postfix daemon. To use Postfix, you also need to configure SASL2 before SMTP can be used to submit e-mail messages. The following are the steps to configure SASL2:

1. The first step is to install the packages libsasl2-2 and sasl2-bin:

```
sudo apt-get install libsasl2-2 sasl2-bin
```

2. Because SASL needs to be run in the directory var/spool/postfix/var/run/saslauthd, run the following commands to create the directory and remove the default directory /var/run/saslauthd:

```
sudo mkdir -p /var/spool/postfix/var/run/saslauthd
sudo rm -rf /var/run/saslauthd
```

   In the foregoing commands, the option -p creates any missing intermediate pathname. The option -rf is used to remove file hierarchies and not to prompt for confirmation.
3. Next, you need to add several variables for activating the daemon saslauthd in the file /etc/default/saslauthd. Enter the following command to edit the file:

```
sudo gedit /etc/default/saslauthd
```

4. After the file is opened, you will add or modify the following four lines of code. The result of editing is shown in Figure 8.17.

```
START=yes
PWDIR="/var/spool/postfix/var/run/saslauthd"
PARAMS="-m ${PWDIR}"
PIDFILE="${PWDIR}/saslauthd.pid"
```

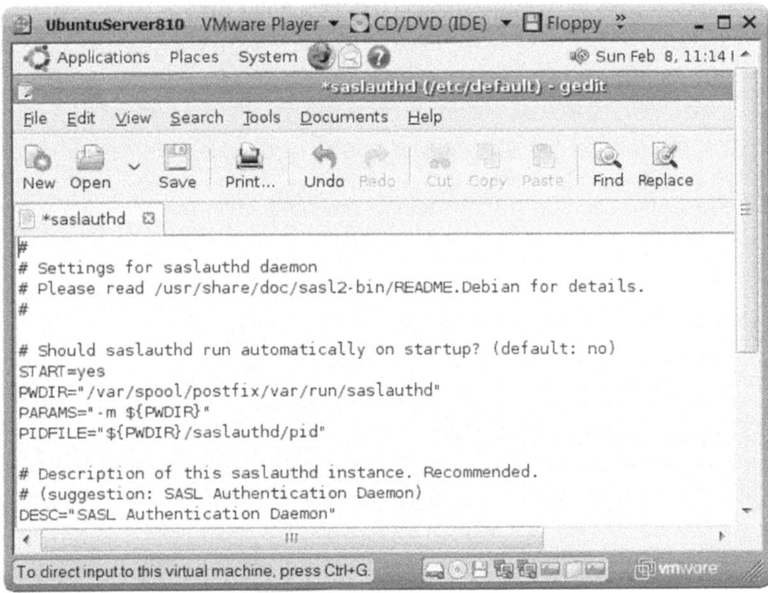

Figure 8.17 Editing saslauthd daemon.

In the preceding code, the variables have the following meanings:

- PWDIR: This variable defines the path to the directory where the files related to the password can be located.
- PARAMS: This variable defines the parameter for SASL authentication. It tells saslauthd which directory to use. The option -m indicates that the path is manually specified.
- PIDFILE: This variable specifies the file that contains the process identification numbers.

5. Your next task is to update the dpkg state of saslauthd. dpkg is a utility used to install, remove, and provide information about the Debian software package. Enter the following command for state updating:

```
sudo dpkg-statoverride --force --update --add root sasl 755
/var/spool/postfix/var/run/saslauthd
```

6. Now, you can run the following command to start the daemon saslauthd:

```
sudo /etc/init.d/saslauthd start
```

7. The last step of the mail transfer agent configuration is to test the settings. Before the testing, you need to make sure that your DNS is working properly. To do so, enter the following command to open the resolver configuration file:

```
sudo gedit /etc/resolv.conf
```

8. After the file is opened, make sure that the following lines are included:

```
search group2.lab
nameserver 192.168.2.1
```

   After the code is entered, click the **Save** menu. Then, click the **File** menu, and select **Quit**.
9. To make sure that your DNS is functioning properly, enter the following command to see if the IP address 192.168.2.1 corresponds to the host name ns1.group2.lab:

```
sudo host 192.168.2.1
```

   You should be able to get the host name ns1.group2.lab displayed on the screen (Figure 8.18).
10. To test the saslauthd daemon with the telnet command, enter the following command:

```
telnet nsl.group2.lab 25
```

11. After Telnet is opened, enter the following telnet command.

```
ehlo nsl.group2.lab
```

12. Enter the command **quit** to exit Telnet.
13. You can now create an e-mail message with the mail transfer agent Postfix, and save the e-mail message to the mailbox. Enter the following command:

```
telnet nsl.group2.lab 25
```

14. To create an e-mail message, enter the following commands and e-mail message:

```
mail from: student@yahoo.com
rcpt to: student@localhost
data
```

```
student@ubuntu-server: ~
File Edit View Terminal Tabs Help
student@ubuntu-server:~$ sudo host 192.168.2.1
1.2.168.192.in-addr.arpa domain name pointer ns1.group2.lab.
student@ubuntu-server:~$ telnet ns1.group2.lab 25
Trying 192.168.2.1...
Connected to ns1.group2.lab.
Escape character is '^]'.
220 ns1.group2.lab ESMTP Postfix (Ubuntu)
ehlo ns1.group2.lab
250-ns1.group2.lab
250-PIPELINING
250-SIZE 10240000
250-VRFY
250-ETRN
250-STARTTLS
250-AUTH NTLM CRAM-MD5 PLAIN LOGIN DIGEST-MD5
250-ENHANCEDSTATUSCODES
250-8BITMIME
250 DSN
quit
221 2.0.0 Bye
Connection closed by foreign host.
student@ubuntu-server:~$
```

Figure 8.18 Testing mail transfer agent postfix.

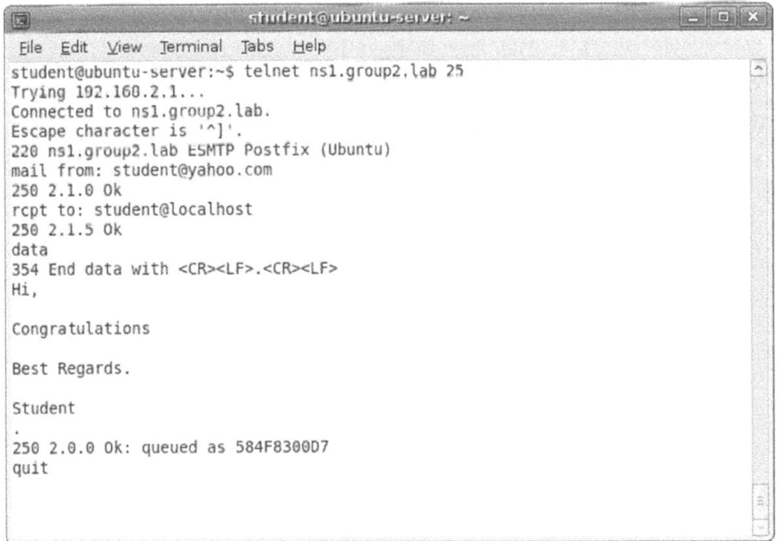

Figure 8.19 Creating e-mail message.

```
Subject:
Hi,
Congratulations
Best Regards.
Student
quit
```

The output for each of the commands is shown in Figure 8.19.

DOVECOT INSTALLATION AND CONFIGURATION

As mentioned at the beginning of this hands-on practice, there are two components in an e-mail server, the mail transfer agent and the mail delivery agent. By following the foregoing steps, you have successfully configured the mail transfer agent. Your next task is to configure the mail delivery agent, which is an IMAP and POP3 server. The IMAP and POP3 server included in Ubuntu is supported by Dovecot. The following are the steps used to install and configure the Dovecot package:

1. You need to make sure that the more secure protocols, IMAPS and POP3S, are included in the file /etc/dovecot/dovecot.conf. First, execute the following command:

   ```
   sudo gedit /etc/dovecot/dovecot.conf
   ```

   After the file is opened, find the following line to make sure that IMAPS and POP3S are included. If not, add these two protocols as shown in the following line:

   ```
   protocols = pop3 pop3s imap imaps
   ```

   Move the cursor down to the section marked as #POP3 specific settings. Make sure the line

   ```
   pop3_uidl_format = %08Xu%08Xv
   ```

   is included. In the preceding line, the symbol %08Xu%08Xv is used to make the UID compatible with other POP servers.
2. Move the cursor down to the line marked by #Mailbox locations and namespaces. Uncomment the following line to specify the format of the mailbox:

   ```
   mail_location = mbox:~/mail
   ```

3. After the file is configured, click the **Save** menu to save the changes. Then, click the **File** menu, and select **Quit**.
4. Now, you can start the Dovecot service by entering the following command:

   ```
   sudo /etc/init.d/dovecot start
   ```

5. To test POP3, enter the following command:

   ```
   telnet localhost pop3
   ```

   If output is similar to Figure 8.20, the configuration is working properly. Enter the command **quit** to exit.

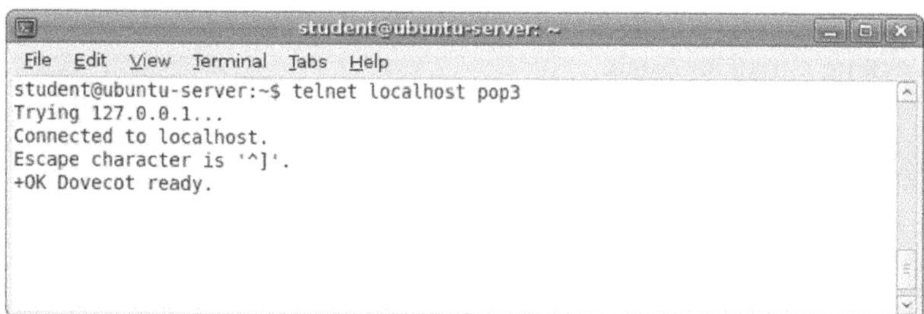

Figure 8.20 Testing Dovecot.

6. Your next task is to configure Dovecot to work with SSL. Enter the following command to open the file dovecot.conf:

   ```
   sudo gedit /etc/dovecot/dovecot.conf
   ```

   After the file is opened, edit the four lines so that they look like this:

   ```
   ssl_cert_file = /etc/ssl/certs/dovecot.pem
   ssl_key_file = /etc/ssl/private/dovecot.pem
   ssl_disable = no
   disable_plaintext_auth = no
   ```

   Click the **Save** menu to save the changes. Then, click the **File** menu, and select **Quit**.

EVOLUTION MAIL CONFIGURATION

At this point, you have configured the mail delivery agent. The two major components of the e-mail server have been successfully configured. Your next task is to configure the e-mail client software on the client machine so that the user can log on from the client machine to use the e-mail service. The e-mail client software included in Ubuntu is called Evolution. Use the following steps to accomplish this task:

1. Log on to the client machine with username **student** and password **ubuntu**.
2. To make sure the DNS service is enabled, enter the following command:

   ```
   sudo host client1
   ```

   You should be able to see that the corresponding IP address is 192.168.2.2.
3. To start Evolution for the configuration, click the **Application** menu, select **Internet**, and then **Evolution Mail**.
4. On the Welcome page, click the **Forward** button to go to the Restore from Backup page.
5. On the Restore from Backup page, click the **Forward** button again to go to the Identity page.
6. On the Identity page (Figure 8.21), type the e-mail address **student@ns1.group2.lab**, and click **Forward** to go to the Receiving Email page.
7. On the Receiving Email page (Figure 8.22), select **POP** in the Server Type drop-down list. You will then be prompted to enter information related to the protocol POP. Enter the IP address **192.168.2.1** in the Server text box, choose **TLS encryption** in the User Secure Connection drop-down list, and select **Password** in the Authentication Type drop-down list. After the information is added, click **Forward** to go to the Receiving Options page.
8. On the Receiving Options page (in Figure 8.23), check the check box for **Leave messages on server**. Click **Forward** to go the Sending Email page.
9. On the Sending Email page (Figure 8.24), you will specify the Server Type as SMTP, the server IP address as **192.168.2.1** and select **TLS encryption** for the Use Secure Connection drop-down list. For the Authentication Type, specify **PLAIN**. Click **Forward** to go to the Account Management page.
10. On the Account Management page, click **Forward** to go to the page Timezone page.
11. On the Timezone page, specify the time zone in your area (Figure 8.25). Click the **Forward** button to go to the page Done.
12. On the Done page, review the information, and click the **Apply** button.
13. The Evolution Dialog box opens automatically. Click the **Send/Receive** button; enter the password **ubuntu**, and click **OK.** Click **Inbox**; then, you will see that the e-mail you created earlier is in the Inbox (Figure 8.26).

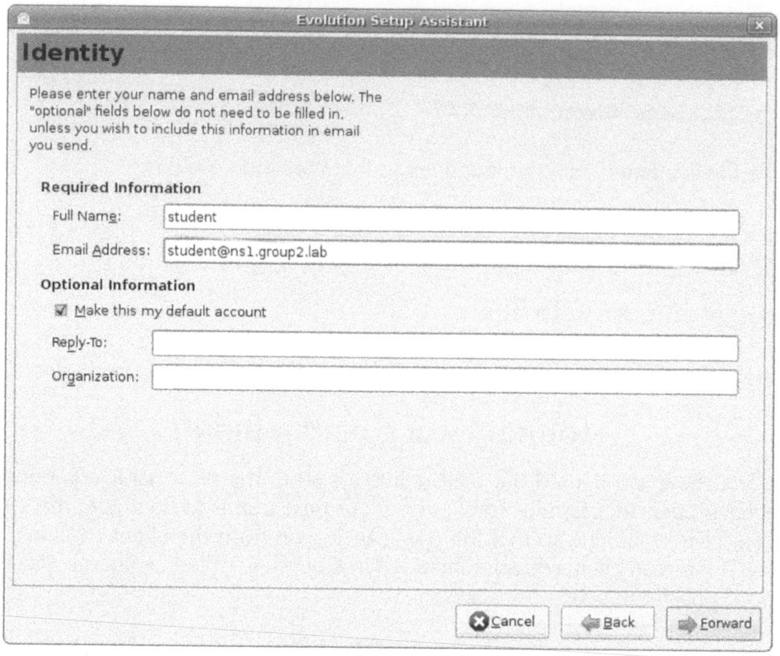

Figure 8.21 Configuration of Identity Page.

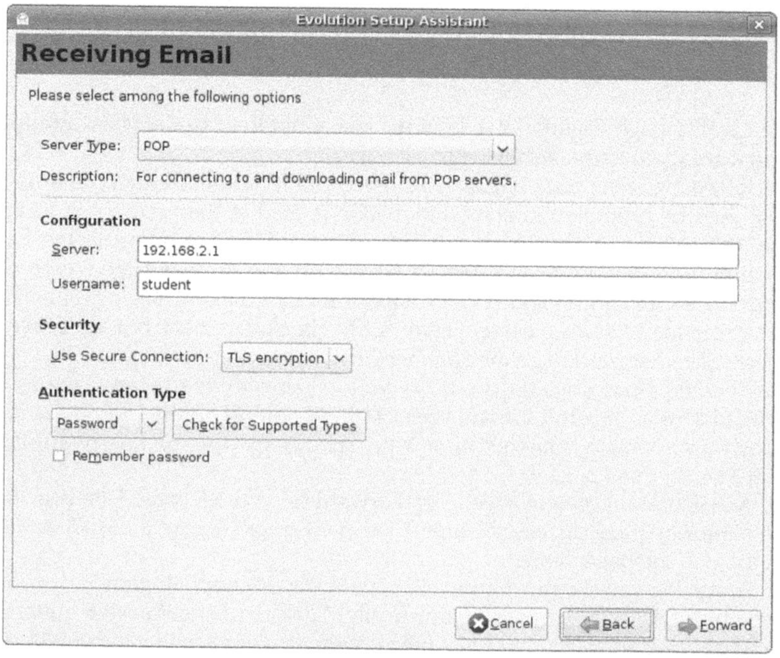

Figure 8.22 Configuration of Receiving Email page.

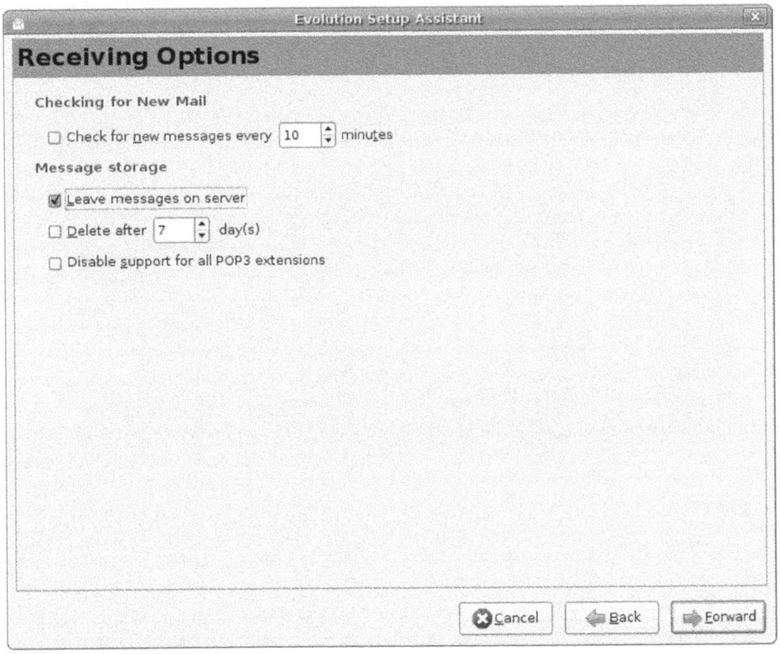

Figure 8.23 Configuration of Receiving Options page.

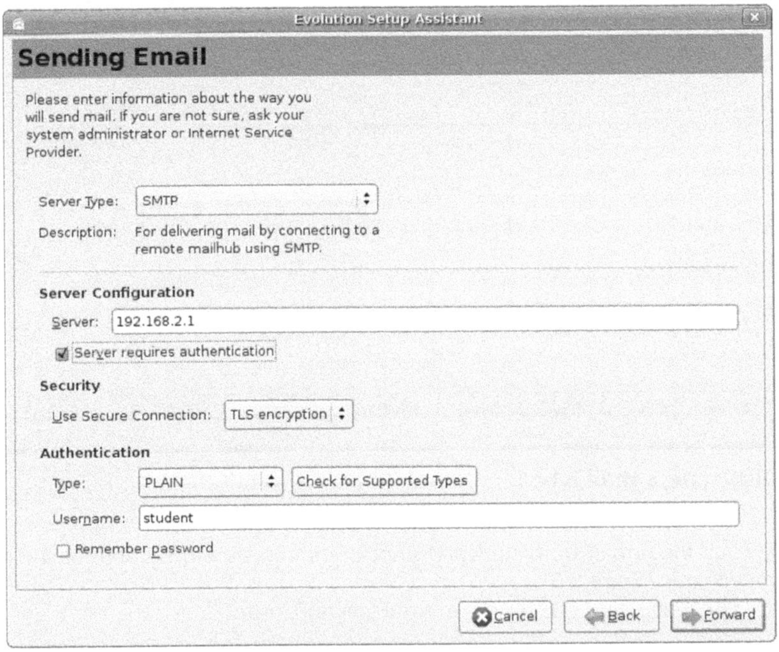

Figure 8.24 Configuration of Sending Email page.

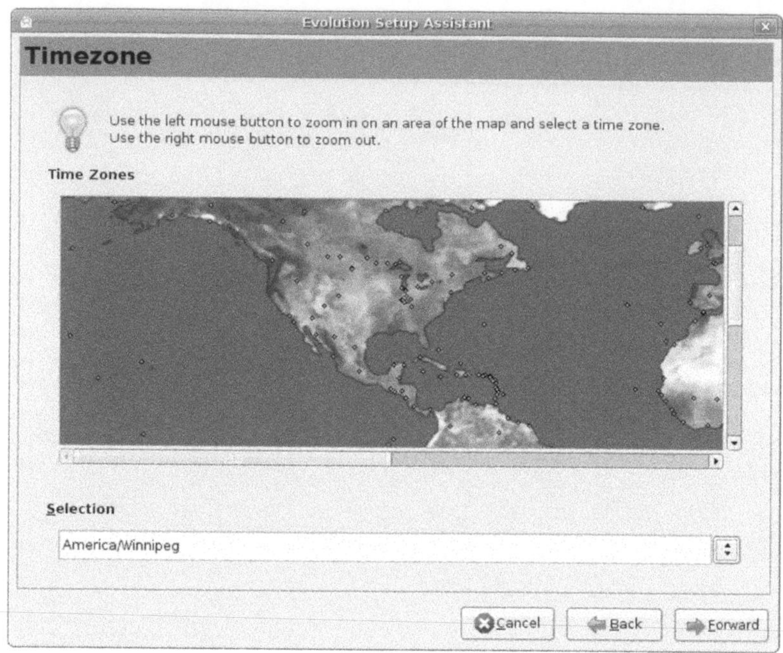

Figure 8.25 Configuration of Timezone page.

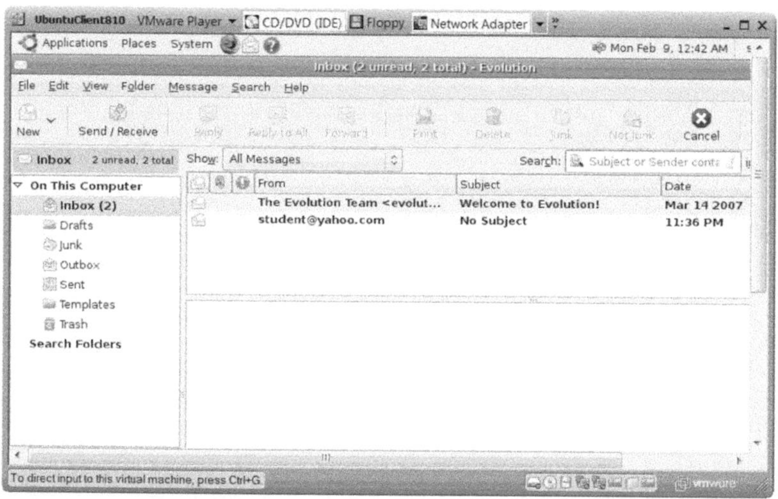

Figure 8.26 Displaying e-mail inbox.

14. Double-click the e-mail from student@yahoo.com; you should be able to see the e-mail content shown in Figure 8.27.
15. Click the **File** menu, and select **Quit** to exit Evolution.

In the hands-on practice, you installed and configured Postfix, which serves as the mail transfer agent and Dovecot, which serves as the mail delivery agent. On the client side, you configured

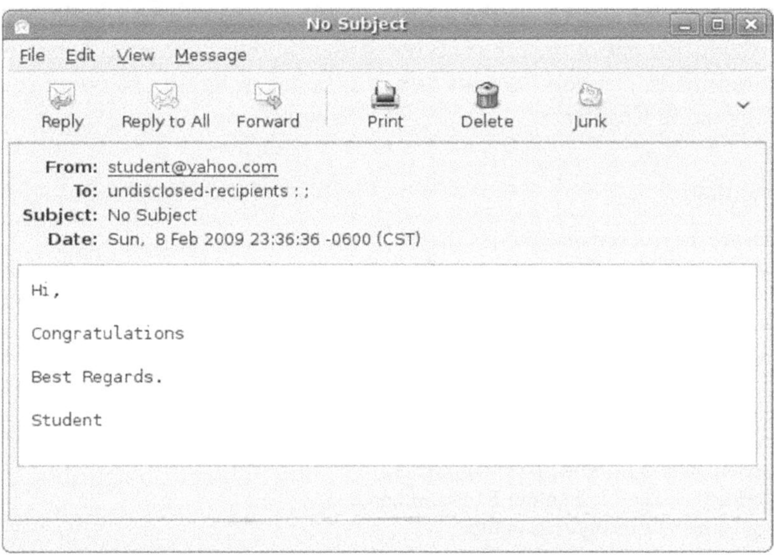

Figure 8.27 E-mail content.

the e-mail client software Evolution Mail so that you can access the e-mail server created by yourself in the earlier steps. At this point, you have successfully set up the e-mail service. Figure 8.27 shows that the e-mail software Evolution Mail can be used to open an e-mail message stored on the server.

8.5 Summary

This chapter discussed several technologies that can be used to provide Internet-related services. One of the main services on the Internet is support for the World Wide Web. The Web server is the key component of the World Wide Web. This chapter explained how the Web server supports Web activities. It also examined the protocols and technologies used to accomplish Web-related tasks. It discussed issues related to the configuration of the Web server. The hands-on practice illustrated the process of installing and configuring the Web server. Through the Web browser, you can access the Web server created in this chapter. This verifies that the Web server is working properly.

The second service introduced in this chapter was the file transfer service. The chapter provided information about File Transfer Protocol (FTP), and demonstrated how FTP is used in sharing files on a network. The hand-on practice in this section illustrated the process of FTP installation, configuration, and management. Through step-by-step instruction, this hands-on practice showed how to access FTP through the FTP client software and through the Web browser.

The last topic was the e-mail service. This chapter covered the major components of an e-mail system. It illustrated how e-mail protocols work and how e-mail messages are submitted to an e-mail server and delivered to e-mail clients. The lists of issues related to e-mail configuration have been provided in this chapter. The hands-on practice illustrated the process of installing and configuring the two main components of the e-mail server, the mail transfer agent and the mail delivery agent. The hands-on practice also illustrated the configuration of the e-mail client software so that it can be used to access the e-mail server. Through the hands-on practice, you gained first-hand experience in setting up the e-mail service, especially, on the server side.

Now that you have learned about these Internet-related services, you will next learn about network security, which is one of the top concerns of users in today's home and enterprise network computing environments. Network security is not to be taken lightly. Network-security-related issues will be explored in Chapter 9.

Review Questions

1. What are the four components of a URL?
2. How does HTTP work?
3. What are the five basic operations performed by HTTP?
4. As a Web server, what can Apache do?
5. In which file can the Apache Web server configuration be done?
6. List the tasks that can be performed by an FTP server.
7. What are the advantages of using the FTP client software package?
8. What are the active mode, passive mode, and extended passive mode?
9. Describe the usage of the ? FTP command?
10. Describe the usage of the mput FTP command?
11. What is the FTP configuration file?
12. What tasks can be accomplished by an e-mail server?
13. What items are included in an e-mail message header?
14. Name three well-known Linux e-mail client software packages.
15. What are the activities involved in an e-mail sending process?
16. What are the activities involved in an e-mail receiving process?
17. What is a mail transfer agent?
18. What is a mail delivery agent?
19. Name three well-known Linux mail transfer agent software packages.
20. What is Transport Layer Security?

Case Study Projects

The following are two networking projects that involve the Web server and e-mail client development:

Case Study Project 8.1. Create a Web server on your home network to host a Web page.
Case Study Project 8.2. Configure the e-mail client software Evolution to access your university or your company's e-mail server.

Chapter 9

Network Security

Objectives

- Understand network security policies, security vulnerabilitics, and security measures.
- Become familiar with some commonly used security technologies.
- Set up network firewalls.
- Install and configure SSL and SSH.

9.1 Introduction

Chapter 8 covered topics related to Internet-based network service. A network, whether it is a wired or a wireless network, is vulnerable to network hackers and network viruses, especially when it is connected the public Internet. A security problem can cause severe damage to an organization's computing environment. Hackers may steal sensitive data, modify the data content in a packet during data transmission, or crash network servers and personal computers. Through the Internet, malicious viruses can be introduced to private networks to disable operating systems, wipe out file systems, jam network traffic, or even shut down an entire network system. Therefore, enforcing security measures to protect a network from viruses and hackers is the first priority.

This chapter will first investigate network security issues, including possible attacks by hackers and computer viruses. It will introduce some commonly used network security technologies and ways to set up firewalls. It will start with some commonly encountered security issues. It will first discuss network security policies. It will examine security vulnerabilities on networks and computer systems.

We will look at problems caused by computer viruses and spyware. Computer viruses can cause various degrees of damage to a network. This chapter will examine the behavior of some commonly known viruses and the damage they can cause to a network system. It will introduce some of the security measures that can block hackers and viruses from invading a private network.

After examining the network security issues, this chapter will introduce several commonly used security technologies, including the Intrusion Detection System (IDS), IP Security (IPSec), Remote Authentication Dial In User Service (RADIUS), Secure Shell (SSH), Secure Sockets Layer (SSL), and Wi-Fi Protected Access (WPA). It will briefly explain how these technologies work and the application of these technologies. Hands-on practice will be provided to illustrate the installation and configuration of SSH and SSL.

The last topic in this chapter is firewalls. This chapter will describe how a firewall can get the job done. Several types of firewalls will be introduced in this chapter. This chapter will also discuss some commonly used firewall architectures. During the hands-on practice, the firewall software, Uncomplicated Firewall (UFW), included in the Linux operating system will be used to demonstrate how to install, configure, and test a firewall.

The discussion will start with security-related issues such as security policies, security vulnerabilities, and security measures in the next section.

9.2 Security Issues

Network security has become the main concern of the network administrator. Once a computer is connected to a network, especially the public Internet, the computer itself and communication with other computers become vulnerable to hackers and computer viruses.

9.2.1 Network Security Policies

Damage caused by a hacker attack or virus infection can be very harmful to an organization's computing environment. Because most hacker attacks and virus infections are through networks, protecting the networks is the first priority. A network system is a complicated system that consists of network devices, operating systems, application software, network protocols, and so on. Developing a network security solution requires knowledge of various areas such as user and computer authentication, data encryption, network service configuration, network protocol security, and so forth. Therefore, we need to plan carefully before we can physically implement a solution for network security. Later, various security measures will be introduced to strengthen the security of networks and computers. To decide when, where, and how to implement these security measures, well-defined security policies should be developed. Security policies identify security threats and regulate network activities. The objectives of security policies are as follows:

- Identifying potential security vulnerabilities
- Identifying what to protect and setting priorities for security protection
- Resolving the conflict between the user's needs and security requirements
- Detailing the rules for confidentiality and the rules for auditing
- Defining the scope of access
- Specifying the responsibilities of users and the security management team members
- Identifying the security measures to be used
- Identifying the knowledge and technology needed for implementing the security measures
- Identifying the software and hardware needed for network protection
- Budgeting the cost for implementing the security measures

The first task in developing a solution for protecting an organization's private network is to investigate potential security vulnerabilities. For example, the computer system can be broken into by hackers and infected by viruses. The data transmitted over the network can be stolen, altered, or destroyed by hackers; they can also be infected by viruses.

9.2.2 Intrusion into Computer Systems

Once a computer is connected to a network, the data stored on the computer are vulnerable in many ways. The following are some of them:

- By trying many different password combinations, hackers are able to log on to a network server through trial and error. The process of repeated attempts to log on to a computer system is called a brute-force attack. This can be easily done by hackers with freely available software.
- Many application server software packages such as Web servers, FTP servers, and database servers have public accounts. If the servers are not properly reconfigured, hackers can log on to these servers through the public accounts to cause some major damage.
- Spyware can be used by hackers to collect information about users. The spyware can be secretly downloaded to victim computers when they are surfing the Web sites set by the hackers.
- Network-enabled application software is often used by hackers to intrude into computers. After the victims open the online application software, the hackers are able penetrate their operating systems. The application software on the server side, such as sendmail and FTP, has some well-known weaknesses. Through these weaknesses, hackers can penetrate a host computer with the permission of a system-level account.
- Hackers can spam a victim's e-mail system with advertisements and viruses. Even worse, hackers can set a spam relay from the victim's computer to harm other computers on the network without being caught.
- Hackers can use Web interactive components such as ActiveX controls and Java applets to bypass firewalls in order to take control of computer systems.
- Hackers can make malicious scripts available on Web sites. Once downloaded and executed on a victim computer, these malicious scripts can cause significant damage to the computer system.
- The bugs in a software package can also be used by hackers as a way to intrude into a computer system. Through these software bugs, hackers may even gain the administrator's privilege.

Most of these security problems are caused by access to the public Internet. Some of these problems may also be caused by attacks that come from internal networks or by unintentional mistakes.

9.2.3 Intrusion into Networks

During data transmission across a network, packets being transmitted are the main target of hackers. The following are some of the methods used by hackers to attack a private network:

- Most of the older network protocols transmit data in cleartext. Hackers can use packet-capturing software to catch data packets. This type of software is called a packet sniffer. Hackers use packet sniffers to capture packets, and to view and process data content such as usernames and passwords carried by the packets.
- Hackers can use a method called IP spoofing to intrude into a network. IP spoofing allows a hacker to gain unauthorized access to a computer system. The hacker first obtains the IP

address of the computer. He then modifies the packet header so that the source address appears to be sent by a trusted host, to gain the trust of the victim computer. Then, the hacker can receive all the packets addressed to the spoofed address and start to communicate with the victim computer. Each time when the victim computer sends packets to a trusted computer, the packets will be forwarded to the hacker's computer.

- Hackers can perform a denial-of-service attack by sending a sequence of requests for a certain service. When the service becomes so busy, it will not be able to respond to any request and therefore shut down the service. The denial-of-service attack employs network protocols such as Hypertext Transfer Protocol (HTTP) or File Transfer Protocol (FTP) to continuously request services from the Web server or FTP server. In this way, it blocks other users from contacting the servers. Protocols such as Transmission Control Protocol/Internet Protocol (TCP/IP) and Internet Control Message Protocol (ICMP) can also be used by hackers to flood the servers with junk network packets or false information.
- In a two-key encryption process, a public key is delivered to the sender through the network to encrypt data before transmission. A hacker can intercept and replace the original public key with his own public key during the public key exchange process. In this way, the hacker can use his own private key to decrypt the message encrypted by the sender, modify the message, and then reencrypt the modified message with the receiver's public key before retransmitting the modified message to the receiver. This type of attack is called a man-in-the-middle attack.

Network security problems are related to many factors in a network-based computing environment. Some of the problems may be caused by network protocols, and others may be due to misconfiguration. Often, well-trained network administrators are required to handle network security problems. Later in this chapter, some technologies will be introduced for solving network security problems.

9.2.4 Computer Viruses

In addition to hacker-related security problems, a computer system or a network can also be infected with computer viruses. Computer viruses can cause significant damage to the computer or the network. The following are some of harmful viruses:

- *Boot virus:* During the computer boot process, this type of virus can load itself by overwriting or replacing the boot program. After the computer system is booted, the virus displays a message on-screen and prevents the user from logging on to the computer.
- *E-mail virus:* As the name indicates, this type of virus is spread through e-mail. The virus can automatically mail itself to all the entries in the victim's e-mail address book. The infection can be propagated so widely that it is very difficult to clean up the infected e-mail system.
- *Java or ActiveX virus:* This type of virus hides behind interactive elements such as the buttons on a Web page. Once a button is clicked by the user, the virus is activated and will take control of the user's computer.
- *Macro virus:* This type of virus hides in the macros used by application software such as the spreadsheet. Once these macros are executed, this type of virus will be activated.
- *Polymorphic virus:* This type of virus can hide its identity by changing its appearance. It appears as a different type of infection. Usually, antivirus software is not able to detect all

types of viruses, so some forms of the polymorphic virus may be able to survive. It is difficult to detect this type of virus on an infected computer.

- *Program virus:* When an executable file is running, this type of virus can be activated. The program virus loads itself into memory and further infects other executable files in the memory, or even spreads itself to other computers through the network.
- *Stealth virus:* This type of virus can hide itself in an ordinary file. It can modify the file size to avoid detection by antivirus software. It can even temporarily replace the infected file with a copy of an uninfected file to trick the antivirus software. Like the polymorphic virus, the stealth virus is very difficult to detect and very costly to correct.
- *Trojan Horse virus:* It often hides in an application file available on some Web sites. Once a user downloads and installs the application file, the Trojan Horse virus will be opened. Once opened, the virus can inflict damage such as annoying the user or wiping out the entire hard disk.
- *Worm:* This kind of virus harms a network by consuming the bandwidth of the infected network. Once a worm gets on a network, it can propagate itself without being carried by a program.

These viruses can get on a computer or network through various ways. Once a computer or network is infected, any of these viruses can do significant damage to the computer system or the network system. Network administrators need to be highly alert about these viruses. In the next section, several prevention methods will be discussed.

9.2.5 Network Security Measures

Based on the vulnerabilities related to hacker intrusions and virus infections, this section will discuss some security measures that resolve some of the security problems. The following are some commonly used security measures:

1. *Properly configuring application software and operating systems:* Application software and operating systems should be configured to use strong passwords and limit the number of times a user can enter an incorrect password. Users should not get more privilege than what they need. When configuring the operating system and application software, reconfigure or remove publicly available accounts. Unused communication ports should be turned off.

   Network-enabled application software is vulnerable to viruses and intrusions of hackers. For example, viruses can infect a database by executing macros or SQL procedures. The e-mail service is vulnerable and can be infected by e-mail viruses or attacked by hackers. Application software such as the media player and text messaging can also pass viruses to computers. Network-enabled application software should be configured not to accept connection requests from anonymous clients.
2. *Timely updating computers with antivirus software and security patches:* It is very important for both network administrators and users to update their computer systems with security patches and antivirus software.
3. *Setting up network firewalls:* A firewall is a network component that links the private network to the public network. It is the first defense of the private network. A properly configured firewall can be used to block communication with certain users, network devices, computer systems, network protocols, network packets, and communication ports. A firewall works like a filter to restrict certain network traffic and only allow communication with trusted

network resources. By using a firewall, the private network can be protected from dangerous Web sites and malicious hackers.

4. *Auditing network activities:* A well-constructed network monitoring and auditing system can effectively detect a hacker's intrusion. Operating systems and some application software such as database management systems support network monitoring and auditing. For example, an auditing tool can be used to set up the auditing of user logins to a computer and access to confidential files.
5. *Educating users:* To prevent viruses from infecting computer systems and private networks, network administrators need to inform users about the danger of computer virus infection. Users need to be informed on how to report computer virus infection and how to properly remove viruses from infected computers. It is very helpful if the network administrators provide users with some tips that can reduce the chances of their computers being infected by viruses. To protect network-enabled application software, users should not execute untrusted macros, Java scripts, ActiveX controls, and other types of code. It is important not to open suspicious e-mail. Users should be allowed to move the suspicious e-mail to the junk mail folder so that the sender's e-mail address can be blocked.
6. *Downloading files with care:* Downloading files from Web sites may introduce various viruses to computers and networks. Installing the infected files will activate viruses or create security holes that allow hackers to penetrate private networks. To reduce the chance of infecting computers with viruses, only download files from trusted Web sites.
7. *Protecting Web servers and Web browsers:* Developed for the public Internet, Web sites play a major role in introducing viruses and hackers to the computers on private networks. The Web server is vulnerable and is frequently attacked by hackers. From a Web site, viruses can be downloaded to a user's computer system. The interactive components on a Web site can also cause the user's computer to be infected. Hackers can find a way to penetrate the user's computer. To reduce the risk of being infected by viruses and attacked by hackers, it is a good idea to prompt users for confirmation before starting the execution of ActiveX, Java applets, scripts, and so on. The network administrator should block suspicious Web sites or other suspicious network resources.
8. *Using secure network protocols:* To protect data integrity and confidentiality, many secure protocols are created to enhance the security of network traffic. For example, the Secure Sockets Layer (SSL) can be used to establish an encrypted link between a Web server and a browser. Secure Shell (SSH) is another protocol used to create a secure connection for remote processing. The protocols are able to encrypt data before sending them out to a network and to enhance the authentication for users and computer systems.

Several security technologies have been discussed. The next section will give more details of these commonly used security technologies.

9.3 Security Technologies

Various security technologies have been created to help network administrators protect their networks. This section introduces six commonly used security technologies, including the Intrusion Detection System (IDS), IP Security (IPSec), Remote Authentication Dial In User Service (RADIUS), Secure Shell (SSH), Secure Sockets Layer (SSL), and Wi-Fi Protected Access. For each of these network security technologies, a brief explanation will be given to help readers to understand how the security technology works. Data that are transmitted over a network can be easily captured by network sniffer software. Without encryption and authentication, the data content in a packet can be read and altered by hackers. It is important to protect the data during transmission. Security technologies are used to enhance the security of network traffic. Hands-on practice will be provided to illustrate how data can be protected during transmission with security technologies such as SSH and SSL.

9.3.1 Intrusion Detection System (IDS)

As mentioned in Section 9.2.5, firewalls are effective in protecting private networks from hackers and viruses. However, some of the application layer attacks and viruses can hide their true identities under the data and activities that are normally accepted by firewalls. Some of the attacks can be done through open ports, which are allowed by firewalls. Also, hackers can use mobile devices and wireless equipment to access private networks. For these situations, an intrusion detection system (IDS) can be used to strengthen network security. The IDS is utility software that can be used to monitor inbound and outbound network traffic. It examines the packets transmitted in and out of a private network and reports security violations to the network administrator. The following are some of the attacks that can be detected by the IDS:

- Port scanning performed by hackers to search for ports used by servers
- Denial-of-service attacks performed by hackers to block network services
- Data-driven attacks, which hide malicious code in the data that are accepted by firewalls
- Mimicry attacks, which hide the malicious sequence of events such as system calls under the guise of normal network activities
- Privilege escalation, which takes advantage of software bugs or design faults to gain more privilege than normally intended
- OS fingerprinting, which can be used by hackers to collect information about the operating systems used in a remote network
- Directory traversals, which take advantage of the lack of control on a Web server to execute commands and access restricted directories
- Web server exploits, which may allow hackers to penetrate a private network while contacting the Web server through Web pages
- Unauthorized logins and access to confidential files by hackers
- Infections by malware such as Trojan horses, Sasser worm, and Gator spyware
- Attacks originating within a private network

To detect the foregoing attacks, an IDS includes sensors to watch network traffic, and a console to manage the sensors, monitor events, and distribute alerts. It also has a central engine to store the data collected by the sensors in a database and to generate alerts based on the data analysis.

Depending on the central engine and the location of the sensors, IDSs can be categorized into several different types. An IDS can be network based, host based, or protocol based. It can also be a passive system or a reactive system. Depending on the detection method, the IDS can be categorized as a misuse detection system or an anomaly detection system. The following list describes these systems:

1. *Network-based system:* In a network-based intrusion detection system (NIDS), the sensors are placed on the border of two networks or at the neutral zone between a private network and a public network, called the demilitarized zone (DMZ). The NIDS sensors capture all the packets flowing through a network and analyze the packets individually to detect malicious packets that are overlooked by firewalls.
2. *Host-based system:* In a host-based intrusion detection system (HIDS), the sensors monitor activities of the host computer. The HIDS analyzes information such as system calls, file system modifications, and file logging collected by the sensors to detect intrusion.
3. *Protocol-based system:* The protocol-based intrusion detection system (PIDS) is typically used to monitor and analyze the content and dynamic behavior of communication protocols such as HTTP or HTTPS. The PIDS is often placed on a Web server.
4. *Application-protocol-based system:* The application-protocol-based intrusion detection system (APIDS) is used to monitor and analyze the activities of protocols used by application servers and programming languages. For example, APIDS is often used to monitor database remote access to detect illegal access to the database server.
5. *Passive system:* In the passive system, the IDS detects and sends alerts to the user after a potential network security violation is detected. The IDS will also log the information.
6. *Reactive system:* In a reactive system, after a potential network security violation is detected, the IDS handles the violation by logging off a user or by reconfiguring the firewall to block malicious network traffic.
7. *Misuse detection:* The misuse detection IDS gathers information from network traffic and analyzes it by comparison with known malicious attacks documented in a database. The advantage of this type of IDS is that a malicious attack can be quickly identified if the attack is known and has been stored in the database. The disadvantage is that the system can only detect known attacks. It also has difficulty detecting viruses that can self-modify their characteristics.
8. *Anomaly detection:* The anomaly detection IDS gathers information from network traffic and compares it with predefined normal network behavior such as the normal traffic load, normal packet size, and so on. The advantage of this IDS is that it can be used to identify unknown attacks if the attacks generate anomalies. Such a system is especially useful in detecting a worm virus because the worm virus needs to scan the network to find security holes, which can generate abnormal network traffic. The disadvantage is that it is not easy to define normal network behavior. It is tedious to define the normal behavior for each of the protocols used by the network. Without an extensive statistical analysis, it is difficult to specify the limits of normal values.

As described in the foregoing, unlike a firewall, which prevents attacks from outside of a private network, an IDS can identify both external and internal attacks. This feature makes the IDS a valuable security technology.

9.3.2 IP Security (IPSec)

IPSec is a set of protocols used for securely exchanging packets at the Internet layer. Because IPSec works at the Internet layer, it can secure almost all the protocols in the layers above the Internet layer. For example, it can provide security for the protocols in the TCP/IP suite as well as the protocols in the application layer. Therefore, there is no need to secure each individual application that uses protocols in the application layer separately. IPSec has three features to keep packet transmission secure:

- Encryption to keep data confidentiality
- Authentication to make sure that the computers or network devices on both ends of the communication are trusted
- Digital signature to prevent the content of a packet from being altered

IPSec supports two encryption modes, tunnel mode and transport mode. Tunnel mode is used to provide encryption for the communication between two networks. Transport mode provides encryption between two hosts.

1. *Tunnel mode:* Tunnel mode is used for the communication between two routers. As shown in Figure 9.1, the two networks are linked through two routers. The hosts in a network do not encrypt the content in a packet. When a router receives a packet, it will encrypt the content and then send the packet to the destination router. On the receiving side, the destination router decrypts the content in the received packet and then delivers the packet to the destination host. All the hosts in one network, even some of the network devices that do not normally support IPSec, can securely communicate with the hosts in another network. However, the communication within a network is not encrypted.

   There are two other modes that tunnel mode can work with. Tunnel mode can work with the Authentication Headers (AH) mode if encryption is not required or the Encapsulation Security Payload (ESP) mode if encryption is required. AH mode authenticates the header of a packet to make sure that both ends of the communication are trusted. In addition, AH mode will add the digital signature and the checksum to make sure that the content carried by a packet is not altered during transmission. As for the encryption, tunnel mode can work with ESP mode to encrypt both the header and the payload of a packet.
2. *Transport mode:* Transport mode is used for the communication between two hosts. As shown in Figure 9.2, each host must support IPSec individually. Before a packet is sent to the destination host, it is encrypted by the sender. Usually, not all hosts are capable of supporting IPSec. For example, some network devices such as printers may not be able communicate with other hosts using IPSec.

   Also, transport mode can work with AH mode if encryption is not required and with ESP mode if encryption is required. If ESP mode is used for encryption, transport mode only encrypts the payload portion of a packet and leaves the header unencrypted.

The description of ESP encryption for transport mode and tunnel mode is illustrated in Figures 9.3 and 9.4. As seen in these figures, tunnel mode encrypts the payload as well as the original header.

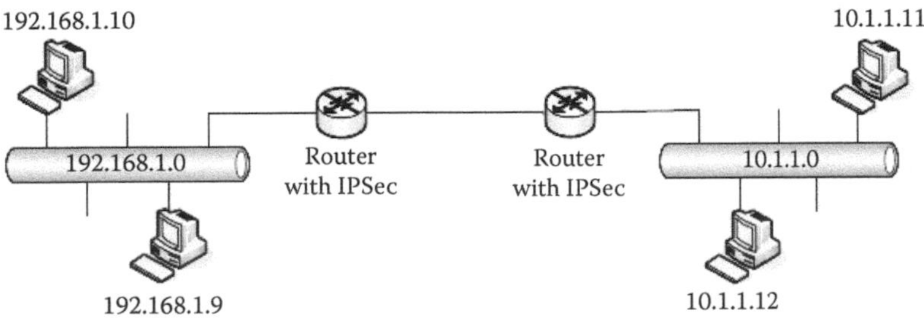

Figure 9.1 Tunnel mode.

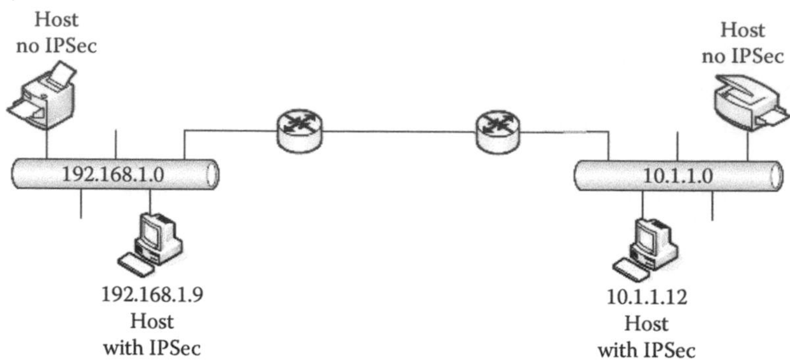

Figure 9.2 Transport mode.

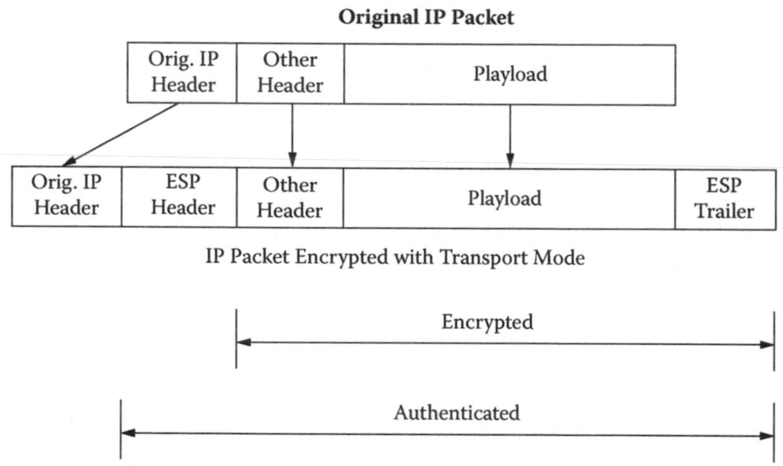

Figure 9.3 ESP encryption for transport mode.

Encryption by tunnel mode is more secure because the original IP header is hidden. With these features, IPSec technology has been widely used by the virtual private network (VPN) to secure the data content when transmitting packets on the public Internet.

9.3.3 Remote Authentication Dial In User Service (RADIUS)

RADIUS is a network protocol designed to centralize the authentication service in a large distributed network managed by ISPs. It can provide the authentication service for remote access mechanisms such as remote dial-up, VPN, and wireless access points. Each server in a large distributed network has its own remote access policies. It is often required that the remote access policies be synchronized. RADIUS simplifies the remote access process, and there is no need to synchronize the remote access policies. RADIUS can also be used to centralize the storage of remote access log files. The process of recording the accesses in log files is also called *accounting*. In addition to centralizing authentication and accounting, RADIUS can also perform tasks to centralize the authorization process. After a user or computer is authenticated, RADIUS can further assign

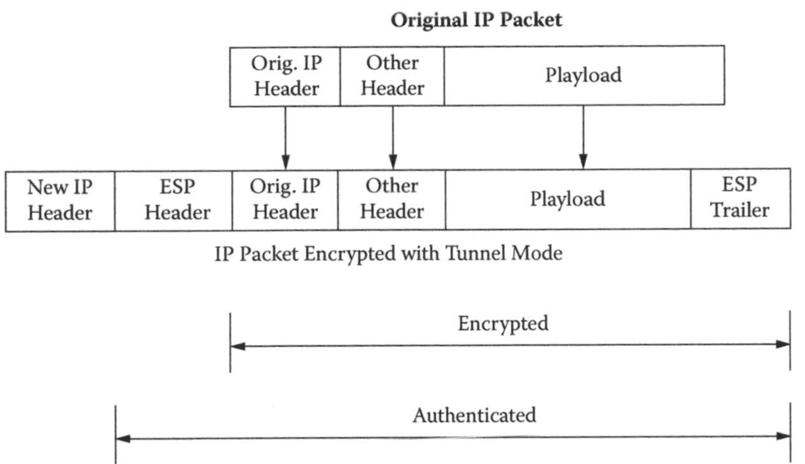

Figure 9.4 ESP encryption for tunnel mode.

privileges to the authenticated user or computer. Therefore, one may say that RADIUS supports the centralized AAA process.

There are two components in RADIUS, the RADIUS client and the RADIUS server. The following are brief descriptions of these two components:

1. *RADIUS client:* The RADIUS client could be a VPN server, a dial-up server, or a wireless access point that takes authentication requests from users or network devices. After it receives an authentication request, which may include the username and password, the RADIUS client forwards the authentication request to the RADIUS server for authentication.
2. *RADIUS server:* After it receives an authentication request from a RADIUS client, the RADIUS server processes the authentication request. Based on the username and password, the RADIUS server can decide if the request should be accepted, denied, or challenged. If the request is accepted, the RADIUS server will authorize the request. Then, the authorization will be sent back to the RADIUS client. With the message sent by the RADIUS server, the RADIUS client can decide whether to allow or deny the connection request from the user or network device. Figure 9.5 illustrates how the RADIUS client and the RADIUS server work together to get the authentication done.

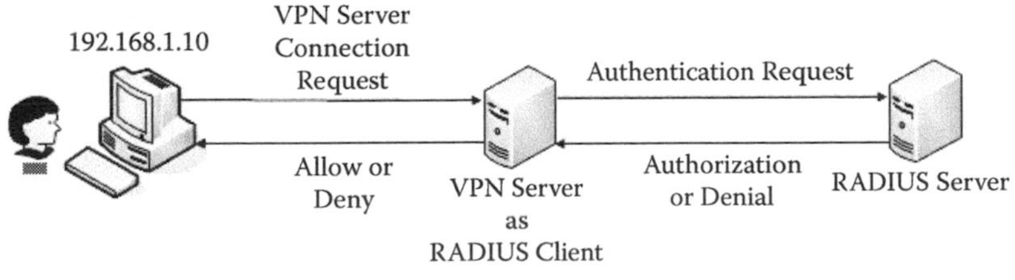

Figure 9.5 Authentication with RADIUS client and server.

9.3.4 Secure Shell (SSH)

Similar to Telnet, SSH is an application layer protocol for remotely logging on to another computer or network device. Telnet transmits data in cleartext, which makes it insecure. SSH is designed to replace Telnet by encrypting data before transmitting them across the Internet. It is important to encrypt the remote logon information, including the username and password. SSH is designed to guarantee confidentiality and integrity for remote logon and file transfer. SSH uses port 22 for communication.

In SSH, asymmetrical encryption is employed, which uses two different keys, the public key and private key. The public key is used to encrypt data by the sender, and the private key is used by the receiver to decrypt the encrypted message. The encrypted message can only be decrypted with the private key. The following text describes the encryption process employed by SSH:

1. To log on remotely to a destination host, the sender and receiver must have SSH enabled. Once SSH is enabled, it generates the public key and private key.
2. When the sender tries to connect to the receiver with SSH, the SSH on the receiver end sends the public key to the sender.
3. After the public key is received, the sender uses the public key to encrypt the remote logon information, including the sender's username and password.
4. The sender sends the encrypted message and his or her own public key to the receiver.
5. After the encrypted message is received, the receiver uses his or her own private key to decrypt the message.
6. To respond to the sender's remote logon request, the receiver uses the sender's public key to encrypt the return message.
7. The receiver sends the encrypted return message to the sender.
8. After the return message is delivered to the sender, the sender uses his or her own private key to decrypt the encrypted return message.

The private key and public key generated by an SSH host are related. Once the message is encrypted by the public key, only the host who issues the public key can decrypt the encrypted message with his or her own private key.

Activity 9.1 Encrypting Network Traffic with Secure Shell (SSH)

In this hands-on practice, you will examine how SSH secures packet transmission. First, you will capture some packets transmitted with Telnet to find out how easy it is for a hacker to get someone's username and password if no encryption is used. This hands-on practice also will show you that after the packets are encrypted with SSH, the information carried by the packets will be hidden from hackers.

Because Telnet will be used for the demonstration, your first task is to make sure that Telnet service is enabled on your server machine. Follow these steps to accomplish the task:

1. Log on to the server machine with username **student** and password **ubuntu**.
2. To install the Telnet daemon, enter the following command in the terminal window:

   ```
   sudo apt-get install telnetd
   ```

3. After successfully installing the Telnet daemon, you need to start the Telnet service with the following command:

   ```
   sudo /etc/init.d/openbsd-inetd restart
   ```

4. To verify that you can access the Telnet service from your client machine, log on to your client machine with username **student** and password **ubuntu**.
5. To access the Telnet service, execute the following command in the terminal window on the client machine:

```
telnet 192.168.2.1
```

6. The Telnet service prompts you to enter authentication information. Enter the username **student** and password **ubuntu**.
7. After successfully connecting to the server machine, you are now logged on to the server machine. To verify this, you can try some commands such as:

```
ls
```

8. You should see files and directories on the server machine in the student's home directory (Figure 9.6).
9. To exit the Telnet service, enter the following command:

```
exit
```

As you can see from the foregoing, Telnet is a convenient tool to remotely log on to a remote computer for performing various tasks. On the other hand, because Telnet transmits the data in cleartext, Telnet is a major security hole in a network. Hackers can easily capture the packets

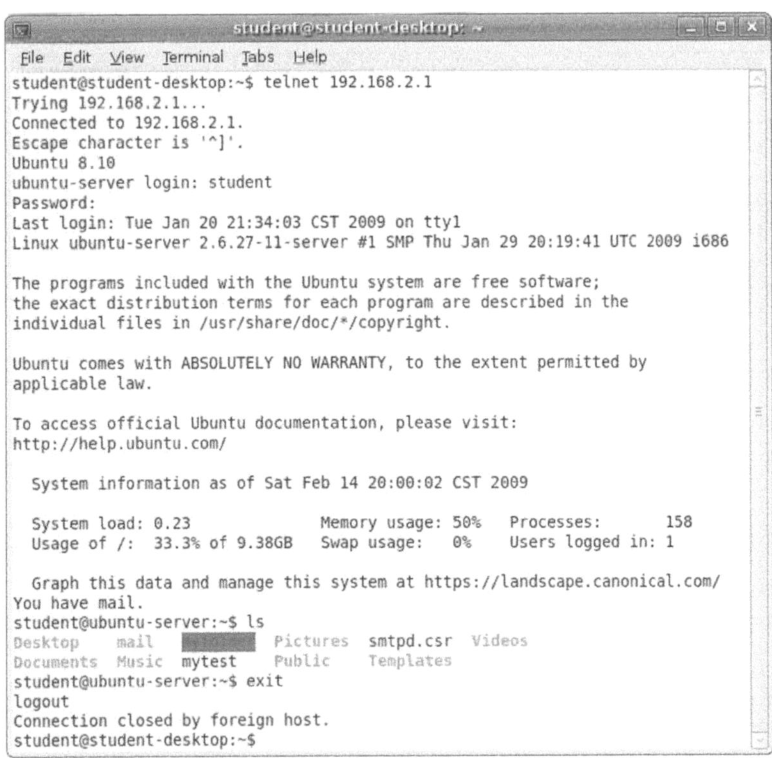

Figure 9.6 Testing Telnet service.

transmitted by Telnet and examine the data content in a packet. This will be demonstrated in the second part of the hands-on practice.

To capture the network traffic, you will need the network monitoring tool called Wireshark. The following steps show you how to install Wireshark on the client machine:

1. To install Wireshark, enter the following command in the terminal window:

```
sudo apt-get install wireshark
```

2. To start Wireshark, enter the following command in the terminal window:

```
sudo wireshark
```

   You will be prompted with a warning message; click **OK** to continue.
3. After Wireshark is opened, you need to specify the NIC through which to capture the packets transmitted on the network. To do so, click the **Capture** menu, and select **Options** from the pop-up menu.
4. Once the Options dialog is opened, in the Interface drop-down list select **eth2**, which is the NIC used to communicate with the server machine (Figure 9.7)
5. Click the **Start** button to start the packet-capturing process.
6. To capture the network traffic generated by Telnet, open a new terminal window on the client machine by clicking the **Applications** menu, **Accessories**, and **Terminal.**
7. Execute the following command to access the Telnet service:

```
telnet 192.168.2.1
```

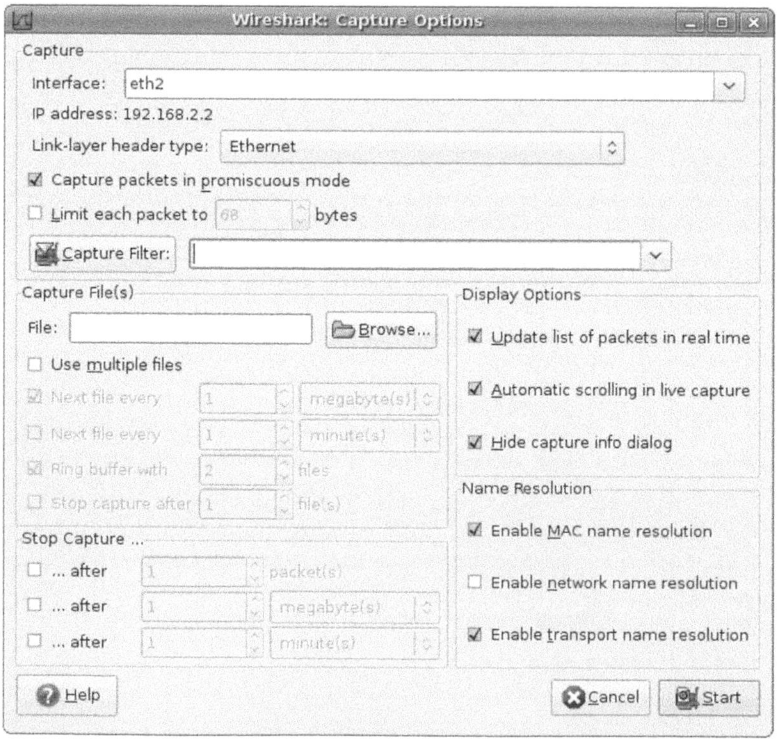

Figure 9.7 Selecting NIC for packet capturing.

8. Enter the username **student** and password **ubuntu**.
9. Enter the following command to exit the Telnet service:

```
exit
```

10. To stop the packet-capturing process, in the Wireshark window, click the **Capture** menu, and select **Stop** from the pop-up menu.
11. Once Wireshark has stopped, you can view the captured packets. To do so, in the top pane of the Wireshark window, try one of the Telnet packets transmitted from the NIC with IP address 192.168.2.1 to the NIC with IP address 192.168.2.2 (Figure 9.8).
12. In the middle pane of the Wireshark window, click the **Telnet** link (Figure 9.8).
13. In the middle and bottom panes, you should see the data content carried by Telnet. In Figure 9.8, the data content is the letter "s." Remember that the username used by Telnet is student.
14. Move down three lines; select the Telnet packet with source IP address 192.168.2.1 (Figure 9.9). Click the link **Telnet** in the middle pane. This time, you should see the letter "t" in the bottom pane in cleartext. Do the same to select another Telnet packet a few lines down in the top pane. Then, you will find the letter "u" in the bottom pane (Figure 9.10). In this way, piece by piece, you will be able to get the username student and password ubuntu.

From this demonstration, it is dangerous to transmit data in cleartext. SSH encrypts the data packet used for remote logins and file transfers. In the following, you will install and configure SSH on the server machine. Then, you will access the server machine from the client machine with SSH and examine if you are still able to view the data content in the captured packets. Follow these steps to accomplish these tasks:

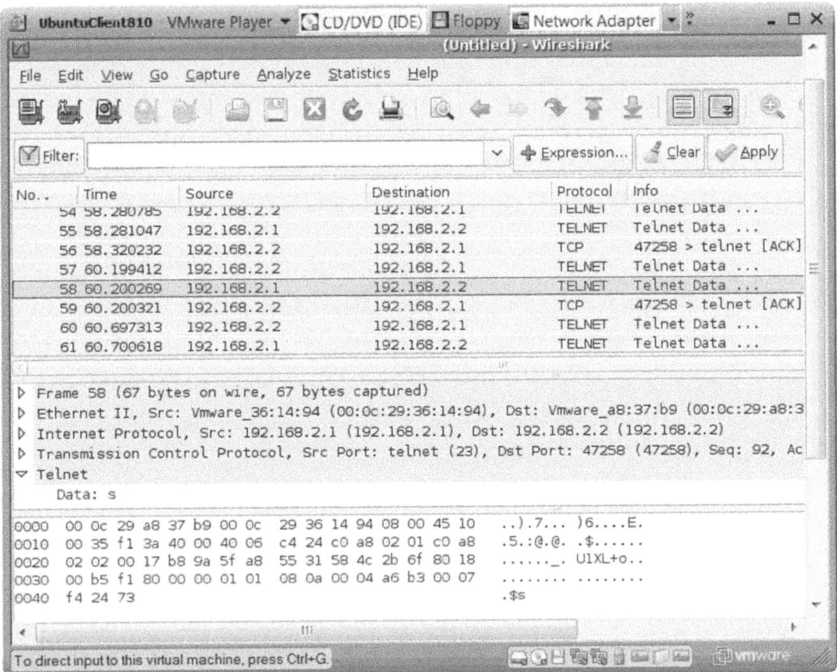

Figure 9.8 Displaying the letter "s" in Telnet packet.

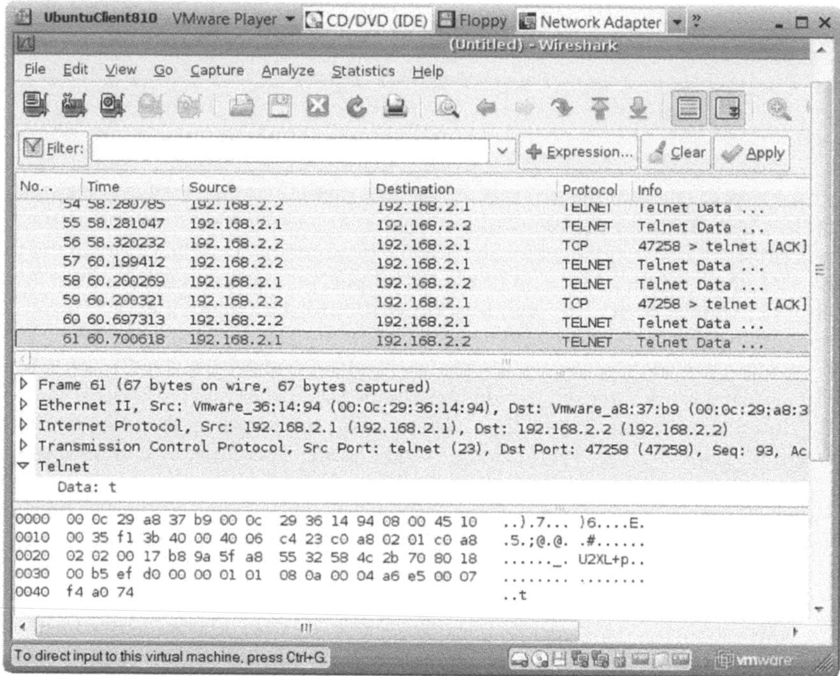

Figure 9.9 Displaying the letter "t" in Telnet packet.

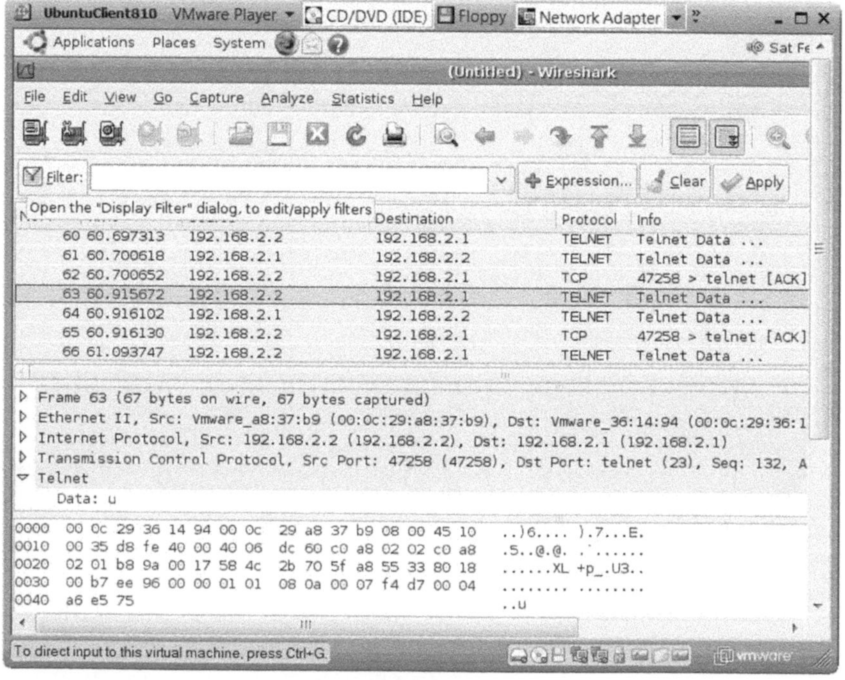

Figure 9.10 Displaying the letter "u" in Telnet packet.

1. Log on to the server computer with username **student** and password **ubuntu**.
2. To install SSH server and client on the server machine, enter the following command:

```
sudo apt-get install openssh-server openssh-client
```

3. After the SSH server and client are installed on the server machine, you may want to test the SSH server to see if it is enabled. To do so, enter the following command:

```
ssh 192.168.2.1
```

4. Enter **yes** to continue the connection. Enter the password as **ubuntu**.
5. After you have successfully logged on to the server machine with SSH, enter the command **exit** to quit the connection.
6. Log on to the client machine with username **student** and password **ubuntu**.
7. By default, the open-client is installed on the client machine. To verify, enter the following command in the terminal window:

```
ssh 192.168.2.1
```

8. Enter **yes** to continue the connection. Enter the password **ubuntu**.
9. After you have successfully logged on to the server machine with SSH, enter the command **exit** to end the connection.
10. If the Wireshark window is still open on the client machine, click the **Start** button to start the packet-capturing process.
11. To capture the network traffic generated by SSH, in the second terminal window on the client machine, execute the following command to access the Telnet service:

```
ssh 192.168.2.1
```

12. Enter the password **ubuntu**.
13. After you have accessed the server machine, enter the following command to exit the SSH:

```
exit
```

14. Click the **Capture** menu on Wireshark, and select **Stop** from the pop-up menu to stop the packet-capturing process.
15. As shown in Figure 9.11, you will see that some encrypted SSHv2 packets are captured. Select one of them on the top pane, and click **SSH Protocol** in the middle pane. In the bottom pane, you will not be able to view the data content.

The foregoing hands-on practice has illustrated that it is vulnerable to use the protocols that transmit data in cleartext. Many of those protocols are still widely used, HTTP being one of them. Next, we will discuss some security measures used to protect the data content carried by HTTP.

9.3.5 Secure Sockets Layer (SSL)

SSL is another protocol that provides authentication and encryption for data transferred over a network. SSL is designed to secure the private data that are to be transferred across the Internet. SSL can be used with any application layer protocols and is optimized for HTTP. Hypertext Transfer Protocol Secure (HTTPS) is commonly known as HTTP over SSL. If a Web server is secured, the Web browser can communicate with the Web server by HTTPS through port 443. Most Internet

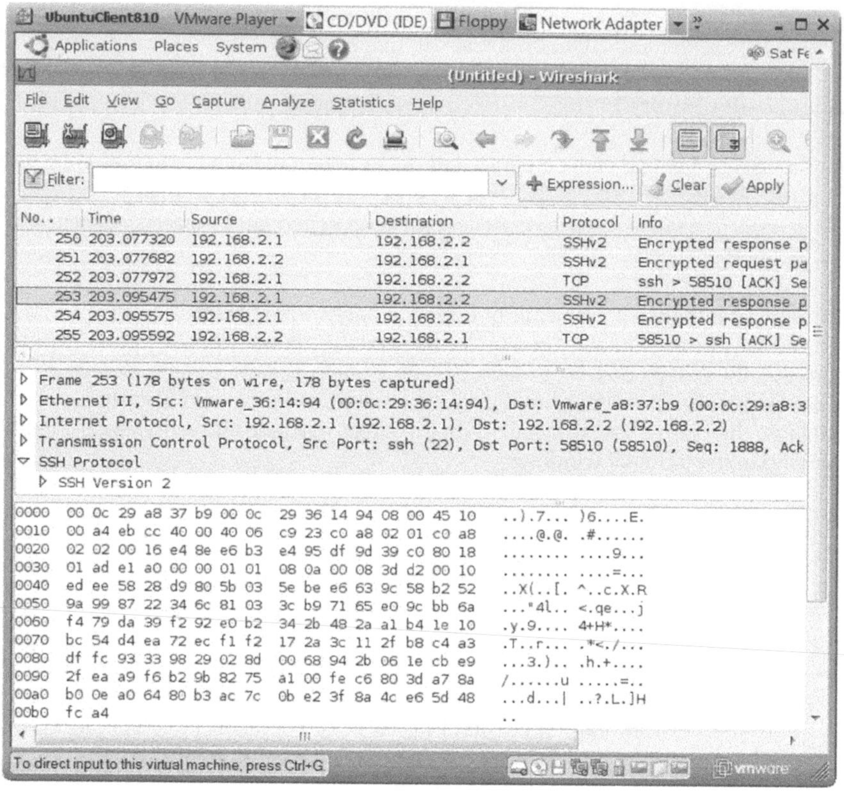

Figure 9.11 Displaying SSHv2 packet.

services use SSL for authentication and encryption. In addition to HTTP, other protocols such as IMAP, FTP, and Telnet, can also use SSL to secure their data content. Before data are transmitted across a network, a client will authenticate the server and negotiate the encryption key with the server. The following are the major steps to apply SSL technology:

1. The company that provides the Internet service installs the SSL service software on the server and generates its own pair of public key and private key.
2. For secure Internet communication, the company that provides the Internet service enrolls in the certification service provided by certification companies such as Thawte or VeriSign.
3. The certification company certifies the identity of the Internet service company and adds certification information to the public key.
4. To access the Internet service provided by the company, the client contacts the server and asks for a connection.
5. The server sends the public key to the client.
6. The client sends the public key to the certification company for verification.
7. The certification company verifies the public key. If the public key is certified, the company will send the confirmation to the client.
8. After the client receives the confirmation from the certification company, the client will accept the server's public key.

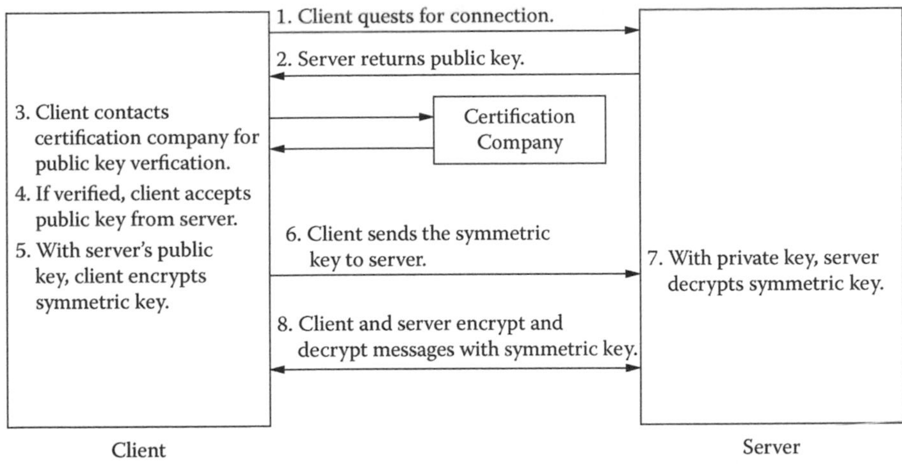

Figure 9.12 SSL authentication and encryption key negotiation process.

9. With the server's public key, the client encrypts a symmetric key that will be used by both the client and the server for data encryption and decryption.
10. The client sends the encrypted symmetric key to the server.
11. The server decrypts the symmetric key with its own private key.
12. From here on, both the client and server will use the symmetric key to encrypt and decrypt data transmitted across the network. The use of the symmetric key can make encryption faster and simpler.

To prevent hackers from guessing a private key, the length of the private key has to be long enough. It is relatively easier for hackers to guess a 40-bit key by using a computer program. SSL currently uses a 128-bit or better private key, which may take longer than a lifetime to guess. Figure 9.12 illustrates the authentication and the encryption key negotiation process.

While SSH introduced earlier is mainly for remote logon and file transfer over a network, SSL is mainly used for transmitting sensitive information such as online banking transactions. SSL is also widely used for online shopping, Web e-mail, and other types of e-commerce activities.

Activity 9.2 SSL Configuration

To secure your Web site, you should use the Secure Sockets Layer (SSL) to encrypt data for communication between the Web server and Web browsers. To use SSL, you need to enable the module mod_ssl. With mod_ssl enabled and configured, a browser can use the prefix https:// at the beginning of a URL to communicate with the Web server. The following steps show you how to enable and configure the mod_ssl module:

1. Log on to the server machine with username **student** and password **ubuntu**.
2. After logging on to the server machine, you need to enable SSL by executing the following command:

```
sudo a2enmod ssl
```

3. After SSL is enabled, you need to reload the Apache Web server by executing the following command:

```
sudo /etc/init.d/apache2 force-reload
```

4. Most of the configuration can be done in the directory /etc/apache2. Use the following command to change the working directory to that directory:

```
cd /etc/apache2
```

5. Your next task is to create an encryption key, which can be done with the following command:

```
sudo openssl genrsa -des3 -out encrypt.key 1024
```

   In this command, the options and keywords have the following meanings:
   - genrsa: It generates an RSA private key.
   - -out: It indicates that the file following this option is an output file.
   - -des3: It means that the encryption is done with the triple DES key.
   - 1024: It is the number of bits in the generated private key. The default is 512 bits. This option should be specified last.
6. The encryption key stored in the file server.key can be used to create a certificate request by executing the following command:

```
sudo openssl req -new -key encrypt.key -out server.csr
```

   In this command, the options and keywords have the following meanings:
   - req: It is the utility used to request a certificate.
   - -out: It indicates that the file following this option is an output file.
   - -new: It means that a new certificate is going to be generated.
   - -key: It specifies the file containing the encryption key.
7. You will be prompted to enter some information about the certificate, such as the address and e-mail of the Web server administrator. Enter the information relevant to yourself for the certificate. When asked to enter the passphrase, enter the password **ubuntu**.
8. In the previous step, you created a certificate request. This certificate request can be used to create a self-signed certificate by executing the following command:

```
sudo openssl x509 -req -days 365 -in server.csr -signkey encrypt.key
-out server.crt
```

   In this command, the options and keywords have the following meanings:
   - x509: It is the utility used to display and sign a certificate.
   - -req: It specifies that the certificate request is used as the input.
   - -days: It specifies the valid days for a certificate. In the preceding command, 365 days are specified. The default is 30 days.
   - -in: It indicates that the file following this option is an input file that contains the certificate information.
   - -out: It indicates that the file following this option is an output file.
   - -signkey: This option specifies that the input file will be self-signed with the key stored in the file following this option.
9. Next, you need to copy the file server.crt to the directory /etc/ssl/certs/ with the following command:

```
sudo cp server.crt /etc/ssl/certs/
```

10. Similarly, you should copy the file encrypt.key to the directory /etc/ssl/private/ with the following command:

```
sudo cp encrypt.key /etc/ssl/private/
```

11. Your next task is to configure the file default-ssl to include the certificate and the encryption key you just created. Use the following command to open the file default-ssl:

```
sudo gedit /etc/apache2/sites-available/default-ssl
```

12. After the file is opened, search for the lines that start with the phrase **SSLOptions**. Uncomment these lines (Figure 9.13).
13. Search for the keyword **SSLCertificateFile**, and change the default directory (Figure 9.14). Also, change the default setting for SSLCertificateKeyFile (Figure 9.14). Save the changes, and quit the editor.
14. Next, you need to restart Apache to allow the configuration to take effect, by executing the following command:

```
sudo /etc/init.d/apache2 restart
```

   If you see the Apache server start successfully, the configuration of the SSL server is complete.
15. You may test the SSL configuration by using the URL https://ns1.group2.lab in the Web browser on the server machine. However, by default, the Firefox browser does not allow a self-signed certificate. You may see an error message (Figure 9.15).
16. To see the default Web page provided by the server machine through the secure connection, you may need to overwrite the Firefox rule by clicking **"Or you can add an exception."**
17. Click the **Add Exception** button. You will see the warning message shown in Figure 9.16. Click the **Get Certificate** button to overwrite Firefox's rule.
18. Click the button **Confirm Security Exception**; you should see the result in Figure 9.17.

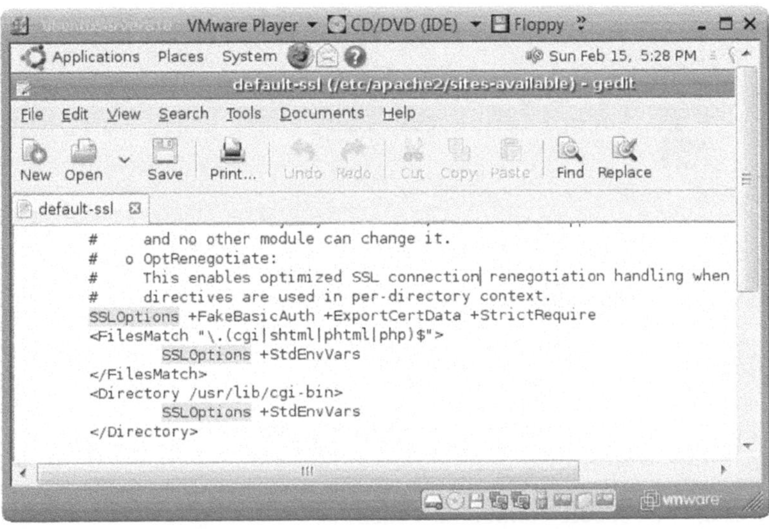

Figure 9.13 Enabling SSL options.

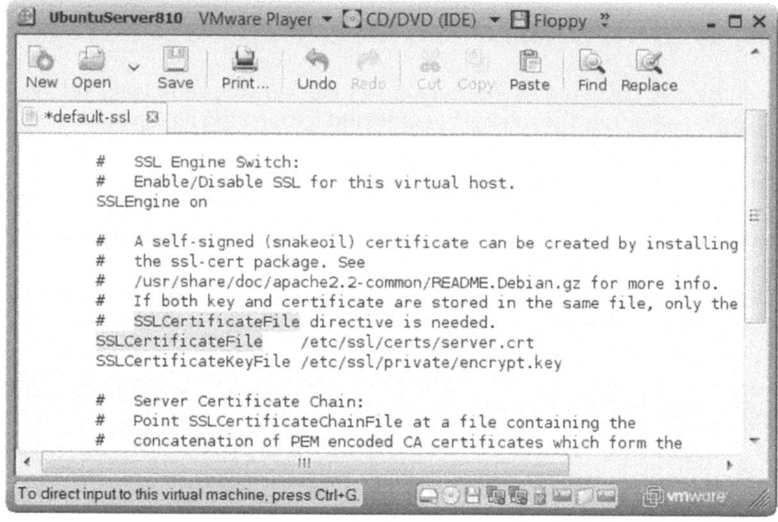

Figure 9.14 Configuration of SSL certificate file.

Figure 9.15 Message that secure connection failed.

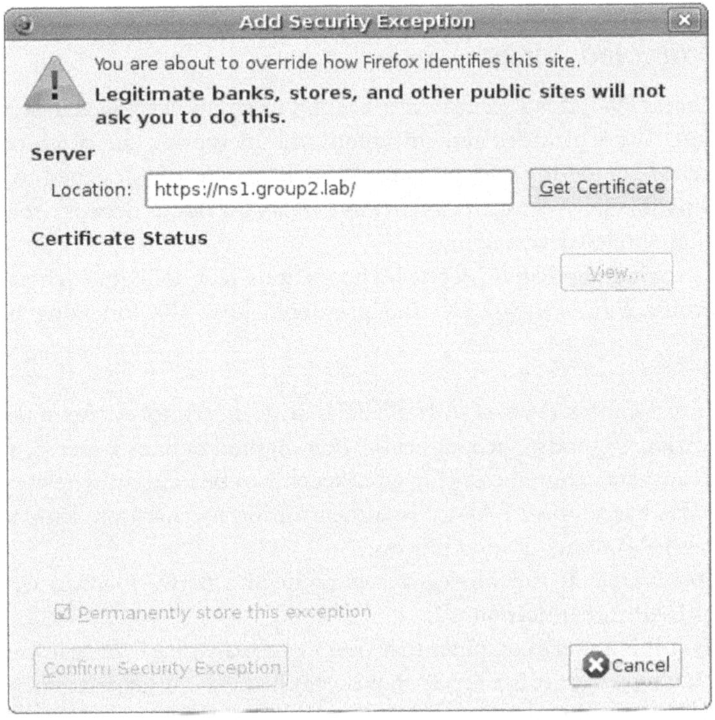

Figure 9.16 Warning message upon clicking the Add Exception button.

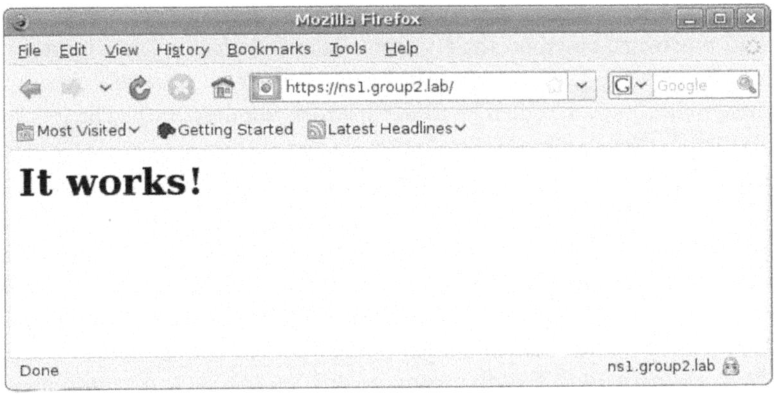

Figure 9.17 SSL configuration.

Now you have completed the configuration for SSL. If certified by the third party, the Web server can provide secure communication with any Web browser across the Internet.

9.3.6 Wi-Fi Protected Access

Wi-Fi Protected Access (WPA) is a security certification program developed to secure Wi-Fi wireless communication. WPA provides authentication and encryption for protecting information exchange in a wireless computing environment. WPA is specifically designed to also work with most wireless-compatible devices, such as wireless NICs and home network routers, except for some first-generation wireless access points.

WPA provides the authentication service with various technologies such as the Extensible Authentication Protocol (EAP), 802.1X, and preshared key. The following briefly describes these technologies:

1. *Extensible Authentication Protocol (EAP):* EAP is an authentication system that includes over 40 authentication methods. Each authentication method defines a specific way to encapsulate the EAP authentication message in a packet. It can be used for wireless as well as wired networks. WPA has adopted EAP as its authentication mechanism. Three components are involved in an EAP authentication process:
   - *EAP authenticator:* It is a wireless access point or a network access server (NAS) that conducts EAP authentication.
   - *EAP client:* It is a user's computer that tries to access an EAP authenticator.
   - *Authentication server:* It is a server that hosts the EAP authentication system, validates the credentials, and authorizes the access to a network. The RADIUS server discussed earlier in this chapter is an example of the authentication server.

   When a client needs to access a network, the client authentication software, which is a supplicant, will contact the authenticator. During the connection phase, the client and authentication server can negotiate on an EAP authentication method. After the authentication method is determined, the authentication message can be processed by the chosen authentication method. The EAP authentication method can be configured to control the authentication conversation. Figure 9.18 illustrates the authentication process.
2. *802.1X:* It is a security standard that supports wireless LAN authentication. 802.1X controls the access to a network based on the result of the authentication. In Figure 9.18, when the EAP client contacts the EAP authenticator for accessing the network resources, the EAP authenticator only allows the client to access network resources if the client is authenticated. 802.1X makes the client only communicate with the authentication server before the client is authenticated. 802.1X can also be configured to enforce the network traffic policy based on the identity of a user or a computer.
3. *Pre-Shared Key (PSK):* PSK is an authentication method based on the fact that both the authenticator and client know the same secret, such as the password. If the authenticator and client enter the same password, the connection is established. The advantage of PSK is its simplicity. PSK does not need an authentication server; this is a desired feature for home or small business networks. The disadvantage of PSK is that it may get intercepted while delivering the pre-shared key to the partner through e-mail or other means.
4. *Wi-Fi Protected Access (WPA):* WPA uses Temporal Key Integrity Protocol (TKIP) for encryption. WPA2 is a newer version of WPA. WPA2 uses the advanced encryption technique called Advanced Encryption Standard (AES). AES is compliant with Federal

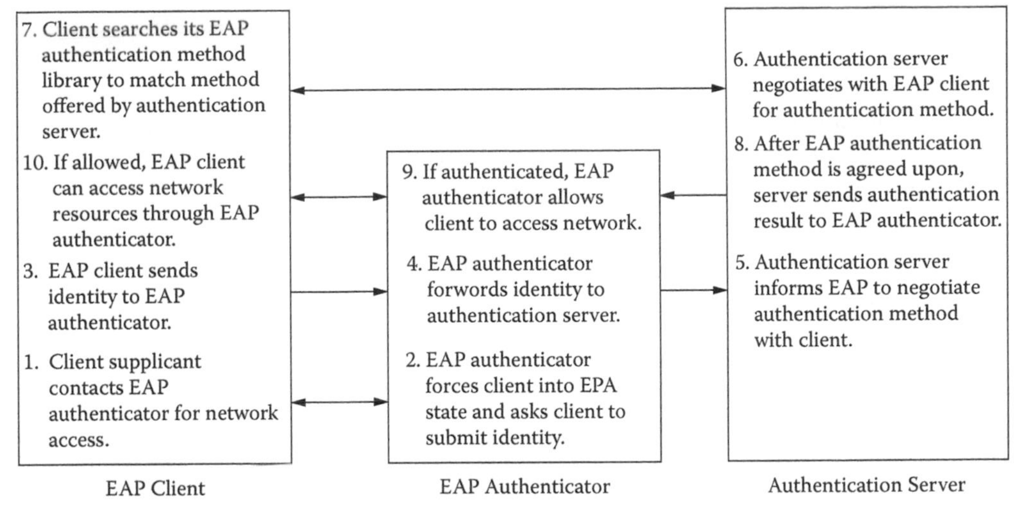

Figure 9.18 EAP authentication process.

Information Processing Standard (FIPS) 140-2, which defines the government security requirements. The AES-based encryption algorithms are considered highly secure and efficient. This advantage makes WPA2 suitable for large corporations and government agencies. Since March 13, 2006, WPA2 certification has been mandatory for all new devices if these devices need to be marked "Wi-Fi Certified." Brief descriptions of TKIP and AES follow.

5. *Temporal Key Integrity Protocol (TKIP):* TKIP is an encryption protocol defined by the IEEE 802.11i specification to address encryption issues related to wireless security. One of the design goals for TKIP is to be backward compatible with some of the older wireless hardware. Therefore, TKIP is built based on the older encryption algorithm called Wired Equivalent Privacy (WEP), which is known for its short key length. TKIP uses a 128-bit encryption key, which is considered very secure. In this way, TKIP is able to work with the wireless devices that support WEP and upgrade the security for these devices. On the other hand, TKIP is not very efficient and does not address all the requirements of Federal Information Processing Standard (FIPS) 140-2. Therefore, IEEE 802.11i has specified another encryption standard called Advanced Encryption Standard (AES).
6. *Advanced Encryption Standard (AES):* As an encryption standard, AES was released by the National Institute of Standards and Technology (NIST) in the year 2001. The following are some of the design goals to be met by AES:
   - AES is designed to secure sensitive but unclassified government documents.
   - AES is designed to address all the requirements specified by Federal Information Processing Standard (FIPS) 140-2.
   - The encryption key used by the AES algorithm should be able to support encryption keys with different lengths. The AES encryption key can be configured to use 128, 192, or 256 bits.
   - The AES algorithm should be free for everyone to use.
   - AES should be easily implemented with hardware or software.
   - Running the AES algorithm should take little computing resources so that it can run on mobile devices or smart cards.

After extensive investigation, NIST adopted the algorithm called Rijndael, written by Belgian cryptographers Joan Daemen and Vincent Rijmen, as the Advanced Encryption Standard (AES). By meeting these design goals, AES has become one of the most popular encryption standards. It offers efficient and reliable encryption that meets security standards approved for government use. It has been adopted by WPA2 as the encryption standard. However, the implementation of AES requires newer hardware.

9.4 Network Firewalls

In the Section 9.3, several technologies to protect network traffic with authentication and encryption were introduced. Firewalls use a different approach: they block harmful network traffic from spreading to private networks and computers. A firewall itself is a piece of software or a hardware device used as a filter to block harmful network traffic. A server machine can also be configured to host firewall software to protect private networks. When properly configured, firewalls can be used to protect private networks from the threats caused by hackers and viruses:

- Firewalls can protect servers from denial-of-service attacks.
- Firewalls can block hackers from accessing network-based application software.
- Firewalls can be used to stop e-mail spam.
- Firewalls can be used to prevent hackers from logging on to the computers in a private network.
- Firewalls can be used to check the content of macros, which may be used by hackers to steal sensitive information or cause a system to crash.
- Firewalls can prevent computer virus infection.

Several approaches can be used by firewalls to accomplish these jobs. The following are some of the mechanisms used by a firewall:

- *Filtering packets:* Based on the protocol, communication ports, source and destination addresses, and so on, a firewall can decide if a packet is allowed to pass the firewall to the private network.
- *Connecting clients to services:* A firewall can serve as a proxy server that creates and controls a process which links a client to a service.
- *Inspecting packet state:* Similar to the packet filtering mechanism, the inspecting packet state mechanism can be used to verify IP addresses, ports, and protocols. In addition, it can record protocol behavior and maintain records about the data and the connection state between the sender and receiver. By having the ability to "remember" the status of a connection and data transmission, the mechanism provides better protection than that provided by the packet filtering mechanism.

In order to use firewalls to protect private networks and computers, you need to know the issues related to firewall rules that are used as the guideline for properly configuring the firewalls. The next section discusses the firewall-rule-related issues.

9.4.1 Firewall Rules

In the online teaching and e-commerce environment, various Internet-based services are set to allow students and customers to interact with the servers located on private networks. Accessing the servers through the public Internet creates the risk of introduction of computer viruses and hacker attacks to private networks. A firewall that links a private network to a public network is configured in various ways to protect the private network. When a firewall is enabled and configured on a router, the private network is protected from outside intruders. However, the firewall does not prevent insiders from intruding into individual computers on the private network. Some highly protected hosts on the private network are also guarded by their own firewalls to prevent untrusted access even from the internal network.

In general, there are fewer constraints on outbound network traffic. Most of the time, outbound traffic is allowed. However, inbound traffic should be closely examined. A set of rules should be used to control how users access services. The configuration of the firewall will be based on this set of rules to protect the private network. The firewall rules specify the following:

- Which network services are allowed or not allowed to receive or send packets through the firewall
- Which network communication ports should be blocked or allowed to pass network traffic
- Which network protocols are accepted or denied by the private network or computer
- Which source addresses or destination addresses should be accepted or denied
- Which host names or domain names should be accepted or denied
- Which key words or phrases in the message carried by a packet should be accepted or denied
- Which connection state should be accepted or denied

The commonly seen network-related services are e-mail service, remote access services such as VPN and Telnet services, Internet phone service, file transfer service, naming service, routing service, error reporting service, Web service (used to share data across the network), and many other client-server-based services. Firewall rules should be ranked based on how restrictive a rule is. The most restrictive rule should be implemented first, and the least restrictive rule should be implemented last. Also, in general, the network administrator starts with a minimum set of network services and then carefully adds more services if they are absolutely necessary.

Each network uses specified protocols to exchange messages with other networks. These protocols communicate through dedicated ports. Based on the services provided, a firewall needs to specify a set of rules about ports and protocols to be allowed by the firewall for information exchange. Table 9.1 lists some services, protocols used by the services, and their dedicated communication ports.

When a service is enabled, the related ports and protocols should be configured accordingly. To be more secure, the network administrator may dedicate one server machine to host one service. Then, he or she will configure the firewall to allow network traffic with certain protocols for certain servers and deny this type of network traffic for other servers. In this way, a network problem with one type of service will not spread to other network services. It is important that the server hosting the firewall be isolated. Even from the inside of a private network, access to the firewall server should be very limited. Only the network administrator who manages the firewall

Table 9.1 Protocols Used by Network Services

Service	*Protocol*	*Port*
E-mail	SMTP, IMAP, POP3	25, 143, 110
File transfer	FTP	21
VPN	PPTP, L2TP	1723, 1701
Remote access	Telnet	23
Web service	SOAP	Vendor specific
Web browsing	HTTP, HTTPS	80, 443
Error reporting	ICMP	No port is used
Network management	SNMP, LDAP	161, 389
Routing	RIP, BGP	520, 179
Network security	SSH, SSL	22, 443
Dynamic IP address	DHCP	67, 68
Internet phone	H323, H248, H501, MGCP, SIP, etc.	1718, 1719, 1720, 2517; 2944; 2099; 2427; 5060

is allowed to access the firewall server with a specific device such as a smart card. The server that hosts the firewall should not have other network-based application software installed. In this way, no network traffic can pass through the application software to access the private network. The Web server is also vulnerable. Most of the attacks on it are from the Internet. It is better to keep the Web server outside of the firewall to prevent hackers from using HTTP, which is insecure, to access the other services on the private network.

By default, some firewalls come with their ports open. In such cases, the better practice is to close all the ports and only then open the ports that are required by the enabled services. By doing so, the network administrator can ensure that no unnecessary port is open to cause security concerns. Similarly, the network administrator should deny network traffic that is not currently used by the private network but is enabled by default.

As demonstrated in earlier hands-on practice, Telnet is vulnerable to hackers. To protect confidentiality, Telnet should be banned from accessing hosts in the private network and the servers hosting network services. Also, there is no reason to allow users to ping servers and other hosts in the private network from the public Internet. Network administrators should consider turning off ICMP services and blocking ICMP traffic from passing through the firewall.

When setting up the firewall filter, IP addresses can be used to identify the source and destination of the network traffic. The firewall can be configured to block network traffic based on the source IP address of a host or a network segment. The firewall can also be configured to block network traffic carrying the destination IP address of a highly protected server. Similarly, the name of a host or a domain can also be used to identify the source and destination of the network traffic.

By inspecting the message carried by a packet, the firewall can decide whether to allow the packet to pass through the firewall based on the key words or phrases included in the packet. The firewall can also be configured to examine the header of a packet and decide based on the content included in the header whether to allow the traffic to go through or deny it permission to pass through. The firewall can remember the state of the information exchange. For example, it can record the state of a connection and, therefore, it can determine if an inbound packet is responding to an outbound packet. The firewall rules can determine the acceptance of a packet based on its state, such as if the packet is used to start a new connection, is used to respond to a request, is used to terminate a connection, or is not part of the current connection.

Even though a private network or an individual computer is protected by a firewall, you need to keep in mind that a properly configured firewall can only reduce the risk to a certain degree. As time goes on, hackers may find new ways to penetrate private networks and new viruses will be created to infect network services. The network administrator should always keep up with network security upgrades and prepare a well-defined rescue plan to rebuild a private network once it is attacked or infected.

9.4.2 Firewall Types

Depending on the tasks performed by firewalls, they can be briefly categorized as three different types: the packet filtering firewall, stateful packet inspection firewall, and application proxy firewall. The following are descriptions of each type of firewall:

1. *Packet filtering firewall:* A packet filtering firewall works at the IP layer in the TCP/IP network architecture. The packet filtering firewall is the first-generation firewall. It has been known since 1988. It is commonly implemented on a router. Its implementation cost is low, and it has less negative impact on network performance. The packet filtering firewall is commonly used to implement simple firewall rules. The packet filter is configured to check the following attributes of a packet:
   - Source and destination IP addresses
   - Communication ports used by the application layer protocols
   - Protocols used for information exchange activities

   The packet filtering firewall compares these attributes against a set of predefined firewall rules. Depending on the result of the comparison, the firewall may allow a packet to pass through the firewall, reject the packet and send a message to inform the sender that the packet has been rejected, or simply drop the packet without informing the sender. The advantages of the packet filtering firewall are as follows:
   - Because the packet filtering firewall is running at the IP layer, it is application independent and has very little processing overhead.
   - It does not require additional configuration from clients.
   - It is easy to implement the packet filtering firewall with hardware or software at minimum cost.

   The packet filtering firewall has some disadvantages, as shown in the following list:
   - It is a complex process to define firewall rules for the packet filtering firewall. It often requires a thorough understanding of the requirements and vulnerabilities of the underlying network.
   - The packet filtering firewall is vulnerable to attacks such as IP spoofing and buffer overruns.
   - The packet filtering firewall makes decisions based on IP addresses, ports, and protocols. It does not verify other characteristics such as connection state and user authentication.

This makes it difficult to detect hidden attacks such as ICMP tunneling by which hackers can hide malicious code in a legitimate ICMP packet.

- If allowed, external clients can directly access the hosts in a private network through the packet filtering firewall. The direct access may cause some security concerns.

2. *Stateful packet inspection firewall:* It is the second-generation firewall and has been known since 1990. By providing a stateful inspection engine, the stateful packet inspection firewall is an improved version of the packet filtering firewall. In addition to filtering packets at the IP layer, it also examines the encapsulated headers from the application layer and the transport layer. Also, besides using the criteria IP address, port, and protocol, the stateful packet inspection firewall uses the data and connection state as its acceptance criteria. The following are some of the data and connection states used by the stateful packet inspection firewall:
   - The data content of packets
   - Whether an incoming packet is relevant to the outgoing packet
   - Whether a packet is part of the existing connection
   - Whether a packet is for starting a connection
   - Whether a packet is for terminating a connection

   The state records are stored in a table and are used to compare the state information provided by the packet. In this way, the stateful packet inspection firewall can detect packets sent by hackers from normal packets. The stateful packet inspection firewall has the following advantages:
   - By being able to operate at the IP layer, the stateful packet inspection firewall is application independent and has very little processing overhead.
   - The stateful packet inspection firewall is able to perform some advanced tasks such as conducting content filtering and reassembling packets before forwarding them to a private network.
   - By inspecting, recording, and evaluating the additional dynamic characteristics of a packet, the stateful packet inspection firewall can determine the connection state between sender and receiver, and therefore can detect unauthorized access by a hacker.
   - By screening the data content in the packets, the stateful packet inspection firewall can determine if the application layer protocol behaves properly.

   There are a few disadvantages of the stateful packet inspection firewall:
   - Defining firewall rules for the stateful packet inspection firewall is a complex process, and it is difficult to test these rules.
   - If allowed, external clients can directly access the hosts on the private network through the stateful packet inspection firewall. The direct access makes the hosts on the private network vulnerable to attacks.
3. *Application proxy firewall:* As the name indicates, the application proxy firewall operates at the application layer in the TCP/IP network architecture. It is the third-generation firewall, and has been known since 1991. The application proxy firewall pays attention to the format of the data carried by packets. Before allowing a packet to pass through the firewall, the application proxy firewall examines the protocol dedicated for a service. By applying the firewall rules, the application proxy firewall can decide whether to accept the packet. If the packet is accepted, the application proxy firewall reassembles the packet and forwards it to the dedicated server that provides the service. The application proxy firewall has the following advantages:

- The application proxy firewall does not allow external users to directly access the host in the private network.
- The application proxy firewall ensures that only the dedicated protocols are allowed and the reassembling of the packets can get rid of some of the hidden problems.
- The application proxy firewall is able to filter the data content stored in the payload of a packet.
- The characteristics of an application service can be used by the application proxy firewall as the criteria of acceptance.
- The application proxy firewall can provide a user authentication service. It can also integrate the authentication service provided by the operating system on a host.
- The application proxy firewall can record user activities and network traffic.

Some disadvantages of the application proxy firewall are listed in the following:

- For each protocol to be handled by the firewall, the firewall and the application software must be specially programmed so that the firewall is aware of the proxy of the protocol. When the protocol is updated, the proxy program should also be updated accordingly.
- Working at the application layer, the application proxy firewall can generate a large amount of process overhead. Network performance can be significantly impacted by the firewall.
- The application proxy firewall is vulnerable to the denial-of-service attack.

In the foregoing text, three types of firewalls were introduced. Each type has its own advantages and disadvantages. Often, the distributions of the Linux operating system provide firewall software. The configuration of the firewall software will be discussed later in this section.

9.4.3 Firewall Architectures

To protect a private network, firewalls are used to separate it from the public network. An organization's private network may be protected by multiple firewalls. These firewalls form a secure perimeter. There are several ways to construct a secure perimeter with these firewalls for better protection. Among many possible firewall architectures, three are now described:

1. *Simple firewall architecture:* The simplest method is to place the firewall at the border of the private network and the public network. All network traffic must go through the firewall to reach the private network. Figure 9.19 illustrates this kind of architecture.

   This simple firewall architecture has some weaknesses. While supporting Internet-based services such as e-mail and Web browsing, the e-mail server and Web server must be either placed in the private network or hosted by the firewall server itself. As mentioned in the firewall rule section, it is not a good idea to let the firewall server host other application server software, which may open a security hole to attacks or viruses. If the application servers are placed in the private network, the firewall has to allow the computers on the Internet to directly communicate with the application servers in the private network, which is not safe either. To overcome the weaknesses, some other firewall architectures have been proposed.
2. *Demilitarized zone (DMZ) firewall architecture:* To prevent direct access to the application servers located in the private network, the network administrator may create a DMZ, which is a network located outside the private network. The application servers will be placed in the DMZ. Although the DMZ is located outside the private network area, it is not in the public

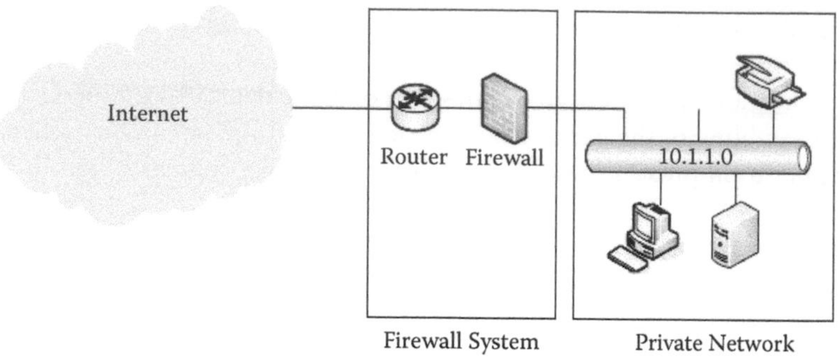

Figure 9.19 Simple firewall architecture.

network area. It is still a private network, but valuable information will not be stored on the application servers in that area. Figure 9.20 illustrates the DMZ firewall architecture.

3. *Screened subnet firewall architecture:* In the DMZ firewall architecture, the DMZ and the private network are constructed on different network segments. The communication between DMZ and private network can be done through a router, as displayed in Figure 9.20. The screened subnet firewall architecture is designed to isolate the DMZ from the private network. This can make it harder for a hacker to attack the private network. Figure 9.21 illustrates the architecture of the screened subnet firewall.

Each of the foregoing firewall architectures may also have a few variations. Interested readers can find more detailed information about firewalls in any network security book.

Activity 9.3 Firewall Configuration

In this hands-practice, you will learn how to configure a firewall on the server machine. By default, Ubuntu 8.10 includes the firewall software called Uncomplicated Firewall (UFW). However, the firewall software may not be enabled on your computer. Your first task is to enable the firewall service. After the firewall is enabled, you can practice on how to configure the firewall to

- Allow and block network traffic through a port
- Accept and deny a protocol
- Enable and disable a firewall service

To verify if the firewall service is enabled on the server machine, perform the following steps:

1. Log on to the server machine with username **student** and password **ubuntu**.
2. To verify if UFW is enabled, enter the following command:

   ```
   sudo ufw status
   ```

   If you receive the message "firewall not loaded," you need to enable the firewall.
3. To enable UFW, enter the following command:

   ```
   sudo ufw enable
   ```

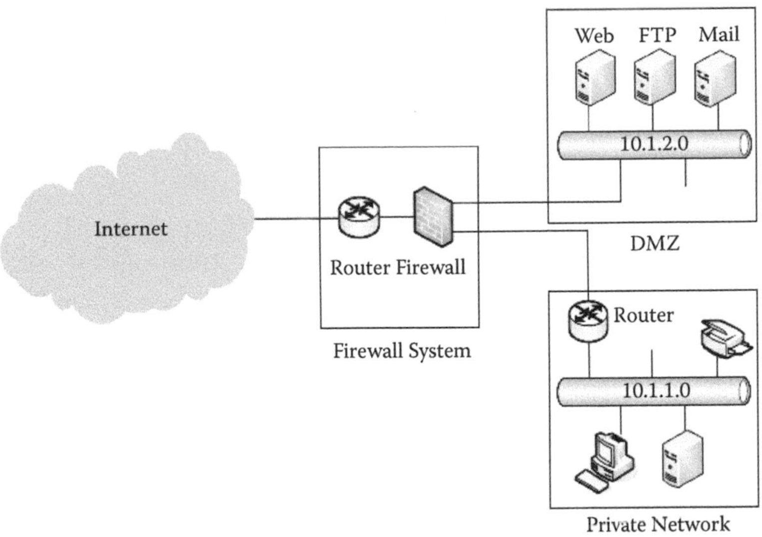

Figure 9.20 Demilitarized zone (DMZ) firewall architecture.

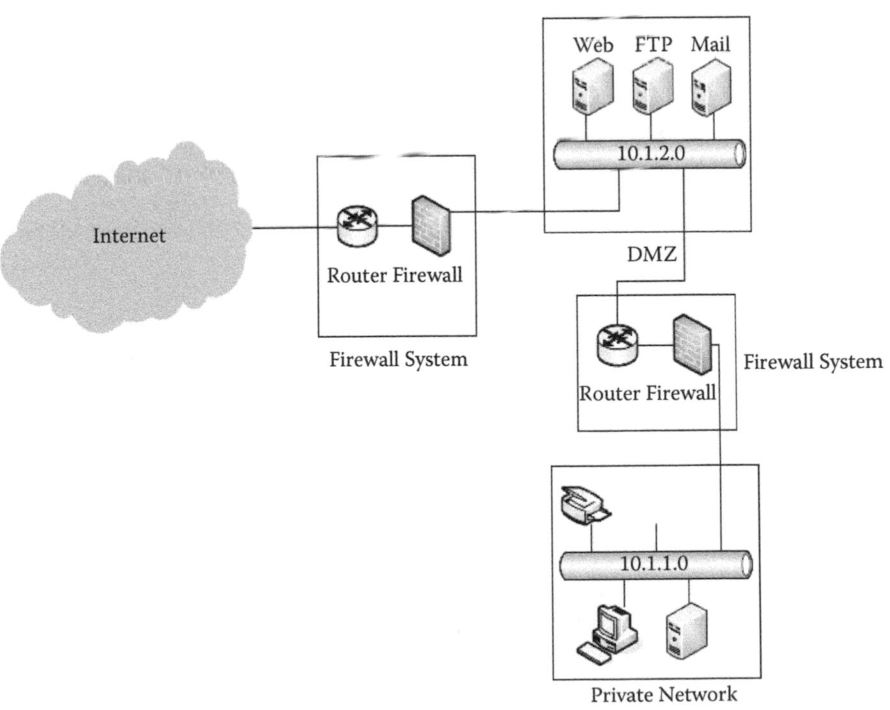

Figure 9.21 Screened subnet firewall architecture.

4. To allow communication through port 21, enter the following command:

```
sudo ufw allow 21
```

5. To remove the communication rule, enter the following command:

```
sudo ufw delete allow 21
```

6. To allow the communication through port 21 and accept UDP, enter the following command:

```
sudo ufw allow 21/udp
```

7. To remove it, enter the following command:

```
sudo ufw delete allow 21/udp
```

8. To deny the protocol SMTP, enter the following command:

```
sudo ufw deny smtp
```

9. To remove the rule, enter the following command:

```
sudo ufw delete deny smtp
```

10. Finally, to disable the firewall, enter the following command:

```
sudo ufw disable
```

This hands-on practice has demonstrated how to configure the firewall UFW on the Ubuntu Linux operating system. Several simple examples have been used to show how to enable and disable the UFW firewall service, and how to add and delete firewall rules. In order to effectively set up a firewall, you need to have a solid understanding of ports, protocols, and network services. Once the firewall rules are determined, the UFW package can be used to implement firewall rules on the Ubuntu Linux operating system.

9.5 Summary

This chapter discussed some network-security-related issues. Security has the highest priority in network management. In order to effectively protect networks and computer systems, it is necessary to create clearly defined network security policies that are used as a guideline in dealing with security issues. To be able to prevent attacks from hackers and computer viruses, network administrators must know how hackers and computer viruses intrude into networks and computer systems. This chapter provided information about various hacker attacks and computer viruses. After examining these attacks, this chapter discussed some security measures to prevent attacks from hackers and computer viruses. For organizations that conduct e-commerce or online teaching, the benefit of enforcing these security measures is huge.

Various security-related technologies have been invented to protect network traffic. This chapter discussed six of them, including Intrusion Detection System (IDS), IP Security (IPSec), Remote Authentication Dial In User Service (RADIUS), Secure Shell (SSH), Secure Sockets Layer (SSL), and Wi-Fi Protected Access (WPA). These technologies provide the mechanisms for data encryption, user and computer authentication, and network monitoring.

Firewalls are the first defense for protecting a network. This chapter addressed the issues related to firewall rules. The firewall rules can be set up based on the network services, related communication ports, protocols, data content, and connection states. Various types of firewalls have been introduced in this chapter to implement firewall rules. Properly placing a firewall in a network system can significantly affect the effectiveness of the firewall. This chapter presented several commonly used firewall architectures and discussed their advantages and disadvantages.

Now that we have addressed the network-security-related issues, our next task is to look at other network-management-related topics. These topics will be covered in Chapter 10.

Review Questions

1. List the issues that need to be addressed by the security policies.
2. What is a brute force attack?
3. How is spyware used by hackers to steal valuable information?
4. How do hackers use e-mail to attack computer systems?
5. What do hackers do with packet sniffer software?
6. What is IP spoofing?
7. What is a denial-of-service attack?
8. Explain why it is difficult to deal with a stealth virus.
9. Describe how a Trojan horse virus works?
10. What is a computer worm?
11. How do we protect a Web server and a Web browser?
12. List the attacks that can be detected by the IDS.
13. What can IPSec do to keep packet transmission secure?
14. Describe how RADIUS works.
15. When compared with Telnet, what is the advantage of SSH?
16. State the difference between SSH and SSL.
17. What are the three components involved in an EAP authentication process?
18. Briefly describe three types of firewall mechanisms discussed in this chapter.
19. What are the advantages and disadvantages of a stateful packet inspection firewall?
20. Briefly describe three types of firewall architectures covered in this chapter.

Case Study Projects

The following are two networking projects that enhance security measures.

Case Study Project 9.1. Install and configure SSH for your home network so that you can remotely access one of the hosts on your home network with SSH.

Case Study Project 9.2. Implement the DMZ firewall architecture for your home network so that your home network is separated from the DMZ, which includes a Web server.

Chapter 10

Network Resource Management

Objectives

- Understand directory services.
- Manage network user accounts.
- Understand Linux kernel.
- Manage network device resources.

10.1 Introduction

Chapter 9 discussed topics related to network security, which is the top concern of network administrators. In addition to keeping networks secure, network administrators perform other tasks such as setting up directory services for user and computer management. They also need to maintain network devices, and the kernel components and drivers related to those network devices. These are the tasks performed by network administrators on a daily basis.

The Linux operating system provides a multiuser and multitasking computing environment. It allows multiple users to log on to the same computer system simultaneously. Users, based on their roles, will be assigned different priorities and permissions. To assist the management of users and groups, the Linux operating system includes various tools for user account management. In this chapter, we will investigate what needs to be done for user account management. Then, the Linux user management tools will be introduced. The Linux operating system supports the directory service for more sophisticated user and computer management. This chapter will discuss the directory service and illustrate the use of the directory service for user account management through hands-on practice.

Network device resources are programs used to manage network devices. In Linux, the commonly used network device resources are the Linux kennel, device driver, and daemon. This chapter will provide information about the commonly used network device resources and explain what tasks can be performed with these resources. Linux utilities used to manage the network device resources will be introduced in this chapter. The hands-on practice on using the utility udev for network device resource management will be presented. This chapter will also include hands-on practice for creating a customized kernel for adding new network functionalities.

Next, the discussion will start with the issues related to network user account management. Both user account management and directory services will be covered in the next section.

10.2 User Account Management

As a network operating system, Linux can host thousands of user accounts and provide tools to manage these user accounts. The following topics are related to the management of users:

- User account management
- User group management
- Directory services

Information about user counts, groups, and directory services will be given first, followed by an introduction to some management tools.

10.2.1 User Management

To log on to a Linux computer, a user needs to have a user account on the computer. To identify a user who is permitted to log on to a Linux machine, a user ID is created whenever a new user account is created. Usually, there are two types of users, regular users and system users:

- *System users:* They are users who enable other users to use services and applications safely and effectively. System users manage operating systems and other application software. They also manage regular users' accounts and services.
- *Regular users:* They are users who are allowed to access certain applications hosted by the Linux operating system. Each regular user has a home directory for storing personal data. The home directory is protected by user IDs and passwords to create a safe computing environment.

Denoted by UID, a user ID is an integer used to uniquely identify a user. A UID is usually automatically generated by the computer when a new user account is created. It can also be manually assigned to a user by the system administrator. Normally, UIDs can be categorized as follows:

- *0–99:* Reserved for the Linux operating system administrators. The root user always has the UID 0.
- *100–499:* Reserved for system users, who manage services and application programs.
- *500 and above:* Reserved for regular users. Some of the Linux distributions may start UID from 1000 for regular users.

In Linux, regular users' information is stored in the files /etc/passwd and /etc/shadow. Although the file name passwd may indicate that the /etc/passwd file probably contains users' passwords, in fact, the encrypted users' passwords are stored in the file /etc/shadow. Only the root can read and modify the content of the file /etc/shadow.

Table 10.1 User Account Management Commands

Command	*Description*	*Example*
`id`	Shows the currently effective user IDs and group IDs	`id`
`cat`	Displays the information in a file	`cat /etc/passwd`
`logname`	Displays users' logon names	`logname`
`w`	Lists the users currently logged on to Linux and the programs run by each user	`w`
`who`	Lists the users currently logged on to Linux and the location from which each user logged on	`who`
`whoami`	Shows the currently effective user ID	`whoami`
`finger`	Lists information about a user, including the full name, default shell, when the user last logged on, and so on	List information about the user student: `finger student`
`useradd`	Creates a new user account	Create a new user account with the home directory /home/student: `useradd -m student`
`passwd`	Changes a user's password	Change the password for the user account student: `passwd student`
`userdel`	Deletes an existing user account	Delete the account and the home directory of the user student: `userdel -r student`
`usermod`	Modifies a user's ID, standard shell, home directory, and group for an existing user account	Change UID for the user student: `usermod -u 1009 student`

User accounts can be either managed by GUI tools or commands. The GUI tools may vary from one Linux distribution to another. The commands are more portable among Linux distributions and other UNIX like operating systems. The commands commonly used to manage user accounts are listed in Table 10.1.

10.2.2 Group Management

The Linux operating system uses groups to manage users who have the same privileges. With groups, user management can be simplified. For example, let us suppose the student group contains thousands of student accounts. To modify the privilege for all the student accounts, the administrator can simply modify the privilege for the student group instead of modifying the privilege for each individual student account.

Table 10.2 Group Management Commands

Command	*Description*	*Example*
`groupadd`	Can be used to create a new group	Create a new group called lab with the group ID 150: `groupadd -g 150 lab`
`groupdel`	Deletes a group	Delete the group called lab: `groupdel lab`
`groupmod`	Modifies the settings of a group	Add the user student to the lab group: `groupmod -A student lab`
`chgrp`	Changes a group so that it has access to a file or directory	Allow the lab group to access the file report.doc: `chgrp lab report.doc`
`groups`	Lists all the groups to which the current user belongs	`groups`
`newgrp`	Allows the current user to log on to a new group	Let the current user log on to the lab group: `newgrp lab`
`vigr`	Uses the vi editor to safely edit the /etc/group file	`vigr`

In Linux, every user belongs to a group. When a new user account is created, Linux automatically assigns the user account to its group. A group created in this way is called a private group. Users can also be assigned to a special-purpose group such as a senior group. The special-purpose groups are called public groups. The owner of a group and the root user can change the privilege of the group. A user can be assigned to multiple groups. The primary group assigned to a user is listed in the file /etc/passwd. Each group can be identified by its group id (GID). Information about the group is stored in the file /etc/group.

Linux also includes several commands for group management. Table 10.2 lists some of commonly used group management commands. In addition to the commands used to manage user accounts and groups, Linux also supports the centralized network user-and-resource management tools such as the directory service, which will be covered in the next section.

10.2.3 Directory Service Management

In an enterprise-level network, network users and resources are spread out in many geographical locations. Users are supposed to access these network resources from any computer linked to the network. To manage users and network resources for the Internet-based network, one may consider implementing the directory service to help the network administrator manage network users and resources. The directory service can be critical for managing any medium-sized or large organization. It serves as a database to store the information about network users, computers, shared directories, and other network services. The directory service performs the following management tasks:

- Storing and categorizing the data about network users and resources
- Managing documents and computer programs
- Configuring user privileges
- Setting permissions to network resources
- Adding or removing users, groups, and network resources
- Authenticating network users for accessing network services

When it is used for authentication, the directory service allows every user to log on to any computers and services on the network as if he or she had an account on all the computers in the network. Once a user logs on to a computer in the network, all of the user's personal data in the home directory will be available on that computer.

Linux distributions include directory service packages that can be used by the administrator to set up his or her own directory service. Among these packages, Lightweight Directory Access Protocol (LDAP) is commonly used to implement the directory service. LDAP is the lightweight version of Directory Access Protocol (DAP), a standard version of directory services. OpenLDAP is an LDAP package for the Linux/UNIX operating system. OpenLDAP consists of a number of software packages. The following are the packages included in OpenLDAP:

- *Stand-alone LDAP daemon (slapd):* It is used as a server to handle LDAP connection requests. The configuration of slapd can be done in the file /etc/openldap/slapd.conf.
- *Stand-alone LDAP update replication daemon (slurpd):* It is a daemon that works with slapd to provide replication service.
- *Utilities:* They are a number of utilities used to interact with the LDAP server.
- *Libraries:* They are files used to implement the LDAP protocol.

In addition, OpenLDAP supports the following features:

- Simple Authentication and Security Layer (SASL), Transport Layer Security (TLS), and Secure Sockets Layer (SSL).
- Internet Protocol Version 6 (IPv6) for the next-generation network protocol.
- Interprocess communication (IPC) for the communication within a system for better security.

The user accounts and other entries are placed by LDAP hierarchically in a treelike structure. The root record is placed on the top of the tree. The parent-level nodes on the tree represent higher-level organizations, and the child-level nodes represent lower-level organizations. Each entry on the tree belongs to one of the following two types:

- *Container:* This entry is an inner node of the tree. From this entry, there are child entries branching out. The value at a container node can be the name of an organization or the name of a department.
- *Leaf:* The leaf entry is placed at the end of each branch. Under the leaf, there is no child entry. Each leaf entry can be an individual user or network resource.

Figure 10.1 demonstrates the LDAP tree structure. The tree in Figure 10.1 is also called the directory information tree (DIT). In Figure 10.1, the symbols have the following meanings:

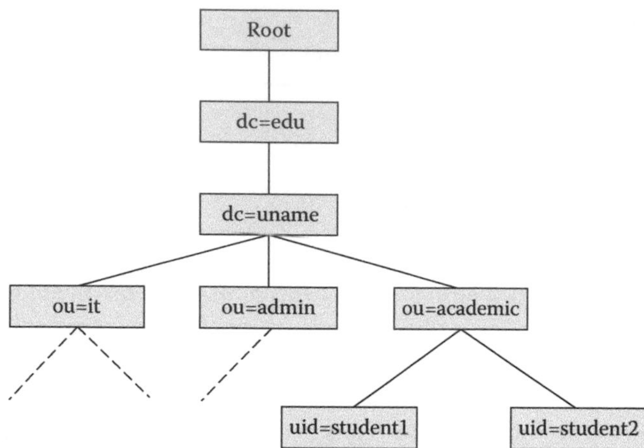

Figure 10.1 LDAP tree structure.

Table 10.3 Terms Used in LDAP Technology

Term	*Description*	*Example*
dn	The path to a distinguished node is called distinguished name (dn)	dn: uid=student1,ou=academic, dc=uname,dc=edu
rdn	The name of the node along the path to an entry is called a relative distinguished name (rdn)	rdn: uid=student1 or rdn: ou=academic
cn	Common name	cn=John Smith
o	Organization name	o=uname.edu
c	Country name	c=us
l	Locality	l=main campus
sn	Surname	sn=Smith

- *dc:* Domain component
- *ou:* Organization unit
- *uid:* User ID

Table 10.3 lists some other terms used in LDAP technology.

As shown previously, LDAP can be used to help quickly locate users, files, and network resources through its tree structure. LDAP runs in the client-server structure. When a client is connected to the LDAP server, he or she can perform the following tasks using the tools provided by the LDAP client software:

- Searching and retrieving entries on the DIT
- Adding new entries to the DIT
- Modifying existing entries on the DIT
- Deleting entries on the DIT

Due to its rich features for network user and resource management, LDAP is also used to manage network-based application software such as database servers and e-mail servers. Major hardware and software vendors such as Microsoft, Novell, and Cisco all support LDAP technology.

Activity 10.1 User Management with LDAP

In this hands-on activity, you will learn how to set up LDAP for user authentication. You will set up LDAP to store user information such as usernames, passwords, user IDs, and other information. To practice, you will perform the following tasks:

- Installing the LDAP server
- Populating the LDAP DIT
- Configuring the LDAP client
- Testing LDAP for user authentication

Your first task is to install the LDAP server slapd, LDAP utility ldap-utils, and LDAP database management tool db4.2-util with the following steps:

1. Log on to your server machine with username **student** and password **ubuntu**.
2. If you have not done so, you may need to update the Linux operating system by entering the following command:

   ```
   sudo apt-get update
   ```

3. Enter the following command to install the LDAP server, LDAP utility, and LDAP database management tool:

   ```
   sudo apt-get install slapd ldap-utils
   ```

4. You will be prompted to enter the LDAP administrator's password (Figure 10.2). Normally, for security reasons, you should use a password that is different from the password used by the root user. Enter the password **ubuntuadmin,** which is different from the one for root. Press the **Tab** key to move the cursor to **<Ok>,** and then press the **Enter** key.
5. When asked to confirm the password, type the password **ubuntuadmin** again. Press the **Tab** key to move the cursor to **<Ok>** and then press the **Enter** key to continue the installation process.

After the LDAP server and the utility tools are installed, your next task is to do some configuration. The following steps show you how to get the job done:

1. Ubuntu Linux provides the ldap configuration utility dpkg-reconfigure. Execute the following command in the terminal window to start the configuration utility:

   ```
   sudo dpkg-reconfigure slapd
   ```

2. You will be asked if you want to omit the openldap server configuration. Press the **Enter** key to accept the default selection **No.**
3. On the next page, you will be asked to specify the DNS domain name. Enter **ns1.group2.lab** as the DNS domain name (Figure 10.3). After you have entered the DNS domain name, press the **Tab** key to select **<Ok>,** and press the **Enter** key to move to the next page.

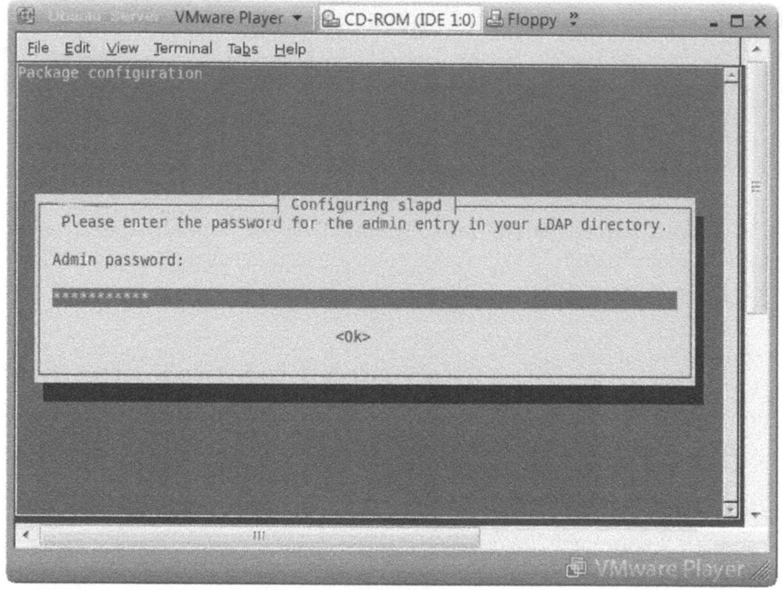

Figure 10.2 LDAP administrator's password.

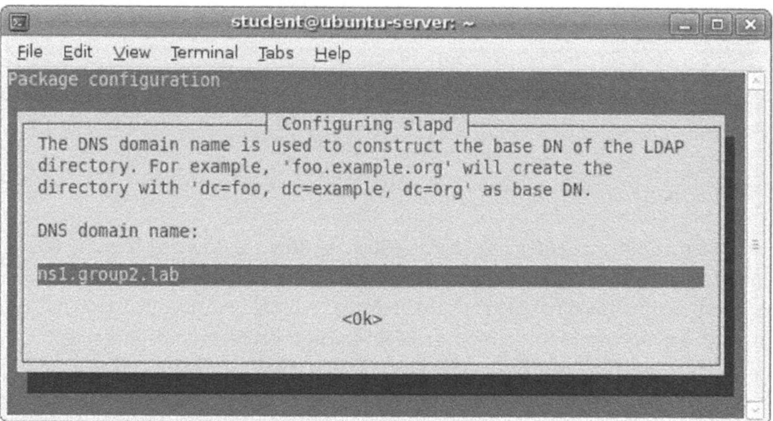

Figure 10.3 Configuration of DNS domain name.

4. You will be asked to enter the organization name. You may use group2 as the company name (Figure 10.4). Press the **Tab** key to select **<Ok>,** and press the **Enter** key to move to the next page.
5. On the this page, you are informed about the back-end database; press the **Tab** key to select **<Ok>,** and press the **Enter** key to move to the next page.
6. This page allows you specify the back-end database. Press the **Tab** key to accept the default selection **HDB** and to select **<Ok>;** then press the **Enter** key to move to the next page.
7. This page asks if you want the database to be removed when slapd is purged; use the Tab key to select **Yes** (Figure 10.5). Press the **Enter** key to move to the next page.
8. On the next page, you will be asked to enter the administrator's password. Enter the password **ubuntuadmin** used for the installation earlier. Press the **Tab** key to select **<Ok>,** and press the **Enter** key to move to the next page.

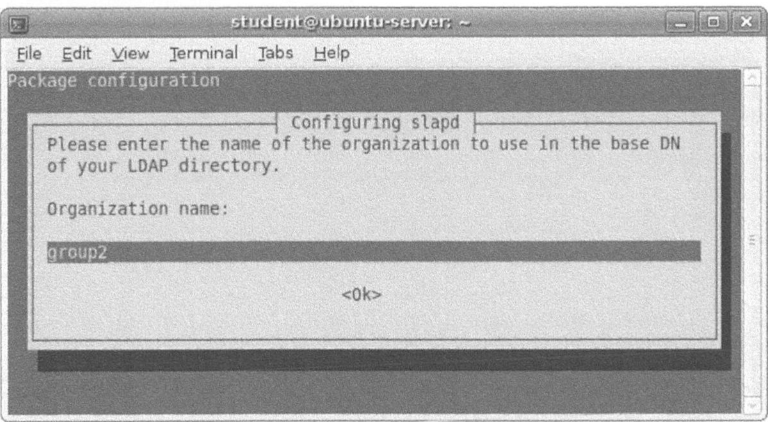

Figure 10.4 Configuration of organization name.

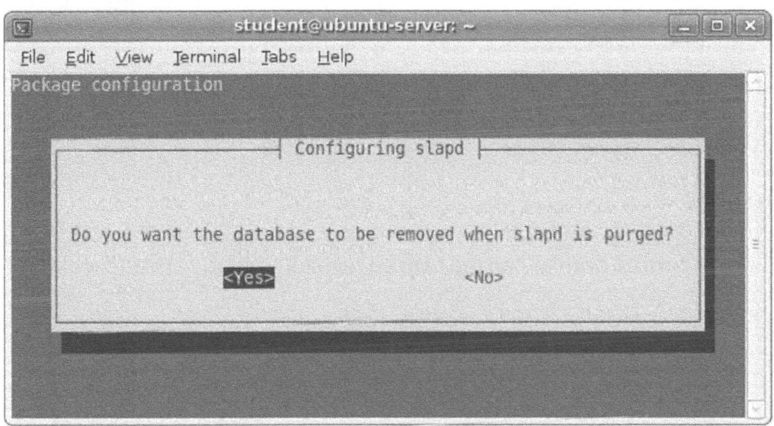

Figure 10.5 Configuration of slapd.

9. Retype the password **ubuntuadmin**. Press the **Tab** key to select **<Ok>,** and press **Enter** to move to the next page.
10. This page informs you about the older version of LDAP. After reading the message, press the **Enter** key to move the next page.
11. This page asks you if the older version of LDAP should be allowed. Accept the default **No**, and press the **Enter** key to complete the configuration.
12. Now, you have completed the configuration for slapd. Next, you need to edit the file /etc/ldap/ldap.conf by executing the following command:

```
sudo gedit /etc/ldap/ldap.conf
```

13. Modify the setup for the entries BASE and URI, and accept the default for the other entries (Figure 10.6). Click the **Save** menu. To exit the file, click the **File** menu, and select **Quit**.
14. Restart the LDAP server by executing the following command:

```
sudo /etc/init.d/slapd restart
```

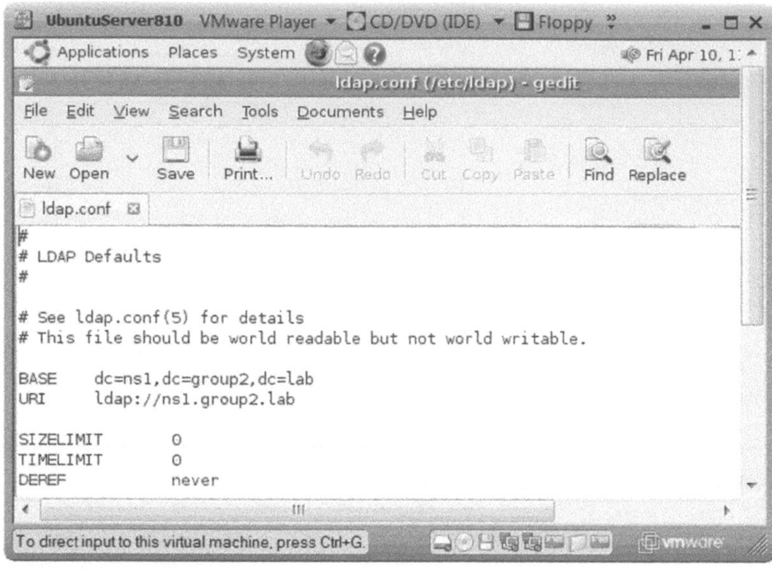

Figure 10.6 Content of ldap.conf.

15. To test your LDAP server, enter the following command:

```
ldapsearch -x -b dc=ns1,dc=group2,dc=lab
```

ldapsearch is the tool used to find the ldap entries stored in the LDAP directory. The option -x is used for simple authentication, and the option -b is used to start the search at the point search base instead of the default search starting point. As expected, two LDAP entries are displayed on the screen (Figure 10.7).

```
student@ubuntu-server: ~
File Edit View Terminal Tabs Help
# ns1.group2.lab
dn: dc=ns1,dc=group2,dc=lab
objectClass: top
objectClass: dcObject
objectClass: organization
o: group2
dc: ns1

# admin, ns1.group2.lab
dn: cn=admin,dc=ns1,dc=group2,dc=lab
objectClass: simpleSecurityObject
objectClass: organizationalRole
cn: admin
description: LDAP administrator

# search result
search: 2
result: 0 Success

# numResponses: 3
# numEntries: 2
student@ubuntu-server:~$
```

Figure 10.7 Searching LDAP server.

Now the LDAP server is up and running. To populate the LDAP directory with information about user accounts and other network resources, you need to create a user account and use the migration tool to add the user account to the LDAP directory. The following steps accomplish this:

1. First, you will create a user with name **studenta** and password **ubuntu** for testing purposes later. To do so, execute the following command:

```
sudo useradd -d /home/studenta -m studenta
```

   In the useradd command, the option -d is used to specify the new user's home directory, and the option -m is used to create the new user's home directory if it does not already exist.
2. To assign the password to studenta, enter the following command:

```
sudo passwd studenta
```

   When prompted, enter the password **ubuntu**.
3. To verify, execute the following command:

```
sudo cat /etc/passwd
```

   You should be able to see that the user studenta is created in the file /etc/passwd (Figure 10.8).
4. Execute the following command to install the migration tools:

```
sudo apt-get install migrationtools
```

5. After the migrationtools package is installed, change to the directory /usr/share/migrationtools/ with the following command:

```
cd /usr/share/migrationtools/
```

6. You need to edit the migration configuration file migrate_common.ph by executing the following command:

```
sudo gedit migrate_common.ph
```

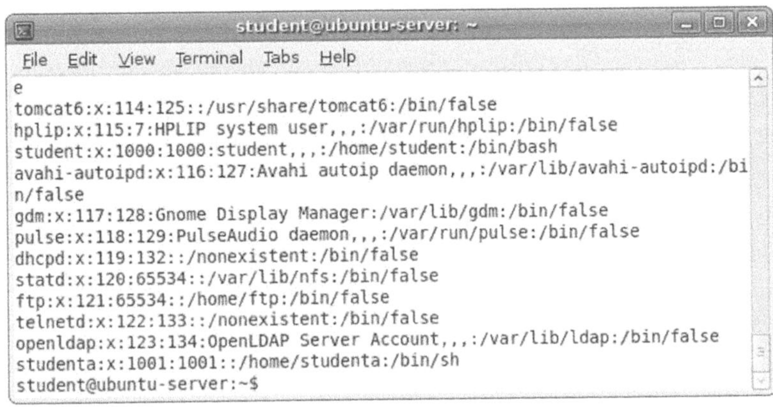

Figure 10.8 Information for user studenta.

7. Change the default DNS service and base with the following two lines:

```
$DEFAULT_MAIL_DOMAIN="ns1.group2.lab";
$DEFAULT_BASE="dc=ns1,dc=group2,dc=lab";
```

To save the change, click **Save**. Then, click the **File** menu, and select **Quit**.

8. To run the migration command, you need the root user's privilege. Run the following command:

```
su -
```

Enter the password **ubuntu,** and press the **Enter** key.

9. Run the following command to change the directory:

```
cd /usr/share/migrationtools/
```

10. The ldif files are used to populate the LDAP directory. Execute the following commands to create the ldif files to populate the directory:

```
./migrate_base.pl > base.ldif
./migrate_group.pl /etc/group group.ldif
./migrate_passwd.pl /etc/passwd passwd.ldif
```

You now have the ldif files that can be used to populate the LDAP directory. Before you can do that, you need to clean the base.ldif file generated by the migrationtools utility, because the migrationtools utility adds extra suffixes to the base.ldif file. You need to edit the base.ldif file to remove those extra suffixes, because they may cause errors. Run the following command in the terminal window:

```
nano base.ldif
```

After the file is opened, delete the first two blocks (the darkened blocks shown in Figure 10.9) by using the **Delete** key. After these two blocks are deleted, press **Ctrl+X**, then **Y**, and then the **Enter** key to save the change.

11. Before you can populate the LDAP directory, you also need to make sure that the DNS service on your server computer is working properly. To do this, enter the following command to test:

```
host ns1.group2.lab
```

You should be able to get the corresponding IP address 192.168.2.1. If not, you may need to edit the file /etc/resolv.conf by entering the following command:

```
nano /etc/resolv.conf
```

Make sure that the following two lines of code are included:

```
search group2.lab
nameserver 192.168.2.1
```

Press the key combination **Ctrl+X** to exit the file.

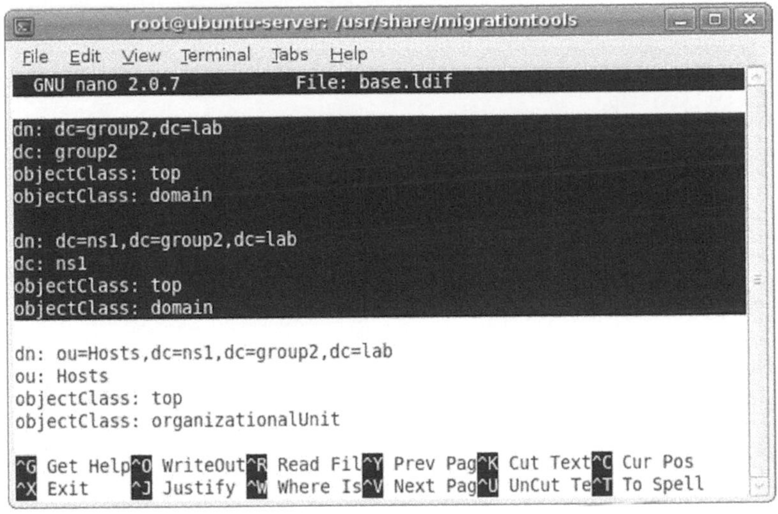

Figure 10.9 Deleting extra blocks.

12. You can now populate the LDAP directory with the ldif files created in the previous step with the following commands:

```
ldapadd -D "cn=admin,dc=ns1,dc=group2,dc=lab" -x -W -f base.ldif
ldapadd -D "cn=admin,dc=ns1,dc=group2,dc=lab" -x -W -f passwd.ldif
ldapadd -D "cn=admin,dc=ns1,dc=group2,dc=lab" -x -W -f group.ldif
```

    You will be prompted to enter the password for the DIT root. Enter the password **ubuntuadmin,** and press the **Enter** key.

    The options used in the foregoing commands have the following meanings:

    - -D: This option is used to identify the administrator.
    - -x: This option is used to specify that SASL is not used.
    - -W: This option is used to prompt for password.
    - -f: This is used to specify the ldif file that contains the data for the DIT population.

13. After the LDAP directory is populated, you may run the following ldapsearch command to view the records loaded to the LDAP directory:

```
ldapsearch -x -b dc=ns1,dc=group2,dc=lab
```

    As expected, the entry about the user studenta is added to the LDAP directory (Figure 10.10).

14. After you have successfully displayed the LDAP records, enter the command **exit** to quit the root user environment.

You have now populated the LDAP directory with the user accounts stored in the ldif files. Your next task is to access the LDAP service from your client machine. Follow these steps to configure the client machine:

1. Log on to the client machine with username **student** and password **ubuntu**.
2. After you have logged on to the client computer, your first task is to install some LDAP client packages. To do so, enter the following command:

```
sudo apt-get install libnss-ldap libpam-ldap nscd
```

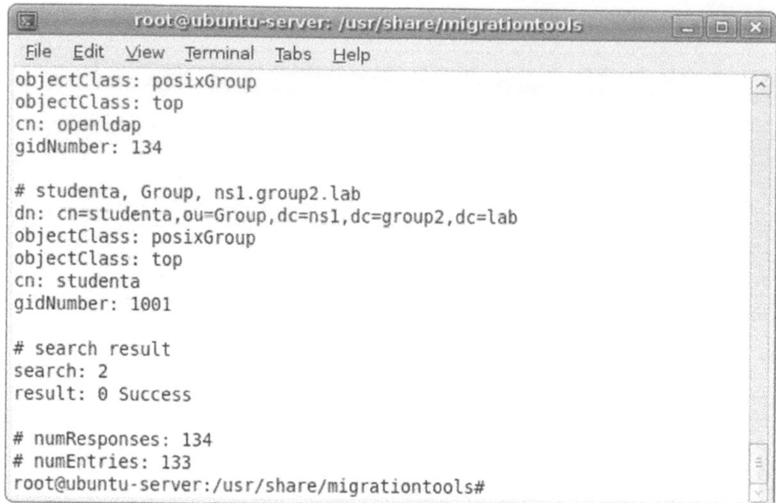

root@ubuntu-server: /usr/share/migrationtools
File Edit View Terminal Tabs Help
objectClass: posixGroup
objectClass: top
cn: openldap
gidNumber: 134

studenta, Group, ns1.group2.lab
dn: cn=studenta,ou=Group,dc=ns1,dc=group2,dc=lab
objectClass: posixGroup
objectClass: top
cn: studenta
gidNumber: 1001

search result
search: 2
result: 0 Success

numResponses: 134
numEntries: 133
root@ubuntu-server:/usr/share/migrationtools#

Figure 10.10 LDAP searching result.

The installed packages can perform the following tasks:

- *libnss-ldap:* This package allows LDAP to be used as a naming service.
- *libpam-ldap:* This package allows Pluggable Authentication Modules (PAM) to authenticate users through LDAP. PAM provides a common authentication API for different applications.
- *nscd:* This is a daemon used to look up passwords, groups and hosts, and caches for LDAP authentication.

3. When prompted to enter the LDAP server Uniform Resource Identifier (URI), enter the server's IP address 192.168.2.1 (Figure 10.11). Press the **Tab** key to select **<Ok>**, and press the **Enter** key to go to the next page.
4. The next page will prompt you to enter the distinguished name of the search base. Enter the following domain name, which is shown in Figure 10.12:

```
dc=ns1,dc=group2,dc=lab
```

   Press the **Tab** key to select **<Ok>**, and press the **Enter** key to go to the next page.
5. The next page will ask you to specify the version of LDAP to use. Accept the default version, LDAP Version 3. Press the **Enter** key to go to the next page.
6. This page will ask if you want to make the local root the database admin. Accept the default option **Yes**. Press the **Enter** key to go to the next page.
7. This page will ask you if the LDAP database requires login. Accept the default option **No**. Press the **Enter** key to go to the next page.
8. On this page, you will be asked to set up the LDAP root account. Enter the root account information **cn=admin,dc=group2,dc=lab** (Figure 10.13). Press the **Tab** key to select **<Ok>**, and press the **Enter** key to go to the next page.
9. The next page prompts you to enter the password for the LDAP root account. Enter the password **ubuntuadmin**. Press the **Tab** key to select **<Ok>**, and press the **Enter** key to finish the installation.
10. Your next task is to edit the file /etc/ldap.conf. To do this, execute the following command:

```
sudo gedit /etc/ldap.conf
```

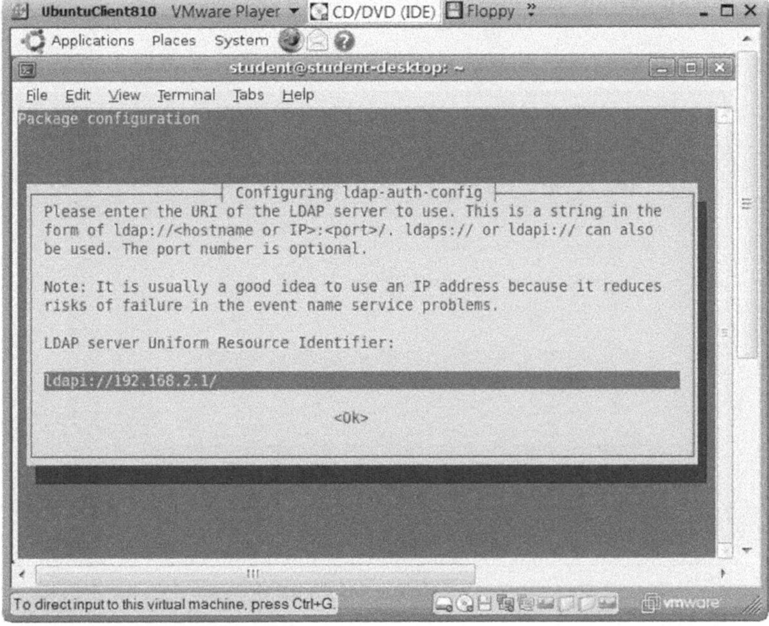

Figure 10.11 LDAP server URI.

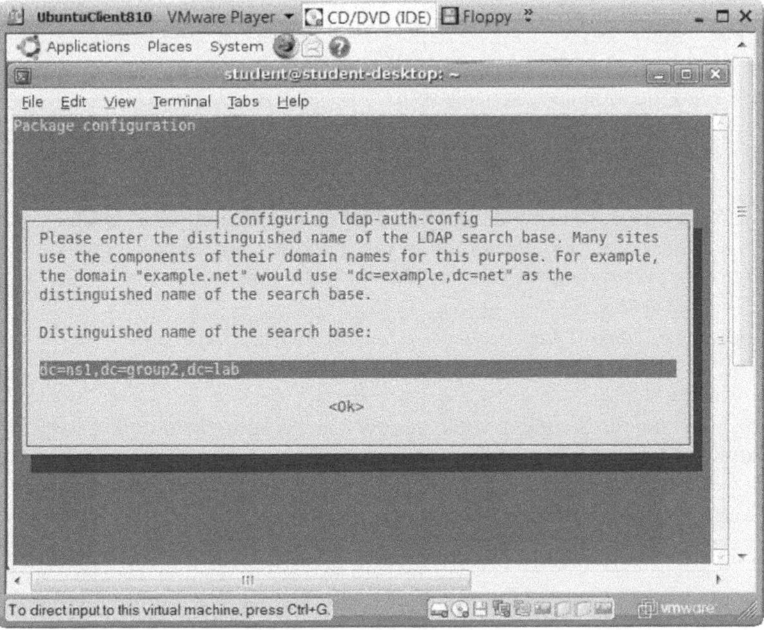

Figure 10.12 Distinguished name of search base.

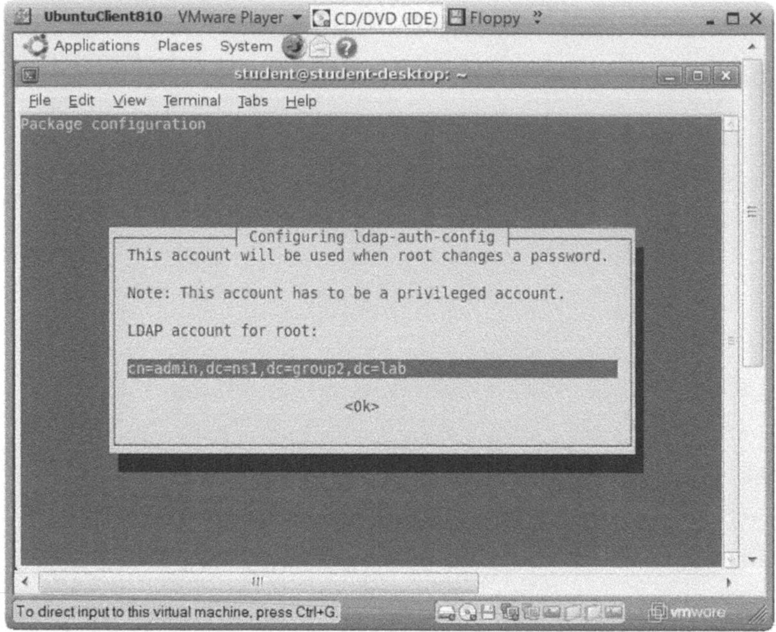

Figure 10.13 LDAP root account.

11. After the file is opened, make sure that following two lines are modified as follows. The line #host 127.0.0.1 is changed to

    ```
    host LDAP_SERVER_IP 192.168.2.1
    ```

    The line #bind_policy=hard is changed to

    ```
    bind_policy=soft
    ```

    Click the **Save** menu. To exit the file, click the **File** menu, and select **Quit**.
12. There is another copy of ldap.conf file in the directory /etc/ldap/. To replace this one with the one configured in the previous step, use the following commands:

    ```
    sudo cp /etc/ldap/ldap.conf /etc/ldap/ldap.conf.bak
    sudo cp /etc/ldap.conf /etc/ldap/ldap.conf
    ```

13. After the ldap.conf file is copied, you can now run the auth-client-config script by executing the following commands:

    ```
    sudo auth-client-config -t nss -p lac_ldap
    sudo pam-auth-update ldap
    ```

    The option -t specifies the type of the file, and the option -p specifies the profile to be used by PAM and the system configuration file nsswitch.conf.
14. To make sure that the /home directory is created when logging on to the client machine, run the following command:

```
sudo gedit /etc/pam.d/common-account
```

After the file is opened, append the following line to the end of the file:

```
session required pam_mkhomedir.so umask=0022 skel=/etc/skel silent
```

Save the change. To exit the file, click the **File** menu and select **Quit**. If there is no error, you can now test the LDAP authentication."

15. Before testing, make sure that the DNS service is working properly by entering the following command:

```
host client1.group2.lab
```

You should be able to get the corresponding IP address 192.168.2.2. If not, you may need to edit the file /etc/resolv.conf as shown in the previous steps.

16. Log out from the client machine.
17. To test the LDAP service, you need to log on to the client machine with username **studenta** and password **ubuntu**. This user account was created on the server machine earlier in this hands-on practice.
18. To verify that you are indeed logged on as user studenta, click the **System** menu. Then, select **Administration** and **Network Tools**, and click the tab **Finger**. You should be able to see the output shown in Figure 10.14. As shown in Figure 10.14, the current user is studenta.

In this hands-on practice, you have learned quite a bit about LDAP. You configured the LDAP server and populated it with the information from the existing system databases. After you configured the LDAP server, you configured the client machine for user authentication. The user studenta created on the server machine can log on to the client machine through the LDAP authentication service as though the user studenta has an account on the client machine.

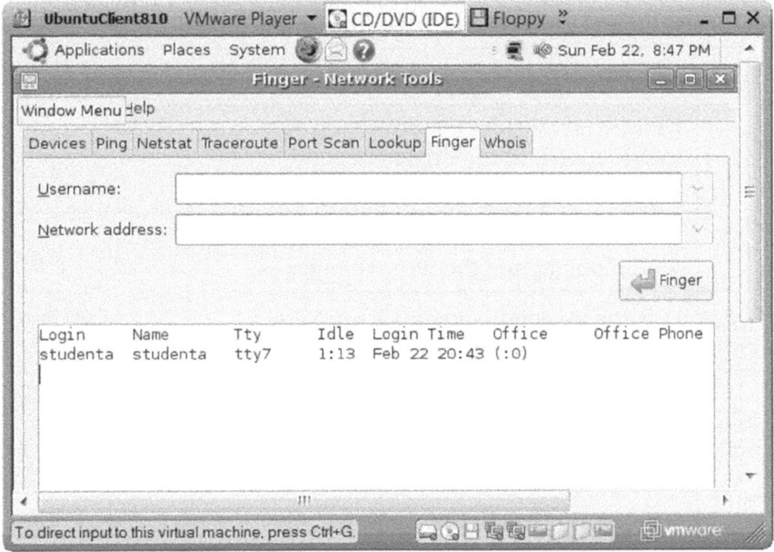

Figure 10.14 Log in as studenta.

10.3 Network Device Resource Management

A network includes various network hardware devices such as network interface cards, USB devices, network printers, and so on. Drivers are developed for these network devices so that the operating system and application software can communicate with them. One of the primary tasks performed by the Linux kernel is managing device drivers. Daemons running in the background can be used to respond to network requests and hardware activities. The drivers and the daemons used to manage these network devices are called network device resources. Various utilities are included in the Linux operating system to help network administrators manage network device resources. This chapter explains how the kernel and daemons can be used for network device resource management and introduces some of the commonly used network device resource management tools.

10.3.1 Viewing Device Information

On a Linux computer, you can view hardware information through commands as well as GUI tools. Table 10.4 lists some of the commands that are commonly used to display the hardware information.

Figure 10.15 illustrates network-related information returned by the command hwinfo, and Figure 10.16 displays the information returned by the command udevinfo. There are also some GUI utilities that can be used to display information about hardware devices. Specifically, Ubuntu provides several GUI-based device management utilities:

- hardinfo
- Control Center
- Gnome Device Manager
- KDE HAL Device Manager

Table 10.4 Commands for Displaying Device Information

Command	*Description*	*Example*
`hwinfo`	Detects and displays hardware device information and the drivers needed to run these devices	`hwinfo --network`
`mount`	Displays the currently mounted devices, the mount points, and the file system types	`mount`
`less /proc/devices`	Lists the devices used on a Linux system	`less /proc/devices`
`less /proc/ioports`	Lists the I/O ports used by a Linux system	`less /proc/ioports`
`lspci`	Lists PCI devices used by a Linux system	`lspci`
`lshal`	Displays the database of hardware devices used by a Linux system	`lshal`
`udevinfo`	Displays device path information	`udevinfo -a -p /sys/class/net/eth2`

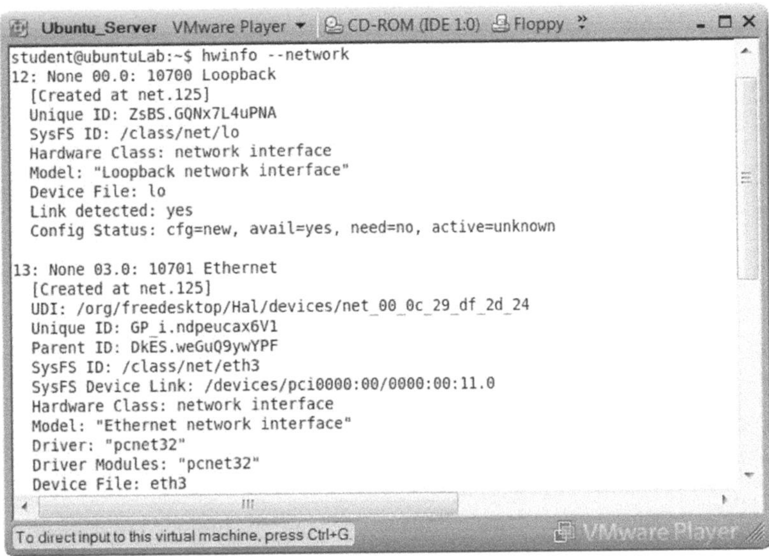

Figure 10.15 Displaying network device information with command hwinfo.

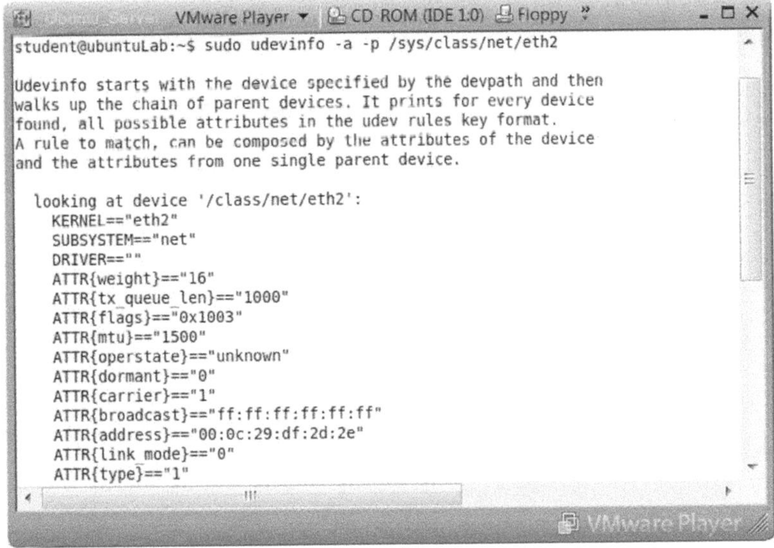

Figure 10.16 Displaying information on NIC eth2 with command udevinfo.

The device management GUI utility, hardinfo, can be used to find information about hardware used by a computer system. Figure 10.17 illustrates the hardinfo GUI window displaying information about PCI devices such as the USB controller and Ethernet controller.

Another commonly used utility that can be used to display and manage hardware devices is the Control Center provided by the Ubuntu Linux operating system. Figure 10.18 illustrates the hardware management tools, such as Hardware Drivers and Hardware Testing, included in the Control Center utility.

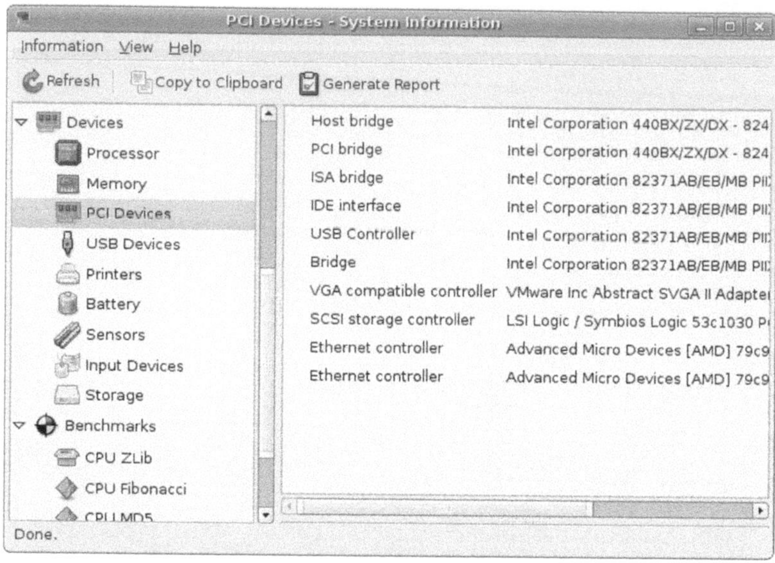

Figure 10.17 PCI device information provided by hardinfo.

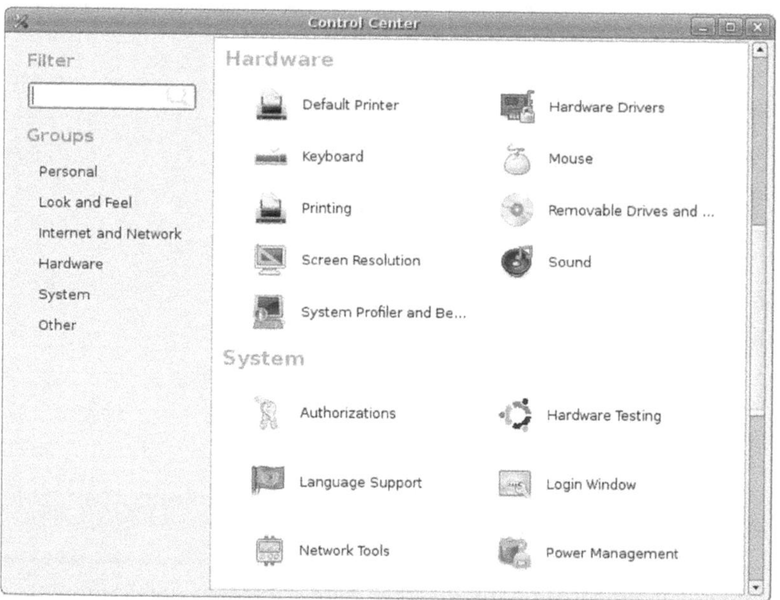

Figure 10.18 Hardware management tools included in Control Center.

For device management, Ubuntu provides another utility called Gnome Device Manager, which can be used to manage hardware devices. In Figure 10.19, the summary information about the Ethernet Network Controller, including the Model, Vendor, and Connection, is displayed in the Device Manager window.

The Hardware Abstraction Layer (HAL) is another utility that provides an abstract view of hardware. HAL can be used to manage a list of existing devices, and displays information about

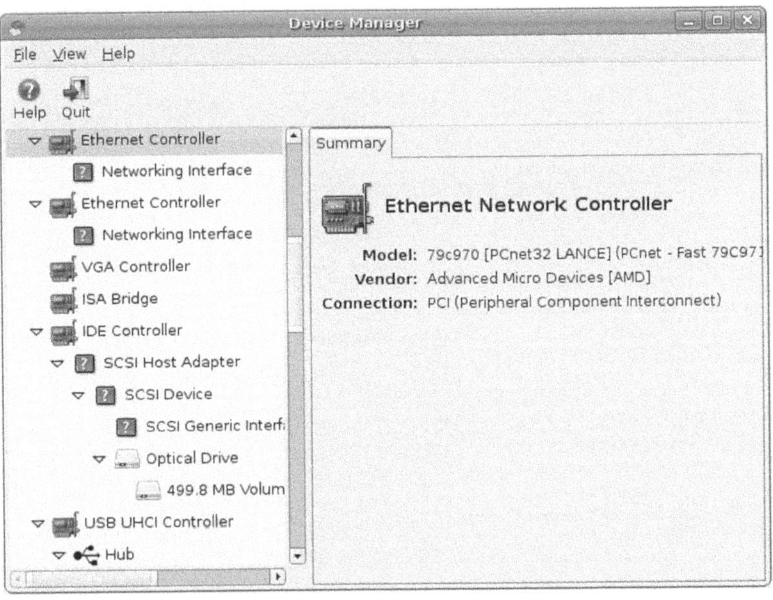

Figure 10.19 Ethernet network controller information displayed in Device Manager.

the devices. With HAL, you can add a new device and connect it to a computer system without modifying every application that uses the device. Figure 10.20 displays the network interface information in kde-hal-device-manager.

10.3.2 Device Management Daemons

Daemons are programs that run in the background. They are used to perform functions in response to events such as network requests and hardware activities. Some daemons are used to manage network devices. Daemons can also run some scheduled tasks. The Linux operating system includes a variety of device management daemons. Among them, udev and HAL are two commonly used ones. In Linux, files related to devices are stored in the folder /etc/dev. As Linux supports more and more devices, there could be a large number of files in the directory /etc/dev. To avoid accumulating too many device files in the /etc/dev directory, Linux now dynamically detects devices, generates device files as needed, and saves them to the directory /etc/dev. Each time a computer system starts, the needed device files are recreated. udev is used to detect and generate device files, and HAL is used to provide information about the devices. HAL is also used to manage the configuration of removable devices such as USB card readers and CD-ROMs.

10.3.2.1 Hardware Abstraction Layer (HAL)

Usually, applications such as desktop environments have no knowledge of available devices. When an application requests a device, it sends the request to a daemon such as HAL, which provides information about the availability of the device. The HAL daemon dynamically interacts with the device objects stored in a device database. HAL also provides the device information used by a management program such as fstab-sync. The fstab-sync program dynamically modifies the content, such as the mount points and other options, in the fstab file. The HAL configuration and

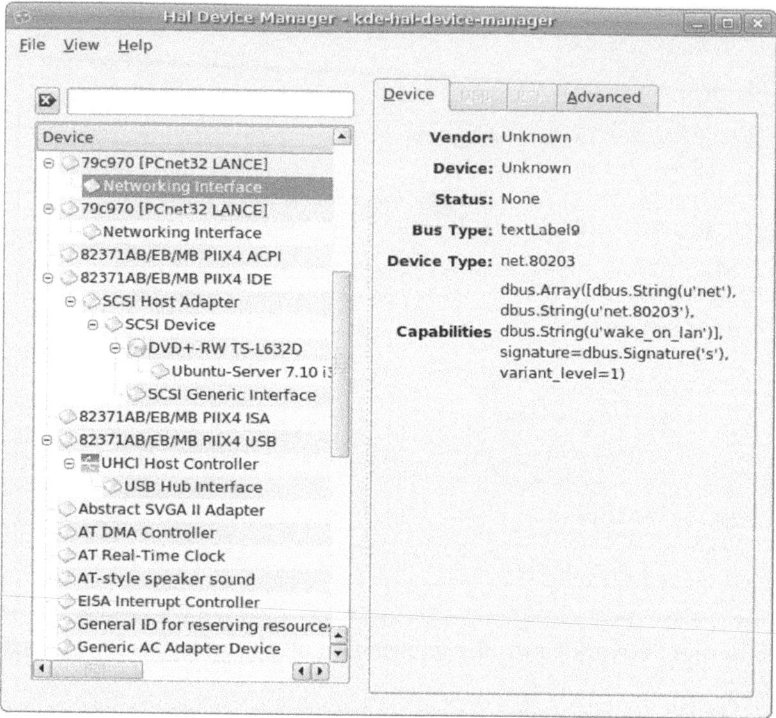

Figure 10.20 Network interface information displayed in kde-hal-device-manager.

properties are managed by the device information files, which have the extension fdi and which are stored in the directories such as /usr/share/hal/fdi/, /usr/lib/hal/fdi/, and /etc/hal/fdi/. There are three subdirectories: information, policy, and preprobe. The descriptions of these three directories are as follows:

- *information:* The information subdirectory contains vendor and product information regarding the devices. A typical file in this subdirectory is 10freedesktop, provided by freedesktop.org.
- *policy:* The policy subdirectory has communication rules such as hot plug policies or storage policies for the devices. A typical file in this subdirectory is 10osvendor, provided by a Linux distribution or the system administrator.
- *preprobe:* The preprobe subdirectory handles unusual devices. It contains the preprobe policies for such devices. A typical file included in this subdirectory is 10-iphone.fdi.

The fdi files contain the rules on how to access device information and the options on detecting and assigning devices. Under the fdi directory, there are some subdirectories with names starting with numbers such as 10, 20, or 30. The lower the number, the higher the priority. The rules in files with lower numbers override the rules in the files with the higher numbers. For example, Figure 10.21 illustrates the information included in the file /usr/share/hal/fdi/information/20thirdparty/20-libmtp7.fdi.

The file illustrated in Figure 10.21 has information for communication with Media Transfer Protocol (MTP)-aware devices. MTP is the protocol often used by USB portable devices.

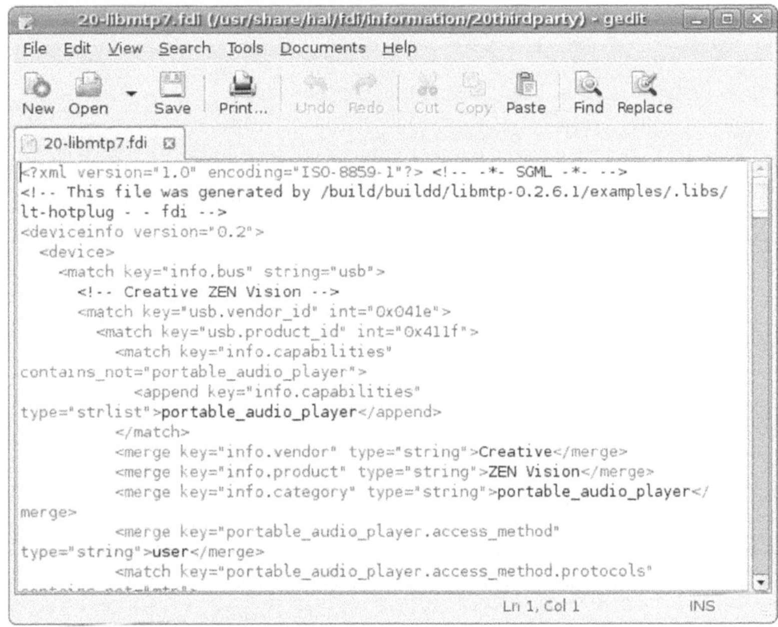

Figure 10.21 fdi file content.

10.3.2.2 User Device (udev)

This is another commonly used device management daemon. During the system booting process, udev starts to detect devices. After a device is detected, information about the detected device will be saved to the udev database. By following a set of predefined rules, udev generates a device file and places it in the directory /etc/dev. It can detect kernel services that are added to or removed from the operating system. It can also be used to detect hot-plug devices.

The rules used by udev are kept in the files stored in the directory /etc/udev/rules.d/. The rules are used to set up symbolic links to the devices. For example, Figure 10.22 displays the content in the file /etc/udev/rules.d/05-udev-early.rules.

As shown in Figure 10.22, each rule consists of a set of key–value pairs separated by commas. There is at least one match key and one assignment key in each rule. For example, in Figure 10.22, the match key is KERNEL==”[0-9]*:[0-9]*”. The equality operator == must be used for the match key. The assignment key is WAIT_FOR_SYSFS=”ioerr_cnt”. The assignment operator = must be used for the assignment key. The match key is used to identify the device. After the device is matched, the assignment key is used to apply the rule.

The existing rules are predefined for the devices supported by Linux. One should not alter any of these predefined rules. You may, however, create your rule files in the directory /etc/udev/rules.d/.

Activity 10.2 Renaming Network Interface Card

In this hands-on practice, you are going to rename the NIC of your server machine. For example, if your current server machine has the NICs eth2 and eth3, in this hands-on activity, you can rename

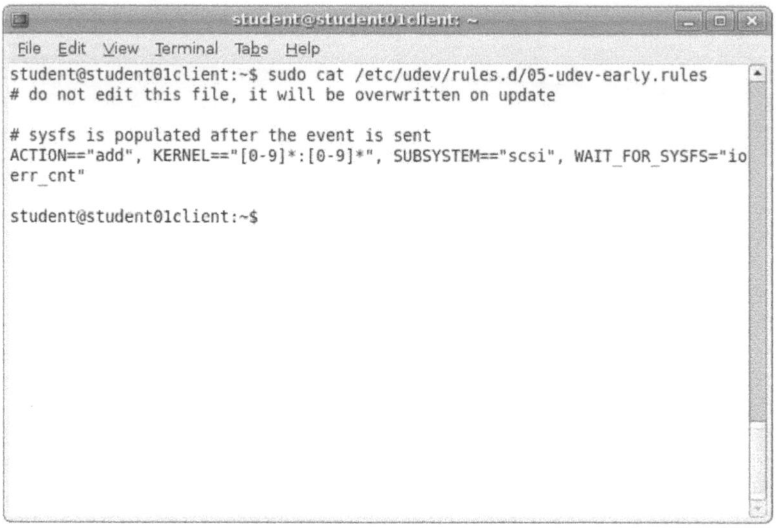

```
student@student01client: ~
File Edit View Terminal Tabs Help
student@student01client:~$ sudo cat /etc/udev/rules.d/05-udev-early.rules
# do not edit this file, it will be overwritten on update

# sysfs is populated after the event is sent
ACTION=="add", KERNEL=="[0-9]*:[0-9]*", SUBSYSTEM=="scsi", WAIT_FOR_SYSFS="io
err_cnt"

student@student01client:~$
```

Figure 10.22 Rules in file /etc/udev/rules.d/05-udev-early.rules.

them as card2 and card3 with udev. For those of you who have eth0 and eth1 as the NICs' names, you may consider renaming them with different names such as card0 and card1. The following are the steps you may follow to get the job done:

1. Log on to the server machine with username **student** and password **ubuntu**.
2. To view information about the eth0 NIC, execute the following command in the terminal window:

   ```
   udevinfo -a -p /sys/class/net/eth0
   ```

   You will get something similar to the information displayed in Figure 10.23.

   Note that the hardware address for the eth0 NIC is 00:0c:29:36:14:8a. You may have a different hardware address.
3. Run the following command to get information about the eth1 NIC:

   ```
   udevinfo -a -p /sys/class/net/eth1
   ```

   The hardware address for the eth1 NIC is 00:0c:29:36:14:94. Again, you may have a different hardware address for the eth1 NIC. The option -a is used to print all the properties of the specified device, and the option -p specifies the path to the device file.
4. Your next task is to create a rule file /etc/udev/rules.d/10-nic.rules by executing the following command:

   ```
   sudo gedit /etc/udev/rules.d/10-nic.rules
   ```

5. Enter the following rules in the file:

   ```
   KERNEL=="eth*", SYSFS{address}=="00:0c:29:36:14:8a", NAME="card0"
   KERNEL=="eth*", SYSFS{address}=="00:0c:29:36:14:94", NAME="card1"
   ```

   You need to use your hardware addresses in the preceding command. Click the **Save** menu. To exit the file, click the **File** menu, and select **Quit**.

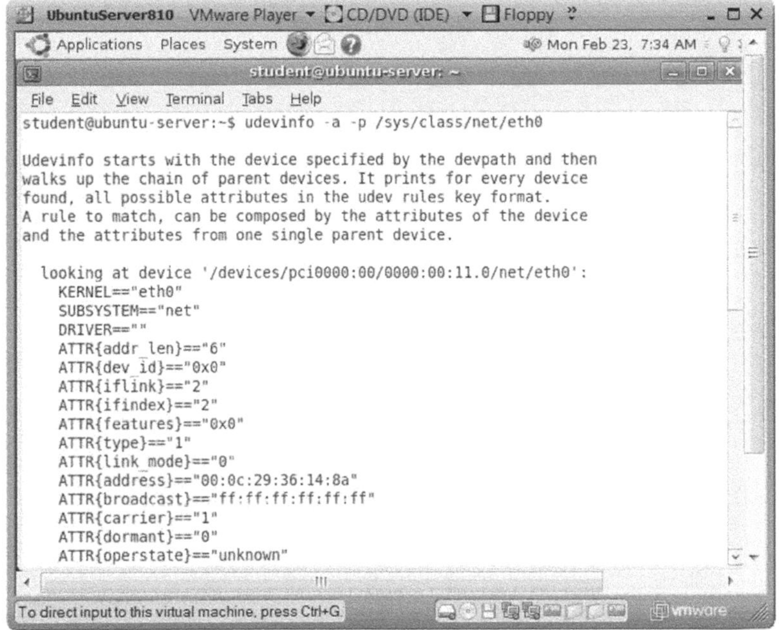

Figure 10.23 Information about NIC eth0.

6. Next, you will update the NIC configuration in the file /etc/network/interfaces. Enter the following command to edit the file:

```
sudo gedit /etc/network/interfaces
```

After the file is opened, change all the eth0 keywords to **card0** and all the eth1 keywords to **card1**. Click the **Save** menu. To exit the file, click the **File** menu, and select **Quit**.

7. To reload the network drivers, you need to restart the server machine by entering the following command:

```
sudo reboot
```

8. After the system is rebooted, you can verify the changes to the NIC names by executing the following command:

```
sudo ifconfig
```

You should be able to see that the names of the NICs have changed (Figure 10.24).

9. To avoid confusion in the later hands-on activities, you may want to get the original configuration back. Open the file /etc/udev/rules.d/10-nic.rules, and comment out both lines in Step 5. Also, open the file /etc/network/interfaces, and change all the card keywords to **eth**. Save the file, and quit the editor. Then, reboot the system.

In the foregoing hands-on practice, the udev rules have been used to rename the network interface cards. As you can see, it is convenient to use udev for managing network hardware devices. While writing the udev rules, you have used the match key KERNEL=="eth*". The kernel is one of the key components of a computer's operating system for managing the system's resources. The next section will introduce the kernel and its management.

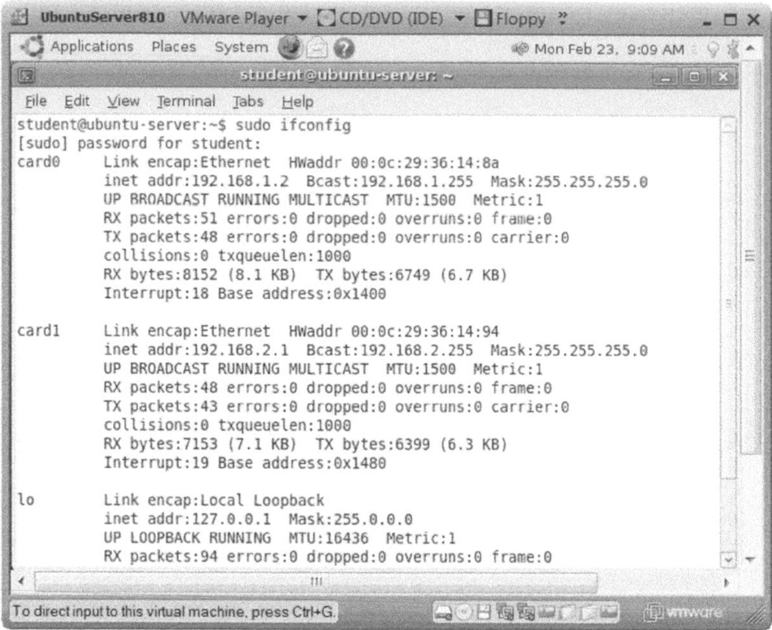

Figure 10.24 Renaming the NIC.

10.3.3 Kernel Management

The kernel is a central component of the Linux operating system. The primary function of the Linux kernel is to manage the system's resources, such as the network devices available for the system's processes. In general, the Linux kernel has the structure shown in Figure 10.25.

By default, the Linux kernel includes a wide range of drivers for hardware devices. These drivers can be directly compiled into the kernel or loaded as kernel modules. The kernel modules can be loaded into the kernel after the computer system is booted. Various kernel management utilities, some of which are command based and others GUI based, are developed for kernel management. Table 10.5 lists some commonly used command-based kernel management tools.

In addition to these commands, Linux also includes various utilities to help network administrators with kernel management. The following are some of the kernel management packages included in the Ubuntu Linux operating system:

- *adjtimex:* This is a utility that is used to display or set the kernel time variables for standalone or intermittently connected computers.
- *Dynamic Kernel Module Support (DKMS):* It is used for installing and updating kernel modules.
- *dphys-kernel-packages:* The term dphys stands for Debian Powered Hosts Yet Simple. This utility can be used to generate many variants of kernel packages and modules.
- *lcap:* It can be used to remove some capabilities in the kernel to tighten the security of Linux machines.
- *loadlin:* It loads a Linux kernel image system under DOS or some earlier versions of Windows operating systems. It replaces the current DOS or Windows operating system with the Linux operating system without altering the existing DOS or Windows system files.

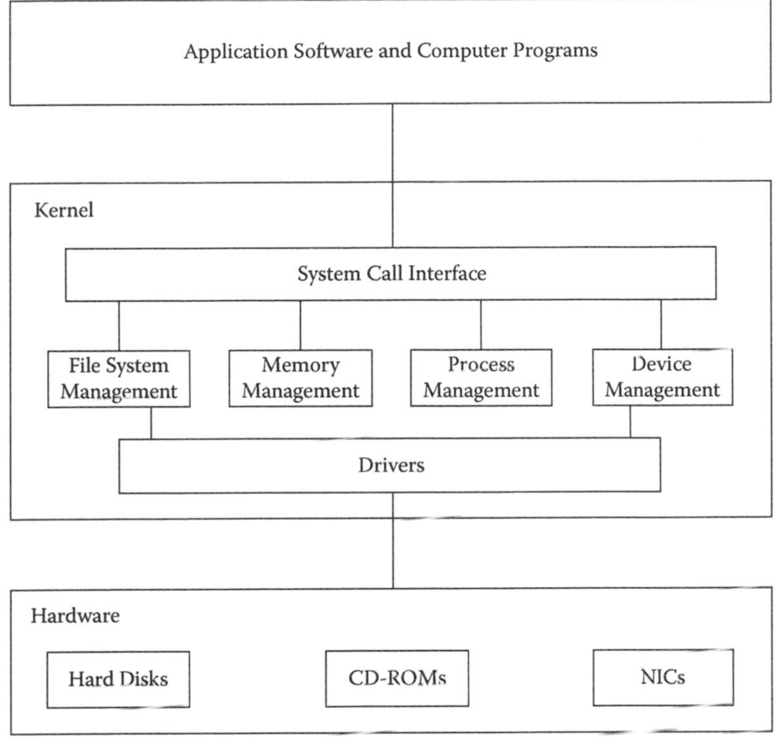

Figure 10.25 General kernel structure.

- *mkrboot:* It makes bootable disks that contain both a kernel and a root image.
- *Module-Init-Tools:* This is a package that includes tools used for managing Linux kernel modules. With this package, you can load, insert, and remove kernel modules for Linux.
- *socklog-run:* It can be used to provide system and kernel logging services for network-based logging.
- *systune:* This program performs kernel tuning for better performance without recompiling the kernel.
- *udev:* It is a rule-based device and kernel event manager. It provides a set of tools and daemons to deal with events generated by devices and the kernel.

The configuration of the kernel can also be done with GUI-based utilities. The commonly used GUI-based utility for kernel configuration is xconfig. Figure 10.26 illustrates the xconfig user interface.

In the xconfig user interface, there are three panes. The pane on the left-hand side displays the tree structure of the items available for kernel configuration. The upper-right pane displays kernel configuration options for the item selected in the left pane. The lower-right pane displays help information for configuration of the selected item.

Another GUI-based kernel configuration tool is menuconfig. It is a keyboard-based GUI editor. It is often used by users who are comfortable using keys instead of using the mouse. Figure 10.27 shows the menuconfig user interface.

Table 10.5 Kernel Management Commands

Command	*Description*	*Example*
`modinfo`	Displays information regarding a specified module	To display the information of the module cdrom: `modinfo cdrom`
`dmesg`	Lists the messages for the last kernel startup	To view the startup messages one screen at a time: `dmesg | less`
`lsmod`	Lists the existing modules currently loaded in the kernel	`lsmod`
`insmod`	Inserts a specified module into the kernel	To insert the module cdrom: `insmod cdrom`
`rmmod`	Removes a specified module from the kernel when no hardware is currently connected to it	To remove the module cdrom: `rmmod cdrom`
`modprobe`	Adds or removes modules to or from the kernel	To install the kernel module wgs200: `modprobe wgs200`
`depmod`	Discovers dependencies among modules	To discover all dependencies in the kernel with version number 2.6.27: `depmod -a 2.6.27`

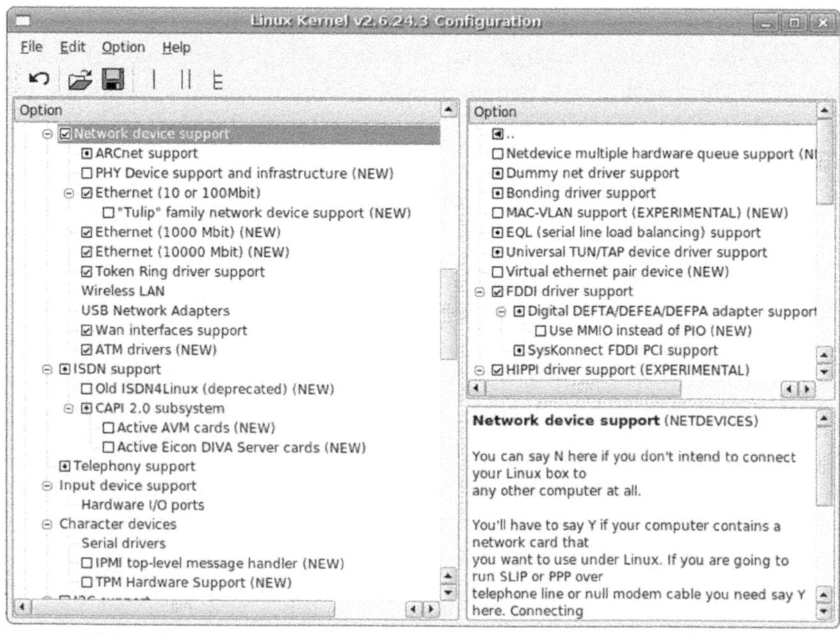

Figure 10.26 xconfig user interface.

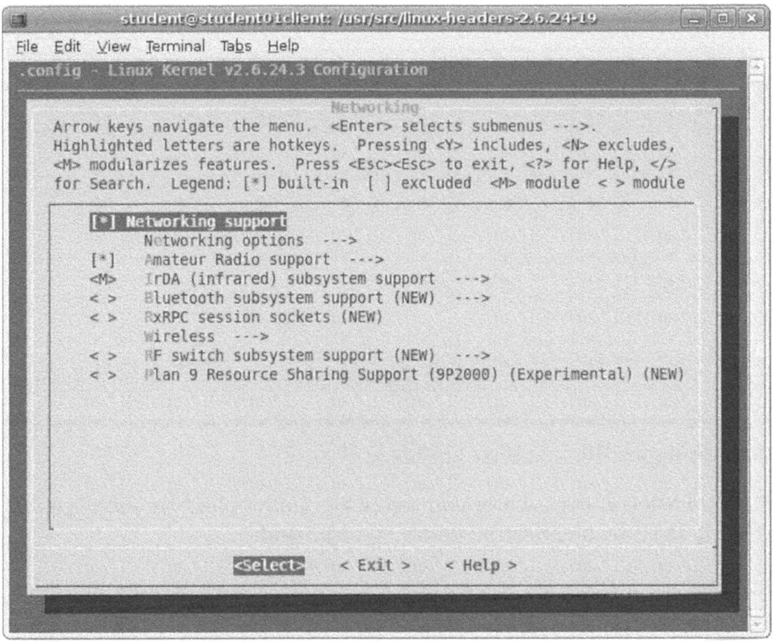

Figure 10.27 menuconfig user interface.

Activity 10.3 Customizing the Kernel

In this hands-on practice, you are going to customize the kernel for the Ubuntu Linux operating system by adding support for IPv6 multiple routing tables, which are useful for IPv6-based mobile devices. This hands-on activity will be performed on the client machine. The following shows the steps to perform the task:

1. Log on to your client machine with username **student** and password **ubuntu**.
2. The first thing you need to know is which version of Linux kernel is running on your machine. To do so, enter the following command:

   ```
   uname -r
   ```

   This command displays the version number on the screen. For example, you may see 2.6.27-9-generic for the kernel.
3. In the next step, you will need to install several software packages. If you have the 2.6.27-9-generic kernel installed on your computer, you will need to install the following packages:
   - *linux-source-2.6.27:* Linux kernel source for version 2.6.27.
   - *kernel-package:* A utility for building Linux kernel-related Debian packages.
   - *libncurses5-dev:* Developer's libraries and docs for ncurses, which are libraries for updating character screens with reasonable optimization.
   - *fakeroot:* A utility for creating a fake root environment that removes the need for the root while building a package.

   To install these packages, execute the following command:

   ```
   sudo apt-get install linux-source-2.6.27 kernel-package libncurses5-
   dev fakeroot
   ```

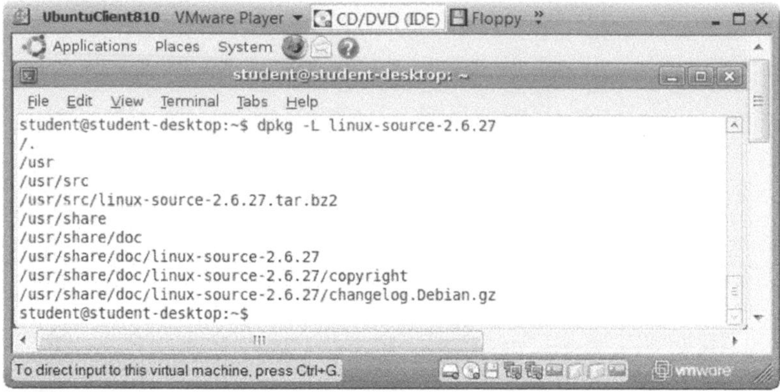

Figure 10.28 Searching for the installed zip file.

4. After the installation is completed, you will unzip the installed zip file. First, you will find where the zip file is by entering the following command:

   ```
   dpkg -L linux-source-2.6.27
   ```

   The option -L lists the files installed on your computer system during the installation process in previous step. As shown in Figure 10.28, you will see that the zip file linux-source-2.6.27.tar.bz2 is stored in the directory /usr/src/.
5. Now, change the working directory to /usr/src/ by executing the command

   ```
   cd /usr/src
   ```

6. After you have changed the working directory to /usr/src/, your next task is to decompress the zip file with the following two commands:

   ```
   sudo bunzip2 linux-source-2.6.27.tar.bz2
   sudo tar xvf linux-source-2.6.27.tar
   ```

   The option xvf is used to extract the files verbosely. The first command is used to decompress the .bz2 file, and the second command is used to create a new archive file.
7. In this step, you will compile a customized kernel. You do not need to create the kernel from scratch. You can make a copy of the currently existing kernel, and edit the copy. To make a copy of the existing kennel, execute the following command:

   ```
   sudo cp /boot/config-2.6.27-9-generic /usr/src/linux-source-2.6.27/.
   config
   ```

   Note that 2.6.27-9-generic is the kernel version obtained from Step 2 in this hands-on activity.
8. You are now ready to edit the kernel with a GUI kernel management utility such as menuconfig. To do so, you will first change the working directory by executing the following command:

   ```
   cd /usr/src/linux-source-2.6.27
   ```

   After the working directory is changed, execute the following command to start the GUI utility:

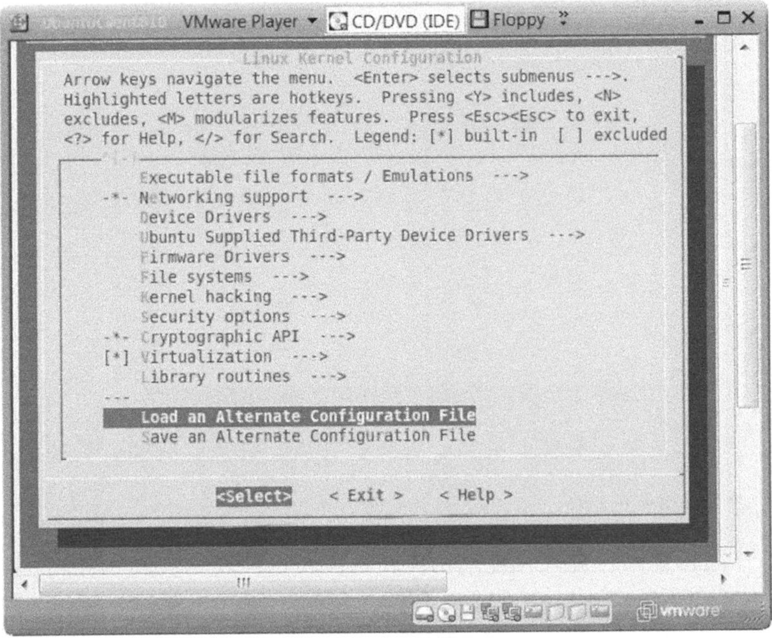

Figure 10.29 Loading alternate configuration file.

```
sudo make menuconfig
```

9. Move the cursor using the arrow key to select the link **Load an Alternate Configuration File** (Figure 10.29), and press the **Enter** key.
10. When prompted to specify the configuration file, make sure that .config is in the text box and the cursor is at **<Ok>** (Figure 10.30). Press the **Enter** key to select the configuration file.
11. Because IPv6 is in the networking category, use the arrow key to select **Networking support** (Figure 10.31), and press the **Enter** key.
12. Under the Networking support category, select **Network options** (Figure 10.32), and press the **Enter** key.
13. Under the Networking options category, use the arrow key to move the cursor to the item **The IPv6 protocol**, and press the **Enter** key.
14. Under "The IPv6 protocol" (Figure 10.33), select **IPv6: Multiple Routing Tables**. Press the space bar to select the item. Do the same to select **IPv6: source address based routing**.
15. Use the **Tab** key to move the cursor to **<Exit>**, and press the **Enter** key. Do the same three more times. Then, select **<Yes>,** and press **Enter** to complete the kernel editing process.
16. After editing the kernel, your next task is to compile the edited kernel. First, you need to execute the following command to get ready for the compilation:

```
sudo make clean
```

17. Next, run the following command to compile the kernel:

```
sudo fakeroot make-kpkg -initrd -append-to-version=-custom kernel_
image kernel_headers
```

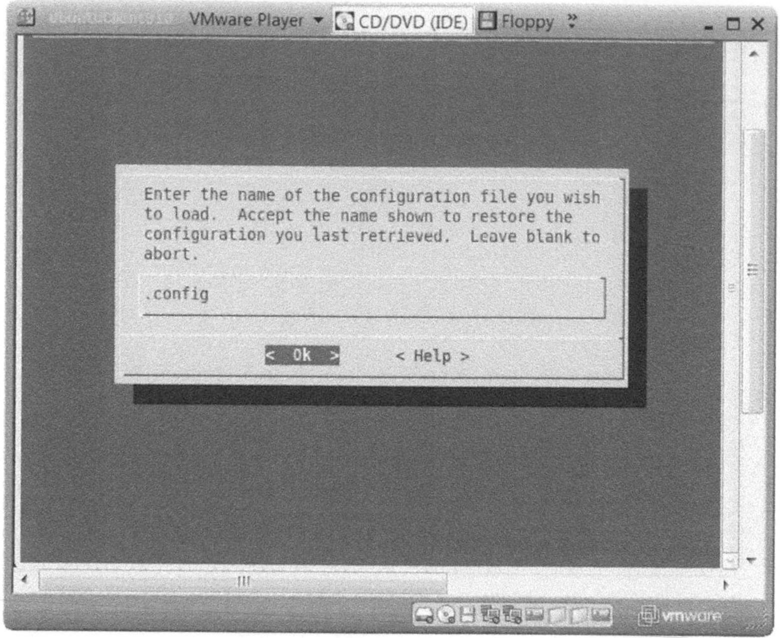

Figure 10.30 Selecting configuration file.

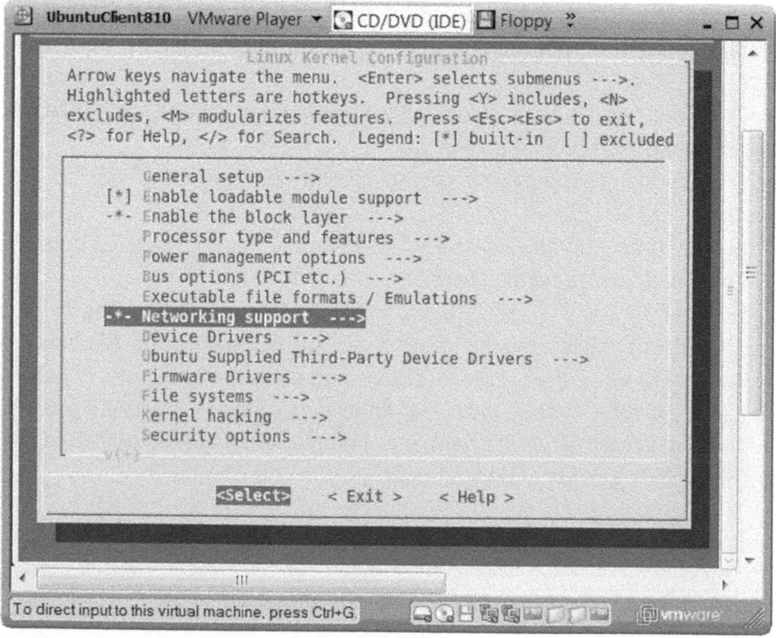

Figure 10.31 Selecting networking support category.

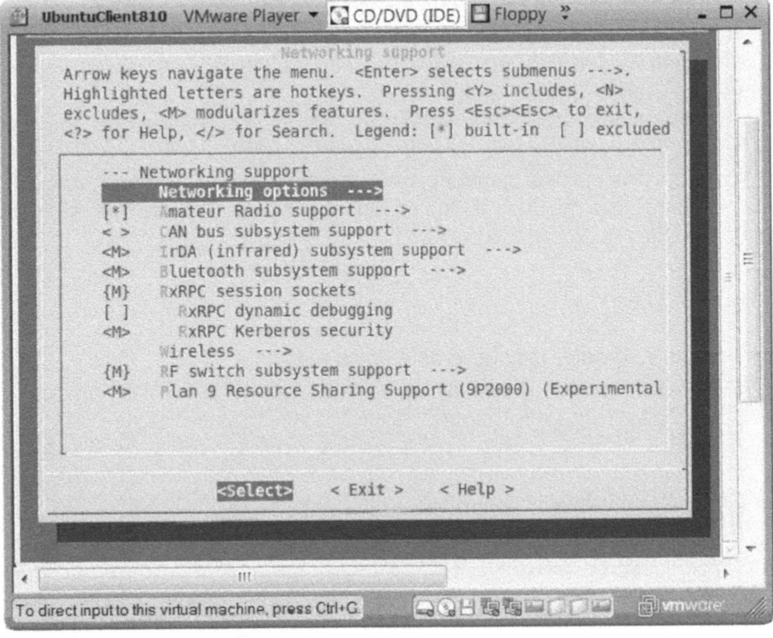

Figure 10.32 Selecting networking options category.

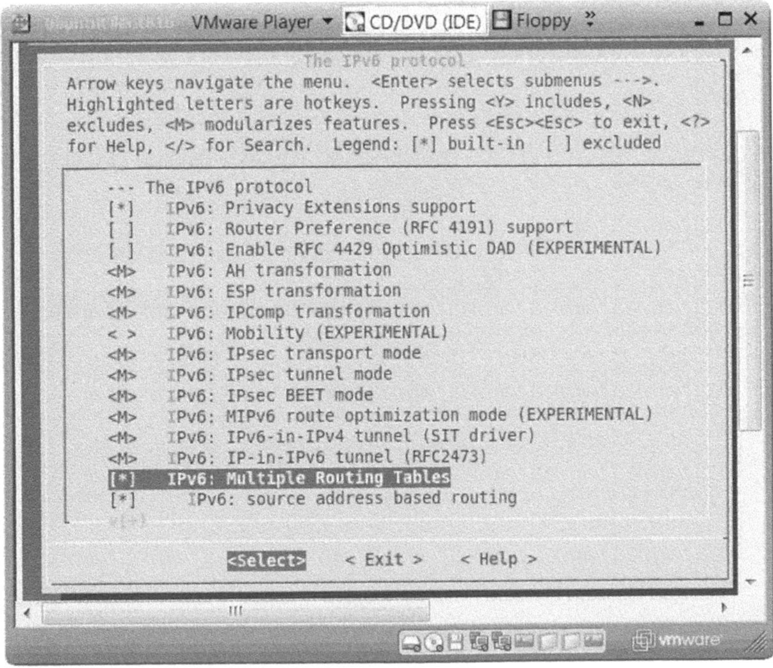

Figure 10.33 Selecting IPv6 routing-related items.

The compilation process will take some time to complete. The following are the meanings of the options and variables used in this command:

- make-kpkg: It is used to build Debian kernel packages from the Linux kernel source.
- –initrd: It is used to load a kernel.
- –append-to-version: The value after this option is appended to the value of the EXTRAVERSION variable present in the kernel Makefile.

18. The compilation process will generate two .deb files in the directory /usr/src. The .deb extension indicates that the file is a Debian binary package. Run the following command to display the two files shown in Figure 10.34:

```
ls /usr/src/*.deb
```

The files on your computer may have different names.

19. Use the following command to change the working directory to /usr/src/:

```
cd ..
```

20. Run the following two dpkg -i commands to install those two .deb files:

```
sudo dpkg -i linux-image-2.6.27.10-custom_2.6.27.10-custom-10.00.
Custom_i386.deb
sodu dpkg -i linux-headers-2.6.27.10-custom_2.6.27.10-custom-10.00.
Custom_i386.deb
```

21. After these two binary packages are installed, reboot the system by executing the following command:

```
sudo reboot
```

22. After the system is rebooted, the customized kernel is ready. To verify, execute this command:

```
uname -r
```

The customized kernel with version number 2.6.27.10-custom should be displayed on your screen (Figure 10.35).

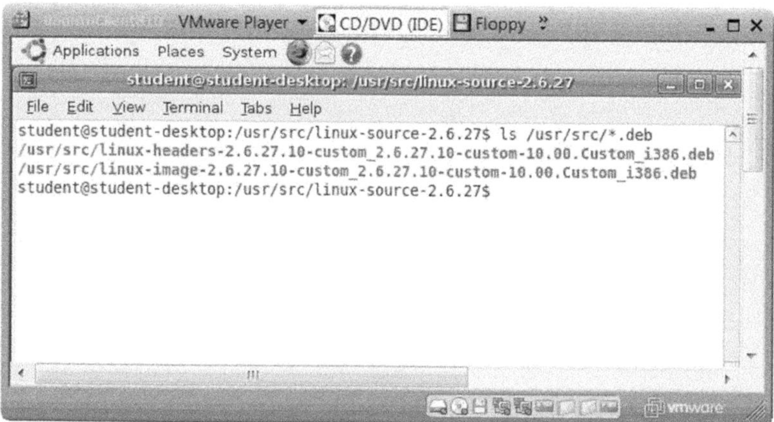

Figure 10.34 Displaying Debian binary package files.

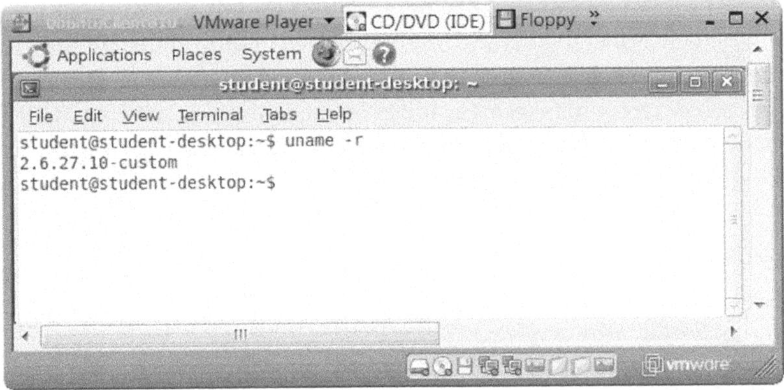

Figure 10.35 Customized kernel.

This hands-on practice demonstrated how to create a customized kernel, compile it, and install it. To avoid creating a kernel from scratch, a copy of the existing kernel was modified to include the new features for IPv6. The keyboard-based GUI kernel management utility was used to customize the kernel. Then, the kernel was installed and recompiled. From that point on, Linux operating system will use the customized kernel for its operation.

This section covered three topics. The first section was about the utilities, command-based and GUI-based, that are used to view network device resource information. The second topic was about the daemons used for managing network device resources; the HAL and udev daemons were discussed under this topic. A hands-on activity was given to demonstrate how to use udev to change the name of an Ethernet card. The third topic related to kernel management. A hands-on activity was used to illustrate the process of managing network resources with the kernel.

10.4 Summary

This chapter discussed issues related to the management of user accounts and network device resources. In order to allow users to log on to any of the computers on a network, the directory service is used to store and manage network user accounts. Although the Network File System (NFS) can be used for managing network user accounts, it is only used for Linux networks. LDAP, on the other hand, supports users who log on to network computers running other operating systems. In addition, LDAP can also deal with various centrally controlled network-based services such as the e-mail service and database service. By storing authentication data in a database, LDAP is more efficient and reliable.

After explaining how the directory service works, this chapter provided a hands-on activity on creating a directory service to allow users to log on to any computer on the network. Through the directory service, a user with the user account created on the server machine can log on to a client machine as if the user has an account created on the client machine.

Managing drivers and other network device resources is a task performed by the network administrator daily. This chapter briefly discussed some of the topics related to network device resource management. It examined several utilities provided by Linux for managing network device resources. This chapter introduced some utilities used to view information about network devices. It also illustrated how to use the daemons to rename the network interface card through the hands-on practice.

The Linux kernel is a key component of Linux. This chapter has introduced some commonly used kernel management utilities. A hands-on activity was used to illustrate how to modify the kernel to include more network resources in the Linux operating system. During the hands-on activity, the GUI-based kernel management utility menuconfig was used to modify the kernel. The hands-on activity also illustrated the process of compiling and installing a modified kernel for Linux.

Review Questions

1. What are system users and regular users?
2. Normally, how are users categorized?
3. Describe the command cat, and give an example to demonstrate its use.
4. Describe the command finger, and give an example to demonstrate its use.
5. What is the advantage of using groups?
6. How do you add the user student to the group club?
7. What tasks can be performed by a directory service?
8. Name some packages included in OpenLDAP, and describe how they are used.
9. What are the features supported by OpenLDAP?
10. Explain the symbols such as dc, ou, and uid used in the LDAP tree structure.
11. What tasks can be performed by the LDAP client software?
12. Describe the command lshal, and give an example to demonstrate its use.
13. Describe the command udevinfo, and give an example to demonstrate its use.
14. Name some GUI-based network device management utilities included in the Ubuntu Linux operating system.
15. What are the three subdirectories under the directory fdi, and what information is included in each of the subdirectories?
16. Describe the command dmesg, and give an example to demonstrate its use.
17. Describe the command modprobe, and give an example to demonstrate its use.
18. What is udev?
19. What is menuconfig?
20. Which utility can be used to build Linux kernel-related Debian packages?

Case Study Projects

The following are two networking projects that involve network resource management:

Case Study Project 10.1. Install and configure a directory service for your home network. Demonstrate that you can log on to any of the computers on your home network by using a user account created on the server machine on your home network.

Case Study Project 10.2. Rename an Ethernet NIC on one of the client machines on your network with the utility udev. Give a meaningful name such as “client” for the NIC.

Chapter 11

Wireless Networks

Objectives

- Investigate Linux-compatible wireless products.
- Install and configure wireless devices.
- Use Linux wireless network utilities.
- Develop wireless network services.

11.1 Introduction

In general, as far as GUI and application software support is concerned, the open source operating system Linux is competitive with commercial operating systems, especially Ubuntu Linux, which supports an adequate GUI-based desktop computing environment. However, Linux has a relatively difficult time dealing with wireless networking. The main reason is that some wireless products are proprietary, and their vendors are unwilling to share their drivers with Linux.

To help users develop a wireless network, this chapter will cover topics related to wireless network technologies and the construction of a Linux wireless network. This chapter will briefly discuss wireless technologies and wireless network devices. It will specifically examine Linux-compatible wireless devices, the usage of wireless network utilities provided by the Linux operating system, and wireless product installation and network configuration.

This chapter will first introduce wireless network technologies, including Wi-Fi, WiMAX, and Bluetooth. These wireless technologies use different wireless transmission media and are used to handle different jobs. This chapter will briefly describe how each of them works and what tasks they can accomplish.

Second, this chapter will introduce wireless network devices such as wireless network routers and wireless network interface cards. It will give a brief description of device characteristics and functionalities, and how they work.

Next, this chapter will investigate some Linux-compatible wireless devices. Finding Linux-compatible wireless devices is the key to success. Major Linux distributions and other Linux organizations provide hardware compatibility information on their Web sites. In this chapter, several of these Web sites will be introduced. Information such as the functionalities of these wireless devices will be summarized. In the hands-on activity, you will practice how to check if the wireless network devices on a computer are compatible with the Linux operating system.

The next topic is about issues related to wireless network device installation and configuration. Wireless network configuration is similar to wired network configuration. Wireless NICs need to be configured so that a computer can be connected to a router and other network devices. Network services such as DHCP and DNS still need to be implemented in a wireless network. On the other hand, the wireless network involves some complexities such as signal acquisition and related security problems. This chapter will provide some solutions to overcome these problems.

In dealing with wireless network complexities, network development utilities are often included in the Linux operating system. This chapter will provide information about these utilities. The commonly used wireless networking commands and GUI tools will be explored, and the hands-on practice will demonstrate how to use these utilities for creating and managing wireless networks.

11.2 Wireless Network Technologies

A wireless computing environment provides flexibility, mobility, maintainability, and scalability. A wireless network can be operated on radio wave, microwave, and infrared. Recently, security for wireless communication has also significantly improved. This section will introduce wireless technologies, such as Wi-Fi, WiMAX, and Bluetooth, that have been developed based on the three commonly used wireless transmission media. The following subsections briefly describe them.

11.2.1 Wi-Fi Technology

Radio waves can be used by many types of wireless equipment such as cellular phones, PDAs, notebook computers with wireless network cards, and so on. Wi-Fi is a radio-wave-based wireless network technology. A Wi-Fi wireless network includes one or more access points that are used to transmit and receive radio signals to and from mobile devices. An access point has a built-in antenna and a radio transmitter for transmitting radio signals. One access point can communicate with as many as 255 mobile devices.

Mobile devices such as notebook computers come with either built-in wireless transmitters or external wireless network adapters. When a user turns on a computer with wireless network capability within the range of an access point, the user will be informed that the network access point is detected. By connecting to the access point, wireless communication can be carried out through the access point and the wireless adapter or built-in wireless transmitter.

In a Wi-Fi wireless network, a data packet is first converted to radio signals by the wireless network adapter and then transmitted into the air through an antenna. Once the radio signals reach the access point, the access point will verify the service set identifier (SSID). If the SSID is certified, the radio signals will be converted back to the data packet, which can then be forwarded to the Internet through a wired connection. Conversely, the data on the Internet can be sent to the access point, which converts the data packet to radio signals and transmits the signals into the air. Then, a wireless network interface card takes the radio signals and converts them back to the data packet. Figure 11.1 illustrates two Wi-Fi wireless networks as part of the Internet.

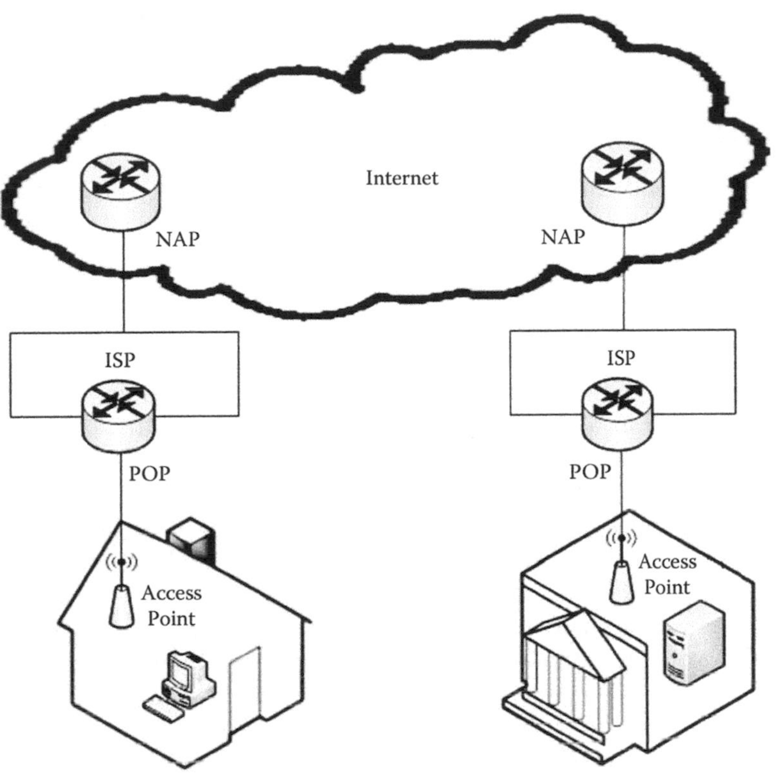

Figure 11.1 Wi-Fi wireless networks.

Table 11.1 Wi-Fi Standards

Standard	*Frequency (GHz)*	*Transmission Rate (Mbps)*	*Maximum Range (m)*
802.11b	2.4	11	38 (indoor) 140 (outdoor)
802.11g	2.4	54	38 (indoor) 140 (outdoor)
802.11n	2.4 5	300	70 (indoor) 250 (outdoor)

Wi-Fi technology is defined based on the IEEE 802.11 standards, which set the data transmission rates and other low-level operations carried out by Wi-Fi technology. Table 11.1 lists the common Wi-Fi standards.

As shown in Table 11.1, the 802.11n standard can operate at a higher frequency, which means more data can be transmitted. Therefore, 802.11n has a much higher transmission rate than 802.11b and 802.11g. For Wi-Fi networks, various NICs are built to match the Wi-Fi standards listed in Table 11.1. An 11b wireless NIC is able to handle data transmission up to 11 Mbps, an

11g wireless NIC is able to handle data transmission up to 54 Mbps, and an 11n wireless NIC can handle up to 300 Mbps data transmission.

11.2.2 WiMAX Technology

Having a higher frequency than radio wave, microwave can travel a much longer distance. Microwave is often used by telephone companies to carry long-distance telephone messages. For a wireless network, microwave can cover an entire metropolitan area with high-quality transmission. While Wi-Fi changes how messages are delivered over the last 100 ft of a network, microwave changes how messages are delivered over the last mile. Worldwide Interoperability for Microwave Access (WiMAX) is a well-known microwave wireless network technology. Its proposed downloading rate is 75 Mbps, and its uploading rate is 25 Mbps. The rates may vary depending on the distance and number of users accessing the transmission center. The transmission rates of WiMAX are much higher than the transmission rates supported by the current landline-based Internet connection such as DSL or cable.

To be able to communicate through microwave, a WiMAX system is constructed with a WiMAX transmission tower, which resembles access points of the Wi-Fi technology. The transmission tower communicates with the Internet through a wired connection. It can communicate with other transmission towers through microwave beams with frequency as high as 66 GHz. The high frequency allows the transmission tower to reach another tower 50 km away and to be less interrupted. Conversely, a WiMAX receiver, which can be a built-in component in a notebook computer or built on a WiMAX PC card, communicates with the transmission tower with a frequency of 2 GHz to 11 GHz, similar to that provided by Wi-Fi technology. In this frequency range, the waves can easily get around physical objects such as buildings. However, the waves in this frequency section can only cover a region of a few miles. Figure 11.2 illustrates a WiMAX system.

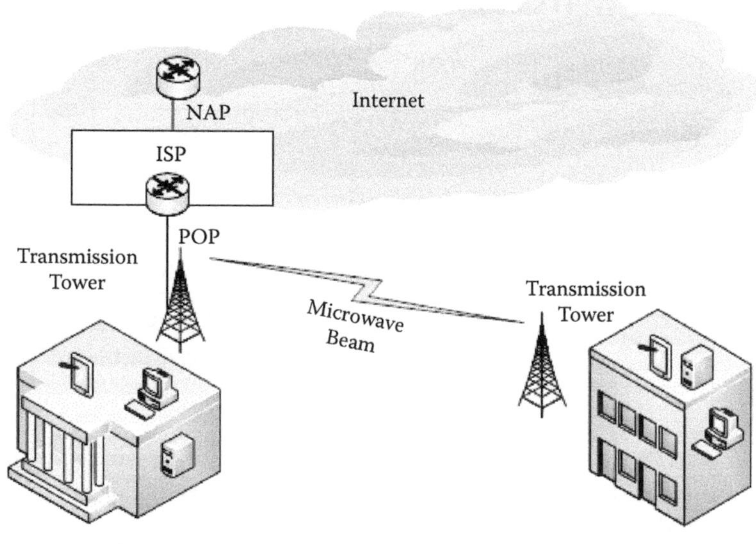

Figure 11.2 WiMAX network.

Table 11.2 Common WiMAX Standards

Standard	*Frequency (GHz)*	*Usage*
802.16	10–66	Supports point-to-point delivery between transmission towers
802.16a	2–11	Supports point-to-multipoint delivery between a transmission tower and individual receivers on network devices
802.16e	2–6	Supports mobility

WiMAX technology is defined around the IEEE 802.16 standards, which are about the operations and properties of a wireless metropolitan area network (MAN). Table 11.2 lists some common WiMAX standards.

To take advantage of WiMAX technology, many WiMAX-compatible computers and network devices, such as WiMAX-compatible notebooks, computers, routers, and network interface cards, have been developed for constructing WiMAX-compatible networks. A WiMAX-compatible notebook computer can pick up signals directly from a WiMAX transmission tower. A WiMAX-compatible router can pick up signals from a WiMAX transmission tower and pass them to the computers connected to the router. The computers can be connected to the WiMAX-compatible router through twisted-pair wires or through radio waves by using Wi-Fi technology.

11.2.3 Infrared

Infrared can be used by devices that transmit data over short distance. Examples of such devices are cordless computer keyboards and mouses, LCD projector remote controls, and so on. Infrared is a point-to-point technology that requires two digital devices to point at each other. This feature makes infrared a more secure but less convenient wireless technology for network use. It cannot communicate with multiple network devices at the same time.

11.2.4 Bluetooth

Similar to infrared, Bluetooth is also a wireless technology for short-distance communication. Unlike infrared, Bluetooth uses radio waves in the frequency range from 2.402 GHz to 2.480 GHz. Such radio waves can move around objects in a room. Although both the Bluetooth and Wi-Fi use a similar frequency range, Bluetooth is less expensive, consumes much less power, has a lower data transmission rate, and travels a much shorter distance. Bluetooth is suitable for a network in which network devices are very close to each other. This type of network is sometimes called a personal area network (PAN), which can usually extend over a distance less than 10 m.

Bluetooth needs much less user attention during data transmission, and it can deal with a variety of mobile devices such as mobile phones, notebook computers, printers, GPS receivers, televisions, digital cameras, PDAs, and video game consoles. Bluetooth can communicate with devices in a different room. In a Bluetooth-enabled network, users do not need to configure network devices for data transmission. A Bluetooth device can advertise all the services provided by the device. If a Bluetooth-enabled device is within the range of another Bluetooth device, the two devices can automatically exchange information to establish a connection. There is no need for the user to initiate the connection.

Bluetooth can automatically detect devices in a room and communicate with up to eight network devices simultaneously. Multiple devices can communicate with a single Bluetooth adapter installed on a computer. Each Bluetooth-enabled device has a Bluetooth transmitter preconfigured by the manufacturer. To prevent the devices from interfering with one another, a technology called spread-spectrum frequency is used so that the Bluetooth devices do not use the same frequency at the same time.

After a device is turned on, the Bluetooth transmitter sends out signals to search and see if there is another Bluetooth-enabled device within its range. After the device gets a response from another device, a connection is established between these two devices. Once the connection is established, it cannot be broken by other devices.

Although it is convenient to let Bluetooth automatically create a connection between network devices, it introduces some security concerns. A hacker can set up a Bluetooth device to create a connection to your mobile device and may send some harmful data to your device. An additional Bluetooth authentication mechanism is usually added to a Bluetooth device. With this authentication mechanism, the user will be prompted to decide if the connection is allowed.

11.3 Wireless Network Devices

To develop a wireless network, you need to first understand the network devices in the wireless environment. The devices included in the wireless network are the wireless router, wireless network interface adapter, wireless network printer, wireless network storage device, Wi-Fi phone, and other wireless mobile devices. These wireless devices are now described:

1. *Wireless router:* A wireless router is a wired router plus a wireless access point. An antenna is used by the wireless router for data transmission. In a wireless local area network, the wireless router distributes network traffic among wired or wireless networks. The router works similarly to how a router in a wired network does. Similar to the router for the wired network, the wireless router serves as a gateway between two networks, wired or wireless. It includes three basic components:
   - Support for the TCP/IP protocol suite
   - Programs that optimize the performance of the wireless router
   - A high-performance digital radio frequency (RF) modem for wireless communication

   Some wireless routers also include other components such as
   - Network Address Translation (NAT) to share Internet connections
   - Firewalls to protect private networks
   - Built-in DSL or cable modems
   - Ethernet ports for wired network devices

   To construct a wireless local area network at home, the wireless router should include a wide-area network port used to connect to the DSL or cable modem and one or more Ethernet ports for the wired network. Because the wireless router will be used to connect to the Internet, typically, a firewall should be included in the wireless router. Nowadays, wireless routers are often built with the 802.11g or 802.11n wireless technology. 802.11n wireless technology allows wireless transmission at 2.4 GHz and 5 GHz rates. In an overcrowded environment with many wireless networks, a dual-band wireless router should be considered. Older wireless technologies such as 802.11b and 802.11g operate at 2.4 GHz; transmission at 2.4 GHz often gets dropped. Here, consider using a dual-band wireless router that can also run up to 5 GHz. This frequency is less crowded. The communication range of a wireless router is less than 40 m in an open area. It can be much shorter if the radio waves are blocked by walls. In such cases, you may consider using a wireless range extender for a wider communication range.

2. *Wireless network interface adapter:* To communicate with an access point, each computer should have one of the following NICs:
   - A built-in wireless transceiver included in a notebook computer
   - A USB wireless network interface card
   - A wireless network interface card that can be plugged into the PCI bus in a desktop computer
   - A PCMCIA network interface card for a notebook computer

   Once a wireless network interface card is properly installed and configured, the card should be able to communicate with the access point. Sometimes, multiple wireless networks may be detected by the wireless network interface card. After selecting the dedicated wireless network, the user will be prompted for user authentication.
3. *Wireless network printer:* In a wireless network, multiple wireless computers and portable devices can share the same printer without wiring them in the network. The wireless network printer allows wireless-enabled notebook computers, PDAs, and other portable devices to print files anywhere in a house or a building. The printer may use Wi-Fi or Bluetooth technology for data transmission. With Wi-Fi technology, users can print their files within 100 m with a transmission rate of 54 Mbps or better. With Bluetooth technology, users can use the wireless network printer within 10 m with a transmission rate of 22 Kbps or better. Some wireless network printers also include security software and various ports for USB, SD, CompactFlash, and Memory Stick devices.
4. *Wireless network storage:* A wireless network storage device is a data storage center where data can be moved in and out through a wireless network. A wireless storage device may include the following components:
   - One or more hard drives
   - Wireless access point
   - Wireless network devices such as wireless network interface cards
   - Network attached storage (NAS) application software such as network configuration software, network security software, software for RAID configuration, remote access control software, and user management software
   - Network device drivers for wireless and wired network devices developed for different operating systems

   Some wireless storage devices are specially designed for portable devices. These wireless storage devices allow users to share music, video, or data files between PCs and portable devices. They can be used in the Bluetooth or Wi-Fi network environment. The size of this type of wireless storage device is small enough to fit in a pocket. Some portable devices such as iPhones can also be turned into a wireless network storage device.
5. *Wi-Fi phone:* A Wi-Fi phone is a type of wireless phone. Unlike a cell phone, which communicates through a cellular phone network, a Wi-Fi phone communicates through VoIP and Wi-Fi technologies. The technology called Voice over WLAN (VoWLAN) is used to deliver voice over a wireless network. VoWLAN transfers a voice message from a wireless-enabled

device to an access point. Then, from the access point, the message is sent to a VoIP gateway or an IP Private Branch Exchange (PBX) switch, which can convert the VoIP voice message to a traditional telephone voice message, or vice versa. From there, the voice message, will be sent to the destination through VoIP. To communicate with VoIP, a Wi-Fi phone can either use the existing VoIP service provided by a company such as Skype, or use the VoIP service provided by a Wi-Fi phone company.

Because some areas may not have Wi-Fi access points, some Wi-Fi phones are built to run in dual modes; this kind of phone is also called the cell-Internet phone. When there is no Wi-Fi access point, the phone can use the cell phone network. On the other hand, when using the phone in a concrete building, the signals for the regular cell phone can be significantly weaker. In this case, the Wi-Fi phone mode may perform better and avoid dropping phone calls. The switch between the cell and Wi-Fi is done automatically.

6. *ExpressCard:* A wireless network allows notebook computers, PDAs, and other handheld devices to be moved around within the range of the wireless network. To improve mobility, various PC cards have been created for connecting to portable peripheral devices such as external hard drives, wireless network interface cards, TV tuners, and so on. The ExpressCard is the new-generation card for computer system modular expansion. It delivers better performance, reliability, and compatibility for both notebook and desktop computers. It can achieve better performance by using the serial data interface to directly communicate with the system chipset. The size of an ExpressCard is smaller than an older CardBus card. It uses less power and runs 2.5 times faster than CardBus cards. Its hot-swappable feature allows users to swap devices without rebooting the system.

   With the ExpressCard, users can add external hard disks, memory, multimedia devices, and wireless network devices. The ExpressCard plays an important role in the broadband wireless network. It allows users to access the broadband data service provided by telecommunication service companies. In Linux, the ExpressCard can be implemented with either PCI Express or USB. Therefore, it is handled by the PCI subsystem or by the USB subsystem.

In a wireless network, these devices communicate with each other directly or through an access point. Therefore, communication between two wireless network devices can be set up in two different modes specified by the 802.11 standards:

- *Infrastructure mode:* With this mode, wireless devices communicate through access points. This is the default mode.
- *Ad-hoc mode:* With this mode, wireless devices communicate with each other without any access point.

The infrastructure mode is efficient for an office environment where no wire is used to connect the computers. Figure 11.3 illustrates a wireless network that operates in the infrastructure mode.

After an access point is installed, it sends out signals regularly to broadcast access information such as its ID and other characteristics. When a wireless device comes to the receiving range of the access point, to initiate a connection, the wireless device sends a request to the access point. When the access point receives the request, it will compare its ID with the ID in the request. If there is a match, the access point responds with a synchronization message and its traffic load information. After the wireless device receives the response, it calculates the distance between itself and the access point. Based on the distance, the wireless device can estimate the traffic load and quality

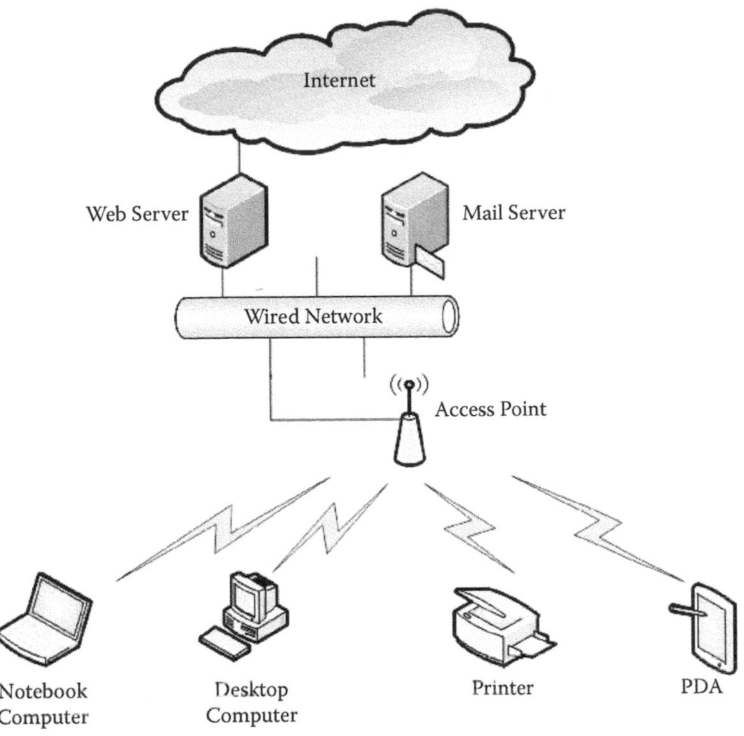

Figure 11.3 Wireless network operating in infrastructure mode.

of the transmission. An access point can be either a piece of hardware or can be built by using a Linux machine.

In the ad-hoc mode, wireless devices communicate with each other directly. Therefore, the ad-hoc mode is also called the peer-to-peer mode. Figure 11.4 illustrates the ad-hoc mode. In the ad-hoc mode, wireless devices communicate directly with each other without requiring an access point. Because no access point is required, it is relatively easy to set up a wireless network in the ad-hoc mode for exchanging data or playing multiplayer games in a small network. The main disadvantage of the ad-hoc mode wireless network is its weak scalability.

Wireless network devices provide mobility solutions for universities and companies. However, not all wireless network devices are compatible with Linux. Before installing a wireless network device, you should make sure that it can be identified by Linux. The compatibility issues will be discussed in the next section.

11.4 Linux-Compatible Wireless Network Devices

The first step in putting together a wireless network is to verify that the wireless network devices installed on each computer are compatible with Linux. Because Linux is an open source product, some proprietary companies do not release drivers for Linux. Therefore, Linux may not be able to support some wireless network devices. This starts our discussion on how to search for information on Linux-compatible wireless network devices. By examining the chipset used by a wireless

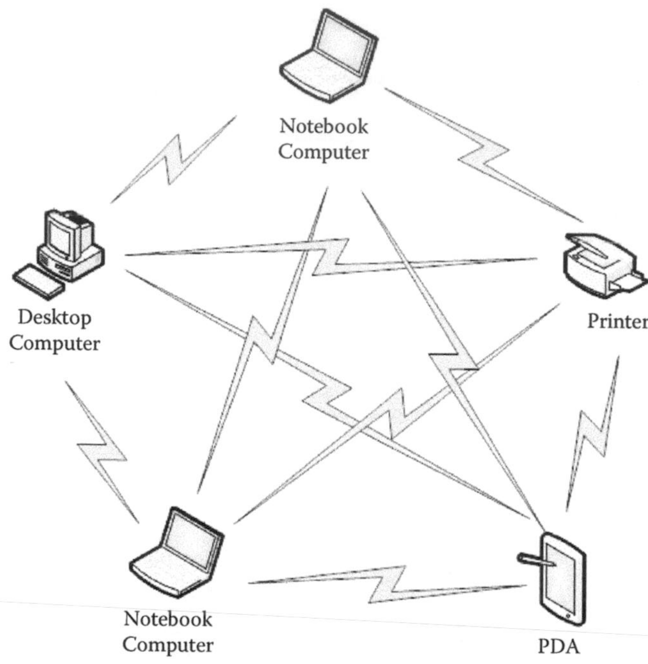

Figure 11.4 Wireless network operating in ad-hoc mode.

device, you may also find out if the device is Linux compatible. For devices that are not supported by Linux, you may consider using the Linux utility NDISwrapper to make those devices Linux compatible.

11.4.1 Linux Compatibility

Because not all wireless network devices are compatible with Linux, the major Linux distributions provide information about the compatibility of wireless network devices with their distributions. This section will present the wireless network device compatibility information provided by the Ubuntu Linux distribution. Then, it will check some other Web sites that provide information about the compatibility of wireless network devices. Let us start with Ubuntu Linux:

1. *Ubuntu Linux:* One of the improvements in the latest version of Ubuntu Linux is that it is able to solve many wireless network device connection problems. Nowadays, most wireless network devices can work well with Ubuntu. To see which wireless network interface cards can work with the Ubuntu Linux operating system, you can check the following Web site:
   https://help.ubuntu.com/community/WifiDocs/WirelessCardsSupported
   On this Web site, you can find the following information:
   - Ubuntu Linux-compatible network interface cards by manufacturer or name
   - Instructions on finding information about the installed wireless network interface card on your computer
   - The link to the wireless troubleshooting guide
   - The link to an article about open-source-friendly Wi-Fi vendors

- The link to an article about the wireless adapter chipset directory
- The link for reporting bugs

Readers can also find other useful information on this Web site.

2. *Esselbach Storyteller CMS System:* It has a Web site called Linux Compatible, which provides detailed information about hardware and software compatible with Linux. The following is the URL of the Web site:

   http://www.linuxcompatible.org/compatcat3-1-1.html

   This Web site provides comprehensive coverage of Linux compatibility information, for example:
   - The latest hardware and software compatibility information
   - The latest news about Linux and the new archives
   - A list of hardware and software that are compatible with Linux
   - Compatibility ratings
   - Forums for discussing Linux-compatibility-related issues
   - Answers to frequently asked questions
   - Links to other related subjects, such as Linux training courses and Linux-compatible notebook computers

   In the Network category, the Web site lists hundreds of Linux-compatible network devices, including wireless network devices from different hardware vendors. Also valuable are the users' responses to the compatibility issues and their first-hand experience of using Linux compatible hardware and software.
3. *TuxMobil:* TuxMobil has a Web site dedicated to Linux-compatible mobile devices such as notebook computers, PDAs, mobile phones, and so on. This Web site provides Linux mobile device news. It also provides information on the usage of Linux and mobile devices. By following the link Components&AddOns, you can find the Web page Linux Compatibility of Mobile Hardware Components & AddOns. This Web page has the following URL:

   http://tuxmobil.org/hardware.html

   On this Web page, you can find the following information about wireless network device compatibility:
   - *Wireless LAN:* Information includes Linux-compatible application software, USB-based network interface cards, and the how-to instructions. It also includes other resources related to wireless LANs.
   - *Mobile ad-hoc network (MANET):* MANET is a type of wireless ad-hoc network in which mobile routers are capable of self-configuring to adapt to different network environments. The information includes MANET software and hardware.
   - *Wireless LAN access points:* The information includes Linux access points, software access points, application software for access points, user reports on Linux wireless access points, and so on.
   - *Wireless sniffer applications:* A network sniffer is software or hardware used to conduct network data stream analyses. The information includes filter configuration tools, wireless security software, and so on.

   This page also includes information about other wireless technologies such as Bluetooth and infrared. Information about wireless communities is also included in this Web page.

Sometimes you may not find information about the wireless devices you are using. In this case, you may get some clues by examining the chipset and driver used by a wireless device. The issues related to compatibility checking through chipsets and drivers will be covered in the next two subsections.

11.4.2 Wireless Device Chipsets

Drivers of wireless devices are often categorized based on their chipsets. The following are some popular Linux-compatible chipsets used by wireless devices:

- *Hermes:* Made by Agere, Hermes is one of the popular 802.11b chipsets. Most Linux distributions support drivers based on the Hermes chipset.
- *Prism:* Prism is also a widely used chipset for wireless devices. It has been used by over 50 major computer companies for their wireless products.
- *Intel iwl 5000-series:* Intel produces various chipsets for supporting a wide range of Wi-Fi devices. iwl 5000-series chipsets are developed for a family of IEEE 802.11a/b/g/draft-n wireless network devices. These devices can run in both the 2.4 GHz and 5.0 GHz spectra and deliver up to 450 Mbps of bandwidth.
- *Atheros AR9001:* Atheros provides the dual-band 2.4/5 GHz chipset for universal wireless connectivity to any 802.11 network. AR9001 chipsets are designed for the 802.11n wireless network solution.
- *Broadcom AirForce:* Lately, the Broadcom AirForce chipset has become Linux compatible. It supports the Linux 2.6.24 kernel or the later versions of Linux kernels. The AirForce chipset is used for the 802.11 b/g family of wireless devices.
- *Ralink:* Ralink chipsets are Linux compatible. They support Wi-Fi standards such as IEEE 802.11n, 802.11a/b/g, and 802.11b/g. Many wireless equipment companies use Ralink chipsets for their wireless devices.

There are many other Linux-compatible chipsets. The foregoing chipsets are just a few examples. You can find more detailed information in the Web sites listed in Section 11.4.1. The type of chipset used by a wireless network device is a good indicator that tells if the device is Linux compatible. This is because some manufacturers may use different chipsets for the same model. Therefore, sometimes wireless devices of the same model may or may not be compatible with Linux.

Information about the chipset used by a wireless device can be obtained by using the tools included in Linux. For example:

- *lspci:* This tool can be used to display chipset information about a PCI bus and the devices connected to it.
- *cardctl ident:* It can display chipset information about PCMCIA-H or CardBus-based wireless devices.
- *dmesg:* This tool can display chipset information about USB-based wireless devices.

Once the chipset information is obtained, you can check the Web sites mentioned in Section 11.4.1 to find out if the chipset is compatible with Linux.

11.4.3 Wireless Device Drivers

As mentioned earlier, computer programs communicate with wireless devices through drivers. Drivers for wireless devices can either be compiled into the kernel or loaded as kernel modules. A kernel module can be loaded while the operating system is running. The loading of a kernel module does not require rebooting the system. Because the drivers are updated frequently, loading the drivers as kernel modules is preferred. In this way, you can avoid frequently rebuilding the entire kernel, which is a time-consuming process.

Most Linux distributions include some drivers for wireless devices. In some situations, the driver for a wireless device may not be included in a specific Linux distribution. In this case, you may need to build the driver with available driver resources. You may also need to build a driver when you want to convert a Linux box to an access point. Various driver resources have been developed for Linux-compatible chipsets. The following are some of them:

- *orinoco_cs:* This type of driver is best known for the Hermes chipset. It can be used in a wide range of wireless devices.
- *Host AP:* This driver can be used for the Prism2/2.5/3 chipset.
- *iwlagn:* The driver iwlagn was developed to support Intel WiFi Link 5000 Series wireless devices.
- *ath9k:* The ath9k driver was developed for the Atheros AR5008 and AR9001 family of chipsets.
- *b43:* This kind of driver is for the Broadcom AirForce chipset.
- *Ralink:* A list of Ralink drivers is provided for Linux-compatible wireless devices, for example, RT2870USB for USB-based network devices and RT2860PCI for PCI devices.

The foregoing drivers are supported by the latest Linux kernel. Usually, the latest version of a driver may not be the best. It may not have been fully tested, and there could be bugs in the driver's source code.

Sometime a wireless network device is simply not supported by Linux. The Linux operating system installed on a computer cannot detect the wireless network device or the detected device fails to function properly. This is often caused by a missing device driver; sometimes, the existing driver may not be specifically written for the device. The next section will introduce a utility that is used to deal with wireless network devices that are not compatible with Linux.

11.4.4 NDISwrapper

As mentioned earlier, network device drivers produced by some proprietary wireless device companies are not available to Linux. Often, there are no instructions on how to write the drivers for the devices either. To be able to use the drivers developed by proprietary wireless device producers, Linux developers have created the open source software called NDISwrapper, which allows a UNIX like operating system to use the drivers developed for the Microsoft Windows operating systems.

Network Device Interface Specification (NDIS), created by Microsoft and 3Com, is an application interface that enables a network interface card to establish network connections with different network protocols such as TCP/IP and IPX. With NDIS, a network protocol can be bound to a network interface card driver. To use the network device drivers developed for Windows operating systems, NDISwrapper implements the Windows kernel and NDIS, and then dynamically links the device driver to NDIS. However, NDISwrapper is far from perfect. It does not guarantee that it will work for every driver created for Windows. It may also stop or crash Linux.

Table 11.3 NDISwrapper Command Options

Option	*Description*	*Example*
`-a`	Forces NDISwrapper to use a specified driver for a given device	`ndsiwrapper -a 1234:5678 wdriver` Assume that 1234:5678 can be a device id and wdriver is the driver.
`-e`	Removes an installed driver	`ndsiwrapper -e wdriver`
`-h`	NDSIwrapper help option	`ndsiwrapper -h`
`-i`	Installs a specified device driver	`ndsiwrapper -i wdriver.inf`
`-l`	Displays the installed drivers	`ndsiwrapper -l`
`-m`	Loads NDSIwrapper module configuration to the kernel	`ndsiwrapper -m`
`-ma`	Loads NDSIwrapper module alias configuration for all the devices to the kernel	`ndiswrapper -ma`
`-mi`	Loads NDSIwrapper module installation specification for all the devices to the kernel	`ndiswrapper -mi`
`-r`	Removes an installed driver	`ndsiwrapper -r wdriver`
`-v`	Reports version information	`ndsiwrapper -v`

NDISwrapper is designed to work with two files, the .inf and .sys files, which are used to form Windows drivers. If a driver is named wdriver, then the two files will be named wdriver.inf and wdriver.sys. These two files will be stored in the directory /etc/ndiswrapper/mydriver/. The drivers can also be delivered by using a zip file.

The NDISwrapper commands provide a few options to perform some operations on these files. Table 11.3 includes some of the NDISwrapper command options.

There are also some NDISwrapper graphical front-end utilities such as Ndisgtk and NdisConfig. Ndisgtk can be used to activate a built-in wireless network interface card, PCMCIA wireless network interface card, and USB wireless interface card. Figure 11.5 shows the Ndisgtk graphical front-end.

This subsection has introduced the utility NDISwrapper for handling devices created for Windows operating systems. It listed the options for the command ndiswrappper and illustrated its usage with examples. The NDISwrapper graphical front end Ndisgtk was also introduced.

To identify if a wireless device is compatible with the Linux operating system, you can first go to the Web sites given earlier. If there is no match, you may try to install the NDISwrapper package, and use NDISwrapper to connect to the wireless network device.

11.5 Wireless Network Configuration Tools

This section will discuss some configuration-related issues and tools used to get the configuration job done.

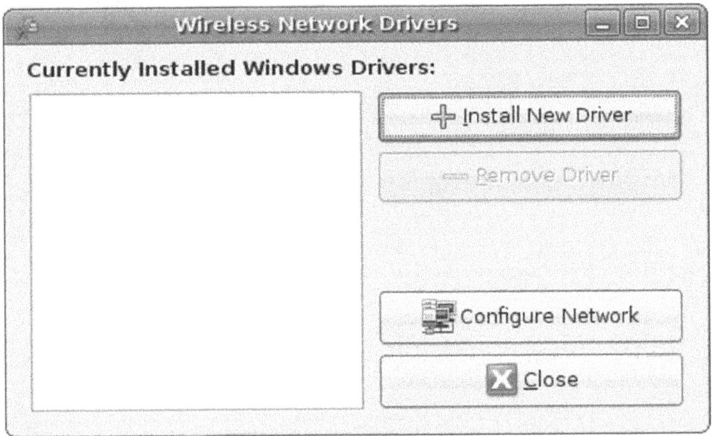

Figure 11.5 Ndisgtk graphical front end.

11.5.1 Viewing Wireless Network Device Information

During a configuration process, the first task is to collect information about the wireless network device. Several commands can get the job done. Table 11.4 lists some of the commonly used commands to display information about the wireless network interface devices installed on a host computer.

Figure 11.6 shows the result after executing the command lshw -short.

The command lshw displays information about the hardware devices that lshw can find. Sometimes, lshw may miss some hardware devices. In such cases, you may try the command lspci to see if information about the network controller can be found.

Table 11.4 Commands for Displaying Device Information

Command	*Description*	*Example*
`hwinfo`	It detects and displays the hardware device information and drivers needed to run the devices.	To display information about network devices, use `hwinfo -network`
`lshw`	It is a subset of hwinfo. It displays information about the hardware configuration of a Linux system.	To get a quick view of all the hardware the command can find, use `lshw -short`
`lspci`	It displays information about all the PCI buses and the devices connected to them.	To display information about the devices and the relations among them on a tree diagram, use `lspci -t`
`lsusb`	It displays information about all the USB buses and the devices connected to them.	To display the USB device hierarchy on a tree diagram, use `lsusb -t`

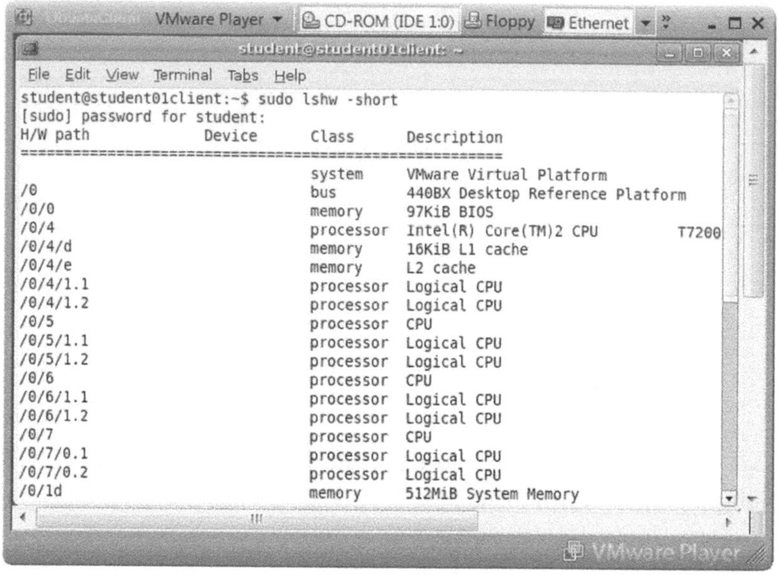

```
File  Edit  View  Terminal  Tabs  Help
student@student01client:~$ sudo lshw -short
[sudo] password for student:
H/W path              Device      Class          Description
======================================================
                                  system         VMware Virtual Platform
/0                                bus            440BX Desktop Reference Platform
/0/0                              memory         97KiB BIOS
/0/4                              processor      Intel(R) Core(TM)2 CPU         T7200
/0/4/d                            memory         16KiB L1 cache
/0/4/e                            memory         L2 cache
/0/4/1.1                          processor      Logical CPU
/0/4/1.2                          processor      Logical CPU
/0/5                              processor      CPU
/0/5/1.1                          processor      Logical CPU
/0/5/1.2                          processor      Logical CPU
/0/6                              processor      CPU
/0/6/1.1                          processor      Logical CPU
/0/6/1.2                          processor      Logical CPU
/0/7                              processor      CPU
/0/7/0.1                          processor      Logical CPU
/0/7/0.2                          processor      Logical CPU
/0/1d                             memory         512MiB System Memory
```

Figure 11.6 Device information.

11.5.2 Configuration of Wireless Network Devices

If a device is natively supported by Linux (meaning that the device is on the compatible list), the device driver or its kernel module is often loaded automatically. On the other hand, if the device is not on the Linux compatibility list, you may need to load its kernel module before using the device. Therefore, after the device is detected, you may want to perform the following tasks:

- Verify that the device's kernel module has been installed and the hardware chipset is supported natively by the Linux kernel.
- If the hardware chipset is not supported by the Linux kernel, the device's kernel module will not be available. You should install NDISwrapper, which allows you to enable some of the drivers created for Windows operating systems.
- If the hardware chipset is supported by Linux but the device's kernel module is not loaded, the kernel module might be missing. In such cases, you may search for the kernel module that matches the hardware chipset on the Internet.
- If the required kernel module can be found, download and install the kernel module.

Table 11.5 lists some commands that can be used to configure wireless devices.

Some GUI-based network management utilities are available. Wicd is one of them. During the configuration of wireless networks, Wicd can be used to perform the following tasks:

- Detect access points in surrounding areas
- Display wireless network signal strengths
- Illustrate network activities
- Configure network interface cards for both wired and wireless networks
- Enforce encryption schemes such as WEP, WPA, and WPA2 for wireless networks

Table 11.5 Wireless Configuration Commands

Command	*Description*	*Example*
`lsmod`	It lists all the currently installed kernel modules.	lsmod
`modprobe`	It installs and removes a kernel module.	To install the module cdrom, use `modprobe -r cdrom`
`dpkg`	The dpkg commands are used for installing and removing packages.	To install the package ndiswrapper-utils*.deb, use `dpkg -i ndiswrapper-utils*.deb`
`ifconfig`	It is used to configure and manage network interface cards.	To display information about the wireless NIC wlan0, use `ifconfig wlan0`
`ifup`	It is used to bring up a network interface card.	To bring up the wireless NIC wlan0, use `ifup wlan0`
`iwconfig`	Similar to ifconfig, iwconfig is dedicated to wireless NICs. It can be used to set parameters such as the frequency of a wireless NIC.	To set a network ID to distinguish your wireless network from others, use `iwconfig eth0 nwid mynetwork`
`iwlist`	It displays information about wireless NICs, such as available channels, frequencies, and transmission rates.	To scan for the information of the NIC eth1, use `iwlist eth1 scan`
`iwpriv`	It is used to modify parameters and set specifications for drivers.	To use shared key authentication for an Atheros chipset Wi-Fi card using the madwifi driver, use `iwpriv ath0 authmode 2`
`iwspy`	It is used to observe the link quality of a list of nodes.	To collect information about the signals and noise for the link to the wireless NIC wlan0, use `iwspy wlan0`
`dhclient`	It is used to configure the DHCP client.	To obtain an IP address from the DHCP server, use `dhclient`

Figure 11.7 displays the Wicd Manager dialog.

If the hardware chipset is supported by Linux, the configuration process is straightforward. Many Linux distributions such as Ubuntu and Red Hat Linux include GUI tools to allow users to configure wireless devices. For example, to set up a wireless network to access the Internet, the following tasks need to be done:

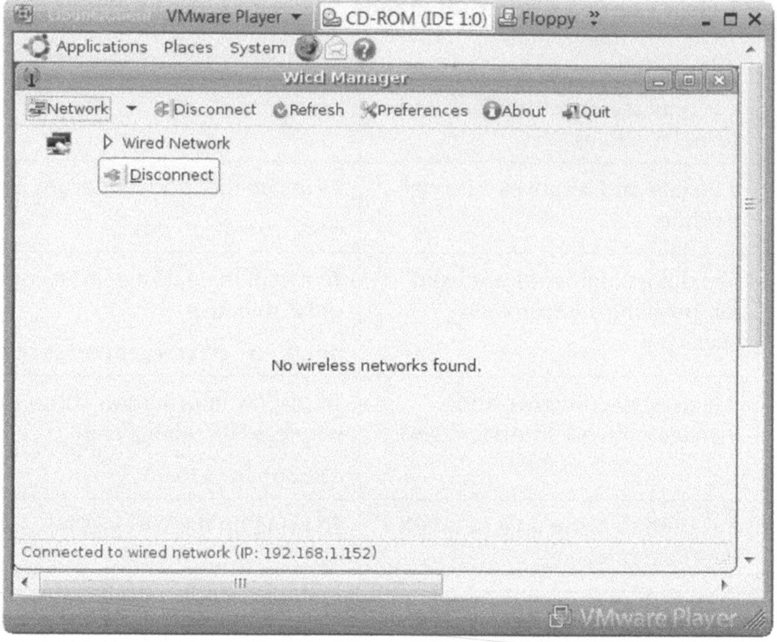

Figure 11.7 Wicd Manager dialog.

- Connect the wireless router to the Internet modem provided by the ISP.
- Configure the wireless router by specifying the wireless network name, the wireless encryption method such as WEP or WPA, the administrative authentication, and the connection to the ISP.
- Make sure that either the computer supports the wireless connection or an external Linux wireless network interface card is installed.
- Search for the available wireless access points.
- Specify which access point to use and connect to it.

In many cases, the hardware chipset is not compatible with Linux. Then, you need to get NDISwrapper up and running. To do so, you will first download and install the NDISwrapper module. Many Linux distributions such as Ubuntu have preinstalled NDISwrapper. However, to make it work, some additional steps may be required. For example, for the installation of some versions of Ubuntu Linux, you may need to perform the following tasks:

- Enable the multiverse and universe repositories. The repositories are used for software installation. By default, the repository used for the installation of NDISwrapper may not be enabled.
- Install the NDISwrapper graphical front-end Ndisgtk.
- Use the command dpkg to install packages such as ndiswrapper-common and nidswrapper-utils.
- Use the modprobe command to enable the NDISwrapper module.
- If the driver for a wireless network device is not already installed on Linux, search for the Windows driver for the device.
- After the driver is found, extract the .inf and .sys files, and place these two files in a directory.

- Install the files to NDISwrapper with the ndiswrapper command with the option -i, and verify the installed driver with option -l.
- Use the command modprobe to install the utility NDISwrapper.

After the module NDISwrapper is installed, you may want to verify that the driver is working. The following are some tasks that should be carried out to check if the installed driver does what it is supposed to do:

- If the wireless network device is a network interface card, verify that it is up and running by using a network management utility, for example, a GUI-based network management utility such as Wicd, the command ifconfig, or the command iwconfig.
- If the wireless network interface card cannot be detected, try to bring it up with the command ifup.
- Set the parameters of the network interface card with the command iwconfig or a GUI utility such as Wicd.
- If the wireless NIC does not receive an IP address from the DHCP server, run the command dhclient or use a GUI network management utility to obtain a dynamic IP address.
- To test the network connection, ping the wireless router's IP address. If the connection to the wireless router is working properly, try to ping one of the known Web sites on the Internet.

Sometimes, connection problems may be caused by firewalls or other security measures. When there is a connection problem, you should check the firewalls or temporarily disable the security measures. After the connection problem is fixed, make sure you enable the firewalls and other security measures.

Some Linux distributions include GUI tools for configuring NDISwrapper. For example, Ndisgtk is one of the commonly used GUI tools. Figure 11.8 illustrates the dialog for the configuration of NDISwrapper. This GUI tool allows users to install drivers designed for Windows operating systems. It can also be used to configure networks.

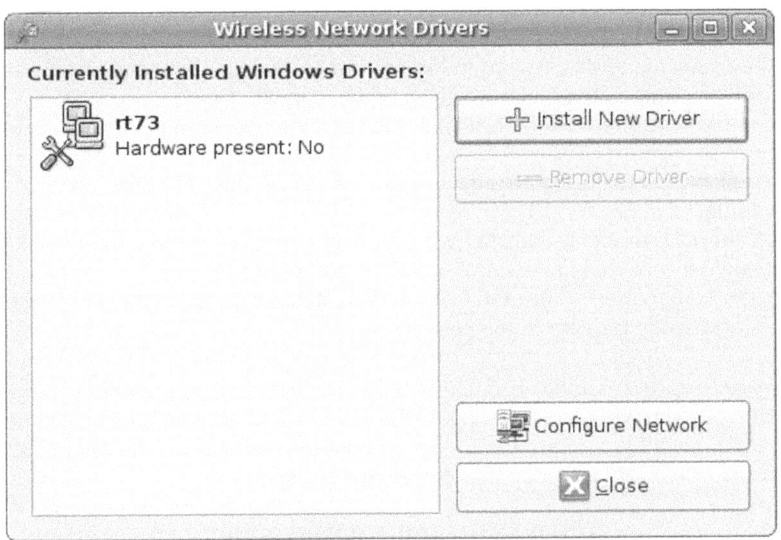

Figure 11.8 Dialog for NDISwrapper GUI configuration tool Ndisgtk.

Now that we have reviewed the tools for constructing a Linux wireless network, we will next employ these tools through a hands-on activity.

Activity 11.1 Implementation of Wireless Home Network

The previous sections have discussed wireless network devices, Linux compatibility issues, and issues related to the configuration of wireless routers and network interface cards. To better understand Linux wireless networks, it is necessary to actually create a wireless network with Linux. In this activity, you will implement a wireless network with Ubuntu Linux installed on a virtual machine. The following are the tasks to be performed in the hands-on practice:

- Install a wireless router for the wireless home network.
- Search for a Linux-compatible wireless network interface card
- Install and configure the Linux-compatible wireless network interface card
- Test the wireless home network.
- Troubleshoot any wireless network problem.

Now, you will start the hands-on activity with the installation of a wireless router for your home network.

WIRELESS ROUTER INSTALLATION

The first task in constructing a wireless home network is to install a wireless router. Most wireless routers are platform independent and can be purchased from local electronic stores or online. The installation of a wireless router is a fairly simple process, and involves the following steps:

1. Assemble the wireless router, and turn off the DSL modem provided by your ISP.
2. Follow the instructions to connect the wireless router to the computer and DSL modem with network cables (Figure 11.9).
3. Power the DSL modem on. After the modem stabilizes, power on the wireless router. It will take a minute for the wireless router to complete the checking process.
4. Start the Web browser, and enter the URL for the router configuration page. The URL should be included in the manual of the wireless router.
5. Enter the username and password to log on to the configuration page. The username and password for configuration page are given in the manual.
6. Specify the wireless network name (SSID) such as mynetwork, and choose a security option such as WPA (Figure 11.10).
7. You may also want to configure the wireless router IP on the LAN side; a typical configuration is displayed in Figure 11.11.
8. Turn off the DSL modem, then the wireless router, and then the computer. Remove the cable that connects the wireless router and the computer.
9. Restart the DSL modem. After the DSL modem stabilizes, restart the wireless router. The router is now ready for your home network.

At this point, you have successfully accomplished the installation of your wireless router. After the wireless router is set, you will need to configure the wireless NIC for your Linux client machine. As mentioned earlier, not all the wireless NICs are compatible with Linux. The following paragraph describes how to search for Linux-compatible wireless NICs.

LINUX-COMPATIBLE WIRELESS NIC

Dealing with wireless NICs that come with your Windows host computers could present a challenge. Some wireless NICs may not have a Linux driver. Sometimes, the configuration of

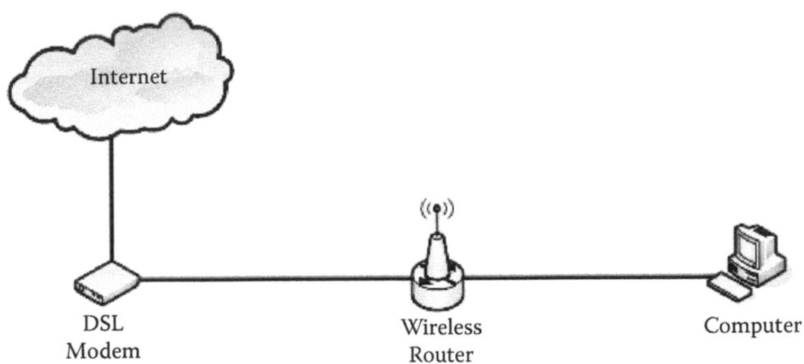

Figure 11.9 Network for wireless router configuration.

WIRELESS LAN

Wireless Radio : Enabled

MAC Address : 00:24:01:35:33:24

Network Name (SSID) : mynetwork

Channel : 1

Security Mode: AUTO (WPA or WPA2) –PSK

Figure 11.10 Wireless router configuration.

LAN

MAC Address : 00:24:01:35:33:24

IP Address : 192.168.0.1

Subnet Mask : 255.255.255.0

DHCP Server : Enabled

Figure 11.11 LAN configuration for wireless router.

NDISwrapper for these NICs can be tricky as well. If a wireless NIC on a host computer does not have a Linux driver, a more common solution is to purchase a Linux-compatible NIC for the virtual machines on that computer. Ubuntu Linux supports a wide range of wireless NICs. The best place to search for wireless NICs supported by Ubuntu Linux is from the following Web site:

https://help.ubuntu.com/community/WifiDocs/WirelessCardsSupported

If you are interested in using a Linksys USB NIC, click the Linksys link on the preceding Web site. The important feature to look for is the ability to work out of the box. Such an NIC can save you a lot of configuration time and reduce the frustration of not being able to get the wireless NIC up

WUSB54GC

See WifiDocs/Device/LinksysWUSB54GC

Chipset	Driver	Supports network install?	Supported in installed system?	Works "out of the box"	Comments	Last Updated
RAlink RT2571W/RT2671	No	Yes	Yes	Works out of box with Gutsy and Hardy. If not, see WifiDocs/Device/LinksysWUSB54GC		2008-06-01
rt73usb	rt73	?	Yes?	Yes	Works out of the box with Feisty 7.04, Gusty 7.10, Hardy 8.04	20-08-2008
rt73usb	rt73usb	?	Yes	Yes	Works out of the box with Intrepid 8.10	2008-11-04

Figure 11.12 Ubuntu Linux-compatible wireless NIC.

and running. Under the USB section, you will find the popular model WUSB54GC, which works "out of the box" (Figure 11.12).

As illustrated in Figure 11.12, the driver used in this wireless USB NIC is rt73 or rt73usb. The driver rt73usb is installed on the Intrepid 8.10 version of Ubuntu Linux and works out of the box. This wireless NIC supports USB 2.0 with a transmission rate up to 54 Mbps. It is compatible with 802.11g and 802.11b standards. It also supports up to 128-bit WEP and WPA encryption.

Based on the information displayed in Figure 11.12, you can search for a suitable wireless NIC online or from local electronic stores. After you purchase a Linux-compatible wireless NIC, you are ready to install and configure the NIC for your wireless home network.

INSTALLATION OF WIRELESS NIC

It only takes a few steps to install a USB-based wireless NIC. The following are the step-by-step instructions for installing the Linksys WUSB54GC wireless network interface card:

1. Because our hands-on project is developed on a virtual machine with Ubuntu Linux as the guest operating system, you need to first make sure that the USB port is active on the guest operating system. To verify this, plug the Linksys WUSB54GC NIC into one of the USB ports on your host computer. Then, log on to the client virtual machine with username **student** and password **ubuntu**.
2. Execute the following command:

   ```
   sudo lsusb
   ```

   If everything works correctly, you will see the output shown in Figure 11.13. If there is a problem, you may need to enable the wireless USB adapter on your virtual machine by selecting the wireless USB adapter from the device list that has the icon >> on top of the virtual machine.

   Figure 11.13 shows that the USB port works fine. It illustrates that a Linksys WUSB54GC 802.11g adapter with the driver ralink rt73 is in the USB drive.

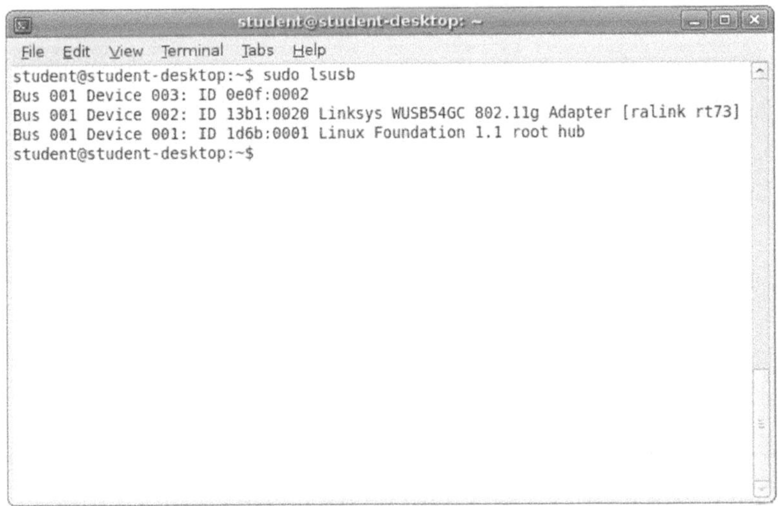

Figure 11.13 Checking USB port.

3. Once you have confirmed that the USB port works properly, you want to make sure that the wireless NIC is working properly. To do so, execute the following command:

   sudo iwconfig

   You should get the output shown in Figure 11.14.

   The output indicates that the wireless NIC wlan0 is recognized. However, the NIC is not associated with any access point.
4. To connect to an access point, click the **Network Management** icon, which is the icon with two monitors on top of the screen. One of the access points is the wireless server mynetwork installed in the previous step. The configuration is shown in Figure 11.15.

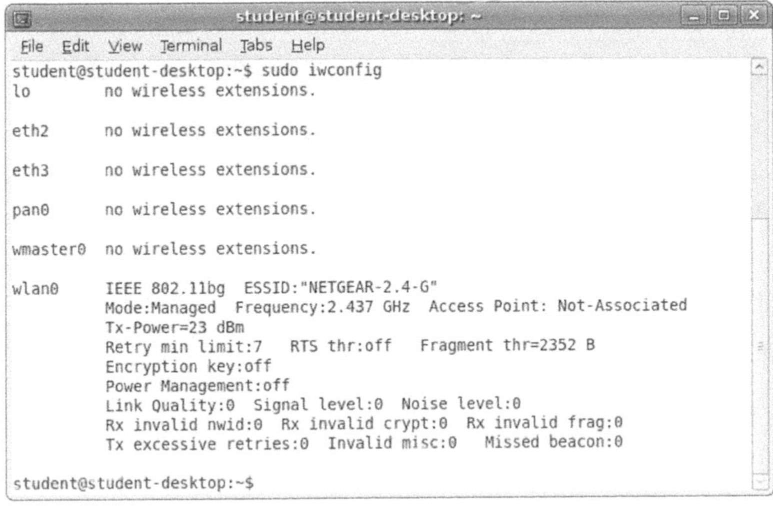

Figure 11.14 Testing wireless NIC.

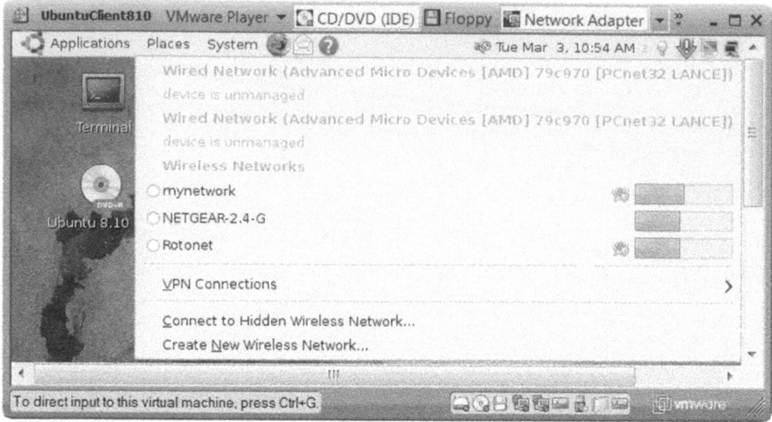

Figure 11.15 Connecting to access point mynetwork.

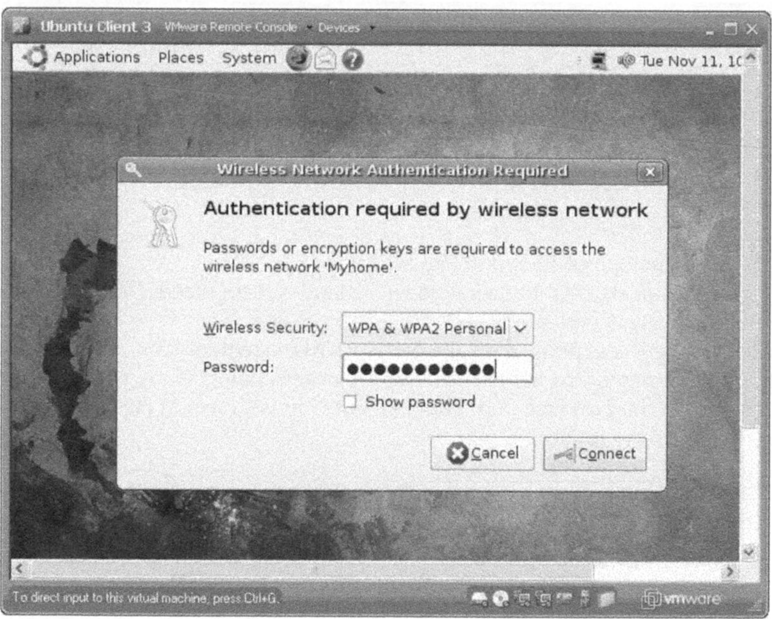

Figure 11.16 Access point authentication.

5. Select the option **mynetwork**. As shown in Figure 11.16, mynetwork is a WPA-protected access point. You are prompted to enter a password. Enter your password for the access point (Figure 11.16). Then, click the **Connect** button.

   If everything works fine, you will get a message to inform you that the wireless network connection is enabled.

The key to successfully installing a wireless NIC is to use a Linux-compatible NIC that works out of the box. Otherwise, you may end up with a long and hard battle to get the wireless NIC up and running. Your next task is to verify that the newly developed wireless network is working properly.

TESTING THE WIRELESS NETWORK

To check if the wireless NIC is able to communicate with the access point, you may use the ifconfig command to see if the NIC can get a dynamic IP address from the access point. The following steps are used for testing:

1. To verify that the wireless NIC gets a dynamic IP address, execute the following command:

   ```
   sudo ifconfig
   ```

   If the wireless NIC is successfully connected to the access point, the NIC should get its IP address from the access point (Figure 11.17).

   Figure 11.17 shows that the wireless NIC wlan0 does get the IP address from the access point, which indicates that the connection to the access point is running properly.
2. Besides using the command ifconfig, you can also use a GUI tool to verify that the NIC gets a dynamic IP from the access point. To do so, click **System**, **Administration**, and **Network Tools.** From the Network device drop-down list, select the **Wireless Interface (wlan0),** and you should be able to see the IP information shown in Figure 11.18. Figure 11.18 also shows that the wireless NIC gets the IP address 192.168.0.102 from the wireless router.
3. To get more detailed information about the wireless connection, you can execute the following command:

   ```
   sudo iwlist scan
   ```

   From the execution result shown in Figure 11.19, the access point to which the wireless NIC is currently connected has the name mynetwork and the hardware address 00:24:01:35:33:24. The radio frequency used for the communication is 2.412 GHz, and the communication channel is 1. There is also a lot of other useful information displayed in Figure 11.19.
4. At this point, your wireless home network should be up and running. You may test the wireless Internet connection by entering the URL http://www.ubuntu.com/ in the Firefox Web browser. The Ubuntu Web site should be displayed (Figure 11.20).

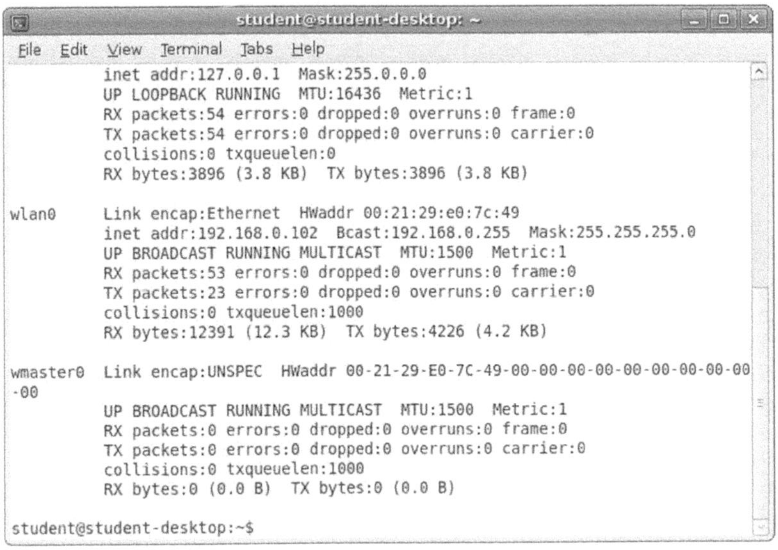

```
student@student-desktop: ~
File  Edit  View  Terminal  Tabs  Help
          inet addr:127.0.0.1  Mask:255.0.0.0
          UP LOOPBACK RUNNING  MTU:16436  Metric:1
          RX packets:54 errors:0 dropped:0 overruns:0 frame:0
          TX packets:54 errors:0 dropped:0 overruns:0 carrier:0
          collisions:0 txqueuelen:0
          RX bytes:3896 (3.8 KB)  TX bytes:3896 (3.8 KB)

wlan0     Link encap:Ethernet  HWaddr 00:21:29:e0:7c:49
          inet addr:192.168.0.102  Bcast:192.168.0.255  Mask:255.255.255.0
          UP BROADCAST RUNNING MULTICAST  MTU:1500  Metric:1
          RX packets:53 errors:0 dropped:0 overruns:0 frame:0
          TX packets:23 errors:0 dropped:0 overruns:0 carrier:0
          collisions:0 txqueuelen:1000
          RX bytes:12391 (12.3 KB)  TX bytes:4226 (4.2 KB)

wmaster0  Link encap:UNSPEC  HWaddr 00-21-29-E0-7C-49-00-00-00-00-00-00-00-00-00
-00
          UP BROADCAST RUNNING MULTICAST  MTU:1500  Metric:1
          RX packets:0 errors:0 dropped:0 overruns:0 frame:0
          TX packets:0 errors:0 dropped:0 overruns:0 carrier:0
          collisions:0 txqueuelen:1000
          RX bytes:0 (0.0 B)  TX bytes:0 (0.0 B)

student@student-desktop:~$
```

Figure 11.17 Result of executing ifconfig command.

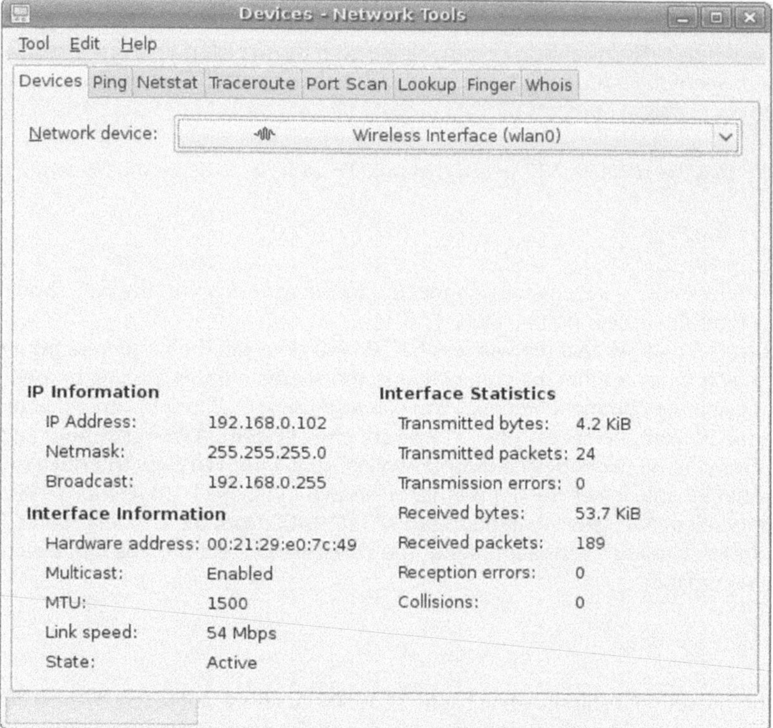

Figure 11.18 IP information for wireless interface (wlan0).

For some of you, problems could occur during the wireless network construction process. The following subsection discusses some commonly encountered problems.

TROUBLESHOOTING

The configuration described earlier should allow you to access the Internet. If there is a problem, you need to turn off the computer, the wireless router, and the DSL modem. Then, restart these devices in this sequence: DSL modem, wireless router, and then your computer.

Another problem you may run into is that no wireless network is shown on the screen of Figure 11.15. Make sure that the USB wireless NIC is working properly. You may verify this by checking if the NIC is working on the host computer. If the NIC is working fine on the host computer, you need to make sure that the USB port is connected on the virtual machine. The following are the steps to make sure that the USB port is connected to your virtual machine:

1. If you have VMware® virtual server downloaded and installed, start the virtual server.
2. Once the virtual server is started, open the virtual machine used to construct the wireless network.
3. To connect the USB port on the virtual machine, click the USB icon (Figure 11.21).
4. Then, select **Linksys Compact Wireless-G USB Adapter**.
5. Ensure that the USB device is connected and you are able to see the options that allow you to select the wireless network (Figure 11.15).

As mentioned earlier, if a Linux-compatible wireless NIC was used, the error is most likely from the virtual machine. Once the problem in the virtual machine is fixed, you should be able to connect to the Internet.

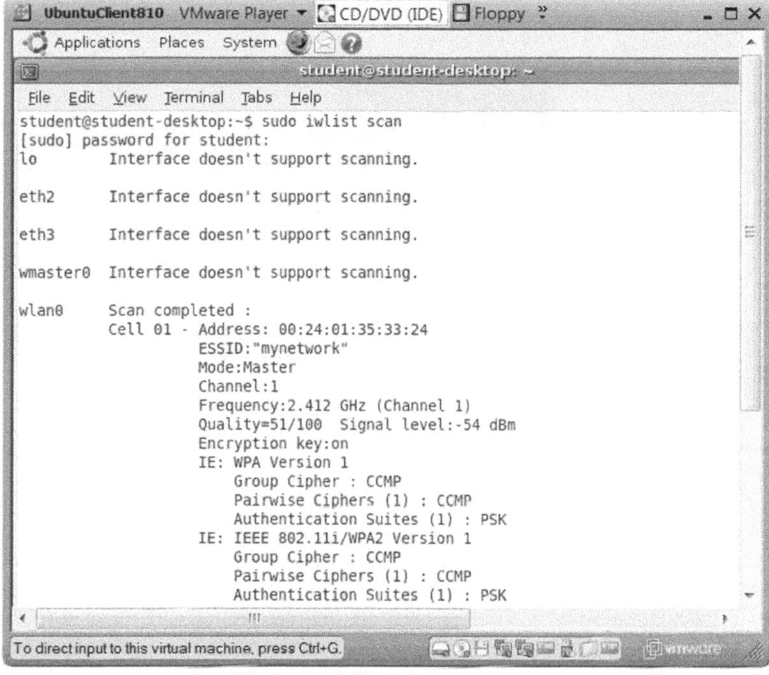

Figure 11.19 Wireless connection information.

Figure 11.20 Testing Internet connection.

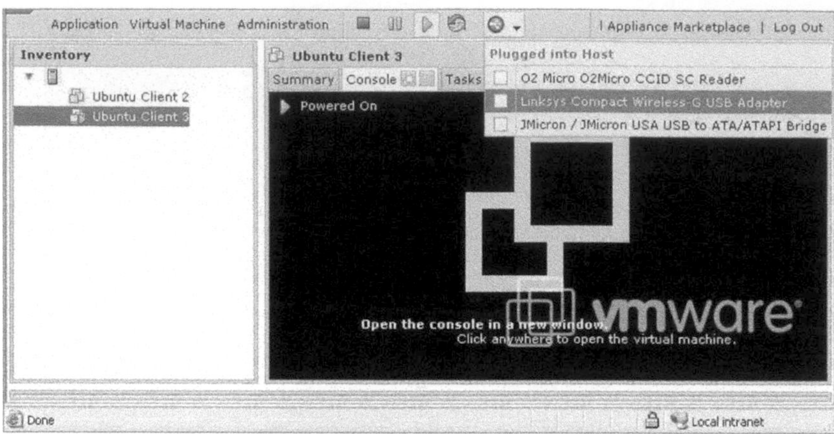

Figure 11.21 Connecting to USB port.

This hands-on practice has demonstrated how to implement a wireless network with Linux-compatible wireless network devices. It walked you through the installation and configuration of the wireless router as well as the configuration of the wireless network interface card. The key to successful configuration of a wireless network interface card is to make sure that the network interface card is Linux compatible. This activity demonstrated how to find Linux compatibility information. It also showed how to test a Linux wireless network. In addition, it provided some information about troubleshooting a wireless network.

11.6 Summary

This chapter covered topics related to the implementation of wireless networks with Linux-compatible wireless devices. One of the difficulties of implementing a Linux wireless network is that wireless device vendors are reluctant to let Linux use their proprietary drivers.

This chapter provided tips on where to find compatibility information about wireless network devices. It presented information about Linux-compatible chipsets and drivers created for these chipsets. For those devices that have no Linux-compatible drivers, the NDISwrapper technology allows Linux to use drivers developed for proprietary wireless network devices. Although NDISwrapper cannot solve all the compatibility problems, it does allow Linux to use some of the drivers developed exclusively for Microsoft Windows operating systems.

In this chapter, some tools were introduced for implementing Linux wireless networks. For example, several tools are for viewing information about wireless devices, and others are wireless network configuration tools.

The last part of this chapter was the hands-on practice on implementing a wireless home network. Through this hands-on practice, readers will be able create a wireless network at home. Detailed instructions on setting up a wireless router and wireless network interface card are included in this hands-on practice.

Now that you have learned about Linux wireless networks, your next task is to learn about mobile networks. The next chapter will introduce Linux-based mobile devices. It will examine the mobile Linux operating system used by these devices.

Review Questions

1. What is Wi-Fi?
2. What are the transmission rates and maximum ranges for the IEEE 802.11 standards?
3. What is the difference between Wi-Fi and WiMAX?
4. Describe the usage of the 802.16 protocols.
5. What is a wireless router and what are the components included in a wireless router?
6. What is the advantage of using a dual-band wireless router?
7. What types of network interface cards can be used by a computer to communicate with an access point?
8. What technology is used by a Wi-Fi phone that communicates with others and how does this technology work?
9. What are the advantages of using the ExpressCard?
10. What are the infrastructure mode and ad-hoc mode?
11. What are the advantages and disadvantages of using the ad-hoc mode?
12. Describe five popular Linux-compatible chipsets.
13. What tools can be used to obtain information about wireless devices?
14. Describe five popular Linux-compatible drivers for wireless device chipsets.
15. What is NDISwrapper and why is it important to Linux?
16. Which NDISwrapper command option allows you to install a specified device driver?
17. What can you do with the command hwinfo?
18. What tasks should be performed after a wireless network device is detected?
19. What can you do with the command iwconfig?
20. To set up a wireless network to access the Internet, what tasks need to be performed?

Case Study Projects

The following are two networking projects that involve wireless network implementation:

Case Study Project 11.1. Implement a wireless network at home.
Case Study Project 11.2. Configure your Linux box as an access point.

Chapter 12

Mobile Networks

Objectives

- Investigate mobile Linux operating system.
- Classify mobile network devices.
- Understand mobile network communication.
- Configure mobile network services.

12.1 Introduction

Mobile networks include components such as mobile devices, operating systems and application software, and communication mechanisms and services. Linux plays an important role in mobile computing. It has been used as the operating system for many mobile devices. This chapter will cover topics related to how Linux can be used in a mobile network. It will also introduce different types of mobile devices and explain how a mobile device communicates with other mobile devices in a mobile network. Brief introductions to mobile network systems will be given in this chapter. We will also discuss some commonly provided services for mobile communication. Some of the issues related to the installation and configuration of mobile devices and the mobile Linux operating system will be discussed during the hands-on practice.

The discussion will first focus on mobile Linux. This chapter will introduce different distributions of mobile Linux and compare the features provided by them. The mobile Linux distributions to be introduced in this chapter are Android, LiMo, LiPS, OpenMoko, and Ubuntu Mobile. This chapter will also discuss some commonly used application software and system management utilities included in mobile Linux.

Then, this chapter will introduce various mobile devices such as personal digital assistant (PDA), mobile Internet device (MID), converged mobile device (CMD), portable media player (PMP), and portable navigation device (PND). It will discuss the features supported by these devices. The emphasis will be on Linux-compatible mobile devices.

Next, this chapter will introduce mobile networks. It will cover various mobile networks, from first-generation mobile networks to mobile networks beyond the third generation. Several commonly used mobile network standards will be discussed briefly. This chapter will also explain how mobile devices can communicate with each other in a mobile network.

The hands-on practice will illustrate a mobile device installation process on a Linux computer and will look at Ubuntu Mobile Linux. The Ubuntu MID virtual machine image will be installed and configured. Then, applications supported by the Ubuntu Mobile Linux operating system will be explored.

12.2 Mobile Linux

Chapter 11 mentioned that the wireless computing environment is less friendly to open source products such as Linux due to proprietary companies' unwillingness to provide drivers for open source products. The situation for the mobile environment is even worse. In the PC industry, different brands of hardware or software are more tolerant of other brands. For example, both Linux and Windows can be installed on the same computer. However, for the mobile computing environment, the device makers usually make their own hardware and software. They do not have to consider compatibility of software produced by another company. The proprietary device makers tightly control the mobile computing environment. Among the well-known operating systems used by mobile devices, Linux is not a predominant operating system. This situation makes Linux compatibility issues more challenging. Unless a mobile device company supports Linux, Linux will not be able to get the driver from the company. Without drivers, Linux will not be able communicate with the hardware.

In addition to competing proprietary mobile operating systems, different Linux distributions also compete among themselves. There is no standard for mobile Linux. A Linux distribution that runs on one mobile device may not run on another device. The incompatibility among Linux distributions makes application software development and testing more difficult. More work needs to be done to develop a standard so that all Linux distributions can benefit from it, so Linux can be in a better position to compete with proprietary software.

Although the mobile computing environment is challenging for Linux, many mobile device makers still find Linux appealing due to its excellent flexibility and usability. The following are some of the Linux features that make it suitable for mobile devices:

- *Cost:* The cost of Linux for mobile devices is relatively low. The mobile device companies only need to modify the existing Linux operating system to fit the needs of their mobile devices. Therefore, the development of mobile devices does not need to start from scratch.
- *Usability:* Linux is a widely used open source operating system. A mobile device with the Linux operating system installed can easily communicate with computers and network devices supported by Linux. Also, there is a wide range of open source application software for the user to choose from. No proprietary product can own this large number of application software packages. Linux can be easily integrated into the computation platforms used by consumer electronic and automotive devices.
- *Flexibility:* Linux can be built to fit into a CD or even into a floppy disk. This is a desirable feature for mobile devices. Linux can be built to consume minimum system resources. Mobile Linux does not require a lot of CPU speed and RAM. It can also be built to consume only a small amount of electricity.

In addition, Linux is supported by a large community of Linux developers and users. Records have shown that Linux has been very successful in running embedded mobile devices.

Due to these great features, Linux has attracted support from a large number hardware companies such as Motorola, NEC, Panasonic Mobile Communications, Samsung Electronics, and Intel Corporation. With the support of major hardware companies, Linux will become the operating system used by many more mobile devices. The following introduces some commonly used mobile Linux distributions such as Android, LiMo, LiPS, OpenMoko, and Ubuntu Mobile Linux:

1. *Android:* Android is an operating system plus an application software development platform. It is an open source product and allows mobile device makers to develop their own application software for mobile phones. Android was initiated by Google. Later, it has been continuously developed by the Open Handset Alliance, which consists of over 30 hardware, software, and telecom companies. The Android package includes three major components: the operating system, middleware, and application software. The Linux-based mobile operating system in Android is used to handle the following tasks:
   - *File system management:* The mobile Linux operating system can be used to manage the file system used to control the data storage service for mobile devices.
   - *User account and security management:* One of the main tasks performed by the operating system is to protect the system from hackers and viruses. The operating system also manages user accounts so that multiple users can work on the same device.
   - *Memory management:* The operating system manages memory by allocating and deallocating memory for the Linux kernel, file system, process, and so on. The operating system can also be used to manage the cache in a mobile device.
   - *Process management:* The operating system can be used to start, execute, and stop a process, which is a program running on the CPU and memory.
   - *Network management:* The operating system can be used to manage network interface cards and routing properties so that mobile devices can be integrated into networks.
   - *Software and service management:* The operating system can also be used to manage application software and services such as system logging, Internet search, and product price comparison, and voice communication.

   The application software supported by Android includes an e-mail client, Short Message Service (SMS) program, calendar, maps, browser, contacts, and so on. These applications in Android are all written in the Java programming language and run on Dalvik, which is a virtual machine optimized for low memory requirements. The Dalvik Virtual Machine is also called the Android runtime. The application development platform also includes programming languages such as Java. With the programming languages, third-party application software developers can create utilities and services for mobile devices. The application development platform also includes the components such as the following:
   - *Activity Manager:* With Activity Manager, the developer can specify the life cycle of applications.
   - *Content providers:* With content providers, an application is able to share data provided by other applications. Content providers can also be used to share data within an application.
   - *Location Manager:* With Location Manager, one is able to access the system location service, which is an application to retrieve the updates of a device's geographical location periodically.

- *Package Manager:* By using Package Manager, a developer can retrieve information related to application packages.
- *Resource Manager:* With Resource Manager, an application can access noncode resources, which may include localized strings, graphics, and layout files.
- *Telephony Manager:* Telephony Manager informs users about telephony services on the device.
- *Notification Manager:* In an application, Notification Manager displays warnings on the status bar.
- *View System:* Views are used to build GUI objects such as lists, grids, text boxes, buttons, and embeddable Web browsers.
- *Window Manager:* Window Manager can be used to specify the properties of a window environment, such as the background, title area, default key processing, and so on.
- *Extensible Messaging and Presence Protocol (XMPP):* XMPP is an open source routing protocol that can be used to build social network projects.

The Java programming language and the foregoing application development components provide a development environment for developers to create application software to meet the requirements of mobile device makers. To further help developers, Android also includes various built-in libraries. According to the Open Handset Alliance, the following are some included libraries:

- *3D Libraries:* The 3D Libraries implement OpenGL ES 1.0 APIs, which include a set of 3D graphics designed to be used by mobile devices such as mobile phones, PDAs, and video game consoles.
- *FreeType:* The FreeType library is an implementation of a font rasterization engine that converts text and images into a matrix of pixels (i.e., bitmap).
- *LibWebCore:* LibWebCore is a Web browser engine that supports the Android browser or an embeddable Web view.
- *Media libraries:* Media libraries provide essential support for playing, streaming, and recording of many popular audio and video files formatted in MPEG4, H.264, MP3, AAC, AMR, JPG, and PNG formats.
- *Scalable Graphics Library (SGL):* SGL is a 2D graphics engine that can be used to generate an image from a previously created model.
- *SQLite:* SQLite is a lightweight relational database management system. It can be integrated into an application.
- *Surface Manager:* Surface Manager can be used to assemble graphic layers and manage the display subsystem.
- *System C Library:* The System C Library tuned for embedded Linux-based devices performs system calls as well as processes tasks that do not require Linux kernel support.

The application development platform also includes utilities such as the device emulator and Eclipse IDE for software development.

Due to these features, a number of well-known mobile phone companies have developed their mobile phones based on Android. The mobile devices will be discussed in Section 12.3.

2. *LiMo:* LiMo stands for Linux Mobile. LiMo is another Linux-based operating system plus application development platform for mobile devices. LiMo is supported by the LiMo Foundation organized by companies such as Motorola, NEC, NTT DoCoMo, Panasonic Mobile Communications, Samsung Electronics, and Vodafone. CompaLiMo has three main components: kernel space, middleware, and application. A description of these components follows:

- *Kernel Space:* The kernel space includes the Linux kernel, device drivers, and modem interfaces.
- *Middleware:* It is the main focus of the LiMo Foundation. The middleware includes components related to security, registry, conflict management, frameworks for networking, database, multimedia, messaging, and other applications. The management components and frameworks are designed to guarantee the consistency amoung the partners of the LiMo Foundation. The middleware supports all the phone handsets produced by the partners of the LiMo Foundation.
- *Application:* LiMo also provides application software development kits (SDKs). The SDKs enable application developers to create mobile phone applications in an Eclipse IDE software development environment. Individual partners of the LiMo Foundation develop their own applications such as the user interface and Web tablet. Application developers can add their own functionalities to the objects provided by the middleware.

Unlike Android, which provides a complete solution for mobile devices, LiMo is focused on the middleware and allows mobile device companies to add their own applications. LiMo may assist the management of drivers and modem interfaces. The development of the Linux kernel is the task for the Linux community.

3. *LiPS:* The LiPS Forum, which stands for Linux Phone Standards Forum, is an organization for helping accelerate the adoption of Linux in fixed, mobile, and converged devices. It also promotes interoperability across Linux-based mobile devices. Mobile device companies, phone service companies, and consumers can benefit from the standards proposed by LiPS in the following ways:
   - Service companies can roll out their services faster.
   - Mobile device makers can produce new Linux-compatible devices in a shorter time.
   - Software companies can develop application software for a unified platform and therefore reduce the development time and cost.
   - Consumers can buy new software and install it on any mobile device that adopts the LiPS standards, just as they have been doing in the PC world.

   Unlike Android and LiMo, LiPS does not provide the actual software for LiPS members. Its goal is to create specifications in each layer of the mobile device software to promote interoperability across Linux-based mobile devices.
4. *OpenMoko:* OpenMoko is a project that creates open source cell phone software that runs on Linux-compatible mobile device hardware. The OpenMoko project provides OpenMoko Linux, which is a Linux operating system optimized for mobile devices. It also creates open source hardware whose hardware design information is released to the public. Unlike Android and LiMo, OpenMoko gives more flexibility to end users to allow them to modify the operating system, application software, and hardware for improvement.
5. *Ubuntu Mobile Linux:* Ubuntu, a Linux operating system producer, has proposed Mobile Linux, which is a project specially designed for mobile Internet devices (MIDs) and smartphones. Ubuntu Mobile Linux fully supports the Intel Atom CPU, which is specially designed for mobile devices. The following are some of the features supported by Ubuntu Mobile Linux:

   - Ubuntu Mobile Linux provides a Web 2.0 application development environment called Asynchronous JavaScript and XML (AJAX).
   - Ubuntu Mobile Linux is able to run a variety of Web 2.0 applications such as Facebook, DailyMotion, MySpace, and YouTube.

- Ubuntu Mobile Linux supports a full range of touch screen applications.
- Ubuntu Mobile Linux provides application developers with programming languages such as Java, Python, Flash, and HTML.
- Ubuntu Mobile Linux has strong support for creating and managing audio, video, and graphic materials.
- Ubuntu Mobile Linux allows users to have real-time conversations with each other on the Internet through VoIP or instant messaging.
- With Ubuntu Mobile Linux, mobile device producers can implement digital TVs and digital cameras on mobile devices.
- Ubuntu Mobile Linux can be used to support GPS devices.
- Ubuntu Mobile Linux allows developers to quickly set up discussion groups, sites for blogging, and other Web-based social software.
- Ubuntu Mobile Linux allows users to play online games.
- Ubuntu Mobile Linux is optimized for mobile devices. It uses limited system resources. It is able to run on 256 MB RAM with a 2 GB flash drive. Its power consumption is low.
- Ubuntu Mobile Linux allows the user to modify the source code for better functionality, flexibility, and extensibility.

Unlike Android, LiMo, and OpenMoko, which put more emphasis on mobile devices such as cell phones, Ubuntu Mobile Linux is a good choice for high-end mobile devices such as MIDs and smartphones. With the aforementioned features mentioned, Ubuntu Mobile Linux can also be used by a wide range of embedded systems, included in a piece of hardware such as a DSL router. This means that Ubuntu Mobile Linux allows a mobile device to communicate with wired computers and network devices. On the other hand, Ubuntu Mobile Linux is not often installed in mobile devices such as low-end cell phones.

In the foregoing, several commonly used mobile Linux operating systems and application development platforms were introduced. These Linux distributions target various mobile devices. The next section will introduce several types of mobile devices used for mobile communication.

12.3 Mobile Devices

Handheld communication devices such as handheld computers, Internet accessing devices, and cell phones are called mobile devices. Usually, these devices are small enough to fit in a pocket. Mobile devices have network functionalities so that they can communicate through Wi-Fi or mobile networks. Various operating systems and application software, proprietary or open source, have been developed for mobile devices. The open source operating system Linux is the heart of many mobile devices. It has been used to run the following mobile devices:

- *Personal digital assistant (PDA):* A PDA is a handheld computer. Various computer application software packages can run on the PDA. In addition to hosting computer software, the PDA can also be used as a smartphone, GPS device, digital camera, and media player.
- *Mobile Internet device (MID):* An MID is also a multimedia-capable handheld computer designed for wireless Internet access. With rich multimedia functionalities, an MID is also a good device for entertainment. It is bigger than a PDA but smaller than an ultra-mobile PC.

- *Converged mobile device (CMD):* A CMD is a mobile phone operated by a sophisticated operating system. The smartphone is a CMD. It is common for a CMD to include a digital camera, an MP3 player, a GPS, and a slot for adding a memory card.
- *Portable media player (PMP):* A PMP can be used to store and play digital media, including audio and video content. A PMP may include a user interface displayed on an LCD screen, a hard drive or flash memory for storing multimedia data, an FM radio, and a recording device.
- *Portable navigation device (PND):* A PND may include a GPS having a built-in map, a voice-guidance system, text-to-speech navigation, a voice-recording device, and so on. It is common that a PND also includes a graphic viewer, a digital camera, digital music, games, or a satellite radio.

As a computing device, a mobile device often includes a microprocessor and RAM to carry out the computation. Intel Corporation is one of the semiconductor companies that produce processors for mobile devices. The Atom processor is specially designed for mobile devices. It is compact and power efficient, and is suitable for ultramobile PCs, MIDs, and smartphones. There are other types of processors based on the Advanced RISC Machine (ARM) structure. Due to their very low power consumption, ARM processors are widely used in mobile devices such as PDAs, PNDs, cell phones, and game systems.

12.4 Mobile Network

The previous chapter discussed the Wi-Fi-based wireless network, which allows wireless devices to access the Internet through an access point. To be able to access the Internet or communicate with another wireless device, a wireless device must be located in an area where it can directly communicate with the access point. For Wi-Fi, mobility is only limited to the area surrounding the access point. This makes the Wi-Fi technology suitable for homes, hotels, restaurants, and offices. For the user who is in a moving car or in a sports stadium, Wi-Fi technology is not adequate. The user who is on the move needs a different type of telecommunication technology that can provide this kind of service. The mobile network system is such a technology designed for this purpose.

12.4.1 Mobile Network System

To be able to communicate with people on the move, one needs to use a radio-based mobile network. A mobile network is divided into a large number of geographic ranges called cells. Within each cell, there is a base station, which is connected to a Public Switched Telephone Network (PSTN) or wireless service provider. A mobile device has a low-power transceiver, which is enough to communicate with the base station in the cell. Its transmission range is no more than 8 to 13 km. Each base station has a transmitter, receiver, and control unit. Figure 12.1 illustrates a mobile network.

Each hexagon in Figure 12.1 represents a cell. The actual coverage pattern may vary depending on the geographical shape of the region. A geographic area such as a city can be covered by multiple cells. This allows radio frequencies to be reused in different cells. In this way, a mobile network allows millions of users in a city to call each other simultaneously with a limited radio frequency range. For an area that has more cell phone users, such as the downtown area in a large city, there should be more small cells to cover the area. On the other hand, a rural area should be

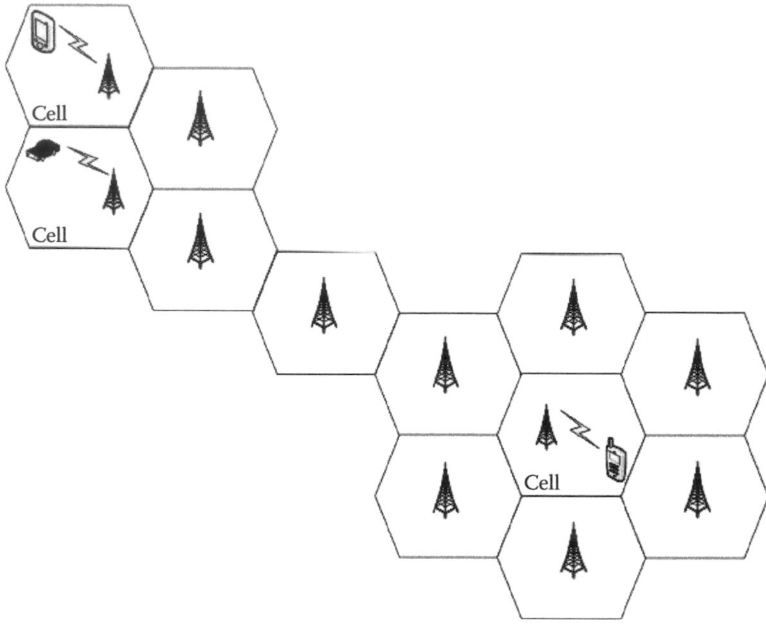

Figure 12.1 A mobile network.

covered by fewer cells. Cell sizes can vary from 100 m in diameter in a highly concentrated urban area to 30 km in a rural area where there are much fewer subscribers. The base station transmission power is adjusted so that its impact on adjacent cells is minimized.

A mobile network system can be characterized by the following features:

- While a mobile device in a mobile network communicates with others, it has the choice to communicate on different radio channels depending on the signal strength. A mobile network system supports 1664 or more channels for mobile devices to choose from.
- While on the move, a mobile device can switch from one cell to another cell automatically without interrupting the user's operation.
- The mobile network allows a user to talk to another user on the other end, while at the same time listening to what the other user has to say. That is, two users can talk simultaneously. This feature is called full-duplex capability. The mobile network implements the full-duplex feature by using two different frequencies, one for sending and the other for receiving the signals.
- It is possible to switch from a mobile network to a Wi-Fi network by changing the specifications of the radio waves.

As shown in Figure 12.1, a cell can have as many as six neighbors. The adjacent cells are assigned different frequencies to avoid interference. Thus, to make sure that each cell uses a different frequency range from its neighbors, one cell should use only one-seventh of the total available frequencies. The number of total available frequencies depends on the mobile system used by the mobile network.

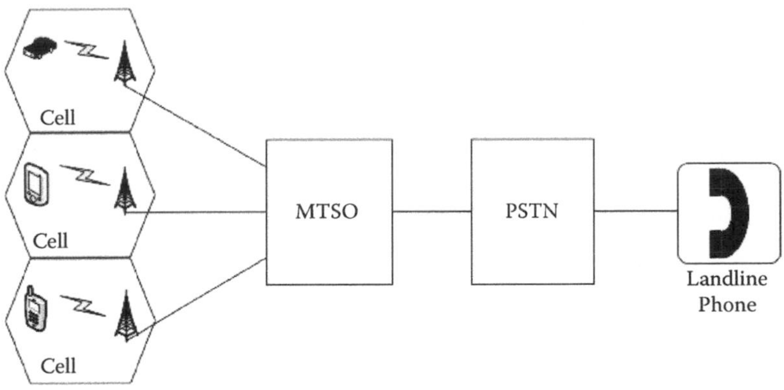

Figure 12.2 A mobile network system.

A mobile device's calling process consists of the following steps:

1. Within each cell, when a mobile device is turned on, the device searches for a base station.
2. The base station with the strongest signal is selected. The selected base station has a connection to a switch. Each telephone company has its own switch in a population center and is managed by a central office called the mobile telephone switching office (MTSO).
3. Through the selected base station, the mobile device registers itself with a unique identification number to the mobile phone switching office.
4. The mobile device places a call by entering the receiver's telephone number.
5. Through the PSTN, the receiver is contacted and the return message is sent back to the PSTN.
6. The receiver listens to the incoming call from the switch.
7. The MTSO identifies the base station connected to the caller and returns the message to the caller.

Figure 12.2 shows a mobile network system, including the MTSO and PSTN.

In general, each base station includes a radio transceiver and a base station controller that acts based on the commands sent to it from the MTSO. A call may come from any of the base stations in the surrounding cells. A mobile device will communicate with the base station that has the strongest signal. While the mobile device is moving, the signal strength may change. The mobile device is designed in such a way that it can change from one base station to another seamlessly to always communicate with the base station with the strongest signal.

A mobile device includes a radio transceiver, a signal processor, and a subscriber identity module. The subscriber identity module needs to be specified before the mobile device can communicate with a base station.

The MTSO unit in Figure 12.2 may perform the following tasks:

- It connects the landline PSTN system to the mobile phone system.
- It monitors the relative signal strengths reported by base stations in response to a mobile device request. It switches from one base station to another base station to achieve the best reception.
- The MTSO includes a handoff management unit that manages the switching of the coverage responsibility as a mobile device moves from one cell to another cell.

- It authenticates user accounts.
- It handles the billing process according to the calling statistics.
- It also handles worldwide roaming.

To handle the foregoing tasks, the MTSO often includes the following components:

- It has a routing and switching unit, which is designed to handle IP traffic. This unit also delivers VoIP, VPN, and multimedia services.
- It includes a Radio Network Controller (RNC), which carries out mobility management tasks. It can be used to track base stations and mobile devices.
- It also includes the interface to connect to the PSTN, which is a collection of interconnected voice telephone networks owned or operated by a telecommunication company.
- A digital-to-analog converter (DAC) is included for converting digital information back to the analog form.
- It has an authentication center (AUC), which is used to handle authentication and encryption for each subscriber.
- Depending on the mobile network system, there may be other components included. Various databases are also included in the MTSO to store the subscribers' and visitors' information.

In its short history, the mobile network system has improved significantly. It has progressed from an analog cell phone system to a high-speed digital cellular system integrated with the high-speed broadband Internet service.

Table 12.1 lists the features of each generation of the mobile network system. The table lists some commonly used technologies for different generations of the mobile network system. Not all of the technologies are listed in Table 12.1. Detailed coverage of these technologies is beyond the scope of this book. 4G technology is still under development. The commercial implementation of 4G is expected after the year 2010. The transmission bit rate is expected to reach 1 Gbps.

The following sections will review some of the technologies developed at each major stage of mobile network development.

12.4.2 First-Generation Mobile Network

The first generation (1G) of mobile technology is an analog wireless cell phone technology introduced in the 1980s. The two commonly used 1G systems are Advanced Mobile Phone Service (AMPS) and Nordic Mobile Telephone (NMT). The analog technology has some significant weaknesses. It is easily interfered by noise and has no protection against eavesdropping. Only a limited number of users can use the mobile network simultaneously. Due to these weaknesses, many cell phone service companies no longer support 1G technology. As a comparison base for the later technologies, the following briefly describes AMPS technology.

Advanced Mobile Phone Service (AMPS) is a cellular system developed by Bell Labs and was first introduced in 1983. By introducing the cell concept, AMPS allows the same frequency to be reused in different cells. It assigns a voice channel to a cell phone handset based on the signal strength. AMPS technology has the following specifications:

- It uses two radio frequency bands for communication. The first frequency band is called the base station transmission band and ranges from 869 MHz to 894 MHz. The base station transmission band is used to transmit signals from a base station to a mobile device. The second frequency band is called the mobile unit transmission band and ranges from 824 MHz to 849 MHz. The mobile unit transmission band is used to transmit signals from a mobile device to a base station.

- AMPS technology uses separate frequencies called channels for each conversation. The bandwidth for each voice channel is 30 kHz, so (894 MHz – 869 MHz)/30 kHz = 832, which means that AMPS supports about 832 channels within the transmission band.
- The radius for a cell can range from 2 km to 20 km.
- The data transmission rate is 10 Kbps.
- The maximum transmission power for each mobile device is 3 W.

Table 12.1 Features of Each Generation of the Mobile Network System

Generation	*Technology*	*Feature*
First Generation (1G)	Advanced Mobile Phone Service (AMPS)	An analog mobile phone system developed by Bell Labs. The transmission bit rate is less than 10 Kbps.
	Nordic Mobile Telephone (NMT)	An analog mobile phone system used mostly in Europe. Again, the transmission bit rate is less than 10 Kbps.
Second Generation (2G)	Global System for Mobile Communica-tions (GSM)	GSM is the most popular mobile phone system, used by over 3 billion people. It is a digital system. The bit rate ranges from 9.6 Kbps to 64 Kbps.
	North American Digital Cellular (IS-95)	It is the first CDMA-based digital cellular standard. CDMA technology allows several radios to share the same frequency. The bit rate for IS-95 is 1.2288 Mbps.
	North American Digital Cellular (IS-136)	IS-136 is also known as Digital AMPS. When compared with IS-95, IS-136 has more functionalities such as text messaging, and so on. The bit rate for IS-136 is 48.6 Kbps.
Third Generation (3G)	Universal Mobile Telecommunications System (UMTS) including UMTS W-CDMA, and UMTS-TDD	UMTS is the third-generation mobile phone system; it is fast and provides mobile applications such as Internet browsing, mobile TV, and video calling. For example, the bit rates for the UMTS family of mobile networks range from 384 Kbps to 16 Mbps. The bit rate for UMTS W-CDMA is 384 Kbps, and the bit rate for UMTS-TDD is 16 Mbps.
	Code Division Multiple Access (CDMA) 2000 including EV-DO, EV-DV, and 1xRTT	CDMA2000 is a 2.5G/3G mobile phone system that provides multiple access for digital radio, voice, data, and signaling data. The transmission bit rate ranges from 0.144 Mbps to 3.1 Mbps.
Pre-Fourth Generation (4G)	HSDPA/HSUPA, HSPA+, and Worldwide Interoperability for Microwave Access (WiMAX)	The HSPA family is the successor of UMTS. Mobile WiMAX is used for portable devices such as smartphones, game terminals, MP3 players, and so on. The WiMAX download bit rate can be up to 70 Mbps for short distances and 10 Mbps at 10 km.

In 1G technology, each voice channel can only be used by one user at a given time. A 1G system such as AMPS supports 832 frequencies. Among these 832 frequencies, 42 are used for control. Therefore, there are 832 – 42 = 790 frequencies available. Each communication channel uses two frequencies for sending and receiving signals. Therefore, there are 395 channels available. Each cell allows 56 voice channels (395 ÷ 7). For an analog mobile phone, at a given time, each voice channel can only be used by one user. This means that 56 users can use their cell phones simultaneously within a cell.

When a mobile device user places a call, AMPS operates in the following sequence:

1. The caller keys in the receiver's phone number then presses the Talk button.
2. The receiver's phone number and caller's authentication information are sent to the MTSO through a base station.
3. The MTSO authenticates the caller and verifies the receiver's phone number.
4. If the authentication is successfully completed, the MTSO issues a message to the caller to indicate the connection is established.
5. The MTSO contacts the receiver by ringing the receiver's phone number.
6. If the receiver responds to the call, the MTSO establishes the communication channel and initiates the billing process.
7. After the caller or receiver ends the call, MSTO releases the channel and completes the billing process.

As mentioned earlier in this chapter, analog technology has some serious weaknesses. It has been widely replaced by digital technology, which is second-generation mobile network technology. The second-generation mobile network will be discussed next.

12.4.3 Second-Generation Mobile Network

The second generation (2G) of mobile network technology was launched in the 1990s. It is based on digital technology. Digital mobile devices convert the analog signals to binary signals, which can be represented with 0's and 1's. Digital technology uses radio frequencies in a different way. It allows the frequencies to be dynamically shared by a number of users. Therefore, more users can operate simultaneously within a cell with digital mobile devices.

Digital signals can be easily compressed to reduce network traffic and use radio frequencies more efficiently. In addition, the digital mobile network provides encryption, and error detection and correction functionalities to improve the security and quality of data transmission. The number of users supported depends on the bit rate used by each user. In addition to cell phone services, the 2G mobile network introduced data services such as text messaging. Due to these advantages, digital technology has been adopted by almost all mobile network equipment companies and service carriers.

In 2G, there are two types of channel access technologies, Time Division Multiple Access (TDMA) and Code Division Multiple Access (CDMA). TDMA and CDMA can be distinguished by the multiplexing methods used by them.

Multiplexing allows multiple users to share a single communication channel. One of the commonly used multiplexing methods is frequency division multiplexing (FDM), which assigns each user a fixed frequency that carries voice or data signals. In this way, multiple users can share the

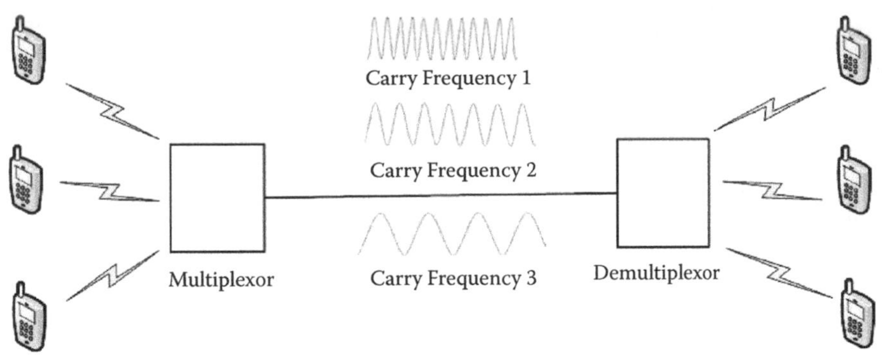

Figure 12.3 Frequency division multiplexing.

same communication channel by using frequencies to distinguish signals sent by users. FDM works like a radio broadcasting system where multiple radio stations can broadcast at the same time and each of them has its own fixed frequency to carry the broadcasting signals to its audience. Figure 12.3 illustrates frequency division multiplexing.

FDM has some problems when used in a mobile network system. First, when interference occurs within the bandwidth used by signals, it could totally destroy the signals. This phenomenon is called catastrophic interference. Also, using a fixed frequency to carry signals is not secure. Hackers can easily intercept the signals carried by a specific frequency. One idea to solve the interference problem is to use multiple frequencies to send the signals simultaneously. So, at a given time, one frequency may have an interference problem while other frequencies may still work. Also, to minimize the security vulnerability, frequencies used to transmit signals should be varied according certain predefined rules.

As the name indicates, the multiplexing method used by TDMA is based on time division multiplexing (TDM), which allows multiple users to take turns to send out signals in different time slots. Figure 12.4 illustrates the TDM process.

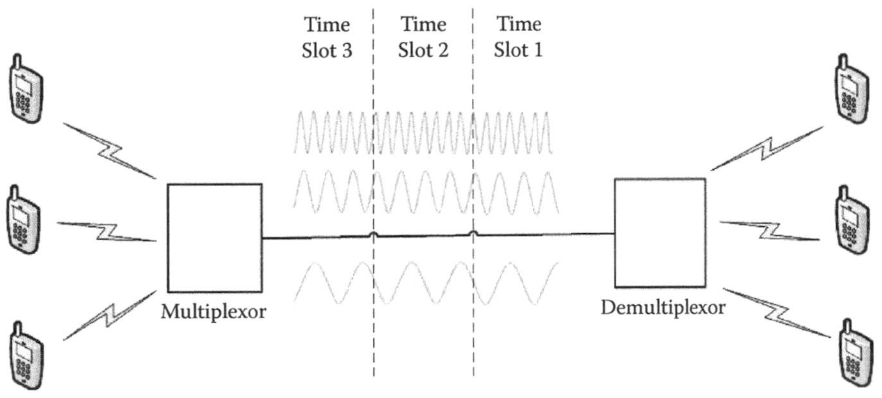

Figure 12.4 Time division multiplexing.

During the time division process, the multiplexer receives signals from each user, breaks each signal into small segments, and then transmits the signal segments at the assigned time slots. Within each time slot, multiple frequencies can be used to transmit the signals. For example, Frequency 1 and Frequency 2 can be used by Time Slot 1, Frequency 2 and Frequency 3 can be used by Time Slot 2, and so on. After the signal segments reach the destination, the demultiplexer reassembles these signal segments according to the time slots used to transmit them. Then, the reassembled signals are forwarded to the dedicated receivers. To optimize performance, the time slots can be adjusted automatically according to the network traffic and the number of the users on the network.

CDMA uses codes for multiplexing. CDMA technology distinguishes multiple transmitters by assigning each of them a special code. During the CDMA multiplexing process, the analog audio signals of each dialog are first chopped into digital signals. These digital signals are then labeled with code to indicate which dialog they are from. The digital signals are then carried by carrier frequencies to the destination. A commonly used scheme to assign a piece of a digital signal to a frequency is called frequency hopping. With frequency hopping, frequencies used to carrier digital signals change abruptly and frequently. Between two hops, a frequency remains the same for a short time, often a fraction of a minute. It is possible that the digital signals are carried by every one of the carry frequencies in the full 1.25 MHz bandwidth of the CDMA channel running at the 800 MHz or 1.9 GHz band.

For security reasons, the way to assign digital signals to the carry frequencies may vary according to a predefined pattern that only the demultiplexer knows. The pattern is usually generated by a frequency-versus-time mathematical function. In this way, it makes it difficult for hackers to intercept the content being transmitted over a mobile network. There is no time slot assigned to each of the multiple users. The users in the conversation are identified by the code assigned to that conversation. In this way, multiple users can share the same physical transmission medium at any time. This is an efficient way to use the communication bandwidth. Unlike other access methods where the frequency is held by a user even if the user is not talking at the moment, the method of CDMA can use that moment to transmit someone else's conversation. The illustration of CDMA is given in Figure 12.5.

Mobile network systems such as Global System for Mobile Communications (GSM), IS-136, and iDEN are TDMA based. On the other hand, the mobile network system IS-95 is an example

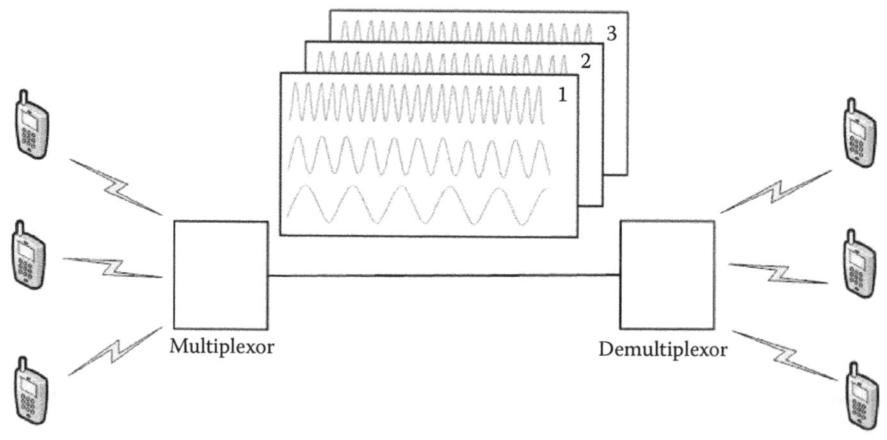

Figure 12.5 Code division multiplexing.

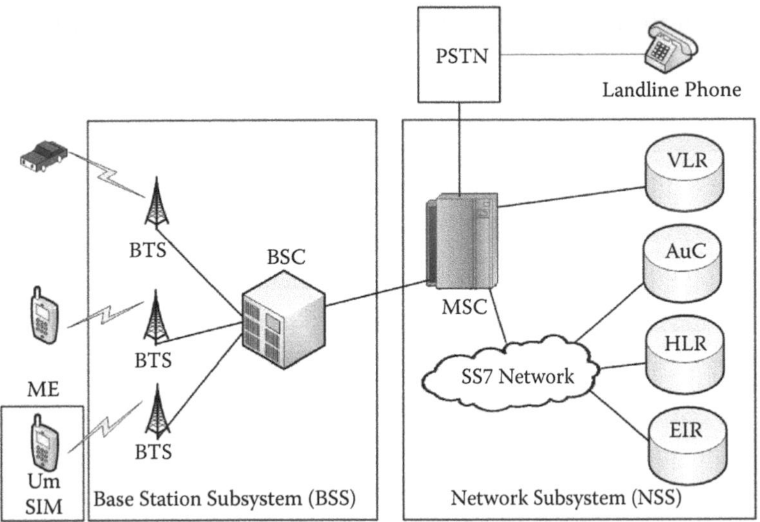

Figure 12.6 GSM network architecture.

of a CDMA-based mobile network system. The following briefly describes some 2G mobile network systems:

1. *Global System for Mobile Communications (GSM):* GSM is a TDMA-based mobile network system. It is the most popular mobile network system. In the worldwide cell phone market, GSM has about 80% of the market share, which means that over 3 billion people are using GSM. Figure 12.6 shows the GSM network architecture.

   The terminology used in Figure 12.6 have the following meanings:

   - *ME:* Mobile equipment. In Figure 12.6, ME is a cell phone handset.
   - *Um:* Um is the air interface. It is involved in call control, report management, location update, and so on.
   - *SIM:* Subscriber identity module. A SIM is a smart card that is detachable from the ME unit. The subscriber's identification information and phone book are stored in the SIM. When a subscriber switches a cell phone handset, the SIM card can be put in the new handset so that the same subscriber identification can be used on the new handset.
   - *BTS:* Base transceiver station. A BTS is a piece of equipment used for transmitting and receiving radio signals.
   - *BSC:* Base station controller. A BSC controls the handoff of the communication from one BTS to another BTS by keeping track of the signal strength and handling the allocation of radio channels.
   - *MSC:* Mobile switching center. An MSC links a mobile network system to the PSTN. It controls the handoff between two different base station subsystems. It performs user authentication and account validation. The MSC also handles worldwide roaming.
   - *SS7:* Signaling System 7. SS7 is a set of telephone signaling protocols for controlling the PSTN phone call establishment. It also handles billing, routing, and short message service (SMS).
   - *VLR:* Visitor location register (VLR) is a database that stores and maintains information about subscribers who are in the region currently controlled by an MSC. It also stores

information about the Location Area Identity (LAI), which identifies the region where the ME is currently located.

- *HLR:* Home location register. An HLR is a database that stores and maintains detailed information about each qualified subscriber, including all the information carried by each SIM card.
- *AuC:* Authentication center. An AuC is used to assist the MSC in handling authentication when a subscriber attempts to connect to the GSM mobile network. Only after a subscriber is authenticated is an HLR allowed to manage the information on the subscriber's SIM. An HLR also holds the encryption keys.
- *EIR:* Equipment identity register. An EIR is a database that keeps track of information about stolen mobile phones. It can be used to prevent calls from stolen mobile phones and defective base stations.

GSM technology allows a subscriber to switch carriers but still keep the same cell phone. The subscriber can also select a cell phone from many different handset makers. GSM even provides a worldwide emergency telephone number for emergencies. In addition to the basic structure illustrated in Figure 12.6, the newer versions of GSM also add more components. For example, the General Packet Radio Service (GPRS) technology includes the packet switching protocols that enable the high-speed wireless Internet access service. Enhanced Data Rates for GSM Evolution (EDGE) is another component added to a newer version of GSM. EDGE improves the GSM data transmission rate up to 384 Kbps. It is also capable of delivering multimedia to mobile devices.

2. *IS-136:* IS-136 is also known as Digital AMPS (D-AMPS). D-AMPS, developed in the 1990s, is considered a TDMA-based mobile network system. As the name indicates, D-AMPS is developed from the analog technology AMPS by digitally compressing the voice signals. D-AMPS uses the existing AMPS channels. Each channel is divided into three slots; this means that the D-AMPS mobile network allows three times more simultaneous calls within each cell. Due to the added authentication and encryption functionalities, D-AMPS is more secure than its predecessor, AMPS. In addition, D-AMPS also provides the text messaging service. To release the AMPS spectrum to the largest 2G GSM mobile network and the next-generation mobile network UMTS, D-AMPS was terminated in 2008.
3. *Integrated Digital Enhanced Network (iDEN):* iDEN, developed in the 1990s, is also a TDMA-based mobile network system. Compared with D-AMPS, iDEN can accommodate more subscribers within a given spectral space. With iDEN technology, three or six users can share the same communication channel. iDEN has a special feature called Push-to-Talk, which has the fastest connection speed. Another technology supported by iDEN is the trunked radio system, which is a computer-controlled radio system that allows a talk group to talk together regardless of frequency. The two-way communication provided by the trunked radio system has been used by many public service departments such as fire departments, traffic control departments, and police departments.

In the foregoing, several TDMA-based mobile network systems were introduced. TDMA is a predominant channel access technology used by mobile network systems. Another commonly used channel access technology is CDMA. IS-95 is one of the CDMA-based mobile network systems. The following briefly describes IS-95.

4. *Interim Standard 95 (IS-95):* IS-95 technology is known by its brand name, cdmaOne. IS-95 has a similar architecture to GSM. When compared with AMPS, CDMA has about 8 to 10 times more capacity than AMPS. IS-95 also has better security and data transmission speed. IS-95 allows several users to share the same frequency. This means that more

subscribers can be served in a small cell. When more and more subscribers turn on their mobile devices, the signals degrade gradually. The power control feature allows the mobile devices near the base station to communicate with lower power to save power consumption. For devices away from the base station, more power can be used for better communication quality. With this feature, a CDMA cell can be made much bigger.

During communication, IS-95 uses the technique called frequency division duplex (FDD), which transmits two types of signals, forward link transmission and reverse link transmission. The first type of signal is from a network to a mobile device, and the second type of signal is from a mobile device to a network. Forward link transmission uses the bandwidth 824 to 849 MHz, and reverse link transmission uses the bandwidth 869 to 894 MHz. Forward link transmission supports four different types of channels:

- *Pilot channel:* From a base station, each CDMA carrier continuously sends out pilot signals so that a mobile device can identify the base station. IS-95 manages the handoff based on the pilot signals that reach the mobile device.
- *Synchronous channel:* It is used to synchronize the timing between a mobile device and a base station.
- *Paging channel:* It is used to page a mobile device to tell the subscriber that there is an incoming call.
- *Traffic channel:* During communication, the traffic channel is assigned to a subscriber to transmit voice and data with a transmission rate up to 9.6 Kbps. The traffic channel supports a variable transmission rate to accommodate different types of data and voice transmission.

Reverse link transmission supports two types of channels, the access channel and traffic channel. The following briefly describes these two channels:

- *Access channel:* It is used by a mobile device to dial the network or respond to paging.
- *Traffic channel:* During communication, the reverse traffic channel is assigned to a subscriber to transmit voice and data with a variable transmission rate up to 9.6 Kbps.

As shown earlier, the reverse transmission link does not transmit the pilot signals from a mobile device. This improves the performance of reverse transmission.

When moving from one cell to another cell, a mobile device needs to decide which base station it should communicate with. The decision depends on which base station provides the most powerful signals. The process of switching from one base station to another base station is called handoff, or handover. There are two commonly used handoffs, hard handoff and soft handoff. These are now described:

5. *Hard handoff:* While switching from one base station to another, the hard handoff process turns off communication with the source base station and then turns on communication with the target base station. This type of handoff is also known as the break-before-make handoff.
6. *Soft handoff:* The soft handoff process keeps the connection to the source base station while trying to connect to the target base station. After the connection to the target base station is established, the connection to the source base station can then be turned off. Therefore, this type of handoff is also known as the make-before-break handoff. While processing the soft handoff, the mobile device is connected to more than one base station simultaneously. It can either use the best signal to communicate or combine the signals from all the connections to produce a better signal.

In general, the implementation of hard handoff is relatively simple on the analog or 2G TDMA-based network mobile system: the frequencies used by different base stations are switched. During the hard handoff process, the time taken to switch frequencies is very short. Usually, for the 2G

TDMA-based mobile network, the user will hardly notice the switching process. The disadvantage of hard handoff is that it is possible that the communication between a mobile device and a base station may be terminated if the hard handoff fails. To prevent termination, the mobile device implementing the hard handoff often includes software that can start a process to reconnect to the source base station if it is not able to connect to the target base station. The reconnecting process may cause a temporary interruption.

On the other hand, soft handoff provides better quality compared to hard handoff. The chance of termination is very small. However, the implementation of soft handoff has a higher cost. A more complicated mobile device is needed to handle soft handoff. In general, no analog and 2G TDMA-based mobile network system have implemented soft handoff. On the other hand, 2G CDMA-based mobile network systems have implemented soft handoff because it is relatively inexpensive to implement on a CDMA-based mobile network system. Also, it is necessary for CDMA-based mobile network systems to use soft handoff to overcome near-far interference, which causes signals with less power to be undetectable. The CDMA-based mobile network system allows two or more communication channels to be used simultaneously. Subscribers far away from a base station may get weaker signals. The near-far effect may prevent these subscribers from communicating with the base station. This is why the CDMA-based mobile network system often includes a power management system to strengthen signals from mobile devices located far away from a base station.

Besides high cost, another disadvantage of soft handoff is that there are fewer communication channels available during the handoff process because the soft handoff process does not release the communication channel to the source base station before the target base station is connected.

In the foregoing, two commonly used 2G mobile network systems, TDMA and CDMA, have been introduced. In summary, Table 12.2 briefly compares these two technologies.

2G mobile network technology has been widely used for cell phones. However, a better technology that integrates the cell phone service and IP data service has emerged. It is third-generation mobile network technology. The next section will discuss 3G technology.

12.4.4 Third-Generation Mobile Network

The third generation (3G) of mobile network technology was originally specified by the 3rd Generation Partnership Project (3GPP). 3G combines the cellular service with the Internet Protocol (IP) service to create a new communication environment. It allows users to access both the cellular service and the Internet anywhere and anytime. With 3G technology, a variety of services such as the digital phone, video call, e-mail, IPTV, VoIP, online gaming, and Internet surfing can be converged. 3G technology also allows users to remotely access an organization's private network with proper authentication. In this way, students can work on their lab projects or collaborate with other students even when they are on the move.

To be able to handle voice traffic as well as data traffic, a 3G mobile network uses wideband radio technology, which allows more users to log on simultaneously. Wideband radio technology is optimized for high-speed Internet service, multimedia service, as well as voice service. The IMT-2000 standard created by the International Telecommunications Union (ITU) defines the characteristics of 3G technology. The following are some of the characteristics specified by IMT-2000:

- IMT-2000 specifies that the spectrum used by 3G should be between 400 MHz and 3 GHz. It specifies a minimum transaction bit rate of 2 Mbps for stationary or walking users, and 348 Kbps in a moving vehicle.

- IMT-2000 specifies that the 3G system support a wide range of interfaces and technologies. The 3G mobile network accommodates three access technologies, FDMA, TDMA, and CDMA, which are used to access five different radio interfaces: IMT-DS, IMT-MC, IMT-IC, IMT-SC, and IMT-FT.
- IMT-2000 specifies that the 3G service be compatible with existing 2G systems. 3G can be evolved from current radio technology to provide higher-speed capabilities. The migration from 2G to 3G should be seamless and effective.
- The 3G system specified by IMT-2000 should be scalable. It should allow growth in new services, users, and coverage areas.
- The initial investment for implementing 3G system should be small. The affordability of 3G is intended for broad adoptions.

Table 12.2 Comparisons between TDMA and CDMA

Factor	*TDMA*	*CDMA*
Requirements on mobile devices	A TDMA mobile device runs simple software. Thus, it has fewer requirements from TDMA.	A CDMA mobile device runs complex software to handle soft handoff. Therefore, it needs to be more sophisticated.
Range of coverage	The TDMA mobile network system has a smaller cell size. The maximum cell size is less than 18 km in radius.	CDMA can cover a bigger area. A mobile device can reach a base station 60 km away.
Battery life	The TDMA transmitter does not consume any power when there is no actual data transmission even though the mobile device is turned on. However, on average, a TDMA mobile device may consume more power.	The CDMA transmitter uses power constantly. However, on average, CDMA uses less power due to its power control function. It also uses less power to reach longer distances.
Transmission quality	Because hard handoff is used, the temporary interruption may reduce the quality of the underlying transmission. TDMA has a clarity in voice comparable to that of CDMA. TDMA has a hard limit on the number of users in a cell. Beyond that limit, users cannot make a connection.	Because soft handoff is used, CDMA suffers from fewer dropped calls. The voice clarity is similar to that of TDMA. CDMA has no hard limit on the number of active users in a cell. However, the quality may go down if there are too many active users in the same cell.
International roaming	Due to the large market share, TDMA is more internationally accepted than CDMA.	CDMA has a much smaller market share and, therefore, it has lower roamability.
Cost of service	The TDMA-based service costs less. It does not need a patent fee. Also, the use of the SIM card allows the user to switch handsets freely.	CDMA is a patented product. Extra fees are paid for the usage. CDMA is also carrier specific. It is not convenient to switch handsets.

Based on the IMT 2000 standard, 3G has the following features:

- 3G technology supports multiple communication formats such as cellular, satellite, wired LAN, wireless LAN, and wireless WAN.
- The voice quality has been greatly improved by 3G technology.
- The 3G mobile network is able to transfer data at 3 Mbps. Some of the newer 3G mobile networks have improved the data transmission rate up to 16 Mbps, and the data transmission rate keeps improving. The 3G network is capable of transferring large multimedia files over the Internet.
- 3G technology enables global roaming seamlessly.
- The wired network and wireless network can be fully integrated with 3G technology, which supports both packet-switched and circuit-switched data transmission.
- 3G mobile devices can be used to perform broadband-based tasks such as video conferencing, video streaming, playing online games, watching TV, listening to music, and faxing documents.
- Compared with 2G, 3G mobile technology offers much better security. It allows the mobile equipment to authenticate the network to which the device is connecting. It also provides better encryption.

3G technology integrates a wide range of services to support data transmission by different types of applications, including the Internet, cellular, and multimedia services.

- *Cellular service:* 3G provides services for delivering voice and video telephony data.
- *Multimedia service:* 3G provides data streaming services for delivering multimedia data for video conferencing and webcasting.
- *Internet service:* With the Internet service provided by 3G, users can surf the Web, play online games, and remotely access databases.
- *E-mail service:* 3G technology can transfer e-mail data as well as data generated by text messaging.

The IP data service supported by 3G technology allows subscribers to access the Internet through the mobile network. Through the broadband Internet service provided by a mobile network carrier, the subscriber can also send and receive e-mail, download and upload files, and browse Web sites. Unlike Wi-Fi, the 3G mobile network allows subscribers to access the Internet service wherever the cell phone service is available. A wireless wide area network (WWAN) can be used to achieve this goal. After a subscriber dials up to a WWAN, the data transmission can be done through the IP data network technology provided by the 3G mobile network. The WWAN is also very secure. The wireless data transmission in the WWAN is protected by both encryption and authentication.

Subscribers can access a WWAN in several ways. The following are some of them:

- To log on to the Internet service through a mobile network, some mobile network service carriers offer the traditional PC card, ExpressCard, and USB card for those subscribers who use notebook computers to access the Internet.
- Some notebook computers may already have mobile network access capability. For example, Qualcomm's Gobi technology has been adopted by many notebook computer vendors to allow users to access mobile networks provided by many leading mobile network service carriers.

- Some cell phones and PDAs can also access the Internet through a Wi-Fi access point or through a computer that is connected to the Internet. Such a method is called tethering, which can be used by mobile devices in places where the mobile network service is not available, or when it is too costly to download a large file through a mobile network.
- Mobile devices in an office can share the Internet service provided by mobile network service carriers through a WWAN router. With broadband-like speeds, the WWAN router offers a cost-effective means of Internet access for virtually any remote location that DSL or broadband cable cannot reach.

In 2001, the first 3G mobile network was released for commercial use in Japan. Since then, more and more 3G mobile networks have been made available for commercial use. The early releases of 3G technology include Universal Mobile Telephone Service (UMTS), which is implemented over existing GSM networks and CDMA2000, which is implemented over existing CDMA networks. Later, the much improved UTMS-TDD was released. The following subsections briefly describe these 3G technologies.

12.4.4.1 Universal Mobile Telephone Service (UMTS)

UMTS, developed in Europe, is also known as 3GSM. The name indicates that UMTS is the 3G successor of the popular GSM mobile technology. Depending on the environment of the usage, the UMTS data transmission rates are defined as follows:

- For the satellite and rural outdoor environment, the transmission rate is 144 Kbps.
- For the urban outdoor environment, the transmission rate is 384 Kbps.
- The data transmission rate for the indoor environment is 2048 Kbps.

The data transmission rates have been improved in the later versions of UMTS-based technologies. UMTS technology is constructed on three domains; Core Network (CN), UMTS Terrestrial Radio Access Network (UTRAN), and User Equipment (UE). Figure 12.7 illustrates the structure of UMTS.

1. *Core Network (CN):* CN performs three major tasks. The first task is to control data traffic. It switches and routes data traffic to the dedicated destinations. The second task is to enforce security measures. The third task is to carry out network and information management. With CN, the UMTS radio access network can exchange data with the Gateway Earth Station (GES) radio access network for satellite communication. CN is also used to connect to various backbone networks such as the Internet, PSTN, and Integrated Services Digital Network (ISDN). CN consists of three major components: the circuit switching domain, packet switching domain, and IP multimedia system (IMS). The following briefly describes these three components:
   - *Circuit switching domain:* Circuit switching is a connection-oriented method of data transmission. It is mostly used to deliver voice data by telephone companies. In the circuit switching domain, a piece of data is passed to its destination through a pre-established route.

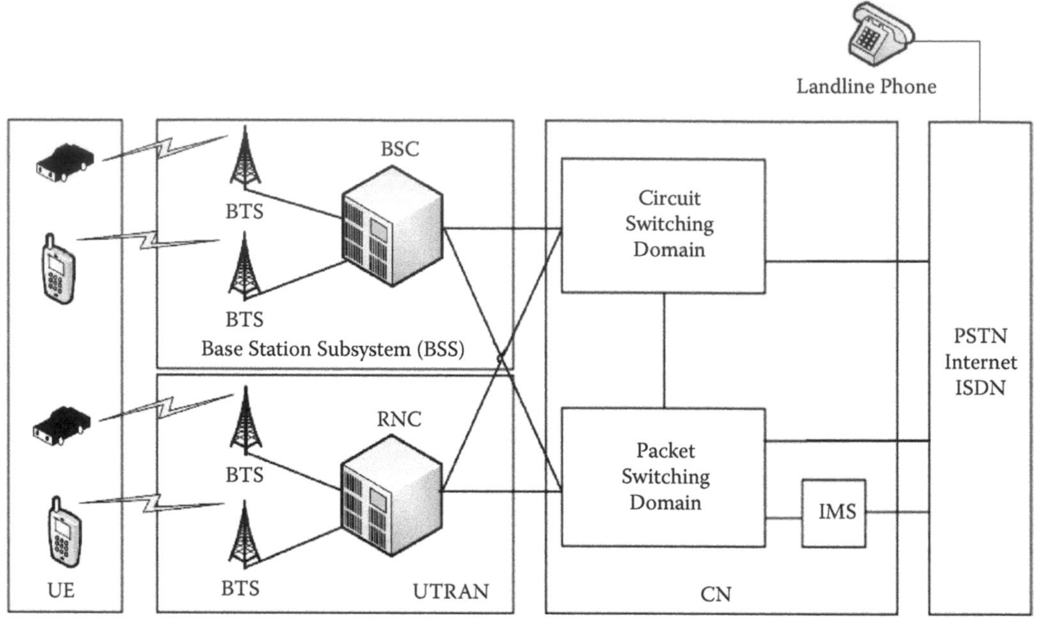

Figure 12.7 UMTS structure.

- *Packet switching domain:* Packet switching is a connectionless method of data transmission. It is mostly used for computer networks. In the packet switching domain, a piece of data is passed to its destination through whichever route is available.
- *IP Multimedia System (IMS):* It can be used to provide multimedia services. It is used by mobile devices to access multimedia and voice applications.

It is important for all the aforementioned three major components to collaborate with each other. A 3G mobile network needs to accommodate all types of data. The network technology Asynchronous Transfer Mode (ATM) is used to handle the UMTS core transmission. ATM is designed to handle data transmission services for various types of data. ATM technology has the following features that can enrich mobile networks:

- *Support for a wide range of services:* ATM provides services for voice, video, and other data.
- *Support for various networks:* ATM can be used as a LAN technology as well as a WAN technology.
- *Support for all types of subscribers:* ATM is designed to support globalized communication. Its goal is to allow a pair of subscribers to communicate with each other from anywhere and at anytime, no matter what types of subscribers they are.
- *Support for all types of computing devices:* ATM supports various computing devices, from small and low-end cell phones to large and sophisticated supercomputers.

CN handles two types of security, Mobile Application Part (MAP) security and IP security. MAP security protects the SS7 protocol, which has no security protection for itself. IP security provides IPSec technology for authentication and encryption at the packet level.

CN also provides services for user account and subscription management. It includes databases such as EIR, HLR, VLR, and AUC for subscriber account management and subscriber authentication. The database Number Portability DataBase (NPDB) included in CN can be used to enable subscribers to keep their old phone numbers after they change their mobile network carriers. Another component, Gateway Location Register (GLR), can be used to monitor, manage, and optimize inbound roaming traffic.

2. *UMTS Terrestrial Radio Access Network (UTRAN):* UTRAN is a radio access network and is used to connect CN to user equipment (UE). It consists of base stations and radio network controllers (RNCs). The base station in the 3G technology is called Node B. The RNC is used to allocate channels, digitize or reassemble signals, manage handoffs, control power settings, and enforce security with authentication and encryption. Node B is used to receive and send signals from UE, modulate and demodulate signals, and check and correct transmission errors. UE communicates with base stations. A radio network controller (RNC) controls one or more base stations. UTRAN may include one or more radio network controllers, which communicate with CN. UTRAN communicates with UE and CN with four different interfaces. The description of these interfaces is given in the following:
   - *Iu interface:* It is the interface between the radio network controller and core network. It has two different instances, Iu-CS and Iu-PS. Iu-CS is used to connect to the circuit switching domain, and Iu-PS is used to connect to the packet switching domain. This interface is used to establish, manage, and release radio access bearers that provide communication links between radio network controllers and CN.
   - *Iur interface:* It is the interface between two radio network controllers. This interface is mainly used for soft handoff. It also handles tasks such as radio resource management and synchronization.
   - *Iub interface:* It is the interface between a base station and a radio network controller. This interface is used to deliver the service offered to a subscriber. There are two components in the Iub interface. The first one is the radio network control component, and the second one is the connection establishment component.
   - *Uu interface:* It is the interface between a base station (Node B) and UE. UE uses this interface to manage the information received or sent to a base station.

   Figure 12.8 illustrates the UTRAN structure. URTAN performs tasks similar to those done by a base station subsystem (BSS). The use of UTRAN separates a 3G mobile network

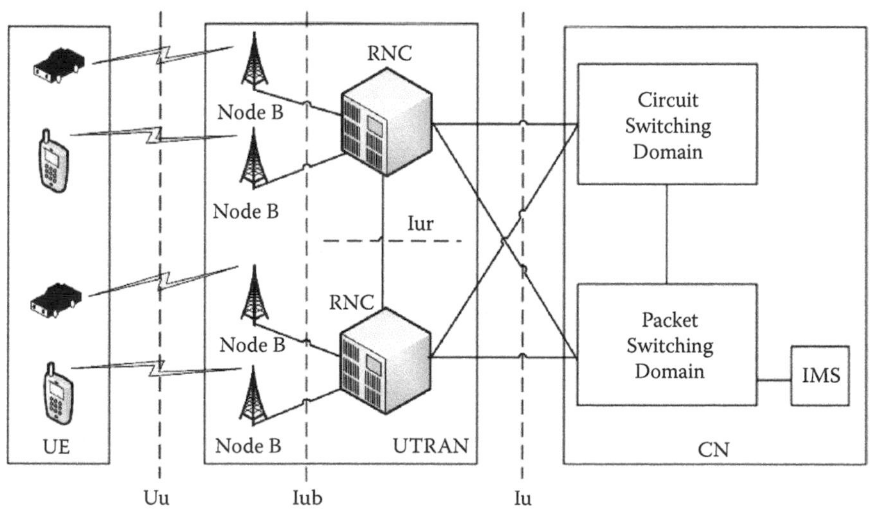

Figure 12.8 UTRAN structure.

from a 2G mobile network. UTRAN is built around an IP-optimized CN, and it is able to carry all types of network traffic such as voice, video, and other types of data. In addition, UTRAN supports both frequency division duplex (FDD) and time division duplex (TDD) radio interfaces for higher bandwidth and better voice quality. With FDD, different frequencies are used for uplink and downlink. Therefore, FDD makes the transmission of symmetric traffic more efficient. For asymmetric traffic, TDD can dynamically adjust the data transmission rates for uplink traffic and downlink traffic to optimize performance.

3. *User Equipment (UE):* Similar to mobile equipment (ME) in the GSM mobile network, UE is a mobile device. The difference is that UE can handle various types of data, support a variety of application software, and transmit data at a much faster rate. UE consists of two major components, the radio frequency (RF) subsystem and the baseband signal processing subsystem. The following is a brief description of these two units:
   - *RF unit:* This unit handles the sending and receiving of signals to and from the antenna of a UE device. The circuits for the receiver and transmitter are built in this unit. The RF unit also performs signal modulation. The signals received by the RF unit will be forwarded to the baseband signal processing unit.
   - *Baseband signal processing unit:* This unit consists of two parts, the application-specific integrated circuit (ASIC) and memory. The unit handles tasks such as analog-digital signal conversion and conditioning.

Similar to the ME in the GSM mobile network, UE contains a SIM card called the USIM, which stores a variety of identification information including

- International Mobile Subscriber Identity (IMSI)
- Temporary Mobile Subscriber Identity (TMSI)
- Mobile station ISDN (MSISDN)
- International Mobile Station Equipment Identity (IMSEI)
- Public Land Mobile Network (PLMN)

In addition to storing identification information, the user can also use the USIM to perform several other functions, such as the following:

- The user can store phonebook information on the USIM so that the phonebook messages do not get lost after the phone is changed.
- The user can update USIM-specific information over the air.
- The USIM can be used for user authentication.
- The user can download new application software on the USIM, and so on.

UE communicates with three counterparts: Node B, RNC, and CN. UE can perform the following tasks while dealing with different counterparts:

a. *Communicating with Node B:* UE communicates directly with Node B. Node B and UE together handle the signal-processing-related tasks, including the following:
   - Signal measurements, including signal strength, signal and noise ratio, and signal quality
   - Error detection and correction with the error correction code
   - Signal modulation for converting signals to messages
   - Power control

b. *Communicating with RNC:* UE communicates with RNC for connection- and base-station-selection-related issues. The tasks performed during the communication include the following:
   - Working with RNC for handoff management
   - Participating in the encryption and decryption process
   - Sending the measurements of signal strengths to RNC for base station selection
   - Participating in the Radio Resource Control (RRC) process for connection establishment and release
   - Performing acknowledged transmission for reliable communication

c. *Communicating with CN:* UE communicates with CN for mobility management. It performs the following mobility management activities:
   - Sending the current location information to CN
   - Participating in the bearer negotiation for the best connection
   - Together with CN, enforcing security measures such as checking International Mobile Equipment Identity (IMEI), registering locations, and identifying CN with reciprocal authentication

Now, three major components of UMTS have been discussed. As mentioned earlier, UMTS is a widely accepted 3G mobile technology. Another 3G technology, CDMA2000, is also well known. The next section will cover the CDMA2000 mobile network system.

12.4.4.2 CDMA2000

CDMA2000 is a 3G mobile network technology developed on top of the 2G technology, CDMA. CDMA2000 is backward compatible with CDMA telephony systems such as IS-95. Standardized by 3GPP, the CDMA2000 family has several different versions. Evolved from CDMA, the first commercial version was first launched by South Korea's Telecom in the year 2000, and therefore was named CDMA2000 1x (or IS-2000). A CDMA2000 1x mobile network consists of CDMA2000-compatible mobile devices, multicarrier BTSs, a BSC, an MSC, packet-switched data network (PSDN), and PSTN. Figure 12.9 illustrates the structure of a CDMA2000 1x mobile network.

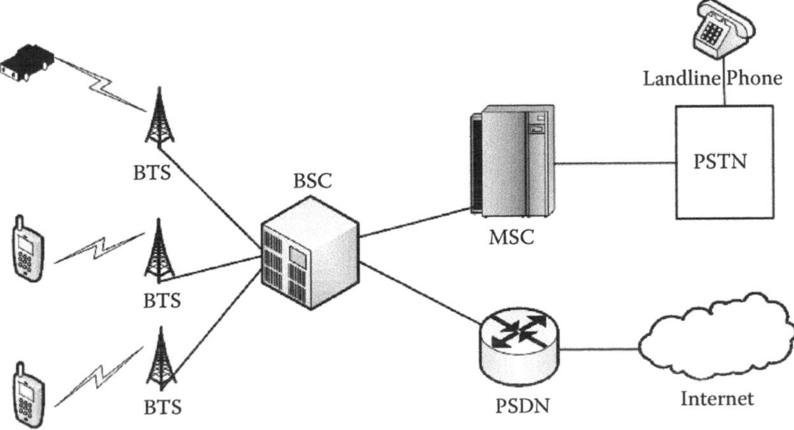

Figure 12.9 CDMA2000 1x mobile network structure.

Table 12.3 Specifications of CDMA2000 Standards

Standard	*Features*	*Downlink Rate*	*Uplink Rate*
CDMA2000 1xEV-DO Revision 0	1. Broadband data transmission rate 2. IP network compatibility 3. Broadband applications: IPTV, MP3 music, VPN, 3D online games	2.45 Mbps	0.15 Mbps
CDMA2000 1xEV-DO Revision A	1. Support for an advanced quality-of-service (QoS) mechanism 2. 20% more network capacity to support more users 3. Low latency 4. Improved data transmission rates 5. Support for all-IP networks 6. More broadband applications: VoIP, push-to-talk, push-to-media, multicasting, and video conferencing	3.1 Mbps	1.8 Mbps
CDMA2000 3x (1xEV-DO Revision B)	1. Support for multiple EV-DO Revision A channels 2. Improved data transmission rates 3. Improved performance of multimedia applications	4.9 Mbps × number of channels used	1.8 Mbps × number of channels used
CDMA2000 EV-DV	1. Support for concurrent operations of voice users and data users within the same channel 2. Lowered cost on mobile network construction.	3.1 Mbps	1.8 Mbps

For the 1x version, there are standards such as CDMA2000 1xEV-DO, which stands for 1x Evolution Data Optimized; CDMA2000 1xEV-DV, which stands for 1x Evolution Data and Voice; and CDMA2000 3x, which is a multicarrier evolution from Rev A. Table 12.3 lists specifications for these CDMA2000 standards.

Table 12.3 shows that every version of CDMA2000 provides adequate data transmission rates for Internet access. Therefore, CDMA2000 is very suitable for users who require high-speed Internet access through mobile networks. Because CDMA2000 can efficiently use the bandwidth, it delivers very high voice quality for its voice service. It is also capable of transmitting a large amount of data; therefore, it is a good choice for multimedia-based applications. By combining data and voice services, CDMA2000 can also reduce the cost of mobile network development and allow developers to get better returns for their investments. Because of the backward compatibility with CDMA, the implementation of CDMA2000 mobile networks will not interrupt the operation of an existing CDMA mobile network. Because of these advantages, CDMA2000 is often a favorite choice for a 3G mobile network.

12.4.5 Mobile Network beyond Third Generation

Since 2006, many mobile network service companies have updated their UMTS mobile networks to the High Speed Packet Access (HSPA) family of mobile network standards. HSPA can provide download speeds as high as DSL. It covers much larger areas than Wi-Fi. HSPA has two standards, High Speed Downlink Packet Access (HSDPA) and High Speed Uplink Packet Access (HSUPA). HSDPA can achieve up to 14.4 Mbps download transmission rate. It is designed to handle multimedia data on mobile devices. The upload transmission rate is about 384 Kbps, which is not very impressive. HSDPA is also backward compatible with older versions of mobile communication technology such as UMTS. High Speed Uplink Packet Access (HSUPA) is a standard specifically designed for better upload transmission. It can achieve up to a 5.76 Mbps upload transmission rate, and its download transmission rate is similar to that of HSDPA.

HSPA includes authentication and encryption mechanisms for securing data communication over wireless networks. It is very hard for hackers to break the security system provided by HSPA. Therefore, HSPA is often used for applications such as mobile banking and other wireless services that transmit sensitive data on mobile devices.

In this HSPA family, HSDPA and HSUPA are commercially available. HSPA+, also known as Evolved HSPA, was first tested on a commercial network in 2008. The features and data transmission rates of HSDPA, HSUPA, and HSPA+ are listed in Table 12.4.

Some high-speed cellular services that advance the 3G mobile network system are under development. Technologies such as Long Term Evolution (LTE) and the 4G version of Worldwide Interoperability for Microwave Access (WiMAX) are IP-based telecommunication technologies for moving data across wireless networks. These technologies allow wireless devices to be used similar to how cell phones are used. Each mobile phone can be considered an access point.

Table 12.4 HSPA Family: Features and Data Transmission Rates

Standard	*Features*	*Downlink Rate (Mbps)*	*Uplink Rate (Mbps)*
HSDPA	1. Faster data transmission rates 2. Higher streaming quality 3. More reliable video telephony 4. Backward compatible with UMTS to lower the implementation cost	14.4	0.384
HSUPA	1. Improved uplink transfer speed 2. Good for collaboration-intensive applications	14.4	5.76
HSPA+	1. Very high data transmission rates 2. Support for the packet-only mode for both voice and data 3. Backward compatible with HSDPA to lower the implementation cost 4. Easier to be updated to the next-generation Long Term Evolution (LTE) mobile network	42	11.5

As mentioned in Table 12.4, HSPA+ paves the way for the next-generation mobile network technology Long Term Evolution (LTE). LTE is the fourth-generation mobile network technology, scheduled to be commercially available in 2010. The following are its proposed features:

- LTE plans to support up to 326.4 Mbps downlink data transmission rate and 172.8 Mbps uplink data transmission rate.
- The LTE cell boundary can reach as far as 100 km with acceptable performance.
- LTE supports an all-IP packet switching network. This feature simplifies the LTE network structure, so that it can transmit a large volume of data. The all-IP network uses less network equipment, which means that LTE reduces data traffic latency and network construction cost.
- LTE is backward compatible with 3G mobile network technologies such as UMTS. It is even compatible with mobile network technologies such as cdmaOne or CDMA2000. This feature makes it less expensive to upgrade from 3G to 4G.
- LTE uses the orthogonal frequency division multiplexing (OFDM) scheme, which is a multicarrier frequency division multiplexing (FDM) method. OFDM offers high spectral efficiency, and it is robust against interference and less sensitive to errors.
- LTE can operate in different frequency bands. This feature allows the service to be deployed in the spectrum chosen by a service carrier to achieve better performance. The bandwidth used for the LTE service is also scalable from 1.25 MHz to 20 MHz. This gives service carriers freedom to design their mobile networks to meet the individual requirement of each network.
- By supporting the technology Multicast Broadcast Single Frequency Network (MBSFN), LTE is capable of delivering Mobile TV.
- LTE supports Multiple Input Multiple Output (MIMO) technology for transmitting data. MIMO technology can use multiple channels to send and receive data independently. In this way, LTE's data transmission rate can be increased several times, and the transmission quality can also be improved.

Due to the foregoing features, LTE has been chosen by a majority of mobile service carriers for their future upgrades. Not only will those service carriers currently running GMS or HSPA upgrade to LTE, but also many service carriers currently running CDMA or CDMA2000.

Another 4G technology is based on WiMAX technology. WiMAX allows users who are on the move to access the Internet wherever the cell phone services are available. The technology can combine the services of LAN, WAN, and the mobile phone. The version of WiMAX that supports the mobile network is Mobile WiMAX, which is based on the open standard IEEE 802.16e. IEEE 802.16e meets the 3G IMT-2000 requirements and, therefore, Mobile WiMAX is qualified as a 3G mobile network technology.

The version of WiMAX designed for 4G mobile networks is called WiMAX II. WiMAX II is based on the standard IEEE 802.16m, which is expected to be available by the end of 2009. WiMAX II is designed to meet the IMT-Advanced standard so that it can qualify as a 4G technology. The following lists some of the features of WiMAX II:

- WiMAX II is designed to support data transmission rates up to approximately 100 Mbps for high mobility and up to 1 Gbps for low mobility.
- WiMAX II can also use a scalable spectrum ranging from 1.25 MHz to 20 MHz, which expands a channel four times broader than what is currently used by today's mobile WiMAX.
- WiMAX II is able to use 4x4 MIMO technology for data transmission, which means that WiMAX II can transmit data through four transmitting and four receiving antennas independently.

- WiMAX II supports real-time gaming, TV broadcasting, and video streaming over high-definition screens.
- WiMAX II supports the OFDM scheme for high spectral efficiency, and it is robust to interference and less sensitive to errors.
- WiMAX will significantly reduce the latency for transmitting data from a radio access network to an IP network.
- WiMAX II supports enhanced power saving management to reduce the power consumption of mobile devices and applications.
- WiMAX II has the ability to self-manage base stations and mobile devices for reducing interference and improving the coordination of neighboring base stations.

From these features, one can see that WiMAX is compatible with LTE. When compared with LTE, WiMAX II has some pros and cons. The openness of Mobile WiMAX makes it less expensive than LTE. However, most mobile service carriers traditionally prefer the proprietary way of doing business. Also, the mobile network frequency spectra have largely been used by GMS and HSPA. The upgrade to LTE can continue to use these spectra. In some areas, there are not many frequency spectra left for Mobile WiMAX and WiMAX II.

The technology of mobile network is undergoing rapid change. Data transmission on mobile networks is becoming faster and faster, and mobile devices are becoming more and more sophisticated. Many useful features have been added to mobile devices. This chapter has merely provided a brief introduction. Detailed coverage of mobile networks is beyond the scope of this book. Readers can get more detailed information on this area from books that cover mobile networks.

Activity 12.1 Mobile Device Support by Ubuntu Linux

Ubuntu 8.10 and later versions are designed to provide better support for mobile devices. In addition to supporting Wi-Fi based wireless devices, Ubuntu Linux also supports 3G mobile devices. This feature of Ubuntu Linux allows users who travel frequently to access the Internet from their mobile devices through mobile networks. Ubuntu Linux works very well with the mobile devices used in a 3G mobile network such as USB mobile network devices and mobile phones. The tool NetworkManager included in Ubuntu Linux can automatically detect devices used in a 3G mobile network. NetworkManager can also be used to manage the mobile devices. In the following, a simple hands-on activity is used to illustrate how Ubuntu Linux works with a USB dongle modem to access the mobile broadband service:

1. Like Wi-Fi manufacturers, not all mobile device manufacturers provide Linux drivers for their devices. Therefore, the first task is to identify Linux-compatible mobile devices. You may find Linux-compatible mobile devices from the following Web site:

   https://wiki.ubuntu.com/HardwareSupport

   For example, to search for Linux-compatible 3G mobile modems, on this Web site, click the link **modems** and then click the link **HardwareSupportComponentsModem**. You should be able to see a few Linux-compatible modems listed on the Web page shown in Figure 12.10.
2. Suppose that you have a Huawei E220 3G mobile network modem. Plug the modem into the USB port on your host computer. Then, log on to your server virtual machine with username **student** and password **ubuntu**.
3. The Ubuntu Linux operating system should be able to detect the device; it will then prompt you to select a device (Figure 12.11). Click the device **Huawei USB Mass Storage Device** to install it.

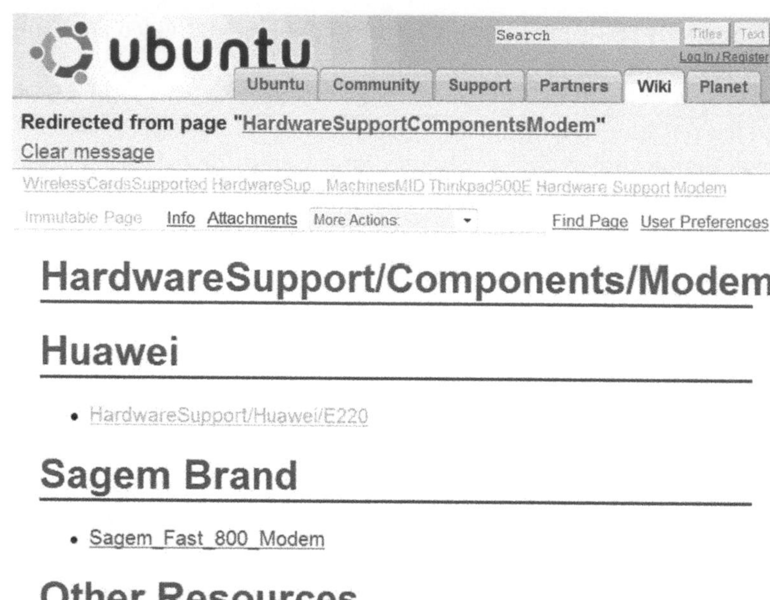

Figure 12.10 Linux-compatible 3G mobile network modems.

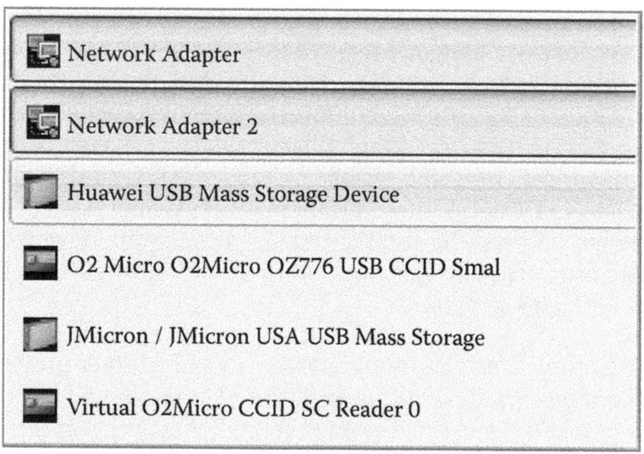

Figure 12.11 Available devices on server machine.

4. As mentioned earlier, the tool NetworkManager can be used to manage mobile devices. For a demonstration, click the **NetworkManager** icon on the top-right corner of your computer screen. You should see the **Configure** option under the item Mobile Broadband (Figure 12.12).
5. Click the option **Configure** to start the Mobile Broadband Connection wizard. On the Welcome page, click the **Forward** button.
6. The Service provider page allows you to select the service provider to which you are currently subscribing the mobile service. Let us say you are using the T-Mobile (Web) service. Select the **T-Mobile (Web)** service plan, and click the **Forward** button (Figure 12.13).

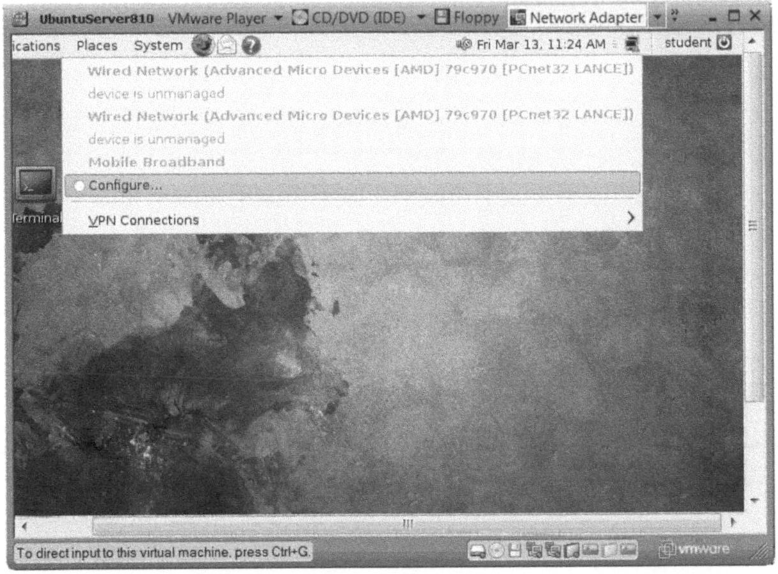

Figure 12.12 Configuration of mobile devices with NetworkManager tool.

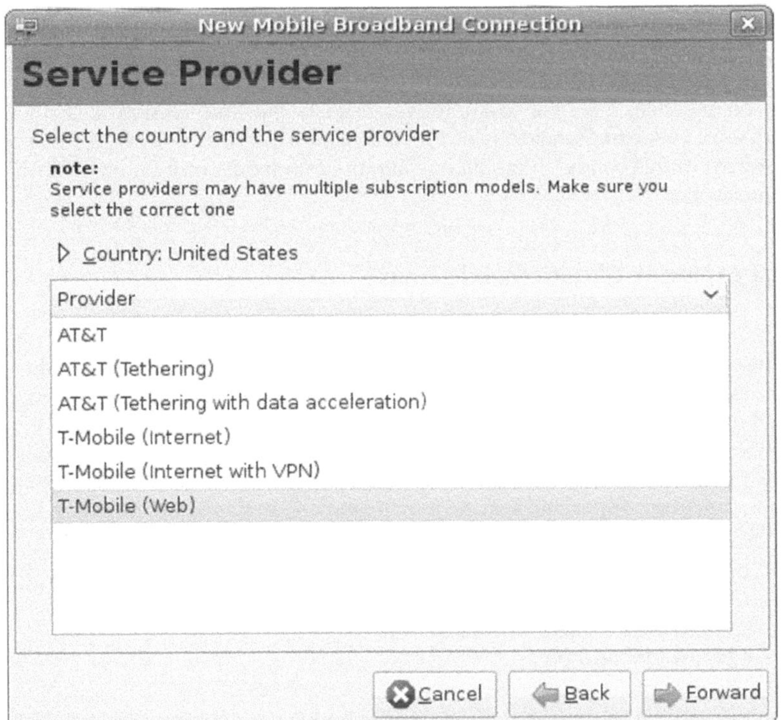

Figure 12.13 Service provider configuration.

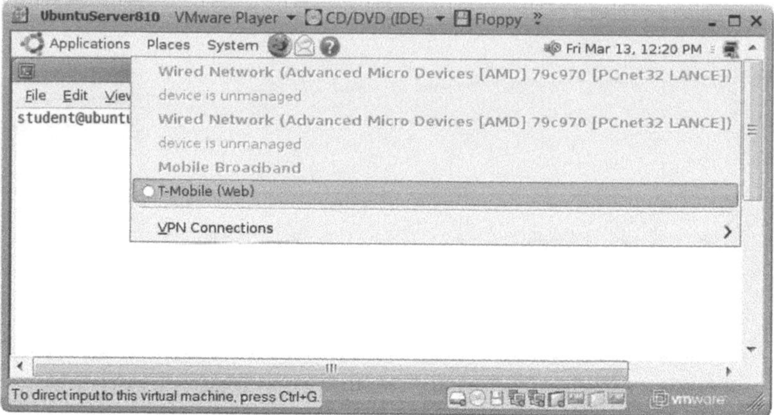

Figure 12.14 Verification of mobile broadband service configuration.

7. On the summary page, you can verify the configuration. If the configuration is correct, click the **Apply** button to complete the configuration.
8. To verify, click the **NetworkManager** icon on the top-right corner of your computer screen. You should be able to see the T-Mobile (Web) option under the item Mobile Broadband (Figure 12.14).
9. To link to the mobile service provider, you may need to provide authentication information by using the tool Network Configuration. To do so, click the **System** menu, then **Preferences,** and **Network Configuration**. Under the Mobile Broadband tab, you can enter the authentication information provided by your mobile broadband service provider.

In this hands-on practice, a simple example was used to illustrate Ubuntu Linux's support for mobile broadband. NetworkManager is a convenient tool used to detect and manage mobile devices. As shown in this hands-on practice, Ubuntu Linux works well with the devices used in a 3G mobile network.

Activity 12.2 Exploring Ubuntu Mobile Linux

Ubuntu Linux supports mobile networks in many ways. Ubuntu Linux 8.10 and later versions support 3G mobile broadband. The network configuration GUI utility can recognize the 3G broadband card, and the user can configure the 3G connection by following the configuration wizard. In addition, Ubuntu has a mobile version of Linux called Ubuntu Mobile Linux, which is designed mainly for smartphones and mobile Internet devices (MIDs). To allow users to experiment with Ubuntu Mobile Linux, Ubuntu provides a KVM virtual machine image that simulates the Ubuntu MID computing environment. In this hands-on practice, you will perform the following tasks:

1. Enable your computer to run a virtual machine.
2. Install a KVM virtual machine.
3. Download the Ubuntu MID KVM image.
4. Explore Ubuntu Mobile Linux.

Our hands-on practice will start with the task of configuring your computer so that you can run a KVM virtual machine.

CONFIGURATION OF BIOS

To run the KVM virtual machine on your computer, you need to configure the BIOS to enable virtualization. Running the KVM virtual machine requires that your computer have adequate memory and CPU power. The virtual machines used for all the hands-on practice in the previous chapters may not be able to run the KVM virtual machine on top of them. What we are going to do in this hands-on practice is run Ubuntu on a DVD directly. In this way, Ubuntu is able to use all the resources of your PC. To do so, you need to configure the BIOS so that your PC can boot from the CD/DVD drive first. The BIOS configuration varies slightly from PC to PC. The following example is based on a DELL notebook computer:

1. Turn on your computer. As soon as it starts, you will be asked if you want to get into Setup mode. In this example, press **F2** to get into Setup mode. (The key may be different for another brand of computer.)
2. In Setup mode, change the boot sequence to force the system boot from the CD/DVD drive first. You will also need to find virtualization and enable it.
3. Insert the Ubuntu Linux installation DVD in the CD/DVD drive.
4. Press the **Esc** key to complete the BIOS configuration. Select the **Save/Exit** button, and press the **Enter** key.
5. After leaving Setup mode, the system continues to boot. You will be prompted to choose how to run Ubuntu. To run the Ubuntu Linux operating system on the live DVD, choose the option **Try Ubuntu without any change to your computer,** and then press the **Enter** key.
6. After the system is booted up, the Ubuntu Linux operating system is ready to use. To run from the live DVD, you do not need to enter the username and password.
7. Your next task is to test if your computer supports the KVM virtual machine. To do so, execute the following command in the terminal window:

   ```
   egrep '(vmx|svm)' --color=always /proc/cpuinof
   ```

8. If nothing is present on-screen after you execute the preceding command, your computer cannot run the KVM virtual machine.

INSTALLATION OF KVM VIRTUAL MACHINE

Once you have verified that your computer is able to run the KVM virtual machine, your next step is to install it. To do so, follow these steps:

1. The first step is to update your Ubuntu Linux operating system by entering the following command:

   ```
   sudo apt-get update
   ```

2. To install the KVM virtual machine, execute the following command:

   ```
   sudo apt-get install kvm
   ```

GETTING KVM UBUNTU MID IMAGE

After installing the KVM virtual machine, your next task is to download the KVM Ubuntu MID image. The following steps show how to accomplish the task:

1. Double-click the Firefox Web browser icon on the Ubuntu Linux desktop.
2. Enter the following Web address, and press the **Enter** key:

   ```
   http://cdimage.ubuntu.com/mobile/releases/hardy
   ```

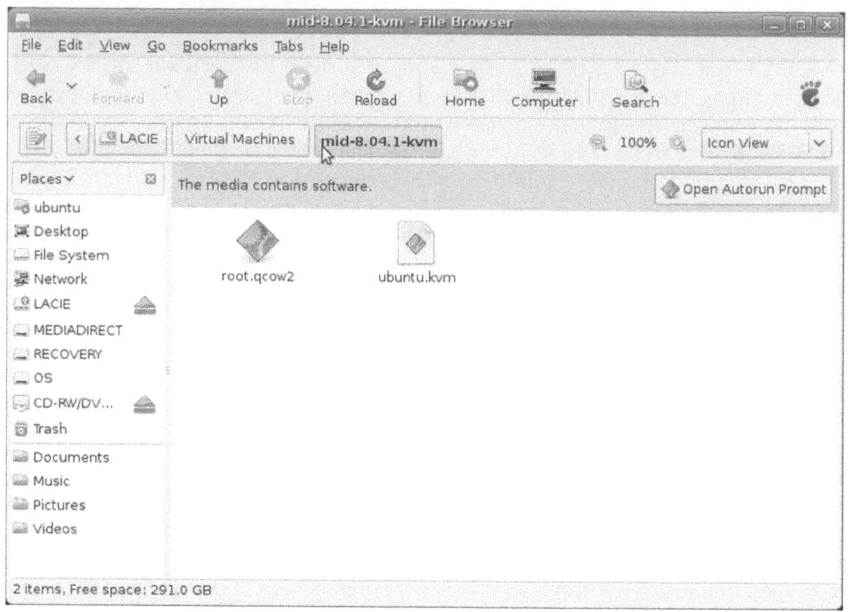

Figure 12.15 Ubuntu MID image files.

3. Once the Web site is opened, click the link **KVM (Kernel Virtual Machine) image**.
4. Select the option **Open with Archive Manager (default),** and then click **OK**.
5. After the file is downloaded, you will see the folder mid-8.04.1-kvm on your computer screen. Right-click the folder **mid-8.04.1-kvm,** and select **Extract** on the pop-up menu.
6. You will see two files that are extracted (Figure 12.15). The file root.qcow2 is the KVM image file. The file ubuntu.kvm is the script to run the image file.
7. Double-click the file ubuntu.kvm to run the KVM virtual machine image. You will have the Ubuntu MID image (Figure 12.16).

EXPLORATION OF UBUNTU MOBILE LINUX

With the Ubuntu MID image, you will be able to explore the application software provided by Ubuntu Mobile Linux. For example, if you want to create an account for the Ekiga softphone service, you can follow these steps.

1. Before you start to explore Ekiga on the Ubuntu MID image, you need go to the Ekiga Web site to create a user account (Figure 12.17).

   After you have created the account, write down the username and password, which will be used for the configuration later.
2. Find the Ekiga icon on the Ubuntu MID Image, and double-click on it. You should be able to get the Configuration Assistant wizard shown in Figure 12.18.
3. Click the **Forward** button to go to the Personal Information page. Enter the username, for example, **Mark Student** (Figure 12.19).
4. Click the **Forward** button to go to the ekiga.net Account page (Figure 12.20). Enter the username and password created in Step 1.
5. Click the **Forward** button to go to the Connection Type page. Keep the current setting shown in Figure 12.21.

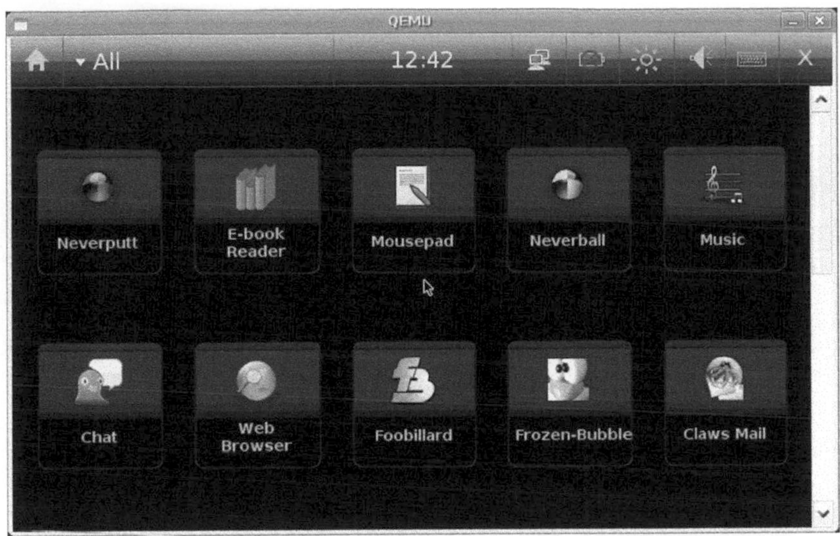

Figure 12.16 Ubuntu MID image

6. Click the **Forward** button to go to the NAT Type page. Depending on the network setup, you may or may have NAT.
7. After the NAT detection process is completed, click the **Forward** button to go to the Audio Manager page. Accept the default audio manager **ALSA** (Figure 12.22).
8. Click the **Forward** button to go to the Audio Devices page. Accept the default audio devices (Figure 12.23).
9. Click **Forward** to go to the Video Manager page. If you want to use a Web camera, you can choose **V4L** as the video manager (Figure 12.24).
10. Click **Forward** to go to the Video Devices page. Your computer may or may not have video devices.
11. Click **Forward** to complete the configuration.

After the configuration is completed, your MID should be able to use the softphone to call another user who also has an account with Ekiga through VoIP.

In this hands-on practice, you have learned how to run the KVM Ubuntu MID virtual image on you PC. This hands-on practice altered the BIOS configuration to allow your PC to run the KVM virtual machine. It also showed how to install the virtual machine KVM, and how to download and use the KVM Ubuntu MID image. The last part of this hands-on activity illustrated the use of the application software included in the Ubuntu Mobile Linux operating system by configuring the Ekiga softphone service.

12.5 Summary

This chapter covered topics related to mobile networks. It first explains the role played by Linux in a mobile network system. Linux has been considered by many as a compact, low-cost, and versatile operating system. Due to these features, Linux has been widely accepted as an operating system for mobile devices. Mobile device producers and mobile network service carriers have teamed up to develop Linux operating systems that are suitable for the mobile computing environment. This

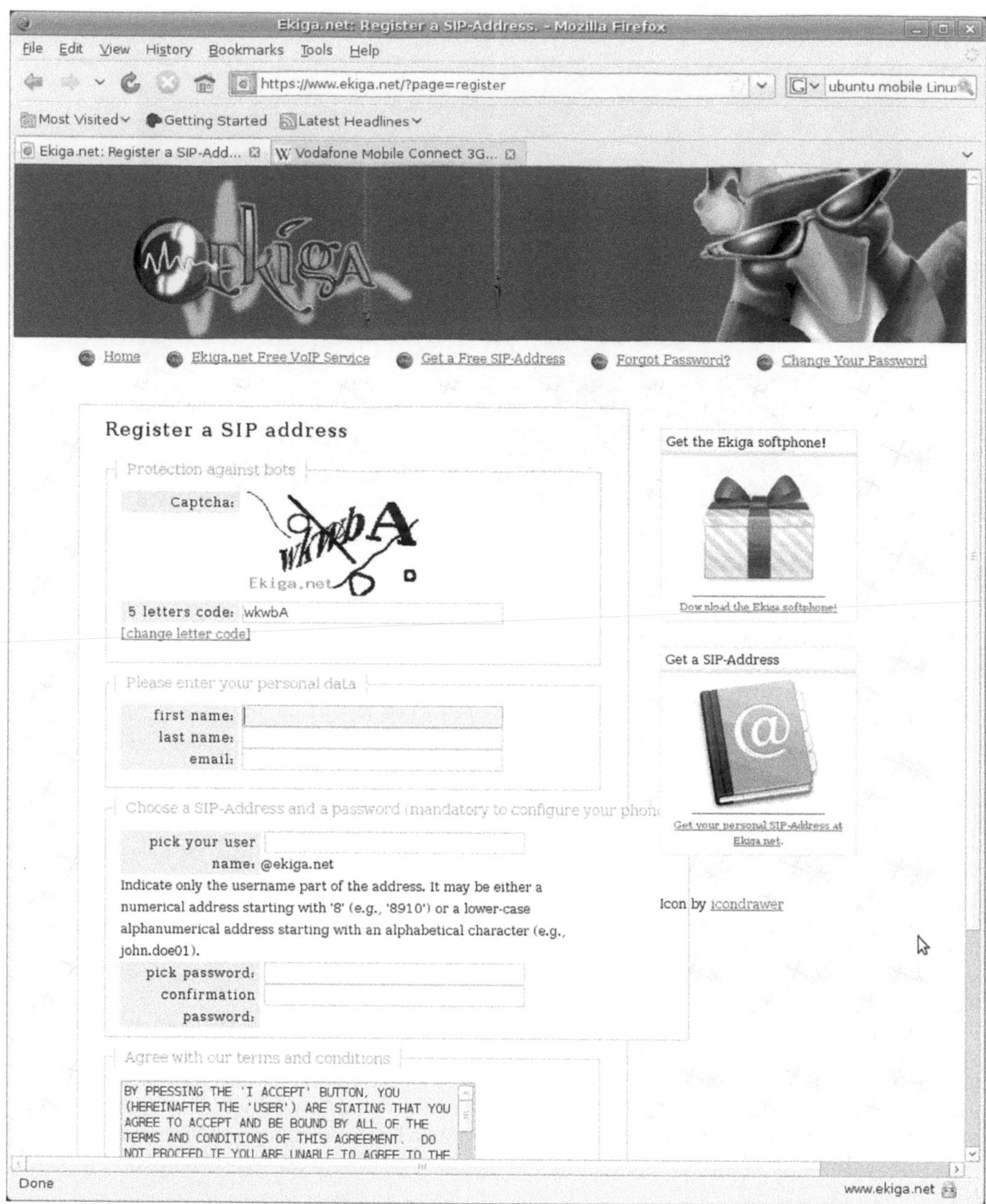

Figure 12.17 Ekiga user account registration.

chapter introduced some mobile Linux organizations and several well-known Linux operating systems such as Android, LiMo, LIPS, OpenMoko, and Ubuntu Mobile Linux.

This chapter introduced different kinds of mobile devices such as personal digital assistant (PDA), mobile Internet device (MID), converged mobile device (CMD), portable media player (PMP), and portable navigation device (PND). As mentioned in this chapter, the mobile devices

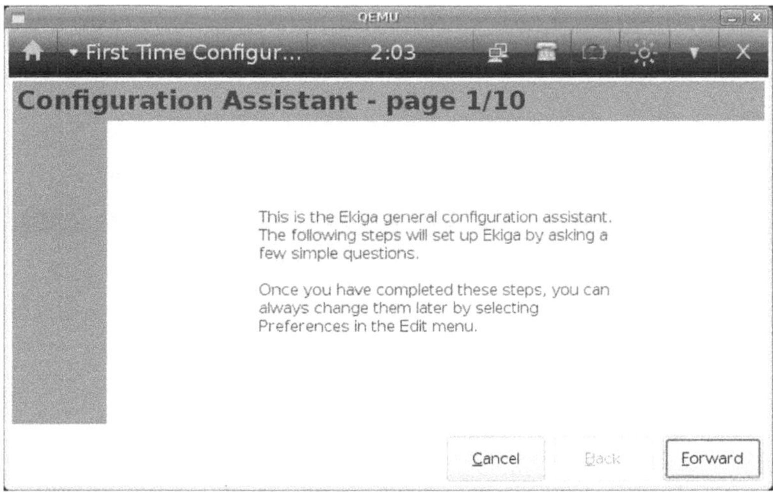

Figure 12.18 Ekiga Configuration Assistant wizard.

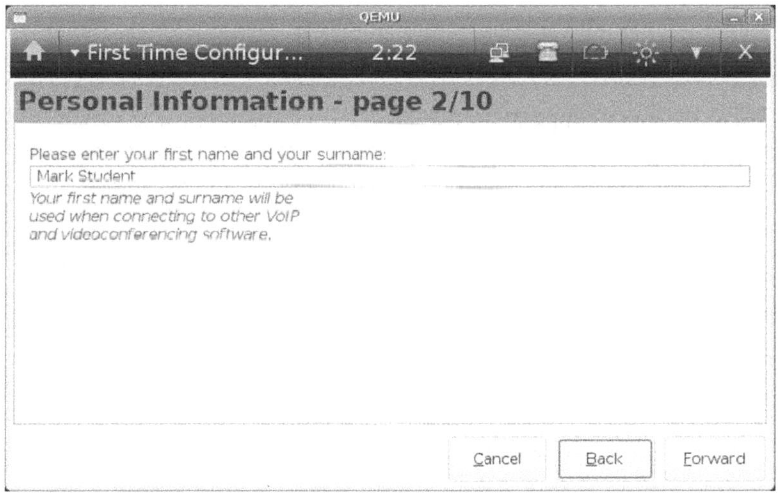

Figure 12.19 Personal Information page.

in each category may provide similar functionalities. Today's mobile devices are sophisticated and are able to handle both voice and data transmission.

This chapter also introduced several well-known mobile network systems. It compared the features provided by the mobile network technologies of 1G, 2G, 3G and the mobile network technologies beyond 3G. Mobile network concepts and structures have also been discussed in this chapter. By explaining how mobile networks work in each generation, this chapter showed how mobile networks migrate from 1G to 4G.

The last part of this chapter was the hands-on practice on installing and configuring the Ubuntu MID virtual machine image. Through this hands-on practice, readers will be able to explore the features provided by a mobile Linux operating system.

QEMU
First Time Configur...
2:30
ekiga.net Account - page 3/10
Please enter your username:
studentmark@ekiga.net
Please enter your password:
The username and password are used to login to your existing account at the ekiga.net free SIP service. If you do not have an ekiga.net SIP address yet, you may first create an account below. This will provide a SIP address that allows people to call you.
You may skip this step if you use an alternative SIP service, or if you would prefer to specify the login details later.
Cancel
Back
Forward

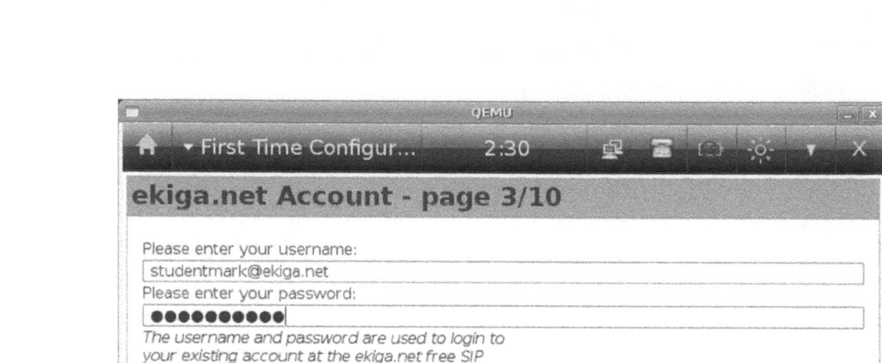

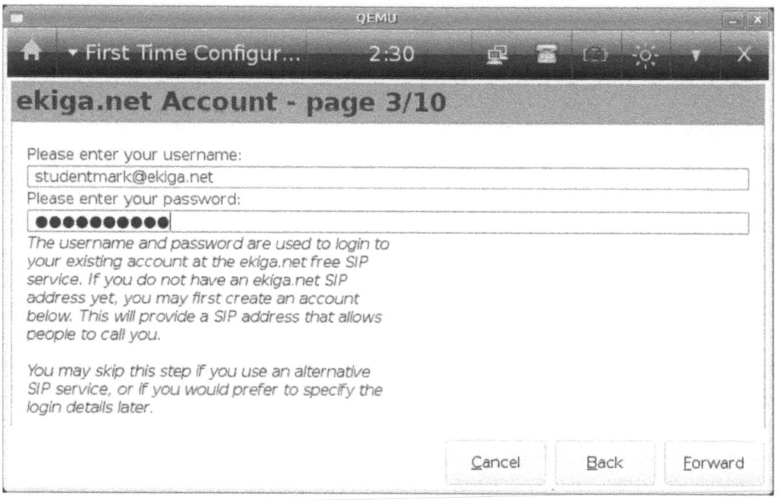

Figure 12.20 Ekiga.net Account page.

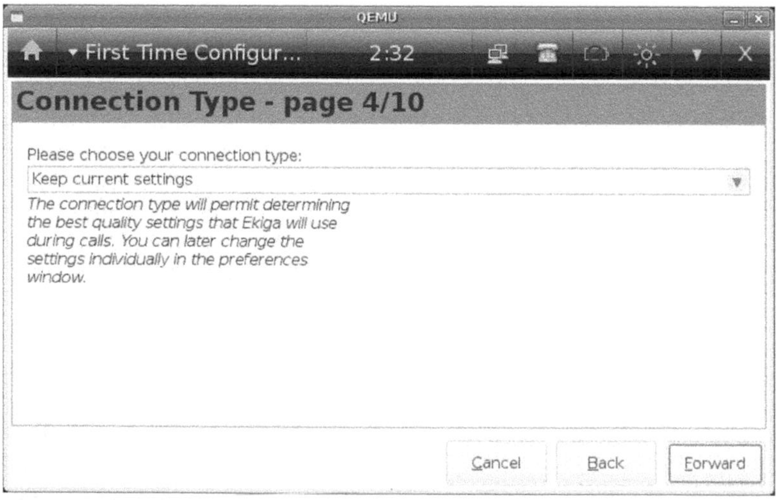

QEMU
First Time Configur...
2:32
Connection Type - page 4/10
Please choose your connection type:
Keep current settings
The connection type will permit determining the best quality settings that Ekiga will use during calls. You can later change the settings individually in the preferences window.
Cancel
Back
Forward

Figure 12.21 Connection Type page.

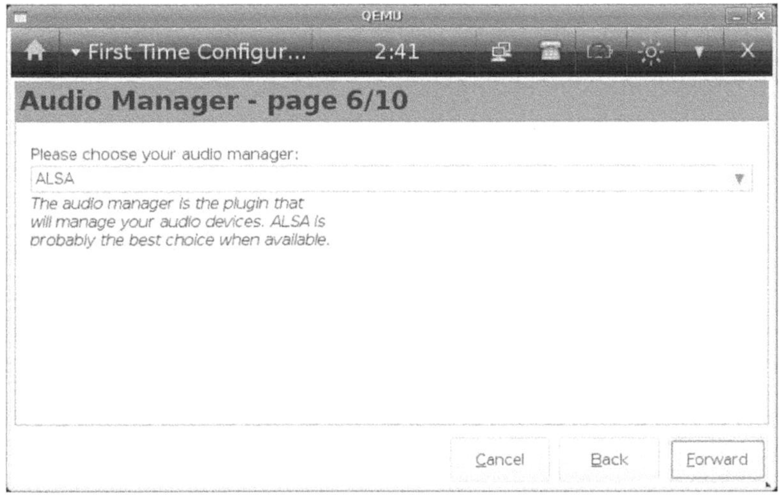

Figure 12.22 Audio Manager page.

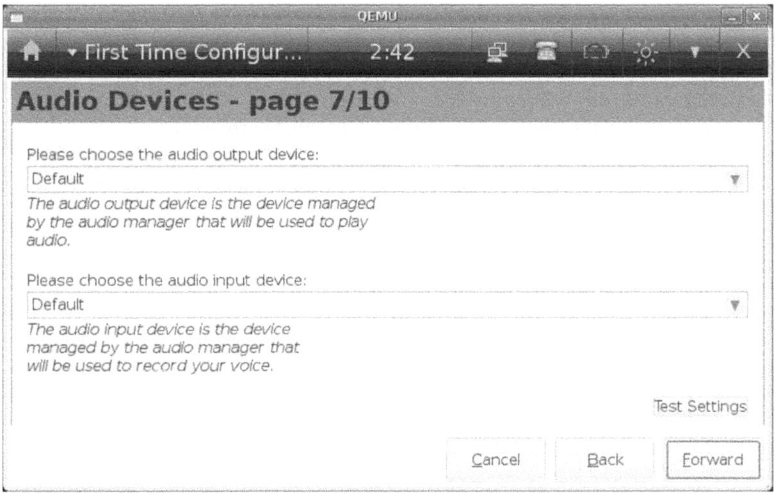

Figure 12.23 Audio Devices page.

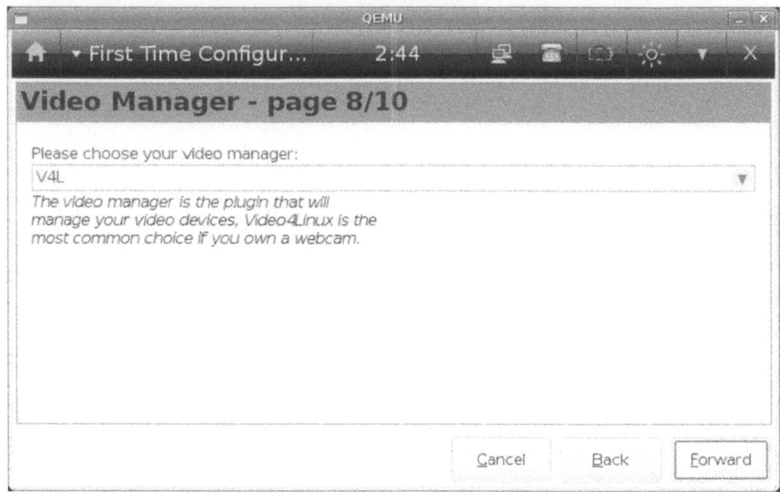

Figure 12.24 Video Manager page.

Review Questions

1. What Linux features make it a suitable operating system for mobile devices?
2. What tasks can be handled by the Android Linux operating system?
3. Name some application software supported by the Android Linux operating system.
4. What is the difference between Android and LiMo?
5. What is open source hardware?
6. List the features supported by Ubuntu Mobile Linux.
7. What is a PDA and what do you do with it?
8. What is an MID and what features does it have?
9. What is a CMD and what functionalities does it have?
10. List some of the features supported by the microprocessors Atom and ARM.
11. Why does a cell use only one-seventh of the total available frequencies?
12. What tasks can be accomplished by an MTSO?
13. When compared with 1G technology, what are the advantages provided by 2G technology?
14. What problems does FDM have?
15. How does CDMA technology handle multiplexing?
16. What is an MSC and what can it do?
17. What is soft handoff and what is the benefit of using it?
18. List the features provided by 3G technology.
19. What are the advantages of CDMA2000?
20. What are the improvements in HSPA technology over UMTS technology?

Case Study Projects

The following are two networking projects that involve mobile network devices.

Case Study Project 12.1. Demonstrate how to configure a 3G cell phone for accessing the class Web site.

Case Study Project 12.2. Demonstrate how to configure a PDA to access the class Web site.

Index

E

F

O

P

R

S

T

Milton Keynes UK
Ingram Content Group UK Ltd.
UKHW020825141024
449569UK00008B/562

9 781420 091595